NINTH EDITION

TECHNICAL ANALYSIS OF STOCK TRENDS

CRC Press
Taylor & Francis Group
6000 Broken Sound Parkway NW, Suite 300
Boca Raton, FL 33487-2742

© 2007 by Taylor & Francis Group, LLC
CRC Press is an imprint of Taylor & Francis Group, an Informa business

No claim to original U.S. Government works
Printed in the United States of America on acid-free paper
10 9 8 7 6 5 4 3 2 1

International Standard Book Number-10: 0-8493-3772-0 (Hardcover)
International Standard Book Number-13: 978-0-8493-3772-7 (Hardcover)

Library of Congress Cataloging-in-Publication Data

Edwards, Robert D. (Robert Davis), 1893-
     Technical analysis of stock trends / Robert D. Edwards, John Magee, W.H.C. Bassetti. -- 9th ed.
          p. cm.
     Includes bibliographical references and index.
     ISBN 0-8493-3772-0 (alk. paper)
     1. Investment analysis. 2. Stock exchanges--United States. 3. Securities--United States. I. Magee, John, 1901- II. Bassetti, W. H. C. III. Title.

HG4521.E38 2006
332.63'20420973--dc22   2006045096

Visit the Taylor & Francis Web site at
http://www.taylorandfrancis.com

and the **CRC Press Web site at**
http://www.crcpress.com

NINTH EDITION

TECHNICAL ANALYSIS OF *STOCK TRENDS*

ROBERT D. EDWARDS

JOHN MAGEE

W.H.C. BASSETTI

CRC Press
Taylor & Francis Group
Boca Raton   London   New York

AMACOM

AMERICAN MANAGEMENT ASSOCIATION
New York • Atlanta • Brussels • Chicago • Mexico City • San Francisco
Shanghai • Tokyo • Toronto • Washington, D.C

Preface to the 9th Edition

Warp speed universe. Warp speed financial markets. The 8th Edition of this classic book appeared when it seemed that the millennium and paradise had been achieved and that, like McKay's tulipomania, the price of stocks would rise forever and men would rush from the world over and pay whatever price was asked for what-was-its-name.com, Internet.groceries, or ihype.com or icon.com or gotcha.com. And, feature this, *Dow 36000*. The bubble was just in the process of bursting, of course. Before it burst fabulous fortunes were made by roller blader and scooter tycoons and by young geeks with nothing but chutzpah and a laptop. One of my favorite stories is of the young entrepreneur who said "Why don't I deserve it (the $100MM he made in the IPO)? I've devoted three years of my life to this project." (Now dead.)

Now many of those people are in prison and the hangover lingers on. Lying, cheating, and stealing on all sides. From Enron to Arthur Anderson. Billions, if not trillions into a black hole. As all this developed I warned of the impending collapse in the John Magee Investment Letters on the web. There was nothing magic or brilliant about seeing what was going on. Perspective and perception came from applying the lessons taught in this book by Edwards and Magee. Like Benedict XVI (in a different area) I am a humble worker in their vineyard.

I press on attempting to modernize (where necessary) and extend their work, fit it to the modern situation and make it even more useful to current day traders and investors.

In this ongoing labor of love I have been immeasurably assisted by my graduate students and colleagues at Golden Gate University in San Francisco. In constant interaction with them, I have been stimulated to see important aspects of Edwards and Magee's work and develop and emphasize these elements in my teaching and in this new edition.

Specifically, both long-term and short-term traders will find important new material in this edition. In my graduate seminars I have seen the power of what Magee called the "Basing Points" procedure and so have extended the treatment of this material. My interest in and respect for Dow Theory have recently increased as the result of a paper done with Brian Brooker for the Market Technicians Association ("Dissecting Dow Theory"). Material from that paper will be found in this edition. Short-term traders and futures speculators will appreciate extensive new material on commodity trading. These traders have been entirely too influenced by mechanical number-driven systems of recent years and need to restore perspective by mastering the material in this book.

It was never the intent of this book to forecast or analyze current markets. Rather it's purpose was, and is, to learn from history and the past so as to be better able to deal with the present and the future. Current markets are analyzed (and forecast?) at the John Magee website. Nonetheless, the very process of keeping current involves picturing issues and instruments in play. The major indices themselves in 2005 were in play, and gold, silver and oil. We don't know how they will pan out. But we can make an analysis with *the data we have*. For this is the situation the analyst is faced with every day. He doesn't know how it will turn out. But, by following the methods and principles taught in this book he can put himself on the right side of the probabilities.

This is no idle remark. The power and effectiveness of classical chart analysis can be seen by examining how it performed in the past at critical times. At the John Magee Technical Analysis website the following comment was made in January 2000:

> Dow: The Dow can expect to find support at 10000 and is buyable, but in small commitments or portions of a portfolio or additions thereto. We expect to see it in a very large seesaw from 9-12000 for some time and would hedge at the high end and increase commitments and lift hedges on oversold conditions at the low end.

In November 2000 the following comment was made:

> November 18, 2000
>
> There is really only one chart pattern of significance in these markets, and that is the big one, more than 12 months long now, and the pattern is a big serpent, whipping back and forth, and as Shakespeare said, signifying nothing. Nothing that is but more of the same. How will we know when it signifies something? Well we won't really know till we know, but we'll let you know when we know. So we would continue to pick likely shorts and employ short term trading strategies for traders, and hedge at interim tops and lift the hedges at bottoms. Based on the chart picture and last week's anemic behavior we would not trade for bounces in the NASDAQ. If anything it is a short, but a risky one.

These past letters, dramatically illustrating the effectiveness of the methods of this book, may be found online through links at the address specified below. Your editor, personally, is not a genius for having made these analyses. It is the method that is to credit, and any number of my graduate students can make the same analyses, as can any alert chart analyst.

The reader should not skip the prefatory material to the 8th Edition. The same practices outlined there have been followed in this edition. Magee said the reader should not skim through this book and put it on his library shelf. Instead it should be read and reread and constantly referred to. And so the reader should, yes, so he should.

Richard Russell, the dean of Dow Theory Analysts, has reportedly said that the price of the Dow and the price of gold will cross in coming years. He has also remarked that the S&P appears to evince a 10-year head-and-shoulders pattern. Robert Prechter believes we are at the crest of the tidal wave and the tsunami cometh.

Dow 36000. Dow 3000. This book contains the best tools to cope with whatever the future holds.

W.H.C. Bassetti
San Francisco, California

A Special Note Concerning Resources on the Web

In the age of instant and easy (and free) access to information on the Internet it would be foolish to ignore the opportunities available to interact with the material of this book. So the reader will find numerous free materials that augment the book at www.edwards-magee.com/nf05/ninthedition.html. For example, when the reader learns in Chapter 28 of the Basing Points Procedure he will be able to go to the website and print out a PDF of material that he can place beside Figure 210.1 for instant and easy cross reference, instead of having to turn pages constantly back and forth from the chart to the keys and commentary, or having to bend the book into pretzels at a copy machine. In general, wherever references are made in the text to the website it is for this purpose, to give the reader easy and flexible usage of the material. And, likewise, at this address the reader will find links to past letters that show how the method functioned in real time in real markets.

A Special Note about Dow Theory

Senator Everett Dirkson said one time that trying to get U.S. Senators herded together and moving in one direction was like trying to transport bull frogs in a wheelbarrow. Trying to synchronize the signals of the various Dow Theory analysts is a similarly challenging proposition. No Ayatollah exists to issue the final fatwa as to whether the signal is valid. Always one to abhor a vacuum I have organized a committee at Golden Gate University to evaluate pronouncements of signals and opine as to whether the signals are valid. This committee may be contacted at the addresses found in Resources and at cbassetti@ggu.edu.

Acknowledgments for the Ninth Edition

For professional assistance: Jack Schannep, Robert W. Colby, Curtis Faith, Greg Morris and John Murphy, Tim Knight and Chi Huang.

For assistance at Taylor & Francis: Richard O'Hanley, Raymond O'Connell, Pat Roberson, Andrea Demby, and Roy Barnhill.

For research assistance and manuscript preparation: Brian Brooker and Grace Ryan, my fearsomely bright and efficient teaching and research assistants. And my inimitable technical assistant, Samuel W.D. Bassetti.

At Golden Gate University for ongoing support and assistance: Professor Henry Pruden, Barbara Karlin, Janice Carter, Tracy Weed and Cassandra Dilosa.

Special appreciation goes to makers of software packages and their supportive executives for software used in the preparation of this and previous editions.

John Slauson
Adaptick
1082 East 8175 South
Sandy, UT 84094
www.adaptick.com

Steven Hill
AIQ Systems
P.O. Box 7530
Incline Village, NV 89452
702-831-2999
www.AIQsystems.com

Alan McNichol
Metastock
Equis International, Inc.
3950 S. 700 East, Suite 100
Salt Lake City, UT 84107
www.equis.com

Bill Cruz, Ralph Cruz, Darla Tuttle
Tradestation
Omega Research
14257 SW 119th Avenue
Miami, FL 33186
305-485-7599
www.tradestation.com

Tim Knight, Chi Huang
Prophet Financial Systems, Inc.
658 High Street
Palo Alto, CA 94301
www.prophet.net
http://tradertim.blogspot.com

Greg Morris, John Murphy
Stockcharts.com, Inc.
11241 Willows Road, #140
Redmond, WA 98052
www.stockcharts.com

Preface to the Eighth Edition

Here is a strange event. A book written in the mid-20th century retains its relevancy and importance to the present day. In fact, Technical Analysis of Stock Trends remains the definitive book on the subject of analyzing the stock market with charts. Knock-offs, look-alikes, pale imitations have proliferated in its wake like sea gulls after a productive fishing boat. But the truth is they have added nothing new to the body of knowledge Edwards and Magee originally produced and Magee refined up to the 5th edition.

What accounts for this rare occasion of a book's passing to be a classic? To be more, in fact, than a classic, to be the manual or handbook for current usage?

To answer this question we must ask another. What are Chart formations? Chart formations identified and analyzed by the authors are graphic representations of unchanging human behavior in complex multivariate situations.

They are the depiction of multifarious human actions bearing on a single variable (price). On price converge a galaxy of influences: fear, greed, desire, cunning, malice, deceit, naiveté, earnings estimates, broker need for income, gullibility, professional money managers' need for performance and job security, supply and demand of stocks, monetary liquidity and money flow, self-destructiveness, passivity, trap setting, manipulation, blind arrogance, conspiracy and fraud and double dealing, phases of the moon and sun spots, economic cycles and beliefs about them, public mood, and the indomitable human need to be right.

Chart formations are the language of the market, telling us that this stock is in its death throes; that stock is on a rocket to the moon; that a life and death battle is being waged in this issue; and in that other, the buyers have defeated the sellers and are breaking away.

They are, in short, the inerasable fingerprints of human nature made graphic in the greatest struggle, next to war, in human experience.

As Freud mapped the human psyche, so have Edwards and Magee mapped the human mind and emotions as expressed in the financial markets. Not only did they produce a definitive map, they also produced a methodology for interpreting and profiting from the behavior of men and markets. It is difficult to imagine further progress in this area until the science of artificial intelligence, aided by yet unimaginable computer hardware, makes new breakthroughs.

If It Is Definitive, Why Offer a New Edition?

Unlike Nostradamus and Jules Verne (and many current investment advisors), the authors did not have a crystal ball or a time machine. Magee did not foresee the electronic calculator and made do with a slide rule. And while he knew of the computer, he did not anticipate that every housewife and investor would have 1000 times the power of a Whirlwind or Univac I on his (her) desk (cf. Note on Gender). In short, the March of Time. The Progress of Science. The Inexorable Advance of Technology.

Amazingly, the great majority of this book needed no update or actualization. Who is to improve on the descriptions of chart formations and their significance?

But insofar as updates are necessary to reflect the changes in technology and in the character and composition of the markets, that is another story. Human character may not change, but in the new millennium there is nothing but change in the character and composition of the markets. And while regulatory forces might not be completely in agreement, the majority of these changes have been positive for the investor and the commercial user. Of course, Barings Bank and some others are less than ecstatic with these developments.

An Outline of the Most Important Additions Made to This Book to Reflect Changes in the Times, Technology, and Markets

Generally speaking, these additions, annotations, and updates are intended to inform the general reader of conditions of which he must be aware for investing success. In most cases, because of the enormous amount of material, no attempt is made to be absolutely exhaustive in the treatment of these developments. Rather the effort is made to put changes and new conditions in perspective and furnish the investor with the resources and proper guide to pursue subjects at greater length if desired. In fact, an appendix has been provided, entitled Resources, to which the reader may turn when he has mastered the material of the book proper.

The stubborn individualist may realize investment success with the use of this book alone (and paper, pencil, ruler, and chart paper (cf. Section on TEKNIPLAT™ chart paper).

Technology

In order to equip this book to serve as a handbook and guide for the markets of the new millennium, certain material has been added to the text of the 5th and 7th editions. Clearly the astounding advances in technology must be dealt with and put in the context of the analytical methods and material of the original. To achieve success in the new, brave world, an investor must be aware of and utilize electronic markets, the Internet, the microcomputer, wireless communications, and new exchanges offering every kind of exotica imaginable.

The advanced investor should also be aware of and understand some of the developments in finance and investment theory and technology — the Black–Scholes Model, Modern Portfolio Theory, Quantitative Analysis. Fortunately, all these will not be dealt with here, because in truth one intelligent investor with a piece of chart paper and a pencil and a quote source can deal with the markets, but that is another story we will explore later in the book. Some of these germane subjects will be discussed sufficiently to put them in perspective for the technical analyst, and then guides and resources will be pointed out for continued study. My opinion is that the mastery of all these subjects is not wholly necessary for effective investing at the private level. What need does the general investor have for an understanding of the Cox–Ross–Rubinstein options analysis model to recognize trends? The Edwards–Magee model knows things about the market the CRR model does not.

Trading and Investment Instruments

The new universe of available trading and investment instruments must be taken into account. The authors would have been in paradise at the profusion of alternatives. In this future world, they could have traded the Averages (one of the most important changes explored in this book); used futures and options as investment and hedging mechanisms; practiced arbitrage strategies beyond their wildest dreams; and contemplated a candy store full of investment products. The value and utility of these products would have been immeasurably enhanced by their mastery of the charting world of technical analysis. As only one example, one world-prominent professional trader I know has made significant profits selling calls on stocks he correctly analyzed to be in down trends, and vice versa — an obvious (or, as they say, no-brainer) to a technician, but not something you should attempt at home without expert advice. Techniques like this occasioned the loss of many millions of dollars in the Reagan Crash of 1987.

Changes and Developments in Technical Analysis

Have any new chart patterns (that is to say, changes in human behavior and character) emerged since the 5th edition? Not to my knowledge, although there are those who take the same data and draw different pictures from them. How else could you say that you had something new! different! better!? There are other ways of looking at the data which are interesting, sometimes valuable, and often profitable, which goes to prove that many are the ways and gateless is the gate to the great Dow. Point and figure charting have been used very effectively by traders I know, and candlestick charting depicts data in interesting ways. Furthermore, since Magee's time, aided by the computer, technicians have developed innumerable, what I call, number-driven technical analysis tools: (the puzzlingly named) stochastics, oscillators, exponential and other moving averages, etc., etc., etc. It is not the intent of this book to explore these tools in depth. That will be done in a later volume. These concepts are briefly explored in an appendix supplied by Richard McDermott, editor of the 7th edition.

I have also made additions to the book (Chapter 18.1) to give a perspective on long-term investing, since Magee specifically addressed the second part of the book (on tactics) to the speculator. I have substantially rewritten Chapters 24 and 42 to reflect current ideas on portfolio management and risk management. I have expanded on the idea of rhythmic trading — an idea which is implicit in the original. I have expanded the treatment of runaway markets so that the Internet stocks of the 1990s might be put in perspective (Chapter 23).

And then, paradigms. Paradigms, as everyone should know by now, are the last refuge of a fundamentalist when all other explanations fail.

Paradigm Changes

Whenever the markets, as they did at the end of the 20th century, depart from the commonly accepted algorithms for determining what their prices ought to be, fundamentalists (those analysts and investors who believe they can determine value from such fixed verities as earnings, cash flow, etc.) are confronted with new paradigms. Are stock prices (values) to be determined by dividing price by earnings to establish a reasonable price/earnings (p/e) ratio? Or should sales be used, or cash flow, or the phase of the moon, or — in the late 1990s, should losses be multiplied by price to determine the value of the stock? Technicians are not obliged to worry about this kind of financial legerdemain. The stock is worth what it can be sold for today in the market.

The Crystal Ball

Investors will get smarter and smarter, starting with those who learn what this book has to say. The professionals will stay one step ahead of them, because they are preternaturally cunning and because they spend all their time figuring out how to keep ahead of the public, but the gap will narrow. Software and hardware will continue to advance, but not get any smarter. Mechanical systems will work well in some areas, and not in others. Mechanical systems are only as good as the engineer who designs them and the mechanic who maintains them. Buying systems is buying trouble. Everyone should find his own method (usually some variant of the Magee method, in my opinion). All good things will end. All bad things will end. The bag of tricks with which the insiders bilk the public will get smaller and smaller. New and ingenious procedures will be developed by the insiders. The well of human naiveté is bottomless. For every one educated, a new one will be born in a New York minute. It is deeply disturbing at the turn of the century that the owners of the NASDAQ and the NYSE should be thinking of going public. Could there be any more ominous sign that enormous changes are about to occur?

Vigorous development of the systems, methods, procedures, and philosophy outlined in this book is about the only protective shield I know of to guard against inimical change.

W.H.C. Bassetti
San Geronimo, California
January 1, 2001

About the Editorial Practices in This Eighth Edition

Needless to say, one approaches the revision of a classic work with some trepidation. Every critic and reader has his or her (cf. Note on Gender) opinion as to how revision should be done — whether the authors' original text should be invisibly changed as though they had written the book in 2000 instead of 1948 and were omniscient, or whether errors and anachronisms were to be lovingly preserved, or footnoted, or... etc., etc. (I have preserved Magee's favorite usage of "etc., etc., etc." against the protestation of generations of English composition teachers because I like its evocation of an ever-expanding universe.)

Notwithstanding every reader's having an opinion, I am certain all critics will be delighted with the practices followed in this 3rd millennium edition of the most important book on technical analysis written in the 2nd millennium.

Integrity of the Original Text

By and large, the 5th edition has been the source of the authors' original text Amazingly, almost no stylistic or clarifying emendation has been necessary to that edition. This is a tribute to the clarity, style, and content of the original — one might almost say awesome, if the word were not in such currency on "Saturday Night Live" and the "Comedy Channel." Considering that it was written in the middle of the last century, and considering its complex subject, and considering that the markets were one tenth of their present complexity, awesome may be the appropriate word. No change or update has been necessary to the technical observations and analysis. They are as definitive today as they were in 1950.

While I have preserved the authors' original intent and text, I have taken the liberty of rearranging some of the chapters. Novices wishing to learn manual charting will find the appropriate chapters moved to appendices at the back of the book, along with the chapters on Composite Leverage and Sensitivity Indexes.

About Apparent Anachronisms

Critics with limited understanding of long-term trading success may think that discussions of "what happened in 1929" or "charts of ancient history from 1946" have no relevance to the markets of the present millennium. They will point out that AT&T no longer exists in that form, that the New Haven has long since ceased to exist as a stock, that many charts are records of long-buried skeletons. This neglects the value of the charts as metaphor. It ignores their representations of human behavior in the markets which will be replicated tomorrow in some stock named today.com or willtheynever-getit.com. Even more important, it ignores the significance of the past to trading in the present. I cite here material from Jack Schwager's illuminating book, The New Wizards of Wall Street. Schwager, in conversation with Al Weiss: "Precisely how far back did you go in your chart studies?" Answer: "It varied with the individual market and the available charts. In the case of the grain markets, I was able to go back as far as the 1840s." "Was it really necessary to go back that far?" Answer: "Absolutely. One of the keys in long-term chart analysis is realizing that markets behave differently in different economic cycles. Recognizing these repeating and shifting long-term patterns requires lots of history. Identifying where you are in an economic cycle — say, an inflationary phase vs. a deflationary phase — is critical to interpreting the chart patterns evolving at that time."

Identification of Original Manuscript and Revisions

True believers (and skeptics) will find here virtually all of the original material written by Edwards and Magee, including their charts and observations on them. Changes and comments introduced by editors since the 5th edition have been rearranged, and, when appropriate, have been identified as a revision by that editor.

Maintaining this policy, where updates to the present technological context and market reality were necessary, the present editor has clearly identified them as his own work by beginning such annotations with "EN" for Editor's Note. Figure insertions are identified as "x.1, x.2."

Absolutely Necessary Revisions

Not too long ago my youngest son, Pancho, overheard a conversation in which I referred to a slide rule. "What's a slide rule, Dad?" he asked. Well, needless to say the world has, in general, moved on from the time of Edwards and Magee when instead of calculators we had slide rules. Where time has made the text useless, moot, or irrelevant, that problem has unobtrusively been corrected.

Where the passage of time has made the text obsolete, I have either footnoted the anachronism and/or provided a chapter-ending annotation. These annotations are marked in the text with "EN" also. It is absolutely essential to read the annotations. Failure to do so will leave the reader stranded in the 20th century.

In some cases, these annotations amount to new chapters — for example, trading directly in the averages was difficult in Magee's time. Nowadays if there is not a proxy or option or index for some Index or Average or basket of stocks, there will be one in less than a New York minute (which, as everyone knows, has only 59 seconds). This new reality has resulted in major additions to this new edition. These are detailed in the Foreword. Major chapter additions necessary to deal with developments in technology and finance theory have been clearly identified as this editor's work by designating them as interpolations, viz., Chapter 18.1 (with the exception of Chapter 23, which I have surreptitiously inserted).

Absolutely Necessary Revisions Which Will Have Arisen in the Thirty Minutes Since This Editorial Note Was Written

In a number of instances, the book relayed information which, in those days of fixed commissions and monopolistic control by the existing exchanges, remained valid for long periods of time, for instance, brokerage commissions and trading costs. It is no longer possible to maintain such information in a printed book because of the rate of change in the financial industry. It must now be filed and updated in real time on the Internet. Consequently, readers will be able to refer to the Internet for this kind of ephemeral data. The general importance of the ephemera to the subject is always discussed.

About Gender

I quote here from my foreword to the 2nd edition of Magee's General Semantics of Wall Street, (charmingly renamed according to the current fashions, Winning the Mental Game on Wall Street):

> ### About Gender in Grammar
>
> Ich bin ein feminist. How could any modern man, son of a beloved woman, husband of an adored woman, and father of a joyful and delightful daughter not be? I am also a traditionalist and purist in matters of usage, grammar, and style. So where does that leave me and my cogenerationalists, enlightened literary (sigh) men (and women) with regards to the use of the masculine pronoun when used in the general sense to apply to the neuter situation?
>
> In Dictionary of Modern American Usage, Garner notes: 'English has a number of common-sex general words, such as person, anyone, everyone, and no one, but it has no common-sex singular personal pronouns. Instead we have he, she, and it. The traditional approach has been to use the masculine pronouns he and him to cover all persons, male and female alike... . The inadequacy of the English language in this respect becomes apparent in many sentences in which the generic masculine pronoun sits uneasily.'

Inadequate or not it is preferable to s/he/it and other bastardizations of the English language. (Is it not interesting that "bastard," in common usage, is never used of a woman, even when she is illegitimate?) As for the legitimacy of the usage of the masculine (actually neuter) pronoun in the generic, I prefer to lean on Fowler, who says, 'There are three makeshifts: first as anybody can see for himself or herself; second, as anybody can see for themselves; and third, as anybody can see for himself. No one who can help it chooses the first; it is correct, and is sometimes necessary, but it is so clumsy as to be ridiculous except when explicitness is urgent, and it usually sounds like a bit of pedantic humor. The second is the popular solution; it sets the literary man's (!) teeth on edge, and he exerts himself to give the same meaning in some entirely different way if he is not prepared to risk the third, which is here recommended. It involves the convention (statutory in the interpretation of documents) that where the matter of sex is not conspicuous or important the masculine form shall be allowed to represent a person instead of a man, or say a man (homo) instead of a man (vir).'

Politically correct fanatics may rail, but so are my teeth set on edge; thus, I have generally preserved the authors' usage of the masculine for the generic case. This grammatical scourge will pass and be forgotten, and weak-willed myn (by which I intend to indicate men and women) who pander to grammatical terrorists will in the future be seen to be stuck with malformed style and sentences no womyn will buy. What would Jane Austen have done, after all?

About Gender in Investors

As long as we are on the subject of gender, we might as well discuss, unscientifically, gender in investors. Within my wide experience as a trading advisor, teacher, and counselor, it strikes me that the women investors I have known have possessed certain innate advantages over the men. I know there are women gamblers. I have seen some. But I have never seen in the markets a woman plunger (shooter, pyramider, pie-eyed gambler). I have known many men who fit this description. I have also noted among my students and clients that as a group women seem to have more patience than men as a group. I refer specifically to the patience that a wise investor must have to allow the markets to do what they are going to do.

These are wholly personal observations. I have made no study of the question and can't speak to the entire class of women investors — and do not personally know Barbra Streisand (who I understand is a formidable investor, especially in IPOs). But just as I believe that the world would be better off if more women ran countries and were police officers, I expect that the world of finance will benefit from the steadily increasing number of women investors and managers.

A Crucial Question — Sensitivity Indexes and Betas

Long before the investment community had formalized the beta measure — the coefficient measuring a stock's volatility relative to the market — Magee and Edwards were computing a Sensitivity Index, which, for all practical purposes, was the same thing. Readers interested in this aspect of their work may find references in Resources which will enable them to obtain betas to plug into the Composite Leverage formula with which Magee intended to determine risk levels. The old appendix on Sensitivity Indexes has been consigned to Appendix A, along with the chapter on Composite Leverage, both originals of which have been emended to reflect current practices in finance theory and practice.

Betwixt and Between, 1/8 of a Dollar or 12.5 Cents

As this edition went to press the financial services industry was once again threatening to implement decimals in stock prices. Pricing in eighths has endured long past its time because it was in the self-interest of the financial industry — it allowed brokers and market makers to enforce larger bid–ask spreads and fatten their profit margins. The importance for this book, and for traders, is what will happen as full decimalization occurs. Often in these pages, Magee will recommend placing a stop 1/8 off the low or high, or placing progressive near stops in eighths. We do not yet know what the psychological interval will be in the new era. It may be 12.5 cents, or more psychologically, 10 cents, or for gaming purposes, 9 or 11 cents. This remains to be seen. As all the charts in this book are in the old notation that usage has been preserved in this edition.

The Editorial "I"

Readers will quickly note that the "Editorial We" of Edwards and Magee has been replaced by the first person voice — or, the "Editorial I" or perhaps the "Professorial I." Well, there were two of Edwards and Magee, and there is only one of me. So my text is immediately noticeable as mine, and the reader may discriminate quickly. As for the use of "I" as an expression of ego, the reader is assured that after 40 years in the market the editor has no ego left to promote. Perhaps the best way to put the editor's sense of importance in perspective is to quote Dr. Johnson's definition of lexicographer from his dictionary. Some people might have thought Johnson self-important in creating the first English dictionary. His definition of his trade put that right. "Lexicographer: a writer of dictionaries. A harmless drudge." An editor is something like the same.

As this book goes to the printer, the publisher, recognizing the importance of the work done on this edition, will credit the Editor as co-author of the 8th Edition. John Magee would be pleased. We had a cordial master–student relationship, and nothing pleases a Zen master more than to transfer the dharma to a passionate student.

Acknowledgments

In General:
John Magee, for his ever-patient tutoring.
Blair Hull, for teaching me the mercurial nature of options.
Bill Dreiss, for teaching me the nature of trading systems.
Art von Waldburg, respected colleague and discoverer of the Fractal Wave Algorithm.
Fischer Black, who should have lived to get the Nobel Prize.
Bill Scott, friend and fellow trader.

For specific support and assistance in the preparation of this 8th edition: Professor Henry Pruden, Golden Gate University, San Francisco, for invaluable support and advice.

Martin Pring; Lawrence Macmillan; Mitch Ackles, Omega Research Corporation; Carson Carlisle; Edward Dobson; David Robinson; Shereen Ash; Steven W. Poser; Lester Loops, late of Hull Trading Company; Tom Shanks, Turtle.

At St. Lucie Press, the dedication and support of the publisher, Drew Gierman, and Production Associate, Pat Roberson, have been invaluable, as has been the dedication of Gail Renard, the Production Editor.

And special acknowledgment to my Research Assistant, Don Carlos Bassetti y Doyle.

Special appreciation goes to makers of software packages used in the preparation of this and previous editions:

AIQ Systems
P.O. Box 7530
Incline Village, NV 89452
702-831-2999
www.AIQsystems.com

Metastock
Equis International, Inc.
3950 S. 700 East, Suite 100
Salt Lake City, UT 84107
www.equis.com

Tradestation
Omega Research
14257 SW 119th Avenue
Miami, FL 33186
305-485-7599
www.tradestation.com

In Memoriam

This book is a memorial for John Magee, who died on June 17, 1987. John Magee was considered a seminal pioneer in technical analysis, and his research with co-author, Robert D. Edwards, clarified and expanded the ideas of Charles Dow, who laid the foundation for technical analysis in 1884 by developing the "Averages," and Richard Schabacker, former editor of Forbes in the 1920s, who showed how the signals, which had been considered important when they appeared in the averages, were applicable to stocks themselves. The text, which summarized their findings in 1948, was, of course, *Technical Analysis of Stock Trends*, now considered the definitive work on pattern recognition analysis. Throughout his technical work, John Magee emphasized three principles: stock prices tend to move in trends; volume goes with the trend; and a trend, once established, tends to continue in force.

A large portion of *Technical Analysis of Stock Trends* is devoted to the patterns which tend to develop when a trend is being reversed: Head-and-Shoulders, Tops and Bottoms, "W" patterns, Triangles, Rectangles, etc. — common patterns to stock market technicians. Rounded Bottoms and Drooping Necklines are some of the more esoteric ones.

John urged investors to go with the trend, rather than trying to pick a bottom before it was completed, averaging down a declining market. Above all, and at all times, he refused to get involved in the game of forecasting where "the market" was headed, or where the Dow–Jones Industrial averages would be on December 31st of the coming year. Rather, he preached care in individual stock selection regardless of which way the market "appeared" to be headed.

To the random walker, who once confronted John with the statement that there was no predictable behavior on Wall Street, John's reply was classic. He said, "You fellows rely too heavily on your computers. The best computer ever designed is still the human brain. Theoreticians try to simulate stock market behavior, and, failing to do so with any degree of predictability, declare that a journey through the stock market is a random walk. Isn't it equally possible that the programs simply aren't sensitive enough or the computers strong enough to successfully simulate the thought process of the human brain?" Then John would walk over to his bin of charts, pull out a favorite, and show it to the random walker. There it was — spike up, heavy volume; consolidation, light volume; spike up again, heavy volume. A third time. A fourth time. A beautifully symmetrical chart, moving ahead in a well-defined trend channel, volume moving with price. "Do you really believe that these patterns are random?" John would ask, already knowing the answer.

We all have a favorite passage or quotation by our favorite author. My favorite quotation of John's appears in the short booklet he wrote especially for subscribers to his Technical Stock Advisory Service: "When you enter the stock market, you are going into a competitive field in which your evaluations and opinions will be matched against some of the sharpest and toughest minds in the business. You are in a highly specialized industry in which there are many different sectors, all of which are under intense study by men whose economic survival depends upon their best judgment. You will certainly be exposed to advice, suggestions, offers of help from all sides. Unless you are able to develop some market philosophy of your own, you will not be able to tell the good from the bad, the sound from the unsound."

I doubt if any man alive has helped more investors develop a sound philosophy of investing on Wall Street than John Magee.

Richard McDermott
President, John Magee, Inc.
September 1991

Preface to the Seventh Edition

More than 100 years ago, in Springfield, MA, there lived a man named Charles H. Dow. He was one of the editors of a great newspaper, The Springfield Republican. When he left Springfield, it was to establish another great newspaper, The Wall Street Journal.

Charles Dow also laid the foundation for a new approach to stock market problems.

In 1884, he made up an average of the daily closing prices of 11 important stocks, 9 of which were rails, and recorded the fluctuations of this average.

He believed that the judgment of the investing public, as reflected in the movements of stock prices, represented an evaluation of the future probabilities affecting the various industries. He saw in his average a tool for predicting business conditions many months ahead. This was true because those who bought and sold these stocks included people intimately acquainted with the industrial situation from every angle. Dow reasoned that the price of a security, as determined by a free competitive market, represented the composite knowledge and appraisal of everyone interested in that security — financiers, officers of the company, investors, employees, customers — everyone, in fact, who might be buying or selling stock.

Dow felt that this market evaluation was probably the shrewdest appraisal of conditions to come that could be contained, since it integrated all known facts, estimates, surmises, and the hopes and fears of all interested parties.

It was William Peter Hamilton who really put these ideas to work. In his book, The Stock Market Barometer, published in 1922, he laid the groundwork for the much-used and much-abused Dow Theory.

Unfortunately, a great many superficial students of the market never understood the original premise of the "barometer" and seized on the bare bones of the theory as a sort of magic touchstone to fame and easy fortune.

Others, discovering that the "barometer" was not perfect, set about devising corrections. They tinkered with the rules of classic Dow Theory, trying to find the wonderful formula that would avoid its periodic disappointments and failures.

Of course, what they forgot was that the Averages were only averages at best. There is nothing very wrong with the Dow Theory. What is wrong is the attempt to find a simple, universal formula — a set of measurements that will make a suit to fit every man, fat, thin, tall, or short.

During the 1920s and 1930s, Richard W. Schabacker reopened the subject of technical analysis in a somewhat new direction. Schabacker, who had been financial editor of Forbes Magazine, set out to find some new answers. He realized that whatever significant action appeared in the average must derive from similar action in some of the stocks making up the average.

In his books, Stock Market Theory and Practice, Technical Market Analysis, and Stock Market Profits, Schabacker showed how the "signals" that had been considered important by Dow theorists when they appeared in the Averages were also significant and had the same meanings when they turned up in the charts of individual stocks.

Others, too, had noted these technical patterns. But, it was Schabacker who collated, organized, and systematized the technical method. Not only that, he also discovered new technical indications in the charts of stocks; indications of a type that would ordinarily be absorbed or smothered in the averages, and, hence, not visible or useful to Dow theorists.

In the final years of his life, Richard Schabacker was joined by his brother-in-law, Robert D. Edwards, who completed Schabacker's last book and carried forward the research of technical analysis.

Edwards, in turn, was joined in this work in 1942 by John Magee. Magee, an alumnus of the Massachusetts Institute of Technology, was well oriented to the scientific and technical approach.

Edwards and Magee retraced the entire road, reexamining the Dow Theory and restudying the technical discoveries of Schabacker.

Basically, the original findings were still good. But with additional history and experience, it was possible to correct some details of earlier studies. Also, a number of new applications and methods were brought to light. The entire process of technical evaluation became more scientific.

It became possible to state more precisely the premises of technical analysis: that the market represents a most democratic and representative criterion of stock values; that the action of a stock in a free, competitive market reflects all that is known, believed, surmised, hoped, or feared about that stock; and, therefore, that it synthesizes the attitudes and opinions of all. That the price of a stock is the result of buying and selling forces and represents the "true value" at any given moment. That a Major Trend must be presumed to continue in effect until clear evidence of Reversal is shown. And, finally, that it is possible to form opinions having a reasonably high probability of confirmation from the market action of a stock as shown in daily, weekly, or monthly charts, or from other technical studies derived from the market activity of the security.

It is important to point out that the ultimate value of a security to the investor or trader is what he or she ultimately receives from it. That is to say, the price the investor gets when it is sold, or the market price obtainable for it at any particular time, adjusted for dividends or capital distribution in either case. If, for example, he or she has bought a stock at $25 a share, and it has paid $5 in dividends and is now bid at $35, he or she has realized an accrued benefit of $5 plus $10, or $15 in all. It is the combination of dividends and appreciation of capital that constitutes the total gain.

It seems futile to try to correlate or compare the market value of a stock with the "book value" or with the "value" figured on a basis of capitalized earnings or dividends, projected growth, etc. There are too many other factors that may also affect the value, and some of these cannot easily be expressed in simple ratios. For example, a struggle for control of a corporation can as surely increase the value of its securities in the market as a growth of earnings. Again, a company may lose money for years and pay no dividends, yet still be an excellent investment on the basis of its development of potential resources as perceived by those who are buying and selling its stock. For the market is not evaluating last year's accomplishments as such, it is weighing the prospects for the year to come.

Then, too, in a time of inflation, a majority of stocks may advance sharply in price. This may reflect a depreciation in the purchasing power of dollars more than improvement in business conditions — but it is important, nonetheless, in such a case to be "out of dollars" and "into" equities.

As a result of their research from 1942 to 1948, Edwards and Magee developed new technical methods. They put these methods to practical use in actual market operation. And, eventually, in 1948, these findings were published in their definitive book, Technical Analysis of Stock Trends.

This book, now in its seventh edition, has become the accepted authority in this field. It has been used as a textbook by various schools and colleges, and is the basic tool of many investors and traders.

In 1951, Edwards retired from his work as a stock analyst and John Magee continued the research, at first, independently, and then from January 1953 to March 1956 as Chief Technical Analyst with an investment counseling firm.

Meanwhile, beginning in 1950, Magee started on a new road, which, as it turned out, was destined to open up virgin fields of technical market research.

Using the methods of Dow, Hamilton, Schabacker, and Edwards as a base, he initiated a series of studies intended to discover new technical devices. These investigations were long and laborious, and, often, they were fruitless. One study required four months of work, involved hundreds of sheets of tabulations, many thousands of computations, and proved nothing.

But from this type of work, eventually in late 1951, there began to emerge some important new and useful concepts — new bricks to build into the structure of the technical method.

The new devices are not revolutionary. They do not vitiate the basic technical approach. Rather, they are evolutionary and add something to the valuable kit of tools already at hand. The new studies often make it possible to interpret and predict difficult situations sooner and more dependably than any other method previously used.

Mr. Magee has designated these newest technical devices the Delta Studies. They are basically an extension and refinement of the technical method. There is no magic in the Delta Studies. They do not provide infallible formulas for sure profits at all times in every transaction, but they have proved eminently successful over a period of years in practical use in actual market operations, as an auxiliary to the methods outlined in the book, Technical Analysis of Stock Trends.

Through his technical work, John Magee emphasized these three principles:

1. Stock prices tend to move in trends.
2. Volume goes with the trends.
3. A trend, once established, tends to continue in force.

A large portion of the book, Technical Analysis of Stock Trends, is devoted to the patterns that tend to develop when a trend is being reversed. Head-and-Shoulders, Tops and Bottoms, "W" Patterns, Triangles, Rectangles, etc., are common patterns to stock market technicians. Rounded Bottoms and Drooping Necklines are some of the more esoteric ones.

Magee urged investors to go with the trend, rather than trying to pick a Bottom before it was completed, or averaging down in a declining stock. Above all, and at all times, he refused to get involved in the game of forecasting where "the market" was headed, or where the DJIA would be on December 31st of the coming year. Rather, he preached care in individual stock selection regardless of which way the market "appeared" headed. Finally, his service recommended short positions as regularly as it did long positions, based simply on what the charts said.

Richard McDermott
Editor and Reviser
Technical Analysis of Stock Trends, Seventh Edition
January 1997

Preface to the Fifth Edition

During the 16 printings of the fourth edition of Technical Analysis of Stock Trends, very few changes have been made in the original text, mainly because the lucid presentation of market action by the late Robert D. Edwards covered so thoroughly the basic and typical market action of common stocks. There has seemed no reason, for example, to discard a chart picture illustrating some important technical phenomenon merely because it occurred several or many years ago.

Instead, over the various printings of the book, pages have been added showing similar examples, or in some cases entirely new types of market action taken from recent history; but these demonstrate mainly that the inherent nature of a competitive market does not change very much over the years, and that "the same old patterns" of human behavior continue to produce much the same types of market trends and fluctuations.

The principal change in this fifth edition, and it is a spectacular improvement, is that practically all of the chart examples drawn to the TEKNIPLAT scale have been redrawn and new plates of these have been substituted. In the course of this work, several minor errors of scaling, titling, etc., previously undiscovered, came to light and have been corrected.

The difficult work of revision was initiated in our charting room by two ambitious teenagers, Anne E. Mahoney and Joseph J. Spezeski, who took on the entire job of preparing the finished drawings and making necessary corrections. This enormous project was undertaken and carried through by these two young people spontaneously. In order to free them entirely from other distractions, their regular charting work was taken over for a period of months by the rest of the chartroom staff, so that a great deal of credit is due to the fine efforts of the entire chartroom group.

John Magee
December 3, 1966

Preface to the Fourth Edition

In the several years since publication of the first edition of this work, "the stock market goes right on repeating the same old movements in much the same old routine." Nearly all of the technical phenomena outlined in the first edition have appeared many times since then, and we see no reason to expect that these habits of stocks will change materially in the years ahead, barring revolutionary changes in the economy, such as the abolishment of the free market entirely.

Since the basic nature of the market has not changed appreciably, it has been unnecessary to make sweeping alterations in the text of Part One: Technical Theory. The previous edition has been very carefully restudied, and revisions have been made where they were called for to bring the material up to date. In Part Two: Trading Tactics, more extensive changes were needed, due to the more specific nature of the material and some differences in the present margin requirements, trading rules, etc. Also, there have been some improvements in the application of technical methods at the tactical level, and these have been incorporated in this section.

Somewhat less emphasis has been put on the use of stop-loss orders, since their need is not so great in the case of the experienced trader as it might be with the novice. The principle of always following the Major Trend has been modified to achieve better protection of capital through balance and diversification. In line with avoiding "all-out" situations, with their consequent dangers, the idea of using an Evaluative Index has been introduced, and this concept has modified somewhat the tactics of following the Major Trend. It also has a bearing on the Composite Leverage or determination of total risk.

Type for the entire book has been reset in this edition. The illustrative charts originally used have been, in the main, retained, since they demonstrate the various points very well, but a new chapter includes a number of additional charts taken from the market history of recent years, showing how the same phenomena continue to appear again and again.

The appendix on the Sensitivity Indexes has been completely recomputed, and extended to cover a broad list of the more important issues. The arduous labor of determining these index figures was undertaken by Frank J. Curto and Marcella P. Curto. Material help in proofreading and revision for this edition was given by Beverly Magee and Elinor T. Magee.

John Magee
January 1, 1957

Preface to the Second Edition

It is, needless to say, gratifying to the authors of this treatise to report that not only has a large first edition been exhausted (although it was originally assumed that it would suffice for many years), but also that the demand for copies has been increasing at a rather astonishing pace during the past 6 months without any "promotion" except word-of-mouth recommendation from one investor to another.

In preparing this new edition, a careful perusal of everything that was written in the previous printing, checked by the market events of the past 24 months and compared with all of the additional chart data accumulated during that period, resulted in the not unexpected, but nevertheless mildly surprising conclusion that nothing whatever of real consequence needed to be changed or amplified. Hence, only minor revisions of an editorial nature have been made.

It would have been interesting to augment our already copious illustrations with a number of charts from current months of market action, but costs of engraving and printing have risen to such a distressingly high level that any additions of that sort would, it was found, be prohibitively expensive. Aside from their novelty, they would add nothing to the book; they would only be substituted for other charts of precisely the same nature and significance, and fully as pertinent to present day conditions.

The stock market, as I wrote in the original Foreword, "goes right on repeating the same old movements in much the same old routine. The importance of a knowledge of these phenomena to the trader and investor has been in no whit diminished." We see the same forecasting patterns developing on the charts today that we have seen over and over again for the past twenty years. Neither the mechanics nor the "human element" of the stock market has changed, and there is no reason to think that they will.

Robert D. Edwards
May 1, 1951

Foreword

This book has been written for the layman rather than for the Wall Street professional. But, it assumes that the reader is already possessed of at least an elementary knowledge of the nature of stocks and bonds, that he has had some dealings with a broker and some familiarity with the financial pages of his newspapers. Hence, no attempt is made herein to define common stock market terms and procedures. Every effort, however, has been exerted to explain, in full, the theories and the terminology of our specific subject, technical market analysis.

Part One is based, in large part, on the pioneer researches and writings of the late Richard W. Schabacker. Students of his Technical Analysis and Stock Market Profits (the latest revision of which is now out of print was made in 1937 by the present writer and Albert L. Kimball) will find in the pages of this section much that is familiar and, except for the illustrations, only a little that is really novel. It has been a matter of surprise, in fact, to the authors and other students of market technics that all the new controls and regulations of the past several years, the new taxes which have placed a heavy handicap on successful investors, the greatly augmented and improved facilities for acquiring dependable information on securities, even the quite radical changes in certain portions of our basic economy, have not much altered the "pattern" of the stock market.

Certain of the evidences of pool manipulation which used to appear on the charts are now seldom seen. A few of the price formations which formerly were quite common, now appear rarely or may have lost much of their practical utility for the trader; they have been omitted from this text. Others have altered their habits slightly, or their consequences to a degree (but not their fundamental nature), which has, of course, been noted herein. The distressing thinness of the market at times — one of the undoubted effects of regulation — has resulted in a few more "false moves," more spells of uninteresting (and unprofitable) inactivity. But, in the main, the market goes right on repeating the same old movements in much the same old routine. The importance of a knowledge of these phenomena to the trader and investor has been in no whit diminished.

Part Two, which has to do with the practical application of these market patterns and phenomena, with the tactics of trading, is all new. For more than 15 years (his total market experience extends back nearly 30 years), John Magee has invested and traded exclusively via the technical theory, kept thousands of charts, made hundreds of actual trades, tested all sorts of applications, audited and analyzed methods, tactics, and results from every conceivable angle, depended on his profits for his living. His contribution is that of one who has tried and knows.

It may well be added here — and will be often repeated in the following pages — that the technical guides to trading in stocks are by no means infallible. The more experience one gains in their use, the more alive one becomes to their pitfalls and their failures. There is no such thing as a sure-fire method of "beating the market"; the authors have no hesitancy in saying that there never will be. Nevertheless, a knowledge and judicious application of the principles of technical analysis does pay dividends — is more profitable (and far safer) for the average investor than any other of the presently recognized and established approaches to the problems of buying and selling securities.

Robert D. Edwards
July 1948

Contents

part one

Technical Theory

chapter one

The Technical Approach to Trading and Investing

Few human activities have been so exhaustively studied during the past century, from so many angles and by so many different sorts of people, as has the buying and selling of corporate securities. The rewards which the stock market holds out to those who read it right are enormous; the penalties it exacts from careless, dozing, or "unlucky" investors are calamitous. No wonder it has attracted some of the world's most astute accountants, analysts, and researchers, along with a motley crew of eccentrics, mystics, and "hunch players," and a multitude of just ordinary hopeful citizens.

Able brains have sought, and continue constantly to seek, for safe and sure methods of appraising the state and trend of the market, of discovering the right stock to buy and the right time to buy it. This intensive research has not been fruitless — far from it. There are a great many successful investors and speculators (using the word in its true sense, which is without opprobrium) who, by one road or another, have acquired the necessary insight into the forces with which they deal and the judgment, the forethought, and the all important self-discipline to deal with them profitably.

In the course of years of stock market study, two quite distinct schools of thought have arisen, two radically different methods of arriving at the answers to the trader's problem of *what* and *when*. In the parlance of "the Street," one of these is commonly referred to as the *fundamental* or statistical, and the other as the *technical*. (In recent years a third approach, the cyclical, has made rapid progress and, although still beset by a "lunatic fringe," it promises to contribute a great deal to our understanding of economic trends.)

The stock market fundamentalist depends on statistics. He examines the auditors' reports, the profit-and-loss statements, the quarterly balance sheets, the dividend records, and policies of the companies whose shares he has under observation. He analyzes sales data, managerial ability, plant capacity, the competition. He turns to bank and treasury reports, production indexes, price statistics, and crop forecasts to gauge the state of business in general, and reads the daily news carefully to arrive at an estimate of future business conditions. Taking all these into account, he evaluates his stock; if it is selling currently below his appraisal, he regards it as a buy. *(EN9: And, no surprise, the buyer's name is Warren Buffet, and he buys the company, not the stock, for while this is an excellent way to buy companies it is not a very good way to buy stocks.) EN: Read Robert Prechter's summation of the fundamental methodology as an amusing endnote at the end of this chapter.*

As a matter of fact, aside from the greenest of newcomers when they first tackle the investment problem, and to whom, in their inexperience, any other point of view is not only irrational but incomprehensible, your pure fundamentalist is a very rare bird. Even those market authorities who pretend to scorn charts and "chartists" utterly are not oblivious to the "action" chronicled by the ticker tape, nor do they conceal their respect for the Dow Theory which, whether they realize it or not, is, in its very essence, purely technical.

Definition of Technical Analysis

The term "technical," in its application to the stock market, has come to have a very special meaning, quite different from its ordinary dictionary definition. It refers to *the study of the action of the market itself* as opposed to the study of the goods in which the market deals. *Technical Analysis* is the science of recording, usually in graphic form, the actual history of trading (price changes, volume of transactions, etc.) in a certain stock or in "the Averages" and then deducing from that pictured history the probable future trend. *EN: With the advent of the computer, many schools of technical analysis have arisen. Number-driven technical analysis, e.g., moving average studies oscillators, etc., attempts to completely objectify the analysis of the markets. The work of Edwards and Magee is the embodiment and definition of "classical technical analysis." See Appendix C.*

The technical student argues thus: it is futile to assign an intrinsic value to a stock certificate. One share of United States Steel, for example, was worth $261 in the early fall of 1929, but you could buy it for only $22 in June of 1932! By March 1937, it was selling for $126 and just 1 year later for $38. In May of 1946, it had climbed back up to $97, and 10 months later, in 1947, had dropped below $70, although the company's earnings on this last date were reputed to be nearing an all-time high and interest rates in general were still near an all-time low. The book value of this share of U.S. Steel, according to the corporation's balance sheet, was about $204 in 1929 (end of the year); $187 in 1932; $151 in 1937; $117 in 1938, and $142 in 1946. This sort of thing, this wide divergence between presumed value and actual price, is not the exception; it is the rule. It is going on all the time. The fact is that the real value of a share of U.S. Steel common is determined at any given time solely, definitely, and inexorably by supply and demand, which are accurately reflected in the transactions consummated on the floor of the New York Stock Exchange.

Of course, the statistics which the fundamentalists study play a part in the supply–demand equation — that is freely admitted. But there are many other factors affecting it. The market price reflects not only the differing value opinions of many orthodox security appraisers, but also all the hopes and fears and guesses and moods, rational and irrational, of hundreds of potential buyers and sellers, as well as their needs and their resources — in total, factors which defy analysis and for which no statistics are obtainable,

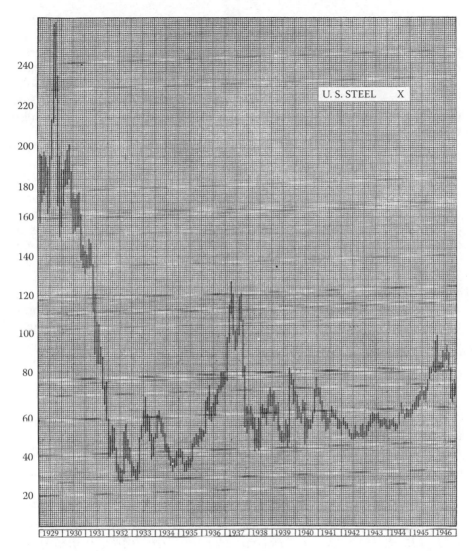

FIGURE 1. Monthly price ranges of U.S. Steel common from January 1929 to December 1946. Compare the great swings in the market price for this stock — from 1929 (extreme high, 261¾) to 1932 (extreme low, 21¼), from 1932 to 1937, from 1937 to 1938, from 1942 to 1946 — with its book values for those years as cited on the previous page.

but which are nevertheless all synthesized, weighed, and finally expressed in the one precise figure at which a buyer and a seller get together and make a deal (through their agents, their respective stock brokers). This is the only figure that counts.

Moreover, the technician claims, with complete justification, that the bulk of the statistics which the fundamentalists study are past history, already out of date and sterile, because the market is not interested in the past or even in the present! It is constantly looking ahead, attempting to discount future developments, weighing and balancing all the estimates and guesses of hundreds of investors who look into the future from different points of view and through glasses of many different hues. In brief, the going price, as established by the market itself, comprehends all the fundamental information which the statistical analyst can hope to learn (plus some that is perhaps secret from him, known only to a few insiders) and much else besides of equal or even greater importance.

All of which, admitting its truth, would be of little significance were it not for the fact, which no one of experience doubts, that prices move in trends and trends tend to continue until something happens to change the supply–demand balance. Such changes are usually detectable in the action of the market itself. Certain patterns or formations, levels or areas, appear on the charts which have a meaning, and can be interpreted in terms of probable future trend development. They are not infallible, it must be noted, but the odds are definitely in their favor. Time after time, as experience has amply proved, they are far more prescient than the best-informed and most shrewd of statisticians.

The technical analyst may go even further in his claims. He may offer to interpret the chart of a stock whose name he does not know, so long as the record of trading is accurate and covers a long enough term to enable him to study its market background and habits. He may suggest that he could trade with profit in a stock knowing only its ticker symbol, completely ignorant of the company, the industry, what it manufactures or sells, or how it is capitalized. Needless to say, such practice is not recommended, but if your market technician is really experienced at his business, he could, in theory, do exactly what he claims.

Should the reader, at this point, find the technical approach to trading or investing, as explained in the foregoing, completely abhorrent, perhaps he had better close the book now. For it is primarily the technical approach, the science of technical analysis, with which the remainder of the book deals.

EN: The Elliott Wave Theory: Perspective and Comments*

This week we had the pleasure of attending the December meeting of the Market Technicians Association of New York.

Long-term subscribers will remember the MTANY as the organization which honored John Magee with its "Man of the Year" award in 1978. The speaker was Robert Prechter, publisher of "The Elliott Wave Theorist," an investment advisory which bases its forecasts on interpretations of R.N. Elliott's work on the stock market....

Of primary interest to SAS subscribers are Prechter's comments on technical analysis itself. The Elliott Wave Theory, it must be remembered, is really no more than a "catalog" of stock market price movements, laid one on top of the other, so

* From the John Magee Market Letters, December 15, 1984.

to speak, until a grand, underlying, and enduring pattern is observed; in short, pure technical analysis. Among Prechter's definitions and observations regarding fundamental analysis are the following:

1. *"First let's define 'technical' versus 'fundamental' data…technical data is that which is generated by the action of the market under study."*
2. *"The main problem with fundamental analysis is that its indicators are removed from the market itself. The analyst assumes causality between external events and market movements, a concept which is almost certainly false. But, just as important, and less recognized, is that fundamental analysis almost always requires a forecast of the fundamental data itself before conclusions about the market are drawn. The analyst is then forced to take a second step in coming to a conclusion about how those forecasted events will affect the markets! Technicians only have one step to take, which gives them an edge right off the bat. Their main advantage is that they don't have to forecast their indicators."*
3. *"What's worse, even the fundamentalists' second step is probably a process built on quicksand…. The most common application of fundamental analysis is estimating companies' earnings for both the current year and next year, and recommending stocks on that basis…. And the record on that basis alone is very poor, as Barron's pointed out in a June 4 article, which showed that earnings estimates averaged 18% error in the 30 DJIA stocks for any year already completed and 54% error for the year ahead. The weakest link, however, is the assumption that correct earnings estimates are a basis for choosing stock market winners. According to a table in the same Barron's article, a purchase of the 10 DJIA stocks with the best earnings estimates would have produced a 10-year cumulative gain of 40.5%, while choosing the 10 DJIA with the worst earnings estimates would have produced a whopping 142.5% gain."*

We enjoyed Prechter's polished exposition of a technical approach different from our own. As for his observations about fundamental analysis, we simply couldn't agree more.

chapter two

Charts

Charts are the working tools of the technical analyst. They have been developed in a multitude of forms and styles to represent graphically almost anything and everything that takes place in the market, or to plot an "index" derived therefrom. They may be monthly charts on which an entire month's trading record is condensed into a single entry, or weekly, daily, hourly, transaction, "point-and-figure," candlestick, etc. They may be constructed on arithmetic, logarithmic, or square-root scale, or projected as "oscillators." They may delineate moving averages, proportion of trading volume to price movement, average price of "most active" issues, odd-lot transactions, the short interest, and an infinitude of other relations, ratios, and indexes — all technical in the sense that they are derived, directly or indirectly, from what has actually been transacted on the exchanges.

With most of these, fortunately, we shall not need to concern ourselves at all; they are of interest only to the full-time economic analyst. Many of them have derived from a completely futile (so far, at least) endeavor to discover some one "mechanical" index or combination of indexes which will always, automatically, without ever failing or going wrong, give warning of a change in trend; such, in our experience, are often confusing and sometimes downright deceptive at a most critical juncture. This book, however, is designed for the layman, the business or professional man who cannot spend all his hours on his investing or trading operations, but to whom these operations are, nevertheless, of sufficient importance or interest to warrant his devoting at least a few minutes a day to their study and management. *(EN9: In retropsect an underestimation of the importance of the work. In the 21st century the best professionals are acutely aware of the importance of trend analysis and use this work as their text book.)* The theories and methods outlined herein will require only the simplest form of stock chart — a record of the price range (high and low), closing price, and volume of shares traded each day. These daily graphs will be supplemented, for certain purposes which will be discussed farther on, by weekly or monthly charts, which for most stocks can be purchased ready-made and which are easily generated by almost all commercially available investment software.

Nearly all the illustrations throughout the following pages are examples of such daily charts. They are easy to make and maintain manually, requiring only a supply of graph or cross-section paper (almost any kind can serve), a daily newspaper which gives full and accurate reports on stock exchange dealings, a sharp pencil, and a few minutes of time. *EN: Alternatively, numerous data services are available for use with computer software packages, not to mention Internet sites (which are mentioned in Resources). The use of this technology eliminates the burden of manual chart keeping altogether. If there is a drawback to this technology it might be in the loss of the "feel" the investor gets through manual charting.*

It is customary in preparing ordinary daily stock charts to let the horizontal axis represent time, with the vertical cross-lines (or as some prefer, the spaces between them) from left to right thus standing for successive days. The vertical scale is used for prices, with each horizontal cross-line then representing a specific price level. Space is usually provided at the bottom of the sheet to plot volume, i.e., the number of shares which change hands each day. The newspapers publishing complete stock market reports give the day's turnover or volume (exclusive of odd-lot transactions which may for our present purpose be disregarded), the highest and lowest price at which each stock sold during the day, the closing price (which is the price at which the last sale effected during the day was made), and usually the opening or first sale price. On our charts, the daily price range is plotted by drawing a vertical line connecting the points representing the high and the low. Then a short horizontal "tick" is added, either crossing the vertical range line or extending out to the right from it, at the level of the closing price. Sometimes all transactions in a stock during a day take place at one and the same price; the high, low, and close are thus all on a level and the only mark on our chart will then be the horizontal dash representing the closing figure. Volume is depicted by drawing a vertical line up from the base line of the chart.

The opening price need not be recorded.* Experience has shown that it seldom, if ever, has any significance in estimating future developments, which is all that ordinarily should interest us. The closing price is important, however. It is, in fact, the only price which many casual readers of the financial pages ever look at. It represents the final evaluation of the stock made by the market during the day. It may, of course, be registered in the first hour of trading, provided no other sales are subsequently effected, but, it becomes, nevertheless, the figure upon which a majority of prospective traders base their plans for the following day. Hence, its technical significance, which will appear in various contexts in later chapters.

Different Types of Scales

Many specific suggestions as to the details of charting are deferred for discussion in the second section of this book, but there is one chart feature which may well be considered here. Until recent years, nearly all stock price

---

* *EN: Edwards considered the opening price unimportant. Some technicians, myself included, do observe it to be of use. And in some charting systems it is indispensable, for example, candlestick charting where it is accorded enormous importance.*

charts were kept on the common form of graph paper ruled to what is known as plain or arithmetic scale. But more and more chartists have now come to use what is known as semilogarithmic paper, or sometimes as ratio or percentage paper. Our own experience indicates that the semilogarithmic scale has definite advantages in this work; most of the charts reproduced in this book employ it. The two types of scale may be distinguished at a glance by the fact that on arithmetic paper, equal distances on the vertical scale (i.e., between horizontal lines) represent equal amounts in dollars, whereas on the semilogarithmic paper, they represent equal percentage changes. Thus, on arithmetic paper the distance between 10 and 20 on the vertical scale is exactly the same as that from 20 to 30 and from 30 to 40. On the logarithmic scale the difference from 10 to 20, representing an increase of 100%, is the same as that from 20 to 40 or from 40 to 80, in each case representing another 100% increase.

Percentage relations, it goes without saying, are important in trading in securities. The semilogarithmic scale permits direct comparison of high- and low-priced stocks and makes it easier to choose the one offering the greater (percentage) profit on the funds to be invested. It facilitates the placing of stop-loss orders. Area patterns appear much the same on either type of paper but certain trendlines develop more advantageously on the ratio scale. Almost anyone can quickly become accustomed to making entries on semilogarithmic paper. We recommend its use. However, its advantages are not so great as to require one to change, one who, because of long familiarity and practice, prefers an arithmetic sheet. Such percentage calculations, as may seem to be required, can, after all, be made on another sheet or in the head and the results then entered on the arithmetic chart if a record is desired.

Several firms specializing in the manufacture of graph paper and other engineers' and architects' supplies now offer sheets specifically designed for stock charting, on which heavier lines to define the business week mark each sixth day on the time scale, and the price scale is subdivided into eighths to represent the standard fractions of the dollar in which stocks are traded on all American exchanges. *(EN9: Eighths went the way of the New Haven and now decimals reign.)* These sheets are available in various sizes and with either arithmetic or logarithmic price and volume scales. *EN: This paper of course is only of interest to the manual chartist, as modern software, as detailed in Appendix D on Resources, enables the computer chartist to easily switch between price scales and methods of charting. References to such paper are also found there.*

On weekly charts, each vertical line represents a week's trading. The price range for the week is plotted thereon and usually the total volume, but the closing price may or may not be omitted. The range extends, of course, from the highest price at which the stock sold on any day during the week to the lowest price at which it sold on any day; these two extremes might, and sometimes do, occur on the same day, but the weekly chart makes no distinction as to day. Monthly charts are prepared in the same way but do not, as a rule, record volume. These two — often referred to as long-term or major charts — are used chiefly for determining important Support and

Resistance Levels and marking long-term trends. Weekly charts — if the reader prefers to keep his own — can be posted easily from the Sunday morning editions of those daily newspapers (e.g., *The New York Times* or *Barron's Business and Financial Weekly*) that publish a summary of the previous week's transactions.

In concluding this chapter on the construction of the charts that we shall study in succeeding chapters, it can well be said that there is no special virtue, certainly no magic, in the chart itself. It is simply a pictorial record of the trading history of the stock or stocks in which we may be interested. To the man possessed of a photographic memory, no chart work is necessary; his mind records all the necessary data — he carries his charts in his head. Many of the expert "tape-readers" who have no use for charts are gifted with that rare memory talent which renders reference to graphic records unnecessary. But most of us are not so blessed; to use the chart is necessary and useful because it lends itself conveniently to the type of analysis which indicates future probabilities.

There is a saying on Wall Street to the effect that "there is nothing wrong with charts — the trouble is with the chartists," which is simply another way of expressing the truth that it is not the chart itself but its interpretation that is important. Chart analysis is certainly neither easy nor foolproof. Yet, it is not at all uncommon for some casual investor who has no idea whatever of market technics to pick up a chart by chance and see in it something which he had not hitherto suspected, something perhaps which saves him from making an unfavorable commitment.

If you have never used stock charts, never paid much attention to them, you may be surprised at some of the significant things you will quickly detect as soon as you begin to study them seriously.

EN9: Surprise and astonishment are the words to describe the reactions of even professionals when they are fully exposed to a coherent presentation of the methods of Edwards and Magee. I have often commented that no understanding of other (non-chart) methods of technical analysis is possible without a firm grasp of the concepts and principles of this book.

Some other comments are worth noting relevant to Edwards' discussion above. For manual charting semi-log remains the superior scale. Given the ease of changing scale and time frames on Internet sites (e.g., prophet.net and stockcharts.com) and in the stand alone software one may switch from a close up of a month to a long range perspective of years. In this process it is important to maintain perspective. Multiyear log charts of large ranges lose graphic importance at the top as chart intervals shrink. This distortion must be countered by breaking the time frame into smaller increments. So instead of 5 years of a chart which spans a range of 10 to 200 we look at five charts of a year each as well as the 5-year chart.

chapter three

The Dow Theory

The Dow Theory is the granddaddy of all technical market studies. Although it is frequently criticized for being "too late," and occasionally derided (particularly in the early stages of a Bear Market) by those who rebel at accepting its verdicts, it is known by name to nearly everyone who has had any association with the stock market, and respected by most. Many who heed it in greater or lesser degree in determining their investment policies never realize that it is purely and simply "technical." It is built upon and concerned with nothing but the action of the stock market itself (as expressed in certain "averages"), deriving nothing from the business statistics on which the fundamentalists depend.

There is much in the writings of its original promulgator, Charles H. Dow, to suggest that he did not think of his "theory" as a device for forecasting the stock market, or even as a guide for investors, but rather as a barometer of general business trends. Dow founded the Dow–Jones Financial News Service and is credited with the invention of stock market averages. The basic principles of the theory, which was later named after him, were outlined by him in editorials he wrote for *The Wall Street Journal*. Upon his death in 1902 his successor, as editor of the *Journal*, William P. Hamilton, took up Dow's principles and, in the course of 27 years of writing on the stock market, organized them and formulated them into the Dow Theory as we know it today.

Before we proceed to an explanation of the theory itself, it will be necessary to examine the stock *averages* which it employs. Long before the time of Dow, the fact was familiar to bankers and businessmen that the securities of most established companies tended to go up or down in price together. Exceptions — stocks that moved against the general financial tide — were rare, nor did they as a rule persevere in that contrary course for more than a few days or weeks at a time. It is true that when a boom was on, the prices of some issues rose faster and farther than others, and when the trend was toward depression, some stocks declined rapidly while others would put up considerable resistance to the forces that were dragging the market down, but the fact remained that most securities tended to swing together. (They still do, needless to say, and always will.)

This fact, as we have said, has long been commonly known and accepted — so completely taken for granted that its importance is usually overlooked. For it is important — tremendously important from many angles in addition to those which come within the province of this volume. One of the best of all reasons for a student of market technics to start with the Dow Theory is because that theory stresses the *general market trend*.

Charles Dow is believed to have been the first to make a thorough effort to express the general trend (or, more correctly, level) of the securities market in terms of the *average price* of a selected few representative stocks. As finally set up in January of 1897, in the form which has continued to date, and used by Dow in his studies of market trends, there were two Dow–Jones Averages. One was composed of the stocks of 20 railroad companies only, for the railroads were the dominant corporate enterprises of his day. The other, called the Industrial Average, represented all other types of business, and was made up, at first, of only 12 issues. This number was increased to 20 in 1916 and to 30 on October 1, 1928.

The Dow Averages

The stocks included in these two Averages have been changed from time to time in order to keep the lists up to date and as nearly representative as possible of their respective groups. Only General Electric, of the present 30 industrial stocks, was included in the original Industrial Average, and that was dropped at one time (in 1898) and subsequently reinserted. In 1929, all stocks of public utility companies were dropped from the Industrial Average and a new Utility Average of 20 issues was set up; in 1938 its number was reduced to 15. The 20 rail, 30 industrial, and 15 utility stocks are now averaged together to make what is known as the Dow–Jones Stock Composite. The history of these Averages, the various adjustments that have been made in them and their method of computation, is an interesting story in itself which the reader may want to look up elsewhere. *EN: Cf. Resources for references. Note also that there is now a proliferation of Dow–Jones Averages.* For our present purpose, it remains only to add that the Dow Theory pays no attention to the Utility or Composite Averages; its interpretations are based on the Rail and Industrial Averages only. *EN: "Rails" now known as "Transportation."*

In recent years, the values of the Dow–Jones Averages have been computed for the end of each hour of trading as well as the end of the day. *EN: Now computed in real time and available over the Internet. These hourly figures are published in* The Wall Street Journal *as well as on all market tickers. In fact presently the Averages are computed in real time, a necessity for options and futures trading which takes place based on them.* The Wall Street Journal also prints in each issue a summary of the important highs and lows of each average by date for the preceding two or three years. Their daily closing prices are reported in many other metropolitan daily newspapers.

Basic Tenets

To get back to the Dow Theory itself here are its basic tenets:

1. **The Averages Discount Everything (except "Acts of God")** — Be-
    cause they reflect the combined market activities of thousands of
    investors, including those possessed of the greatest foresight and the
    best information on trends and events, the Averages in their
    day-to-day fluctuations discount everything known, everything fore-
    seeable, and every condition which can affect the supply of or the
    demand for corporate securities. Even unpredictable natural calam-
    ities, when they happen, are quickly appraised and their possible
    effects discounted.

2. **The Three Trends** — The "market," meaning the price of stocks in
    general, swings in trends, of which the most important are its *Major*
    or *Primary* Trends. These are the extensive up or down movements
    which usually last for a year or more and result in general appreci-
    ation or depreciation in value of more than 20%. Movements in the
    direction of the Primary Trend are interrupted at intervals by *Second-
    ary* Swings in the opposite direction — reactions or "corrections" that
    occur when the Primary Move has temporarily "gotten ahead of
    itself." (Both Secondaries and the intervening segments of the Pri-
    mary Trend are frequently lumped together as Intermediate Move-
    ments — a term which we shall find useful in subsequent discus-
    sions.) Finally, the Secondary Trends are composed of *Minor* Trends
    or day-to-day fluctuations which are unimportant to Dow Theory.

3. **The Primary Trends** — These, as aforesaid, are the broad, overall,
    up and down movements which usually (but not invariably) last for
    more than a year and may run for several years. So long as each
    successive rally (price advance) reaches a higher level than the one
    before it, and each Secondary Reaction stops (i.e., the price trend
    reverses from down to up) at a higher level than the previous reac-
    tion, the Primary Trend is *Up*. This is called a *Bull Market*. Conversely,
    when each Intermediate Decline carries prices to successively lower
    levels and each intervening rally fails to bring them back up to the
    top level of the preceding rally, the Primary Trend is *Down* and that
    is called a *Bear Market*. (The terms *Bull* and *Bear* are frequently used
    loosely with reference, respectively, to any sort of up or down move-
    ments, but we shall use them in this book only in connection with
    the Major or Primary Movements of the market in the Dow sense.)
    Ordinarily — theoretically, at least — the Primary is the only one of
    the three trends with which the true long-term investor is concerned.
    His aim is to buy stocks as early as possible in a Bull Market — just
    as soon as he can be sure that one has started — and then hold them
    until (and only until) it becomes evident that it has ended and a Bear

Market has started. He knows that he can safely disregard all the intervening Secondary Reactions and Minor Fluctuations. The trader, however, may well concern himself also with the Secondary Swings, and it will appear later on in this book that he can do so with profit.

4. **The Secondary Trends** — These are the important reactions that interrupt the progress of prices in the Primary Direction. They are the Intermediate Declines or "corrections" which occur during Bull Markets, the Intermediate Rallies or "recoveries" which occur in Bear Markets. Normally, they last for 3 weeks to many months, and rarely longer. Normally, they retrace from one third to two thirds of the gain (or loss, as the case may be) in prices registered in the preceding swing in the Primary Direction. Thus, in a Bull Market, prices in terms of the Industrial Average might rise steadily, or with only brief and minor interruptions, for a total gain of 30 (or 300) points before a Secondary Correction occurred. That correction might then be expected to produce a decline of not less than 10 points and not more than 20 points before a new Intermediate Advance in the Primary Bull Trend developed.

Note, however, that the one third/two thirds rule is not an unbreakable law; it is simply a statement of probabilities. Most Secondaries are confined within these limits; many of them stop very close to the halfway mark, retracing 50% of the preceding Primary Swing. They seldom run less than one third, but some of them cancel nearly all of it.

Thus we have two criteria by which to recognize a Secondary Trend. Any price movement contrary in direction to the Primary Trend that lasts for at least 3 weeks and retraces at least one third of the preceding net move in the Primary Direction (from the end of the preceding Secondary to the beginning of this one, disregarding Minor Fluctuations) is labeled as of Intermediate Rank, i.e., a true Secondary. Despite these criteria, however, the Secondary Trend is often confusing; its recognition, its correct appraisal at the time it develops and while it is in process, poses the Dow theorist's most difficult problem. We shall have more to say about this later.

5. **The Minor Trends** — These are the brief (rarely as long as 3 weeks — usually less than 6 days) fluctuations which are, so far as the Dow Theory is concerned, meaningless in themselves, but which, *in toto*, make up the Intermediate Trends. Usually, but not always, an Intermediate Swing, whether a Secondary or the segment of a Primary between successive Secondaries, is made up of a series of three or more distinguishable Minor Waves. Inferences drawn from these day- to-day fluctuations are quite apt to be misleading. The Minor Trend is the only one of the three trends which can be "manipulated" (although it is, in fact, doubtful if under present conditions even that can be purposely manipulated to any important extent). Primary and

Secondary Trends cannot be manipulated; it would strain the resources of the U.S. Treasury to do so.

Right here, before we go on to state a sixth Dow tenet, we may well take time out for a few minutes to clarify the concept of the three trends by drawing an analogy between the movements of the stock market and the movements of the sea. The Major (Primary) Trends in stock prices are like the tides. We can compare a Bull Market to an incoming or flood tide which carries the water farther and farther up the beach until finally it reaches high-water mark and begins to turn. Then follows the receding or ebb tide, comparable to a Bear Market. But all the time, during both ebb and flow of the tide, the waves are rolling in, breaking on the beach, and then receding. While the tide is rising, each succeeding wave pushes a little farther up onto the shore and, as it recedes, does not carry the water quite so far back as did its predecessor. During the tidal ebb, each advancing wave falls a little short of the mark set by the one before it, and each receding wave uncovers a little more of the beach. These waves are the Intermediate Trends, Primary or Secondary, depending on whether their movement is with or against the direction of the tide. Meanwhile, the surface of the water is constantly agitated by wavelets, ripples, and "cat's-paws" moving with or against or across the trend of the waves — these are analogous to the market's Minor Trends, its unimportant day-to-day fluctuations. The tide, the wave, and the ripple represent, respectively, the Primary or Major, the Secondary or Intermediate, and the Minor Trends of the market.

Tide, Wave, and Ripple

A shore dweller who had no tide table might set about determining the direction of the tide by driving a stake in the beach at the highest point reached by an incoming wave. Then if the next wave pushed the water up beyond his stake he would know the tide was rising. If he shifted his stake with the peak mark of each wave, a time would come when one wave would stop and start to recede short of his previous mark; then he would know that the tide had turned, had started to ebb. That, in effect (and much simplified), is what the Dow theorist does in defining the trend of the stock market.

The comparison with tide, wave, and ripple has been used since the earliest days of the Dow Theory. It is even possible that the movements of the sea may have suggested the elements of the theory to Dow. But the analogy cannot be pushed too far. The tides and waves of the stock market are nothing like as regular as those of the ocean. Tables can be prepared years in advance to predict accurately the time of every ebb and flow of the waters, but no timetables are provided by the Dow Theory for the stock market. We may return to some points of this comparison later, but we must proceed now to take up the remaining tenets and rules of the Theory.

Major Trend Phases

6. **The Bull Market** — Primary Uptrends are usually (but not invariably) divisible into three phases. The first is the phase of *accumulation* during which farsighted investors, sensing that business, although now depressed, is due to turn up, are willing to pick up all the shares offered by discouraged and distressed sellers, and to raise their bids gradually as such selling diminishes in volume. Financial reports are still bad — in fact, often at their worst — during this phase. The "public" is completely disgusted with the stock market — out of it entirely. Activity is only moderate but beginning to increase on the rallies (Minor Advances).

    The second phase is one of fairly steady advance and increasing activity as the improved tone of business and a rising trend in corporate earnings begin to attract attention. It is during this phase that the "technical" trader normally is able to reap his best harvest of profits.

    Finally, comes the third phase when the market boils with activity as the "public" flocks to the boardrooms. All the financial news is good, price advances are spectacular and frequently "make the front page" of the daily papers, and new issues are brought out in increasing numbers. It is during this phase that one of your friends will call up and blithely remark, "Say, I see the market is going up. What's a good buy?" — all oblivious to the fact that it has been going up for perhaps two years, has already gone up a long ways, and is now reaching the stage where it might be more appropriate to ask, "What's a good thing to sell?" In the last stage of this phase, with speculation rampant, volume continues to rise, but "air pockets" appear with increasing frequency; the "cats and dogs" (low-priced stocks of no investment value) are whirled up, but more and more of the top-grade issues refuse to follow.

7. **The Bear Market** — Primary Downtrends are also usually (but again, not invariably) characterized by three phases. The first is the *distribution* period (which really starts in the later stages of the preceding Bull Market). During this phase, farsighted investors sense the fact that business earnings have reached an abnormal height and unload their holdings at an increasing pace. Trading volume is still high, though tending to diminish on rallies, and the "public" is still active but beginning to show signs of frustration as hoped-for profits fade away.

    The second phase is the Panic Phase. Buyers begin to thin out and sellers become more urgent; the downward trend of prices suddenly accelerates into an almost vertical drop, while volume mounts to climactic proportions. After the Panic Phase (which usually runs too far relative to then-existing business conditions), there may be a fairly long Secondary Recovery or a sideways movement, and then the third phase begins.

This is characterized by discouraged selling on the part of those investors who held on through the Panic or, perhaps, bought during it because stocks looked cheap in comparison with prices which had ruled a few months earlier. The business news now begins to deteriorate. As the third phase proceeds, the downward movement is less rapid, but is maintained by more and more distress selling from those who have to raise cash for other needs. The "cats and dogs" may lose practically all their previous Bull Advance in the first two phases. Better-grade stocks decline more gradually, because their owners cling to them to the last. And, the final stage of a Bear Market, in consequence, is frequently concentrated in such issues. The Bear Market ends when everything in the way of possible bad news, the worst to be expected, has been discounted, and it is usually over before all the bad news is "out."

The three Bear Market phases described in the preceding paragraph are not the same as those named by others who have discussed this subject, but the writers of this study feel that they represent a more accurate and realistic division of the Primary down moves of the past 30 years. The reader should be warned, however, that no two Bear Markets are exactly alike, and neither are any two Bull Markets. Some may lack one or another of the three typical phases. A few Major Advances have passed from the first to the third stage with only a very brief and rapid intervening markup. A few short Bear Markets have developed no marked Panic Phase and others have ended with it, as in April 1939. No time limits can be set for any phase; the third stage of a Bull Market, for example, the phase of excited speculation and great public activity, may last for more than a year or run out in a month or two. The Panic Phase of a Bear Market is usually exhausted in a very few weeks if not in days, but the 1929 through 1932 decline was interspersed with at least five Panic Waves of major proportions. Nevertheless, the typical characteristics of Primary Trends are well worth keeping in mind. If you know the symptoms which normally accompany the last stage of a Bull Market, for example, you are less likely to be deluded by its exciting atmosphere.

Principle of Confirmation

8. **The Two Averages Must Confirm** — This is the most-often questioned and the most difficult to rationalize of all the Dow principles. Yet it has stood the test of time; the fact that it has "worked" is not disputed by any who have carefully examined the records. Those who have disregarded it in practice have, more often than not, had occasion to regret their apostasy. What it means is that no valid signal of a change in trend can be produced by the action of one Average

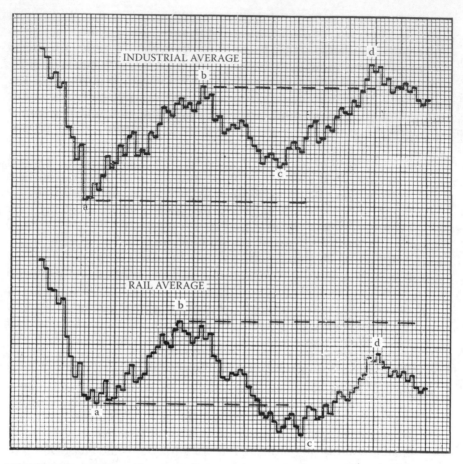

DIAGRAM 1.   A hypothetical daily market chart to show how one average may fail to confirm the other's Dow signal. Closing prices, indicated by short horizontal dashes, are connected with vertical lines to make the day-to-day trend easier to follow.

alone. Take, for example, the hypothetical case shown in Diagram 1. In this, we assume that a Bear Market has been in effect for several months and then, starting at **a**, the Industrial Average rises (along with the Rails) in a Secondary Recovery to **b**. On their next decline, however, the Industrials drop only to **c**, which is higher than **a**, and then turn up to **d**, which is higher than **b**. At this point, the Industrials have "signaled" a change in trend from down to up. But note the Rails during this period: their decline from **b** to **c** carried them lower than **a**, and their subsequent advance from **c** to **d** has not taken them above **b**. They have (so far) refused to *confirm* the Industrials and, hence, the Major Trend of the market must be regarded as *still down*. Should the Rails go on to rise eventually above their **b**, then, and then only, would we have a definite signal of a turn in the tide. Until such a development, however, the chances remain that the Industrials will not be able to continue their upward course alone, that they will ultimately be dragged down again by the Rails. At best, the direction of the Primary Trend is still in doubt.

The above illustrates only one of the many ways in which the principle of *Confirmation* applies. Note also that at **c**, it might have been said that the Industrials had thus far not confirmed the Rails in continuing the downtrend — but this had to do only with the continuation or reaffirmation of an existing trend. It is not necessary that the two Averages confirm on the same day. Frequently, both will move into new high (or low) ground together, but there are plenty of cases in which one or the other lags behind for days, weeks, or even a month or two. One must be patient in these doubtful cases and wait until the market declares itself in definite fashion.

9. **"Volume Goes with the Trend"** — Those words, which you may often hear spoken with ritual solemnity but little understanding, are the colloquial expression for the general truth that trading activity tends to expand as prices move in the direction of the prevailing Primary Trend. Thus, in a Bull Market, volume increases when prices rise and dwindles as prices decline; in Bear Markets, turnover increases when prices drop and dries up as they recover. To a lesser degree, this holds for Secondary Trends also, especially in the early stages of an extended Secondary Recovery within a Bear Market, when activity may show a tendency to pick up on the Minor Rallies and diminish on the Minor Set-backs. But to this rule, again, there are exceptions, and useful conclusions can seldom be drawn from the volume manifestations of a few days, much less a single trading session; it is only the overall and relative volume trend over a period of time that may produce helpful indications. Moreover, in Dow Theory, *conclusive* signals as to the market's trend are produced in the final analysis only by price movement. Volume simply affords collateral evidence which may aid interpretation of otherwise doubtful situations. (We shall have much more to say in later chapters about volume in specific relation to other technical phenomena.)

10. **"Lines" May Substitute for Secondaries** — A *Line* in Dow Theory parlance is a sideways movement (as it appears on the charts) in one or both of the Averages, which lasts for 2 or 3 weeks or, sometimes, for as many months, in the course of which prices fluctuate within a range of approximately 5% or less (of their mean figure). The formation of a Line signifies that pressure of buying and selling is more or less in balance. Eventually, of course, either the offerings within that price range are exhausted and those who want to buy stocks have to raise their bids to induce owners to sell, or else those who are eager to sell at the "Line" price range find that buyers have vanished and that, in consequence, they must cut their prices in order to dispose of their shares. Hence, an advance in prices through the upper limits of an established Line is a Bullish Signal and, conversely,

a break down through its lower limits is a Bearish Signal. Generally speaking, the longer the Line (in duration) and the narrower or more compact its price range, the greater the significance of its ultimate breakout.

Lines occur often enough to make their recognition essential to followers of Dow's principles. They may develop at important Tops or Bottoms, signaling periods of distribution or of accumulation, respectively, but they come more frequently as interludes of rest or Consolidation in the progress of established Major Trends. Under those circumstances, they take the place of normal Secondary Waves. A Line may develop in one Average while the other is going through a typical Secondary Reaction. It is worth noting that a price movement out of a Line, either up or down, is usually followed by a more extensive additional move in the same direction than can be counted on to follow the "signal" produced when a new wave pushes beyond the limits set by a preceding Primary Wave. The direction in which prices will break out of a Line cannot be determined in advance of the actual movement. The 5% limit ordinarily assigned to a Line is arbitrarily based on experience; there have been a few slightly wider sideways movements which, by virtue of their compactness and well-defined boundaries, could be construed as true Lines. (Further on in this book, we shall see that the Dow Line is, in many respects, similar to the more strictly defined patterns known as Rectangles which appear on the charts of individual stocks.)

11. **Only Closing Prices Used** — Dow Theory pays no attention to any extreme highs or lows which may be registered during a day and before the market closes, but takes into account only the closing figures, i.e., the average of the day's final sale prices for the component issues. We have discussed the psychological importance of the end-of-day prices under the subject of chart construction and need not deal with it further here, except to say that this is another Dow rule which has stood the test of time. It works thus: suppose an Intermediate Advance in a Primary Uptrend reaches its peak on a certain day at 11 a.m., at which hour the Industrial Average figures at, say, 152.45, and then falls back to close at 150.70. All that the next advance will have to do in order to indicate that the Primary Trend is still *up* is register a daily close above 150.70. The previous intraday high of 152.45 does not count. Conversely, using the same figures for our first advance, if the next upswing carries prices to an intraday high at, say, 152.60, but fails to register a closing price above 150.70, the continuation of the Primary Bull Trend is still in doubt.

In recent years, differences of opinion have arisen among market students as to the extent to which an Average should push beyond a previous limit (Top or Bottom figure) in order to signal (or confirm or reaffirm, as the case may be) a market trend. Dow and Hamilton evidently regarded any penetration, even as little as 0.01, in closing price as a valid signal, but some modern commentators have required penetration by a full point (1.00). We think that the original view has the best of the argument, that the record shows little or nothing in practical results to favor any of the proposed modifications. One incident in June of 1946, to which we shall refer in the following chapter, shows a decided advantage for the orthodox "any-penetration-whatever" rule.

12. **A Trend Should Be Assumed to Continue in Effect Until Such Time as Its Reversal Has Been Definitely Signaled** — This Dow Theory tenet is one which, perhaps more than any other, has evoked criticism. Yet, when correctly understood, it, like all the others we have enumerated, stands up under practical test. What it states is really a *probability*. It is a warning against changing one's market position too soon, against "jumping the gun." It does not imply that one should delay action by one unnecessary minute once a signal of change in trend has appeared. But it expresses the experience that the odds are in favor of the man who waits until he is sure, and against the other fellow who buys (or sells) prematurely. These odds cannot be stated in mathematical language such as 2–1 or 3–1; as a matter of fact, they are constantly changing. Bull Markets do not climb forever and Bear Markets always reach a Bottom sooner or later. When a new Primary Trend is first definitely signaled by the action of the two Averages, the odds that it will be continued, despite any near-term reactions or interruptions, are at their greatest. But as this Primary Trend carries on, the odds in favor of its further extension grow smaller. Thus, each successive reaffirmation of a Bull Market (new Intermediate high in one average confirmed by a new Intermediate high in the other) carries relatively less weight. The incentive to buy, the prospect of selling new purchases at a profit, is smaller after a Bull Market has been in existence for several months than it was when the Primary Uptrend was first recognized, but this twelfth Dow tenet says, "Hold your position pending contrary orders."

A corollary to this tenet, which is not so contradictory as it may at first seem, is: a Reversal in trend can occur *any time* after that trend has been confirmed. This can be taken simply as a warning that the Dow Theory investor must watch the market constantly if he has any commitment in it.

EN: *Modern Market Importance of Dow Theory and Necessity for Moving to a New Composite Market Theory*

Dow Theory has much to recommend it. Concepts embodied within Dow Theory retain their validity to the present day, and retain their importance as the foundation thinking for technical analysis. Concepts of waves, major secondary and minor movements are absolutely descriptive of the reality of the market. Other constructs within Dow Theory

are similarly important — that all information is discounted; that major market move-
ments are like the tide and, as it were, raise all boats; that trends tend to continue.
These are not just theoretical musings, but observations of reality.

In addition to its technical validity the Dow has now taken on a mythic
dimension. It now has a symbolic function which interacts with its originally
intended purpose. Dow and Hamilton saw their measurement of the market as an
economic barometer for the entire economy. Its use as a tool for investing in the
market came later.

In the opinion of this editor, the Dow Theory is no longer adequate to its original
purpose — or even to its secondary purpose. It is a simple theory propounded in a
simple time. Expounders of Dow Theory have implicitly recognized the necessity
for evolutionary changes to the doctrine with the addition of the Rails (now Trans-
portations) and the Utilities ad infinitum. Thirty stocks may have been sufficient
originally to reflect the American economy. No one would deny that simple paradigm
must be changed to reflect an economic structure geometrically more diverse than
that of Dow and Hamilton. Entering the 21st century, the American and Global
economy require more sophisticated econometrics than the Dow alone.

For that reason I now consider that in order to fulfill the functions of the old
Dow we now must consider a variety of averages and indexes to measure the state
of the market — not to mention the economy, which is another question, although
not altogether another question, but at least another question. Magee foreshadowed
some instruments of great value to this end in his writings, specifically on the Magee
Evaluative Index (Chapter 38), which may be used for the entire market, and not
just for one summary index or average. The value and power of this tool are still
little used and understood.

In 21st century markets, there are not just broad tides and markets flowing in
one direction as they might on Magee's Cape Cod. Instead the currents, rip tides,
and cross currents are like the economy of the country, moved West. They are now
symbolized by the Pacific Ocean roaring in and out of San Francisco Bay. While
the Dow is in a secondary Downtrend, the broader S&P 500 is going to new highs,
and while they are both whipping sideways, the NASDAQ is rocketing into space.
For this reason, I now believe that only a composite of the three indexes can express
the true state of the markets as a whole. And, in addition, to dissect the entrails of
the market, the Magee Evaluative Index should be run across the three indexes.

The Dow Theory required that the Rails and Industrials move in harmony in order
to signal Bull or Bear Markets. In this century, there is a similar need for harmonic
convergence among the averages to indicate to us the state of the markets as a whole.

When all three indexes agree in the direction of their trends, up or down or
sideways, Bulls may assumed to be safe in general, and vice versa for Bears. Failure
of the three to be in harmony is a clear sign of mixed markets and advises one to
arrange his bets and portfolio to correspond with economic uncertainty. Capital
should flow naturally to the area which is most productive. What reason is there to
ride the Dow down when the NASDAQ is raging up? If the investor follows the
philosophy of this book, he will never sit passively through an extended Downtrend.
At the very least, he will be hedged, if not outright short. (As Edwards and Magee
preferred and as this editor prefers.)

chapter four

The Dow Theory in Practice

EN9: The casual and careless reader will shake his head at this chapter and ask why on earth the Editor has not excised it from the book. The Editor has not deleted the chapter because, like old-fashioned cod liver oil, it is good medicine. It will appeal mainly to the serious student of not just Dow Theory, but of long-term investing. If the reader has absolutely no interest in Dow Theory or long-term investing he may skip over this chapter and return to it in his old age, when he is wiser.

At this point, the reader, if he has little previous knowledge of the stock market, may be suffering a mild attack of mental indigestion. The Dow Theory is a pretty big dose to swallow at one sitting. We departed deliberately in the foregoing chapter from the order in which its principles are usually stated in an effort to make it a little easier to follow and understand. Actually, not all of the 12 tenets we named are of equal import. The essential rules are contained in 2, 3, 4, 5, 8, 10, and 11. Number 1 is, of course, the basic assumption, the philosophical justification for these rules. The other points (6, 7, 9, and 12) furnish "background material," as the news reporters might put it, which aid in interpretation. Theoretically, one should, by strict adherence to the essential rules alone, accomplish just as much as he could with the added collateral evidence.

But the utilization of Dow Theory is, after all, a matter of interpretation. You may memorize its principles verbatim and yet be confounded when you attempt to apply them to an actual market situation. We can better organize our knowledge of the theory and acquire some understanding of its interpretation by following through a few years of market action and seeing how it looked at the time through the eyes of a Dow theorist. For this purpose, we may well take the period from late 1941 to the beginning of 1947, since this covers the end of one Bear Market, an entire long Bull Market, and part of another Bear Market, and includes examples of most of the market phenomena with which the Dow Theory has to deal.

Five Years of Dow Interpretation

Figure 2 is a condensed chart of the course of the two Dow Jones Averages from January 1, 1941, to December 31, 1946, on which most of the Minor Trends have been disregarded but all the recognized Intermediate Swings (Primary and Secondary) have been indicated. Certain portions of this history will be supplemented by complete daily charts in connection with our detailed discussion which follows.

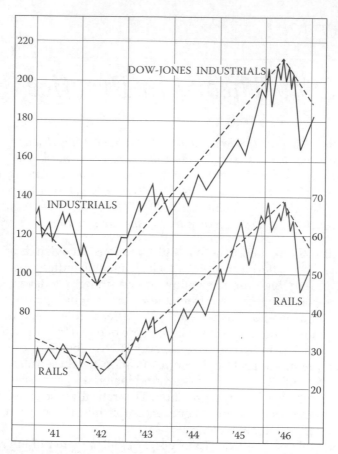

FIGURE 2. "Swing" *(EN: OR Wave)* chart showing all the Intermediate and some of the more extensive Minor Trends of the Dow–Jones Industrial and Rail Averages, January 1941 to December 1946. Industrial price scale left, Rails right.

The year 1941 opened with the stock market in a Minor Rally. A Primary Bear Market had been signaled when prices collapsed in the spring of 1940, and that Bear Market was still in effect. After the May Panic had ended, a Secondary Recovery swing, which lasted for more than 5 months, had regained more than half of the ground previously lost by the Averages, carrying the Industrials from their closing price of 111.84 on June 10 to 138.12 on November 9 and the Rails from 22.14 on May 21 to 30.29 on November 14. (During this long Bear Market Secondary, incidentally, volume tended to increase on rallies, which encouraged many who did not hold strictly to first principles to believe that this rise was the beginning of a new Bull Trend, illustrating the point we cited under "Volume" in Chapter 3.) From the November highs, however, the trend turned down again. Then a Minor Rally developed, as we have said, at the end of the year, reaching its peak on January 10 at 133.59 in the Industrials and 29.73 in the Rails. From there, prices fell again to 117.66 and 26.54, respectively, on February 14.

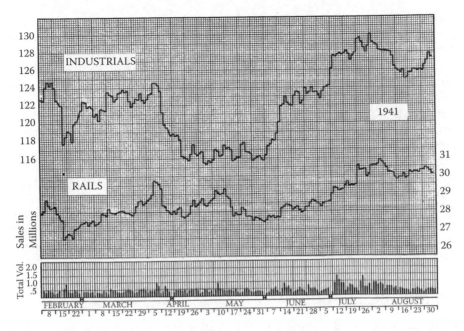

FIGURE 3.   Closing price levels of the Dow–Jones Industrial and Rail Averages, February 1 to August 31, 1941, and total daily market volume. Vertical lines show net daily change from one closing level to next.

The First Severe Test

The next few months will be particularly interesting for us to trace because they put the Dow Theory to a real test. Figure 3 shows the daily ranges and closing prices of the two Averages and total daily market volume for the 7 months from February 1 to August 31, 1941. Before we examine it in detail, however, let us first review the situation on February 14. The Bear Market lows to date had been registered in May–June, 1940. Thereafter, an extended Intermediate Recovery had advanced the Industrial Average 26.28 points and the Rail Average 8.15 points. This had been followed by a 3-month decline of 20.46 and 3.75 points, respectively, and this decline, incidentally, had consisted of three well-defined Minor Waves. In duration, and in extent of price change with respect to the previous swing — 46% in the Rails and nearly 78% in the Industrials — this downswing qualified as an Intermediate Trend, and now prices were turning up again. Dow theorists were on the alert. If both Averages could continue their rise to levels above their high closes of the previous November (138.12 and 30.29), that action would constitute a signal of a new Primary Bull Market, and reinvestment of funds withdrawn from stocks in May 1940 would be at once in order. Also, it would then be necessary to go back and label the May–June lows of 1940 as the end of a Bear Market, the advance to November as the first Primary Swing in the new Bull Market, and the decline to February as its first Secondary

Reaction. But note that Rule 12 of our preceding chapter applied here; the presumption was that it was still a Bear Market until a definite signal to the contrary appeared.

Let us now turn again to Figure 3 and see what actually did happen. The Industrials rallied for 6 weeks, reaching 124.65 on April 3. The Rails got up to 29.75 on the same date, registering double the percentage gain of the Industrials, but both Averages were still below their November highs. Then the Industrials slipped off within 2 weeks, and had broken down below their February low and drifted down to close at 115.30 on May 1. This Average was, therefore, still in an Intermediate Downtrend. But the Rails, meanwhile, were staging a different sort of performance. They dropped back from their April 3 high for 2 weeks, but held at 27.72, rallied smartly and then sold off again to 27.43 on May 31. The picture became at once even more interesting. Here was a Divergence between the two Averages, a failure to confirm; the Rails, after two opportunities, were refusing to confirm the Industrials in the latter's downtrend.

Failure to Confirm

When prices began to work upward in June, many commentators seized upon this "failure to confirm" as a Bullish omen and the wishful thinkers again talked Bull Market. There is an unfortunate tendency in "the Street" to overstress any such divergence, particularly when it can be twisted into a favorable sign. The fact is that, in Dow Theory, the refusal of one Average to confirm the other can never produce a positive signal of any sort. It has only negative connotations. Divergences sometimes occur at Reversals in the Major Trend — there have been several instances in market history, in which, perhaps, the most remarkable occurred way back in 1901 and 1902, and we shall soon inspect another — but they also occur with equal frequency at times when no Major Reversal is developing, and the instance we are discussing here was one of the latter.

So the situation at the end of May in 1941 was precisely the same to the Dow theorist, insofar as the Major Trend was concerned, as it had been on February 14. The June–July rally topped out in the Rails at 30.88 on August 1, and in the Industrials at 130.06 on July 28 (compare these figures with their 1940 November highs) and prices then declined at an accelerating pace which culminated, temporarily, in the "Pearl Harbor" Panic. This took the Industrial Average below its previous Bear Market low (111.84 on June 10, 1940), although the Rails, again, did not follow. They had, however, by this time, broken below their previous (February 14) Intermediate Bottom by a liberal margin.

The next period of importance began in April 1942. We can skip any detailed chart of the months between December and April because they posed no Dow Theory problems. After a Minor Rally in the Rails in January, prices simply drifted lower and lower, but it was increasingly evident that trading volume did not expand on the dips (Minor Declines). Liquidation

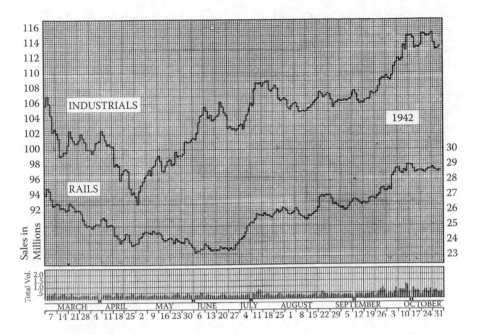

FIGURE 4. Daily closing price levels of the Dow–Jones Industrial and Rail Averages from March 2 to October 31, 1942, and total daily market volume. This period saw the beginning of a 4-year Major Bull Market.

was drying up; the boardrooms were void of customers; the atmosphere was typical of the last stages of a Bear Market.

Figure 4 shows the daily action of the Averages from March 2 to October 31, 1942. New lows (since 1940) were registered in both in late April, at 23.72 on April 24 in the Rails and at 92.92 on April 28 in the Industrials. Shortly thereafter, a notable Divergence developed, when, after rallying for only 7 days, the Railroad Index began to slip off while the other Average kept right on going up. Trading activity remained at a low ebb (there was no sustained volume increase, in fact, until late September). On June 1, the Rails dropped to another new low and on the 2nd closed at 23.31. On June 22, it looked as though the Industrials were going to be pulled down again, but only a few days later, the best rally in months got started, taking the Industrials to new highs and more than recovering all of the April–May loss in the Rails. Activity also speeded up briefly, with one day registering a greater turnover than the market had enjoyed in any session since early January. *EN9: Note this warning sign. The ringing of an alarm clock.*

Signs of Major Turn

Again the Dow theorists were very much on the alert. An advance of Intermediate proportions was obviously under way. Until proved otherwise, it had to be labeled a Secondary within the Bear Market which was still presumably in effect, but that Major Downtrend had by now run for nearly 3 years — nearly as long as any on record — and its last decline had shown no selling pressure whatever, simply a dull drift. This presumed Secondary might turn out to be, instead, a new Primary; hopes for such a denouement had been blighted 12 months earlier under somewhat similar circumstances, but this time prices were lower and there was a different "feel" to the market. The general news offered little encouragement, but the Dow Theory does not concern itself with any news other than that made by the market itself (which discounts all other kinds of news). In any event, there was nothing to do but wait and see — let the market, in its own time and way, state its own case.

In early July, the Industrials started to "mark time"; for 11 weeks, they fluctuated within a 5-point range, building a typical Dow Line from which they emerged on the upside in late September. The Rails pushed up to a new high for the move at the same time, and by November 2, both Averages had surpassed their Rally Tops of the preceding January. At this stage, some Dow theorists were willing to announce that a Bull Market had been signaled. Their arguments, aside from points of a nontechnical nature or having nothing to do with Dow Theory, were:

1.   The conspicuously low level of volume at the April–June Bottom, typical of the end of a Bear Swing. (True and cogent.)
2.   The Rail Average had refused to follow the Industrials into new Major low ground at that time. It had held above its closing level of May 1940. (Also true, but of questionable significance. More about this later.)
3.   The Industrials had constructed a Line and gone up out of it. (Again true, but the Line was somewhat short to have, beyond a doubt, major import.)
4.   The Rail Average had for 4 months produced successively higher Minor Tops and Bottoms. (And this also was true but did not permit of positive differentiation from a Bear Market Secondary.)

The more conservative Dow theorists were not yet convinced. They maintained that this uptrend had yet to undergo the test, bound to occur sooner or later, of an Intermediate Reaction. They admitted that the picture was most encouraging, but called attention to the fact that, except for Point 1, it was no better than that of November 1940. Let's follow along through the next 5 months. Figure 5 shows the daily market action from November 1, 1942, to June 30, 1943.

The Bull Signal

After reaching 29.28 at their close on November 2, the Rails declined in almost a straight line for 6 weeks to 26.03 on December 14. This move indubitably rated as an Intermediate in duration, and it had "given up" more than half of that Average's entire advance from the June 2 low point. The

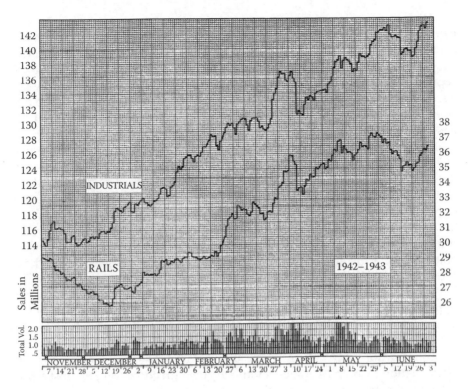

FIGURE 5. Daily closing price levels of the Dow–Jones Industrial and Rail Averages from November 2, 1942, to June 30, 1943, and total daily market volume. This chart follows and should be compared with Figure 4. The decline in the Rail Average during November and early December produced the first test of the Major Trend since the preceding June. When this Index recovered and, on February 1, 1943, closed above its November 2 high, a Primary Bull Market was thereby signaled according to Dow Theory.

Industrial Index, however, held stoutly in another narrow Line throughout November, December, and January. From December 14, the Rails turned up, and finally, on February 1, 1943, closed at 29.55, out above their previous Intermediate Top of 29.28 recorded the previous November. By then, the Industrials had also moved up into new high ground. This development at last satisfied every strictest requirement of Dow Theory; a new Primary Bull Market was in force. Trading volume had also been expanding on each Minor Advance during the fall and winter months, but its evidence was not needed; the price action alone was conclusive. The Rails had produced the necessary sequence of higher Intermediate Tops and Bottoms. In the Industrials, Lines had served the purposes of the theory as substitutes for Intermediate Reactions.

It was necessary now to relabel the up-move from April–June to November of 1942 as the first Primary Swing in a Bull Market. The decline of the Rails from November 2 to December 14 was now recognized as the first Secondary within that Major Trend.

We may turn back for a moment at this point to comment on the performance of the Rail Index in June 1942. Because it held then above its low of May 1940, some commentators have maintained that the Bull Market should really have been dated from that former year as representing the last "confirmed" lows. This strikes us as rather impractical hair-splitting. Regardless of the 1.17 higher level in the Rail Average in June 1942, a genuine Bull Move did not start until that time. We suspect that before many years have passed, Dow theorists will have occasion greatly to regret the importance which has since been assigned to the Rails' "failure to confirm" in the spring of 1942. Remember, such a Divergence does not and cannot produce a positive signal; at the time of its occurrence, it can serve merely to negate or cast in doubt the implications of the other Average; only subsequent action in the opposite direction can establish the existence of a change in trend. If the Rails' decline in May 1942 had carried them below 22.14, but their subsequent action had followed the course which it actually did, point for point but at a lower level, a Bull Market Signal would nevertheless have been given at the very same time, not one day later and not one day sooner.

Moreover, a Divergence does not necessarily imply that a move of consequence in the opposite direction will ensue. We have already examined one comparable instance (in the spring of 1941) which resulted otherwise. Logically, also, if a failure to confirm such as occurred in 1942 is to be taken as an indication of a turn in trend, then its opposite, i.e., confirmation or reaffirmation by both Averages, should argue with equal force against a turn in trend. Yet the simple truth is that many more Major Reversals have come when the Averages were in agreement than when they were divergent. We have no wish to belabor the point or waste the reader's time, but we do feel that he should be warned against the wishful thinking that every "failure to confirm" seems to inspire when the market is in a Bear Trend.

To return to our history, the Averages closed at 125.88 and 29.51, respectively, on the day following our conclusive Bull Market Signal in February 1943. Theoretically, there is where an investor who followed the Dow Theory strictly would have bought his stocks. (Those who were satisfied that the Primary Trend was up in November 1942 bought with Averages around 114.60 and 29.20.) It was reasonable to assume that this Bull Market, which as yet showed few of the usual characteristics of the second phase and none whatever of the third phase, would continue for some time to come. The next 4 months produced no market developments that required interpretative attention, and we can move on to the events of July. Figure 6 charts the action from July 1, 1943, to January 31, 1944.

The First Correction

After closing at 145.82 on July 14, 1943, the Industrial Average drifted off. The Rails pushed up to a new high (38.30) 10 days later, but the Industrials refused to join in the rally and then both indexes cracked down sharply for 7 sessions. Turnover increased and the decline was the greatest that had

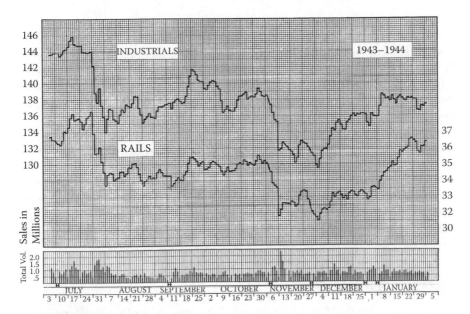

FIGURE 6. Daily closing prices of Dow–Jones Industrial and Rail Averages, and total market volume, July 1, 1943, to January 31, 1944.

occurred in the Bull Market up to that date. But, everyone realized that the market, after several months of quite persistent advance, was "entitled to a correction." In neither duration nor extent could this down move be qualified as more than a Minor Trend. Next ensued 3 months of desultory fluctuation with little net progress in either Average. The Industrials pulled up to 141.75 on September 20 and then drifted off again, while the Rails struggled back to 35.53 on October 27. Another quick break developed in early November, culminating in a high-volume shakeout which cut the value of the Industrials by 3.56 points and the Rails by 1.75 on November 8. Prices rallied a little and sold off again, reaching new lows (since early spring) on November 30 — Industrials 129.57 and Rails 31.50.

There was no question now but that a full-fledged Secondary Reaction had developed. The problem for Dow interpreters was whether more than that was involved. If the first drop in July could be construed as an Intermediate Trend in itself, and the August–October action as another Intermediate Swing, then the November break would signal a Bear Market. As a matter of fact, no Dow theorist, so far as we know, gave very serious consideration to any such interpretation. The July break, as aforesaid, did not rate as an Intermediate in either duration or points retraced; the whole move from July to November 1943 had to be regarded as all-of-a-piece, all one Secondary Reaction. The real Major Trend test would come on the next advance, whenever that should develop; if that failed to top the July peaks, and prices thereafter declined to new lows, a Bear Market would indeed be in effect.

The decision was long deferred. Prices began again to move up, but the advance in the Industrials was slow and grudging. The Rails forged ahead more rapidly and pushed through their July Top on February 17, 1944, going on to a Minor Peak at 40.48 on March 21. The Industrial Average attained 141 on March 13, but still nearly 5 points below its "signal" level, faltered and fell back. Here was another striking case of "failure to confirm." For those who chose to assign grave significance to such developments, it could have only a very Bearish meaning. But all it did mean, in fact, was that continuation of the Primary Bull Move had not as yet been confirmed. Only if both Averages now declined and closed below their respective November 30 Bottoms would the new high registered by the Rails alone in February have to be disregarded and a Primary Bear Market announced. In brief, the situation at the end of March was no different, so far as its Major Trend implications were concerned, from what it had been in early January before the Rails pushed through.

Bull Trend Reaffirmed

The situation remained in doubt (but subject always to that basic presumption of the Dow Theory which we named as Number 12 in the preceding chapter) until June 15, 1944, when the Industrials finally came through to close at 145.86. It had taken them 4 months to confirm the Rails, almost a full year to reaffirm the Primary Uptrend. The effect of this "signal" on traders was electric; trading volume increased by 650,000 shares on the following day as prices jumped another full point.

The following 12 months need no detailed discussion as they produced nothing in the way of market action to give a Dow theorist any concern. Prices drifted off irregularly for 9 weeks after mid-July but their net loss was of minor proportions, and they then climbed with only brief interruptions to 169.08 in the Industrial Index on May 29, 1945, and 63.06 in the Rail Index on June 26, 1945. We should take a brief look at the period which followed, not because it illustrates anything new in our study, but because it takes in the surrender of Japan and the end of fighting in World War II.

Figure 7 covers the 7 months from May 1 to November 30, 1945. The Industrials held steady for 4 weeks while the Rails were making the spurt to their June 26 Top. On June 28, with nothing in the newspaper headlines to account for such a radical trend change, prices broke sharply and turnover climbed to nearly three million shares, the highest day's total for the Bull Market up to that time. But the Industrial Average gave ground reluctantly thereafter, and by June 26, at 160.91 had given up less than 5% of its top price. The Rails shook down rapidly, however. The Hiroshima bomb was dropped on August 5 and Japan surrendered on the 14th. The Industrials were now rallying up from their July 26 low, but the Rails couldn't hold and plunged again, hitting bottom finally (for this move) on August 20 at 51.48, for a loss of more than 18% of their June peak value.

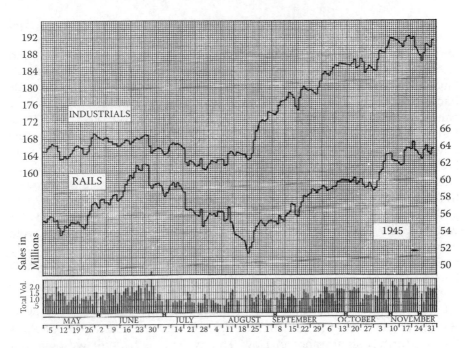

FIGURE 7. Daily closing price levels of the Dow–Jones Industrial and Rail Averages from May 1 to November 30, 1945, and total daily market volume. This period, which saw the end of World War II, produced only a moderate Secondary Correction in the Primary Bull Market, which had already run for 3 years from its beginnings in April/June, 1942.

The Rails Falter

Before we go on with our examination of the market action here, it is interesting to note that, up to this point, the Rail Average had been the "hero" of our story. Starting with its refusal to go down to a new Bear Market low in June of 1942, it was the spearhead of each important advance, had staged the most spectacular rallies, had gained 170% in value as compared with the Industrials' 82%. In retrospect, the explanation is obvious: the railroads were the chief business beneficiaries of the war. They were rolling up profits, paying off indebtedness, and reducing their fixed charges at a rate unheard of in this generation (and probably never to be seen again). While the "public's" eye was on the traditional and better publicized "war industries," the market began, as far back as Pearl Harbor, to shrewdly appraise and discount this unprecedented harvest for the Rails. But from here on, the picture changes and the Rails become the laggards. As we look back now, it is just as obvious that, with equal shrewdness, the market began in July of 1945 to discount a change in their fortunes. An illuminating demonstration of the basic assumption (Tenet Number 1) in Dow Theory!

Turning back to our chart, prices began to push up again with renewed vigor after August 20. Both Averages had experienced a Secondary Reaction and now Dow theorists had to watch closely to see if the Primary Uptrend would again be reaffirmed by their going to new highs. The Industrials "made the grade" when they closed at 169.89 on August 24, but the Rails had much more ground to recover and were running into offerings as they came up in succession to each of the Minor Bottom levels of their June–August downtrend (a phenomenon to which we shall devote some attention later on in the chapter on Support and Resistance). Not until early November 1945 were they able to confirm the signal of the Industrials by closing above 63.06. At this point, the Averages had, once again, announced that the Primary Bull Market was still in force. It had now lasted for three and a half years — longer than most Bull Markets, and "third phase" signs were rapidly appearing. The public was buying, the boardrooms were crowded, stock market news was making the front pages of even small city newspapers, the "cats and dogs" were being whooped up, business was booming.

With both Averages in new high ground and the Bull Market reaffirmed, all previous low points could now be disregarded. For example, the 160.91 Bottom of July 26 in the Industrials and the 51.48 of August 20 in the Rails had no further significance in Dow Theory. This is a point we have not stressed heretofore, but it is important. It might, indeed, be added to our set of rules in the preceding chapter were it not implicit in the basic tenets. Once a Primary Trend has been confirmed or reconfirmed, the past is forgotten and everything hinges on future action. At the end of 1945, with "third phase" symptoms rife, the action of the market had to be followed with redoubled vigilance. The third phase could last for 2 more years (as it did in 1927 to 1929) or be concluded at any moment. Our next chart (Figure 8) carries us through May 1946.

The Spring of 1946

The market went through a Minor Setback in late December, a development which has come to be expected as the normal pattern for that month and which is usually attributed to "tax selling" — and stormed ahead again in January 1946. Daily volume on January 18 exceeded 3 million shares for the first time in more than 5 years. During the first week of February, prices "churned" with little net change. Extreme high closes were registered during this period by the Rail Average at 68.23 on February 5, and by the Industrial Average at 206.97 on February 2. On February 9, both started to slide off, pulled back sharply from the 13th to the 16th, and then broke in a selling wave that ran to a climax on February 26 with closings at 60.53 and 186.02, respectively. The loss in the Industrials was the greatest in points (20.95) they had suffered during the entire Bull Market; in the Rails, it was exceeded only by their July–August decline of the previous year. It amounted to a little

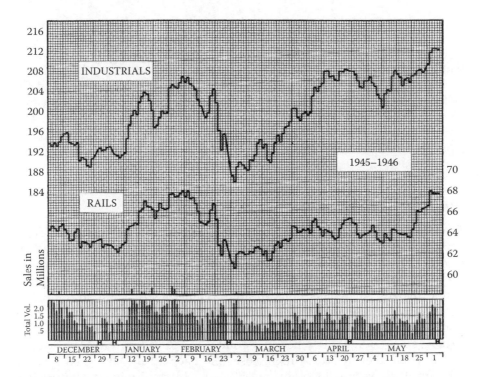

FIGURE 8. Daily closing price levels of the Dow–Jones Industrial and Rail Averages from December 1, 1945, to May 31, 1946, and total daily market volume. Noteworthy features of this period included the extremely high volume which prevailed during January and February as compared with lower turnover in April and May, and the laggard performance of the Rails when the Industrial Average pushed up to a new high in April and again at the end of May. At the latter date, the February lows were still the critical downside "signal" levels according to the Dow Theory.

more than 10% in the former and 11% in the latter, and gave up a little less than half of their advances from the 1945 summer lows. The decline was 3 weeks old on February 26. It was an unqualified Intermediate — in Dow Theory a Secondary Reaction presumptively within the still existing Major Uptrend.

Labor troubles were dogging the steel and motor industries in 1946 from early January on, and a coal strike was looming. The February break was attributed to those news developments, but the ruling cause was more likely the discontinuance of margin trading. The Federal Reserve Board had announced in January that after February 1, stocks could be bought only for full 100% cash. The late January up-fling was featured by the "little fellow" seizing his last chance to buy on margin. (Those who participated in this scramble will doubtless regret it for a long time yet to come.) Professionals seized the opportunity to unload their trading commitments, but the "little fellow" was now temporarily out of funds; his brokerage account was quickly "frozen." Under the circumstances, as we look back, it is amazing that a more extensive Panic did not then eventuate.

But the Dow theorist was not concerned with causes. The Bull Market had been reaffirmed by both Averages in early February, canceling all previous "signal" levels. Bullish Forces were still evidently in effect because the February 26 lows held and prices began to recover. The Industrials came back quickly, and by April 9 had closed in new high ground at 208.03. The Rails dragged. When the market showed signs of weakening at the end of April, the Rail Average was still nearly 5 points below its early February high. Was this another "failure to confirm" to worry about?

Final Up Thrust

The late February Bottoms were now the critical points on the downside; if both Averages should decline below the Intermediate Low closes then recorded, before the Rails could make a new high above 68.23 (in which event the Bullish Signal of the Industrials would be canceled), a Bear Market would thereby be signaled. But, despite a miner's strike and an imminent rail workers' strike, the market turned firm again in mid-May and put forth a surprising rally which swept the Industrial Index up to 212.50 on May 29, 1946 — a new Bull high by nearly 6 points. The Rails failed in May by only 0.17 to equal their February high close, slid back a trifle, and then pushed through at last on June 13 to close at 68.31, thereby confirming the Industrials in their announcement that (as of that date) the Primary Trend was still up. The February lows (186.02 and 60.53) now ceased to signify in Dow Theory, but keep those figures in mind because they are involved in an argument which raged among Dow students for months thereafter.

Figure 9 overlaps the preceding picture, taking up the market's action on May 4 and carrying it forward to October 19, 1946. Trading volume, it may be noted, in late May and early June did not come up to the levels of either the late January to early February Top or the late February Bottom; the market appeared to be losing vitality, an ominous, although by no means, decisive manifestation. Prices began to fall off rapidly immediately after the Rail Confirmation on June 13. The Industrials rallied for 2 weeks in early July, but the Rails continued to decline; the Industrials broke again on July 15 and the two Averages continued their slide until they stood at 195.22 and 60.41 at the close on July 23.

There, as it subsequently developed, was the end of that particular Intermediate Swing — one which in accord with our Rule 12 had to be labeled a Secondary Reaction in a Bull Market until proved otherwise. The market swung up again. It climbed slowly and steadily, but with turnover running well under a million shares, until exactly 3 weeks later, the Industrials at 204.52 (August 13) had regained a little more than half of their June–July loss and the Rails at 63.12 (August 14) a little more than a third of theirs. This advance, therefore, had met the minimum requirements of an Intermediate Trend. If prices could continue to rise and eventually push

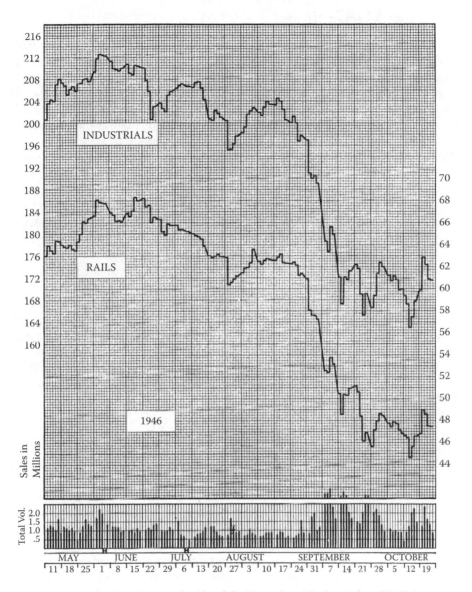

FIGURE 9.   Daily closing price levels of the Dow–Jones Industrial and Rail Averages from May 4 to October 19, 1946, and total daily market volume. This chart overlaps Figure 8. Compare the closing price of the Rail Average on June 13 with its February 5 high close. This June action nullified the previous Dow Theory importance of the February lows. Note significant change in volume pattern after May, especially during the August rally.

through their May–June Tops, the Major Bull Trend once again would be reaffirmed. But if they should now turn down and fall below the July 23 closing levels, that action would signal a Reversal of the Primary Trend.

The Bear Market Signal

That the situation was critical was evident in the volume chart. Ever since the end of May, turnover had tended not only to increase on the declines but, what was much more important, to dry up on the rallies. Compare Figure 9 with 7 and 8, and you can see how conspicuous this phenomenon had become by mid-August. Prices did turn down, with activity increasing on the breaks, and on August 27, the closing prices, 191.04 for the Industrials and 58.04 for the Rails, told a sad story. The Averages had spoken: a 4-year Bull Market had ended, and a Bear Market was under way. A Dow investor should have sold all his stocks on the following day (at approximately 190 and 58 in terms of the two Averages).

To clear the record, it was necessary for the Dow theorist now to go back and mark the May 29 and June 13 highs in the Industrials and Rails, respectively, as the end of the Bull Market. The June–July decline then became the first Primary Swing in the new Bear Trend, and the July 23 to August 14 advance became the first Secondary Recovery within the Major Downtrend. A second Primary Swing was now in process of development.

You will have noted in the foregoing that a Bear Market was signaled as soon as both Averages penetrated their July 23 lows. Let us return now and take up that argument which we mentioned on the preceding page. Some students of Dow Theory refused to recognize the new high of June 13 in the Rail Average as a decisive reaffirmation of the Bull Trend. The previous close should be bettered by at least a full point (1.00), many argued, in order to confirm the signal previously given by the Industrials; the margin of only 0.08 was inconclusive. But this opinion, if accepted, had logical consequences which later proved embarrassing. For, if the Bull Market had not been reaffirmed in June, then the critical levels on the downside remained at 186.02 in the Industrials and 60.53 in the Rails, the February 26 Bottoms. Therefore, a Bear Market could not be "called" until those prices had been penetrated downside by both Averages. This view acquired a large following, especially among those who were not interested in "hair splitting" theory but wanted "to give the market every chance in view of the still improving fundamentals."

The market did, of course, proceed to break its February lows, and by that time, the Panic (second phase) was on. Obviously, in this case, the orthodox "any-penetration-whatever" school had all the best of it; they had sold out at least 13 points higher up in terms of the Industrial Index (at least 6 in the Rails). Six weeks later, on October 9, 1946, to be exact, this second Primary Intermediate Swing ended at Industrials 163.12, Rails 44.69, and another Intermediate Recovery Move started.

Before closing this history of 6 years of Dow Theory interpretation, we might note that the June 13 high in the Rail Average furnishes a perfect illustration of the rule that a trend can change any time after it has been confirmed or reaffirmed, also of the diminishing odds in favor of continuance with each successive reaffirmation of the Primary Trend.

The Dow Theory's Defects

Our readers, we suspect, heaved a deep sigh of relief when they closed the preceding chapter on a difficult, tedious, and, at times, confusing subject. Some may even wish at this point that the Dow Theory had never been conceived. Others doubtless spotted one or more of its real or supposed defects and have questions to ask. Before we proceed to more interesting chart matters, we had better devote a few pages to clearing them up.

First, let's take up the charge of "second guessing" which is so often flung at writers on Dow Theory. It is a charge which will continue to crop up so long as opinions differ among Dow theorists at critical periods (which, unfortunately, is often the case). Even the most experienced and careful Dow analysts find it necessary occasionally to change their interpretations when a stand first ventured is rendered untenable by some subsequent action of the market. They would not attempt to deny it — but, they say, in the long run, surprisingly little is lost by such temporary misinterpretations. Many of them publish their comments regularly and can refer you to the printed files of opinions and advice expressed before and during the event, as well as after it. As for the preceding chapter of this book, the reader, if he cares to check such records, will find that the interpretations given therein (aside from the remarks made "in retrospect" and so labeled) were precisely the interpretations published at the time by the best established Dow analysts. *EN9: While, in the modern age Richard Russell (dowtheoryletters.com) is probably senior in terms of reputation, a host of other Dow Theorists (actually trying to round them up is like herding cats) inhabit the scene, among them Jack Schannep (thedowtheory.com) and Richard Moroney (dowtheory.com) who must be taken into account when consulting the sacred-chicken bones. Robert W. Colby (robertw-colby.com) is currently doing interesting work in Dow Theory. Note that it is the chicken which is sacred, and the bones only secondarily.*

The Dow Theory Is "Too Late"

This is a more valid objection. It is sometimes expressed in the rather intemperate statement that "the Dow Theory is a sure fire system for depriving the investor of the first third and the last third of every Major Move, and sometimes there isn't any middle third!" Or, to give a specific example:

A Primary Bull Market started in 1942 with the Industrial Average at 92.92 and ended in 1946 at 212.50, for a total gain of 119.58 Average points, but the strict Dow theorists could not buy until the Industrials were up to 125.88 and couldn't sell until prices had already declined to 191.04, thus capturing, at best, only about 65 points, or not much more than half of the total move. This specific statement cannot be disputed. But the answer to the general objection is "Try and find a man who first bought his stocks at 92.92 (or even within 5 points of that level) and stayed 100% long throughout the intervening years, and finally sold out at 212.50, or within 5 points thereof." The reader is welcome to try; he will, in fact, find it very difficult to locate even a dozen who did as well as the Dow Theory.

A still better answer, since it comprehends all of the hazards of every known kind of Bull and Bear Market to date, is the overall dollars and cents record of the past 60 years. We are indebted to Richard Durant for permission to reprint the following computation of what would, in theory, have resulted if a fund of only $100 could have been invested in the stocks of the Dow–Jones Industrial Average on July 12, 1897, when a Primary Bull Market was signaled by the Dow Theory, and those stocks were thereafter sold and repurchased when, and only when, the Dow Theory had definitely confirmed a change in the Major Trend (see Table 1).

In brief, an investment of $100 in 1897 would have become $11,236.65 in 1956 simply by buying the Industrial Average stocks each time the Dow Theory announced a Bull Market and holding them until the Dow Theory announced a Bear Market. During this period, the investor would have made 15 purchases and 15 sales, or about 1 transaction every 2 years on average.

The record is not perfect. It shows one losing transaction and three instances where reinvestment would have been made at a higher level than the preceding liquidation. But, at that, it hardly needs defending! Also, it takes no account of commissions and transfer taxes, but neither does it include the dividends the investor would have received during the time he held his stocks; the latter would, needless to say, have added many more dollars to the fund.

For the enlightenment of the man who believes in "just buying good stocks and putting them away," compare the above results with the best that could have been done by buying shares only once at the lowest price recorded by the Industrial Average during these entire 50 years and selling them only once at the highest. $100 invested at the all-time low, 29.64 on August 10, 1896, would have become only $1,757.93 at the all-time high, 521.05, 60 years later on April 6, 1956, as against the $11,236.65 derived from the straight Dow Theory program.

EN: This record of the Dow Theory is updated to the year 2006 in Chapter 5.1.

The Dow Theory Is Not Infallible

Of course, it isn't. It depends on interpretation and is subject to all the hazards of human interpretive ability. But, again, the record speaks for itself.

Table 1. The Dow Theory's 60-Year Record

Original fund $100.00	Date	Industrial average price	Percent gain	Proceeds
Invested	July 12, 1897	44.61		
Stocks sold	December 16, 1899	63.84	43.1	$143.10
Proceeds reinvested	October 20, 1900	59.44		
Stocks sold	June 1, 1903	59.59	0.3	143.53
Proceeds reinvested	July 12, 1904	51.37		
Stocks sold	April 26, 1906	92.44	80.0	258.35
Proceeds reinvested	April 24, 1908	70.01		
Stocks sold	May 3, 1910	84.72	21.0	312.60
Proceeds reinvested	October 10, 1910	81.91		
Stocks sold	January 14, 1913	84.96	3.7	324.17
Proceeds reinvested	April 9, 1915	65.02		
Stocks sold	August 28, 1917	86.12	32.5	429.53
Proceeds reinvested	May 13, 1918	82.16		
Stocks sold	February 3, 1920	99.96	21.7	522.74
Proceeds reinvested	February 6, 1922	83.70		
Stocks sold	June 20, 1923	90.81	8.5	567.17
Proceeds reinvested	December 7, 1923	93.80		
Stocks sold	October 23, 1929	305.85	226.1	1849.54
Proceeds reinvested	May 24, 1933	84.29		
Stocks sold	September 7, 1937	164.39	95.0	3606.61
Proceeds reinvested	June 23, 1938	127.41		
Stocks sold	March 31, 1939	136.42	7.2	3866.29
Proceeds reinvested	July 17, 1939	142.58		
Stocks sold	May 13, 1940	137.50	(Loss 3.6)	3727.10
Proceeds reinvested	February 1, 1943	125.88		
Stocks sold	August 27, 1946	191.04	51.9	5653.71
Proceeds reinvested	October 2, 1950	228.94		
Stocks sold	April 2, 1953	280.03	22.3	6911.01
Proceeds reinvested	January 19, 1954	288.27		
Stocks sold	October 1956	468.70	62.6	11,236.65

The Dow Theory Frequently Leaves the Investor in Doubt

This is true in one sense and not in another. There is never a time when the Dow Theory does not afford a presumptive answer to the question of the direction of the Primary Trend. That answer will be wrong for a relatively short time at the beginning of each new Major Swing. There will also be times when a good Dow analyst should say, "The Primary Trend is still presumably up, but it has reached a dangerous stage, and I cannot conscientiously advise you to buy now. It may be too late."

Frequently, however, the above objection simply reflects the inability of the critic mentally to accept the fundamental concept that the Averages discount all the news and statistics. He doubts the Dow Theory because he cannot reconcile its message with his own ideas, derived from other sources, of what stocks should do. The theory, needless to say, is usually more nearly right.

This criticism in other cases reflects nothing but impatience. There may be weeks or months (as, for example, during the formation of a Line) when the Dow Theory cannot "talk." The active trader quite naturally rebels. But patience is a virtue in the stock market as elsewhere — in fact, essential if serious mistakes are to be avoided.

The Dow Theory Does Not Help the Intermediate Trend Investor

This is perfectly true. The theory gives little or no warning of changes in Intermediate Trend. Yet, if a fair share of these can be captured, the profit amounts to more than can be derived from the Primary Trend alone. Some traders have worked out supplementary rules based on Dow principles which they apply to Intermediate Movements, but these have not proved to be satisfactory. The remainder of our book is devoted to a better approach to this problem.

The Dow Theory is a mechanical device, designed to tell the direction of the Primary Market Trend, which is important because, as we said at the beginning of this study, most stocks tend to go with the trend. The Dow Theory does not and cannot tell you which individual stocks to buy, aside from those stocks which make up the averages themselves. That, again, is a problem for the remainder of this book.

EN: An Old Criticism, obsolete in Modern Markets. The Dow Theory does not tell you which stocks to buy. True at the time Edwards wrote this. But in modern markets the investor can buy substitute instruments which almost perfectly mimic its behavior (DIA). As it is possible to trade in surrogates for the Dow Averages in present markets, see Chapter 15.1.

chapter 5.1

The Dow Theory in the 20th and 21st Centuries

As may be seen in the following table, replacing the table from Chapter 5, the Dow Theory continued to provide its user an advantage over the unaware Buy-and-Hold Investor. From its original investment of $100 in 1897 the Theory investment would have grown to $345,781.94 by December 31, 2005, with the long trade still open. The table below shows the details, including the post-2000 bust drawdown. To my mind this table is a powerful demonstration of the power of methodical technical investing.

By contrast, the investment of $100, if bought at the low, 29.64, and sold at the historic high, 11762.71, in January 2000 would have grown to $39,685.03.

	A Signal	B M/D/Y	C Average Price	D % Change	E Lor	F Long Side Δ%	G ng Side Capital	H Side Accumulated
2	Invested (Buy)	7/12/1897	44.61					100.00
3	Sell	12/16/1899	63.84	43.1%		43.11%		143.11
4	Buy (Reinvest)	10/20/00	59.44	-6.9%				
5	Sell	6/1/03	59.59	0.3%		0.25%	0.36	143.47
6	Buy (Reinvest)	7/12/04	51.37	-13.8%				
7	Sell	4/26/06	92.44	79.9%		79.95%	114.70	258.17
8	Buy (Reinvest)	4/24/08	70.01	-24.3%				
9	Sell	5/3/10	84.72	21.0%		21.01%	54.24	312.41
10	Buy (Reinvest)	10/10/10	81.91	-3.3%				
11	Sell	1/14/13	84.96	3.7%		3.72%	11.63	324.05
12	Buy (Reinvest)	4/9/15	65.02	-23.5%				
13	Sell	8/28/17	86.12	32.5%		32.45%	105.16	429.21
14	Buy (Reinvest)	5/13/18	82.16	-4.6%				
15	Sell	2/3/20	99.96	21.7%		21.67%	92.99	522.19
16	Buy (Reinvest)	2/6/22	83.7	-16.3%				
17	Sell	6/20/23	90.81	8.5%		8.49%	44.36	566.55
18	Buy (Reinvest)	12/7/23	93.8	3.3%				
19	Sell	10/23/29	305.85	226.1%		226.07%	1,280.78	1,847.34
20	Buy (Reinvest)	5/24/33	84.29	-72.4%				
21	Sell	9/7/37	164.39	95.0%		95.03%	1,755.51	3,602.84
22	Buy (Reinvest)	6/23/38	127.41	-22.5%				
23	Sell	3/31/39	136.42	7.1%		7.07%	254.78	3,857.62
24	Buy (Reinvest)	7/17/39	142.58	4.5%				
25	Sell	5/13/40	137.5	-3.6%	L	-3.56%	(137.44)	3,720.18
26	Buy (Reinvest)	2/1/43	125.88	-8.5%				
27	Sell	8/27/46	191.04	51.8%		51.76%	1,925.70	5,645.88
28	Buy (Reinvest)	10/2/50	228.94	19.8%				
29	Sell	4/2/53	280.03	22.3%		22.32%	1,259.93	6,905.80
30	Buy (Reinvest)	1/19/54	288.27	2.9%				
31	Sell	10/1/56	468.7	62.6%		62.59%	4,322.39	11,228.19
32	Buy (Reinvest)	5/2/58	459.56	-2.0%				
33	Sell	3/3/60	612.05	33.2%		33.18%	3,725.71	14,953.90
34	Buy (Reinvest)	10/10/61	706.67	15.5%				
35	Sell	4/26/62	678.68	-4.0%	L	-3.96%	(592.30)	14,361.60
36	Buy (Reinvest)	11/9/62	616.13	-9.2%				
37	Sell	5/5/66	899.77	46.0%		46.04%	6,611.47	20,973.07

	A	B	C	D	E	F	G	H
38	Buy (Reinvest)	1/11/67	822.49	-8.6%				22,648.13
39	Sell	10/24/67	888.18	8.0%		7.99%	1,675.06	
40	Buy (Reinvest)	10/1/68	942.32	6.1%				21,626.18
41	Sell	2/25/69	899.80	-4.5%	L	-4.51%	(1,021.94)	
42	Buy (Reinvest)	10/27/69	860.28	-4.4%				19,328.52
43	Sell	1/26/70	768.88	-10.6%	L	-10.62%	(2,297.66)	
44	Buy (Reinvest)	9/28/70	758.97	-1.3%				22,207.29
45	Sell	7/28/71	872.01	14.9%		14.89%	2,878.76	
46	Buy (Reinvest)	2/10/72	921.28	5.7%				22,241.76
47	Sell	3/27/73	922.71	0.2%		0.16%	34.47	
48	Buy (Reinvest)	11/5/74	674.75	-26.9%				26,446.84
49	Sell	10/24/77	802.32	18.9%		18.91%	4,205.08	
50	Buy (Reinvest)	6/6/78	866.51	8.0%				25,833.37
51	Sell	10/19/78	846.41	-2.3%	L	-2.32%	(613.47)	
52	Buy (Reinvest)	5/13/80	816.89	-3.5%				30,333.47
53	Sell	7/2/81	959.19	17.4%		17.42%	4,500.10	
54	Buy (Reinvest)	10/7/82	965.97	0.7%				38,683.91
55	Sell	1/25/84	1231.89	27.5%		27.53%	8,350.44	
56	Buy (Reinvest)	1/21/85	1261.37	2.4%				72,226.30
57	Sell	10/15/87	2355.09	86.7%		86.71%	33,542.39	
58	Buy (Reinvest)	1/7/88	2051.89	-12.9%				90,437.67
59	Sell	10/13/89	2569.26	25.2%		25.21%	18,211.37	
60	Buy (Reinvest)	6/4/90	2935.19	-4.2%				86,569.59
61	Sell	8/3/90	2809.65	-4.3%	L	-4.28%	(3,868.08)	
62	Buy (Reinvest)	12/5/90	2610.40	-7.1%				281,467.56
63	Sell	8/4/98	8487.31	225.1%		225.13%	194,897.98	
64	Buy (Reinvest)	9/15/98	8024.39	-5.5%				361,940.08
65	Sell	9/23/99	10318.59	23.6%		28.59%	80,472.52	
66	Buy (Reinvest)	11/8/01	9587.52	-7.1%				344,547.36
67	Sell	6/25/02	9126.8	-4.8%	L	-4.81%	(17,392.72)	
68	Buy (Reinvest)	8/21/02	8957.23	-1.9%				295,538.04
69	Sell	9/24/02	7683.13	-14.2%	L	-14.22%	(49,009.33)	
70	Buy (Reinvest)	11/5/02	8678.13	13.0%				276,905.60
71	Sell	1/24/03	8131.01	-6.3%	L	-6.30%	(18,632.44)	
72	Buy (Reinvest)	5/2/03	8582.68	5.6%				345,781.94
73	Mark to Market	12/30/05	10717.5	24.9%		24.87%	68,876.34	

I am indebted to Jack Schannep of *The Dow Theory.Com* (www.thedowtheory. com) for the data recapitulated here. At that URL an enlightening exposition of the Theory and its record may be found — much more complete than that which is found here outside of Edwards' magisterial presentation.

Minor discrepancies are acknowledged within these and others' data, a point which will be raised by purists. This is occasioned by disagreements within the priestly circles of those who keep the sacred records. That is, not all theorists are in 100% agreement as to the exact date or nature of the signals. (Some will say the reentry date of October 1, 1956, should have been October 7, 1957, for example.) Meaning, of course, that some judgment is involved in interpretation of the entrails. The Dow Theory is not a 100% objective algorithm, just as chart analysis is not reducible to an objective algorithm. (I am allowed to jest at the priesthood as I am a junior acolyte in these matters. It would not be seemly for the uninitiated to burlesque.)

In brief, an investment of $100 in 1897 would have become $345,781.94 simply by buying the Industrial Average stocks each time the Dow Theory announced a Bull Market and holding them until the Dow Theory announced a Bear Market, then selling.

The Technical Investor would have had this amount in pocket marked to market at the end of 2005 as opposed to the $39,685.03 of his dozing counterpart, or the Trust Department of the Rip Van Winkle Bank of Sleepy Hollow. And, in addition, he would not have been deliquidified during Bear Markets.

Whether or not the Dow Theory retains its validity over the market as a whole, there can be no question that it still calls the turn for its sector of the market, which as Jack Schannep correctly notes, has five times the capitalization of the NASDAQ.

As Mark Twain observed, everybody talks about the Dow Theory, but nobody does anything about it. Perhaps that is not precisely what Twain said, but close enough for government work. As further inquiry into the inner workings of the Theory I have initiated a series of studies of the record with Brian Brooker, MS Finance, Golden Gate University. Following are some of the results of our study, from the monograph, *Dissecting Dow Theory*.

	A Signal	B M/D/Y	C Average Price	D % Change	E Loss	G Acc Profits	H Duration	I Bull	J Bear
2	Invested (Buy)	7/12/1897	44.61			100	0		
3	Sell and Short	12/16/1899	63.84	43.1%		143	887	887	
4	Buy (Reinvest)	10/20/00	59.44	-6.9%		153	308		308
5	Sell and Short	6/1/03	59.59	0.3%		153	954	954	
6	Buy (Reinvest)	7/12/04	51.37	-13.8%		175	407		407
7	Sell and Short	4/26/06	92.44	79.9%		314	653	653	
8	Buy (Reinvest)	4/24/08	70.01	-24.3%		390	729		729
9	Sell and Short	5/3/10	84.72	21.0%		472	739	739	
10	Buy (Reinvest)	10/10/10	81.91	-3.3%		488	160		160
11	Sell and Short	1/14/13	84.56	3.7%		506	827	827	
12	Buy (Reinvest)	4/9/15	65.02	-23.5%		625	815		815
13	Sell and Short	8/28/17	86.12	32.5%		828	872	872	
14	Buy (Reinvest)	5/13/18	82.15	-4.6%		866	258		258
15	Sell and Short	2/3/20	99.96	21.7%		1,053	631	631	
16	Buy (Reinvest)	2/6/22	83.7	-16.3%		1,224	734		734
17	Sell and Short	6/20/23	90.81	8.5%		1,329	499	499	
18	Buy (Reinvest)	12/7/23	93.8	3.3%	L	1,285	170		170
19	Sell and Short	10/23/29	305.85	226.1%		4,189	2147	2147	
20	Buy (Reinvest)	5/24/33	84.29	-72.4%		7,224	1309		1309
21	Sell and Short	9/7/37	164.39	95.0%		14,089	1567	1567	
22	Buy (Reinvest)	6/23/38	127.41	-22.5%		17,258	289		289
23	Sell and Short	3/31/39	136.42	7.1%		18,478	281	281	
24	Buy (Reinvest)	7/17/39	142.58	4.5%	L	17,644	108		108
25	Sell and Short	5/13/40	137.5	-3.6%	L	17,015	301	301	
26	Buy (Reinvest)	2/1/43	125.88	-8.5%		18,453	994		994
27	Sell and Short	8/27/46	191.04	51.8%		28,005	1303	1303	
28	Buy (Reinvest)	10/2/50	228.94	19.8%	L	22,449	1497		1497
29	Sell and Short	4/2/53	280.03	22.3%		27,459	913	913	
30	Buy (Reinvest)	1/19/54	283.27	2.9%	L	26,651	292		292
31	Sell and Short	10/1/56	468.7	62.6%		43,332	986	986	
32	Buy (Reinvest)	5/2/58	459.56	-2.0%		44,177	578		578
33	Sell and Short	3/3/60	612.05	33.2%		58,835	671	671	
34	Buy (Reinvest)	10/10/61	706.67	15.5%	L	49,740	586		586
35	Sell and Short	4/26/62	678.68	-4.0%	L	47,770	198	198	

	A	B	C	D	E	G	H	I	J
36	Buy (Reinvest)	11/9/62	616.13	-9.2%		52,173	197		197
37	Sell and Short	5/5/66	899.77	46.0%		76,191	1273	1273	251
38	Buy (Reinvest)	1/11/67	822.49	-8.6%		82,735	251		251
39	Sell and Short	10/24/67	888.18	8.0%		89,343	286	286	343
40	Buy (Reinvest)	10/1/68	942.32	6.1%		83,897	343		343
41	Sell and Short	2/25/69	899.80	-4.5%	L	80,111	147	147	244
42	Buy (Reinvest)	10/27/69	860.28	-4.4%	L	83,630	244		244
43	Sell and Short	1/26/70	768.88	-10.6%	L	74,745	91	91	245
44	Buy (Reinvest)	9/28/70	758.97	-1.3%		75,708	245		245
45	Sell and Short	7/28/71	872.01	14.9%		86,984	303	303	197
46	Buy (Reinvest)	2/10/72	921.28	5.7%	L	82,069	197		197
47	Sell and Short	3/27/73	922.71	0.2%		82,197	411	411	588
48	Buy (Reinvest)	11/5/74	674.75	-26.9%	L	104,285	588		588
49	Sell and Short	10/24/77	802.32	18.9%		124,002	1084	1084	225
50	Buy (Reinvest)	6/6/78	866.51	8.0%	L	114,081	225		225
51	Sell and Short	10/19/78	846.41	-2.3%	L	111,435	135	135	572
52	Buy (Reinvest)	5/13/80	816.89	-3.5%		115,321	572		572
53	Sell and Short	7/2/81	959.19	17.4%	L	135,410	415	415	462
54	Buy (Reinvest)	10/7/82	965.97	0.7%		134,453	462		462
55	Sell and Short	1/25/84	1231.89	27.5%		171,466	475	475	362
56	Buy (Reinvest)	1/21/85	1261.37	2.4%	L	167,362	362		362
57	Sell and Short	10/15/87	2355.09	86.7%	L	312,481	997	997	84
58	Buy (Reinvest)	1/7/88	2051.89	-12.9%		352,710	84		84
59	Sell and Short	10/13/89	2569.26	25.2%		441,643	645	645	234
60	Buy (Reinvest)	6/4/90	2935.19	14.2%	L	378,742	234		234
61	Sell and Short	8/3/90	2809.65	-4.3%	L	362,543	60	60	124
62	Buy (Reinvest)	12/5/90	2610.40	-7.1%		388,253	124		124
63	Sell and Short	8/4/98	8487.31	225.1%		1,262,344	2799	2799	42
64	Buy (Reinvest)	9/15/98	8024.39	-5.5%		1,331,196	42		42
65	Sell and Short	9/23/99	10318.59	28.6%		1,711,789	373	373	777
66	Buy (Reinvest)	11/8/01	9587.52	-7.1%		1,833,069	777		777
67	Sell and Short	6/25/02	9126.8	-4.8%	L	1,744,982	229	229	57
68	Buy (Reinvest)	8/21/02	8957.63	-1.9%		1,777,403	57		57
69	Sell and Short	9/24/02	7683.13	-14.2%	L	1,524,581	34	34	42
70	Buy (Reinvest)	11/5/02	8678.13	13.0%		1,722,021	42		42
71	Sell and Short	1/24/03	8131.01	-6.3%	L	1,613,454	80	80	98
72	Buy (Reinvest)	5/2/03	8582.68	5.6%	L	1,523,829	98		98
73	Mark to Market	12/30/05	10717.5	24.9%		1,902,859	849	849	
74						Totals	39493	25115	14378

It seems obvious that the risk characteristics of Dow Theory investing are unique, and I will belabor the obvious. The Buy-and-Hold Investor mentioned above for comparison with the Dow Theory Investor not only realized less profit over the period of his investment; he also experienced greatly expanded risk over the life of the investment. At first blush all the profits garnered by the Reversing Investor in the table above represent risk actually experienced by the Buy-and-Hold Investor. But that is only first blush. A little deeper thought reveals that the true extent of the Buy-and-Hold Investor's risk is measured by maximum drawdowns over any given period of time. It is not necessary to theorize about this question. The measurement is empirical.

When viewed in perspective these risks are startling. From the top in 2000 to the low in 2002 a 39% drawdown occurred. Is this disquieting? A 41% drawdown occurred during the Reagan crash of 1987. A mere bagatelle. The drawdown from 1929 to 1932 was 89%. Of course such things are unlikely to happen again. The big guys would step in and support the market.

Clearly the way to reduce market risk to zero is to be out of the market. Less obviously, or perhaps blatantly, the second most important way to reduce risk is to be right the trend — or not to be wrong. And in fact because of the nature of the Theory much time is spent on the sidelines by the Dow Investor. A natural reduction of risk. In fact of the total days from 1897 to 2006, 39,493, the Dow Investor spent 14,378 (or about 37% of the time) days at the beach or at the S&L. But his accumlated profits have not been credited with interest as this is a "pure" study.

As will be readily apparent Table 1.2 is much richer in data than just the duration of investments in the long side of the market. Acting on the maxim (my own) that it is unwise to invest on only one side of the market I have computed the accumulated profits gained by trading the Dow long and short. After all the market goes down as well up, and for a reversing system a liquidation of longs is a signal to go short. If the record on the long side is impressive, showing accumulated profits to 2006 of $345,781.94, how much more impressive is the accumulated profit of $1,902,859 garnered from trading both sides of the Dow, long and short.

The reader who listens carefully will hear the meta message here. For the great majority of investors it is the long run which is important. In the "right now" culture of the Internet and the computer and get rich quick one wonders if there are still such investors, outside of the very rich and very intelligent. Perhaps there are still a few aged readers of early editions of this book. And, not to despair, perhaps some new converts.

In Figures 9.1 and 9.2 I practice what I preach. I post historical Dow Theory buy and sell signals on the Dow chart. I am constantly urging students and clients to take the chart of an issue they have done poorly (or well) in and post their trades on it. The mere examination of this kind of chart should be an enlightening experience. When this exercise is accomplished the investor may see whether in fact he is operating according to

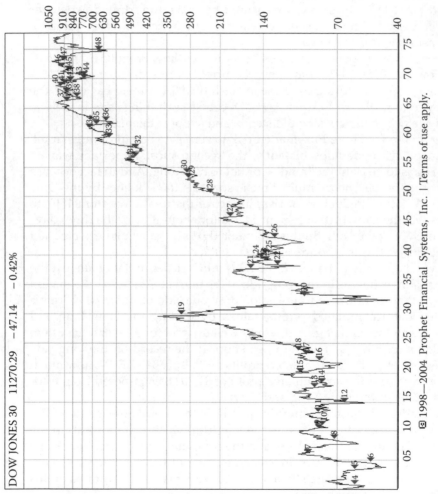

DOW JONES 30   11270.29   – 47.14   – 0.42%

Ⓒ 1998—2004 Prophet Financial Systems, Inc. | Terms of use apply.

FIGURE 9.1. To my knowledge the only charts existing of the performance of the Dow Theory from beginning to 2006. The numbers on the charts of the Dow in figures 9.1 and 9.2 are keyed to the row numbers of Tables 1.1 and 1.2. In the tables the reader may see the exact date and price of the Dow Theory transaction by finding the matching number. Thus, Number 19 represents the sale of the portfolio on November 23, 1929 at 305.85 during the Great Crash.

$INDU (Dow Jones Industrial Average Index)

03/23/2006 11:54 PM EST (all, monthly)

DOW JONES 30 11270.29 −47.14 −0.42%

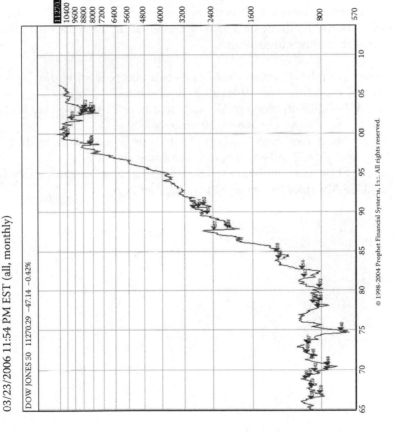

FIGURE 9.2. The second half of graphic representation of the timing of Dow Theory signals from beginning to 2006. Note Number 82.

sound methods. Sound Methods being, in the opinion of this book and this Editor, mid- to long-term trend following methods.

Further, these charts of the Dow Theory method may be compared with Figures 210 and 210.1 showing the use of Basing Points and the reader will have extensive cases of two methods for following the market in addition to the chart analysis methods prevalent thoughout the book.

Robert W. Colby (robertwcolby.com), a member of the Market Technicians Association (mta.org), in a paper published by that organization (and available at his website), explored many objective algorithms for duplicating the performance of Dow Theory. Among these is a naturalistic channel breakout algorithm which I find worth further investigation. I will quote the rules here without further comment, reminding the reader that no (repeat NO) system should EVER be backed with money until the trader has exhaustively vetted it. Colby's algorithm:

1. Enter Long (Buy) when INDU rises to a new 9-trading day high and TRAN rises to a new 39-trading day high.
2. Close Long (Sell) when INDU falls to a new 22-trading day low and TRAN falls to a new 166-trading day low.
3. Enter Short (Sell Short) when INDU falls to a new 22-trading day low and TRAN falls to a new 166-trading day low.
4. Close Short (Cover) when INDU rises to a new 36-trading day high and TRAN rises to a new 32-trading day high.

chapter six

Important Reversal Patterns

In our discussion of certain deficiencies in the Dow Theory from the point of view of the practical trader, we mentioned the fact that it did not tell us what specific stocks to trade in. *(EN9: Obviously no longer a problem as the investor may buy the DIA and trade the Average like a stock.)* A conservative and wealthy investor, more interested in safety than maximum profit, can solve this problem by making up a comprehensive and thoroughly diversified list of sound, well-seasoned "blue chip" issues and handing his broker an order to buy the lot when the Dow Theory signals a Bull Trend. Some of his selections will do better than others; some may "go sour," but wide diversification will ensure his getting a fair Average result. Better results should be obtained if we can find a way to select for purchase the most favorably situated issues at any given time, and can manage to sell them promptly and switch to others whenever the prospects for the first have been fully discounted.

There is the possibility, too, of increasing our gains if we can, at times, buy with safety earlier in an uptrend than the Dow theorist does, and sell before the market has reacted far enough to give a Dow Bear Signal.

We mentioned also the fact that the Dow Theory is of little or no assistance in trading on the Intermediate Trends. There is obviously more money to be made if we can get the benefit of all of each up move without having to write off some of our profits in each reaction. Or if we can profit both ways by trading on both the "long side" and "short side" of the market.

Finally, although all stocks tend to move with "the market" as typified in the Averages, there are in fact wide variations in the price paths of individual issues. An average, after all, is just that, a device for expressing in one figure a diversity of other figures. A Primary Bull Market ended in the Dow–Jones Industrial Average on May 29, 1946; but United Air Lines registered its highest price in December 1945; General Motors saw its peak in January 1946; Goodyear in April, DuPont in June, and Schenley in August. Is there a way of capitalizing on these Divergences?

Technical analysis of the charts of individual stocks definitely answers the first and most important of these four problems, the matter of selection. It frequently, but not always, gives us a running start on the Dow Theory; it also, in large part, takes care of the question of the Intermediate Trend, although there are certain reservations as to policy and risk in connection with both these points which will be taken up in due course. Finally, careful technical analysis should, in nearly every case, get us out of a stock that "tops out" ahead of the Averages long before it has suffered any considerable decline, often in time to transfer funds to other issues which have yet to complete their advances.

Just as the Averages constantly discount all known and foreseeable factors affecting the future of security prices in general, in the same way does the market action of an individual issue reflect all the factors affecting its individual future. Among these factors, and, expressed in its chart, are the general market conditions which influence all stocks to a greater or lesser degree, as well as the particular conditions applying to the particular stock, including the operations of "insiders."

Let us assume right from the start that you, the reader, are not a member of that mysterious inner circle known to the boardrooms as "the insiders." Such a group — genuinely entitled to be called insiders, thoroughly informed on every fact, figure, and development that might determine the fortunes of a certain corporation — may exist from time to time, may influence the market price of its stock *(EN9: and wind up in prison)*. But it is fairly certain that there are not nearly so many "insiders" as the amateur trader supposes, and that they do not cause one tenth of the market movements for which the public blames them. It is even more certain that insiders can be wrong; they would, in fact, be the first to admit it. Frequently, their plans are upset by some development which they could not foresee, or by some blind force which puts to scorn all expert estimates of value. Any success they have, however, can be accomplished only by buying and selling on the floor of the Exchange. *(EN9: No longer strictly true. Insiders sold stock to their companies in the tulip bubble which went unreported publicly for up to a year. Still, only an isolated problem.)* They can do neither without altering the delicate poise of supply and demand which governs prices. Whatever they do is sooner or later reflected on the charts where you, the "outsider," can detect it. Or detect, at least, the way in which the supply–demand equation is being affected by insiders' operations plus all other prevailing market factors. So, you don't need to be an insider in order frequently to ride with them.

Important Reversal Patterns

Stock prices move in trends. Some of those trends are straight, some are curved; some are brief and some are long-continued; some are irregular or poorly defined and others are amazingly regular or "normal," produced in a series of action and reaction waves of great uniformity. Sooner or later, these trends change direction; they may reverse (as from up to down) or they may be interrupted by some sort of sideways movement and then, after a time, proceed again in their former direction.

In most cases, when a price trend is in the process of Reversal, either from up to down or from down to up, a characteristic area or "pattern" takes shape on the chart, becomes recognizable as a Reversal Formation. Some of these chart pictures are built and completed very quickly, while others may require several weeks to reach a stage where one can surely say that a reversal of trend is definitely indicated. Speaking in broad generalities, the greater the Reversal Area — the wider the price fluctuations within it, the longer it takes to build, the more shares transferred during its construction — the more important its implications. Thus, roughly speaking, a big Reversal Formation suggests a big move to follow and a small pattern, a small move. Needless to say, the first and most important task of the technical chart analyst is to learn to know the important Reversal Formations and to judge what they may signify in terms of trading opportunities.

There is one recognized Reversal Pattern which appears and is completed within a single day's trading, and is, in consequence, named the "One-Day Reversal." There are times when it has great significance as calling a halt, at least temporarily, to any up or down move, but in its ordinary manifestations it does not imply much of an immediate move in the opposite direction. It is a useful pattern and we shall have more to say about it later. But the price formations from which extensive new trends proceed take time to build. One does not bring instantly to a stop a heavy car moving at 70 miles an hour and, all within the same split second, turn it around and get it moving back down the road in the opposite direction at 70 miles an hour.

Time Required to Reverse Trend

But we do not need to lean on a racing automobile analogy to explain why it takes time (and volume and price action) to produce an important Trend Reversal. The logic of it is plain enough, if we take but a moment to examine it. We can do so most easily by describing what might have (and, doubtless, many times has) happened in specific terms. Suppose a certain well-informed and well-financed coterie *(EN9: A congerie of mutual funds, for example.)* decides that the shares of a certain company, now selling around 40, are cheap, that this company's affairs are progressing so satisfactorily that, before long, it will attract the attention of many investors and its stock will be in demand at much higher levels, perhaps at 60 or 65. Our group realizes that if they manage their market operations skillfully, if nothing unforeseen intervenes to upset their calculations, they can "take" 20 points out of the situation. So they proceed to buy in all offerings, going about this business as quietly as possible, until they have accumulated their "line," which may run to several thousand shares and represent practically all of the current floating supply of the issue. Then they wait. Presently, professionals become suspicious and the rumor circulates that there is "something doing in PDQ," or other canny bargain hunters discover the company's bright prospects, or chart analysts detect the signs of accumulation in the stock's action. Buyers now find that the stock is scarce; there are few offerings on the books and they have to raise their bids to get it. An advance starts.

The up-move gathers momentum as more and more traders are attracted by rising prices. It is helped along by the good reports (higher earnings, increased dividend, etc.) which our group knew were to be expected. Eventually, prices approach the level at which they had planned to take profits. But this operation, the "distribution" of their holdings, may require even more patient and skillful handling than did the accumulation. Suppose they have 20,000 shares to unload. They cannot throw all on the market at once; to do so would defeat their own ends immediately and, perhaps, permanently. They must feed their line out little by little, trying to avoid attention, feeling their way along and never permitting a surplus of offerings to kill the demand. If activity in their stock has reached a level of, say, 2000 shares transferred daily, they may be able to dispose of 500 shares a day from their holdings without bringing the price down. (They will be competing, sooner or later, with others who have followed their play, who bought lower down and will be ready to take profits as soon as the advance shows signs of weakening.) So they start to sell when the rising Trend appears to have attained maximum momentum, or as it nears their price objective, but well before it has reached its probable limit, and they push out their shares as rapidly as buyers will take them.

Before long, as a rule — before they have distributed their entire line — a lull in demand will occur. Perhaps prospective buyers sense the increase in supply. A reaction develops. Our group quickly ceases selling, withdraws its offers, perhaps even buys back a few shares to support prices if they threaten to drop too far. With supply temporarily held off the market, the decline halts and the advance resumes. Our group lets it proceed this time until it carries prices into new high ground; this reassures other holders and brings in more buyers. As soon as the pot is once again merrily boiling, distribution is started anew and, if the maneuver has been well directed, completed in perhaps 2 or 3 weeks, before the second wave of demand has been exhausted.

Our group is now out of its stock with a nice profit; its 20,000 shares have passed into other hands. If they gauged the market correctly and distributed their line at a price about as high as the situation would bear, demand will have been satiated for a long time to come. Prices will probably first drift back to somewhere near the level where they were supported on the previous dip, then rally feebly on the strength of a little new buying from traders who were waiting for just such a Minor Reaction, meet sales from other traders who failed to seize the opportunity to take their profits on the preceding volume Top and are now anxious to get out, and then break down into a decline of Intermediate or Major proportions.

You can see now why, under one specific set of circumstances, a Top area, a chart pattern of distribution, takes time and volume to complete. But, it doesn't matter whether we have to deal with the highly organized operations of a single group of insiders or of an investment syndicate or, as is more often the case, with the quite unorganized activities of all the investors variously interested in an issue. The result is pretty much the same. Distribution, which is simply the Street's way of expressing the process of supply overcoming demand, takes time and a change in ownership (turnover) of a large number of shares. And it is amazing to see how these patterns of distribution, which hereafter we shall find it simpler to refer to as "Tops," tend to assume certain well-defined forms. Most of the same pattern forms appear also as "Bottoms," in which manifestation they signify accumulation, of course, instead of distribution.

The Head-and-Shoulders

If you followed closely and were able successfully to visualize how the foregoing example of distribution would appear on a chart, you saw a Head-and-Shoulders Top Formation. This is one of the more common and, by all odds, the most reliable of the Major Reversal Patterns. Probably you have heard it mentioned, for there are many traders who are familiar with its name, but not so many who really know it and can distinguish it from somewhat similar price developments which do not portend a real Reversal of Trend.

The typical or, if you will, the ideal Head-and-Shoulders Top is illustrated in Diagram 2. You can easily see how it got its name. It consists of:

A. A strong rally, climaxing a more or less extensive advance, on which trading volume becomes very heavy, followed by a Minor Recession on which volume runs considerably less than it did during the days of rise and at the Top. This is the "left shoulder."

B. Another high-volume advance which reaches a higher level than the top of the left shoulder, and then another reaction on less volume which takes prices down to somewhere near the bottom level of the preceding recession, somewhat lower perhaps or somewhat higher, but, in any case, below the top of the left shoulder. This is the "Head."

C. A third rally, but this time on decidedly less volume than accompanied the formation of either the left shoulder or the head, which fails to reach the height of the head before another decline sets in. This is the "right shoulder."

D. Finally, decline of prices in this third recession down through a line (the "neckline") drawn across the Bottoms of the reactions between the left shoulder and head, and the head and right shoulder, respectively, and a close below that line by an amount approximately equivalent to 3% of the stock's market price. This is the "confirmation" or "breakout."

Note that each and every item cited in A, B, C, and D is essential to a valid Head-and-Shoulders Top Formation. The lack of any one of them casts in doubt the forecasting value of the pattern. In naming them, we have left the way clear for the many variations that occur (for no two Head-and-Shoulders are exactly alike) and have included only the features which must be present if we are to depend upon the pattern as signaling an important Reversal of Trend. Let us examine them in greater detail.

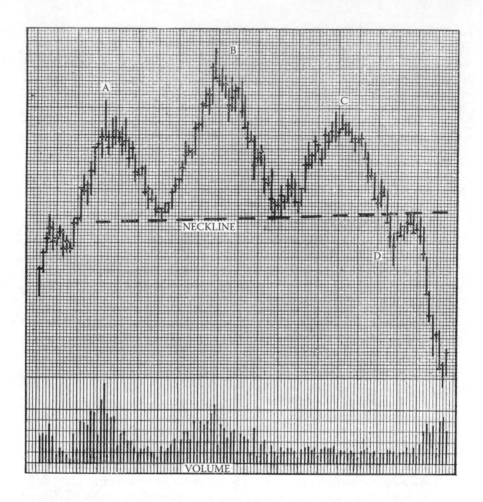

DIAGRAM 2. A hypothetical daily stock chart — price in the upper part and volume at bottom — drawn to show how an ideal Head-and-Shoulders Top Reversal Formation would develop. A, B, C, and D refer to essential features listed on the previous page.

Volume Is Important

First, the matter of volume. It is always to be watched as a vital part of the total picture. The chart of trading activity makes a pattern just as does the chart of price ranges. The two go together and each must conform to the requirements of the case. But note also that volume is relative. When we speak of high volume, we mean a rate of trading notably greater than has been customary in that particular stock during that particular period under examination. The exact number of shares traded is not important, nor will it ordinarily signify anything for our purposes to compare a daily volume of, say, 6500 shares in Radio Corporation with 500 in Bohn Aluminum and

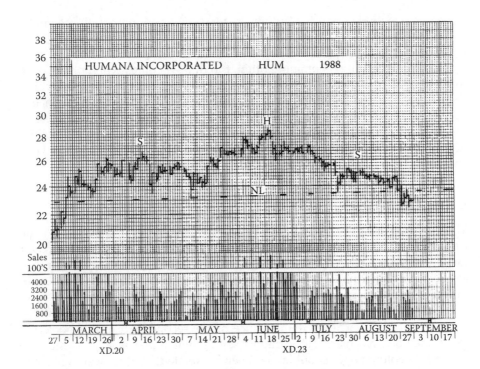

FIGURE 10. Starting in March, "HUM" formed a broad Head-and-Shoulders Top pattern on the daily chart. August's decline penetrated the neckline by 3%, confirming the Reversal Pattern. The minimum objective for the Head-and-Shoulders Top would be 18.

Brass. The former may be very low and the latter very high as judged by the proper technical criterion which is, in each case, the average recent activity in the same issue. In the case of a Head-and-Shoulders Top, we have said that high volume attends the making of the left shoulder; so, this means that activity on the rise to and at the Top of the left shoulder should be greater than on the preceding rally waves in the same issue, then a Minor Recession on dwindling activity, and then a new advance on high volume. The action thus far does not differ from what we should expect of normal wave development within a continuing uptrend. In these respects, any two typical, successively higher waves in an advance may, as you can see, become the left shoulder and head, respectively, of a Head-and-Shoulders Reversal.

The first suggestion that a Head-and-Shoulders is really developing may come when the volume record shows that activity accompanying the most recent Top was somewhat less than on the one preceding it. If this volume disparity is conspicuous, and if it becomes evident from the way prices are receding that the second and higher rally has ended, then the chart should be tabbed with a "red" signal and further developments closely scrutinized. But such a preliminary warning does not always appear, nor should it be taken as conclusive when it does appear. Roughly estimated, about one third of all confirmed Head-and-Shoulders Formations show more volume on the left shoulder than on the head, another third show about equal volume, and the final third show greater volume on the head than on the left shoulder.

Another warning — or, more often, the first — comes when prices drop in the course of the second reaction (i.e., from the head) below the level of the Top of the left shoulder. Such action, as we shall see later on in our specific study of Support and Resistance levels, is significant of weakness in the price structure. So far it is Minor; it may be only temporary; it is certainly not conclusive. Nevertheless, when this occurs, put a double red tab on your chart.

Breaking the Neckline

The real tip-off appears when activity fails to pick up appreciably on the third rally, the right shoulder. If the market remains dull as prices recover (at which stage you can draw a tentative "neckline" on your chart) and if, as they approach the approximate level of the left shoulder Top and begin to round over, volume is still relatively small, your Head-and-Shoulders Top is at least 75% completed. Although the specific application of these pattern studies in trading tactics is the province of the second part of this book, we may note here that many stock traders sell or switch just as soon as they are sure a low-volume right shoulder has been completed, without waiting for the final confirmation which we named under D as the breaking of the neckline.

Nevertheless, the Head-and-Shoulders is not complete, and an important Reversal of Trend is not conclusively signaled until the neckline has been penetrated downside by a decisive margin. Until the neckline is broken, a certain percentage of Head-and-Shoulders developments, perhaps 20%, are "saved"; i.e., prices go no lower, but simply flounder around listlessly for a period of time in the general range of the right shoulder, eventually firm up, and renew their advance.

Finally, it must be said that, in rare cases, a Head-and-Shoulders Top is confirmed by a decisive neckline penetration and still prices do not go down much farther. "False moves" such as this are the most difficult phenomena with which the technical analyst has to cope. Fortunately, in the case of the Head-and-Shoulders, they are extremely rare. The odds are so overwhelmingly in favor of the downtrend continuing once a Head-and-Shoulders has been confirmed that it pays to believe the evidence of the chart no matter how much it may appear to be out of accord with the prevailing news or market psychology.

There is one thing that can be said and is worth noting about Head-and-Shoulders Formations that fail completion or produce false confirmations. Such developments almost never occur in the early stages of a Primary Advance. A Head-and-Shoulders that does not "work" is a warning that, even though there is still some life in the situation, a genuine turn is near. The next time something in the nature of a Reversal Pattern begins to appear on the charts it is apt to be final.

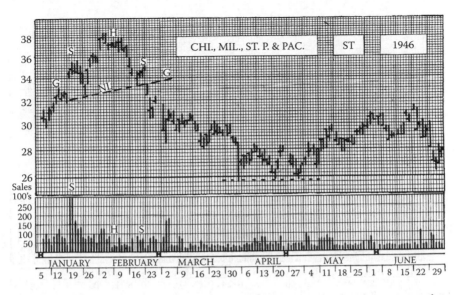

FIGURE 11. Daily chart of Chicago, Milwaukee, St. Paul & Pacific common from January 1 to June 29, 1946. Head-and-Shoulders which topped this issue's Primary Advance in February was unmistakable despite small size of shoulders (S S). Note volume pattern. Measuring implication (see following pages) of this formation was carried out by April. Rectangular price congestion of March 30 to May 4 is a subject of Chapter 9. "ST" fell to 11½ in October.

Variations in Head-and-Shoulders Tops

There is a tendency, surprising when one thinks of all the vagaries of news and crosscurrents which may influence day-to-day trading, for Head-and-Shoulders Patterns to develop a high degree of symmetry. The neckline tends to be horizontal and the right shoulder tends to resemble the left in price confirmation (although not, of course, in volume); there is a sort of satisfying balance to the overall picture. But symmetry is not essential to a significant Head-and-Shoulders development. The neckline may slope up (from left to right) or down. The only qualification on an up-sloping neckline is that the Bottom of the recession between the head and right shoulder must form appreciably below the general level of the Top of the left shoulder. It is sometimes said that a down-sloping neckline indicates an unusually weak situation. This is so obvious that it is apt to be given even more weight than it deserves. A share of that excessive weakness, it should be noted, will have already been discharged by the time the down-sloping pattern is formed and prices have broken the neckline. The measuring formula which we shall discuss later applies to such situations.

Because of the tendency toward symmetry in shoulder development, some traders, as soon as the neckline has formed, will draw on their charts

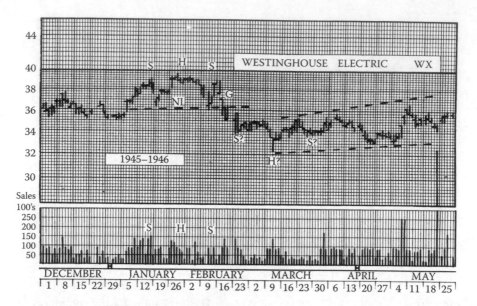

FIGURE 12. Bull Market Top of Westinghouse Electric in 1946 was the "wideswing-ing," powerful type of Head-and-Shoulders (S-H-S). Decline that broke neckline (NL) on February 13 produced a Breakaway Gap (G) discussed in Chapter 12. Measuring formula (see following pages) called for initial decline to 33. The possible Bottom Head-and- Shoulders pattern (S?-H?-S?) formed in March was never completed (see Chapter 7). Note failure of prices to push up through neckline of latter at any time, despite several rally efforts in late spring while general market Averages were actu-ally reaching new high levels. By the following November, "WX" had broken on down to 21½. Study in detail the change in volume pattern after the end of January.

a line parallel to the neckline, extending from the top of the left shoulder through the head and on to the right. This furnishes a guide as to the approximate height that the right shoulder rally should attain and, conse-quently, a selling level. But you will not see very many formations as perfect and symmetrical as our ideal picture, a fact which the several actual exam-ples accompanying this chapter amply illustrate. Either shoulder may, in fact, go higher or take more time than the other. Either or both may come up nearly to the level of the head (but not equal it, else no Head-and-Shoul-ders) or both may fall considerably short of it. If activity attending the right shoulder is abnormally dull, that shoulder is apt to be low but protracted in time. In general, there seems to be a balanced relation between the three elements of price pattern, time, and volume which is practically impossible to express in words or figures, but which one comes with experience to sense in its development. However, there are no "laws" beyond those stated in our A, B, C, and D; within those limits, look for an infinity of minor variations.

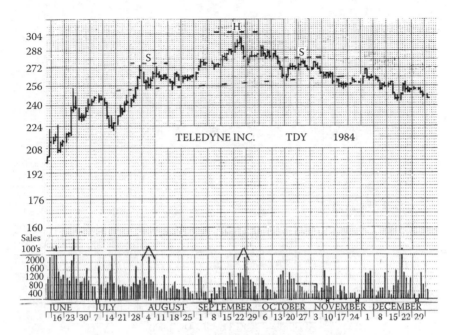

FIGURE 13. A large Head-and-Shoulders Topping Pattern evolved in "TDY" over 5 months, with December's high-volume plunge through the neckline confirming the Trend Reversal. Since this was a very expensive stock, you might have considered buying the April 260 puts instead of selling "TDY" shares outright. Our measured objective in this issue was 44 points from penetration of the 264 neckline, or 220.

Price Action Following Confirmation: The Measuring Formula

The final step, the downside penetration of the neckline, may be attended by some increase in activity, but usually isn't at first. If volume remains small for a few days as prices drift lower, a "Pullback" move frequently ensues which brings quotations up again to the neckline level (rarely through it). Normally, this is the "last gasp"; prices then turn down quickly, as a rule, and break away on a sharply augmented turnover. Whether or not a Pullback Rally will occur after the initial penetration seems often to depend on the condition of the market in general. If the whole market trend is turning down at the same time as our individual issue, which has just completed its Head-and-Shoulders, there will probably be no Pullback; prices instead will tend to accelerate their decline, with activity increasing as they leave the vicinity of the Top. If, on the other hand, the general market is still firm, then an attempt at a Pullback is likely. Also, the odds seem slightly to favor a Pullback if the neckline has been broken before much of a right shoulder

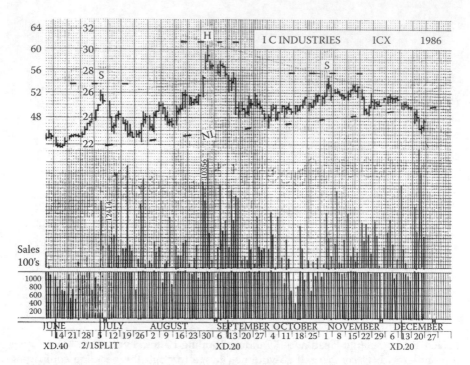

FIGURE 14. "ICX" was in a powerful uptrend for over a decade and gains were spectacular. But the upward momentum began to fade and Topping indications were evident. The August peak fulfilled the objective of the measuring Flag formed during 1985. The August gap to new highs was quickly filled, indicating that it was an Exhaustion Gap. The reaction back to Support, followed by a slow, relatively low-volume rally to the July high, formed a credible right shoulder. The final week's high-volume plunge through the neckline confirmed the Reversal. The minimum objective for the Head-and-Shoulders Pattern was 19¼, the top of the 1985 Flag. A possible alternative cover point was the Bottom of the Flag at 14¼.

developed, but certainly no very sure rules can be laid down. In any event, the Pullback Rally is of practical interest chiefly to the trader who wants to sell the stock short, or who has sold it short and has then to decide where he should place a stop-loss order.

Now we come to one of the most interesting features of this basic Reversal Formation — the indication which it gives as to the extent (in points) of the move which is likely to follow the completion of a Head-and-Shoulders. Measure the number of points down vertically from the Top of the head to the neckline as drawn on the chart. Then measure the same distance down from the neckline at the point where prices finally penetrated it following the completion of the right shoulder. The price level thus marked is the minimum probable objective of the decline.

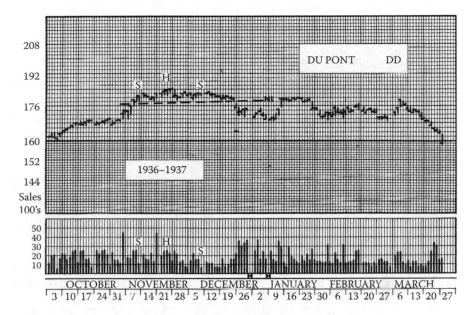

FIGURE 15. Reversal Formations, which develop in important stocks while the general market is still apparently in a strong trend, are often difficult to believe, much less act upon. But they may be highly significant. DuPont topped out in 1936, 4 months ahead of the Averages. Despite its extended right shoulder (but note volume), Reversal implications were clear on December 19. The Pullback of January, meeting supply at the old neckline level, and the second try in March were interesting and typical of such a general market situation. Compare with Figure 12.

Let us hasten to state one important qualification to the Head-and-Shoulders Measuring Formula. Refer back to our original set of specifications for a Head-and-Shoulders. Under A, we required "strong rally climaxing a more or less extensive advance." If the up-move preceding the formation of a Reversal Area has been small, the down-move following it may, in fact probably will, be equally small. In brief, a Reversal Pattern has to have something to reverse. So, we really have two minimums, one being the extent of the advance preceding the formation of the Head-and-Shoulders and the other that derived by our measuring formula; whichever is the smaller will apply. The measuring rule is indicated on several of the examples that illustrate this chapter. You can see now why a down-sloping neckline indicates a "weaker" situation than an up-sloping, and just how much weaker, as well as the fact that more than half of the minimum expected weakness has already been expended in the decline from the Top of the head to the penetration of the neckline.

The maximum indications are quite another matter, for which no simple rules can be laid down. Factors that enter into this are the extent of the

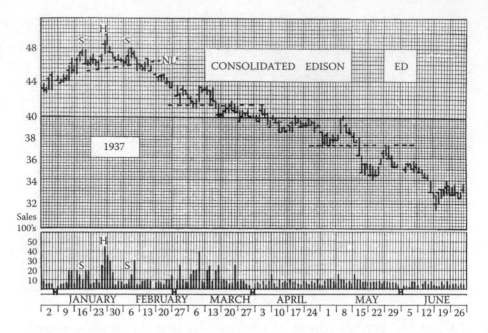

FIGURE 16.   Another 1937 Bull Market Top of Head-and-Shoulders Form, with only one quick Pullback (February 10). In this case, volume increased sharply on February 5 with the initial break through the neckline (NL). Measuring formula was satisfied in March. Study this picture in connection with "ED's" long-range chart (Figure 89) in Chapter 10, and turn back to it later when you come to the Support-Resistance study in Chapter 13.

previous rise, the size, volume, and duration of the Head-and-Shoulders Formation, the general market Primary Trend (very important), and the distance that prices can fall before they come to an established Support Zone. Some of these are topics for later discussion.

Relation of Head-and-Shoulders to Dow Theory

Without doubt, some readers have already suspected that the Head-and-Shoulders Pattern is, in a sense, just an adaptation of the principles of Dow Theory to the action of an individual stock. So it is. The decline of prices from the head to the neckline, the rally to the right shoulder, and then the ensuing decline that breaks the neckline set up a sequence of lower Tops and Bottoms analogous to those which signal a downtrend in Dow Theory. This logical relation of the Head-and-Shoulders to Dow Theory is another reason, in addition to its basic importance, frequency, and dependability, why we have placed it first in our study of Reversal Formations. But it is

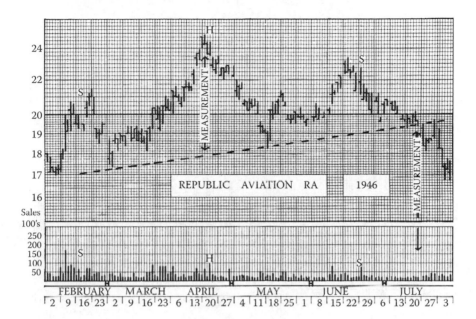

FIGURE 17. The 6-month-long Head-and-Shoulders Top of Republic Aviation in 1946. Such a pattern became a possibility to be watched for when prices broke down in May below the level of the February high (first S). Refer to requirement B. Note also how the Head-and-Shoulders Measuring Formula (Chapter 7) is applied to patterns with up-slanting necklines. Minimum downside requirement here was 12½, reached in November. The quick Pullback on July 27 gave a last good selling opportunity.

more definite, gives advance warnings which are relatively easier to detect, and is quicker with its signals in the case of up-sloping necklines. Also, it requires no specified minimum time for any of its component moves, and no confirmation by another stock or Average.

There are Head-and-Shoulders Bottoms *(EN: An undescriptive term for a bottom formation which I would prefer to call the "Kilroy Bottom." See Figure 23.1)* as well as Tops, with equally important implications. The Bottom Formations will be taken up in our next chapter.

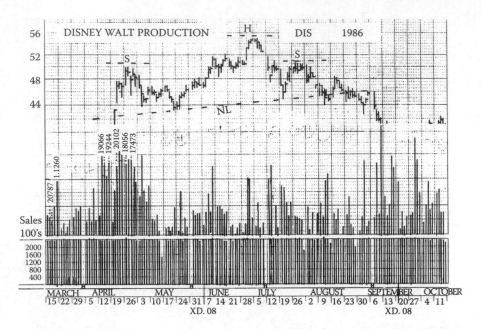

FIGURE 18. After a sharp reaction from its 1983 high, which lasted a year and pushed "DIS" back to long-term Support, the Bulls took over and sent Walt and friends on a trip to the moon. But beginning in April, the rocket began to lose power, and it looked like reentry had begun. Since the big-volume days of spring, this issue etched out a large Head-and-Shoulders Top. High-volume penetration of the neckline by 3% confirmed the Reversal.

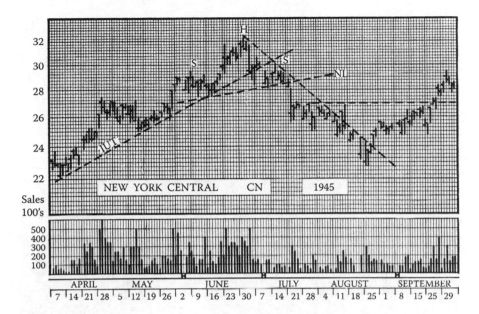

FIGURE 19. New York Central made a Head-and-Shoulders Top in June 1945. Intermediate Up Trendline (IUT) was broken by drop from head on July 5. Minimum measuring implication was carried out at 24 on August 18. Reaction ended a few days later at 22¾. Prices recovered to projected neckline (see September 25), dropped again to 26⅞ in October, and then pushed up, giving "rebuy" signal (on Fan Line construction) at 30 in first week of November. Final Bull Market High was made in January at 35½. The period from August 1945 to February 1946 was difficult for technical traders in this stock. Those who sold at 26–27 in July 1945 could, however, congratulate themselves in May 1947 when "CN" hit 12.

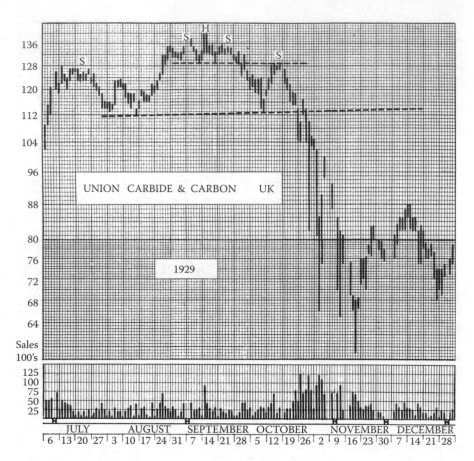

FIGURE 20. The great 1929 Bull Market Top was characterized by many impressive Head-and-Shoulders Formations, of which this is an interesting example. Note the small Head-and-Shoulders Pattern of September, which became the head of a much larger formation of the same character. The Pullback of October 9 to the upper neckline afforded a second chance to get out at 128 to those who did not sell immediately when this first line was decisively penetrated on September 28. The larger pattern "broke" on October 19, with a quick pullback on October 22. Less than a month later "UUK" had lost half its peak value. By 1932 it had fallen to 15½. Although such a catastrophic decline as 1929–32 may never come again, the moral is, nonetheless, plain: Never scorn a Head-and-Shoulders Formation. Patterns such as this merge into the "multiple" types discussed in Chapter 7. Although this example is selected from the 1929 portfolio, they were not at all uncommon mid-20th century. Several modern examples appear in our later pages.

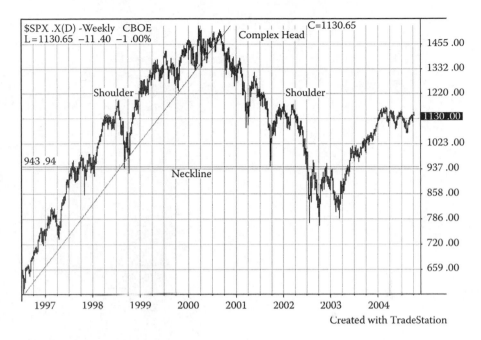

FIGURE 20.1.   A massive Head-and-Shoulders in the S&P? It can clearly be seen here, even when not pointed out by Richard Russell. It is marked on the chart with a complex head. If one took the complex head alone the formation might be said to have fulfilled itself with the bear market of 2001-2002. The long term trendline which was broken in 2000 should have been signal enough that the drunken binge was over. Not to mention numerous Basing Points and/or lower lows. The bull market (or bear market rally of 2004) presents an interpretation problem. The question is has this prolonged rally nullified the massive Head-and-Shoulders? Such an extended penetration of the neckline might imply that we were reading too much into the pattern. And, in 2005, this rally is nose to nose with the huge top resistance made in 1999-2000. the technician is *forced* to conclude that it will take years to overcome this resistance. But remember, as technicians we are obliged to change our analysis as old highs are taken out, and new situations develop.

chapter seven

Important Reversal Patterns — Continued

Head-and-Shoulders (EN: or Kilroy) Bottoms

A formation of the Head-and-Shoulders type may develop at an important Reversal of Trend from down to up. In that case, it is, of course, called a Head-and-Shoulders Bottom, and its price pattern (as compared with a Top) is turned upside down, i.e., it stands on its head. *EN: The present Editor has always been disturbed by the undescriptive nature of the term "Head-and-Shoulders Bottom." And so he has renamed it the "Kilroy Bottom." See Figure 23.1.* The volume pattern is somewhat the same (not turned upside down) as at a Top, but with some important changes in the latter half of the formation, which we shall discuss in detail. We can lay down specifications for it in much the same words as we used for the Head-and-Shoulders Top. Here they are, with the portions that differ in principle from the Top printed in italics.

A. A decline, climaxing a more or less extensive downtrend, on which trading volume increases notably, followed by a Minor Recovery on which volume runs less than it did during the days of final decline and at the Bottom. This is the "left shoulder." *EN9: Or left hand.*

B. Another decline that carries prices below the Bottom of the left shoulder, on which activity shows some increase (as compared with the preceding recovery) *but usually does not equal the rate attained on the left shoulder decline*, followed by another recovery which carries above the Bottom level of the left shoulder and on which activity may pick up, at any rate *exceed that on the recovery from the left shoulder*. This is the "head." *EN9: Or nose.*

C. A third decline on decidedly less volume than accompanied the making of either the left shoulder or head, which fails to reach the low level of the head before another rally starts. This is the "right shoulder." *EN9: Or right hand.*

D. Finally, an advance *on which activity increases notably*, which pushes up through the neckline *(EN9: Or fenceline)* and closes above by an amount approximately equivalent to 3% of the stock's market price, *with a conspicuous burst of activity attending this penetration*. This is the "confirmation" or "breakout."

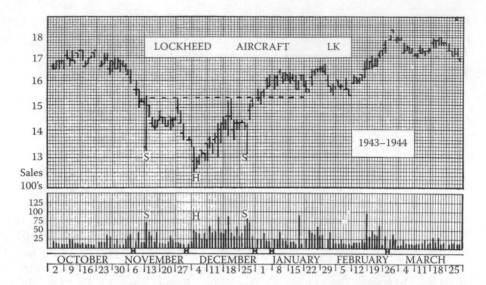

FIGURE 21. After "rounding over" in October 1943 in the last phase of a long decline from 41 in 1940, Lockheed made a conspicuous 2-month Head-and-Shoulders Bottom. Note especially, on the above chart, the volume on the rally in early December and in the first week of January with reference to points B and D on the preceding pages. "LK" dropped back to 15 again in June 1944, then ran up quickly to 23 by November and finally reached 45 in January 1946. One advantage of logarithmically scaled charts is that they expand, and thus call attention to important formations which develop at low price levels, and which would be obscured on an arithmetic scale.

The essential difference between Top and Bottom patterns, you can see, lies in their volume charts. Activity in Head-and-Shoulders Bottom Formation begins usually to show uptrend characteristics at the start of the head and always to a detectable degree on the rally from the head. It is even more marked on the rally from the right shoulder. *It must be present on the penetration of the neckline*, else the breakout is not to be relied upon as a decisive confirmation.

There is an important basic principle of technics involved here which merits further discussion. Wall Street has an old saying that expresses it: "It takes buying to put stocks up, but they can fall of their own weight." Thus, we trust, and regard as conclusive, any price break (by a decisive margin) down through the neckline of a Head-and-Shoulders Top even though it occurs on a light turnover, but we do not trust a breakout from a Head-and-Shoulders Bottom unless it is definitely attended by high volume. A low-volume breakout from a Bottom Pattern may only be premature, to be followed after more "work" around the Bottom levels by a genuine advance, or it may be a "false" move entirely. It pays generally to wait and see. This same distinction in volume development applies to some of the other Reversal Patterns we shall take up farther on.

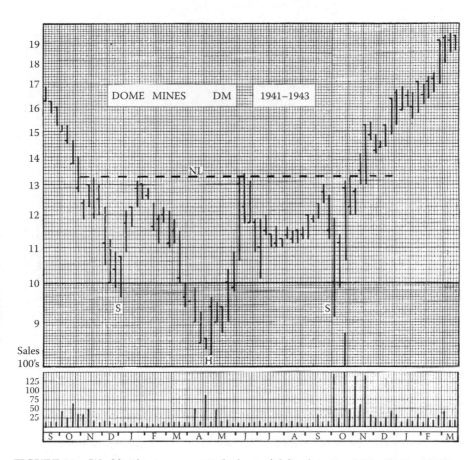

FIGURE 22. Weekly charts are particularly useful for detecting Major Bottom Reversals, since Bottom Formations characteristically take longer to build than Tops. Dome Mines made a typical Head-and-Shoulders base, 13 months long, at its Primary Trend Reversal in 1942. Note volume pattern. (Volume detail, however, is better studied on daily charts.) Dome's powerful Head-and-Shoulders Bottom was "high" enough to be conspicuous on an arithmetic monthly chart. Reached 25 in 1944.

Other differences between Top and Bottom Head-and-Shoulders do not involve any new principles. It can be said that Bottoms are generally longer and flatter, i.e., they take more time in relation to depth of pattern in points than do Tops. This is particularly true when they occur at Reversals in the Primary Trend. The overall volume at Bottoms tends to be less than at Tops, and the turns more "rounded." In the construction of a Head-and-Shoulders Top the activity that goes into the left shoulder usually exceeds that on any preceding rally in the entire uptrend. In a downtrend, on the other hand, there may be Panic Selling in some of the earlier phases of decline, which runs the volume chart up to a mark higher than any that is subsequently registered in the final Bottom Formation. But none of these differences affects our essential Head-and-Shoulders specifications.

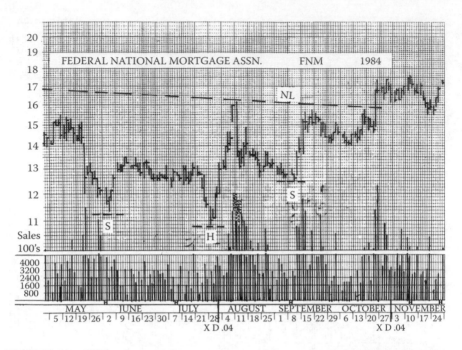

FIGURE 23. With a strong movement toward lower interest rates evident since June, the timing of the low in "FNM" is not surprising. Neither is the massive width (from March through October) of its evolving pattern, which closely matches that of the huge, complex Inverse Head-and-Shoulders Bottom in Treasury Bills (December 1984), September 25, 1984. Even the slight timing lag is appropriate.

The measuring implications of the Head-and-Shoulders Bottom are the same in all respects and are applied in the same way as with Tops. Tendency to symmetry is again the rule, with variations as to slope of neckline, relative size of shoulders about the same as in Tops. Reactions to the neckline following the initial breakout from the Bottom type appear in about the same frequency and proportions as do the Pullback Rallies which follow initial breakdown from the Top type.

Multiple Head-and-Shoulders Patterns

The Head-and-Shoulders Formations we have examined up to this point have been, despite minor variations, relatively simple and clean-cut, consisting of three well-defined elements. We come now to a group of related patterns which carry much the same technical significance but have more elements and are much less clearly defined. These are the Multiple Head-and-Shoulders Tops and Bottoms, also known as Complex Formations. We need not take much of our space to define them or lay down specifications for them, since they may be described quite sufficiently as Head-and-Shoulders Reversals in which either the shoulders or the head, or both, have been doubled or proliferated into several distinct waves.

FIGURE 23.1. *EN: At the risk of being considered a comic (actually, a satirist), I suggest that, though the image is comical, the pattern is more descriptive of the incongruously named "Head-and-Shoulders Bottom" than the present terminology. Left hand equals left shoulder. Right hand equals right shoulder and nose equals head and neckline equals fence line, or, as easily, neckline. I am teaching all of my students to think and use this term, which makes much more sense than the absurd "upside down Head-and-Shoulders Bottom standing on its head." One hundred years from now this contribution to the nomenclature will be accepted as totally descriptive and appropriate and the term "Head-and Shoulders Bottom" will have disappeared from the lexicon.*

Almost any combination is possible, of which only a few can be illustrated in the actual chart examples reproduced with this chapter. Formations of this type appear with fair frequency at Primary Bottoms and Tops, but more often at Bottoms than at Tops. They appear less frequently at Intermediate Reversals.

A common form consists of two left shoulders of approximately equal size, a single head, and then two right shoulders, again of approximately even size and balancing the two on the left. Another is made up of two heads with two or more shoulders on either side. Still another, of which you will usually find several good examples at any Major Market Turn, consists of double shoulders on either side of a head which is itself composed of a small but quite distinguishable Head-and-Shoulders development.

Tendency to Symmetry

We have mentioned the tendency toward symmetry in the simple Head-and-Shoulders Formation. Patterns of the Multiple or Complex type show an even stronger urge toward symmetry — so strong, in fact, that it may be counted on in determining trading policy. If there are two shoulders on the left, there are almost always two on the right of nearly the same size and duration. (Of course, one does not know that a Multiple is in process of formation until its right shoulder becomes evident.) Except in volume, the right-hand half of the pattern is, in the great majority of cases, an approximate mirror image of the left.

Necklines on Multiple Head-and-Shoulders Formations are not always easy to draw, since the reactions between the shoulders and between shoulders

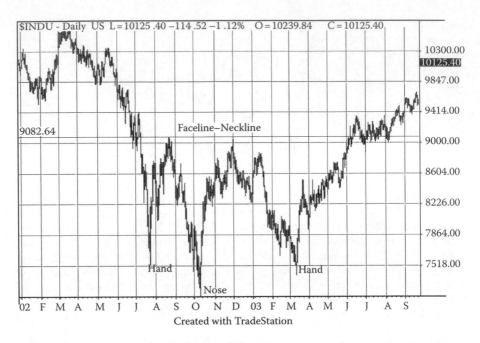

$INDU - Daily US L = 10125.40 −114.52 −1.12%   O = 10239.84   C = 10125.40

Faceline–Neckline

9082.64

Hand

Hand

Nose

10300.00
10125.40
9847.00
9414.00
9000.00
8604.00
8226.00
7864.00
7518.00

'02 F M A M J J A S O N D 03 F M A M J J A S

Created with TradeStation

FIGURE 23.2. A ragged Kilroy (or if from the old school a Head-and-Shoulders) Bottom which ended the bear market (or first phase thereof) of 2001-2002. Some 7½ months in formation it threw a few knuckle balls and curves and looked right up to March 2003 as though it were a bear market rally. Once the neckline was taken out there was no arguing with it. It was a real bottom. It balked at the neckline for a couple of months before becoming the full bull. Complex economic and political realities affected the markets. The terrorist attacks of September 11, 2001, which put paid to the tulipomania of the roaring nineties and the ill-advised tax cuts of the Bush (II) administration. Using the Reagan formula of cut taxes and increase spending and start a war the market was sufficiently stimulated to rally exuberantly. Although the trend line is not drawn here the reader should have no trouble seeing that the break of the long-term down trend as well as the Kilroy Bottom demanding a shifting of gears from bear to bull.

and heads may not stop at levels that all fall on a single line. Up-sloping and down-sloping variants seldom appear in this class of patterns; necklines are almost always very close to the horizontal. Sometimes, it is possible to estimate by simple inspection where the critical line really lies. More often, there are two necklines, an inner and an outer, and no price movement of consequence is to be expected until the outer has been penetrated (which, of course, is simply another expression of that tendency toward symmetry referred to above).

Curiously enough, the "power" of a Multiple Head-and-Shoulders Pattern is more apt to be over- than underestimated. One might think, in view of the length of time and amount of trading entering into its construction, that it would signal a move (in reverse direction to the trend preceding it) of greater extent than the simple Head-and-Shoulders. Yet, in its immediate

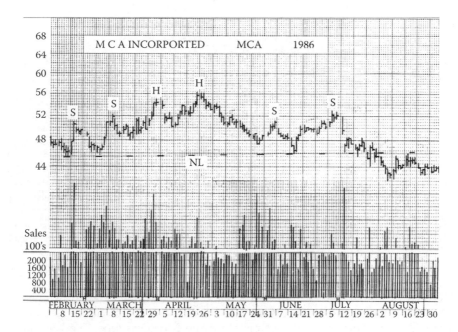

FIGURE 24. "MCA" enjoyed an excellent advance from 1980–1986. But the going became increasingly difficult after the turn of the year, when this issue began to challenge its 1985 high. Although the Bulls did manage to set a new high water mark in April, a series of Pullbacks kept this issue well away from any further tests. Indeed, a large Complex Head-and-Shoulders Top appeared to be unfolding with the Major Neckline penetrated slightly on the sell-off.

consequences, at least, the Complex shows consistently less power. Minimum measuring rules for the two types of formations are the same and are applied in the same manner. The difference between the patterns appears in the price action after the minimum has been reached. The first downswing out of a plain Head-and-Shoulders Top, not counting any early Pullback Rally, will frequently carry out the minimum measuring implications of that pattern quickly and run well beyond it. From a Multiple Top, the first downswing is often more leisurely, and very seldom does it exceed the bare minimum — a probability well worth remembering when you are dealing with an Intermediate rather than a Primary Top. Of course, if the Complex does develop at a turn in the Primary Trend, prices will eventually go much farther, but even then there is usually a strong recovery (or reaction, in the case of a Bottom) from the "minimum rule" level.

A Leisurely Pattern

The volume attending the construction of Multiple Head-and-Shoulders conforms in general to the "laws" we have previously stated and explained for simple Head-and-Shoulders Reversals. During the earlier stages of Multiple

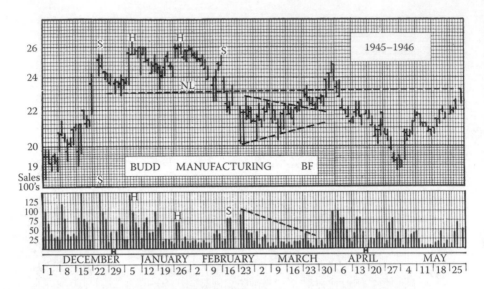

FIGURE 25. An "ideal" Multiple Top made by Budd in 1946, with two heads. Observe accompanying volume. Prices often break away from Complex Formations more reluctantly than from the simple Head-and-Shoulders type. The late March rally, which went back through the old neckline, was greater than normal in that respect, but the general market Averages were pushing to new highs at this time. Re-penetration of a neckline does not, of itself alone, cancel the implications of a Reversal Formation.

Formation development, the volume chart may show much irregularity with little recognizable pattern, but in the latter stages, its correspondence with the Head-and-Shoulders Trend should be plainly seen.

There is something about Multiple Head-and-Shoulders patterns especially pleasing to technical chart followers. Because of their symmetrical tendencies, it is fascinating to watch them evolve to completion. Once completed, however, they may try your patience by their seeming reluctance to "get going" with a new trend. On that account, it becomes easy at times to jump to the conclusion that they have "blown out," i.e., produced a false signal. Actually, except in the matter of extent of move which we have already discussed, they are fully as reliable as the plain Head-and-Shoulders. False moves are relatively rare with both. And in those extraordinary cases when a Complex Formation does go wrong, it still stands, like the plain Head-and-Shoulders, as a warning that the final Reversal is near.

Rounding Tops and Bottoms

The Multiple Formations we have just examined are produced by a sort of extension or proliferation of the ordinary Head-and-Shoulders pattern. Carry this process still further and the Complexes merge into our next class of Reversals, known as Rounding Turns.

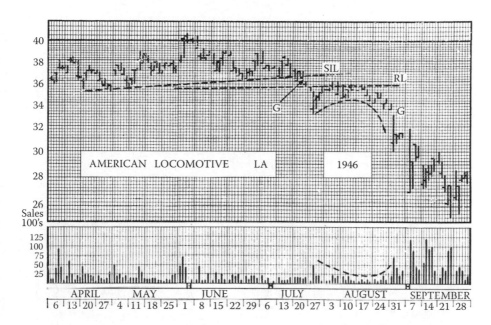

FIGURE 26. The long Multiple Head-and-Shoulders Top made by American Locomotive in 1946 displays very well the sort of volume pattern — irregular, but taking on definitely Bearish character in its latter half — that is normal to this formation. The rounded Bear Market Rally of August (compare price and volume trends) was unable to attain the old neckline, but was stopped at a Resistance (RL) created by earlier Bottom levels (see Chapter 13). G and G mark Breakaway Gaps which were not "covered" (see Chapter 12).

In our first approach to the theory of chart Reversal Patterns, we saw why it takes time and a considerable volume of trading to swing an established trend in prices from up to down or down to up. In the Head-and-Shoulders type of Reversal, the trend surges, struggles, attacks again and again before it finally gives up and retreats. During this struggle, the balance between the forces of supply and demand fluctuates, often wildly, until finally the one overcomes the other. In the Multiple Formations, a similar process goes on but rather less violently and, over a period of time, the progressive change from one force to the other becomes clearly apparent.

The Rounding Turn is a much more simple and logical manifestation of this technical phenomenon. It pictures simply and plainly a gradual, progressive, and fairly symmetrical change in the trend direction, produced by a gradual shift in the balance of power between buying and selling.

If, for example, the buying has been stronger than the selling for some time past, we know that the result will have been a general upward trend in the price of our stock, as indicated by our pictorial chart record of its trading history. So long as the buyers of the stock remain more anxious, more numerous, more aggressive, more powerful than the sellers, that preceding upward trend will continue. Now, however, suppose the selling grows a

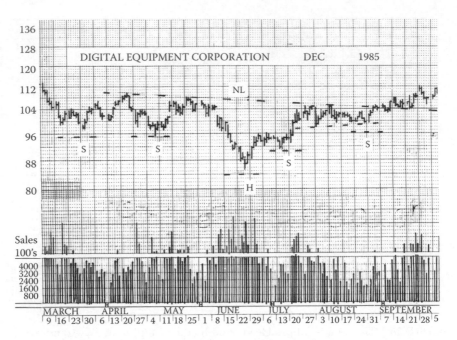

FIGURE 27. From a Head-and-Shoulders Top in February, Digital plunged sharply lower into mid-June, retracting roughly two thirds of the 1983–85 advance. The summer low was the head of a Broad, Complex Head-and-Shoulders *(EN: Or Kilroy)* Bottom. "DEC", however, had already enjoyed a high-volume penetration of the neckline and was, therefore, in a buying position.

little stronger, while the buying either weakens slightly or remains stationary at its previous strength. This slight change in the technical balance will be indicated by a slowing up of the previous advance. As the selling increases in relative power, it will finally become equal to the buying power, with the result that the market level moves neither up nor down but remains for a time quite stationary (except for Minor and insignificant fluctuations).

Assume that the new development continues and the selling pressure grows until it is finally stronger than buying power. Now the balance is moving the other way. There are now more sellers than buyers, and the result will be a gradual decline in the market quotations for the stock. If this change in the balance of power is fairly steady and continues to its logical conclusion, we can see, even without the aid of a chart, that our picture of the price movement for that stock would be one of a long advancing trend slowly beginning to round off, holding in stationary suspense for a time, and then commencing a retreat, reversing the previous upward movement into a new and Accelerating Downward Trend.

Rounding Bottoms are commonly referred to as *Bowl* or *Saucer* Patterns. Rounding Tops are sometimes called *Inverted Bowls*. Despite the logic of their construction, neither type appears as frequently as Head-and-Shoulders Formations. Rounding Bottoms occur most often in low-priced stocks, in an

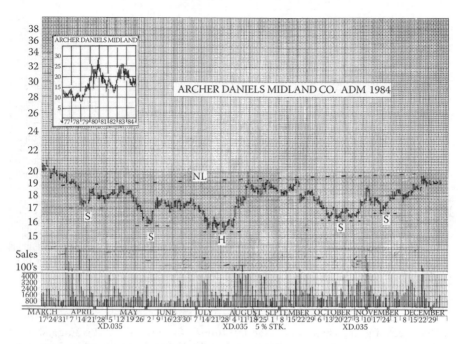

FIGURE 28.   After testing its 1980 high in mid-1983, "ADM" turned sharply lower, retracing roughly 40% of the 1982–83 advance by mid-1984. The summer low, however, appeared to be a Bottom. Indeed, if one looked at the volume pattern from April to November and correlated it with price activity, it was not difficult to make a good case for a Complex Head-and-Shoulders Bottom. A neckline through the closes gave us a go signal on a penetration of 20%.

extended, flat-bottomed form which usually takes many months to complete. There was a host of such developments during 1942 and 1943 among issues selling under $10 a share. (It should be noted here that "Saucer" Bottoms of two or three months' duration also appear frequently, one right after another, in the charts of low-priced issues *during* an extended up-movement. Their characteristics and denotations will be discussed later when we come to *Consolidation.*)

Tops of the Rounding type are very rare among stocks in the lower- and medium-price ranges, but are found occasionally in the charts of those high-priced common stocks which command an AA rating among wealthy investors and do not ordinarily interest the general public. They also appear frequently in the charts of high-grade preferred stocks and quite naturally, because the demand for their shares reflects chiefly two factors — supply of funds seeking conservative investment and interest rates — both of which tend to change very slowly. The speculative appeal which produces wide-swinging price fluctuations is absent in such issues. The same line of reasoning explains why Rounding Tops almost never develop in lower-priced, speculative common stocks; Bull Markets in those are topped off by excited public buying which pays little or no heed to long-range investment considerations.

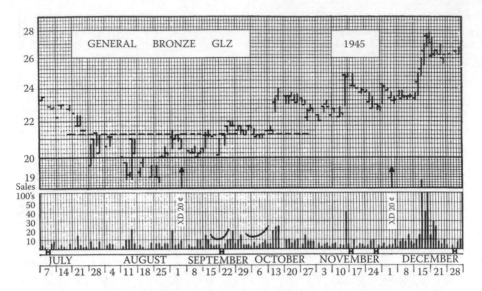

FIGURE 29. An Intermediate Bottom of the Complex class, abnormal in its lack of symmetry but, nonetheless, easy to recognize. Low volume on reactions after head was completed gave usual (and essential) Bullish Confirmation. The sluggish start of the new trend was a common feature of Multiple Head-and-Shoulder Reversals.

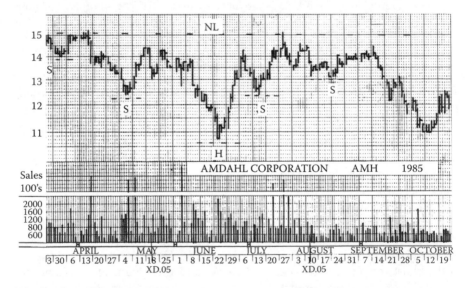

FIGURE 30. The slide in Amdahl occupied the Bears from March–June before a sharp rally gave notice that the Bulls were still alive. After that, a choppy sideways trading range evolved with Support near the Pullback lows established earlier in the year. Overall, there was a fine symmetry to this chart, including volume, which indicated the price action from March to September was actually a Broad Head-and-Shoulders Bottom. Entry was on a 3% breakout of the neckline with a minimum objective of 19¾.

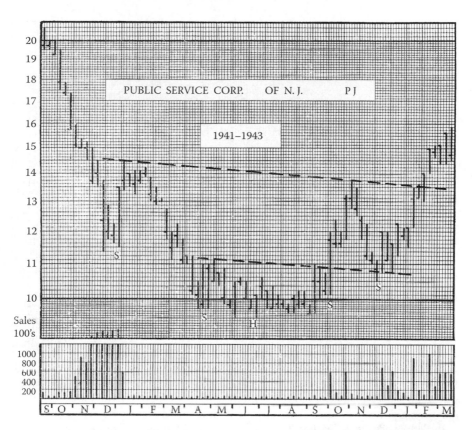

FIGURE 31.   Another variant of the Head-and-Shoulders within a Major Reversal Formation. The smaller Head-and-Shoulders pattern was easily overlooked on the daily chart. Moreover, although it was 6 months long, this pattern in itself did not necessarily imply Primary Reversal. But when it pushed "PJ's" prices up in October through the great supply which had been lodged at 12–13 the previous December, something more than a Secondary Advance could obviously be in prospect. An up-move of consequence was not finally signaled, however, until February 1943 when the upper neckline was penetrated and prices closed at 14. Public Service "threw back" to 12 in November 1943 (to the old neckline exactly), but then advanced steadily to 30. Study this again when you take up Support and Resistance, Chapter 13. This chart reiterates the point that, whereas Top Formations are often completed in a relatively short time, Major Bottoms usually require many months, and call for a great deal of patience. Allowing for the greater time needed, however, most Top Patterns have their counterparts in Bottom Formations.

How Rounding Turns Affect Trading Activity

We have not, as yet, mentioned the volume half of the Rounding Turn picture. It is interesting, as well as meaningful. In the case of Rounding Bottoms, its pattern is usually as clean-cut and decisive as the price pattern. The first step in the gradual conquest of supply by demand, which produces a Rounding

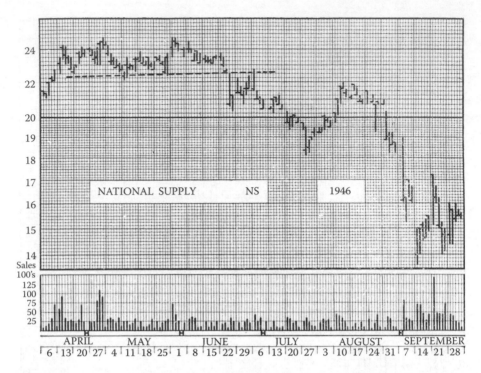

FIGURE 32. Still another form that the Complex Reversal may take. This can be described as a Head-and-Shoulders Pattern with two widely separated heads. Study its volume pattern, noting breakout June 20 and subsequent Pullback. Compare it with Bethlehem Steel's Bottom Reversal shown in Chapter 12, Figure 123.

Bottom, appears as a lessening in selling pressure. Volume, which has been running high, gradually decreases. Demand is still timid, but the pressure on it less; so, while prices still decline, the pace is slower and the trend curves more and more to the horizontal. At the Bottom, with the two forces technically in balance, relatively few transactions are recorded. Then demand begins to increase, and as the price curve turns up, trading becomes more active. Volume accelerates with the trend until often it reaches a sort of climactic peak in a few days of almost "vertical" price movement on the chart.

In such formations, the tips of the volume lines at the bottom of the chart, when connected, will describe an arc that often roughly parallels the arc formed by the price "Bowl" above. These patterns, when they occur *after an extensive decline*, are of outstanding importance, for they nearly always denote a change in Primary Trend and an extensive advance yet to come. That advance, however, seldom carries in a "skyrocket" effect which completes the entire Major Move in a few weeks. On the contrary, the uptrend that follows the completion of the pattern itself is apt to be slow and subject to frequent interruptions, tiring out the impatient trader, but yielding eventually a substantial profit.

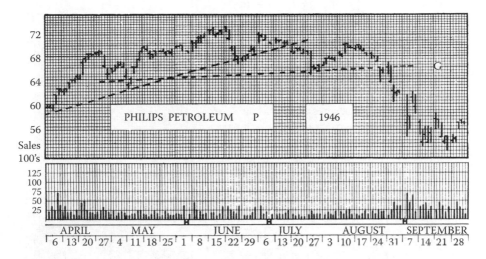

FIGURE 33. Major Top Reversal Patterns in high-priced investment issues are frequently long and "flat." The 1946 Top of Phillips Petroleum could be classified as either a Multiple Head-and-Shoulders or an irregular Rounding Top. An important trendline (Chapter 14) was broken downside in July.

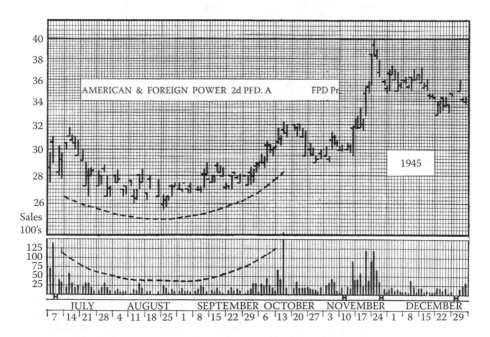

FIGURE 34. The war-end reaction of 1945 in American & Foreign Power 2d Preferred, as well as in many other issues, took the form of a Rounding Bottom. Compare the price and volume trends. By October 4, the implications here were plain to see.

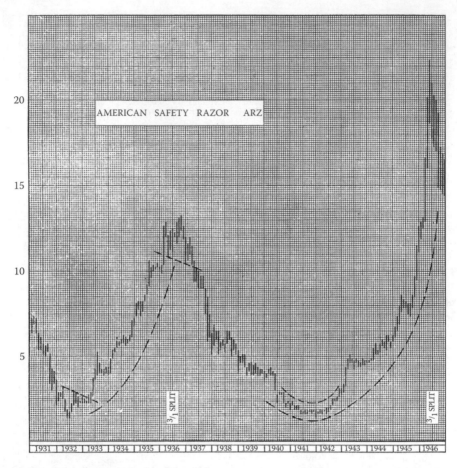

FIGURE 35. Monthly chart, on arithmetic scale. American Safety Razor's 1932 Major Bottom was a Head-and-Shoulders, also its 1936 Bull Top. Its 1942 to 1946 Bull Market started from a Rounding Bottom nearly two and a half years long! Monthly chart study pays.

Let us repeat that trading volume should ebb to an extreme low at the Bottom of a Bowl Pattern if its implications are to be trusted. After prices have passed dead center, however, and begun their first gradual climb with as yet only a slight pickup in activity, something in the nature of a premature breakout may occur. Without warning, a burst of buying may shoot quotations straight up for a day or two. These incidents are by no means rare, but, almost invariably, prices will quickly drop back again into their former channel, and the gradual rounding movement is resumed. There is no particular danger for the trader in these premature bursts but, if he is tempted to jump in on such a sudden showing of strength, he should realize that there probably will still be need for patience. A classic example of this type of premature break appears in one of our accompanying illustrations, Figure 38.

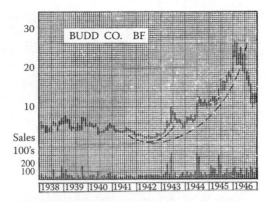

FIGURE 36.   Monthly chart of Budd Company. Note that 1942 was the first year to produce a dull Saucer-shaped Pattern, a Rounding Bottom of Major import. "BF" climbed from below 3 in 1942 to above 26 in 1946.

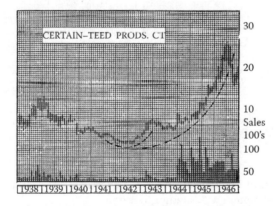

FIGURE 37.   Similar formation in CertainTeed Products, which rose from below 2 in 1942 to above 25 in 1946. Study volume, 1940 to 1945. The up-curving type of Major Bull Trend shown on these charts will be discussed in Chapter 15.

See Chapter 16.1 for some interesting 2005 rounding bottoms.

The Dormant Bottom Variation

There is one sort of Major Bottom chart picture that has been called a *Dormant Bottom*, but which relates logically to our Bowl Pattern, being, in effect, an extreme development of the "extended, flat-bottomed form" to which we have alluded above. It appears characteristically in "thin" stocks, i.e., those in which the total number of shares outstanding or, more particularly, the floating supply of shares is very small. In such issues, a normal day's turnover may be only two or three hundred shares in an active rising market. Finally, weeks and sometimes months will pass during which no sales will

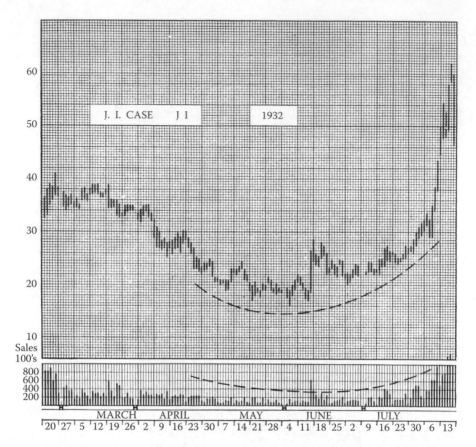

FIGURE 38. A classic example of Rounding Bottom at the Major Trend Reversal of 1932. The jump out of line on June 10 and subsequent return to the Saucer Pattern is a common development in Rounding Bottoms.

be registered for days at a time, or only an occasional lot at a figure which fluctuates within a fractional range. The chart appears "fly specked."

Eventually, there may appear a sudden and usually quite inexplicable flurry of activity. Several hundred shares appear on the tape and prices advance sharply. This "breakout of dormancy" can be a premature move, such as we have noted in connection with typical Rounding Bottoms, to be followed by several more weeks of inactivity, or it can be the first lift in a sort of step-up process with shorter and shorter intervals between each step, until finally a consistent uptrend develops. In any event, it is a signal that we are dealing with an important Accumulation Pattern.

What has happened to form these Dormant Bottoms is easy to guess. With relatively few shares outstanding, and only an occasional lot put up for sale "at the market," investors (perhaps insiders connected with the company) would succeed only in running the price up out of reach if they started to bid for the stock. So they simply "hold a basket under it," as the

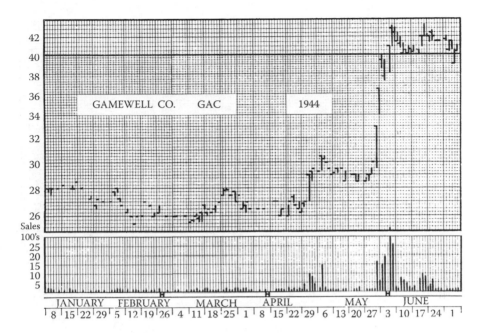

FIGURE 39. An extreme case of "Dormant Bottom." There were many days in the first 4 months during which no shares were traded. A "buy" signal appeared on April 26. Note volume.

saying goes, quickly picking up anything that is offered but never reaching for it, until eventually the tree is shaken clean. Then they may raise their bids a point or so; if that seems to bring out a lot of stock for sale, they go back to their waiting tactics.

Volume Pattern at Tops

The volume pattern on Rounding Tops is seldom as clearly defined as at Bottoms. Indeed, it is apt to be rather high and irregular throughout the entire rounding-over movement in prices. Under close scrutiny, one can usually see some signs of a change from Bullish to Bearish activity in the Minor Fluctuations after the peak has been passed, but the volume warnings do not become conspicuous in most cases until the downtrend has begun to accelerate toward the vertical.

We know of no measuring formula which can be applied to Rounding Turns (except for the minimum qualifications we mentioned in connection with Head-and-Shoulders, i.e., they cannot be counted upon to produce a greater move than the preceding price swing in the opposite direction). But they almost never deceive. Their implications can be roughly estimated from the magnitude of the trends that led to them and the length of time they take in the rounding-over process. The Rounding Turns that often appear on weekly and monthly charts, thus, have major import.

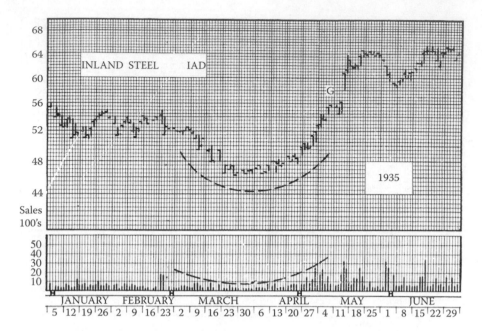

FIGURE 40.   The March 1935 reaction produced many Rounding Bottoms. This one verges on the dormant type. The gap (G), a Breakaway through a Resistance Level, was not closed until late 1937. (See Chapter 12.)

This leads us to the general consideration of weekly and monthly chart patterns. Thus far, we have been speaking in detail of only daily chart developments, but all of the formations we have taken up appear, as well, in the much larger swings into which daily movements are condensed on weekly and monthly charts, and with identical significance. Thus, volume record may not be quite so easy to read (climactic activity may occur on one day of a week and the other days run dull, which would not show at all in the week's total figure) but is less critical — may almost be disregarded. Head-and-Shoulders Tops are particularly plentiful on monthly charts and should be accorded due respect. In fact, any clearly defined pattern, which is built to completion on a weekly or monthly chart, is proportionately significant (bearing always in mind that "a Reversal must have something to reverse").

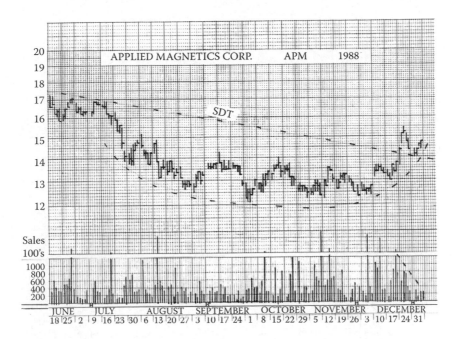

FIGURE 41. In a broad trading range (11–17½) during 1988, "APM" turned down from Resistance in the summer. The reaction, however, was slow, forming a Saucer-like Pattern from July through November on generally Bullish price/volume correlation. Of particular note was the fact that the low point of the Saucer was above the February low, i.e., higher lows were beginning to emerge. The High-Volume Rally through the Short-Term Downtrend Line signaled the start of the next upleg.

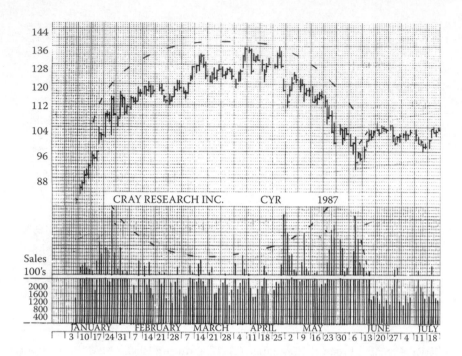

FIGURE 42.   Cray Research, a powerhouse stock for over a decade. Trading at under one dollar in 1976, it reached 135¾ before the late April gap, through the Bottom of a 7-week Diamond, started the decline. However, after the High-Volume Rally in mid-January, "CYR" also managed to form an impressive Rounding Top. The concave volume pattern, clearly evident after the high-volume decline to Support that followed the Diamond breakdown, was particularly significant in illuminating this Topping Pattern.

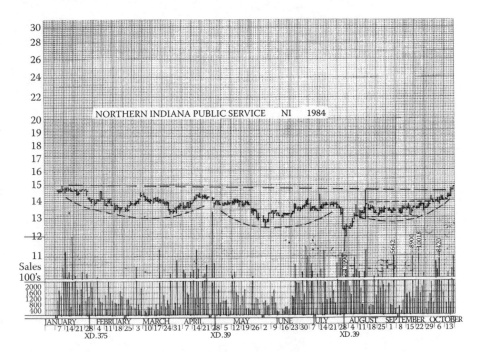

FIGURE 43. 1984. We love the Scalloping tendency of Northern Indiana Public Service. Although it is obviously not a pattern portending rocket-like advance, the technical picture brightens with the high-volume breakout through Resistance at chart end.

chapter eight

Important Reversal
Patterns — The Triangles

We come next to an entirely different family of technical patterns, the Triangles, a group that has not been as well represented on the charts of the decade of the 1940s as it was during the 1920s and 1930s. Their scarcity in that decade is regrettable because they are an intriguing lot with excellent profit potential. (EN: Demonstrating that charts from the 1920s may be intermixed with charts from the 2000s, compare Figures 269 and 269.1.) Before we examine them in detail, however, a quick review of the basic theory, which gives meaning and value to technical analysis, may be appropriate. That theory can be resummarized in the following brief statements.

1. The market value of a security is determined solely by the interaction of supply and demand.
2. Supply and demand are governed at any given moment by many hundreds of factors, some rational and some irrational. Information, opinions, moods, guesses (shrewd or otherwise) as to the future combine with blind necessities in this equation. No ordinary man can hope to grasp and weigh them all, but the market does this automatically.
3. Disregarding Minor Fluctuations, prices move in trends that persist for an appreciable length of time.
4. Changes in trend, which represent an important shift in the balance between supply and demand, however caused, are detectable *sooner or later* in the action of the market itself.

By this time, the fact expressed in the italicized words of the last statement may have begun to raise some misgivings in your mind. The complaint that the Dow Theory is often "late" has already been discussed. The Reversal Patterns studied in the two preceding chapters give no certain signal until after the trend has changed, usually "sooner" as compared with Dow Theory, but never at the absolute top or bottom price. The man who sells a stock as soon as, but not until, a Head-and-Shoulders Top has been completed on its chart may cash in on no more than half of the total decline from its extreme high to extreme bottom, since by the very terms of our measuring formula, the first half of the decline can have taken place before the Top Reversal Formation was finally confirmed.

Make up your mind that there is no help for it. Somebody, of course, managed to sell his shares at the very top eighth of a point on the peak of the "head" (and some poor devil bought them). The seller was just plain lucky! His exploit can be truly compared with a "hole-in-one" in golf. Even a complete duffer occasionally enjoys that thrill. But the more experienced a player, the better satisfied he is to land safely on the green and not too far from the cup. The more experienced an investor, the less concerned he is with getting the last point, or even the last ten points, out of his market commitments.

No one can ever be sure *at the time* that he is selling at the final high. No rules or methods have ever been devised — or ever will be — to ensure buying within fractions of the Bottom, or selling within fractions of the Top. Of course, a man can make certain of buying a stock at its absolute low provided he is prepared to take at that figure every last share offered, even to the entire outstanding issue if necessary. It might, in theory, require as much as $3.7 billion to "put a bottom" under U.S. Steel at 70, *(EN9: ca. 1950s)* in case you are tempted.

The reader, who at this point may think we "protest too much," will see more excuses for the foregoing remarks when we take up the habits of Triangles, for these formations are not always indicative of Trend Reversal. On the contrary, except in certain rather uncommon varieties, they are more apt to signal what may most conveniently be termed *Consolidation*, terminating an up or down move only temporarily and setting the stage for another strong move *in the same direction* later on. (Schabacker called such chart formations "Continuation Patterns.") The reason for including Triangles in this section of our studies under the general heading of Reversal Formations is that they do, at times, develop at periods of Major Trend change, and those are, by all odds, the periods which it is most essential for the investor to recognize.

Symmetrical Triangles

The most common form of a Triangle is composed of a series of price fluctuations, each of which is *smaller than its predecessor*, each Minor Top failing to attain the height of the preceding rally, and each Minor Recession stopping above the level of the preceding Bottom. The result is a sort of contracting "Dow Line" on the chart — a sideways price area or trading range whose Top can be more or less accurately defined by a *down-slanting* boundary line and whose Bottom can be similarly bounded by an *up-slanting* line. This type of Triangle is called a Symmetrical Triangle. If we wanted to make a more accurate application of the language of geometry, we might better call it an Acute Triangle, since it is not at all necessary that its Top and Bottom boundaries be of equal length or, in other words, make the same angle with the horizontal axis. However, there is a very strong tendency in these formations to approximate the symmetrical form; so, the established name will do well enough. This pattern is also sometimes referred to as a "Coil."

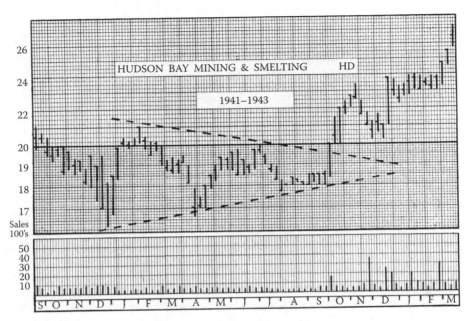

FIGURE 44. A fine Symmetrical Triangle Reversal Formation on a weekly chart. Upper boundary sloping down from February 1942 recovery high at 21 and lower boundary sloping up from "Pearl Harbor" Bottom at 16⅜ converge to an apex at about 18⅜. From this Major Bottom Pattern, "HD" advanced to 45 in 1946. Note shrinkage in volume as pattern formed, and increase as price broke out through Top in October 1942. Breakout came not quite three quarters of the way over from first Top to apex.

While the process of contraction or coiling, which makes up the price action of the Symmetrical Triangle Pattern, is going on, trading activity exhibits a diminishing trend, irregularly perhaps, but nevertheless quite noticeably as time goes on. The converging upper and lower boundary lines of the price formation come together somewhere out to the right (the future in the time sense) of the chart, at the apex of our Triangle. As prices work their way along in narrower and narrower fluctuations toward the apex, volume ebbs to an abnormally low daily turnover. Then, if we are dealing with a typical example, comes the action which first suggested the name "Coil." For suddenly and without warning, as though a coil spring had been wound tighter and tighter and then snapped free, prices break out of their Triangle with a notable pickup in volume, and leap away in a strong move which tends to approximate in extent the up or down move that preceded its formation.

There is seldom any clue given on the one chart containing the Triangle to tell in which direction prices are going to break out of the pattern until that action finally occurs. Sometimes you can get a pretty good idea of what is likely to happen by observing what is going on at the same time in the charts of other stocks (which is an important topic for later discussion), but

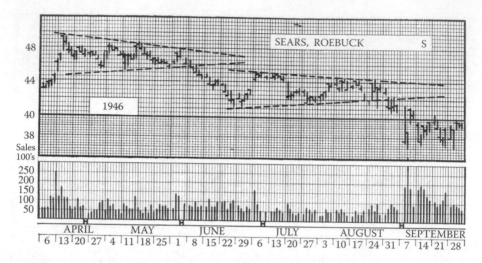

FIGURE 45. Sear's Roebuck made a Symmetrical Triangle Reversal at its Bull Market Top in 1946, and then went into another long Triangle which turned out to be a Consolidation rather than Reversal Formation. (Logarithmic volume scaling minimizes volume variations.) Sell signal was given at 44½ and again at 41. Decline continued to 30½.

often, there is nothing to do but wait until the market makes up its mind which way to go. And "making up its mind" is just what the market seems to be doing when it builds a Triangle; everything about this pattern appears to exemplify doubt, vacillation, and stalling until finally a decision is reached.

Some Cautions About Symmetrical Triangles

A compact, clean-cut Triangle is a fascinating picture, but it has its tricky features. The beginner in technical chart analysis is quite naturally prone to look for Triangles constantly, and will often think he has detected them when, in fact, something entirely different is in the process of development. Remember that it takes two points to determine a line. The top boundary line of a price area cannot be drawn until two Minor Trend Tops have been definitely established, which means that prices must have moved up to and then down away from both far enough to leave the two peaks standing out clear and clean on the chart. A bottom boundary line, by the same token, cannot be drawn until two Minor Trend Bottoms have been definitely established. Therefore, before you can conclude that a Symmetrical Triangle is building, you must be able to see *four* Reversals of Minor Trend. If it comes after an advance in prices, you must have first a Top, next a Bottom, next a second Top lower than the first, and finally a second Bottom higher than the first Bottom (and prices must move up away from the second Bottom before you can be sure it is a Bottom). Then, and only then, can you draw your boundary lines and proceed on the assumption that you have a Symmetrical Triangle.

Another point to remember — and one which does not conform at all to the "coil" simile — is that the farther out into the apex of the Triangle prices push without bursting its boundaries, the less force or power the pattern seems to have. Instead of building up more pressure, it begins to lose its efficacy after a certain stage. The best moves (up or down) seem to ensue when prices break out decisively at a point somewhere between half and three quarters of the horizontal distance from the base (left-hand end) to the apex. If prices continue to move "sideways" in narrower and narrower fluctuations from day to day after the three quarter mark is passed, they are quite apt to keep right on to the apex and beyond in a dull drift or ripple which leaves the chart analyst completely at sea. The best thing to do in such cases is go away and look for something more promising elsewhere in your chart book.

And a third tricky point is that it becomes necessary sometimes to redraw one or both boundaries of a Triangle before it is finally completed (i.e., before prices break out and move away from it in a decisive fashion). This can happen, for example, when, after the first two Rally Tops have established a down-slanting upper boundary line, the third rally starting from the lower boundary pushes up and *through* the original Top line by a moderate margin and then, without developing a recognizable breakout volume on this move, stops short of surpassing the highest level of the preceding (second) pattern Top. When prices subsequently drop back again into pattern, it is necessary to abandon the original upper boundary line and draw a new one across the highs of the first and third rally tops.

How Prices Break Out of a Symmetrical Triangle

Prices may move out of a Symmetrical Triangle either up or down. There is seldom, if ever, as we have said above, any clue as to direction until the move has actually started, i.e., until prices have broken out of their triangular "area of doubt" in decisive fashion. In a very general way, the precepts we have laid down for breakouts from Head-and-Shoulders Formations apply here as well. For example, the margin by which prices should close beyond the pattern lines is the same, roughly 3%. It is equally essential that an *upside* break in prices be confirmed by a marked increase in trading volume; lacking volume, do not trust the price achievement. But a *downside* breakout, again as in the case of the Head-and-Shoulders, does not require confirmation by a pickup in activity. As a matter of record, volume does visibly increase in most cases, but in a majority of down breaks, not to any notable extent until after prices have fallen below the level of the last preceding Minor Bottom within the Triangle, which, as you can see, may be several points lower than the boundary line at the place (date) of the actual breakout.

The curious fact is that a downside breakout from a Symmetrical Triangle which is attended right from the start by conspicuously heavy volume is much more apt to be a false signal rather than the start of a genuine downtrend that

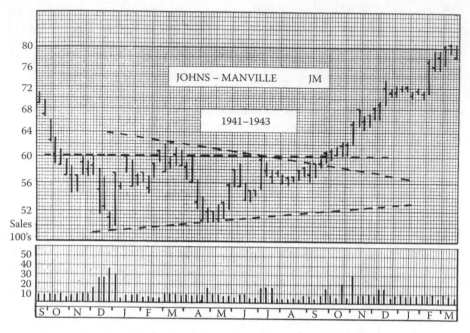

FIGURE 46. Johns-Manville's Primary Trend Reversal in 1942 developed out of a Symmetrical Triangle which had also some aspects of a Head-and-Shoulders Pattern with a long right shoulder. Although this is a weekly chart, the volume here is worthy of detailed study in connection with the price action. "JM" (old stock) advanced more than 100 points in the next 4 years.

will be worth following. This is particularly true if the break occurs after prices have worked their way well out into the apex of the Triangle; a high volume crack then frequently — we might even say usually — develops into a 2- or 3-day "shakeout" which quickly reverses itself and is followed by a genuine move in the *up* direction.

All of the above the reader will have undoubtedly found most disconcerting. Here is a very pretty technical pattern and it cannot always be trusted. Unfortunately, Symmetrical Triangles are subject to *false* moves to a far greater extent than the Head-and-Shoulders or any of the other formations we have discussed or will discuss later. Unfortunately, some of these false moves cannot be identified as such until after a commitment has been risked (although good trading tactics should prevent their occasioning much more than a trivial loss). And, unfortunately again, even a typical shakeout, such as we described in the preceding paragraph, may produce a double cross, proceeding right on down in a genuine decline. No technical chart formation is 100% reliable, and, of all, our present subject is the worst offender.

But most Symmetrical Triangles — lacking an actual statistical count, our experience would suggest more than two thirds of them — behave themselves properly, produce no false signals which cannot be spotted before

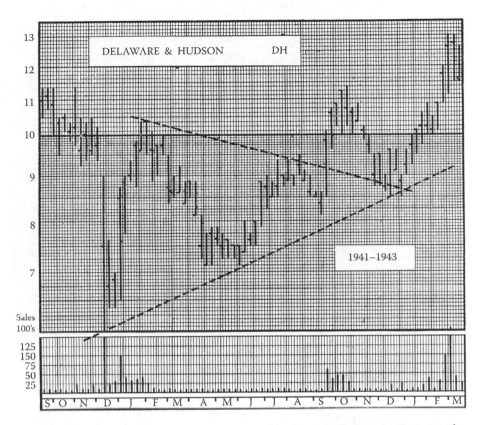

FIGURE 47. Logarithmic price scaling on weekly chart emphasizes important technical developments at low price levels. "DH's" Symmetrical Triangle Bottom started a Bull Market which reached 57 in 1945. Note Throwback to apex of Triangle, a not uncommon development. The apex itself is a strong Support (Chapter 13).

any damage is done. Upside breakouts on high volume may be premature in the sense that prices return to pattern and do some more "work" there before the genuine uptrend gets under way, but they seldom are false. We shall have a little more to say about false signals in this chapter and more later on what we trust will be helpful in developing the experience a trader needs to defend himself against them.

A Typical Triangle Development

The several actual chart examples of Symmetrical Triangles that illustrate this chapter will serve, we trust, to give the reader a working acquaintance with their appearance in various manifestations. Yet it may help to clear up some of the more important points if we describe in detail just how a typical pattern develops step by step. Let us suppose that you are watching a stock on your charts which has climbed, with only the normal, brief hesitations and inconsequential reactions, from around 20 to 30, 32, 35, and is still

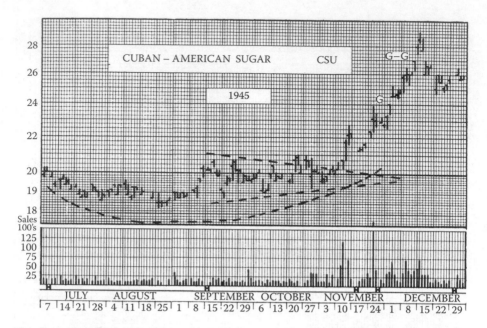

FIGURE 48. Triangles often form as a part of a larger and more important pattern of some other type. Here a symmetrical figure constitutes the latter half of a Rounding Turn. Note premature breakout October 17, return to pattern, and then final break-away on November 8.

moving up. (Let's hope you bought it at 20!) Lower down, its turnover ran between 300 and 600 shares daily, but now, above 30, it has attracted quite a following, and daily volume has increased to around 1000. As it approaches 40, activity shoots up to nearly 2000 shares, the market "churns" between 39 and 40, and then prices begin to drop. As they fall back, you (especially if you own the stock) watch it with some concern, but you know it is hardly likely that it is going to go straight down again to 20; stocks don't act that way. *(EN9: Sometimes they do now, in the 21st century.)* If the trend of this issue has actually been reversed, it should, nevertheless, spend some more time and effort around its top levels, make some sort of a Distribution Pattern.

The decline continues for 10 days with the turnover also declining quite appreciably. By the time prices have worked back to 33, volume is running at about 700 shares daily. At 33, it may pick up again for a single day to 800 or 900 shares, but the reaction stops there, and after a day or two, prices begin to climb again with little change in their turnover rate. In 8 or 9 days, quotations have gotten back into the upper 30s and activity increases and reaches, say, 1200 shares on the day 39 is reached. Instead of going on to 40 or beyond, however, a new reaction sets in and prices drift back to 37. (Perhaps you will find this growing picture easier to visualize if you pencil its development on a scrap of chart paper.) Now it is evident that a second Top has formed at 39; you can now draw a tentative pattern line (there are other names for this, as we shall see later) on your chart across the two

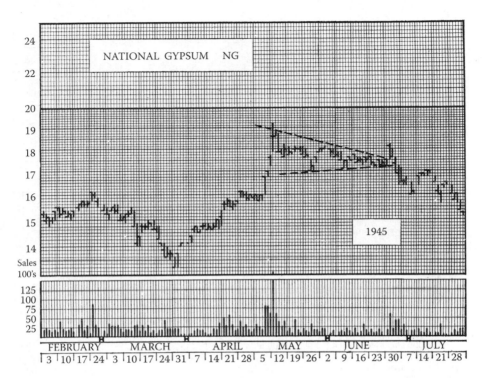

FIGURE 49. Prices in this Symmetrical Triangle squeezed way out into the apex before erupting. Breakout at that stage is unreliable; above is a fair sample of the false moves that occur there. Real move was down.

extreme high ranges (not closing prices) which will slant downward from left to right. So far you have only one Bottom point so you can draw no lines from that. But this second decline brings out even less trading activity than the first. Volume ebbs to 400 shares and the down move halts at 34; the price track "rounds out" and turns up again; trading is very dull, but begins to pick up as 36 is reached.

This action defines a second Minor Bottom and now you can draw a Bottom "tangent," an up-slanting line across the extreme low prices registered on the two reactions, the first at 33 and the second at 34. Your two pattern lines will converge, meeting near the 36½ level about 4 weeks ahead (i.e., to the right) on your chart. You have a Symmetrical Triangle — *but* you don't know whether prices are going to fall out of it eventually or shake off present doubts and push up in a new advance worth following. You can only watch further developments very closely and be prepared to take whatever action is, in due time, indicated.

The second rally picks up a little in activity, attains a daily turnover of about 700 shares, and pushes up to 38 and on for part of a day to 38½. This nudges through the previously drawn pattern line by perhaps a quarter of a point (since each swing is shorter in points traveled and, accordingly, in

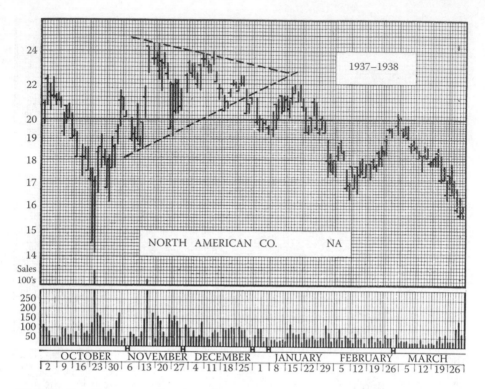

FIGURE 50. Recovery rallies from "Panic" Bottoms are often capped by Triangles, for those are periods in which doubt and indecision are prevalent. The doubt in such cases, however, is usually resolved in favor of renewed decline. "Panic" Bottoms seldom hold. This chart shows a typical Symmetrical Pattern topping the recovery from the famous Selling Climax of October 19, 1937. Note Pullback to apex.

duration). But the volume on this Minor Penetration is less than on the preceding Top (at 39), and buying again ebbs. As the price range line falls back to 37 and 36, you had best now draw a new upper tangent across the first Top at 40 and the last Top at 38½. There is the suggestion here in this slight "lift" that the balance may be swinging slightly to the demand side, but don't count on it. Pinpoint accuracy is not to be expected; Triangles must be allowed some leeway.

On the third reaction, activity dwindles away to the lowest yet. The up-slanting Bottom boundary will be reached at about the 35 level if prices continue their present course. It is worth noting now if they will come all the way down to it this time, because if they don't — if their recession is halted half a point or so above it — that action would give some significance to the previous bulge through the upper boundary. But this doesn't happen; the drift continues right on down to 35, and now volume is running at the rate of only 200 shares daily, less than it ran in the early stages of the original advance above 20. This is a critical spot. The price track flattens out momentarily, turns up feebly but keeps on hitching up, crosses 36½, picks up activity,

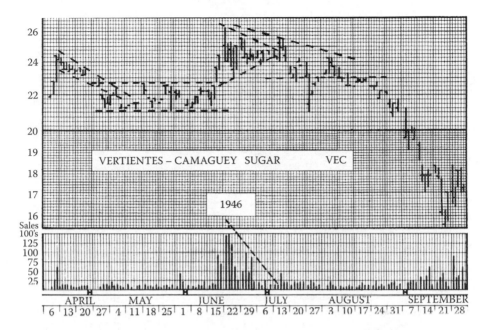

FIGURE 51.   A Major Symmetrical Triangle Top in which prices squeezed out into the apex and then produced a false move upside (see Figure 49). "VEC," as a matter of fact, was a bad actor technically, but this particular breakout would be suspect anyway.

reaches the (new) upper Triangle boundary at 37½ and, on the next day, punches through on a turnover of 1500 shares to close at 39⅛. This is a breakout; the doubt is resolved and (barring a false move, unlikely at this point) the trend is once again up. Note that it was not necessary for prices to surpass the previous high at 40 to produce this signal — that is one of the interesting things about Symmetrical Triangles.

Reversal or Consolidation

But, we started to discuss Symmetrical Triangles as Reversal Patterns, and our example has turned out to be, instead, a *Consolidation* Pattern, i.e., only a sort of resting stage in a continued uptrend. Well, three out of four of these formations will turn out to be just that. The fourth is the dangerous one (if you own the stock). How would it differ?

The example described might have been a Reversal instead of a Consolidation Formation any time up to the point of the decisive breakthrough to 39. If it had been a typical Reversal, the first change would probably have appeared shortly after the final rally started up from the third Bottom at 35. That rally would have petered out at about 36½, and prices would have started to drift back again. Then, with the activity increasing slightly, the Bottom boundary would be penetrated. As quotations dropped to 34, daily

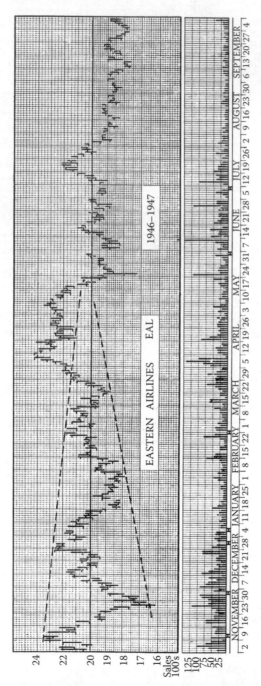

FIGURE 52. The other side of the story — an imposing Symmetrical Triangle which failed badly, although for the alert and experienced technician, there were warnings of something amiss in March and April. Eastern Airlines built, in late 1946 and early 1947, a formation which, so far as price pattern was concerned, left little to be desired. Prices broke out topside decisively in late March. A Throwback in April met normal Support at the upper Triangle boundary. But the subsequent advance fell short, weakened, and finally broke down, producing an "end run" around the apex. Warnings referred to were high and irregular volume, particularly on reactions, in February and March — not characteristic of valid Triangle development — and failure of prices to push up rapidly and vigorously after the April 14 Throwback.

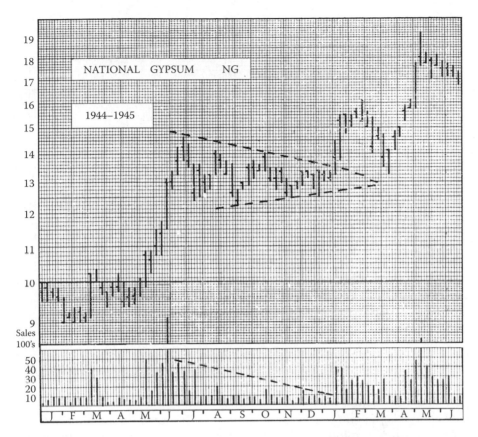

FIGURE 53. A weekly chart. The 7-month Consolidation area of 1944 — in "NG," undefinable at first, developed eventually into a typical Symmetrical Triangle. Two months after the high-volume breakout in January 1945, prices reacted nearly to apex level, then pushed away rapidly. Minimum measuring implications of this Triangle were satisfied at 16.

volume might mount to 600 or 700 shares. Any further decline would constitute a down signal and would result in a further pickup in turnover and an acceleration in the price decline as the stop-loss orders (to be discussed later) spotted under 34 were "touched off."

Before we leave our typical example, we might make some mention of the post-breakout reactions or Pullbacks that sometimes occur. As in the case of the Head-and-Shoulders Formation, the initial breakout move from a Symmetrical Triangle may halt before prices are carried very far away from the pattern and be followed by a Minor Reaction, usually lasting only 2 or 3 days, which will carry quotations back to the nearest pattern boundary. Thus, in our first example in which the break, when it came, took our stock up through the top side to 39⅛, the next day might have seen a push on to 40, and then prices might have backed off again in a couple of days of decreased activity to 37½ or 38. The up-move would then normally be

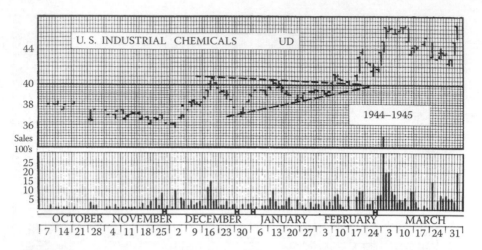

FIGURE 54. A small Symmetrical Triangle which tended toward the "Ascending" type. Note that the higher volume that developed within this pattern in early January came on a rally. This sort of action is fairly typical of very "thin" stocks.

resumed with greater vigor. Downside breakouts are sometimes followed in much the same manner by pullbacks to the lower boundary of the pattern, after which the decline is resumed with an increase in volume. However, these post-breakout reactions occur less often with Triangles than they do with Head-and-Shoulders patterns.

Another matter we might take up, before going on to study the next formation, is the *rationale* of the Symmetrical Triangle. It may help to fix its characteristics in mind if we try to deduce what sequence of events might typically produce it. Of course, any effort of this sort can result only in a gross oversimplification which will not fit all of the Triangle's various man-ifestations, but it is an interesting mental speculation — and one not without benefit to our understanding of the general theory of chart formations. Let us turn back again to our typical example. We started with a stock that ran up rather steadily from around 20 to 40 and then reacted. It is fairly obvious what happened at 40: many investors had substantial paper profits, approaching 100%, at that price. (A "round figure" such as 40, 50, 75, or 100 is apt to become a sort of mental profit objective and, hence, bring in increased selling.) Some of them were ready to cash in and did so, tempo-rarily swinging the technical balance from demand to supply; they sold less freely, of course, as prices receded. Other would-be investors had been attracted to the stock, but too late to "get aboard" below 30. Unwilling to "chase" it up to 40, they welcomed the reaction and, by the time prices had dropped back to 33, enough of them were now ready to buy to swing the balance back again to the demand side of the equation.

Watching the ensuing rally, however, were the owners of the stock who had failed to grab their profits near 40 on the previous advance and had made up their minds to be a little less greedy if given a second opportunity.

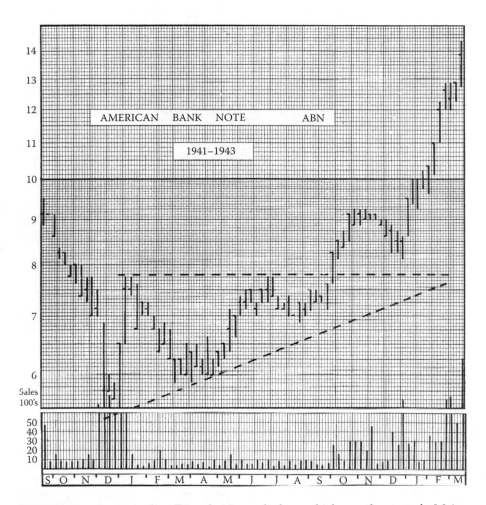

FIGURE 55.   An Ascending Triangle 10 months long which was the start of a Major Bull Trend, carrying "ABN" to 45. Refusal of prices to react to the lower pattern boundary, as here in August 1942, is a frequent development in strong formations, a warning of near completion and breakout.

Their offerings began to come in above 37, say, and were sufficiently copious at 39 to stem the advance at that level. Behind the scenes, we can imagine this process repeated again and again, with new money constantly coming in and meeting supply from owners increasingly anxious to cinch their profits. Eventually, the offerings of the latter are all absorbed, or perhaps withdrawn, and then professionals, as well as hopeful investors, suddenly discover that there is no stock ahead on the books and rush to buy results.

Since the advance (or decline) that follows the completion of a Symmetrical Triangle usually runs to worthwhile trading proportions (we shall discuss measuring implications later), there would be evident advantage to the trader who could tell in advance of the breakout which way prices were

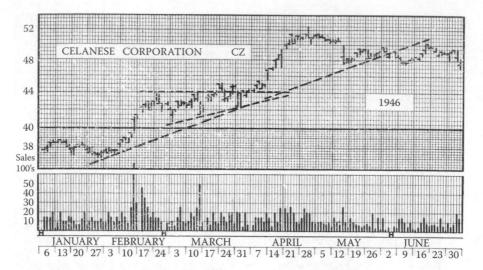

FIGURE 56. Premature breakouts from Right-Angle Triangles, such as appeared in Celanese in March 1946, are temporarily disappointing to the trader who buys on them, but work out all right eventually. Celanese, before its 1946 split, was subject to frequent and peculiar shakeouts, as here on March 9 and 26.

going to move. The odds are, as we have already said, that the new move will proceed in the same direction as the one prior to the Triangle's formation. These odds are greatest, of course, in the *early* stages of either a Primary Bull or Bear Market, with the chances of Reversal increasing as those Major Trends mature. But the charts of other stocks often furnish valuable collateral evidence. Thus, if at the same time you detect a Symmetrical Triangle in process of formation in "PDQ," a majority of your charts are showing Saucers or Head-and-Shoulders Bottoms or Ascending Triangles or some other pattern of typically Bullish import, it is a fair assumption that your Symmetrical Triangle will break out topside. There are times when advance indications of this sort are strong enough to justify taking a position on it.

The Right-Angle Triangles

We mentioned *Ascending* Triangles in the preceding paragraph. The Ascending and Descending are the Bullish and Bearish manifestations, respectively, of our next class of patterns, the *Right-Angle Triangles*. In many respects, in most in fact, they perform like their Symmetrical cousins, but with this very gratifying difference: they give advance notice of their intentions. Hence, their names, for the supposition always is that prices will ascend out of the Ascending form and descend from the Descending form.

The Symmetrical Triangles, as we have seen, are constructed of a series of successively narrower price fluctuations which can be approximately bounded across their Tops by a down-sloping line and across their Bottoms by an up-sloping line. Right-Angle Triangles are distinguished by the fact

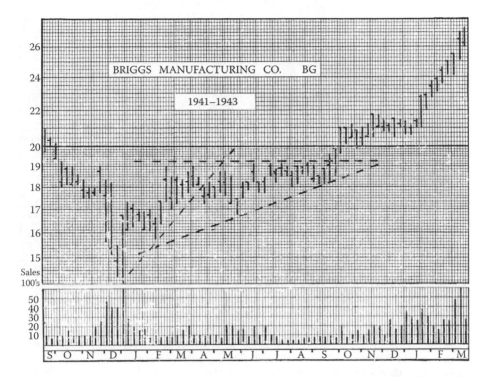

FIGURE 57. A steep recovery from a Panic Bottom (the "Pearl Harbor" selling) flattened out into a fine Ascending Triangle. Note horizontal supply line at 19, above a gradually rising demand line. The breakout at the end of September signaled initiation of an advance of some consequence. It turned out to be a Primary Bull Market which took Briggs up to 53.

that one of their boundaries is practically horizontal, while the other slants toward it. If the top line is horizontal and the bottom line slopes up to meet it somewhere out to the right of the chart (at the apex), the Triangle is of the *Ascending* persuasion. If the bottom line is horizontal and the top line slopes down, the Triangle is *Descending*.

These formations are perfectly logical and easy to explain. The Ascending Triangle, for instance, pictures in the simplest and most normal form what happens when a growing demand for a certain stock meets a large block of shares for sale at a fixed price. If the demand continues, the supply being distributed at that price will eventually be entirely absorbed by new owners looking for still higher levels, and prices will then advance rapidly. A typical Ascending Pattern starts to develop in much the same way as the "ideal" Symmetrical Triangle previously described, with an advance in our certain stock from 20 to 40 where sufficient supply suddenly appears on the market to fill the orders of all buyers and produce a reaction. Sensing the temporary satiation of demand, some owners may dump their holdings on the decline, but offerings are soon exhausted as prices drop back to, say, 34, and renewed demand then stimulates a new rally. This runs into supply

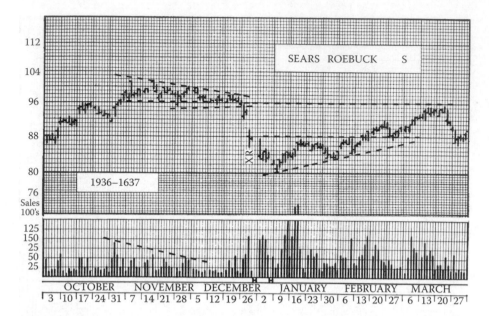

FIGURE 58. Sears' 1936 Bull Market Top was a Symmetrical Triangle, out of which it declined 15 points. An Ascending Triangle then produced an Intermediate Recovery to the Supply Zone (see Chapter 13) at the lower side of the top Triangle. Compare this chart with the 1946 Top in Figure 45.

again at 40, and again, all buyers are accommodated at that level. The second recession, however, carries quotation down only to 36 before another up-move develops. But the pool or inside group that is distributing at 40 still has some of its holdings left to sell, so it may take more time, another backing away and another attack at the 40 line, before the supply there is exhausted and the trend can push along up.

A Planned Distribution

This type of market action evidences a planned campaign by owners of a fairly large quantity of shares to liquidate at a predetermined price. It contains little of the element of doubt that we mentioned as characterizing the Symmetrical Pattern. So long as demand persists, the distributing pool knows it can ultimately cash in its entire line at 40 and need not sell for less. It is equally apparent, so long as demand keeps coming in at higher and higher levels, that, once the supply at 40 has all been absorbed, the market will advance rapidly and easily. As soon as prices break out above 40, those who took over the supply at that figure will feel their judgment has been vindicated and will not be disposed to sell until they, in turn, can register a good profit.

The crux of the matter is, of course, contained in the two preceding sentences. Demand must continue to come in at higher and higher levels;

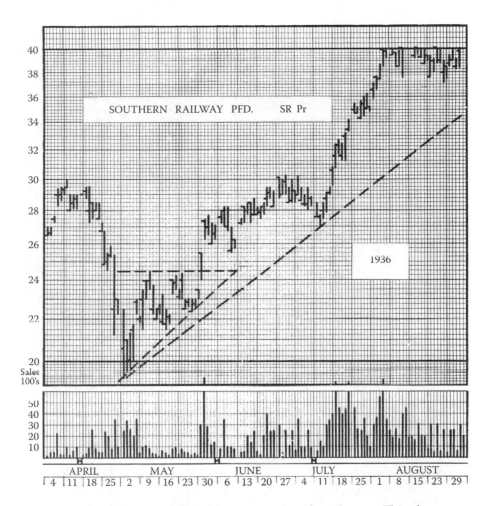

FIGURE 59. An Ascending Triangle at an Intermediate Bottom. This chart runs from April through August 1936. Extreme shrinkage in trading volume during this formation indicated a very strong situation technically.

otherwise, our formation will cease to be an Ascending Triangle. And the overhead supply must eventually be absorbed, permitting an upside break-out. If demand begins to falter any time before the Supply Line (horizontal Top boundary) has been broken through, the ensuing reaction may drop prices down "out of pattern," and then the chart technician is faced with the necessity of revising his chart picture. One might think that such a develop-ment, blasting the earlier promise of the chart, would occur fairly often, but, as a matter of experience, it is surprisingly rare. We say "surprisingly" because it is obvious that in many cases of Ascending Triangle development, the group whose selling creates its Top boundary or Supply Line must believe that level to be just about as high as the stock has any right to go. As holders of a large enough block to influence the market for several weeks,

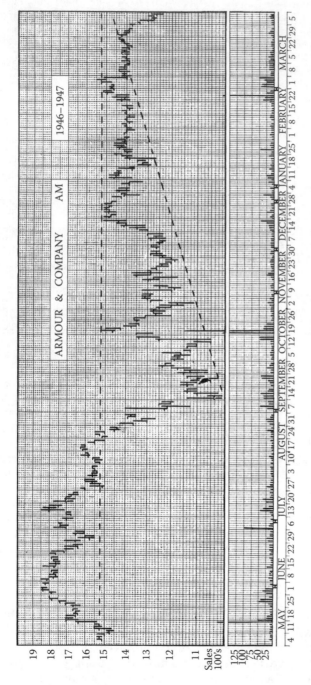

FIGURE 60. One of the early 1947 disappointments (to the Bulls) was the failure of "AM" to break out topside from the long Ascending Triangle depicted above. Here is a case (see page 112) where supply at 15 finally overwhelmed demand. A pattern such as this indicates a potentially strong underlying situation for the long pull. Ordinarily, the consequence of an Ascending Triangle's "failure" of this sort is the development either of an extended Rectangular base within the general range of the Triangle (in this case, 10 to 15), or formation of a Double Bottom at or near the earlier low (in this case near 10). However, "AM" dropped lower after several more attempts to overcome the Major Supply at the 15 level, which was not substantially penetrated until 1955.

and sometimes for months, their judgment is hardly to be scorned. Yet, once it becomes evident that the lower boundary or Demand Line is slanting *up*, the odds are certainly somewhere in the neighborhood of 9–1 that the new buyers will eventually have the best of it.

On occasion, the third reaction or fourth reaction within an Ascending Triangle Formation will break down through the previously established up-slanting Demand Line (lower boundary), but will be halted at the same level as the previous reaction. The pattern from there on is apt to develop as a *Rectangle*, a formation to be discussed in our next chapter, and should be treated as such. (The *tactics* of trading on Ascending and Descending Triangles, including protection against the rare cases of collapse, will be taken up in the second section of this book.)

Descending Triangles

Descending Triangles have a horizontal lower boundary or Demand Line and a down-sloping upper boundary or Supply Line. It is evident that they are created by market conditions just the reverse of those responsible for the Ascending Pattern. Their implications are equally strong and their failures equally rare. Development of a Descending Formation hinges upon a campaign by a group or syndicate (often an investment trust) *(EN9: or Mutual Fund or a takeover group)* to acquire a large block of shares in a certain company at a predetermined price below the market. Their orders are placed and allowed to stand until executed at that level. If the successive rallies therefrom, which their buying generates, are stifled by new supplies of stock for sale at lower and lower levels (thus creating the typical Descending picture on the chart), orders to buy are eventually all filled and quotations break through and on down. The mere breaking of the critical line, which many traders have seen function as a support under the market for a more or less extended period, often shakes the confidence of holders who had not previously considered selling. Their offerings now come on the market and accelerate the decline.

Volume Characteristics Same as Symmetrical Type

The volume section of the Right-Angle Triangle's chart requires little comment. It will ordinarily present a picture practically identical with that accompanying the development of a Symmetrical Triangle. Activity tends to lessen as prices move out toward the apex. In the Ascending Formation, there will usually be a pickup on each rally and an ebb in turnover on each decline within the pattern; in the Descending Formation, the opposite is true, but sometimes not quite so evident. These Minor fluctuations, however, do not affect the overall diminishing trend of volume until the breakout point is reached.

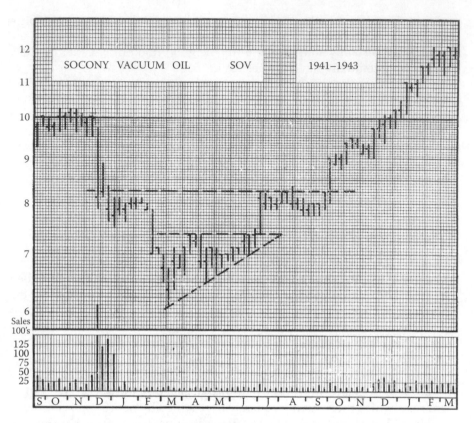

FIGURE 61. The 1942 Bear Market Bottom in Socony–Vacuum was an unusual Head-and-Shoulders formation, the head consisting of an Ascending Triangle. Note increase in volume on the breakout from the Triangle in July and again on the break through the Head-and-Shoulders neckline in October.

As to breakouts also, practically everything we have said about the Symmetrical Triangle will apply as well to the Right-Angle type. Upside breakouts (from an Ascending Pattern, of course) are attended by a conspicuous increase in trading volume; if not, they should be treated as suspect. Downside breakouts (from Descending Patterns) may not evince much of a pickup in activity, but turnover usually speeds up the second or third day out of pattern. Throwback reactions to the pattern's boundary line after a breakout are fairly common; their occurrence seems to depend largely on general market conditions. Thus, if prices break down out of a Descending Triangle in an individual stock at a time when the rest of the market is firm, a Pullback Rally is fairly certain to intervene before any very extensive further decline takes place.

Good, reliable breakouts from Right-Angle Triangles usually occur at about the same stage of pattern completion as they do in Symmetrical Triangles. The earlier the breakout, the less apt it is to be a false move (although false moves from Right-Angle Formations are considerably rarer, it should be noted, than from Symmetrical). In those infrequent cases when prices

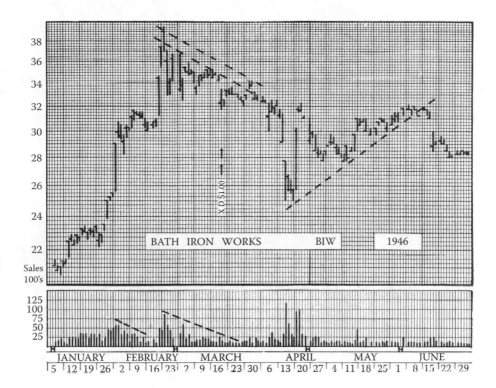

FIGURE 62. Because a dividend of $1.00 went ex on March 14, the lower boundary of this Descending Triangle Top in "BIW" had to be dropped 1 point from 33 and redrawn at 32. Despite the added leeway thus afforded, however, the original pattern implications were quickly carried out. Prices pulled back three times to the new lower boundary line of this Triangle on April 4, April 16, and May 31 — unusual, but explained by the existence of a strong general market uptrend during this period. Whenever a stock goes ex-dividend during the formation of an Area Pattern of any type, the lines bounding that pattern should immediately be adjusted to the new value by lowering them a distance corresponding to the amount of the dividend.

"squeeze" right on out of the apex without producing a definite breakout, the pattern seems to lose much of its power.

Measuring Implications of Triangles

We have stated (in Chapter 6) a minimum measuring rule to apply to price movements developing from a Head-and-Shoulders Formation, and we can lay down a somewhat similar rule for Triangles — one that applies to both the Symmetrical and the Right Angle species. The method of deriving the Triangle formula is not easy to explain in words, but the reader can familiarize himself with it quickly by studying its application on several of the actual examples which illustrate this chapter. Assuming that we are dealing with an up-movement (upside breakout), draw from the Top of the first rally that initiated the

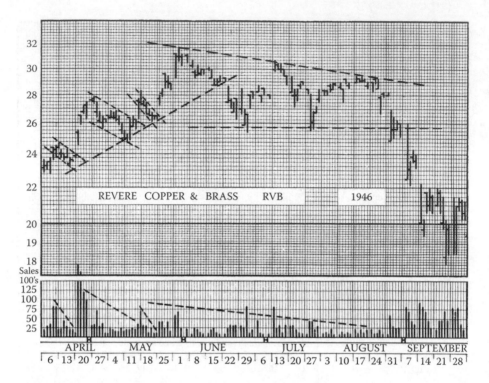

FIGURE 63. On the basis of "fundamentals," Revere was an attractive holding in 1946, which may account for its reluctance to "give up" when the market generally started downhill in earnest in June of that year. Its fluctuations from mid-May to late August constructed a fine, large Descending Triangle, in which, however, Bearish Volume Signals had already appeared in late June and on July 23. The breakout came (with a wide Breakaway Gap) on August 27. Prices clung to the edge of the pattern for 4 days, then collapsed. The small formations outlined in April and May are Flags, to be discussed in Chapter 11.

pattern (in other words, from its upper left-hand corner) a line parallel to the Bottom boundary. This line will slope up away from the pattern to the right. Prices may be expected to climb until they reach this line. Also, as a rule, they will climb, following their breakout from the pattern, at about the same angle or rate as characterized their trend prior to their entering the pattern. This principle permits us to arrive at an approximate time and level for them to attain the measuring line. The same rules apply (but measuring down, of course, from the lower left corner) to a descending move.

Although application of the above formula does afford a fair estimate of the extent of move to be expected from a Triangle, it is neither as definite nor as reliable as the Head-and-Shoulders formula. Do not forget the important qualification that the Triangle has somehow lost a part of its potential strength if the breakout is delayed until prices are crowded into the apex.

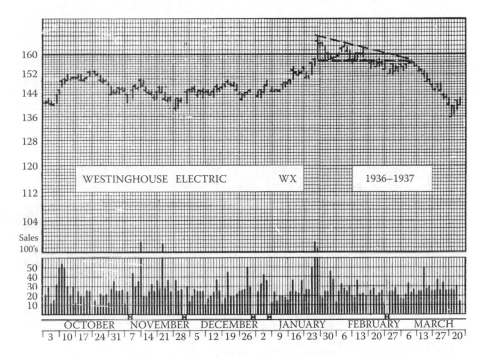

FIGURE 64.   The 1937 Bull Market Top in Westinghouse was this Descending Triangle which started in January and broke on February 15. Prices hung at the lower edge of the Triangle for 4 days, fell away, and then pulled back to its lower line on March 4 at the time when the general market Averages were making their final Bull highs.

This chart, and a number that have preceded it, illustrate an important point for the market technician which may well be restated here: When a large number of individual issues, after an extensive advance, make well-defined Reversal Patterns of plainly Bearish import, break down out of them, and then succeed only in pulling back no farther than their lower boundaries or "Resistance Lines" at a time when the Averages are going on up to new highs, the whole market is in a dangerous condition, and a Major Downturn is imminent. Divergences of this particular sort between many important issues and the Averages seldom develop at Intermediate Turns. The warning is particularly pointed when stocks of the caliber of Westinghouse, DuPont, General Motors, etc., fail to "confirm" new highs in the Averages.

Refer back to Figures 12, 15, 18, and 58, for example, and compare the "timing" in those with the trend of the Averages for the same periods. The Saucer-like Reaction Pattern of October to January in the above chart analyzes into a Complex Head-and-Shoulders Consolidation, a formation which will be taken up in Chapter 11.

Incidentally, "WX" continued on down to 130 in April 1937, made a Rectangle base there, and recovered to 158 (cf. above Descending Triangle) in August, and then fell to 88 in November. Compare this daily chart with the monthly chart of "WX" for 1935 to 1938 in Chapter 15.

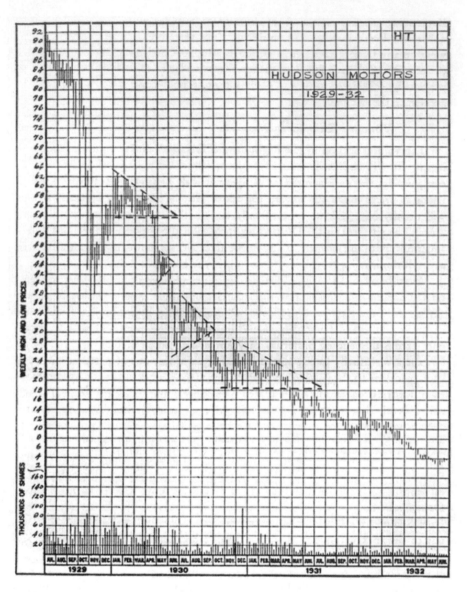

FIGURE 65. A series of Triangles, Symmetrical and Descending, which evolved during the 1929–32 Bear Market in Hudson Motors. Note that at no time during this decline did anything resembling a Major Bottom appear. Note also how each Triangle's measuring implications were carried out before any temporary halt or consequential rally developed. Follow your daily charts for the proper timing of your trading operations, but keep an eye always on the longer-range pictures which evolve on weekly and monthly projections, so as to maintain your perspective on the Major Trend.

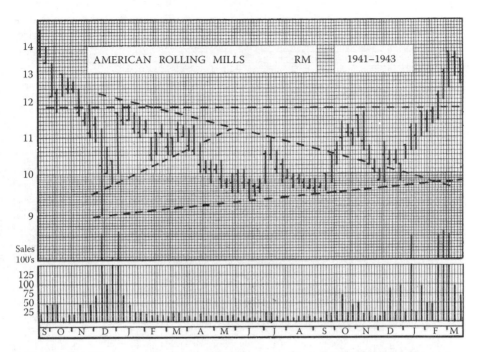

FIGURE 66. The curious, and in its early stages confusing, Major Bottom Formation which American Rolling Mills constructed in 1941–43. The recovery from the "Pearl Harbor Panic" of 1941 ran into a large Symmetrical Triangle which broke out on the downside in April 1942. The subsequent decline satisfied the measuring requirements of that Triangle, but did not carry below the December low. The rally of June and reaction of August–September built the whole area out into another and larger Symmetrical Triangle, out of which prices broke on the upside in September. Then the reaction to the apex of the latter, in December 1942, and the following advance built up into a 15-month Ascending Triangle which constituted the final Major Bottom for a trend that carried prices up eventually to 42 in 1946. The low volume on the June and August–September reactions, the increase on the October markup and, even more, the January 1943 rise and breakout in February were unmistakably of Major Bullish implications. It takes time, remember, to build a foundation for a Bull Market.

Triangles on Weekly and Monthly Charts

We have seen in preceding studies how Head-and-Shoulders Formations may appear on the long-range (weekly or monthly) charts and will have importance commensurate with their size. Triangles also may develop. On weekly charts, their implications are usually clear and dependable, but the coarse Triangular Patterns which can be found on graphs of monthly price ranges, especially the great, loose convergences that take years to complete, had better be dismissed as without useful significance.

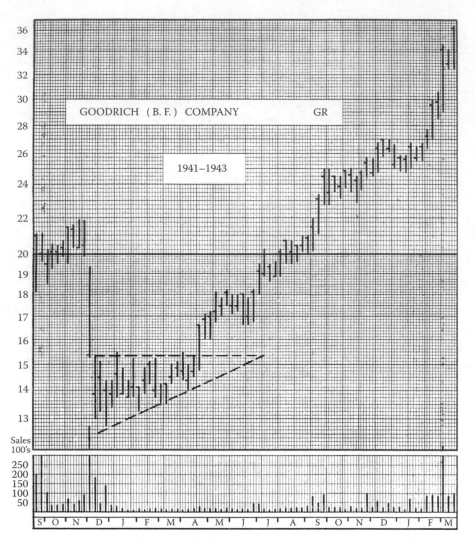

FIGURE 67.   A beautifully compact Ascending Triangle which turned out to be the Major Bear-to-Bull Reversal in Goodrich in 1942. The breakout from this pattern (in April) was not signaled by any extraordinary pickup in activity so far as this weekly record shows (but remember that significant volume detail is often hard to see in a weekly plotting). The Triangle's measuring implications were carried out by the first upswing which reached 18¼ at the end of May. Supply had to be absorbed in the 18 to 21 range (refer back to this chart when you study Support and Resistance in Chapter 13), but a Major Up Signal was given in September when prices erupted through that zone with a conspicuous increase in trading volume.

Other Triangular Formations

There are other patterns of price consolidation or congestion that can be bounded by converging lines and might, therefore, be classified as Triangles.

FIGURE 67.1. A real time chart from prophet.net. The volume blow out in July 2002 drew attention to Ebay and the sloping line was drawn at that time. Although the lines are sloppy and the pattern is ragged it looked at the time like a Descending Triangle with all its implications. But when it broke out of the pattern on emphatic volume in October 2003 the handwriting was on the wall. Ebay was for real. So, what's for real? It could really make money, not just capture free eyeballs, like its Internet brothern and sistern. It actually performed a service of economic benefit to many people. Unlike the Internet fantasy follies. See Figure 104.4 for a longer perspective on Ebay. Lessons for the attentive: power of trendlines; alarm-clock nature of unusual volume; not believing any forecast. Forecast in this case would have been for a downtrend if, as seemed, the pattern was a descending triangle.

But they deviate from the true Triangles of this chapter so markedly in one or more important respect that they are best treated under other headings elsewhere. Such are the Flags, Pennants, and Wedges. Still another group of chart patterns develops between *diverging* boundary lines, on which account they have sometimes been called Inverted Triangles. But their causes, characteristics, and forecasting implications are so radically different that we have chosen to rename them Broadening Formations and discuss them in a later chapter.

The reader may have become dismayed at this point by our frequent recourse to such qualifying adverbs as *usually, ordinarily,* and the like. It cannot be avoided if one wishes to present a true picture of what actually happens. No two chart patterns are ever precisely alike; no two market trends develop in quite the same way. History repeats itself in the stock market, but never exactly. Nevertheless, the investor who familiarizes himself with the historical pattern, with the normal market action, and refuses to be tempted into a commitment in the belief that "this time will be different," will be far and away ahead of the fellow who looks for the exception rather than the rule.

The beginner is proverbially lucky. He will find Triangles, Head-and-Shoulders, or other significant patterns, one after the other, on his charts, watch them develop, and see them carry through with profitable moves according to rule. And then the exception will come along — or he will overlook the larger picture while concentrating on some Minor Pattern development — and suddenly awake to the fact that he is caught in a very bad play. Hence our constant emphasis on the nonconforming movements. Our words of qualification are necessary because technical analysis of market action is not an exact science and never will be.

chapter nine

Important Reversal Patterns — Continued

The Rectangles, Double and Triple Tops

The Triangular Price Formations which we examined in the preceding chapter can be either *Reversal* or *Consolidation* Patterns. In the case of the Right-Angle Triangles, we know as soon as they have attained recognizable form in which direction the trend will (or should) proceed. With the Symmetrical Triangles, we have no way of knowing whether they point up or down until prices finally break away from them, although the odds are, as we have seen, that the previous trend will be continued rather than reversed. In this respect and in many others, our next class of technical formations, the *Rectangles*, resemble the Symmetrical Triangles. There are, in fact, so many points of similarity between them that we can forego any long and detailed discussion.

A *Rectangle* consists of a series of sideways price fluctuations, a "trading area," as it is sometimes called, which can be bounded both top and bottom by *horizontal* lines. A glance at any one of the examples which illustrate these pages will show how it got its name. On rare occasions, you may discover a chart pattern whose upper and lower boundary lines are parallel but either slightly down-sloping or up-sloping. So long as their departure from the horizontal is trivial, they may be treated as Rectangles. You will also find, on occasion, patterns whose boundaries, while nearly horizontal, tend somewhat to converge. These may be considered Rectangles or Symmetrical Triangles; it doesn't matter which, since the "prognosis" will be the same in either case.

If you will give a quick mental review also to the Head-and-Shoulders, the Complex and the Rounding types of formations, you will see how, if you disregard the volume part of their charts, any one of these patterns might merge or grade into a Rectangle. As a matter of fact, however, you will seldom be left in doubt as to proper classification because the circumstances of trading, the type of buying and selling, which produce Rectangles are different and that difference is usually apparent.

We characterized the Symmetrical Triangle as a "picture of doubt." The Rectangle might, with even greater propriety, be called a picture of conflict. Of course, any fairly compact price formation represents conflict in the supply–demand sense. A Head-and-Shoulders Top, for example, portrays a conflict between "strong" sellers and "weak" buyers, with the outcome

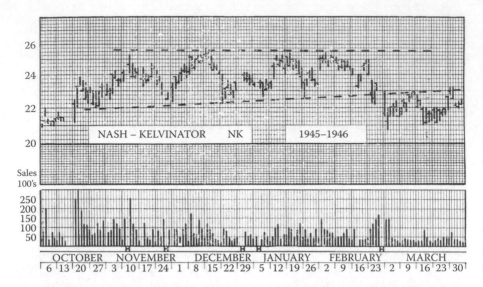

FIGURE 68.   Although its Bottom boundary had a slight tendency to "lift," the formation which put a Top on Nash–Kelvinator in 1946 was an unmistakable 4-month distribution Rectangle. Long and rather loose Rectangular Patterns of the type shown here may not evince constantly and noticeably diminishing volume, but note, nevertheless, the general, though irregular, downtrend in volume from mid-October to mid-February.

already clearly to be seen before the combat has ended. But a Rectangle defines a contest between two groups of approximately equal strength — between owners of the stock who wish to dispose of their shares at a certain price and others who wish to accumulate the stock at a certain lower figure. They bat the ball back and forth (up and down, that is) between them until ultimately, and usually quite suddenly, one team is exhausted (or changes its mind) and the other then proceeds to knock the ball out of the lot. Nobody (often, not even the contestants themselves) can tell who is going to win until one line or the other is decisively broken.

We speak of two groups operating in the development of a rectangular trading area because, under present-day conditions, that is what is usually the fact behind the scenes. This, it should be noted, does not imply "manipulation" in any invidious sense. An investment trust or an estate or, in some cases, an individual heavy stockholder has good and sufficient reasons for selling at the top price (the "Supply Line" of the Rectangle) with no intent to mislead the public. And another investment trust or a group of insiders interested in the company may have equally good and, from their point of view, wise reasons for buying at the bottom price ("Demand Line"). Such are the forces at work in the market at the start of most Rectangular Chart Patterns, but if the "spread" between top and bottom lines is wide enough (say 8–10% of the market value of the stock), the situation may quickly attract a following from quick-turn scalpers and the professional element. Thus, a

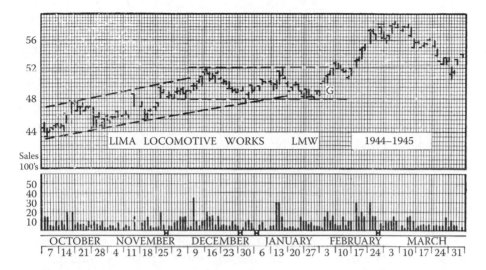

FIGURE 69. Consolidation Rectangles in uptrends have been less common in recent years than during the 1920s and early 1930s. The large price gap (G) in this example is of the "last in pattern" type which we shall come to in Chapter 12. When a gap within a pattern area is followed by breakout from that pattern, as in this case, the gap is seldom quickly closed.

syndicate holding a large block of U.S. Steel may decide to liquidate at 76, while another group decides to invest heavily in "Steel" at 69. The price of X will naturally fluctuate for a time between those two levels. Traders, seeing this, will try to "ride the play," buying at 69 and selling at 76 (perhaps also selling short at 76 and covering at 69). Their operations will tend to accentuate or extend the Rectangle, although the number of shares involved in such "parasitic" trading is seldom great enough to affect the final outcome. As a matter of fact, this type of trading *inside* a Rectangle can be quite profitable at times, especially if protected by judicious stops (see Part Two).

Pool Operations

In times past, before the SEC outlawed the practice, Rectangles were frequently created by the well-organized operations of a single "pool" or syndicate. Such a pool might undertake to accumulate a large block of stock in a certain company with a view to marking it up and taking profits when some piece of good news, of which they had inside knowledge, eventually became public. In order to acquire the desired "line," they would find it necessary first to shake out shares held by other traders and uninformed investors. They might start their campaign by suddenly selling short a few hundred shares in order to quench any current demand and start a reaction. Then, on that reaction to the previously determined accumulation level, they would start to buy, scattering their orders carefully and avoiding any publicity.

Their buying would, sooner or later, engender a rally, but then they would "plant" rumors around the boardrooms to the effect that such-and-such insiders were selling, or that a projected merger was being called off, or a dividend would have to be passed, and, if necessary, they would ostentatiously let out a few of their own recently purchased shares to give color to the rumor. The process might be repeated several times, with the "pool" gradually securing more and more shares on balance, until finally, it had completed its intended line, or could shake out no more of the floating supply. Often, what was going on was fairly evident to the alert chartist back in the 1920s even before the operation was concluded, and perfectly evident, of course, as soon as prices broke out topside from their Rectangle.

But such tactics are no longer permitted. "Wash sales" are strictly condemned. The constant policing of all exchange transactions and prompt investigation by the SEC of any suspicious news or activity in a stock effectually deters the blatant "pool" manipulations of previous years. This probably is the chief reason why Rectangles are nowhere near so common on the charts of the 1950s as they were in the 1920s.

Perhaps we can clear up various details of the Rectangle formation most quickly and easily by comparison with that most nearly related chart pattern, the Symmetrical Triangle, as follows:

Volume — Follows the same rules as in the Triangles, gradually diminishing as the Rectangle lengthens. Any contrary development, unless it be a momentary news flurry, is suspect.

Breakouts — Here also the same rules apply as with Triangles. Review volume requirements, margin of penetration, etc., thereunder.

False Moves — Much less frequent from Rectangles than from Symmetrical Triangles. A clearly defined Rectangle is, in fact, almost as reliable as a Head-and-Shoulders, although not as powerful in its implications.

Premature Breakouts — Slightly more frequent, perhaps, from Rectangles than from Triangles.

(**Note**: both *false moves* and *premature breakouts*, in the sense in which we employ these terms, are indistinguishable at the time they occur from genuine breakouts. Following both false and premature breaks, prices return inside the pattern. But, in the case of a *false* move, the trend ultimately proceeds out of pattern in the *opposite* direction, while in the case of the *premature* move, the trend finally breaks out again and proceeds in the *same* direction.)

Pullbacks — Return of prices to the boundary of the pattern, subsequent to its initial penetration (breakout), takes place more frequently with Rectangles than with Symmetrical Triangles. Our estimate would be that a Pullback or Throwback (the first is the common term for a rally after a downside breakout, and the second for a reaction following

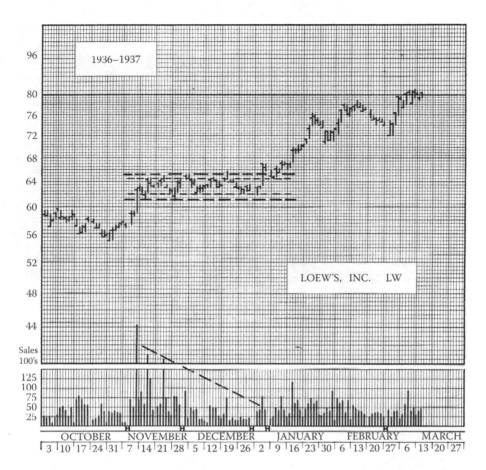

FIGURE 70. A perfect example of Consolidation Rectangle which formed in Loew's near the end of the 1932–37 Bull Market. In this case, a large block of "inside" stock was distributed at 64 to 65 but taken over around 62 by other investors who had the satisfaction of seeing it go on up to 87 the following August. Note Throwback following breakout in January.

an upside breakout) occurs within 3 days to 3 weeks in about 40% of all cases.

Directional Tendency — The Rectangle is more often a *Consolidation* Formation than a *Reversal* Formation, the ratio being about the same as with Symmetrical Triangles. As Reversal Patterns, Rectangles appear more frequently at Bottoms (either Major or Intermediate) than at Tops. Long, thin, dull Rectangles are not uncommon at Primary Bottoms, sometimes grading into the type of Flat-Bottomed Saucer or Dormancy described in Chapter 7.

Measuring Implications — A safe minimum measuring formula for the Rectangle is given by its width. Prices should go at least as far in points beyond the pattern as the difference in points between the top

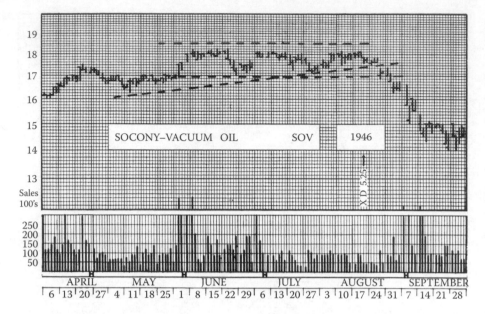

FIGURE 71.   Here is a Rectangle in Socony–Vacuum, a low-priced stock character-ized by fluctuations within a narrow range. After reaching a high of 18¾ in December 1945, it fell back to 15¼ and then rallied in mid-1946 as shown above. In late August, prices broke down through an Intermediate Trendline (see Chapter 14) and 4 days later fell out of the Rectangle. This formation, in conjunction with the earlier and higher Top, implied lower levels for "SOV" for some time to come. See also comment under Figure 72.

and bottom lines of the pattern itself. They may, of course, go much farther. Generally speaking, the brief, wide-swinging forms, which appear nearly square in shape on the chart and in which turnover is active, are more dynamic than the longer and narrower manifesta-tions. Moves out of the latter almost always hesitate or react at the "minimum" point before carrying on.

Relation of Rectangle to Dow Line

The resemblance of this individual stock chart formation, which we have discussed under the name of Rectangle, to the Average formation known to Dow theorists as a "Line" has doubtless occurred to you. Obviously, their rationale and forecasting implications are much the same. But true Rectan-gles with sharply delimited Top (Supply) and Bottom (Demand) boundaries are truly characteristic only of trading in individual issues. Line formations in the Averages are seldom rigorously defined, with successive Minor Heights forming quite precisely at a certain horizontal tangent, and succes-sive Bottoms at a similarly precise horizontal level. If you will examine the separate charts of the issues composing an Average at a time when the

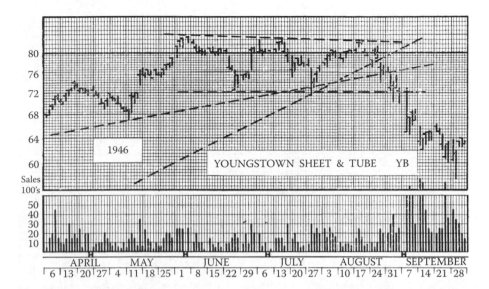

FIGURE 72. Another long, loose Rectangle of Major Reversal implications, somewhat similar to that pictured in Figure 68. Both an Intermediate and Major Up Trendline (to be discussed later) were decisively punctured by "YB" in August, just before its Rectangle broke down. Under Figure 64, we discussed one sort of warning of a Primary Downturn which may be derived from the comparison of individual stock charts with the Averages. Here is another hint: The better-grade steels and oils (see "SOV," Figure 71) frequently hold up, or make stronger Secondary Recoveries, after the Averages have turned down at Major Tops. The Street sometimes speaks of "distribution under cover of strength in the steels."

Average is "making a Line," you are pretty sure to find that some of them are showing an irregular uptrend, others an irregular downtrend, still others may be forming Triangles, and a few may be constructing Rectangles, or what not, but it is the algebraic sum of all these more or less divergent pictures which makes up the Average "Line."

To be sure, there is some tendency on the part of active traders to sell (or buy) stocks when a certain Average reaches a certain figure, regardless of the status of individual issues involved. An investment counsel will occasionally advise his clients, for example, to "sell all speculative holdings when the Dow Industrials reach 500 (*EN: or 5000 or 15000*)." But trading commitments based solely on general Average levels are so seldom followed consistently that they have little effect.

Rectangles from Right-Angle Triangles

In the preceding chapter, we referred to a type of partial "failure" in the development of a Right-Angle Triangle which necessitates reclassifying the Triangle as a Rectangle. Now that we have examined the latter pattern in detail, we need say little more about this phenomenon, except to note that

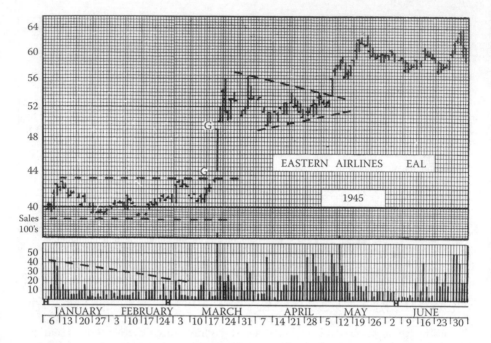

FIGURE 73. The Rectangle in early 1945 in "EAL" was actually the final stage of a nearly 2-year Consolidation in the rise which started around 17 in 1942 and ended above 125 in December 1945. G, G mark gaps (Chapter 12), the first a Breakaway and the second a Measuring Gap which marked the probable objective of the move as 55. When prices reached that level, another Consolidation developed, a Symmetrical Triangle. Neither of these gaps was "closed" during the following 2 years.

the odds appear to be still somewhat in favor of ultimate breakout in the direction originally implied by the incipient Triangle. The fact that there is this slight presumption, however, certainly does not warrant disregard of an opposite breakout from the rectangular reconstruction.

Double and Triple Tops and Bottoms

To some of the old hands in the Street, our relegation of that good old byword, the *Double Top*, to a Minor Position in our array of Reversal Formations may seem almost sacrilegious. It is referred to by name perhaps more often than any other chart pattern by traders who possess a smattering of technical "lingo" but little organized knowledge of technical facts. True Double Tops and Double Bottoms are exceedingly rare; Triple Forms are even rarer. And the true patterns (as distinguished from chart pictures which might mistakenly be called such, but are really assignable to some one of our other Reversal Formations) can seldom be positively detected until prices have gone quite a long way away from them. They can never be foretold, or identified as soon as they occur, from chart data alone.

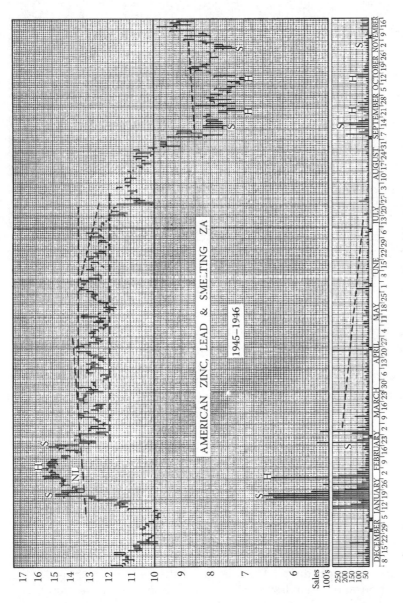

FIGURE 74. An extraordinary, fine, long Rectangle which developed after "ZA" had broken down out of a Head-and-Shoulders Top in February 1946. A perfect opportunity to sell this stock short was given by its Pullback of July 17–18 after prices had broken out of the Rectangle on the 15th. The Multiple Head-and-Shoulders Bottom which it subsequently made from September to November produced a recovery to 11, but prices later fell to 6 in early 1947.

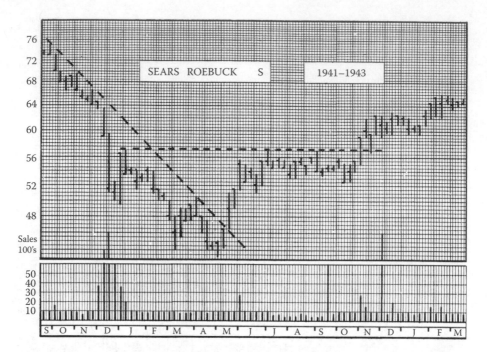

FIGURE 75.   In this weekly chart showing Sears Roebuck's 1942 Bear Market Bottom, a Consolidation Rectangle (June to November) forms the right shoulder of a large "unbalanced" Double Head-and-Shoulders Pattern.

But we are getting ahead of our story. We should first define what we are talking about. A *Double Top* is formed when a stock advances to a certain level with, usually, high volume at and approaching the Top figure, then retreats with diminishing activity, then comes up again to the same (or practically the same) top price as before with some pickup in turnover, but not as much as on the first peak, and then finally turns down a second time for a Major or Consequential Intermediate Decline. A *Double Bottom* is, of course, the same picture upside down. The Triple types make three Tops (or Bottoms) instead of two.

It isn't difficult to skim through a book of several hundred monthly charts and pick out two or three examples of Major Double Tops, perhaps one or two Double Bottoms. One will find cases where stocks made two successive Bull Market Peaks, several years apart, at almost identical levels. Such phenomena stand out, in distant retrospect, like the proverbial sore thumb, which undoubtedly accounts for the undue awe with which the amateur chartist regards them. He neglects, for the moment, to consider the fact that a thousand other issues might have done the same thing, but didn't — that some of these even acted, for a time, as though they were going to Double Top, but then went on through and higher.

Is there any practical utility for the trader or investor in the Double Top concept? Yes, there is, but it will be easier for us to formulate it if we first

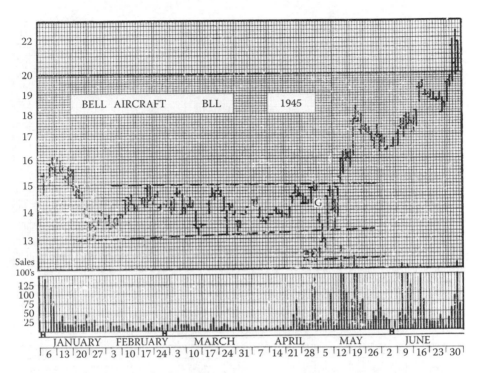

FIGURE 76.   After advancing to 16 in January 1945, "BLL" dropped back to 13 and then constructed a 15-week Rectangle. Note that the down gap (G) on April 30 was caused by a $1.00 dividend going off. The revised bottom line of the pattern, drawn $1.00 lower, was not violated.

consider what is *not* a Double Top. Refer back for a moment to the Ascending Triangles and the Rectangles previously studied. When these start to evolve, almost their first step is the construction of two Tops at an identical level with an intervening recession, and with less volume on the second Top than on the first. In the ordinary course of events, a third Top will develop there, and ultimately, prices will break through and move on up to still higher levels. Thus, we see we must have some rule or criterion to distinguish a true Double Top Reversal Pattern from the Double Tops which do not imply Reversal when they appear as a part of a Consolidation Area in an uptrend.

Distinguishing Characteristics

No absolute and unqualified rule can be laid down to fit all cases involving stocks of different values and market habits, but one relative distinction quickly suggests itself when we study these different kinds of chart formations. It is: if two Tops appear at the same level but quite close together in time and with only a Minor Reaction between them, the chances are that they are part of a Consolidation Area; or, if a Reversal of Trend is to ensue,

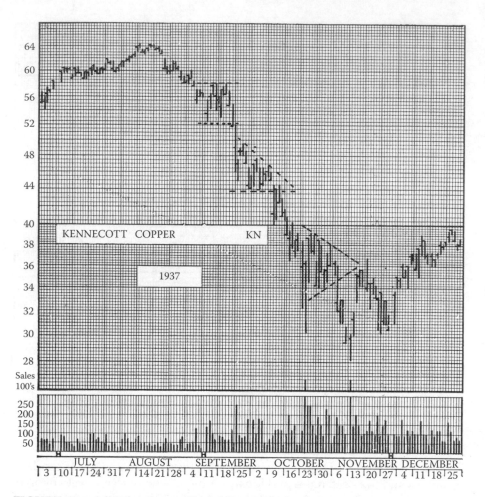

FIGURE 77. A brief and very "high" Rectangle formed in September 1937 in the rapid Bear Market Decline of "KN," followed by a Descending and then a Symmetrical Triangle Consolidation.

that there will first be more pattern development — more "work" done — around those top ranges. If, on the other hand, there is a long, dull, deep, and more or less rounding reaction after the initial peak has appeared, and then an evident lack of vitality when prices come up again to the previous high, we can at least be suspicious of a Double Top.

How deep is deep, and how long is long? Fair questions, to which, unfortunately, it is impossible to give simple, definite answers. But we can attempt approximations. Thus, if the two Tops are *more than* a month apart, they are not likely to belong to the same Consolidation or Congestion Formation. If, in addition, the reaction between the first and second high reduces prices by 20% of their top value, the odds swing toward a Double Top interpretation. But both of these criteria are arbitrary, and not without exception.

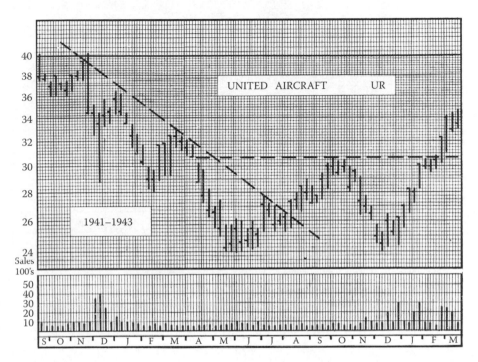

FIGURE 78. This formation, constructed by United Aircraft in 1942, was not completed and could not be called a Double Bottom until prices rose above 31 in February 1943. (See following pages.)

There are cases in which the two peaks have occurred only 2 or 3 weeks apart, and others in which the "valley" between them descended only about 15%. Most true Double Tops, however, develop 2 or 3 months or more apart. Generally speaking, the time element is more critical than the depth of the reaction. The greater the time between the two highs, the less the need of any extensive decline of prices in the interim.

Given the conditions we have specified, viz., two Tops at approximately the same level but more than a month apart on the chart, with somewhat less activity on the second advance than on the first, and a rather dull or irregular and rounding type of recession between them, we can then be suspicious that a Double Top Reversal has actually evolved. Should a small Head-and-Shoulders or Descending Triangle start to develop at the second Top, as is frequently the case, we can be on guard, to the extent of protecting long commitments at once with a close stop or switching to something else with a more promising chart picture.

Yet, even all these signs together are not final and conclusive. The situation can still be saved, and often is. Let us take a look at what is, presumably, going on behind the scenes to create our chart picture up to this point. The first Top on relatively high volume was a normal incident and tells us little except that here, for the moment, demand met with sufficient supply to stop

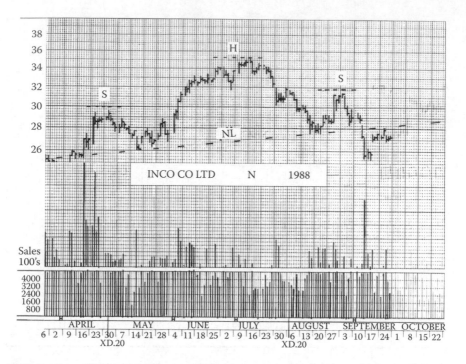

FIGURE 79. INCO quickly recovered from the Reagan Crash of 1987 and by year's end, it was nearly back to its 1987 high; the latter was decisively broken in April 1988. The powerful rally continued to carry "N" higher. But the August reaction, followed by a poor rally in September, created a large Head-and-Shoulders Top. The early September decline broke the neckline to confirm the Reversal and the subsequent Throwback, to Neckline Resistance, was an excellent selling point.

the advance and produce a reaction. That supply may have represented only traders' profit-taking, in which event the trend is likely to push on up after a brief setback. But, when the reaction drifts off lower and lower until it has given up 15% and more of the stock's peak market value, and flattens out without any prompt and vigorous rebound, it becomes evidence that either the demand was pretty well played out on the last advance or that the selling there represented something more than short-term profit cashing. The question then is: did the first high give evidence of important distribution, and is there much more to meet at the same price range?

Nevertheless, as our chart picture shows, demand did finally come in and absorb enough of the floating supply to turn the trend around. When prices pushed up and began to run into selling again near the level of the first Top, that was to be expected on "psychological" grounds; many quick-turn operators naturally would take profits at the old high (perhaps with the intention of jumping right back in at a still higher price if the old high should be exceeded). Hence, a Minor Hesitation there was quite in order. But selling in sufficient quantity to produce another extensive reaction would be quite another matter. We have, by now, established a zone of Supply or

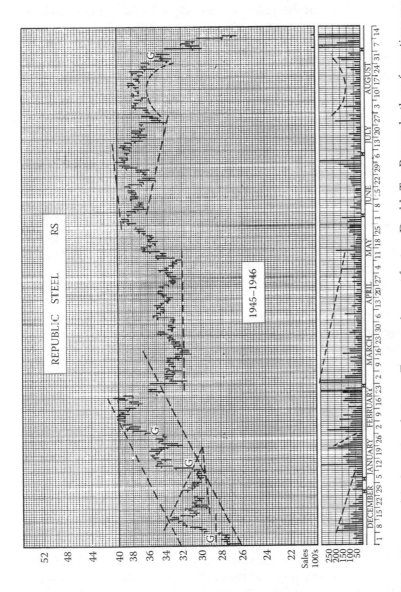

FIGURE 80. Because of the long-time-between-Tops requirement for true Double Top Reversals, these formations can seldom be seen to advantage on a daily chart, but here is a good 1946 example in Republic Steel. Note 5 months and 20% decline between Tops. This chart contains many interesting lesser technical formations also. The "Broadening" Swings (see Chapter 10) in June and July, as the second Top was made, and the rounding rally in August were extremely Bearish in their implications.

Resistance at the peak levels and a zone of Support or Demand at the Bottom of the valley between. The final and decisive question now is: will the "valley" Support reappear and stop the second decline?

The conclusive definition of a Double Top is given by a negative answer to that last question. If prices, on their recession from the second peak, drop through the Bottom level of the valley, a Reversal of Trend from up to down is signaled. And it is usually a signal of major importance. Fully confirmed Double Tops seldom appear at turns in the Intermediate Trend; they are characteristically a Primary Reversal phenomenon. Hence, when you are sure you have one, do not scorn it. Even though prices may have already receded 20%, the chances are they have very much farther to go before they reach bottom.

As to measuring implications, the Double Top affords no formula comparable with that we have attributed to Head-and-Shoulders and Triangle Formations, but it is safe to assume that the decline will continue *at least as far* below the valley level as the distance from peak to valley. It may not be so, of course, in one interrupted slide; on the contrary, considerable time may be required to carry out the full descent in a series of waves. Pullbacks to the "valley" price range, following the first breakthrough, are not uncommon. (Bear in mind the general rule that a Reversal Formation can be expected to produce no more than a retracement of the trend which preceded it.)

One more point: we have said that the Tops need not form at precisely the same level. Use here the 3% rule we have previously laid down as a measuring stick for breakouts. A first Top at 50, for example, and a second at 51½ would come within this limit. Curiously enough, the second peak often does exceed the first by a fraction. The important points are (1) that buying cannot push prices up into the clear *by a decisive margin*, and (2) the Support below is subsequently broken.

Double Bottoms

In identifying a Double Bottom, we can apply all of the precepts we have formulated for the Double Top Pattern, but, of course, upside down. The differences between the two pictures are just what you might expect them to be, having in mind the characteristic differences between Head-and-Shoulders Tops and Bottoms, for example. Thus, the second Bottom is usually conspicuously dull (little trading volume) and is apt to be quite rounded, whereas the second Top in a Double Top is moderately active and nearly as sharp and "spiky" in contour as the first. The rally up from the second Bottom shows an increase in turnover, and volume should pick up to a marked degree as the valley level, or more properly, in this case, the *height* between the two Bottoms, is surpassed. Double Bottoms appear just about as frequently as do Double Tops at Primary Trend Reversals, and Double Bottoms also occur sometimes at the end of Intermediate Corrections in a Major Uptrend.

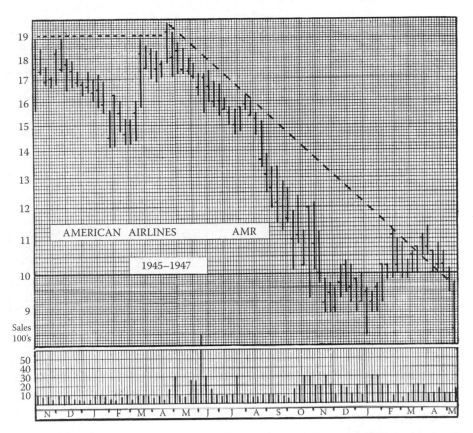

FIGURE 81.   Shares of "AMR," then selling for around 90, were split 5-for-1 in April 1946, resulting in a quick rally to a new high. But the overall aspect of a Double Top with the high made the previous December was nevertheless apparent, and was confirmed when prices broke down through the "valley" level on August 28. Popular buying brought in by "splits" is usually short-lived and only temporarily distorts the broad picture.

If you are familiar with some of the jargon of the Street, it has probably occurred to you that the second low of a Double Bottom is an example of the market action so often referred to as a "test." In a sense, that is just what it is — a test or corroboration of the Support (i.e., demand) which stemmed the first decline at the same level. The *success* of that test is not *proved*, however — and this is a point to remember — until prices have demonstrated their ability to rise on increasing volume above the preceding high (the height of the rally between the two Bottoms). Until such time as that has happened, there is always the possibility that a second test (third bottom) may be necessary, or even a third, and that one of these will fail, with prices then breaking on down into further decline. This thought leads us to our next type of Reversal Formation.

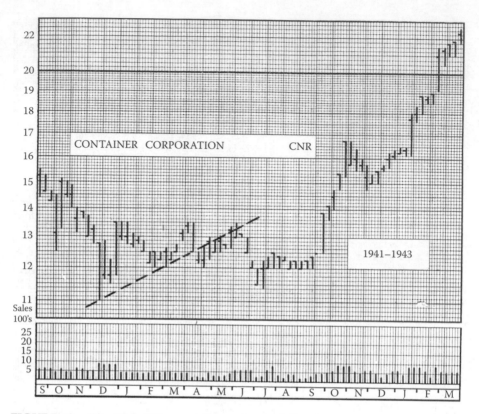

FIGURE 82. The Major Reversal Formation in "CNR" at the start of a Primary Advance which reached 54. Note how an attempt at an Ascending Triangle turned into a Double Bottom.

Triple Tops and Bottoms

Logically, if there are Double Tops, then we might expect that there will also be Triple Tops, which will develop in somewhat similar fashion. Fact is that Reversal Formations, which can only be classed as Triple Tops, do occur, but they are few and far between. Of course, there are many patterns evolved at an important turn from up to down in the trend which contain three Top points, but most of these fall more readily into the category of Rectangles. For that matter, any Head-and-Shoulders Formation, particularly if it be rather "flat," with the head not extending much above the level of the two shoulders, might be called a sort of Triple Top.

The true Triple Top (as distinct, that is, from other types of three-peak formations) carries a recognizable family resemblance to the Double Top. Its Tops are widely spaced and with quite deep and usually rounding reactions between them. Volume is characteristically less on the second advance than on the first, and still less on the third, which often peters out with no appreciable pickup in activity. The three highs need not be spaced quite so

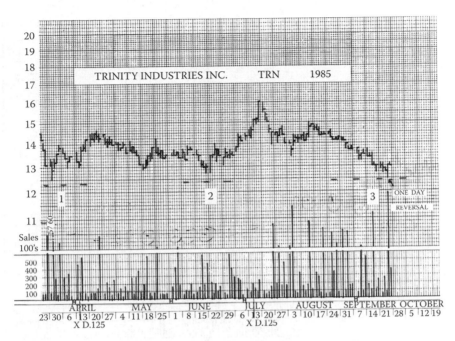

FIGURE 83. Although Trinity Industries did not have the well-formed pattern exhibited by our other recommendations, we found the high-volume plunge, with the low of the day the third test of the year's low, a very beguiling technical situation. Basically, it was a Triple Bottom with a One-Day Reversal to get the uptrend started.

far apart as the two which constitute a Double Top, and they need not be equally spaced. Thus, the second Top may occur only about 3 weeks after the first, and the third 6 weeks or more after the second. Also, the intervening valleys need not bottom out at exactly the same level; the first may be shallower than the second and vice versa. And the three highs may not come at precisely the same price; our 3% tolerance rule is again useful here. Yet, despite all these permissible variations, there should be, and generally is, something suspiciously familiar about the overall picture, something which immediately suggests the possibility of a Triple Top to the experienced chartist.

The *conclusive* test, however, is a decline from the third Top which breaks prices down through the level of the valley floor (the lower one, if the two valleys form at different levels). Not until that has occurred can a Triple Top be regarded as confirmed and actually in effect, since so long as demand persists at the valley price range, the trend can be turned up again. Only in those cases where activity is conspicuously lacking on the third peak and then begins to show Bearish characteristics by accelerating on the ensuing decline is one justified in "jumping the gun."

Triple Bottoms are simply Triple Tops turned upside down, with the same qualifications we noted when we were discussing Double Bottoms. The third low should always be attended by small volume, and the rise therefrom must show a decided increase in turnover and carry prices decisively above

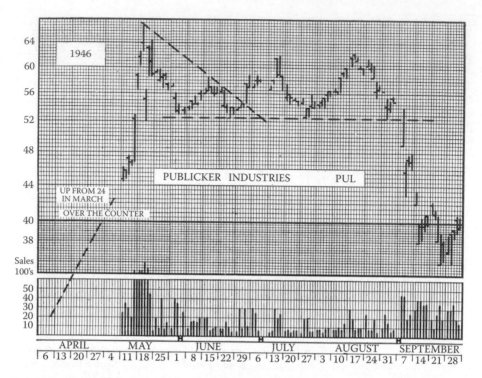

FIGURE 84. Publicker made its Bull Market high only a few weeks after it was listed on the "big board." Then it started to build a Descending Triangle, but pulled up out of it. Final outcome was a Triple Top, completed in August. (See Figures 60 and 82.)

the Tops of the rallies that formed between the Bottoms. One is never justified in "jumping the gun" on a presumed Triple Bottom Formation unless nearly every other chart in the book is in an unmistakably Bullish position. The risk of premature buying is expressed in a saying one sometimes hears in the boardrooms to the effect that "a Triple Bottom is always broken." This is not a true saying. Once a Triple Bottom has been established and confirmed by the necessary up-side breakout, it seldom fails — almost always produces an advance of distinctly worthwhile proportions. But an uncompleted "possible" Triple Bottom chart picture must be regarded as treacherous. Stick to the breakout rule and you will be safe.

Triple Tops are sometimes referred to as "W" Patterns because of their occasional resemblance to that capital letter on the chart. There is a sort of hybrid between the Double and Triple Top, in which the middle one of the three Tops does not attain the height of the first and third, and thus, even more strikingly resembles a "W." For the same reason, Double Tops are sometimes called "M" Formations.

Because the elements in Double and Triple patterns are normally spaced well apart in time, they are often easier to detect and appreciate on a weekly

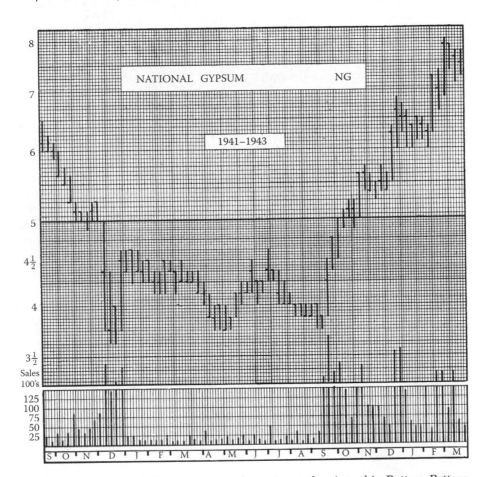

FIGURE 85. In the ordinary course of events, at the time this Bottom Pattern developed in "NG," consisting, as it did, of fluctuations for 10 long months within a range of only 1 full point, most traders would pay no attention to it. Certainly it suggested very little opportunity for short-term profits. On an arithmetically scaled chart, the pattern could hardly be seen. Logarithmic price scaling, however, as we have remarked in an earlier chapter, has the great advantage of bringing to light the percentage importance of significant market action at very low price levels.

Note that this formation qualifies in every detail — spacing between Bottoms, extent in percent of intervening rallies, volume — as a Triple Bottom. Of course, its completion, in October 1942, did not necessarily forecast that "NG" would climb to 33, as it ultimately did. But the fact that many other stocks were making sound Major Bottom Formations at higher price levels at the same time certainly warranted the conclusion that "NG" was on its way up, and that it was a bargain at 5.

chart than on a daily. Monthly graphs disclose numbers of widely spread Double and Triple Bottoms but, on the other hand, are too coarse to reveal many good Double and Triple Top Patterns.

In our foregoing discussion of the Triple Top, we referred to a sort of intuition which comes with experience and enables a technical analyst to recognize the potentialities for Reversal of a certain chart development, sometimes long before it has reached a conclusive stage. This is a not uncommon talent, but it is one that is seldom attained except through searching study and long experience (in which the latter usually involves a few expensive mistakes). The reader of this book need not despair of acquiring "chart sense" and without undue cost — if he will concentrate on his study, watch, check, and double-check every new development on his charts, and "keep score" on himself.

It has been said that chart interpretation is not a *science*, but an *art*. It is not an exact science, to be sure, because it has no rules to which there are not exceptions. Its finer points defy expression in rule or precept. It requires judgment in appraisal of many factors, some of which may seem, at times, to conflict radically with others. But to call it an art, which implies the need for genius, or at least for a high degree of native talent, is certainly improper. Say, rather, that it demands skill, but a skill that can be acquired by anyone of ordinary intelligence.

chapter ten

Other Reversal Phenomena

We have considered so far seven classes of chart patterns which appear at more or less important Reversals of direction in the trend of prices. They were:

1. The Head-and-Shoulders
2. Multiple or Complex Head-and-Shoulders
3. Rounding Turns
4. Symmetrical Triangles
5. Right-Angle Triangles
6. Rectangles
7. Double and Triple Tops and Bottoms
8. One-Day Reversal

Of these, 1, 2, 3, and 7 develop most often at Major Turns, while 4, 5, and 6 occur more frequently at Intermediate Stages. Numbers 1, 2, 3, and 5 give indication *before* they are completed as to which way the price trend is likely to proceed from them. Numbers 4 and 6 give no such indication and, as we have seen, are rather more apt to signal Consolidation or Continuation than Reversal. But all of them can, and on occasion do, appear at both Major Tops or Bottoms. *EN: Number 8 appears typically after out of control moves, up and down.*

We have yet to take up a few other technical patterns which, because of their limited significance, or their rarity, or their doubtful utility to the long-term traders, have been relegated to the end of our Reversal studies.

The Broadening Formations

In concluding our discussion of Triangles in Chapter 8, we mentioned certain types of price congestion or trading areas which have sometimes been called "Inverted Triangles" because, starting with very narrow fluctuations, they widen out between diverging rather than converging boundary lines. Herein, we have chosen to classify them instead as *Broadening Patterns* because, except for that inverted resemblance in superficial appearance, they are quite different in nature and trend implications.

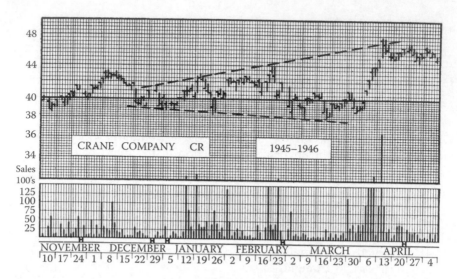

FIGURE 86. The Symmetrical type of Broadening Formation, which develops most frequently in the later and more "excited" stages of a Primary Bull Market, is perfectly exemplified in this Crane Company chart. Note that the Broadening Pattern here started to form in December 1945 after a 10% reaction; if it had formed on Top of a rally, it would have been suspected as a possible Broadening Top. Nevertheless, it carried the usual Bearish implications. "CR" topped out at 49½ in June.

If the Symmetrical Triangle presents a picture of "doubt" awaiting clarification, and the Rectangle a picture of controlled "conflict," the Broadening Formation may be said to suggest a market lacking intelligent sponsorship and out of control — a situation, usually, in which the "public" is excitedly committed and which is being whipped around by wild rumors. Note that we say only that it suggests such a market. There are times when it is obvious that those are precisely the conditions which create a Broadening Pattern in prices, and there are other times when the reasons for it are obscure or undiscoverable. Nevertheless, the very fact that chart pictures of this type make their appearance, as a rule, only at the end or in the final phases of a long Bull Market lends credence to our characterization of them.

Hence, after studying the charts for some 20 years and watching what market action has followed the appearance of Broadening Price Patterns, we have come to the conclusion that they are definitely Bearish in purport — that, while further advance in price is not ruled out, the situation is, nevertheless, approaching a dangerous stage. New commitments (purchases) should not be made in a stock which produces a chart of this type, and any previous commitments should be switched at once, or cashed in at the first good opportunity.

The Broadening Formation may evolve in any one of three forms, comparable, respectively, to inverted Symmetrical, Ascending, or Descending

Triangles. The "Symmetrical" type, for example, consists of a series of price fluctuations across a horizontal axis, with each Minor Top higher and each Minor Bottom lower than its predecessor. The pattern may thus be roughly marked off by two diverging lines, the upper sloping up (from left to right) and the lower sloping down. But these Broadening Patterns are characteristically loose and irregular, whereas Symmetrical Triangles are normally regular and compact. The converging boundary lines of a Symmetrical Triangle are clearly defined as a rule, and the Tops and Bottoms within the formation tend to fall with fair precision on those boundary lines. In a Broadening Formation, the rallies and declines usually do not all stop at clearly marked boundary lines.

Volume During Broadening Formations

Another distinction between Triangle and Broadening Formation is in the volume chart. The construction of a true Triangle is attended, as we have seen, by diminishing activity, starting with high volume on the first Minor Reversal which initiates the pattern, but growing less and less as prices fluctuate in ever smaller waves out toward the apex. Then activity picks up again after prices have broken out of the Triangle, immediately and sharply if the breakout is through the top side. With the Broadening Formation, on the other hand, trading activity usually remains high and irregular throughout its construction. If it develops after an advance, as is almost always the case, the first Minor Reversal which starts the pattern will occur on large turnover, but so will the second rally in the pattern, and the third, and high volume also frequently develops on one or more of its Minor Bottoms. The whole picture — both price and volume — is, thus, one of wild and apparently "unintelligent" swings.

As can easily be seen, under such circumstances, a true breakout from the area may be difficult, if not impossible, to detect at the time it eventuates. The volume part of the chart obviously furnishes no clue, while the very looseness and lack of definition of the price pattern prevents the drawing of any line which surely says, "this far and no farther." (We are referring now to the "Symmetrical" type only of Broadening Formation.) Of course, once prices have run well away, either up or down, from the pattern area, it becomes plain that a breakout has occurred, but by that time, it may be too late to risk a trade on the situation; the move may already have gone too far. What can we do about Broadening Formations then? Well, we have already noted that, nine times out of ten, they carry Bearish implications. They appear most often at or near an important topping out of the trend. Hence, it is reasonably safe to assume that prices, when they finally break away from the formation, will go down, or if they do go up, will very soon turn around and come back down again. Therein lies one answer to the problem of what to do about a Broadening Formation.

In addition, the price action within the formation, in many cases, furnishes an *advance* indication of breakout direction. If the trend is going to break down from the Broadening Area, the last rally within the area may fail to rise as high as its predecessor, thus breaking the sequence of ever higher Tops within the pattern. And, alternatively, if the trend is going to emerge on the top side, the last reaction within the pattern may fail to depress prices as low as the preceding reaction. These "failures" within the pattern occur, as we have stated, in a majority of all Broadening Formations. But note that one cannot be sure of such a significant development (what we have referred to above as a failure, for lack of a better descriptive name) until prices go on and out the other side of the formation or, more precisely, have exceeded the last preceding move in that direction by a decisive margin (our 3% rule again).

A Typical Example

No doubt the foregoing paragraph sounds rather complicated. It will be easier to visualize the development of a "failure" signal if we cite an example using actual price figures. Easier yet, perhaps, if the reader will sketch out our example on a scrap of chart paper. Suppose stock XYZ, after advancing some 30 points on gradually increasing turnover, runs into heavy selling at 62 and reacts to 58. But there is still plenty of interest in the issue; it stops at 58 and then swings up to a new peak at 63. It "churns" there for a day or two and drops back again, this time to 56½ before it is halted by another burst of buying. Its third rally takes it up to 62, where it hesitates and falls back to 59, but is then picked up again and carried on to 65. (By this time, of course, a Broadening Formation has become evident on the chart.) At 65, there is a great show of trading, followed by another reaction which drops quotations quickly back to 60. Support appears there momentarily and prices fluctuate for 3 or 4 days between 60 and 62 and then fall away again, finally to close at 56, with volume running high all through this phase. A fourth rally starts, but now the traders who bought in at 60 on the preceding downswing are frightened and looking for a chance to "get out even," and the advance is stifled at that level. Quotations start to slip and soon are down to 55, *below the previous pattern Bottom*. When this occurs, the "failure" of the preceding rally is confirmed — its failure, that is, to rise above 65 and, thus, carry on the Broadening Movement. The decline below 56, by virtue of that failure, may be regarded as a breakout.

If you followed the foregoing example closely, you will have noted that there can be (and very often are) Minor Fluctuations inside the pattern that do not affect its outcome. Thus, the rise from 56½ to 65 really consisted of 3 moves, first from 56½ to 62, then from 62 back to 59, and, finally, from 59 up to 65. The reaction from 62 had no significance so long as it stopped *above* 56½ and was succeeded by a new rise carrying beyond the previous pattern high, which, in this case, had been 63.

The example just detailed is one of the more common types in which the failure occurs on a rally and the breakout eventuates on the downside. But it could have been converted into the opposite form if the last decline had stopped at 60, and then, instead of fluctuating for a few days between 60 and 62 and breaking down again, had pushed right back up and past 65. That action would have given us a failure on a decline and an upside breakout. (The odds would be, however, that the final Top was not far away.)

The Orthodox Broadening Top

There is one particular manifestation — a special case, as the mathematicians might say — of the Broadening Price Formation whose general nature we have discussed in the preceding paragraphs. This particular form appeared at the 1929 Tops of many of the active and popular stocks of that day, but with less frequency at Bull Market highs since 1929, and rarely at high-volume Tops preceding extensive Intermediate Declines, as in 1933 and 1934. It is known to market technicians under the specific name of *Broadening Top*, and although it conforms to our general descriptions for all Symmetrical Broadening Price Patterns, it has been so precisely defined, and so often cited in technical writings, that we may well take some time to examine it.

The Orthodox Broadening Top has three peaks at successively higher levels and, between them, two Bottoms with the second Bottom lower than the first. The assumption has been that it is completed and in effect as an important Reversal indication just as soon as the reaction from its third peak carries below the level of its second Bottom.

Perhaps we can best see what this formation is like if we examine one of the classic patterns which developed in 1929. Our chart (Figure 87) shows the daily market action (price and volume) of Air Reduction from July 1 to December 31 of that year. We have numbered from 1 to 5 the significant turning points within the Broadening Top which ended that stock's Bull Market in October. A Broadening Price Pattern was not detectable, of course, until prices had started to move up from the second Minor Low (point 4); by then 3 had formed *above* 1, and 4 *below* 2. New highs at 5 (*a* and *b*), followed by the definite downside breakout at B (nearly 6% under 4), completed the pattern and, according to the rules, signaled a Major Reversal Trend. In this case, there can be no doubt as to the importance of the Reversal indication, since, as our chart shows, the price of Air Reduction dropped from above 220 on October 18 to below 80 on November 14, just 4 weeks later, and the final Bottom was not seen until nearly 3 years later in 1932!

There are some fine points of this classic example which should be noted. First, a new high, i.e., a third and higher Top, was made at 5*a* and the subsequent reaction was halted at 195, well above 4, and succeeded by renewed advance. This looked like one of the advance notices ("failures") to which we have referred on a preceding page, portending an upside break-out. But the example before us will serve to emphasize the warning which

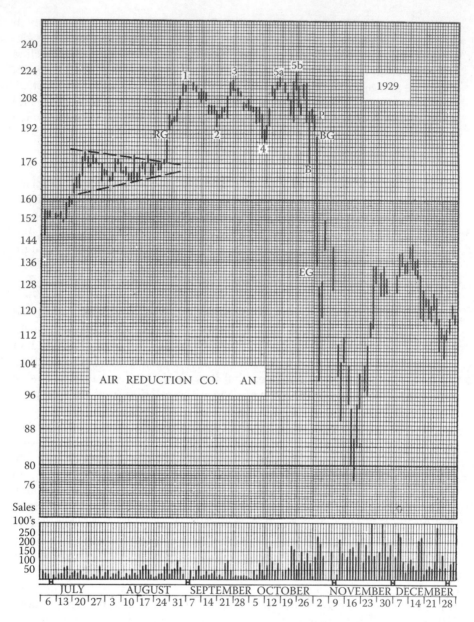

FIGURE 87. Although this particular Major Reversal Formation appeared on the charts over 35 years ago, it is so perfectly developed and on such a large scale that it may well stand as our elementary model for an Orthodox Broadening Top. This pattern in Air Reduction is discussed in detail on previous pages. Note also the Symmetrical Triangle Consolidation of July–August, and the examples of Runaway, Breakout, and Exhaustion Gaps (RG, BG, and EG), which will be taken up in Chapter 12.

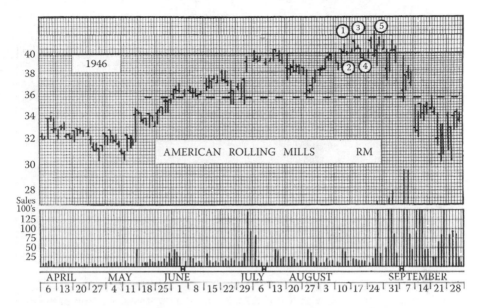

FIGURE 88. A small but perfect 1946 Broadening Top that formed at the end of a 3-month chart pattern which also had overall Broadening (and, hence, Bearish) aspects. The five critical points of Reversal are numbered on the chart. The "breakout" was registered on August 27. The Pullback Rally that followed immediately was strong, but still held within normal bounds. Another interesting Broadening Top of 1946 appears in Figure 217.

we attached thereto — that such an indication is not to be trusted until prices have decisively exceeded the previous Top. At 5*b* Air Reduction was traded briefly at 223, 2 points, but less than 3%, higher than 5*a*, and the day closed with quotations *below* 5*a*. The break on October 24 (to B) took prices more than 3% under the level of 4. Now occurred a development typical of Broadening Tops — a Pullback Rally (to B) retracing about half of the ground lost between the last pattern Top (5*b*) and the end of the initial breakout move (B). Such a recovery (and failure) will be attempted, according to our experience, in at least four out of five Broadening Top Patterns, and may not fail until it has regained two thirds of the preceding decline, although it usually peters out around or even below the halfway mark.

This, as we have said, is a classic example; there were many others at that time. The very fact that so many did evolve at the 1929 peak, which was followed by history's most disastrous losses, probably accounts for the extremely Bearish implications market technicians have ascribed to the Broadening Top Formation. We regard it now with somewhat less awe; its measuring implications are probably no greater than those of a large, high-volume Head-and-Shoulders, but it is a pattern characteristic of the last stages of a Primary Uptrend.

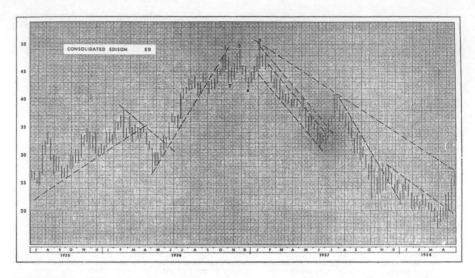

FIGURE 89. When they appear as plain and as compact as this example, Broadening Tops on weekly charts carry very powerful Reversal indications. The Top of the fifth turn in this formation was capped on the daily chart by a Head-and-Shoulders, which was pictured in Figure 16. The dashed lines on the above chart are trendlines — to be discussed in Chapter 14.

The insistence that the third Top (our number 5), when followed by a decline below the second Bottom (our number 4), *completes* the Reversal Pattern may be regarded, in the light of experience, as setting too strict a limitation, since Broadening Formations do, on occasion, go on to make a fourth and higher Top. Yet this rule may be, and usually is, justified by the fact that the overall indications are undeniably Bearish and, hence, one should not wait too long to get out. On the other hand, the requirement that there be a third Top does seem to be justified on the score that Major Reversals are seldom completed until at least three attempts have been made to push prices on in the direction of the previous trend. This is the reason, of course, why pioneer technical students lumped together many formations under the classification "Five-Point Reversals." The Broadening Top is a Five-Point Reversal (our numbers 1 to 5) and, so, obviously is a Head-and-Shoulders. A Broadening Top might, in fact, be called a Head-and-Shoulders with a high right shoulder and a down-sloping neckline.

Why No Broadening Bottoms?

All of the other types of Reversal Formations we have studied thus far can occur as either Tops or Bottoms. They can develop at the end of a decline to turn the trend up, or at the end of an advance to turn the trend down. But this does not seem to be true of the Broadening Formation. It has been assumed in the past that Broadening Bottoms must exist, but the writer has

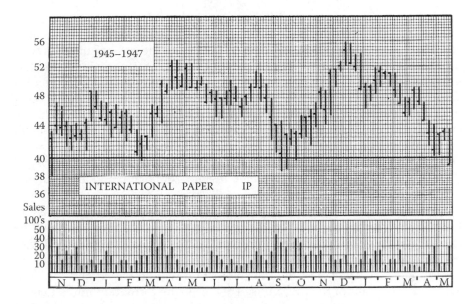

FIGURE 90. Broadening tendencies that appear on monthly charts, or very wide spread (with Tops 5 or 6 months apart) like the above on weekly charts, should not be regarded as significant technical formations. Reversal points in a true Broadening Top should not be more than 2 months apart, as in Figure 89.

never found a good one in his examination of the charts of thousands of individual stocks over many years, and only one or two patterns which bore a resemblance to it in the charts of the Averages. Apparently, the circumstances that create Broadening Formations do not exist after a prolonged decline in prices. This would seem to bear out our earlier characterization of this sort of pattern as suggesting active, excited trading with much public (and, hence, not too well informed or managed) participation. Such conditions are naturally associated with the final phases of a Bull Market.

Right-Angled Broadening Formations

Price patterns of the "Inverted Triangle" shape, having a horizontal Top or Bottom boundary, occur about as often as the symmetrical type, which is to say, not nearly as often as true Triangles, Rectangles, etc. In the mid-20th century, there were very few of them (*EN9: Still scarce in the 2000s*). While the true Right-Angle Triangle with a horizontal top line and up-slanting bottom line is called an Ascending Triangle, just as its counterpart with a horizontal bottom boundary and a down-slanting top boundary is called a Descending Triangle, we cannot apply these terms to the Inverted or Broadening Forms. Generally speaking, Right-Angled Broadening Formations carry Bearish implications, regardless of which side is horizontal, in nearly the same degree as the symmetrical manifestations.

Obviously, however, they differ essentially from Symmetrical formations in one respect: a horizontal side indicates either accumulation or distribution at a fixed price, depending, of course, on which side is horizontal. And it follows, logically, that any decisive break through that horizontal side has immediate forceful significance. Thus, if a Broadening Price Pattern *with a flat top boundary* develops after a good advance, and if prices finally burst up through that top line on high volume and close above it to a conclusive extent (roughly 3%), then it is safe to assume that the preceding uptrend will be resumed and carried on for a worthwhile move. This does happen, although it is rare. The odds favor the opposite, i.e., the eventual victory of the forces of distribution which created the horizontal Top and a breakaway into an extensive decline.

Moreover, if an advance is to ensue from a Flat-Topped Broadening Formation, the chances are that the third reaction in the formation will be attended by much diminished trading activity instead of the continued high or irregular volume which is characteristic of Bearish Broadening Movements, and that either it or the fourth reaction will be halted and reversed *above* the low point of the preceding. This turns the formation into a *Consolidation Head-and-Shoulders*, a Continuation-of-Trend Pattern, which we shall take up in Chapter 11. The message here for the trader owning a stock whose chart begins to develop a Broadening Formation of this type is: watch the third reaction. If it carries below the second and volume does not fall off to a marked degree, sell out on the next rally. (You can always repurchase the same stock if you wish, without much "loss of position" should prices finally and, improbably, recover and push up through the Top.)

Right-Angled Broadening Formations with horizontal lower boundaries (flat Bottoms) almost always break down. Once prices have fallen below the lower boundary line, there is frequently a Pullback Rally to that line, either in a few days or in 2 or 3 weeks, similar to the Pullbacks that so often follow the break down from a Head-and-Shoulders Top.

(Note that the third or fourth rally in a pattern which starts out as a Flat-Bottomed Broadening Formation may fail to carry prices as high as its predecessor, in which case we have a Head-and-Shoulders to deal with. In other words, every Head-and-Shoulders begins as a Broadening Formation. And the statement of that relation takes us logically to our next type of Reversal picture.)

The Diamond

The *Diamond* Reversal Formation might be described either as a more or less Complex Head-and-Shoulders with a V-shaped neckline, or as a Broadening Formation which, after two or three "swings," suddenly reverts into a regular Triangle which is nearly always of the Symmetrical form. So far as the accompanying volume pattern is concerned, the latter is possibly the better description. Its name derives obviously from its pictorial resemblance to the conventional diamond figure.

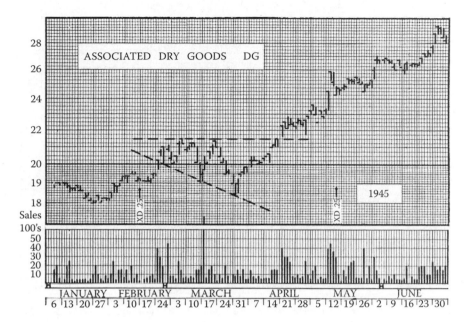

FIGURE 91. Three successive reactions in "DG" in February–March 1945 made successively lower Bottoms, but the intervening rallies came up to the same high (about 21¼), thus forming a Right-Angled Broadening Formation with a horizontal Top (Supply) Line. Penetration of this technically important top line on April 16 was a Bullish signal. The flat-topped type of pattern does not necessarily portray a Bearish situation.

Although it is fairly conspicuous and easily detected when it appears on the charts, the Diamond is not a common pattern. Since its development requires fairly active markets, it rarely occurs at Bottom Reversals. Its "natural habitat" is Major Tops and the High-Volume Tops which precede extensive Intermediate Reactions. Many Multiple Head-and-Shoulders Formations are borderline Diamond cases; i.e., they permit the drawing of slightly bent necklines. The reader is cautioned, however, against trying too hard to make Diamonds out of price patterns of the Head-and-Shoulders type. There is a temptation to do so because a V-shaped neckline may promise to give an earlier (and, hence, more profitable) breakout signal than the straight neckline of the Head-and-Shoulders, but it is much safer to stick to the latter unless the second half of the formation consists of a series of clean-cut, converging Minor Fluctuations which plainly demands definition by converging boundary lines, and unless activity shows some tendency to diminish during this period as it would in a Triangle.

The Diamond requires little further comment. Our illustrations will suffice to acquaint you with its typical details. It carries a minimum measuring implication which, having studied the Head-and-Shoulders and Triangle formulas, you can probably deduce for yourself. Prices should move *at least as far* from the breakout point as the greatest width in points of the pattern

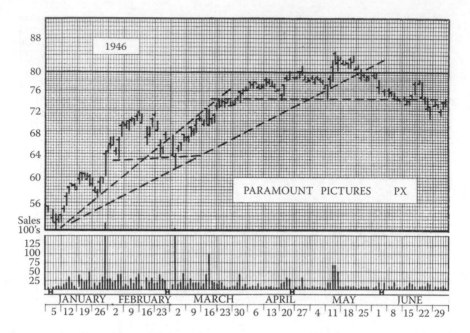

FIGURE 92. The 1946 Top in Paramount Pictures, from which it fell to 46 a year later, was a Right-Angled Broadening Formation with a horizontal bottom line which was "cracked" the first week of June, but not decisively broken until June 20. (This stock was later split 2-for-1.)

from its Top (head) to Bottom (V in neckline). This, it must be emphasized, is a minimum rule and subject only to the usual qualification that a Reversal Formation must have something to reverse. Generally, the new trend carries prices eventually well beyond the minimum measurement.

Wedge Formations

All of the chart formations we have discussed up to this point can and do develop at changes in the Major Trend of prices. A few of them seldom occur at any other than a Major Reversal. We have now to consider three patterns which are ordinarily Minor, or, at most, only Intermediate in their trend implications. They are useful, nevertheless, in trading operations. One of them, the *Wedge*, we have already alluded to (in Chapter 8) as having some resemblance to the Triangles.

The Wedge is a chart formation in which the price fluctuations are confined within converging straight (or practically straight) lines, but differing from a Triangle in that both boundary lines either slope up or slope down. In a Symmetrical Triangle, the Top border slants down, while the Bottom border slants up. In Right Angle Triangles, one boundary slopes either up or down, but the other is horizontal. In a Rising Wedge, both boundary lines slant up from left to right, but since the two lines converge,

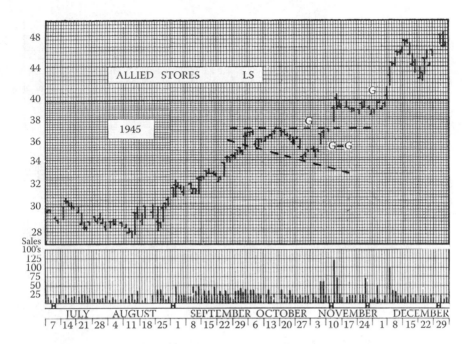

FIGURE 93. Another example of the Flat-Topped type of Broadening Price Pattern that appeared near the end of 1945. "LS" went on up to 63 in 1946. Prices broke out of this formation with a Breakout Gap (G) and another Breakout Gap appeared on December 3. G-G marks an "Island." See Chapter 12 for Gaps.

the lower must, of course, project at a steeper angle than the upper. In a Falling Wedge, the opposite is true.

Superficially, one might think that since an Ascending Triangle, with one horizontal and one up-line, is a Bullish picture, the Rising Wedge, with both of its pattern lines up, should be even more Bullish. But such is not the case. Remember that the flat top of an Ascending Triangle signifies a supply of shares being distributed at a fixed price; when that supply has been absorbed (and the rising lower boundary line indicates that it will be absorbed), the pressure is off and prices will leap forward. In a Rising Wedge, on the other hand, there is no evident barrier of supply to be vaulted, but rather, a gradual petering out of investment interest. Prices advance, but each new up wave is feebler than the last. Finally, demand fails entirely and the trend reverses. Thus, a Rising Wedge typifies a situation which is growing progressively *weaker* in the technical sense.

Of course, it might be said that any advance in prices, no matter what shape it may take on the chart, weakens the technical status of the market. Prospective buyers are — or, at least, should be — more reluctant to pay high prices than low, and owners are more willing to sell at high prices than at low; in other words, any sort of rise tends to increase supply and diminish demand. (While theoretically true, the preceding statement must be qualified by the fact that rising prices actually attract rather than discourage public

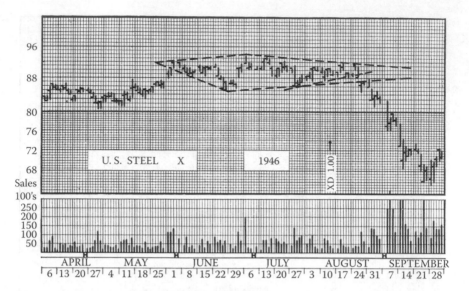

FIGURE 94. The 1946 Bull Market Top in U.S. Steel was a 3-month Diamond which might also be construed as a Head-and-Shoulders.

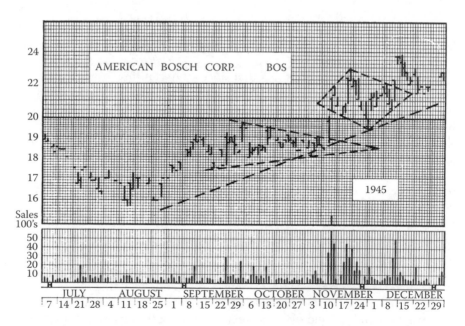

FIGURE 95. A Diamond (November) which broke out topside and thus functioned as Consolidation rather than Reversal.

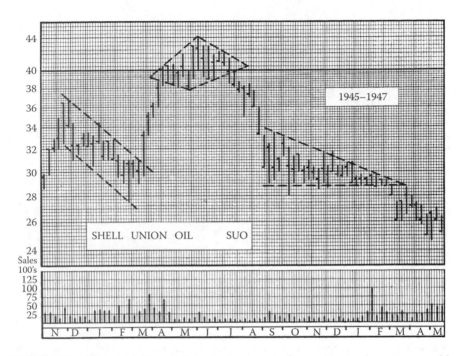

FIGURE 96. Diamond Reversal Formations are often easier to detect on weekly than on daily charts. Trace out the price swings and volume in this May–June 1946 Diamond in Shell. Note also the remarkable Descending Triangle which developed from September 1946 to February 1947, and the March Pullback to its apex, another ideal place to sell short.

buying.) The difference between a Rising Wedge and what might be called a normal Uptrend Channel (of which we shall have more to say later) is that the Wedge sets a sort of limit on the advance. Its converging boundary lines focus on a point near where the advance will halt and reaction set in.

We can state most of the essential facts about the Up-Pointed Wedge Formation in a few short sentences. It can develop either as a sort of Topping-Out Pattern on a previously existing uptrend, or start to form right at the Bottom of a preceding downtrend. It (the Wedge) normally takes more than 3 weeks to complete; a shorter pattern of this shape is nearly always better classified as a Pennant, which we will discuss in the next chapter. Prices almost always fluctuate within the Wedge's confines for at least two thirds of the distance from the base (beginning of convergence) to the apex; in many cases, they rise clear to the apex, and in some, they actually go a short distance beyond, pushing on out at the Top in a last-gasp rally before collapsing. Once prices break out of the Wedge downside, they usually waste little time before declining in earnest. The ensuing drop ordinarily retraces all of the ground gained within the Wedge itself, and sometimes more. Trading volume in a Wedge tends to follow the regular Triangle Pattern, diminishing gradually as prices move up toward the apex of the Wedge.

Created with TradeStation 2000i by Omega Research©1999

FIGURE 96.1. Technicians in the future will look back with amazement at the top which put the exclamation point on the Bull '90s. The most amazing thing being that what was going on at the time was recognizable and subject to analysis with a ruler (Cf. Resources). The analysis furthermore indicated that the party was over (or at least the fat lady was in the process of singing). As Edwards noted the Broadening Top *which had (and has) implications of its own* morphed into a Diamond, which threw off a false signal, breaking out on the upside, which developed into another triangular-like pattern (could be looked at as ragged triangular or ascending — only bottom line shown here), which after a head fake broke down made a modified V-Bottom and returned to the top of what could be looked at as a monster rectangle. The top horizontal line, drawn in August 2000 stops the 2001 rally cold and from there it is a slippery slide to the tragedy of September 11, 2001. It was obvious that the investor had no business being long, and that trading strategy was in order. Was there any prescience in recognizing the mulish sideways trend of the market? None whatsoever. Is all this hindsight? The reader may see for himself by examining the record of how this market was analyzed *at the time* by the John Magee Investment Newsletter in Resources.

The Falling Wedge

Except for the fact that it is pointed down, the *Falling Wedge* appears in all respects like the rising form we have just described. But the price trend that follows its completion differs in character. When prices break out of a Rising Wedge, they usually fall away rapidly, but when they move out of a Falling Wedge, they are more apt to drift sideways or in a dull "Saucering-around" movement before they begin to rise. The Rising Wedge may, therefore, call for quick action to secure profits, while with a Falling Wedge, the trader ordinarily can take his time about making his commitment for the ensuing rise.

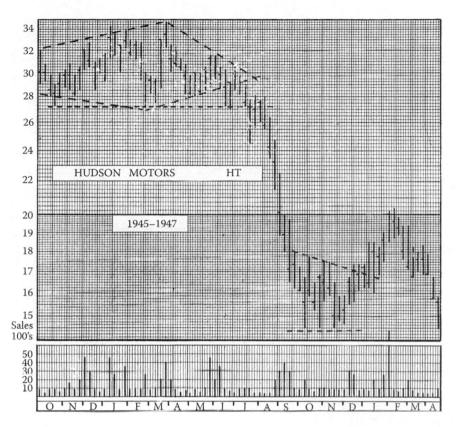

FIGURE 97. Hudson is another stock that ended its Bull Market in 1946 with a Major Diamond which could also be taken as a Complex Head-and-Shoulders. This formation was plain on the weekly chart but hard to see on the daily. Note how the Diamond gave a sell signal about 2 points higher than the Head-and-Shoulders. The 14½ to 17½ area at the end of the year, when construed as a weak Rectangle, was barely fulfilled in February 1947.

Both types should be well defined on the chart. Unless a trend pattern is quite compact with frequent fluctuations, and nicely bounded by lines which clearly converge to a point, and unless their up (or down) slant is marked, the Wedge construction must be considered doubtful. You will find borderline cases where one of the pattern lines so nearly approaches the horizontal in direction that it resembles a Right-Angle Triangle, and the latter would, of course, carry quite different implications for future trend development. It is difficult to lay down any hard and fast rules for distinguishing the two. If one boundary line is *nearly* horizontal, or if the daily *closing* prices tend to fall at about the same level, then the formation is more safely construed as a Triangle. The reader need not let this problem worry him unduly, as he will rarely be left in doubt for long after he has acquired a little experience with charts. One soon gets to recognize the characteristic "symptoms" of the different formations and make correct diagnoses almost instinctively.

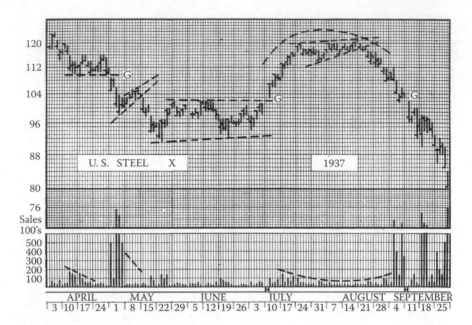

FIGURE 98.   As U.S. Steel approached the Top of its Secondary Recovery in August 1937, its price fluctuations tended to grow narrower, between upward sloping but converging boundaries, while volume diminished. This pattern — a Wedge — carried a definitely Bearish message. The entire swing from July to the end of August was essentially a Rounding Top. The three Gs mark Breakaway Gaps (Chapter 12), the last (September 7) made as prices broke down through a Support Level (Chapter 13).

Wedges on Weekly and Monthly Charts

Most true Wedges are too short-lived (seldom longer than 3 months) to take on a recognizable definition on a monthly chart, but they may be spotted occasionally on the weeklies. Long continued, gradual downtrends, when plotted on arithmetic scale, sometimes assume the Wedge form. Thus, an entire Major Bear Decline on any arithmetic monthly chart may appear like a giant Falling Wedge. This is due to the fact that the up and down fluctuations which compose the Major Swing, while maintaining about the same extent in *percentage*, tend to shorten in terms of points (dollars) as prices move from higher to lower levels. Such Major chart patterns are not, of course, the true Wedges we have discussed herein. When plotted on semilogarithmic scale, these same moves would normally show a Parallel or even slightly widening, instead of Converging, Channel.

Rising Wedges Common in Bear Market Rallies

As a final note, we might add that the Rising Wedge is a quite characteristic pattern for Bear Market Rallies. It is so typical, in fact, that frequent appearance

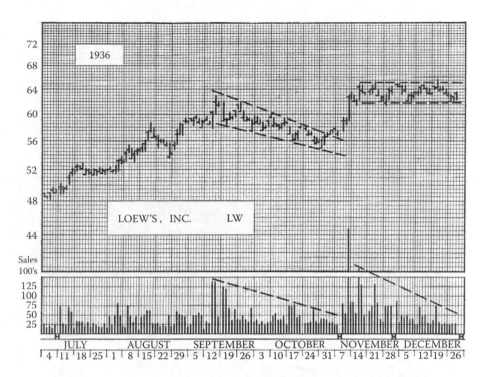

FIGURE 99. An "ideal" Falling Wedge that developed in Loew's in 1936. Note volume trend therein, irregular but generally diminishing. July produced a small Flag (Chapter 11), and at the end of the year, "LW" went into a Rectangle out of which prices "skyrocketed" to 75.

of Wedges at a time when, after an extensive decline, there is some question as to whether a new Bull Trend is in the making may be taken as evidence that the Primary Trend is still down. When a Major Bear Swing ends in a Head-and-Shoulders Bottom, the last Rising Wedge will often appear as prices rally from the left shoulder to the neckline, and just before they break down to the head (final low). A Rising Wedge on an arithmetically scaled weekly chart is almost invariably a Bear Market phenomenon, expressing, as it does, the diminishing vigor which is the normal property of any reaction against a prevailing Primary Trend.

The One-Day Reversal

We referred in Chapter 6 to a price pattern known as the One-Day Reversal. This particular technical Reversal indication, when taken alone, can be accorded only temporary or strong Minor Trend significance. True, it may appear at the very peak of a long advance, forming perhaps on the high day of the head in a Head-and-Shoulders Pattern which will be followed by a long decline, but it can hardly be credited with forecasting that entire decline; all it really signaled was the turn in the "head" itself. A One-Day Reversal

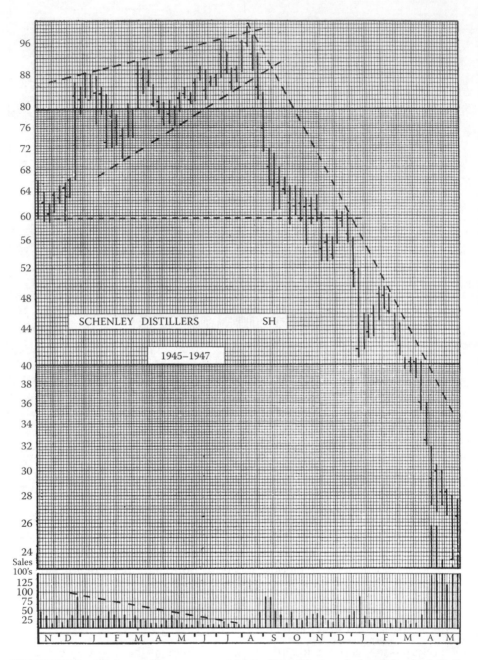

FIGURE 100. Wedges seldom appear at Major Trend Reversals, but Schenley's Bull high in 1946 was made at the end of an 8-month Rising Wedge, plain to see on its weekly chart. The dashed line at 60 marks a Support Level (see Chapter 13) which served to stem the subsequent decline for 9 weeks.

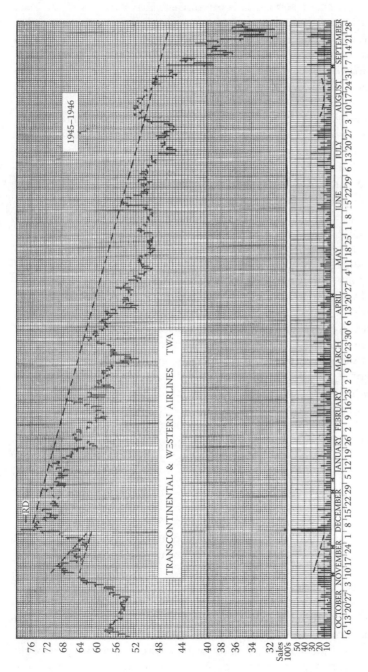

FIGURE 101. There are many interesting and technically significant features in this 12-month daily chart record of "TWA." Note the extraordinary One-Day Reversal, December 3, which marked its Major Top. Although the next 4 weeks produced a sort of poorly formed Descending Triangle, the Reversal Day was the only clear-cut and unmistakable signal to sell. When you study pennants, turn back to this chart for its November Pennant. Its long Intermediate Down Trendline was tentatively broken in August 1946 but without confirming volume (see Chapter 14). Note that at no time during the decline did a "Buy" Pattern appear.

may just as well occur, for example, at the beginning (the first peak) of a Symmetrical Triangle which only Consolidates instead of Reversing the previous uptrend. Even so, it serves, as you can see, to warn us of at least temporary exhaustion of Bullish forces.

On the downside, a One-Day Reversal often appears in magnified and conspicuous form at the end of a Panic Sell-Off, in which case, it usually is referred to as a *Climax Day* or Selling Climax. This manifestation of it has special significance which we shall take up later. First, however, just what is a One-Day Reversal?

It is, to begin with, a day of unusually high volume, exceeding, as a rule, by a notable margin any trading turnover registered in any one market session for several months past. It comes after a fairly long and steady advance (or a similar decline), on which activity has been increasing gradually. Prices push right ahead from the opening gong as if nothing could stop them. Frequently, even the opening sales are so far beyond the previous day's closing level as to leave a large gap on the chart. (We shall discuss gaps later.) The tape runs late, and before the advance (or decline) halts, prices have been carried as far in an hour or two as three or four days would ordinarily take them. But the halt does come finally, maybe at the end of the first hour or perhaps not until late in the day. Then quotations "churn," registering only fractional changes to and fro, with the tape still "fast" and often running late by spurts. Suddenly the trend reverses and prices move just as rapidly in the opposite direction. The session ends with a final burst of activity that puts the price at the close right back where it started the day. There has been an enormous amount of activity, and quotations may have traversed intraday a percentage range of 2 or 3%, but the net change from the previous day at the end of trading is very small.

One-Day Reversals at Tops appear quite often in the charts of individual stocks which are thin (relatively small floating supply of shares), which have had an active advance and have attracted a large public following. They develop rarely in the Averages. Selling Climaxes (One-Day Reversals at Bottoms), on the other hand, are found conspicuously in the Averages at the end of many abnormal or Panic Declines.

One-Day Reversals, as we have already stated, do not carry Major Trend implications. The nimble in-and-out trader can capitalize on them — maybe pick up several points if he has funds available and jumps in at the right moment. But, as a rule, the new trend (i.e., the trend at the close of the day) does not carry very far right away; prices usually "work" around in the nearby ranges for some time and build some sort of area pattern before they move away in a swing of Intermediate proportions. However, the One-Day Reversal, as a phenomenon that occurs frequently within or at the start of more pregnant technical formations, gives an important clue to probable trend developments. In any event, it is an urgent warning to watch closely the chart in which it has appeared to see what pattern of price action may follow and be prepared for the worthwhile move when it comes.

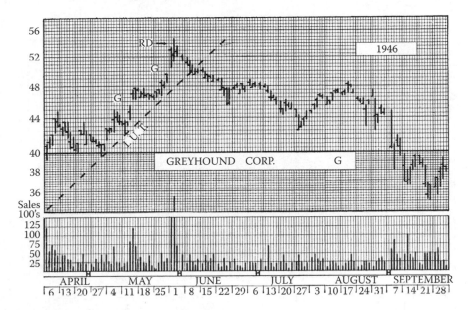

FIGURE 102.   The strong One-Day Reversal which marked Greyhound's 1946 Bull Market high. Note climax volume. A less conspicuous Reversal Day appeared on August 26. It is suggested that the reader go back over all charts in preceding chapters; he will find many Reversal Days of greater or lesser consequence. Many gaps (G) were of measuring type — see Chapter 12.

It is worth noting that the type of false move or shakeout that we described in Chapter 8 as occurring at the apex end of a Symmetrical Triangle often takes the form of a One-Day Reversal.

The Selling Climax

In the "bad old days" when stocks could be bought by putting up as little as 10% of their cost in cash, and there were no restrictions on short selling, professional operators could (and tradition says they often did) organize Bear Raids to shake out weakly margined holdings. By selling short in quantity at a favorable moment when the "public" had gotten itself pretty well extended on the long side, they could break prices down. Brokers then would send out calls for more margin from their "long" accounts, many of whom could not or would not put it up, with the result that their stocks were dumped on the market. That, in turn, produced further declines. The professionals could then step in, cover their shorts with a profit, and secure a line of long stock for the next advance. Bear Raids of this sort were effectively checked by the imposition of the SEC regulations, but margin calls and forced selling will, of course, always exist as a market factor so long as stocks can be bought on margin, and will come into play whenever prices drop extensively following a spree of public buying.

APPLE COMPUTER INC-(Nasdaq NM)   62.72 −0.03 −0.05%

©1998-2004 Prophet Financial Systems, Inc. I Terms of use apply.

FIGURE 102.1.   Apple. 1987 Reagan Crash. Does this plunge appear to be out of the blue? Not really. Numerous signs are given: break of major trendline; short-term momentum down before crash in an environment of extreme top psychology; then the crash itself, the panic selling exhibiting the typical pattern of short covering, then further decline.

Most true Selling Climaxes, if not all, have been produced by distress selling of the type referred to in the preceding paragraph. They have come at the end of rapid and comprehensive declines which exhausted the margin reserves of many speculators and necessitated the dumping of their shares at whatever the market would bring. This process is progressive — feeding upon itself, so to speak — with each wave of forced sales jeopardizing another lot of margined accounts, until, at last, millions of shares are tossed overboard, willy-nilly, in a final clean-up. Such is a Selling Climax in which the total turnover may exceed any single day's volume during the previous swing up. It is a harvest time for traders who, having avoided the Bullish infection at the top of the market, have funds in reserve to pick up stocks available at panic prices.

Obviously, a clean-out day or Selling Climax radically reverses the technical condition of the market, for in its process, shares have passed from weak hands into strong hands at very much lower prices. The ominous weight of potential selling that has been overhanging the market has been removed. And usually the Panic has carried quotations (although only

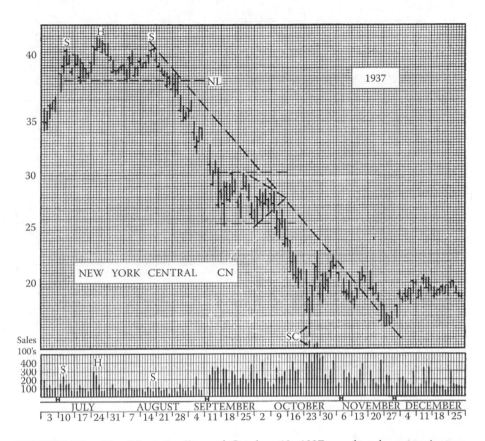

FIGURE 103. The "Panic" selling of October 19, 1937, produced a conspicuous Climax Reversal Day in nearly all leading stocks, as well as in the Averages. This New York Central chart shows, beside the Selling Climax (SC), its Head-and-Shoulders Recovery Top of July–August and a Consolidation Rectangle which ended as a Triangle in early October. "CN" made a final Bear Market low the following March at 10½. On a logarithmic price scale, its down trendline from August was not broken until June 1938.

temporarily, as a rule) well below even conservative values based on current business conditions.

A Selling Climax need not be completed, and the Reversal of Trend actually become evident, within a single day. We have classified it as a variety of One-Day Reversal, but some of them have actually spread out over 2 days, with the decline exhausted and coming to a halt late on the first day, too near the end of the session to permit much recovery. The next day sees an extensive rally right from the opening gong, as it is immediately apparent then, if not late the preceding day, that there are no more distress offerings.

The all-time percentage record for Selling Climaxes is held by October 29, 1929. Prices in terms of the Dow–Jones Industrial Average opened that day practically at their high, 252.38, which was more than 8 points below the

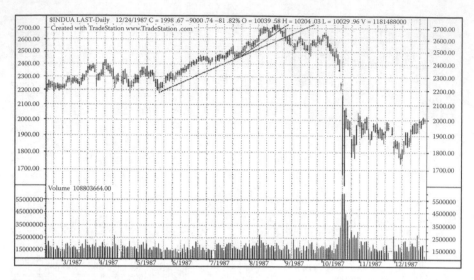

FIGURE 103.1. Dow Industrials, 1987 Reagan Crash. Rumors proliferated — iron-
ically, one that Reagan had Alzheimer's. Proximate cause: professional panic exacerbated by an ill-considered portfolio insurance scheme propagated by academics.
Note that the authoritative (lower) trendline here (75 days) is broken by more than
2% (Magee's suggestion) in early September. The broken upper trendline (25 days)
would have pulled the ripcord for the more agile trader. Savvy investors were
hedging and liquidating through September, and fund managers panicked in October. According to the Brady Report, Hull Trading Co. bought the bottom October 20,
thus saving American capitalism.

previous day's closing level. Panic selling flooded the Exchange from the
start, and before it was over, the Industrial Average had lost 40.05 points!
From that low, 212.33, it rallied in the final 2 hours to 230.07 for a gain of
nearly 18 points, and went on up another 28 points the following day. This
1929 climax set the all-time record also for daily turnover: 16,410,000 shares
were traded in those 5 hours, more than twice as many as in any one day
during the entire preceding Bull Market. But the low level of October 29 was
broken a week later, and the bottom of that particular early phase of the
1929–32 Bear Market was not reached until November 13. *EN: See comments
on the following page on the Reagan Crash of 1987.*

The Panic of 1937 ended with a classic Selling Climax on October 19,
another "Black Tuesday" in stock market annals. The Dow Industrials had
closed at 125.73 the night before. Prices had already fallen without a rally
of consequence from a high of 190 in mid-August, and margin accounts were
nearly all in a precarious situation. The telephones had been worked over-
time the preceding day by brokers demanding additional margin, most of
which was not forthcoming. When the Exchange opened on the 19th, quotations hit the toboggan under a flood of offerings. By 11:30 a.m., with the
Industrial Average around 115, the selling was over and offerings disappeared. An hour later, prices were jumping a point between sales and the

day closed at 126.85, recovering its entire loss. Volume on that climax was 7,290,000 shares, double that of any day at the top of the preceding Bull Market. An intraday high of 141.22 was reached 10 days later, but the Panic Low was subsequently broken on November 20, 1937, and that Bear Market finally ended at 98.95 (Dow–Jones Industrials' closing level) on March 31, 1938.

EN: Compare 1987. No wonder investors have instinctual angst on October 19. In 1987 the Bear returned to create another great Panic — on the very same date. From a high of 2746.65 on August 25 the Dow bungeed to a low of 1616.21 on October 20. The actual full-blown panic took place from October 14 (high 2485.15) to October 20 (low 1616.21) with October 19 and 20 traversing a range of 547.95 points or 25% of the market at that point. Top to bottom 1130 points were lost comprising a percentage retracement of 41%. The more things change the more they stay the same, as André Malraux is said to have remarked. Actually he said it in French, which is more elegant, and expresses the same idea: Plus ça change, c'est plus la meme chose. *Readers should not assume that similar crashes will not occur in the future.*

The foregoing were *general market* climaxes, a phenomenon which, of course, produces (or rather is produced by) simultaneous selling in practically every actively traded individual issue. A Climax Bottom, as a matter of fact, appears in an individual stock chart, as a rule, only as a concomitant of a general market clean-out, although there are cases where some particular and completely unexpected piece of bad news affects one certain company and causes panicky liquidation of its shares alone, terminating with a One-Day Reversal. The *Top* Reversal Day, on the other hand, is normally a manifestation of an individual stock rather than of the general market average.

The two outstanding examples of Selling Climaxes that we have cited above, and numbers of others which have appeared at the conclusion of various Panic Sell-offs, obviously offered extraordinary opportunities for a quick turn to the trader who was smart (or lucky) enough to get in at the bottom. He could cash in a few days later with exceptional profits. Professional operators capitalize on such opportunities. The problem is to recognize the climactic nature of the selling in time to seize the chance — and that isn't as easy as it may have sounded in our discussion. Just to emphasize the possibilities of error, there was a 30-point drop, followed by a 30-point recovery, on a turnover of nearly 13 million shares, on October 24, 1929, but the trader who didn't grab his profits within 48 hours never had another chance to get out even (in terms of the Averages, that is).

But it isn't impossible to recognize a Selling Climax, if you have friends in the Street to keep you informed on the condition of margin accounts and the amount of necessitous selling to be expected. *EN: This information is now not difficult to come by. It is easily obtainable in the general financial press.* The climax comes *after* a decline approaching Panic proportions. The day usually opens with a substantial Downside Gap (opening prices considerably below the previous night's closing); offerings appear too great to be absorbed; prices collapse; the ticker runs late; the market is exceptionally "broad" with nearly

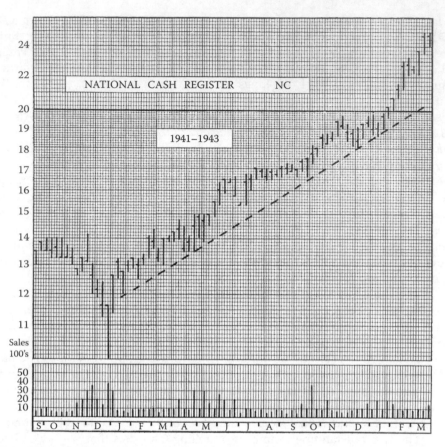

FIGURE 104. The Selling Climax discussed on the preceding pages is typically a 1-day phenomenon, and on only one occasion (April 1939) in history has a general market One-Day Reversal signaled the final low of a Primary Bear Trend (although many individual stocks evinced a Selling Climax on their charts in March 1938).

Occasionally, a weekly chart will produce a formation which might be called a "One-Week Reversal," in some such conspicuous fashion as is shown above in "NC." In this instance, the subsequent rise proves that a Major change in its technical balance occurred in December 1941. Curiously enough, no other obvious Reversal Pattern appeared on the weekly chart at this turn in the Primary Trend of "NC." (Its daily chart showed an Ascending Triangle.) But this example of a One-Week Reversal is not shown to give the idea that such phenomena carry important technical indications. On the contrary, most "Reversal weeks" are followed by very disappointing moves.

every listed stock crowding into the record. Then, some time after 11 a.m., perhaps not until afternoon, the selling appears to dry up; a few issues continue to decline while others begin to climb. Suddenly prices are jumping. That is the time to act. Buy a stock that has been thoroughly depressed but one which normally has at all times a good following (for example, U.S. Steel). Don't hang on too long; take a reasonable profit as soon as it is available and sell, in any event, whenever the recovery shows signs of bogging down.

Remember, a One-Day Reversal is not a dependable Major Trend indicator. Selling Climaxes do not normally occur at the final Bottoms of Bear Markets — weak holdings usually have been shaken out long before that stage is reached. Only one Primary Downtrend in all the record has, in fact, ended with the first Panic Phase, that being the 5-month Bear Market of 1938–39 which was followed by an equally short Bull Market.

One remaining Reversal Formation, the *Island Pattern*, involves the whole subject of *Gaps* which we have not yet had an appropriate occasion to discuss. Gaps will be taken up in detail in Chapter 12, and we will defer the Island Reversal until then.

Short-Term Phenomena
of Potential Importance

Very short-term phenomena — of a one-day or a few days' duration — can sometimes be indicative of not only short-term direction, but also give hints as to longer-term price behavior. Gaps (Chapter 12), and One-Day Reversals (Chapter 10), which have been discussed, belong to this group. Other short-term patterns of interest include *Spikes*, *Key Reversal Days* (sometimes called merely *Reversal Days*), and *Runaway Days* (sometimes called *Wide-Ranging Days*).

Spikes

On the day it occurs, a Spike is not immediately identifiable, for by definition it protrudes head and shoulders above days before and after if it is at or near a Top, and plunges much below the surrounding days if it occurs at a Bottom. So after a day that exhibits an unusually wide range, the subsequent days must be observed to discriminate the day from a Runaway Day. Both are the marks of a far-ranging battle between bulls and bears, with the close giving a clue as to whom the eventual winner will be. The importance of the spike is highlighted by

A. The strength and length of the action which preceded it
B. The close of the day, whether up on a Bottom or down on a Top
C. Its prominence when compared to the days before and after it

An extremely wide-range day at the end of a long bull move which closes down after making unusual new highs might even be construed as a one-day signal. Whether one trades on it or not would depend on his particular style and taste and the nature of his trading — long range, scalping, etc. In fact, the Spike might also be a One-Day Reversal — that pattern where often an opening gap is followed by avid buying which collapses and closes below the opening or at the low of the day. Such action might be compared to an army pursuing a seemingly defeated enemy only to discover the retreat was a ruse, then turning and fleeing the other way in a rout.

FIGURE 104.1. A church spire top in Qualcomm. The December gap might be mistaken for a buy signal, as might be the runaway days, but they are actually hand-engraved invitations to leave the party with near progressive stops ⅛ off the day's low. Also valid—exit on the Key Reversal on day 2 after the gap. How does the trader know this is a blow-off and not a signal to pyramid? By the age, length, state, and slope of the market. When trendlines go vertical, blow-off management must be used. The return to the base of the first runaway day is notification that it is a bull trap. The first bull trap. The second bull trap is the breakout of the triangle in March. A wonderful chart filled with fin de siècle and fin de millennium lessons.

Turn this description on its head and you have a Spike Bottom. It is not infrequent that a Spike will be followed by significant price movement in the opposite direction. Figure 104.1 illustrates a modern Spike. Figures 1 and 35 show some spikes on Edwards' and Magee's charts.

Runaway Days

A Runaway Day is a day that stands out on the chart as having an unusually long range, often opening at the low and closing at the high, or vice versa for bear runaways. Here the enemy has retreated precipitously, or treacherously to draw the bulls into a trap. The holders and sellers cannot or will not satisfy the eager demand of the buyers and so the price transverses perhaps two to three times the daily range. While the agile speculator may jump on this charging train and realize a nice scalp, it is the following days that reveal the true significance. Nice consolidation and continued volume will confirm the day as significant while a tapering of volume and rounding or volatile pullback will call into question its validity. While these days may be taken as hair-trigger buy signals (or sell signals, depending) the return

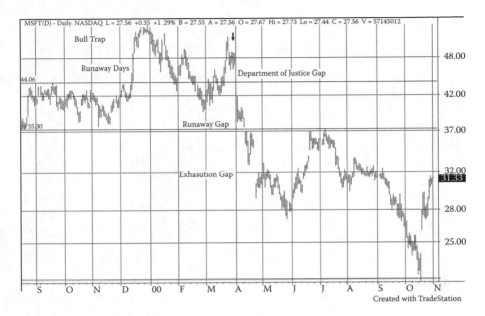

MSFT(D) - Daily NASDAQ L = 27.56 +0.35 +1 .29% B = 27.55 A = 27.56 O = 27.67 Hi = 27.73 Lo = 27.44 C = 27.56 V = 57145012

Bull Trap

Runaway Days

Department of Justice Gap

44.06

35.30

Runaway Gap

Exhaustion Gap

48.00

42.00

37.00

32.00
31.33

28.00

25.00

Created with TradeStation

FIGURE 104.2. Microsoft. A Key Reversal Day in March. Department of Justice breakaway gaps: runaway gaps, exhaustion gaps. Selling climax. As usual, further lows are achieved. A cornucopia of chartist's delights.

of prices to the low of the Runaway Day will probably indicate that the day was a false signal, and that a trade in the opposite direction is shaping up. See Figure 39 for runaways complete with gaps.

Figure 104.2 showing Microsoft in 2000 was one such example where a bull trap precipitated by a Runaway Day with a subsequent collapse foretold the 50% decline in Microsoft stock.

Key Reversal Days

The Key Reversal Day pattern occurs when one sees a new high in an upmove and then a close below the close of the previous day. As a short-term trading signal it has much to recommend it, but like every other technical pattern, judgment and timing are required to profit from it. In a Bull Market there will be some if not many such interim highs marked by Key Reversal Days. On the Key Reversal Day at a major or important Top the trader shorts the stock on the close with a stop at the high of the reversal day, or slightly above. He may then exit on the profit side on the occurrence of a Key Reversal Day in the opposite direction, or on a profit target, or a chart pattern. Or he may, if adventurous, use the trade as the first of accumulating a position for an anticipated Bear Market, adding other positions as more significant patterns occur and as support levels are broken.

This pattern also is useful in trading range markets, as shown in some Internet stocks from 2000, where trading with Key Reversal Days would

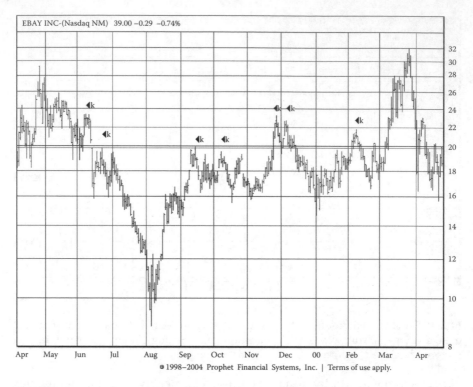

FIGURE 104.3.   Ebay. As Ebay broke its trendline and drifted sideways, it became
a good subject for Key Reversal Day trading. Note several instances.

have allowed the trader to escape *unscathed* in the minicrash of the NASDAQ
in early 2000. (Cf. Figures 104.3 and 104.4 on the following pages for Ebay
and Lucent.)

Of all the Very Short-Term Patterns, Gaps, One-Day Reversals, Key
Reversal Days, Spikes, and Runaway Days, it should be noted that return
of prices to the origination of the formation marks the formation as a false
signal and reason to reverse the trade direction and look for perhaps significant profits.

Clearly these are the tactics of scalpers and speculators, but it does not
hurt the long-term investor to know and understand them.

FIGURE 104.3.1. If you can't deliver groceries electronically what good is the Internet? Meg Whitman (a competent, well, more than competent, CEO) and Ebay found a use for it: The biggest flea market ever invented (and growing every day). Every military commander knows the axiom, Exploit Success! and Ebay exploits and exploits and exploits. Is there a fundamental lesson here for the technician? Absolutely. Although the technician should be able to take a nameless chart and trade it competently (CEO of his own ship) no *real* information or data should be ignored. In this case the real information – that Ebay was an 800 pound gorilla (or flea) – fit the chart perfectly. So Ebay separated itself from a bunch of nags to run long and hard. Handicappers know to always keep an eye on winning jockeys: Whitman. Ellison at Oracle. Moore at Intel. Gates at Microsoft. Jobs at Apple (and Pixar and NEXT and etc., etc., etc...). In 2005 what's to be done with Ebay? Draw a trendline, raise your stops and sell it if it reverses.

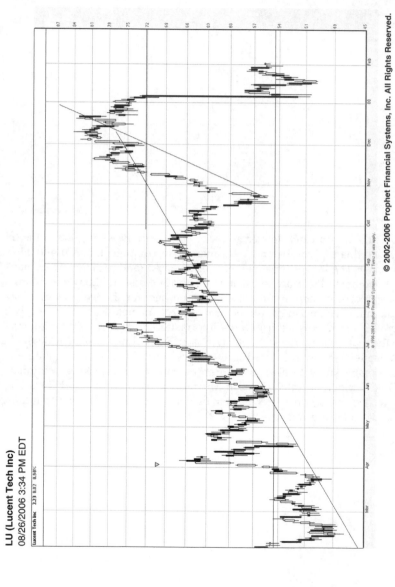

LU (Lucent Tech Inc)
08/26/2006 3:34 PM EDT

FIGURE 104.4. Lucent. Late 20th and early 21st century schizophrenia. Runaway Days, Breakaway Gaps. Maalox is to be prescribed for the investor. Ecstasy for the trader. Reversal Days and short-term tactics win the day when the subject is insane. An excellent example of fitting the trader to the stock. Why would a rational investor own such a stock?

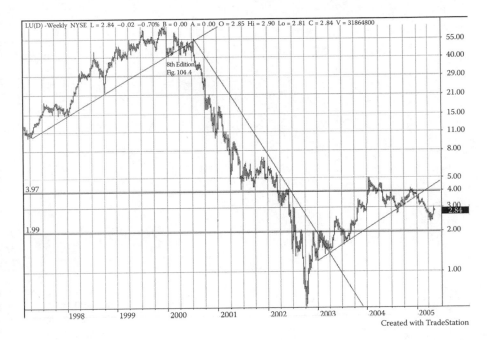

LU(D) -Weekly NYSE L = 2 .84 −0 .02 −0 .70% B = 0 .00 A = 0 .00 O = 2 .85 Hi = 2 .90 Lo = 2 .81 C = 2 .84 V = 31864800

8th Edition
Fig. 104.4

55.00
40.00
29.00
21.00
15.00
11.00
8.00
5.00
4.00
3.00
2.84
2.00
1.00

3.97

1.99

1998   1999   2000   2001   2002   2003   2004   2005

Created with TradeStation

FIGURE 104.4.1. In the caption to Figure 104.4, the editor asked, apparently rhetorically why a rational investor would own Lucent. The picture here shows what happens when apparently rational investors do not set a stop to protect themselves from irrational volatility. The market knows things investors do not know. But it will reveal these things to the most basic of investors if he reads the chart. This chart is added for the 9th Edition to pick up the picture where the 8th left it.

chapter eleven

Consolidation Formations

An army, which has pushed forward too rapidly, penetrated far into enemy territory, suffered casualties, and outrun its supplies, must halt eventually, perhaps retreat a bit to a more easily defended position and dig in, bring up replacements, and establish a strong base from which later to launch a new attack. In the military parlance with which we have all become more or less familiar these past few years, that process is known as *consolidating* one's gains. Although it will not do to overwork the analogy, there is much in the action of the stock market which may be compared to a military campaign. When a stock pushes ahead (up or down) too fast, it reaches a point where the forces that produced its move are exhausted. Then it either reverses its trend (in a Major or Intermediate sense), reacts to a good Support Level, or *Consolidates* its position, in some sort of "sideways" chart pattern composed of Minor Fluctuations, until it has caught up with itself, so to speak, and is ready to go on again.

We already have had occasion to refer to Consolidation Formations in our study of Symmetrical Triangles and Rectangles. We saw how those two chart formations might either reverse the previous trend or Consolidate it in preparation for its continuation. We noted that about three out of four Symmetrical Triangles will turn out to be Consolidations rather than Reversals — and Rectangles in about the same proportion. Even a Flat-Topped Broadening Pattern, constructed at the Top of an Intermediate Advance, may, despite its normally Bearish implications, be converted into a Consolidation or Continuation Formation if its Flat Top is decisively penetrated on the upside.

A Dow Theory Line in the chart of one of the Averages may be either a Consolidation or Reversal Formation, and is rather more likely to be the former than the latter. A Dow Line is, of course, a sort of loose Rectangle. The fact is that almost any sort of sideways price pattern, such as is often termed a "Congestion" or trading area, provided trading volume tends to diminish during its construction (and provided it does not show definite broadening tendencies), usually functions as a Consolidation. But most areas of Trend Consolidation are fairly well defined, taking on a recognizable pattern.

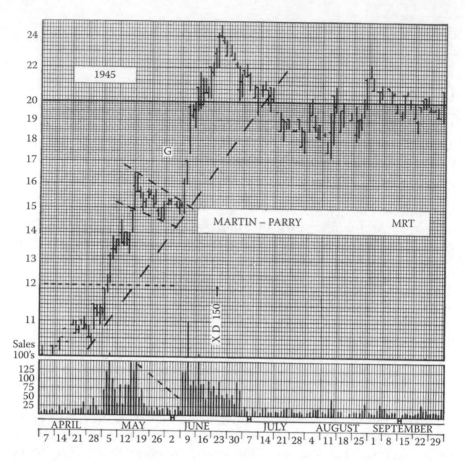

FIGURE 105. This is a typical and practically perfect Flag, constructed May 12 to June 2, 1945, in Martin–Parry. Daily turnover diminished to a low rate as prices settled down for exactly 3 weeks after their swift advance from 11 to 16½, but held up away from the lower boundary line during the third week, and then burst out topside with high volume in another straight-line push from 15 to 21. Study this chart again when you come to the Flag-measuring formula on page 192. The dashes at 12 indicate the upper range of an old Resistance Level (Chapter 13).

Flags and Pennants

We do not need to spend more time here on the Triangles and Rectangles; they have been examined in both their Reversal and Consolidation manifestations in previous chapters. Our first two formations, which are characteristic of Consolidation *only*, are the Flags and Pennants, and they are curiously related in certain aspects, as we shall see, to Triangles, Rectangles, and Wedges.

A *Flag* looks like a flag on the chart. That is, it does if it appears in an uptrend; the picture is naturally turned upside down in a downtrend. It

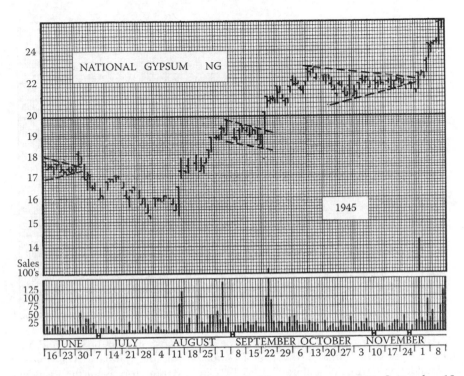

FIGURE 106.   Another typical Flag of 3 weeks' duration, August 30 to September 18. This National Gypsum chart overlaps that in Figure 49, showing the false move at the apex of the May–June Symmetrical Triangle. A buy signal was given when prices pushed up through the old apex level on August 23 with increased volume. Most interesting is the second Symmetrical Triangle which formed in October–November, an almost exact replica of the first, but with a downside false move at its apex. The sharp increase in volume on November 27 left no doubt as to its being a Consolidation rather than Reversal Pattern. "NG" went on up to 33.

might be described as a small, compact parallelogram of price fluctuations, or a tilted Rectangle which slopes back moderately against the prevailing trend. Let us consider the Uptrend Flag first. It usually forms after a rapid and fairly extensive advance which produces a nearly vertical, or at least quite steep price track on the charts. On such moves, volume normally shows a progressive increase until it reaches a high rate. This volume (since every transaction signifies a sale, as well as a purchase) is a warning, of course, that many holders of the stock are taking profits. Eventually the pressure of profit-taking halts the markup. Prices "churn" without further gain and then react two or three points on reduced turnover. A new rally occurs, but fails to equal the previous high or attain the previous top volume. Another reaction carries quotations slightly below the preceding Bottom with further diminution of activity. Then follows a series of similar Minor Fluctuations, each of whose Tops and Bottoms are successively a trifle lower than its predecessor, and with volume shrinking markedly and constantly as the

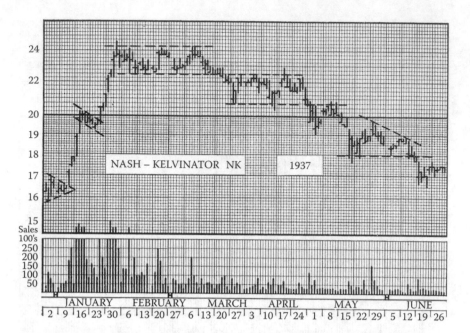

FIGURE 107. Flags of the "Half-Mast" type appear most often in the later and most active stages of a Primary Advance. The above example (January) was the last Consolidation Formation before "NK's" 1937 Bull Market Top. Note the Rectangle Reversal Pattern in March and series of step-down patterns that followed.

pattern develops. On the chart, the initial, steep up-move followed by the compact, sideways, and slightly down-sloping price Congestion Area, which can be roughly bounded, top and bottom, by parallel lines, takes on the appearance of a mast (or halyard) with a flag flying from its peak. Hence, of course, the name of the formation.

Sometimes each rally and setback within the Flag takes 3 or 4 days, rarely more. In other cases, prices will skip back and forth between the upper and lower Flag boundaries in a single day or two, in which event the pattern on the chart consists of an almost solid block of price range lines. The wider the pattern (from top to bottom) the longer time, naturally, it should take for each swing within it to be completed. This process of Minor Fluctuations may continue for only 5 days to a week if the Flag is narrow, or go on for as much as 3 weeks. Daily turnover by that time usually will have shrunk to a relatively low ebb. Then suddenly, prices will erupt with a new burst of activity from the end of the Flag and push straight up again in another advance that practically duplicates the original "mast" atop which the Flag was constructed.

We have spoken of the Flag pattern as being moderately down-slanting, but the very short and "solid" ones will frequently develop horizontally and look like small squares. (On rare occasions a pattern of the Flag type in an uptrend will even slope up a trifle.)

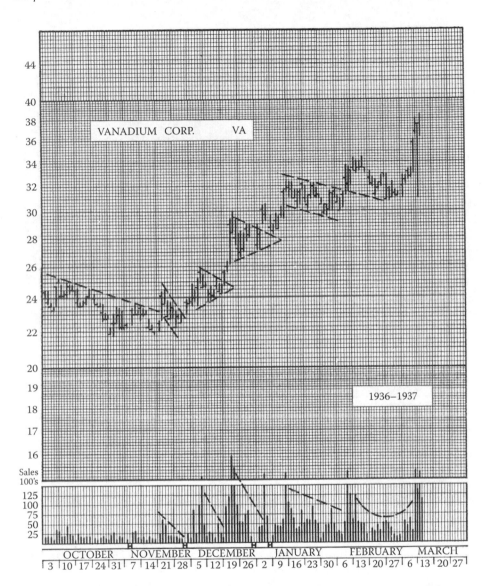

FIGURE 108. Sometimes a stock will make a long series of small Consolidation Patterns in its uptrend, one following right on the heels of another as successive groups of traders buy in while others take their profits on previous purchases. In this sequence of step-ups in Vanadium, the Flag Pattern formed in January 1937 ran a few days over, but the volume breakout of February 4 left no doubt that the trend was still up. A final Top was made at 39½ in March. Note strong buy signal given on December 14. Refer to this record again in connection with Support and Resistance studies in Chapter 13.

Flags form on steep down moves in much the same manner and with precisely the same implications as they do in uptrends. Down Flags, of course, tend to slope up; i.e., they simply invert the picture presented by an

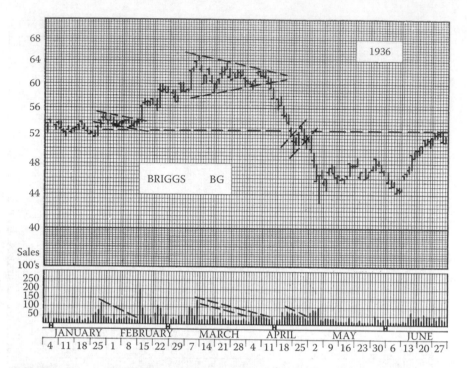

FIGURE 109. A Bull Flag in February and a Bear Flag in April 1936, in Briggs. The Top between was a Symmetrical Triangle. April 30 was a Reversal Day. Prices recovered to 64½ in November 1936, making there a long-term Major Double Top with this March high. The Support–Resistance Zone at 51–53, indicated by dashed line, was still effective in 1946! (See Chapter 13.)

up Flag. Trading volume diminishes during their formation and increases again as prices break down away from them.

The Pennant — A Pointed Flag

The only important difference between a *Pennant* and a *Flag* is that the former is bounded by converging boundary lines rather than parallel. The normal Pennant, in other words, is a small, compact, sloping Triangle. It slants down when it appears in an uptrend, and up in a downtrend. It forms, as a rule, after a rapid advance (or decline), and trading volume shrinks notably during its construction. In fact, activity tends to diminish even more rapidly in a Pennant than in a Flag (which we naturally would expect on account of the progressively shorter fluctuations which compose it), and may drop almost to nothing before the Pennant is completed and prices break away from it in a new and rapid move.

The Pennant might also be described as a short, compact Wedge, characterized by marked diminution of activity. When, as is usual, it slants back against the preceding trend, its forecasting implications are similar to those

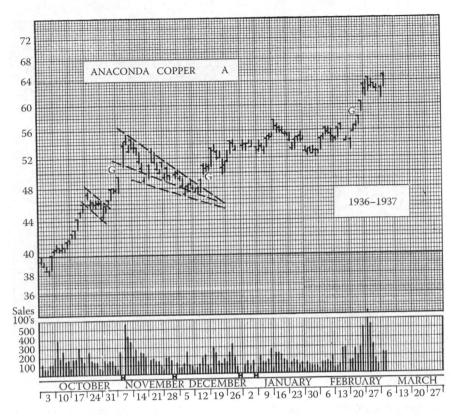

FIGURE 110.   The down-sloping, Converging Price Formation of November 4 through December 9 might be called either a short Wedge or a Pennant. Note small Flag in October; also Runaway Gaps November 4 and February 19, and Breakout Gap December 10.

of the Wedge, in that prices break out of it in a direction opposite to its slant. But there are rarer Minor variations of the Pennant, comparable with those sometimes found in the Flag, in which the price area is very short and "solid" and practically horizontal (like a Symmetrical Triangle), or in which the slope is actually slightly in the same direction as the preceding trend instead of against it. When prices move out of the last named type, they ordinarily do so not in a sudden straight-line breakaway but rather in an accelerating curve with volume increasing gradually instead of abruptly at the break. The whole pattern then resembles a curved horn which runs to a long, slender point. Don't let these variations worry you; there is nothing deceptive about their appearance; their kinship to the more common, normal form is quite apparent.

The Measuring Formula

The same approximate measuring formula applies to the Pennant as to the Flag. They are both "Half-Mast" Patterns which ordinarily form after a fairly

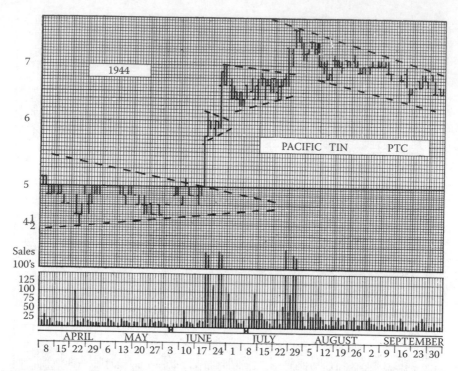

FIGURE 111. An example (in June 1944) of the very brief and compact type of price "Congestion" which can be classed as a Flag. The advance here started at 5 from a 13-month Symmetrical Triangle of which only the last 2 months appear above. The measuring implication (see below) of this tiny Flag was not fulfilled until after prices had undergone a sort of Triangular Consolidation in July.

steady and rapid (steep) price movement. In applying the measuring rule, go back to the beginning of that immediately preceding move, to the point where it broke away from a previous Consolidation of Reversal Formation (or through a significant trendline or Resistance Level, with which later chapters are concerned), a point recognizable as a rule by a quick spurt in activity, and measure from there to the Minor Reversal level at which the Flag or Pennant started to form. Then measure the same distance from the point where prices break out of the Flag or Pennant, and in the same direction. The level thus arrived at is the minimum expectation of this type of Consolidation Pattern. As a matter of fact, advances from Flags or Pennants in an uptrend generally go farther (in terms of points or dollars) than the preceding move, while declines may not carry quite so far. Hence, the formula is best applied on a semilogarithmic chart by measuring actual chart distance rather than by counting points. You can check this by referring to the examples illustrating this study.

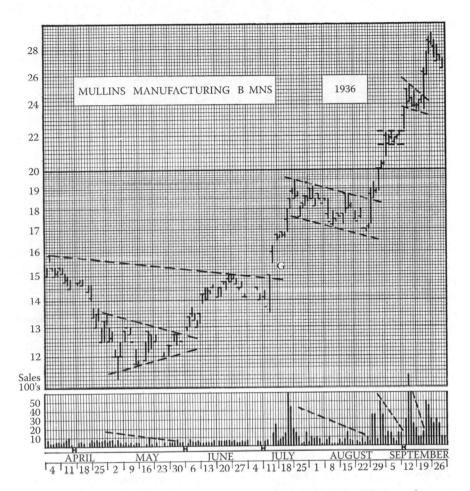

FIGURE 112.   Another example of the series of Flag-type Consolidations that may form in a rapid, third-phase Bull Market Advance. Mullins went from 15 to above 39 in 6 months in 1936, dropped back to 31, and then rose again in March l, 1937, to its previous high, making a Major Double Top. ("MNS" was split 2-for-1 in 1937.)

The July–August Flag ran for 5 weeks — too long to be trusted without additional technical evidence (see point 3 on page 194). The danger in such prolonged formations is either that the breakout, when it finally appears, will fail to follow through, or that prices will keep right on drifting down. For the moment — on August 25 — it looked as though this Flag had "gone stale," but when prices rose above the previous high on August 27, with a smart pickup in volume, purchases were obviously safe.

Reliability of Flags and Pennants

These pretty little patterns of Consolidation are justly regarded as among the most dependable of chart formations, both as to directional and measuring indications. They do fail occasionally, but almost never without giving warning before the pattern itself is completed. All that is necessary to guard against such failures is to strictly apply the tests as to authenticity of pattern which we already have incorporated in their description. These are

1. The Consolidation (Flag or Pennant) should occur after a "straight-line" move.
2. Activity should diminish appreciably and constantly during the pattern's construction, and continue to decline until prices break away from it.
3. Prices should break away (in the expected direction) in not more than 4 weeks. A pattern of this type which extends beyond 3 weeks should be watched with suspicion.

The matter of practical trading on these particular formations will be taken up in the second section of this book, devoted to tactics. But our second test deserves some further comment here. If a pattern begins to develop on the chart which, so far as the price picture alone is concerned, qualifies as a Flag or Pennant, but during which trading volume remains high or obviously irregular instead of diminishing, the outcome is more apt to be a quick reaction against, rather than continuation of, the previous trend. In other words, such high or irregular activity formations are characteristically *Minor* Reversal Areas rather than true Consolidations. Watch the volume half of your chart at all times.

Where They May Be Expected

Flag and Pennant Consolidations are characteristic of fast moves. Therefore, they show up most frequently in the later, dynamic phase of Bull Markets, after the first accumulation and the more orderly early markup stages have passed. Hence, the appearance of these patterns may be taken as a warning that an advance is approaching its final weeks. The rapid phase of a Major Bear Trend, on the other hand, is its second stage, often characterized by almost "vertical" Panic Declines. The Flags and Pennants which develop therein are usually short — completed in a matter of 3 or 4 days rather than weeks. In the late months of a Bear Market, formations that evolve on the charts in the Flag or Pennant similitude often will run too long (4 weeks or more), begin to show an increase in volume on the rallies, and be succeeded by only dull and limited reactions.

In general, it may be said that these particular chart patterns are most common (and most dependable) in uptrends. The appearance, *after* a Major Decline, of price pictures which, at the start, assume the downtrend Flag or Pennant form must be regarded with caution. Unless such developments hold strictly to the limitations we have stated above under the heading of "reliability," do not trade on them.

FIGURE 113. The vertical lines marked "M" show how the measuring formula is applied to a Flag Pattern. Note that the first measurement is taken from the level where the mast leaves the previous "Congestion" up to the peak of the Flag. This same distance is then measured up from the Flag breakout. In "WYO," the formula worked out exactly. Trading commitments should normally have been cashed in above 36 on this move. They might then have been reinstated when it became apparent by April 2 that a Rounding Bottom was completed (note volume) for a new advance.

Flag Pictures on Weekly and Monthly Charts

One of our requisites for a dependable Flag (or Pennant) was that it should not take more than 4 weeks to complete its pattern and break out in a new move. It stands to reason, therefore, that a true Flag cannot show up at all on a monthly chart and barely appears on a weekly chart. You will find price areas on long-range charts, patterns which have taken 8 or 10 weeks to as many months, and sometimes a year or two, in their construction, which assume the shape of a Flag, but do not expect them to function as Flags.

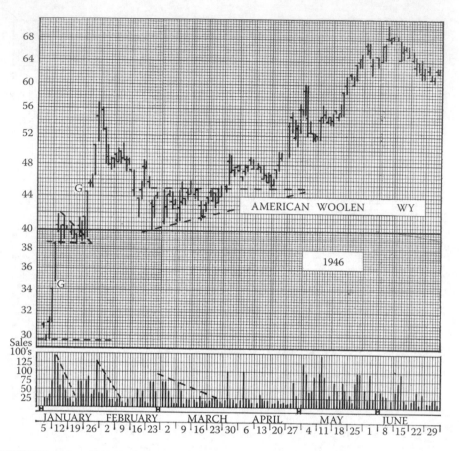

FIGURE 114. A 1946 chart that delighted technicians. Contains a perfect "Half-Mast" Pattern in January, with measuring gaps (G, G) above and below it; a downside Flag in early February (check measurement); a fine Ascending Triangle at the bottom of this reaction, with a Throwback in April, giving an ideal "buy spot."

Examined in detail on a daily chart, these same long areas almost always will be found to contain price formations having entirely different significance. Frequently, what is really a Major *Reversal* Area following a long, rapid advance will look something like a Flag when it is condensed on a monthly chart. So, do not trust such pictures on long-range charts; do not take it for granted that they represent Consolidation for a new rise; find out what the detailed *daily* plotting for the same period says.

Rectangular Consolidations: An Early Phase Phenomenon

In contrast with Flags and Pennants, which are typically last stage Bull Market Concomitants, Consolidations of the Rectangle class are found more often in the earlier phases of Bull Trend evolution. In Major Bear Moves, Rectangles may develop in the first stage just before a Panic Decline, or in

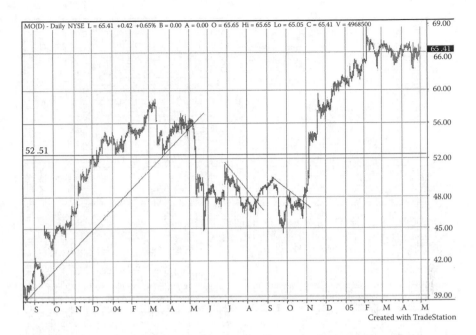

FIGURE 114.1. MO. Talk about your technician's delights. Altria Group throws off some pretty good delights here. A breakaway gap and run days to the downside. A down flagpole with flag. Pattern gaps. But *good* pattern gaps, really interesting. Then a triangle complete with a breakaway and an up flagpole with flag. Of course the nontechnician probably is suffering from nausea at this point. It's an ill roller coaster which bodes ill for everyone. And note well, a completely tradable situation for the alert short-term technician.

the last stage preceding a strictly limited final sell-off. The latter manifestation presumably betokens premature accumulation by interests who feel that prices have already gone low enough to suit their purposes. (They come out all right, of course, if they are able to hold on through the remainder of the Bear Swing and long enough for the next Bull Market to put prices back up again to profitable levels.)

Head-and-Shoulders Consolidations

All our references to the Head-and-Shoulders Formations up to this point (see Chapters 6 and 7) have considered that pattern as typifying a Reversal of Trend, and, in its normal and common manifestation, that is most definitely the Head-and-Shoulders function. But, occasionally, prices will go through a series of fluctuations which construct a sort of inverted Head-and-Shoulders picture, which in turn leads to *continuation* of the previous trend.

There is no danger of confusing such Continuation or Consolidation Formations with regular Head-and-Shoulders Reversals because, as we have said, they are inverted or abnormal with respect to the direction of the price

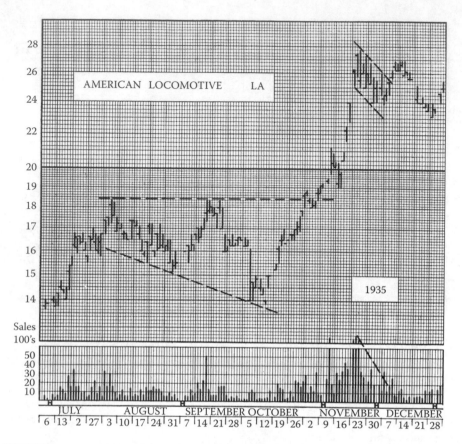

FIGURE 115. A Flag (end of November) which seemed for several weeks to have failed completely. However, prices rose quickly to 36¼ from their December 23 low, thus finally carrying through according to formula. Note Flat-Topped Broadening Formation which started the move.

trend prior to their appearance. In other words, one of these patterns that develops in a rising market will take the form of a Head-and-Shoulders Bottom. Those that appear in decline assume the appearance of a Head-and-Shoulders Top. By the time these price formations are completed (left shoulder, head and right shoulder evident), there is no question as to their implications. But at the head stage, before the right shoulder is constructed, there may be — usually is — considerable doubt as to what is really going on.

The volume pattern in Consolidations of this type does not follow the rule for Reversal Head-and-Shoulders. In a downtrend, for example, the Consolidation Formation resembled in its price contour a Head-and-Shoulders Top, but the attendant volume will diminish instead of increase on the left shoulder and head, as well as on the right shoulder. The same holds true for the "Bottom" Patterns that develop as Consolidation in an advance

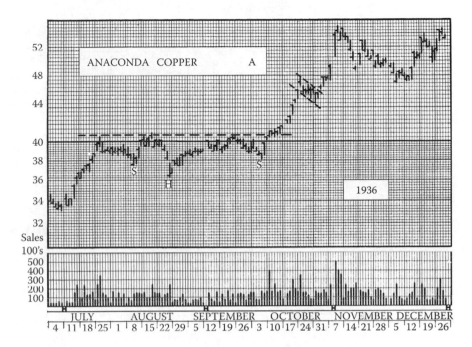

FIGURE 116. Typical of the form that Head-and-Shoulders Consolidation Patterns may take, both as to price pattern and volume, was this development in Anaconda. Measuring formula for the small Flag in October should be applied from the point of breakout through the Head-and-Shoulders neckline.

market. Breakouts, however, resemble in all respects those arising from Reversal Formations.

Head-and-Shoulders Consolidations of the Complex or Multiple-type very seldom appear on the charts. Theoretically, they might, of course, and should be as easy for the chart technician to handle as the simple forms.

The formula for determining the probable minimum price move (beyond the neckline) from a Head-and-Shoulders Reversal Formation was discussed in Chapter 6. To anyone familiar with the verities of stock market trends and the endless variety of pictures that the charts can present, it is amazing how accurately that formula works out, how often the first consequential move away from a Head-and-Shoulders Top or Bottom will carry through to the point (or a little beyond) implied by the measurement of the formation. But, the same formula applied to Consolidation Patterns of the Head-and-Shoulders form does not work out as well. Such patterns are usually quite "flat," and the ensuing move generally extends well beyond the measurement implied thereby, while, in some cases, it may not go quite as far. Consequently, the Head-and-Shoulders formula cannot be applied to Consolidation Areas with assurance that it sets up a definite and dependable objective; one has to look, in these cases, to a variety of other chart indications in order to appraise the probable proportions of the move to follow.

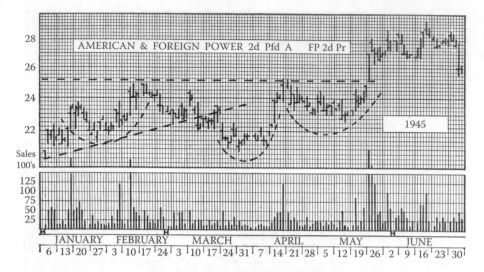

FIGURE 117. A 1945 Head-and-Shoulders Consolidation in which both of the shoulders and the head took a "Saucer" form. Compare price and volume trends. Prices advanced to 31½ in July, came back again to 25½ in August, and then shot up to 40 in November.

Scallops–Repeated Saucers

Our next chart picture differs from the Consolidation Formations previously discussed, in that it does not constitute a more or less definite area of Congestion or fluctuation to which one or more critical boundary lines can be affixed. We could, perhaps, take it up as well in a subsequent chapter under the general heading of normal trend action. Yet it is a pattern so characteristic of certain types of stocks and certain types of markets, and so nearly related to the principle of Consolidation for further advance, that it may better be treated here.

When a stock in which there is a large number of shares outstanding, and in which there is, at all times, a fairly active and "close" market emerges from a long-time Bottom (as exemplified by the past history of Radio Corporation and Socony Vacuum), it will often make a long Major Advance in a series of "Saucers." These successive patterns, each of which resembles, in both price and volume action, the Reversal Formation described in Chapter 7 as a Rounding Bottom, are slightly uptilted. That is, the rising end always carries price a little higher than the preceding Top at the beginning of the Saucer. The net gain accomplished by each Saucering movement will vary from stock to stock, but there seems to be a strong tendency for it to amount to about 10 to 15% of the price of the issue. The total reaction from the left-hand lip of each Saucer to its Bottom level is usually a little greater, from 20 to 30%. And the length (duration) of the Saucers is normally 5 to 7 weeks, rarely less than 3. Thus, overall advance is slow but steady, in much the

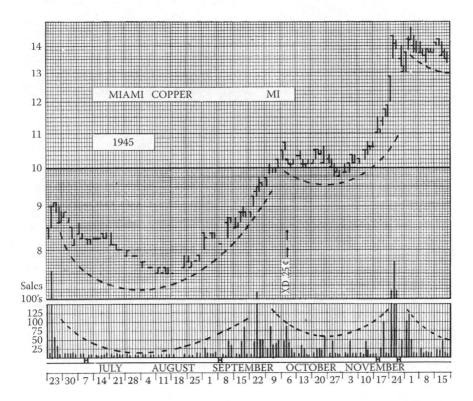

FIGURE 118. Part of a genuine "Scallop" uptrend, typical except for the short duration and relatively small decline in the October Saucer. The next Scallop, which started in December, dropped prices back to 12½ in January, and then carried them to 18½ in February. A 4-month Saucer, from February 1945 to June, preceded this chart. Note position traders found themselves in, who bought at 9 on the "new high volume" in June.

same sense as the progress of the man who eventually got out of the deep well by climbing three steps for each two that he slipped back.

The charts of stocks that take this sort of course show a picture of strikingly similar and Symmetrical Rising Scallops, one succeeding another with little or no pause between. Trading activity runs up to a peak at the latter stage of each Scallop, as the previous high is approached and exceeded, then diminishes into dullness as prices curve down and flatten out at the Bottom of the next Saucer, and picks up again as prices curve up into their next rise.

The trading opportunities afforded by stocks of the Saucering habit hardly require extended comment (although we shall set down some detailed specifications in the second section of this book). The Bottom level of each Scallop is usually easy to detect by watching price trend and volume, and so is the topping out at the end. Yet it is curiously a fact that most "tape watchers" handle such stocks in the wrong way, becoming interested in them and buying when they show activity ("make a new high on volume") and neglecting them entirely when they are in the dull, rounding-out stage of their trends.

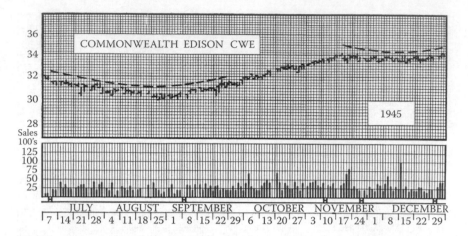

FIGURE 119. Although the Scalloping habit characteristically appears in low-priced issues, it is sometimes found in widely held, semi-investment stocks of medium price, such as "CWE."

(Many boardroom tape watchers scorn charts with unfortunate conse-quences to their capital in the long run. Genuinely expert tape readers — those who are able to show fairly consistent profits in their trades — are really extremely rare. *EN: For "tape readers" substitute "day traders," 99% of whom are unsuccessful.* When you do meet such an individual, you will find that he either, in effect, "carries charts in his head" or else takes a careful look at the record before he buys on a ticker showing activity.)

As a stock with the Scalloping habit finally works up in price to 15 or so, its pattern tends to become less regular; it begins to depart from the smooth, narrow Saucer-like curve of the lower levels. Above 20, it is apt to break away entirely from the Scallop sequence and produce, from there on, more rapid straight-line advances, interspersed with sharp reactions and standard types of Consolidation Formations, which are characteristic at all times of medium- and higher-priced issues. (There are exceptions: Some high-priced preferred stocks for which there is always a market, but whose trends depend almost entirely on the gradual changes in prevailing interest rates and supply of funds for investment, have a persistent Scallop habit in their Primary Upswings.)

We have named rather specific price levels (15 and 20) in the preceding paragraph, but price is not, of course, the sole factor determining the depar-ture of a stock from a Scallop Trend. The only safe assumption is that, once such a habit is detectable, it will be continued until the chart shows a definite divergence from it, and such divergence usually takes first the form of a greater-than-wanted advance arising at the end of one of the Saucers. Con-sequently, if you have previously taken a position in it at a favorable point (near the Bottom of a Scallop), you will unlikely be hurt when the stock finally alters its action.

Very low-priced issues may persist in a Scalloping Trend right up to their Major Bull Tops, and even attempt another Saucer Movement following what turns out to have been the final high, which attempt then fails, of course, to carry out the previous successively higher and higher pattern. Such failures are not difficult to detect; the change from previous pattern appears before any appreciable damage is done to a properly assumed commitment.

Modern vs. Old-Style Markets

We have mentioned in our discussion of Reversal Formations that some of them have appeared less frequently in the charts of the 1960s than they did in prior years, and others more frequently. The same is true of Consolidation Formations. Patterns of the compact, strictly defined sort such as Rectangles and Right Angle Triangles are less common now. Symmetrical Triangles are apt to be somewhat looser than they were in the 1920s and 1930s — not as clean-cut and conspicuous on the charts. Typical profit-taking patterns such as Flags and Pennants seem to be as common as ever, while "normal" trend pictures, including those formations associated with normal trend development (such as Head-and-Shoulders, Rounding Turns, etc.), are more common.

The reasons for these changes are fairly apparent. SEC regulations, higher margin requirements, greater public sophistication, and a more conservative — we might better say more pessimistic   approach to the problems of investment and stock trading generally have all played a part in this evolution. SEC and Stock Exchange vigilance have done away with the flagrant pool manipulations designed to take advantage of the "lambs" of former years. Nowadays, there is even very little of the more "legitimate" sort of syndicate operation planned to facilitate large-scale accumulation or distribution.

It is still possible, of course, for "insiders" to hold back for a limited time, or to prematurely release announcements of good or bad portent with regard to the affairs of a particular corporation, in order to serve their personal strategic purposes. But the stock purchase and sales of officers, directors, and principal owners are now too closely watched to allow a great deal of "skullduggery." (Nevertheless, the average investor had better still be a trifle skeptical as to the probability of any great advance in the market following publication of a good report.)

Collusion between investment advisory services and trading pools has been effectively outlawed. (It is safe to say that it never did exist as flagrantly, even in the 1920s, as many amateur traders seem to think.) The SEC (with the thorough cooperation of the Stock Exchange) polices the investment counsel profession thoroughly, constantly, and most effectively. No well-established investment counsel can afford to indulge in deceptive or collusive practices even if the desire were there. Most of them go far beyond the most reasonable needs to safeguard themselves against any contacts which, however innocent or useful, might be viewed with suspicion.

FIGURE 120. This chart shows the last 5 months of a broad, 13-month Saucer-like Consolidation in "IT," which followed its rapid run up from 3 to 16 in late 1943 and early 1944. "IT" is an erratic actor, and its volume is apt to be particularly deceptive in day-to-day movements. Major Price Patterns in it, however, are dependable. This final phase of its long Consolidation (distribution and reaccumulation) took first the form of a Rectangle (with a premature breakout) and then an Ascending Triangle. Its 1945–46 Bull Market Top was a massive Head-and-Shoulders.

The old-time "plunger" hasn't disappeared entirely, but high margins and regulations preventing "Bear Raiding" have made present-day stock markets relatively difficult and unprofitable for him. The out-and-out board-room gamblers *(EN: Day Traders — whose rushing to and fro probably exacerbates daily volatility.)* still come in, although high margins have cramped them too. In recent years, they have appeared in numbers only in the final stages of Bull Markets. *EN: Note the Day Trading craze that infected the markets in the late 1990s.* Of course, their operations never did affect the charts much except to augment activity.

On the other hand, higher taxes and greater regulation have most certainly not provided safer, closer, or more stable markets for the small investor. Higher margins have not prevented Panic Collapses. If anything, markets have been "thinner" on the downside, more vulnerable to rapid and drastic decline, than they were prior to modern regulation. We still have the very same sort of Bull and Bear Markets, and much the same sort of market trend development, that we had 50 years ago. The surprising thing is not that a

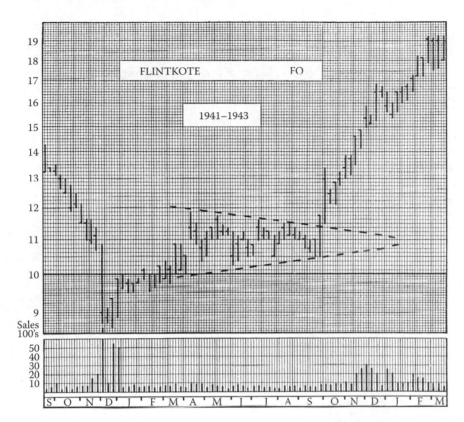

FIGURE 121. There are times when a Consolidation Pattern gives the only good technical signal that a Reversal in an issue's Primary Trend has actually taken place. Although cases of a Major Turn, particularly a Bottom, without some sort of recognizable Reversal Formation on the chart are quite rare, they do occur. This weekly chart of Flintkote illustrates such a phenomenon. A Bear Market low, from which it rose to 47 in 1946, was made at 8⅝ in December 1941. Without developing any important technical foundation on either a daily or weekly chart, its first upswing took it to 11⅞ the following April. From that point, it went into a 6-month Symmetrical Triangle, and then broke out topside at the three-quarters stage on increased volume. This action, plus the fact that it immediately thereafter burst up through an old and highly significant Resistance Level at 12, was sufficient to mark it as being in at least a strong Intermediate if not a full Primary Uptrend.

The combination of technical developments illustrated in this chart — a large Consolidation Pattern forming just under a Major Resistance and then a breakout upside from both — is something to watch for when it appears that a Reversal from a Bear to Bull Trend is due.

Resistance Levels will be discussed in Chapter 13.

few types of chart patterns that were, on occasion, produced by unregulated trading are now less common, but that the great majority of technical phenomena have been practically unaffected. The chart student of 1907 would be quite at home with the charts of 1966. *EN: And with those of 2000. That is why so little change has been necessary to bring Edwards' classic account current to the third millennium. EN9: A note to a note. Pools and manipulators disappear and are replaced by some new pernicious form of skullduggery. Specialists and market makers are hauled before the bar of justice for cheating. In the 21st century hedge funds proliferate like rabbits in Australia. For any exacerbation of volatility they cause they probably make up for in additional market liquidity. The same patterns keep appearing because, computers to the contrary notwithstanding, humans are eventually responsible for pulling the trigger. It does seem that frequently patterns are not so neat as they were "in the old days." Trend lines, especially horizontal lines seem to be more "zones" than hard and fast lines and more judgment might be necessary in interpretation. But everything which Edwards says here might have been written in 2005 instead of in the mid-20th century.*

chapter twelve

Gaps

A *gap*, in the language of the chart technician, represents a price range at which (at the time it occurred) no shares changed hands. This is a useful concept to keep in mind, because it helps to explain some of their technical consequences.

Gaps on daily charts are produced when the lowest price at which a certain stock is traded on any one day is higher than the highest price at which it was traded on the preceding day. When the ranges of any two such days are plotted, they will not overlap or touch the same horizontal level on the chart. There will be a price gap between them. For a gap to develop on a weekly chart, it is necessary that the lowest price recorded at any time in one week be higher than the highest recorded during any day of the preceding week. This can happen, of course, and does, but for obvious reasons not as often as daily gaps. Monthly chart gaps are rare in actively traded issues; their occurrence is confined almost entirely to those few instances where a Panic Decline commences just before the end of a month and continues through the first part of the succeeding month.

Which Gaps Are Significant?

From the earliest days of stock charting, gaps attracted attention. These "holes" in the price trend graph were conspicuous. It was only natural that observers should attach importance to them, should try to assign some special significance to their occurrence. But the result was unfortunate, for there soon accumulated a welter of "rules" for their interpretation, some of which have acquired an almost religious force and are cited by the superficial chart reader with little understanding as to why they work when they work (and, of course, as is always the case with any superstition, an utter disregard of those instances where they don't work). We refer to this situation as unfortunate not so much because the gap "rules" are wrong, but rather because their blind acceptance has barred the way to a real understanding of a gap's implications and the establishment of a more logical basis for its uses in trading.

The most common superstition is that "a gap must be closed." Sometimes it is stated more cautiously in such words as: "If a gap isn't closed in three days, it will be closed in three weeks, and if it isn't closed in three weeks, it will be closed in three months, etc." There are numerous variations, but they all add up to the belief that a gap must be closed, and that the trend is not to be trusted until the gap has been covered. It is the latter inference which leads to error.

Closing the Gap

But first, what is meant by "closing" or "covering" a gap? Suppose a stock in an Advancing Trend moves up day after day, from 20 to 21, 22, 23, 24, and closes one night at the top of its range for that day, at 25. The next morning it opens at 26 and keeps right on moving up from there. This action leaves a 1-point gap, between 25 and 26, on the chart. Then suppose the rise continues to 28, halts there and is followed by a reaction in the course of which prices slip to 28, halts there and is followed by a reaction in the course of which prices slip back to 27, 26, and finally to 25. The return move has carried prices back through the gap area (25–26); the gap has thereby been covered or closed. In brief, a gap is closed when a subsequent price trend comes back and retraces the range of the gap.

Must a gap be closed before prices move very far away from it? Certainly not! Will it be closed eventually? Probably yes. If it is not closed by the next Minor Reaction, there is a chance it will be covered by the next Intermediate Retracement, and if not then, pretty surely by the next great Major Swing in the opposite trend. But that may be years later — hardly a matter of interest to the ordinary trader. The investor who bought Chesapeake and Ohio shares at 260 on October 21, 1929, counting on the closing of the gap which that issue had made on the preceding Friday, 2 points down from 266 to 264, had to wait nearly 7 *years* to get out even! Not until it neared the Top of the next Major Bull Market did CO attain an equivalent market value (65, since it was split 4-for-1 in 1930). In the meantime, he saw his investment shrink in 1932 to less than a sixth of his purchase price. As a matter of fact, there were hundreds of gaps made in the charts of the 1929 to 1930 markets which never have been covered since then, and many of them, it is safe to say, never will be closed.

If you will think the matter over for a moment, you will see that the probabilities we have stated above for a gap's being closed apply just as well to a stock's returning to *any* price range at which it has once been traded, gap or no gap.

Another point: there are thousands of price gaps made in trading — some of them quite wide — which do not appear at all on the standard daily range charts because they are made *during* a single day and not between one day's closing and the next day's opening. Such intraday gaps are ordinarily overlooked entirely; the gap theorists are oblivious of them, although their significance is often greater than that of many *interday* gaps. Practically every emphatic breakout move from a strictly defined Rectangle or Right-Angle Triangle is attended by a gap, but only those few show up on the charts that occur at the day's opening gong.

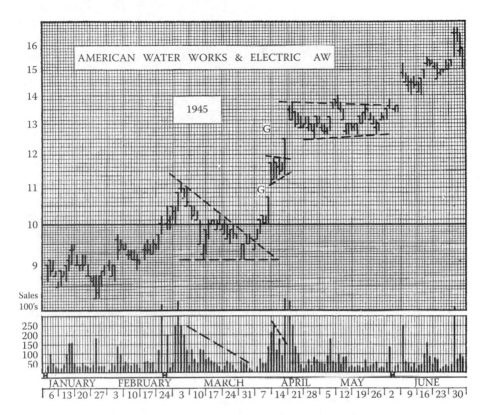

FIGURE 122. The April–June Rectangle on this 1945 chart of "AW" contained a number of insignificant Pattern Gaps. The two larger gaps marked "G" are of the Continuation or Runaway class. Note that prices closed at or near the top on each day that made a gap. Neither of these was closed for 2 years.

Also of interest in this chart is the Descending Triangle, which started to form in March, but was never completed — a deceptive and discouraging picture until the April 7 gap was made.

The Flag of mid-April "measured" the move from 9½ to 14. The gaps measured the two halves of it, on either side of the Flag.

If we seem to have "protested too much" in the foregoing, it is only because we want our readers to study this topic with an open mind, free from preconceived notions as to any mystic qualities which gaps may possess. Turning to the other side of the picture, gaps — some gaps — have technical import. Some gaps are useful to the chart analyst in appraising trend possibilities. Let us see what we can make of them.

Ex-Dividend Gaps

First, however, we must eliminate from consideration the gaps that do *not* mean anything. An eighth-point gap obviously has no technical significance as it represents only the minimum permitted change in price. By the same token, a gap of a quarter of a point or even a half point in a high-priced stock, such as Norfolk & Western (before the split), represents only a normal, in fact close, spread between successive bids. In brief, to carry interest for the chart technician, a gap must be wider than the usual changes in price that occur under normal or prevailing trading conditions. A second class of gaps that have no forecasting implications are those formed consistently and habitually by "thin" issues in the medium- and higher-price brackets. You can spot them easily. If your chart of a certain issue shows numerous gaps as a regular thing, then no one of them is apt to mean anything special.

Finally, gaps that appear on the charts when a stock goes ex-dividend (whether the dividend be in cash, stock, rights, or warrants) possess no trend implications. They are occasioned not by a change in the Supply–Demand relation which governs the trend, but by a sudden and irreversible alteration in the actual book value of the issue.

Eliminating the technically meaningless types named above, we are left with the gaps which occur infrequently (and which are not occasioned by an ex-dividend change in value) in issues that are so closely and actively traded as ordinarily to produce "solid" charts. A 1-point gap, for example, in the chart of New York Central would be an unusual event; it would demand attention; it would presumably have some forecasting significance.

Such gaps, for the purposes of our study, may be divided into four classes: Common or Area Gaps, Breakout Gaps, Continuation or Runaway Gaps, and Exhaustion Gaps.

The Common or Area Gap

This type of gap gets its name from its tendency to occur within a trading area or Price Congestion Pattern. All of the Congestion Formations that we have studied in the preceding chapters — both Reversal and Consolidation types — are attended by a diminution in trading turnover. The more strictly defined sorts — the Triangles and Rectangles — show this characteristic most conspicuously. Moreover, activity in these patterns tends to be concentrated pretty much at or near the top and bottom edges, their Supply and Demand Lines, while the area in between is a sort of "no-man's land." It is easy to see, therefore, why gaps develop frequently within such areas. You will find numbers of good examples of Pattern Gaps in the charts illustrating Chapters 8 and 9.

Such Pattern Gaps are usually closed within a few days, and for obvious reasons, before the Congestion Formation in which they have appeared is completed and prices break away from it. But not always. Sometimes a gap will develop in the *last* traverse of prices across the pattern area just before a breakout, and in such cases, it is not closed for a long time, nor is there any reason why it should be.

The forecasting significance of Common or Pattern Gaps is practically nil. They have some use to the technician simply because they help him recognize an Area Pattern — that is, their appearance implies that a Congestion Formation is in process of construction. If, for example, a stock moves up from 10 to 20, drops back to 17, and then returns to 20, making a gap in the course of that rally, it is a fair assumption that further pattern development will take place between approximately 17 and 20. This is a convenient thing to know and may, on occasion, be turned to profit in short-term trading policy.

Pattern Gaps are more apt to develop in Consolidation than in Reversal Formations. Thus, the appearance of many gaps within an evolving Rectangle or Symmetrical Triangle reinforces the normal expectation that the pattern in question will turn out to be a Consolidation rather than a Reversal Area.

Breakaway Gaps

The Breakaway type of gap also appears in connection with a Price Congestion Formation, but it develops at the *completion* of the formation in the move which breaks prices away. Any breakout through a *horizontal* pattern boundary, such as the Top of an Ascending Triangle, is likely to be attended by a gap. In fact, it is safe to say that most of them are. And, if we consider what goes on in the market to create a Flat-Topped Price Formation, it is easy to see why Breakaway Gaps should be expected. An Ascending Triangle, for example, is produced by persistent demand for a stock meeting a large supply of it for sale at a fixed price. Suppose that supply is being distributed at 40. Other holders of the stock, who may have intended originally to liquidate at 40½ or 41, see quotations come up to 40 time after time, stop there and turn back. They tend, in consequence, either to join the crowd selling at 40, or else to figure that once through 40, prices will go much higher; they may either lower or raise their selling price. The result is a "vacuum" on the books, a dearth of offerings in the price range immediately above the pattern. Hence, when the supply at 40 in our Ascending Triangle example is finally all absorbed, the next buyer of the stock finds none offered at 40⅛ or 40¼ and he has to bid up a point or more to get his shares, thus creating a Breakaway Gap.

As we remarked earlier in this chapter, gaps of this type actually occur on almost every decisive breakout from a Horizontal Congestion, although many of them do not show on the charts because they occur *during* a day and not between one day's close and the following day's opening. Breakaway Gaps also develop at times when prices move out of other types of Reversal or Consolidation Formations; they are not uncommon in connection with Head-and-Shoulders Patterns, for instance, and they even occur on the penetration of trendlines, which we shall discuss in a subsequent chapter.

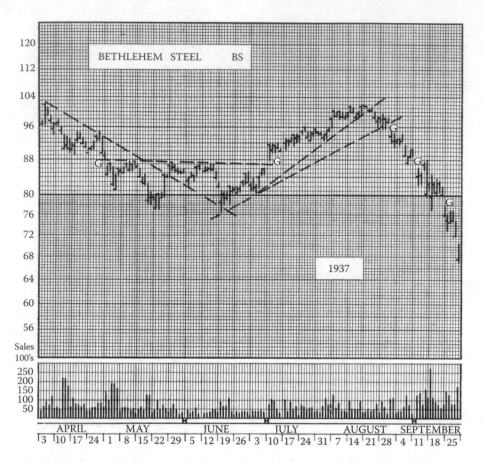

FIGURE 123. The large up-gap made on July 5 in this chart was a typical Breakaway Gap, occurring as prices broke out of the complex base for the July–August Secondary Recovery. (Compare this chart with Figure 32 on page 84.) Another type of Breakaway Gap — through a trendline — occurred on August 26. That of September 7 was primarily due to the "ex-dividend," while that of September 18 was still another type of breakaway — through a Support Level.

The first gap marked, on April 26, must be classified as a Runaway. It made a sort of "Island" of the whole April/June complex base.

What forecasting value can we ascribe to them? First, they serve to call attention to, and emphasize the fact of, a breakout. There can be little doubt that a genuine breakout has eventuated when prices jump out of a pattern with a conspicuous gap. False moves are seldom attended by gaps. Second, they carry the suggestion that the buying demand (or selling pressure, as the case may be) that produced the gap is *stronger* than would be indicated by a gapless breakout. Hence, it may be inferred that the ensuing move will carry prices farther or faster, or both. It does not do to make too much of this point; it is a logical inference and one which has been borne out in the

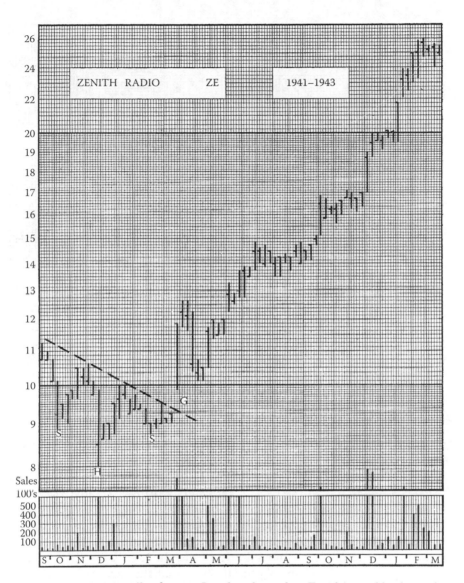

FIGURE 124. A potent Breakaway Gap that showed on Zenith's weekly chart when it broke out of a Head-and-Shoulders Bottom in early 1942. Note that high volume developed beyond the gap, suggesting that it would not be quickly closed. The April reaction stopped short of it. In fact, this gap had still not been closed in 1956, more than 14 years later.

majority of cases, but it has its exceptions and may prove most disappointing on occasion. Nevertheless, *other things being equal*, of two stocks which emerged from Ascending Triangles at the same time, we should choose to buy the one that gapped out over the one that pushed its way out by small fractional steps.

FIGURE 125.   As a matter of interest, this monthly chart of Zenith Radio is reproduced for comparison with the weekly chart on the preceding page. The Head-and-Shoulders Bottom is easily seen.

Except for the presumption of somewhat greater "steam" behind the move, the Breakaway Gap carries no particular measuring implication, nor any other forecasting significance. The next question is: should we expect a Breakaway Gap to be closed within a relatively short time? Or, to put the question in more practical and pragmatic terms: should we defer buying in the expectation that it will be closed before any worthwhile move develops?

In order to give a fair answer to that question, it is necessary to scrutinize closely the volume of transactions before *and after* the gap. If a great many sales were recorded at the takeoff level from which prices jumped the gap, but relatively few as prices moved away from the far side of the gap, then there is a chance — perhaps about 50–50 — that the next Minor Reaction will carry prices back to the edge of the pattern of origin, thus filling the gap. On the other hand, if high volume developed at the *far* side of the gap, and a great many transactions took place there as prices moved on away from the gap, then the chances are remote that any near-term Throwback will close the gap. In such cases, a Throwback reaction is almost always stopped at the *outside* of the gap.

(One is constantly tempted in a work of this sort to employ the words *always* or *never* without qualification. Unfortunately, the authors have *never* been able to discover a rule of techniques to which the market did not, on rare occasion, produce an exception. It is *always* necessary to be on guard against such exceptional developments. Many of them are caused by general market conditions which counteract the technical trend in individual issues. Keep an eye on the charts of the "Averages," as well as the particular issues in which you are interested.)

Where Breakaway Gaps develop intraday, the daily chart cannot, of course, indicate how the day's volume was distributed. In that event, it may be necessary to examine the ticker tape or ask your broker to refer to the published record of individual transactions to which most brokerage firms subscribe. *EN: This data may now be easily obtained. See Appendix D, Resources. EN9: Candlestick charts, now much in use, will allow the analyst to see the intraday breakaway gap.* Lacking any clear-cut volume clue, it is safest to figure that a Breakaway Gap will not be filled until long after the full move implied by the pattern of origin (usually a move of Intermediate Extent in the Dow sense) has been carried out.

Continuation or Runaway Gaps

Less frequent in their appearance than either of the two forms we have discussed above, gaps of the Continuation or Runaway type are of far greater technical significance because they afford a rough indication of the probable extent of the move in which they occur. For that reason they have sometimes been called "Measuring" Gaps.

Both the Common or Pattern Gap and the Breakout Gap develop in association with Price Formations of the Area or Congestion type, the former within the formation and the latter as prices move out of it. The Runaway Gap, on the other hand, as well as the Exhaustion Gap, which we will take up later, is not associated with Area Patterns, but occurs in the course of rapid, straight-line advances or declines.

When a dynamic move starts from an area of accumulation, the upward trend of prices will seem often to gather "steam," to accelerate for a few days, perhaps a week or more, and then begin to lose momentum as supply increases when the very extent of the advance invites more and more profit-taking. Trading volume jumps to a peak on the initial breakout, tapers off somewhat in the middle of the advance, and then leaps up again to a terrific turnover as the move is finally halted. In such moves — and in rapid declines of corresponding character — a wide gap is quite likely to appear at the time when the Runaway is at its height, when quotations are moving most rapidly and easily with relation to the volume of transactions. That period comes normally at just about the halfway point between the breakout which inaugurated the move and the Reversal Day or Congestion Pattern which calls an end to it. Hence, a Continuation or Runaway Gap affords an approximate measurement of the move in which it develops. Its inference is that *prices will go as much farther beyond the gap as they already have gone between* the beginning of the move and the gap, as measured directly (and vertically) on the chart.

Since there is a tendency for advances to run, in terms of points, beyond the price levels arithmetically implied by this rule, and for declines to be

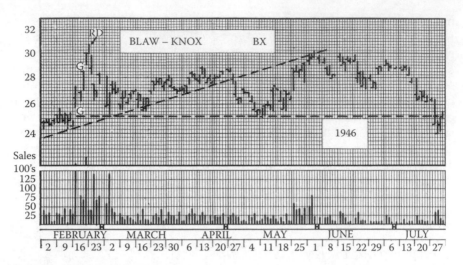

FIGURE 126. The early 1946 daily chart of Blaw–Knox contained a number of interesting technical features. Its spurt from 19 to 25 in December 1945 was followed by a 9-week Rectangle Consolidation, the end of which appears on the chart above. Prices erupted from this Rectangle on February 11 with a typical Breakaway Gap. Four days later, another gap appeared on even greater volume, and prices closed at the top of the day's range. This looked like a Runaway Gap, in which case continuation to 32 was implied according to the "rule" stated below. (Note that the Rectangle "measurement" called for only 31.) On the following day, however, a One-Day Reversal, from 31 back to 30, appeared, and the next session closed the February 15 gap, which now had to be relabeled, tentatively, as an Exhaustion Gap (see page 219). Prices subsequently dropped back to the support of the 9-week Rectangle, rallied grudgingly along an established Intermediate Up Trendline, and broke that on April 24 to return again to the 25 support. In May, another advance took "BK" up once more to 30, where it bumped against the previously broken trendline. That was its last effort; in late July, the "valley" level at 25 was penetrated and a Major Double Top had been completed.

To return to the February 15 gap, this is fairly typical of many cases in which it is impossible to say whether Continuation or Exhaustion is being signaled until 2 or 3 days after the day the gap is made.

more strictly limited, the gap-measuring rule works out particularly well when applied directly on semilogarithmic scale charts. On arithmetic charts, look for a trifle more on the upside and a trifle less on the downside. (In any event, you will be wise to "bank" on something short of the theoretical goal.)

Runaway Gaps are easy to find and identify in retrospect, but our task is to recognize them as such at the time they appear. Of course, there is, obviously, no danger of confusing them with Pattern or Breakout Gaps. With those aside, any gap which shows up in a fast advance or decline *after* prices have moved well away from an Area Formation (or the penetration of an important trendline or break through a potent Support or Resistance Level, which we shall discuss later) may be a Runaway Gap. What then becomes

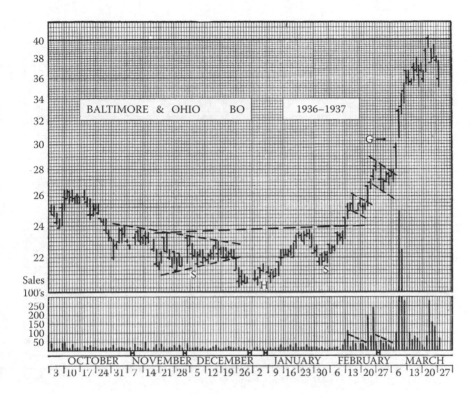

FIGURE 127. A good example of a Runaway Gap which performed according to rule. After reacting from 26½ in late 1936, "BO" formed a Head-and-Shoulders Bottom (the left shoulder was a Triangle) and broke out of it on February 6, 1937. A small Flag formed immediately thereafter, calling for 28. At that level, another Flag developed which signaled 30½ or better. As prices reached this latter goal, however, a gap was made, on March 3, on extraordinary volume. The next two days confirmed this to be a Runaway or Continuation Gap. As such, it implied further advance (measuring from the Head-and-Shoulders neckline) to 37 plus. "BO" made its Bull Market high at 40½ on March 17.

The measuring-gap rule should be used for purposes of "getting out" rather than "getting in." It does not guarantee that a move will continue to the implied limit, but it does give assurance that the move is near an end when the rule has been fulfilled.

necessary is to distinguish it from our next type, the *Exhaustion Gap.* Usually, the price and volume action on the day following the gap furnishes the evidence required for a safe diagnosis.

Two or More Runaway Gaps

But it will be much easier to bring out the characteristics distinguishing Runaway and Exhaustion Gaps when we take up the latter in detail. Before doing so, we must mention those cases where two, and, rarely, even three,

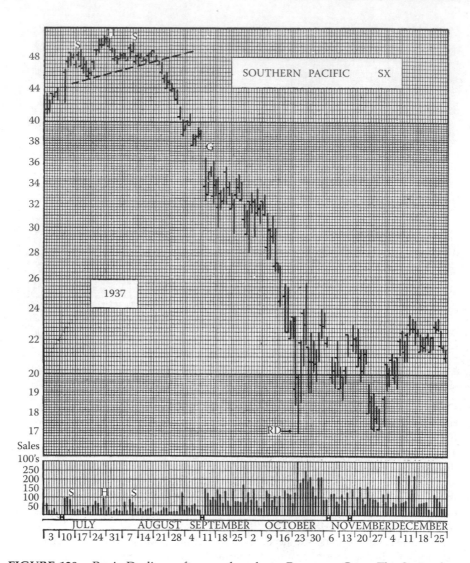

FIGURE 128.   Panic Declines often produce large Runaway Gaps. The September 7 gap in this chart, judged by its size, volume, subsequent action, and the fact that it was made in "new low ground," marked it as of the measuring type. Implied goal was 26 or below. All other gaps in this chart were obviously of the "common" variety.

gaps intervene in a fast move and are evidently all classifiable as of the Continuation or Runaway breed. It doesn't happen often, and is particularly unlikely to appear in the chart of a fairly large and active issue, but one of the thinner stocks in the midst of a "skyrocket" move may go skipping along for 3 or 4 days making gaps between each successive pair. The only question of practical importance that arises in such cases is: where should the halfway measuring point be located? No quick and easy rule can be laid down, but studious inspection of the chart, especially of the volume trend, will usually afford an answer. Remember that halfway in these fast moves tends to come at the stage where prices are moving most easily and rapidly with respect to number of transactions recorded (whence the tendency to gap). If there are *two* gaps, the halfway stage may very likely have been reached somewhere between them. Inspect your chart carefully and try to "average" the picture mentally; look for what appears to be the center of "thinness" and use that for your measuring level. But remember also that each successive gap brings the move inevitably nearer to Exhaustion, so let your judgment lean to the conservative side; do not expect too much of the second or third gap.

Exhaustion Gaps

The Breakout Gap signals the start of a move; the Runaway Gap marks its rapid continuation at or near its halfway point; the Exhaustion Gap comes at the end. The first two of these are easily distinguished as to type by their location with respect to the preceding price pattern, but the last is not always immediately distinguishable from the second.

Exhaustion Gaps, like Runaway Gaps, are associated with rapid, extensive advances or declines. We have described the Runaway type as the sort that occurs in the midst of a move that accelerates to high velocity, then slows down again and finally stops as increasing Resistance overcomes its momentum. Sometimes, however, "skyrocket" trends evidence no such gradual increase of Resistance as they proceed, showing no tendency to lose momentum, but rather continue to speed up until, suddenly, they hit a stone wall of supply (or, in cases of a decline, demand) and are brought to an abrupt end by a day of terrific trading volume. In such moves, a wide gap may appear at the very end, i.e., between the next to the last and the last day of the move. This gets the name of Exhaustion Gap because the trend seems thereby to have exhausted itself in one final leaping spurt.

The best test of whether a gap formed in a rapid, straight-line advance or decline is of the Continuation or Exhaustion type comes on the day after the gap (more precisely, the day which makes the gap), although there are frequently other clues in the preceding chart picture. If trading activity mounts to an extraordinary height during the session following the gap, and particularly if the previous trend in prices does not appear to be carried along at a pace commensurate with that day's activity, the gap is probably of the Exhaustion class. This interpretation is reinforced, in fact, made a virtual certainty, if the day after, the gap develops into a Reversal Day (as described in Chapter 10) with the closing price registered back near the edge of the gap.

Evidence that may be derived from the chart anteceding the gap may be enumerated as follows. If the trend has already carried out the full implications of the price formation or Congestion Area from which it emerged, Exhaustion is more likely than Continuation. By the same token, if the reasonable measuring implications of the pattern of origin are still far short

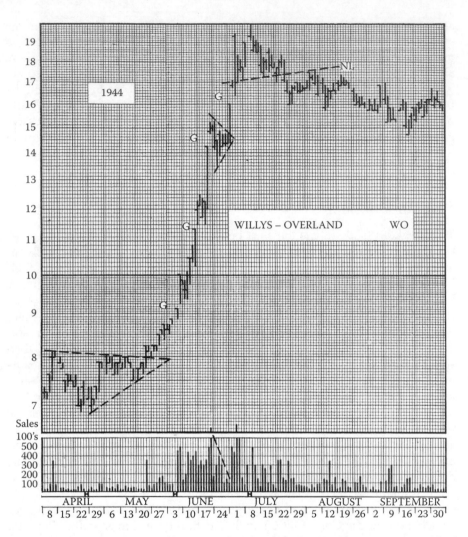

FIGURE 129. The "skyrocket" run-up of Willys–Overland in June 1944 was marked by a number of small gaps. The first two were too small to have much technical significance. The larger gap made June 16 was marked by the "stickiness" of prices on that day as Exhaustion. A small Flag Consolidation ensued. The June 27 gap also acted like an Exhaustion Gap insofar as price action was concerned, but volume had declined instead of climbing to a new peak. On June 28, prices jumped away again, so the June 27 gap was now marked as another Runaway with an implied objective of 18½ plus, which had already been reached. Note the Head-and-Shoulders Reversal that then formed and subsequent Intermediate Reaction.

of attainment, the gap is probably of the Continuation type. An Exhaustion Gap is seldom the first gap in a runaway move; it is usually preceded by at least one Continuation Gap. Thus, you may ordinarily assume (unless the contrary appears from other and more weighty indications) that the first gap

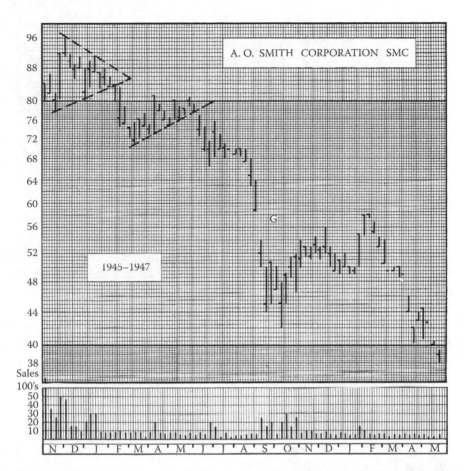

FIGURE 130. "SMC" is a thin stock whose daily chart is usually "full of holes," but this large gap that appeared on its weekly chart in September 1946 evidently possessed technical significance. Treated as a Runaway, and measuring from the 8-week Congestion at 68, it called for a downside objective of 44 or below, which was duly fulfilled.

in a rapid advance or decline is a Continuation Gap. But each succeeding gap must be regarded with more and more suspicion, especially if it is wider than its predecessor.

We have referred to Exhaustion Gaps as *wide* gaps. Width is, of necessity, relative in this study; it is impossible to lay down any exact rules to define wide or narrow. Do not let this bother you too much. Recognition of what constitutes an unusually wide gap for the particular stock you have under observation soon comes with a little charting experience.

Runaway Gaps are usually not covered for a considerable length of time, not, as a rule, until the market stages a swing of Major or full Intermediate proportions in the opposite direction. But Exhaustion Gaps are quickly closed, most often within 2 to 5 days, a fact which furnishes a final clue to

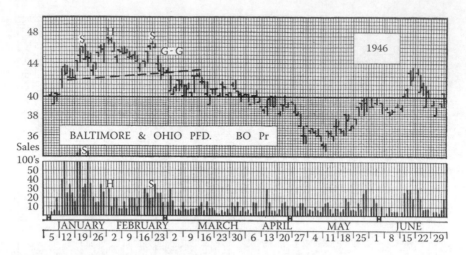

FIGURE 131. A small Island in the right shoulder of the Head-and-Shoulders Top that marked this issue's Major Reversal. The Island served only to emphasize the chart's Bearish implications.

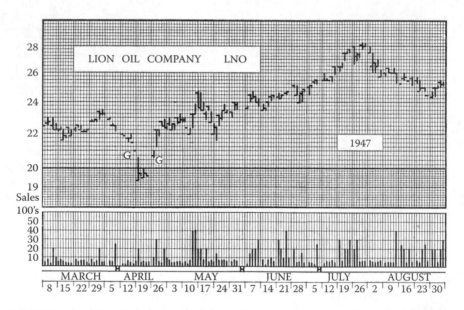

FIGURE 132. Island "shakeouts" are not uncommon in "thin" stocks. Why they should develop as they do is hard to explain, but their forecasting implications are obvious.

distinguish Exhaustion from Continuation, if it should still be needed at that stage. (This, incidentally, upsets the common superstition that all gaps must be closed before the trend can be trusted to continue very far. In the case of the Runaway Gap, it is not closed, but the trend moves right along nevertheless, and often for a surprising distance. In the case of the Exhaustion Gap, the closing of it actually contributes to the signal that the trend has run out.)

An Exhaustion Gap, taken by itself, should not be read as a sign of Reversal, nor even, necessarily, of Reversal at all. It calls "stop," but the halt is ordinarily followed by some sort of area pattern development which may, in turn, lead to either Reversal or Continuation of the move prior to the gap. However, in practically every case, enough of a Minor Reaction or delay ensues from the formation of an Exhaustion Gap, before a new trend is established, to warrant closing out commitments at once. (One can always reenter if it subsequently appears that the previous trend is to be resumed.)

The Island Reversal

We mentioned (at the end of Chapter 10) a Reversal Pattern, the Island, which was to be taken up under the general study of gaps. The Island Pattern is not common, and it is not, in itself, of major significance, in the sense of denoting a long-term Top or Bottom, but it does, as a rule, send prices back for a complete retracement of the Minor Move which preceded it.

An Island Reversal might be described as a compact trading range separated from the move which led to it (and which was usually fast) by an Exhaustion Gap, and from the move in the opposite direction which follows it (and which is also equally fast, as a rule) by a Breakaway Gap. The trading range may consist of only a single day, in which event it normally develops as a One-Day Reversal, or it may be made up of from several days to a week or so of Minor Fluctuations within a compact price zone. It is characterized, as might be expected, by relatively high volume. The gaps at either end occur at approximately the same level (they should overlap to some extent) so that the whole area stands out as an Island on the chart, isolated by the gaps from the rest of the price path.

We have said that an Island does not, of itself, appear as a *Major* Reversal Formation, but Islands frequently develop within the larger patterns at turning points of Primary or important Intermediate consequence, as for example in the head of a dynamic Head-and-Shoulders Top. By the same token, they appear occasionally at the extremes of the Minor Swings which compose a Triangle or a Rectangle (in which event, of course, the gaps that set them off are really better classified as Common or Pattern Gaps).

The reasons why Islands can and do develop — in other words, why gaps can and do repeat at the same price level — will be more apparent when we take up the general subject of Support and Resistance in a later chapter. Suffice it to repeat at this point that prices can move most rapidly and easily, either up or down, through a range where little or no stock changed hands in the past, where, in other words, previous owners have no "vested interest."

FIGURE 133. This Island Reversal Pattern at Bethlehem Steel's Major Top in 1937 is a "classic," yet it was followed by a curious and disturbing abnormality in the strong rally that developed on March 30. Those who sold out on the Island's signal around 95 on March 19 or 20 were startled, and, if they had also sold short, justifiably alarmed when prices jumped up a week later, not only through the second gap level, but well above it. But eventually, as can be seen, everything worked out according to the original forecast.

This incident will serve to illustrate a general principle: when a clear-cut technical pattern of unquestionable significance has been completed on your charts, do not let some apparently contrary development that occurs shortly thereafter lead you to forget or neglect the previous plain signal. Give such situations time to work out.

Figure 123 on page 212 shows the sequel to the above chart and, incidentally, another Island. Compare the volume.

Sometimes the second gap — the Breakaway that completes the Island — is closed a few days later by a quick Pullback or reaction. More often it is not. Rarely, the first gap — the Exhaustion Gap that starts the Island — is covered in a few days before the second gap appears, in which event the Island Congestion takes on a sort of V-Shape (if it is a Top), and there is no

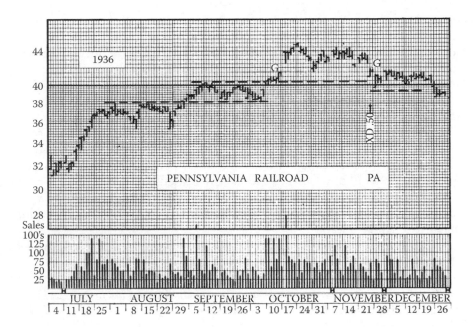

FIGURE 134.   This looked like an Island in "PA," but the second gap was actually attributable to a 50-cent dividend which went ex on November 20, and had, therefore, to be discounted technically. Because of this dividend, it was necessary to lower the Support Line at 40 (see Chapter 13) by half a point. That Support, therefore, was not violated in December, and prices subsequently advanced to above 50 the following March.

clear "open water" across the chart horizontally between the Island and the trends preceding and following it. In any of these variations, however, the interpretation remains the same: the preceding Minor Move should be practically retraced.

An Island Pattern is not easy to trade on, unless it be for a short-term "scalp," as, obviously, a good share of the retracement may already have been accomplished by the time the Island is charted and an order to buy or sell on its indications can be executed. Of course, if the entering gap is recognized as an Exhaustion Gap, the trader who is interested in the stock presumably will take action before the second gap forms and before the Island is in evidence. Perhaps, the greatest utility that Islands have for the chart analyst is that of calling attention to a situation, of putting him on the alert as to its potentialities.

Gaps in the Averages

Gaps appear also in nearly all Averages but, for obvious reasons, with rather less frequency than in the charts of individual issues. While it is not necessary for all of the stocks composing an average to make a gap simultaneously in order to produce a gap in the Average figures, a majority of them must. As might therefore be expected, Common or Pattern Gaps are particularly rare in Average charts, but Breakaway and Runaway types are not uncommon, although small as compared with the size of such gaps in single stocks. Exhaustion Gaps, and, in consequence, Islands, again are rare. The conditions that create an Exhaustion Gap seldom develop in a sufficient number of individual issues at any one time to produce a counterpart in the Averages.

The technical interpretation of gaps in Averages is, in the main, the same as in single stocks. The authors have not found that an Average gap possesses any peculiar potency or significance over and above that attributable to a gap in the chart of any actively and closely traded single issue.

The broader, and hence, most representative market indexes show the fewest and smallest gaps. *EN: On the other hand, the NASDAQ is quite volatile and a good gap producer.*

(It is suggested that the reader review this chapter after he has finished studying the principles of Support and Resistance in Chapter 13.)

EN9: The truth is there is nothing more that need be said about gaps, and the truth also is that no modern examples need be added. But gaps are fun, so see Figure 114.1 and Chapter 16.1 for modern examples.

chapter thirteen

Support and Resistance

The phenomena that we shall study in this chapter are markedly different in kind from those discussed in preceding sections. We shall look now at the stock market from a new angle, and in so doing may find it possible to develop some very practical additional rules to guide us in selecting stocks for purchase or sale, in estimating their potential moves, in foreseeing where they are likely to "run into trouble." As a matter of fact, some experienced traders have built their "systems" almost entirely on the principles of what we here call Support and Resistance, paying no attention to the specific pictorial patterns of price and volume action we have been investigating in preceding pages.

But Support and Resistance phenomena are not, by any means, unrelated to the various patterns and formations previously studied. We have already had occasion to hint at a basic principle of Support and Resistance in our explanation of gaps, and, as you read on, you will find that a number of the other patterns of price behavior are explained thereby, or at least become more readily understood.

The term *Support* is commonly used in the Street. In one or more of its connotations, it must be fairly familiar to the reader. For example, we hear that such-and-such a crowd is supporting XYZ at 50, or is prepared to support the market by buying all stock offered on any 5-point concession. For the purposes of this chapter, we may define *Support* as buying, actual or potential, sufficient in volume to halt a downtrend in prices for an appreciable period. *Resistance* is the antithesis of Support; it is selling, actual or potential, sufficient in volume to satisfy all bids and, hence, stop prices from going higher for a time. Support and Resistance, as thus defined, are nearly but not quite synonymous with demand and supply, respectively.

A *Support* Level is a price level at which sufficient demand for a stock appears to hold a downtrend temporarily at least, and possibly reverse it, i.e., start prices moving up again. A *Resistance* Zone, by the same token, is a price level at which sufficient supply of a stock is forthcoming to stop, and possibly turn back, its uptrend. There is, theoretically, a certain amount of supply and a certain amount of demand at any given price level. (The relative amount of each will vary according to circumstances and determine the trend.) But a Support Range represents a *concentration* of demand, and a Resistance Range represents a *concentration* of supply.

According to the foregoing definitions, you can see that the top boundary of a Horizontal Congestion Pattern such as a Rectangle is a Resistance Level, and its bottom edge a Support Level; the top line of an Ascending Triangle is unmistakably a Resistance Level, etc. But we are more interested now in the reasons why Support or Resistance, as the case may be, can be *anticipated* to appear at certain price ranges. Within reasonable limits, and with a certain few exceptions which we will examine later, it is quite possible to do this. Expert chart readers are able frequently to make some amazingly accurate predictions as to where an advance will encounter Resistance (supply) or where a declining trend will meet Support.

The basis for such predictions — the elementary data from which Support and Resistance theories are derived — is that turnover in any given issue tends to be concentrated at the several price levels where a large number of shares changed hands in times past. Since any level at which a great volume of transactions takes place usually becomes a Reversal point (Major, Intermediate, or Minor) in that stock's trend, it follows naturally that Reversal Levels tend to "repeat." But, here is the interesting and the important fact which, curiously enough, many casual chart observers appear never to grasp: these critical price levels constantly switch their roles from Support to Resistance and from Resistance to Support. A former Top, once it has been surpassed, becomes a Bottom zone in a subsequent downtrend; and an old Bottom, once it has been penetrated, becomes a Top zone in a later advancing phase.

Normal Trend Development

Perhaps we can make this plainer by citing a typical example of normal trend development. Suppose a stock in a Bull Trend moves up from 12 to 24, and there runs into a large volume of selling. The result is a reaction that may take the form of a full Intermediate Correction to, say, 18, or a series of Minor Fluctuations forming a Consolidation Pattern between, say, 24 and 21, the effect being the same in either case. Following this Correction or Consolidation, a new advance gets under way and carries price on up to 30 before running again into supply in sufficient concentration to stifle the move. Now another reaction is evidently due. Again, it may take the form of a sideways Consolidation Pattern or an Intermediate Correction. If the latter, where will that corrective setback be reversed; where, in other words, will it meet Support? The answer is at 24, the level of the first Top in the trend. That is the level (below current quotations) where a large turnover had previously occurred. Then it functioned as Resistance, producing a halt or Reversal in the first upswing; now it functions as Support, stemming and reversing, at least in a Minor sense, the latest downswing.

Why should this be? It will be easier to suggest an answer to that question if we first go on with a similar example of typical action in a downtrend. This time, suppose our stock makes a Major Top and declines from, say, 70 to 50. There, at 50, a temporary Selling Climax occurs; there is a large turnover, prices rally, perhaps slip back for a "test" of 50, and then stage a good recovery to 60. At 60, buying peters out, the trend rounds over, turns down, and accelerates in renewed decline which carries to a new low at 42. Again a wave of buying comes in, and a second recovery swing gets under way. We can confidently expect that this recovery (from 42) will run into strong Resistance at 50. The price level which functioned as a *Support* for the first phase of decline, now that it has been broken through downside by the second phase, will reverse its role and function as *Resistance* to the second recovery move. The former Bottom level will now become a Top level.

Here, we may ask again why this should be so, and now we can suggest an answer. In the example of downtrend action cited in the preceding paragraph, our stock first dropped to 50, ran into considerable volume there, reversed its trend and rallied to 60 with activity dwindling on the rise. A lot of shares changed hands at 50, and for every seller, there was, of course, a buyer. A few of those buyers may have been covering short positions and, having done so, had no further interest in the issue. Others, short-term traders and professionals, may have purchased simply because they sensed a temporary Bottom in the making and hoped to scalp a few points on the ensuing rally; presumably, they (or at least some of them) took their profits and were out before prices broke very far on the next decline But a majority of those who acquired shares at 50, it is safe to say, did so because they thought the stock was cheap at that price, because they figured it had gone low enough. Only a few months ago, it was selling above 70; surely it was a bargain at 50 and could be picked up and put away "for the long term."

The Explanation

Imagine yourself, for the moment, in the place of those new owners. They see prices turn up, reach 55, 58, 60. Their judgment appears to have been vindicated. They hang on. Then the rally peters out, and prices start to drift off again, slipping to 57, 55, 52, finally 50. They are mildly concerned but still convinced that the stock is a bargain at that price. Probably there is momentary hesitation in the decline at 50, and then prices break on down. Briefly, there is hope that the break is only a shakeout to be recovered quickly, but that hope vanishes as the downtrend continues. Now our new owners begin to worry. Something has gone wrong. When the stock gets down below 45, the former bargain doesn't look so good. "Well, I guess I picked a lemon that time, but I won't take a loss in it. I'll just wait until it gets back up to 50 some day where I can get out even (except for expenses), and then they can have it." (Does it sound familiar, by any chance?)

Take the opposite side of the picture — the uptrend process. You, along with many others, bought XYZ at 12, carried it up to 24, decided that was plenty high for it, and cashed in. Thereupon XYZ reacted to 20, and you congratulate yourself on your astuteness. But then, unexpectedly, it turns around and rushes up to 30. Now you don't feel so smart; that was a better stock than you gave it credit for being. You wish you had it back. You will

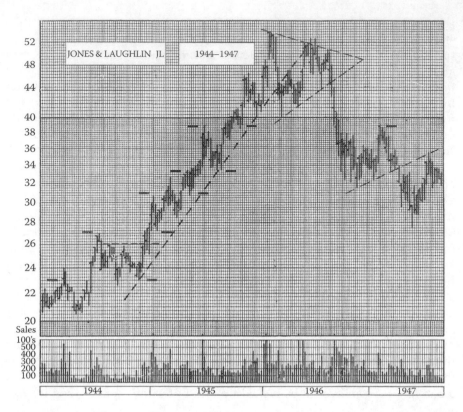

FIGURE 135. Why now was so much time spent, so much "work" done during mid-1945 under 33–34? We cannot see it on this chart, but the previous monthly history shows that the Bottoms of long Congestion Areas were made in this zone in late 1939 and late 1940. These old Bottoms, representing Support, originally, were able to produce some supply (Resistance) 5 years later. Once prices had worked through that supply, however, they were able to rise quickly to 44, and then their subsequent reaction found Support just where you might have expected — at 33–34. Support had turned to Resistance and then to Support again.

We can skip over the next few swings which "followed the rules" and go on to the change in the picture which came with the first notable violation of a Support Level in 1946. Prices had pushed up the first of February nearly to 54, well out above the Tops around 46, formed the previous November. The late February reaction should have "caught Support" around 46 — but it didn't; it crashed on down to the "round figure" 40. This was an ominous (although not necessarily "fatal") development. Thereafter, a massive Symmetrical Triangle was formed and broke downside in September.

The first Panic Decline in the Bear Market is no respecter of Support Levels. This one was no exception, although it is noteworthy that prices "bounced" several times from the important old 33–34 zone. By November, the Top Triangle's measurement had been exactly fulfilled.

You should turn back to this record and study it again after you have read the next 10 or 11 pages.

not pay more for it, but if it comes back down to 24, the price at which you sold, you'll "reinstate your position."

Perhaps you have never been in either of these situations. Perhaps your own reactions wouldn't, in such cases, have been the same as those we have indicated. But, if you have had a fair amount of experience in the market — have some knowledge of the psychology of the "average investor" — you know that the pictures we have described are typical.

At this point you may not be satisfied that we have succeeded in giving an adequate explanation for our basic principle of Support and Resistance Levels. Remember, however, that the supply and demand balance in the market is nearly always a delicate thing. Only a moderate oversupply at any one price will suffice to stifle an advance; only a little extra demand concentrated at a certain level will stem a decline. And remember, further, that other traders are watching the tape — will be quick to sense any change in the situation, and quick to join the parade whenever a change in trend appears to be developing. Consequently, orders to buy or sell a few hundred shares may induce the transfer of several thousand.

Another point worth bearing in mind is that the traders and investors who (because, as we have presumed, of their previous mistakes in either selling or buying prematurely) created Support and Resistance Levels are not necessarily ignorant or inexperienced. On the contrary, we must list them among the wiser and more alert of those who operate in the market. To make one more use of our previous theoretical example of typical downtrend action, those who bought at 50 were certainly smarter than those who bought at the top (70) or on the way down to 50, even though the latter price was broken later on. Giving them credit for somewhat superior judgment, it follows that they may be expected to appraise later developments pretty carefully and display something better than a wooden and stubborn determination to "get out even" when it comes to selling on a Recovery Move. Hence, in a marked Bear Trend "overhanging supply"; i.e., stock bought at higher levels by holders now waiting for a good chance to unload, will begin to come on the market *below* the theoretical Resistance Level. Wise owners will be willing to sacrifice a point or so to avoid getting caught in a worse loss.

By the same token, "sold-out Bulls," when a Major Uptrend is under way, may be willing to pay a point or two more in order to replace the shares they had previously cashed in too soon. Thus, it is characteristic of reactions in well-established (second phase) Bull Markets to drop back only to the very uppermost limits of a Support Range — and for recoveries in established Bear Markets to reach only the lowest edges of Resistance Zones, or perhaps even fail of that by an appreciable margin. We shall have more of this sort of thing to point out later on, but first we must take up two other matters — how to estimate the potential importance of Support and Resistance Zones, and how to locate, more exactly, the centers of axes of such zones.

Estimating Support–Resistance Potential

To go back to first principles, we have seen that the Resistance that an upward move may meet at any given level depends on the quantity of stock over-hanging there — the number of shares previously bought at that price by owners who now would like to get out without loss. Obviously then, *volume* is our first criterion in estimating the power of a Resistance Range. An old Minor Bottom level at which only four or five hundred shares changed hands cannot set up much Resistance to a subsequent advance, but a Selling Climax Bottom where several thousand shares were bought will provide a lot of potential supply after prices, at some later date, have dropped well below it, and then attempt to rise up through it again.

A long Rectangle or a Descending Triangle has a number of Bottoms at the same level. We can get a crude approximation of the amount of Resistance there by summing up the volume of trading on all its Bottoms, but then some discount must be taken for the shares that may have been bought at the Bottom of the pattern in its early stages and then sold near the Top before it was completed. In brief, a single, sharp, high-volume Bottom offers some-what more Resistance than a series of Bottoms with the same volume spread out in time and with intervening rallies.

Another criterion is the extent of the subsequent decline. Or, to put it another way, how far prices will have to climb before they encounter the old Bottom zone whose Resistance potential we are attempting to appraise. Generally speaking, the greater the distance, the greater the Resistance. Suppose PDQ sells off from 30 to 20, "churns" at that level for several days, rallies to 24, and then drifts back down to 19. Investors who picked it up at 20 will not be greatly concerned at that stage. If a rally now develops from 19, there will be little or no disappointed selling at 20. Should prices dip to 18 before the rally starts, there may be some supply forthcoming at 20, but still not a formidable quantity. From 17, Resistance will become evident. In brief, prices have to break far enough below the price at which a trader bought his stock to convince him that he made a bad investment and, hence, that he should sell when he gets a chance to do so without too great a loss.

It is impossible to formulate any precise rule or equation to define how far a decline must proceed to set up Resistance above it. However, do not look for much supply to come out of a Bottom level in the low-middle price ranges (20 to 35) unless the trend later takes quotations more than 10% under it. This 10% rule cannot be applied to very low-priced issues. A man may buy a stock at 5 and see it drop to 4 or 3½ with considerable equanimity despite the fact that he stands a loss of 30% at the latter figure. His "dollar" loss looks small, and he still thinks it will be easy for his stock to get back up to 6 or 7; he is willing to wait.

Another factor enters into and reinforces the "extent of decline" criterion. If our PDQ rallies, as before, from 20 to 24 and then drops rapidly to 12, not

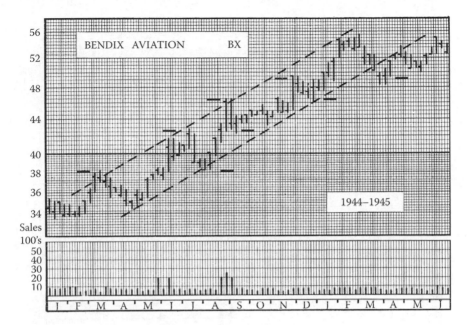

FIGURE 136. Support–Resistance Levels in a long Intermediate Uptrend. The reader will need no guidance in applying the principles stated in this chapter to the Bendix weekly chart reproduced above. Observe that when prices broke down in 1945 through a long trendline, their decline stopped, nevertheless, at the Support set up by the previous November's Top.

only will many of the old owners at 20 be thoroughly disgusted and glad to get out at that price, given an opportunity, but the new owners at 12 will also be pleased to take 20 (66⅔% profit) and quick to do so if they detect any signs of trouble there. New buyers at 18, needless to say, would not be quite so ready to sell at 20.

A third criterion for appraising the Resistance potential at an old Bottom level is the length of time that has elapsed since it was formed and the nature of general market developments in the interim. You will, no doubt, find it reasonable to suppose that an Intermediate Bottom formed in the early stages of a Bear Market will offer relatively little Resistance after prices have fallen far below it, have taken perhaps the better part of a year to make a Major base, and then have gradually climbed up to it again 4 or 5 years later. To some small extent, this is true. A supply only a year or two old is apt to be more effective than one that is 4 or 5 years old, but the latter does not lose all of its potency by any means. In fact, it is often surprising how effective the Resistance will be at a very old Bottom zone, provided it has not been "attacked" in the interim, and provided no changes have been made in the capitalization of the company which might obscure, in the mind of the owner, the original cost of his stock. Under the latter heading, we would put split-ups and large stock dividends, or even an unusually generous cash "melon."

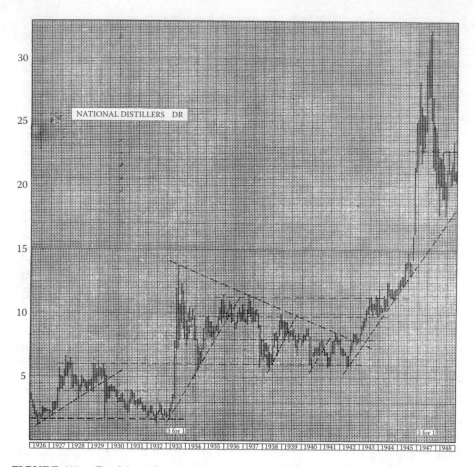

FIGURE 137.   For Major Support–Resistance Level study, monthly charts are most useful. This one presents many points of interest. Observe how important levels are formed and how, once formed, they appear again, and reverse their roles. The price scale shows 1947 values with previous years adjusted for the splits of 1933 and 1946.

We do not mean to imply that an investor is ever actually deceived as to the actual cost of his shares, no matter how they may have been split, or what dividend distribution has been made, but his disappointment (and desire to get out even) may be abated.

If, however, a Resistance Zone has once been attacked — if prices have come back up to it, hit it, and then retreated — some of its power has obviously been removed. Some of its overhanging supply has been used up in repelling the first attack. The next advance, therefore, will have less stock to absorb at that level. Here again, the volume chart may be looked to for some approximation of the amount of Resistance consumed. In any event, it is an odds-on assumption that a third attack at a Resistance Level will succeed in penetrating it.

We have named three criteria — volume, distance away, and time elapsed — to be used in assessing the amount of Resistance to be expected at any given level. At this point, it must be apparent to the reader (and perhaps disappointing) that his own judgment must play a large role in applying them. This cannot be helped. It is impossible to set up an exact mathematical formula for any of them.

But, after all, the problem is not too complicated. The general principles are simple enough and, we believe, easy to understand. We can look back at the charted history and see where, in the last preceding downtrend, a Bottom formed that may produce more or less Resistance when the current advance reaches back up to its range. We have to estimate how much supply resides there, how many shares were bought originally at that price and are still held by owners who may welcome a chance to get out even.

The greatest danger in applying judgment to the measuring of these factors lies in underestimating the amount of Resistance to be expected. Guard against that effort; it is safer always to overestimate it. You may be Bullishly disposed yourself; you may say, "Those fellows who were hung up there in this stock must realize that conditions have improved, and they will not be so anxious now to sell." Don't count on it. Remember that they have been "hung up" for a long time. Even if they are mildly Bullish on the market in general, they may be so disappointed with this particular stock that they want to switch out of it and try something else. (The stubborn and often costly refusal of the average American investor to "take a loss" operates even against timely switching.)

Everything we have said in the foregoing paragraphs about estimating potential Resistance applies as well — but in a reverse direction, of course — to estimating potential Support. The principles are precisely the same, even though the underlying rationale may be less easy to grasp.

Locating Precise Levels

Our next problem to consider is how, in practical day-to-day chart analysis, we can locate as exactly as possible the limits of a Support or Resistance Range, and in many cases, the specific price figure representing the core or axis of such a range. In the theoretical examples we have made up so far to illustrate basic principles, we have used even figures, but in actual trading, the levels are seldom so nicely marked. Even the sharp and relatively patternless Bottom of a Recession may consist of a week of price fluctuations within a narrow range. Perhaps the lowest day of that week's Congestion will appear on the chart as a One-Day Reversal, or there will be 2 or 3 days which "spike" down below the general mass. Here again, although no mathematical rule can be laid down, it is easy to relate the price and volume patterns visually, and by simple inspection, arrive at a near estimate of the figure at which supply in quantity is likely to be forthcoming. Look particularly at the closing levels of the days making up the Bottom Congestion,

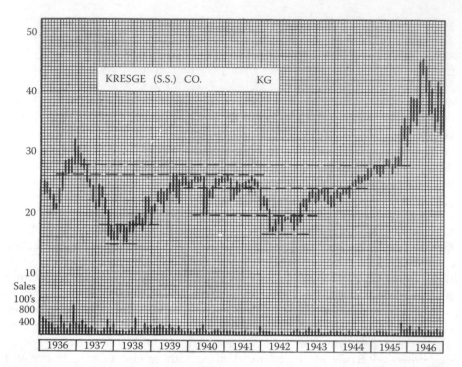

FIGURE 138. Particularly noteworthy in this monthly record is the Resistance met in 1939, 1940, 1941, and even in 1944, at the Bottom level (just above 26), the 3-month Congestion of 1936. Also, the appearance 8 years later (!) in 1945 of Resistance at the Bottom level (28) of the High-Volume Top Congestion of 1936–37.

Prices were able to "skyrocket" when that Resistance was finally overcome. You will find that several additional Support–Resistance Lines might have been drawn on this chart. Note Major Bottom Formations of 1937–38 and 1942.

and average them mentally; this figure is apt to be pretty close to the "center of gravity" of the entire Resistance Area.

Of course, some supply is likely to start coming in as soon as a subsequent advance reaches the bottommost fraction of the Resistance Zone, and more and more will appear as the move pushes up into it. Sometimes, it is possible to predict "to a hair" just how far prices will penetrate a Resistance Range by carefully comparing the vigor (volume of trading) on the advance with the volume registered at various levels in the original formation of the Resistance. This takes experience, but it is experience which you will find quite easy and not at all costly to gain. However, in most cases, it is neither necessary nor particularly desirable to be so exacting.

Nearly every chart in this book shows some example of Support and Resistance phenomena, and the reader should make it a point, when he has finished this chapter, to go back over them and study them all in detail. The practical application of the rules we have been discussing will be greatly clarified. Equally instructive, if you can manage to obtain such a collection, is a study of the Support and Resistance Levels appearing in the monthly charts of all actively traded stocks over a period of 10 years or more. *EN: Easily generated by most currently available software and on the Internet at prophet.net and stockcharts.com.* You will undoubtedly be amazed to see how Tops, Bottoms, and Sideways Congestions tend to form at the same approximate levels in successive Major Swings, while prices move freely and rapidly, up or down, through the ranges between such levels. It is hardly necessary to dwell on the practical dollars-and-cents value of such information which may be derived from the chart history.

And that brings up a matter that we may as well pause to consider here — the kind of charts most useful for locating and appraising Support and Resistance Levels. For near-term Minor Moves, the daily chart is naturally the only source of information, and a daily chart record that extends back for a year or more may, if necessary, be used in the location of levels of Intermediate Trend importance. The writers have found, however, that a daily chart does not give the perspective on the long range which one really needs to determine Major and Intermediate Support and Resistance Zones. It is apt to overemphasize the potential of a recently set up Minor Support (or Resistance) Zone and obscure the importance of a true Intermediate Level. For true perspective, a weekly chart, showing volume as well as price ranges, and covering at least the whole previous Major Bull and Bear cycle, is most desirable. Also, very good results can be obtained with a little study and experience from monthly charts.

To return to our study of Support phenomena, we have had several occasions to refer in previous chapters to a "normal" trend. What we have had in mind might perhaps be better called an "ideal" trend, since, like so many other so-called normal things, it represents a pattern from which the facts of experience frequently deviate. In stock trends, nevertheless, this normal or ideal appears as a fairly common pattern. If it is an uptrend, it consists of a series of zigzags, each "zig" carrying prices to a new high and each "zag" taking them back to the approximate top of the preceding "zig." To illustrate with figures, up to 10, back to 6, up to 15, back to 10, up to 20, back to 15, up to 26, back to 20, etc. Such a move is what technicians refer to as "self-correction" and regard as particularly sound and, hence, likely to be continued. You can see that what it really represents is reaction to the nearest Minor Support Level following each step forward. If you become interested in an issue with such a trend pattern, the normal return to a Support produces a good place to buy.

Significance of Support Failure

Sooner or later, however, a normal Minor Wave Pattern is bound to be broken up. This generally occurs in one of two ways (although there is an infinity of possible variations). In one, prices spurt away in an advance out of all proportion to the previous succession of up waves. Such a move is seldom

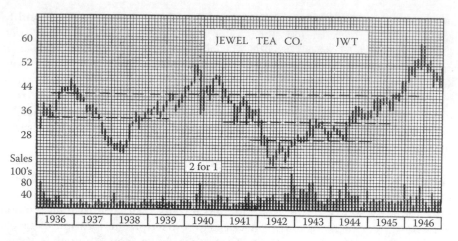

FIGURE 139.   A monthly chart of Jewel Tea Company with its Major Support–Resistance Levels marked. Note reversal of roles.

followed by a reaction to the Support now left far behind, but rather, by the construction of some sort of Area Pattern — which may be either Consolidation or Reversal.

The other type of disruption appears when a reaction does *not* halt and reverse at the level of the previous Minor Top, but sifts on down through that zone, perhaps to the level of the preceding Minor Bottom. This move has "broken its Support," and any such action carries a distinct warning of a change in trend, a particularly emphatic warning if activity shows a tendency to increase as or after the Support is violated. Note that we said *change* in trend rather than Reversal, since the puncturing of a Minor Support Level may signify only a halt for sideways Consolidation. But it may also foretoken an impending Reversal. Either of these is a change.

If you will now call to mind the picture of a typical Head-and-Shoulders Top, you will see that the decline from the head constitutes just such a break in Minor Support since it comes down through the level of the top of the left shoulder, and you will recall that this decline is often the first intimation we have that something in the nature of a Reversal Formation is developing.

Thus, even the violation of a nearby Support Level has a practical meaning in technical chart analysis. The breaking of a Minor Support should always be regarded as the first step in the Reversal of the Intermediate Trend. (If it turns out to be Consolidation only, there will be an opportunity later to reenter an abandoned commitment if desired.) By the same token, the breaking of an *Intermediate* Support Range is frequently the first sign of a Reversal in the *Major* Trend. We do not believe it is necessary to expatiate further on this principle. Recommended trading tactics based thereon are discussed in the second part of this book; Support and Resistance Levels are particularly useful as basing points for stop-loss orders which are discussed there.

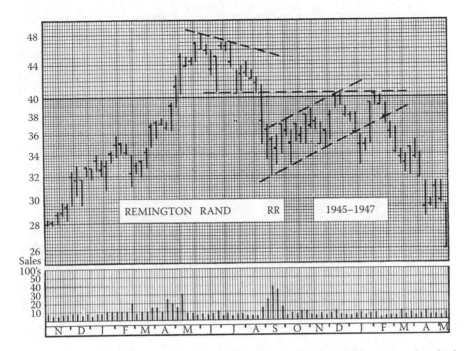

FIGURE 140.   When prices broke down out of the large Descending Triangle which formed on Remington Rand's weekly chart in 1946, the decline might have halted, at least temporarily, around 37 at the level of the 4-week Congestion made in April, and should have "caught Support" at 35–36, the level of the February top. Failure of the latter carried Major Trend significance (see next page). Note later Resistance at 40½.

Popular Misconceptions

The reader will understand, of course, that all we have said here about the breaking of Supports applies, as well, but in reverse direction, to the penetration of Resistance Levels. One more point may well be mentioned before we leave this subject. If you happen to have spent much time in boardrooms, you will have noticed that the concepts of Support and Resistance that are prevalent there are somewhat different from those outlined in this chapter. For example, if X has advanced to 62, reacted to 57, then pushed on to 68, many traders will speak of 57 as being the Support Level, presumably because that was the last price at which X was supported in sufficient strength to turn its trend from down to up. We, however, as you have seen, would name the vicinity of 62 as the Support Range. The distinction is important to grasp, and sometimes extremely important in practical results.

Admittedly, it does not come easy to think of a former Top as denoting the level at which a later Bottom should form, or vice versa; it would seem superficially to be much more logical to relate Top to Top and Bottom to

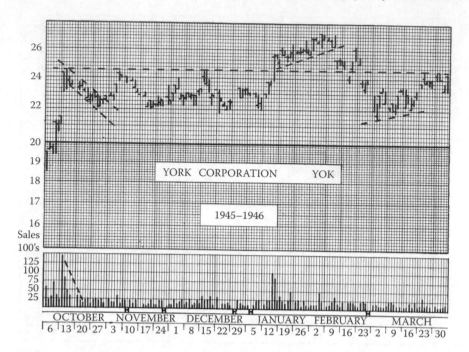

FIGURE 141. York is a relatively thin stock, which normally makes many small, technically meaningless gaps, but its large, high-volume gap of October 8, 1945, demanded attention. It looked like a Runaway Gap, and as such implied continuation to 26½ plus. But prices halted their advance at 24½ and went into a 3-month Rectangle. An upside breakout on January 10, 1946, carried out the minimum measurement of the Rectangle (and October gap); prices then reacted. See sequel in Figure 142.

Bottom. Moreover, it is perfectly true, to use our X example again, that some of the investors who wanted to buy it at 57 might not have succeeded in getting it before the second advance to 68 took it away, and that their buy orders might still stand at 57 or might be reentered on any return to that price. Nevertheless, there is certainly no assurance that such is the case; there is no "vested interest" in X at 57 that will "automatically" bring in new buying. On the other hand, we have seen how there is a sort of vested interest set up at an old Bottom which produces selling (Resistance), and thereby creates a new Top, and at an old Top which produces buying (Support) and thereby creates a new Bottom.

The reader is urged to keep this concept well in mind. Any analytical study of the chart records will quickly show that it is much easier for prices to push up through a former Top level than through the Resistance set up at a previous volume Bottom (and vice versa, of course, with respect to declines). You will find that a little selling may come in at a former high, but usually only enough to cause a brief halt rather than the more or less extensive reactions or Consolidations that develop when the trend comes up against a real Resistance Zone.

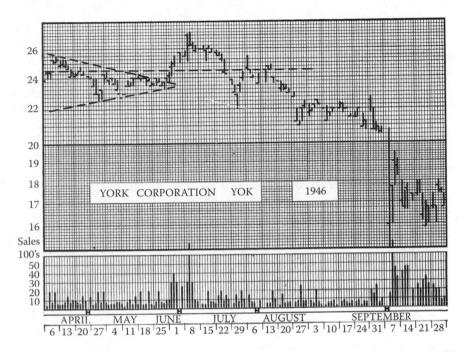

FIGURE 142. The February reaction in Figure 141 met momentary Support at 24; prices bounced far enough to close the February 7 gap, and then broke down through the Rectangle Top-Line Support — technically a distinct warning. Then a Symmetrical Triangle formed, but the breakout came too near the apex, produced only a rally to the former high, and then an "end run." One did not need to wait for the Double Top signal on August 22 to forecast a decline of more than Minor consequence.

The Round Figures

There are certain other levels that may, at times, evidently produce considerable Resistance or Support without any reference to a previous "vested interest." We have in mind the "round" Figures 20, 30, 50, 75, 100, etc. In setting a goal for taking profits when we buy a stock, it is natural for us to think in terms of such round prices. If a low-priced stock has advanced steadily from around 10, it is pretty certain on this account to meet with profit-taking sales at 20, *especially if that figure represents a new high for it for several years.* In fact, any time an issue gets out into new all-time high ground, where there is nothing in its chart history to indicate otherwise, it is a fairly safe bet that Resistance will appear at the round figures. In old and actively traded stocks, such as U.S. Steel *(EN: Or IBM and GE),* the round figures diminish in importance.

Repeating Historical Levels

If, once they had been set up, important Support and Resistance Levels always "worked," we should see Intermediate Tops and Bottoms form at exactly the same ranges year after year in one Bull and Bear cycle after another. As a matter of fact, there is a well-marked tendency for this to occur in old-line, actively traded stock. In General Electric, for example, the 22–24, 34–35, 40–42, and 48–50 zones have been characterized by large turnover (and, consequently, by many Intermediate Reversals of trend), throughout the 1920s to 1950s. In Southern Pacific, there are historical Support and Resistance Zones at 21–22, 28–30, 38–40, and 55–56. In U.S. Steel, 42–45, 55–58, 69–72, 78–80, and 93–96 are conspicuously marked as Reversal Ranges. And many other stocks might be cited. *EN9: While the particular stocks are dead or transmogrified the principle is alive and well.*

Over long periods, however, such Support and Resistance Levels do tend to be gradually modified, broadened, or "blurred," and new ones created. One source of many important new Supply Zones is a Bear Market Panic. For this is the one type of decline that can be counted on to pay no heed whatever to previous underlying Support Zones. Panics (which, as we have seen in our earlier study of Primary Swings in connection with Dow Theory, typify the second phase of Bear Markets), once they get under way, seem to sweep away all potential Support in their calamitous plunges until they exhaust themselves in a general market Selling Climax. And that climax may or may not come at a level that bears a relation to some previously established Support. To use U.S. Steel again as an example, the 1937 Panic Decline took the stock down through its 93–96 range, hesitated briefly at the 78–80 level, and then plunged through 69–72 and 55–58 to stop just above 50. In the 1946 Panic, X again broke swiftly through 78–80 and 69–72 to halt at 66.

When there is a large turnover at a Panic Bottom in any given stock, that level acquires a strong "vested interest" for the future, and will usually furnish conspicuous Resistance to a subsequent advance (after another Bear Market Decline has taken quotations below the Panic Level).

This discussion of Panics brings us back to a consideration of Support and Resistance performance at other stages of the Primary Trend — a matter on which we stated early in this chapter we should have more to say. Bearing in mind the relation of Resistance to volume, it is easy to see why in a long drawn out, but otherwise typical Bear Swing, in which trading interest diminishes to a very low ebb as the final low is approached, the next to the last Intermediate Bottom may produce relatively little supply, and consequently, only a small reaction when the new uptrend reaches its level. Add to this the fact that many of the buyers in the last stages of a Major Decline are deliberate scale-down investors who fully expect prices will go lower and, hence, are not easily shaken out. The slow progress so often seen in the first part of a new Primary Bull Market is due not so much to overhead Resistance as to lack of impatient public bidding.

The Recovery Trends that follow precipitous Bear Market Panics usually exhaust themselves, for obvious reasons, long before they get back up to the last Resistance Level left behind in that Primary Downswing (which is usually the Bottom of the first Intermediate Decline from the extreme Top of the cycle), but they often meet supply at a lower Resistance Zone set up *in the preceding Bull Market*. Look way back on your charts, therefore, when sizing up the prospective advance in such situations.

A further thought along that line is: there is no law that requires an advancing trend to keep right on climbing until it reaches a distant overhead Supply Zone. It is true, as a corollary which we have already mentioned to our Support and Resistance Theory, that prices can and do rise easily through a price range where no Bottoms or Congestion Areas have formed in previous downtrends, but if the first established Resistance Level is a long ways above, the advance may exhaust itself before it gets there. Heavy supply *may* come in for other reasons at a lower level. Think, then, of a distant Resistance Level as a maximum possibility rather than as a certain goal. However, between two stocks whose purchase you are considering, you should select the one which, other things being equal, has the "thinner" track overhead, can rise farther before it encounters a charted Supply Zone.

Pattern Resistance

We can revert now to some of the Minor phenomena discussed in connection with Reversal and Consolidation Patterns in earlier chapters. Take gaps, for instance. You will now see why it is easy and, hence, quite in order for a reaction that comes soon after a gap has been made to slip back and close that gap. There is no "vested interest" whatever in the range through which prices skipped to form the gap on the chart. You will also see why such a reaction may stop short and reverse as soon as it has closed the gap, *provided* there was a high-volume turnover in the price range immediately preceding the gap. Such is usually the case with a Breakaway Gap.

Any gap, for the same reason, is easy to close once a reaction starts prices moving back in that direction, if it is not too far away and if there are no intervening Resistance Levels to stop the reaction before it gets there. In the case of a Runaway Gap, however, there is no reason why a reaction should halt as soon as it has covered the gap range; on the contrary, it will probably continue on through the "thin" price track that preceded the gap.

Pullbacks and Throwbacks — the quick return moves which we noted as developing so often shortly after a breakout from a Head-and-Shoulders or other Area Pattern — exemplify the principles of Support and Resistance. When prices break down, for example, out of a Descending Triangle, the horizontal lower boundary of the formation, which was originally a Demand Line, promptly reverses its role and becomes a Resistance Level. Any attempt to put prices back up through it, therefore, after a decisive breakout, is stopped by supply at or near the line. By the same token, the neckline of a Head-and-Shoulders Top, which was a Demand Line, becomes a Resistance Level after it has been broken. The Top or Supply Line of a Rectangle becomes a Support after prices have pushed above it on volume and by a decisive margin.

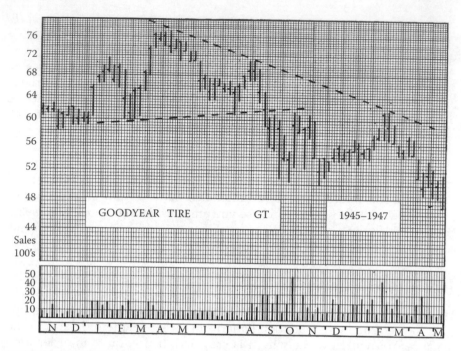

FIGURE 143. We first discussed Pullbacks in connection with the Head-and-Shoulders in Chapter 6 and refer to them again in this chapter (page 243) as Support–Resistance phenomena. At least one Pullback to the neckline (after the breakout) occurs in the great majority of cases. Many Head-and-Shoulders Formations produce two, the first within a few days after the breakout and before prices have gotten very far away, and the second weeks later, sometimes after the minimum measurement of the Head-and-Shoulders has been fulfilled. Goodyear saw the unusual number of four Pullbacks to its 1946 neckline — the first two weeks after the August breakout, another in October, a third in November, and a fourth in February 1947, which met the Double Resistance of the neckline and the down trendline (Chapter 14) projected from the 1946 April head and August right shoulder.

Earlier in this chapter, in our discussion of the three criteria for appraising the amount of Resistance to be expected at a former Bottom level, we named "distance away" as one of them and stated as a general rule that prices should have gone at least 10% beyond that level in a medium-priced stock before much Resistance would be set up. This 10%-away rule does not apply, however, in the case of a Throwback to a well-defined area formation, when it follows shortly after a breakout. All that is necessary to establish strong Resistance to such moves at the pattern boundary is a conclusive breakout.

The Symmetrical Triangle has a different sort of Support and Resistance "field." You will recall that the first Reversal point in the formation of a Symmetrical Triangle (a Top, if it forms on a rising trend, or a Bottom if on a decline) is normally accompanied by high trading volume, but that activity

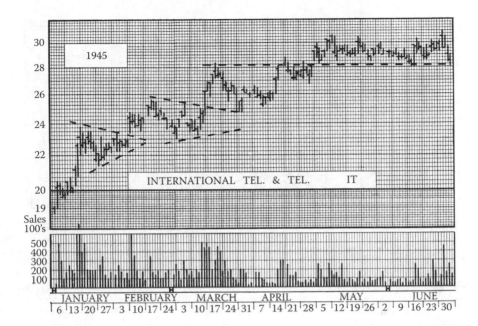

FIGURE 144. Several examples of the support "field" of the Symmetrical Triangle appear in this 1945 daily chart of "IT." Following the belated February 5 breakout from the first Triangle, prices returned on the 9th to the level of the mid-January Top, but then suffered a more extensive reaction, which came down on February 26 to the Triangle's apex level. This was a critical juncture. The apex point itself is a strong Support (or Resistance), but its level becomes weaker as time passes. In this case an "end run" might have been developing. Stop-loss orders should always be entered under an apex level (see Chapter 27). Here the apex held, however, and prices went into another "Coil," breaking out topside on March 10. Their next reaction was supported, as was to be expected after an early breakout like this, at the Top Pattern Line.

The price track from mid-March to the end of April fell into an Ascending Triangle Pattern, the top boundary of which functioned as Support in June but was broken in July. Refer back to Figure 120, page 204.

diminishes rapidly on succeeding fluctuations within its converging boundaries. Consequently, once prices have broken out of the Triangle and have proceeded well beyond the level of the pattern's first Reversal point, that level, because of the volume of shares traded there, becomes a Support (or Resistance) against a subsequent reaction. But, if the breakout move does not carry beyond the Triangle's first Reversal Level by a clear margin, any Throwback will probably bring quotations back to the extended (sloping) pattern boundary, and if the reaction does not occur until the trend has worked out to or beyond the Triangle's apex, then the Throwback usually will not meet Support (or Resistance) until it has carried back to the level of the apex. The apex, in brief, represents the concentration level or *axis* of the Triangle's Support and Resistance.

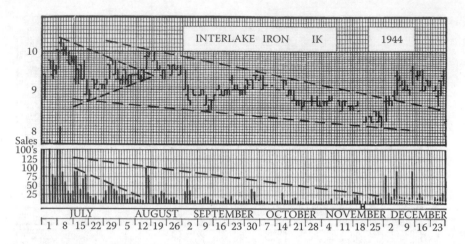

FIGURE 145. In this instance, a belated upside breakout (August 10) from a Symmetrical Triangle failed quickly and the subsequent reaction, after holding for several days at the apex level, finally broke down for an "end run." Thereafter, note that the apex level turned into a Resistance against Recovery Moves.

The intersection of the two converging boundary lines of a Symmetrical Triangle has sometimes been called a "cradle." The axis Support (or Resistance) is strongest near the cradle point and gets weaker as the axis line (apex level) is extended out to the right on the chart (i.e., as time passes). Thus, if a late breakout move fails to carry prices very far from the Triangle area, and the trend then peters out, flattens, and begins to react *after* the cradle point has been passed in terms of time, its action, as it reaches the axis line, must be closely watched. (A stop-loss order may be indicated here.) Should the axis Support fail to hold, the reaction may plunge through and accelerate in a more extensive swing, which has aptly been termed an "end run around the line."

Volume on Breaks Through Support

On those occasions when prices fail to retreat when they hit a Resistance (or Support) Range, but, after perhaps holding there for several days, push on through, there is nearly always a sudden acceleration and a marked pickup in volume. This may be taken as confirmatory evidence of a decisive break and, consequently, an indication that the move will carry on. The reasons for this volume increase are obscure. Some say, "It takes volume to overcome Resistance," which is true enough, but the volume usually comes *after* the Resistance has been penetrated. Therefore, others say, "The volume is evidence that technicians see what has happened and are now jumping in." But that line of thought, in the authors' opinions, also has little to substantiate it. (We shall have more to say about the questionable influence of technicians on the trend later on.) Many of the arguments over volume change vs. price

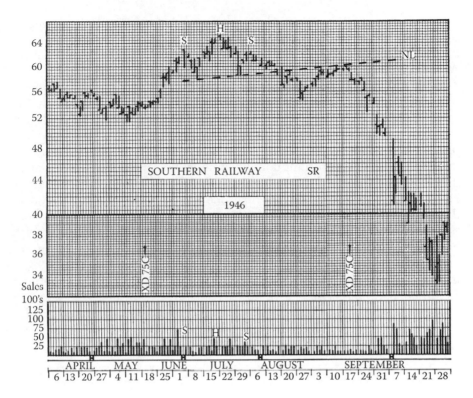

FIGURE 146. Here is a typical case of two Pullbacks to a Head-and-Shoulders neckline, the first immediately after the breakout and the second 3 weeks later. Note that the initial breakthrough "bounced" from the early April Top Support, and the late July decline met Support at the general April–May Congestion Area. But what this chart illustrates, particularly, is how volume increases when a good Support Range is penetrated. Note the decided pickup on August 27, when the April–May area was left behind.

change savor of the old hen-or-egg riddle. In any event, causes for many technical phenomena, such as this one, may be left to the academicians, provided the practical implications are clear.

Support and Resistance in the Averages

As has been the case with nearly every other technical phenomenon we have studied, the principles of Support and Resistance apply, with suitable allowances, to Averages as well as to individual stocks. Since an Average reflects the combined charts of the majority of the issues that compose it, but with a minority of them frequently evincing quite divergent patterns, it follows naturally that Support and Resistance Zones in the Averages cannot be as sharply and narrowly construed. Minor Tops and Bottoms in the Averages, particularly, are less dependable as Resistance Levels. Clearly defined and important Intermediate Reversals, however, since they nearly always represent Reversals in the entire market (practically all stocks), will normally produce strong Resistance (or Support, as the case may be) in the subsequent Average Trend.

When the Averages break down through a Support Level, but one or more stocks, at the same time, hold firm at or above their corresponding individual Supports, there is a presumption that those particular stocks are in a stronger position than others to participate in the next recovery. The phrase "other things being equal" should be added, however, for there are qualifications to this presumption which must be considered. For instance, it may be that the stock that has resisted decline will, for that very reason, be less attractive to new buyers than one which broke drastically and is, therefore, now purchasable at a more "attractive" price.

Many of the claims made regarding future prospects for stocks that have, by one criterion or other, previously evinced "better-than-Average" or "worse-than-Average" market performance permit argument either way. It is safest to treat all such relative performance indications as only one minor factor to be appraised in the overall chart picture.

chapter fourteen

Trendlines and Channels

One of our basic tenets in this system of technical stock chart analysis — indeed, a fact which any neophyte can quickly verify for himself by inspection of the market records for whatever period he chooses — is that *prices move in trends*. The market in general, and the many stocks which compose it, do not jump up and down in an altogether random fashion; on the contrary, they show definite organization and pattern in their charted course.

Prices move in trends. These trends may be either up or down or sideways (horizontal). They may be brief or of long duration. They may be classified as Major (Primary), Intermediate (Secondary), or Minor, according to the rules of Dow Theory, or as Horizontal Line Formations. (The distinction between a short Intermediate and an extended Minor Trend is often more difficult to make with individual stocks than it is with the Averages, but it is not so important.) But sooner or later, trends change; they may change by reversing from up to down or down to up, and they may also change direction without reversing as, for example, from up to sideways and then perhaps to up again, or from a moderate slope to a steep slope, and vice versa.

Profits are made by capitalizing on up or downtrends, by following them until they are reversed. The investor's problem is to recognize a profitable trend at the earliest possible stage of its development and then later to detect, again as quickly as possible, its end and Reversal. The Reversal of any important trend is usually characterized, as we have already seen, by the construction of some sort of joint price and volume pattern — in brief, of a Reversal Formation.

The Trendline

All of the foregoing statements regarding trends have been expressed or implied in earlier chapters of this text. It is our purpose now to examine trends, as such, more closely, to see how they may be plotted most effectively on the charts, and determine to what extent they can be used to reinforce or supplement the technical forecasts derived from our other chart formation and Support–Resistance studies — sometimes to furnish even earlier forecasts or warnings of change.

One of the first discoveries a new student is likely to make when he begins to inspect stock charts with a critical eye is that nearly all Minor and most Intermediate Trends follow nearly straight lines. A few readers will, perhaps, dismiss this as perfectly natural, something to be taken for granted. But the majority become increasingly amazed and excited as they delve deeper. Not only the smaller fluctuations, but, frequently, also the great Primary Swings of several years' duration appear on the charts as though their courses had been plotted with a straight-edge ruler. This phenomenon is, in truth, the most fascinating, impressive, and mysterious of all that the stock charts exhibit.

If we actually apply a ruler to a number of charted price trends, we quickly discover that the line which most often is really straight in an uptrend is a line connecting the lower extremes of the Minor Recessions within those trends. In other words, an advancing wave in the stock market is composed of a series of ripples, and the Bottoms of each of these ripples tend to form on, or very close to, an upward slanting straight line. The Tops of the ripples are usually less even; sometimes, they also can be defined by a straight line, but more often, they vary slightly in amplitude, and so any line connecting their upper tips would be more or less crooked.

On a Descending Price Trend, the line most likely to be straight is the one that connects the *Tops* of the Minor Rallies within it, while the Minor Bottoms may or may not fall along a straight edge.

These two lines — the one that slants up along the successive wave Bottoms within a broad up-move and the one that slants down across successive wave Tops within a broad down-move — are the basic trendlines.

It is unfortunate that a more distinctive name for them has never been devised than the threadbare word "line," which has so many other uses and connotations. A few analysts have called them "tangents," a term that has the advantage of novelty, but, because it is a distinct perversion of the true meaning of the word *tangent*, confuses many readers even more. Perhaps tangent will eventually become established in this new sense. However, we shall be satisfied herein with the overworked "line," but can give it some distinctiveness in its present context by joining it to trend in the one word "trendline."

Trendlines, you may have heard it said, "are made to be broken," but that is one of those exasperatingly sententious remarks which fails to clarify anything. Of course they are broken; they are all always broken, ultimately, and some very shortly after they are set up. The problem is to decide which breaks (i.e., penetrations by a price movement) are of important technical significance and which are of no practical consequence, requiring possibly only a Minor Correction in the drawing of the original trendline. There are no 100% certain, quick answers to this problem; the significance of some penetrations cannot be determined as soon as they appear, but must await confirmatory indications from other chart developments. In a great majority of instances, however, an important break — one that requires a prompt review and possibly a revision of trading policy — is easy to recognize.

FIGURE 147. A series of Intermediate Trendlines drawn to illustrate the "basic" principle (see below) on a weekly chart of Atlantic Refining, extending from January 1944 through August 1947. Observe that each up trendline required two distinct Bottom points to determine it, and each down trendline, two Tops. In some cases, the two determining points were formed only a few weeks apart, as in August and September 1945. The Bottom points that fixed the early 1946 up trendline, on the other hand, were months apart — February and June.

Many other experimental lines might have been drawn on this chart originally, including several uptrends whose Intermediate authority was questionable because they were "too steep" — as in early 1944, late 1945, and early 1946.

Only final trendlines are shown here.

There are here also some interesting examples of Pullbacks (after trendline penetration) which are discussed on the following pages. Note July 1944, April 1945, September 1945, and May 1947.

How Trendlines Are Drawn

But first, how are trendlines drawn? A straight line is mathematically determined by any two points along it. In order to draw a trendline, therefore, we require two determining points — two established Top Reversal points to fix a Down Trendline and two established Bottom Reversal points to fix an Up Trendline. The principle here is the same as the one we laid down in our specifications for drawing Triangle boundary lines in Chapter 8. The fact is that boundary lines of Triangles and Rectangles, as well as necklines of Head-and-Shoulders Formations, are simply special types of trendlines.

Suppose we start with a Major Bottom point and describe how a series of Up Trendlines might develop therefrom. To make this first illustration simple, let us assume that the Bear Market Bottom in our stock consisted of a Rectangle area between 6½ and 8, and that the last move in this formation arose from the 6½ level, broke through the pattern's Top at 8, and proceeded to 9. From 9, prices reacted to 8 and then headed back up again. As soon as this last rally had gone far enough to leave the dip to 8 showing in the clear as a Minor Bottom, we could draw our first Up Trendline because we then had two Bottom points, the second (8) higher than the first (6½), to fix its slope. This would be a Minor Up Trendline. We would rule it in lightly on our chart in pencil, and extend it on up and ahead for, perhaps, a week or more. (It will help you to visualize our example if you sketch it on a scrap of chart paper.)

To proceed, suppose prices push up to 10, then move sideways for a few days, or dip slightly, until they have approached and touched, once more, our extended Minor Trendline. Then they start to move up in a third advance, but run into supply again without making much progress, quickly make a fourth contact with the trendline, hesitate, and then break down through it. If prices now close clearly below the line, and if, in addition, there has been some pickup in trading volume evident on the penetration, we may conclude that our first Minor Trend is completed, and that our stock either will build some sort of Consolidation Pattern before it stages another advance, or will suffer a more extensive "Correction" than any of the brief dips it registered during its first Minor Upswing.

The whole Minor Uptrend we have described as an example in the foregoing paragraphs might well have run its course in 2 weeks, and our first trendline would then have been very steep — too steep, obviously, to hold for any very long period of time. Now, let us assume that a series of downward fluctuations produces the more extensive correction which we have foreseen as one probability following the trendline break, and that this carries prices back to the Support Level set up at the Top of the original Rectangle, i.e., at 8. (From our previous Support–Resistance studies, we would recognize this as a prime "buy spot.") Assuming that subsequent developments pursue a normal course, prices should not linger long at 8, but should start promptly on a new series of advancing fluctuations. As soon as this becomes evident and the new Bottom at 8 is "in the clear," we can rule in a new trendline across the original base point at 6½ and the new point at 8. This should be, and probably is, an *Intermediate* Up Trendline which will not be penetrated for several weeks, and maybe for several months, until the Intermediate Advance tops out.

Then, if that Intermediate Top takes the form of a Head-and-Shoulders Reversal Pattern, our Intermediate Up Trendline may be broken by the recession from the top of the head to the neckline. As a rule, however, the final advance in a strong Intermediate Move accelerates far enough away from the extended trendline to leave room (to the right on the chart) for

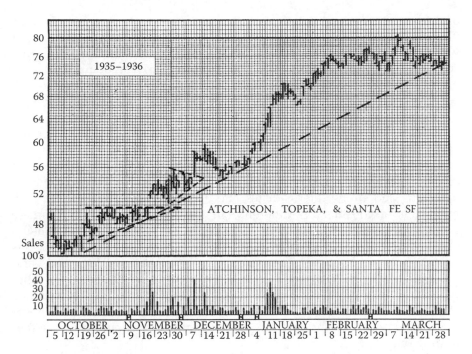

FIGURE 148. This 1935–36 daily chart of Atchison illustrates how the latter part of a long, strong Intermediate Advance may accelerate away from its trendline. (Notice the action in late January and early February.) Prices dropped back to 66 in April 1936 after this Up Trendline was broken at the end of March. Note also that at the point where the December 1935 reaction met Support, the trendline coincided with a Triangle apex level. Such "coincidences" appear frequently in technical studies.

considerable pattern construction before the line is again touched and penetrated. Hence, the actual puncturing of the trendline is more apt to occur either on the decline from the right shoulder to the neckline, or at about the same time as prices break down through the neckline to complete the Head-and-Shoulders signal. It is surprising to see how often the two lines, neckline and trendline, are broken *simultaneously*. In other instances, and there are many of them also, in which the trendline is the first to be punctured, perhaps shortly after prices turn down from the right shoulder, we do not have to wait for a neckline break but can take action at once. Here is one type of trendline indication which produces a working signal a little earlier, and often at a much more favorable price level, than is given by the completion of a Reversal Formation.

Arithmetic vs. Logarithmic Scale

By this time, the more mathematically inclined among our readers must have begun to ponder the difference between trendlines projected on the ordinary or arithmetic scale and on the logarithmic or ratio scale. A series of points which fall on a perfectly straight, up-sloping line on arithmetic chart paper will, when transferred to a semilogarithmic sheet, produce a curved line that rises sharply at first and then gradually rounds over. And points which fall on a straight line on a semilogarithmic sheet will produce an accelerating curve on an arithmetic sheet, a line which slants up more and more steeply the farther it is projected.

As a matter of fact, this variance is of little or no importance in defining Minor Trends, since they seldom run far enough for the dissimilar characteristics of the two types of scales to become effective. And the same holds true for average Intermediate Moves of normal slope. But when it comes to very long and strong Intermediates, the divergence may become marked, may make a considerable difference in the time and level of ultimate trendline penetration. Therein lies one of the strongest reasons for using semilogarithmic paper in charting stocks for technical analysis. But let us postpone further discussion of this point until we take up Major Trends, and go on now with the Intermediate Lines which are much the same on either type of scale. And, for the present, let us concentrate on Intermediate *Uptrends*. (Intermediate Moves are emphasized rather than Minor for the obvious reason that the latter are of little practical importance in either trading or investing.)

To go back to first principles, and granting that price advances trend up in more or less straight lines, it follows that if we can find and draw the lines that accurately define those trends, they will serve two purposes, as follows:

1. When the trendline is broken (i.e., when prices drop down through it in decisive fashion), it signals that the advance has run out. It calls time for the intermediate-term trader to sell out that issue, and look for reinvestment opportunities elsewhere.
2. When a small Top Reversal Pattern forms on the chart of an issue well up and away from that issue's Intermediate Up Trendline, so that there apparently is room for the downside implications of the Reversal Formations to be carried out *before* the trendline is violated, then the intermediate-trend trader may well decide to ignore the small Reversal Pattern. He can hold on so long as the trendline holds.

The advantages of the first-named trendline function are obvious. Those of the second, though less obvious to the inexperienced, are equally important to the investor who has learned that it is an expensive practice to switch out of every holding as soon as it shows evidence of a Minor Setback, provided the chance of further Intermediate Advance still exists.

To accomplish these purposes it is necessary, as we have said, to find and draw the line that accurately defines the Intermediate Trend, and then to recognize when that line has been broken in decisive fashion. Our earlier

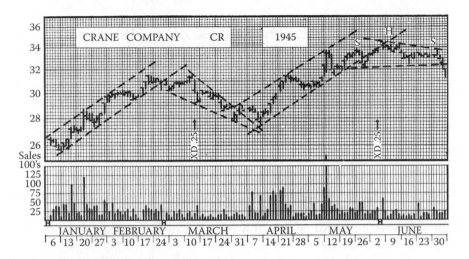

FIGURE 149. Trendlines which defined the short-term swings in Crane Company in 1945. Note that three Bottoms formed on the first up-line and that the third rally (late February) in this advance failed to reach a line drawn across the earlier Tops parallel to the Basic Trendline. A failure of this sort frequently precedes a break in the trend. The same thing happened at the end of the second uptrend in late May. "Failures" and the use of parallel or "Return" Lines will be discussed later in this chapter.

The downtrend in March assumed Wedge form. Observe how the April 6 reaction met Support at its previously penetrated Top line. In June, a rally met Resistance at the previously broken Up Trendline. Such Pullbacks are common. The small Complex Head-and-Shoulders in June was never completed, since prices did not break down out of it by the required margin.

quick review of how a trendline is constructed did not attempt to cover these points thoroughly.

Tests of Authority

Here are some of the tests which may be applied to judge the technical validity, the authority, of an Up Trendline:

A. The greater the number of Bottoms that have developed at (or very near) a trendline in the course of a series of Minor Up Waves, the greater the importance of that line in the technical sense. With each successive "test," the significance of the line is increased. A first and tentative Up Trendline can be drawn as soon as two Bottoms have formed, the second higher than the first, but if prices move back to that line a third time, make a third Bottom there and start a renewed advance, then the validity of that line as a true definition of the trend has been *confirmed* by the action of the market. Should a fourth Bottom later form on it, and prices move up away from it again, its value as a trend criterion is very considerably enhanced, etc.

B. The length of the line, i.e., the longer it has held without being penetrated downside by prices, the greater its technical significance. This principle, however, requires some qualification. If your trendline is drawn from two original Bottoms which are very close together in time — say, less than a week apart — it is subject to error; it may be too steep or (more often) too flat. If the latter, prices may move away from it and stay high above it for a long time; they may then turn down and have declined well along in an Intermediate Correction before the trendline thus drawn is reached. But if the trendline has been drawn from Bottoms which are far enough apart to have developed as independent wave components of the trend you are trying to define, with a good rally and "open water" between them, then it is more apt to be the true trendline. Greater weight should be given to the number of Bottoms that have formed on a trendline (Test 1) than to its length alone (Test 2).

C. The angle of the trendline (to the horizontal) is also, to some degree, a criterion of its validity as a true delimiter of Intermediate Trend. A very steep line can easily be broken by a brief sideways Consolidation move — as, for example, by a compact Flag forming on an advance of the "mast" type — only to have prices shoot up again in another extensive advance. Such steep lines are of little forecasting value to the technician. The flatter, more nearly horizontal the trendline, the more important it is technically and, in consequence, the greater the significance of any downside break through it.

But "steep," as applied to stock trends, is a relative term, and one which, we must frankly confess, defies exact definition. Experience, which can only be gained by studying many charts and by actually building and working with them over a period of many months, brings an almost intuitive ability to distinguish between a trendline which is "too steep to hold" and one whose angle of rise is reasonable and should be maintained until such time as the trend is actually reversed from Intermediate Up to Intermediate Down. Trend slopes will vary from stock to stock according to their characteristic market habits. They will vary also according to the stages of the Primary Cycle — tending to become somewhat steeper in its later phases. The more chart history you have on any particular issue in which you are interested, the better able you will be to judge its present trend.

(The foregoing statement, we might remark, applies to the interpretation of most other technical patterns and phenomena as well as to trendlines.)

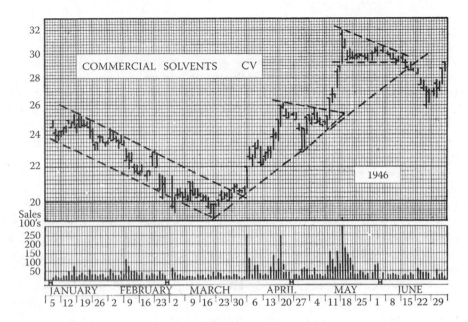

FIGURE 150. Intermediate Downtrend and Uptrend in Commercial Solvents in 1946. Note the increased volume on the March 30 penetration of the basic Down Trendline (and, at the same time, a breakout from a small Head-and-Shoulders Bottom). The drop through the lower parallel at the end of February had no technical significance. The Up Trendline from the March low was broken on June 14, simultaneously with a breakout from a Descending Triangle which, as it turned out, was the final Bull Market Top.

One clue to relative steepness is afforded to those who employ the TEKNIPLAT semilogarithmic chart sheet, which has been used for most of the illustrations in this book. When projected on this scale, Intermediate Uptrends on the daily charts, in the great majority of issues selling in the 10 to 50 range, rise at an angle of approximately 30 degrees to the horizontal. Some will be a trifle flatter, some a trifle steeper, but it is surprising to see how often the trendline falls very close to the 30-degree slope in stocks of average volatility and activity. Thin, highly speculative issues and heavy investment stocks offer exceptions, the former usually steeper and the latter flatter. The semilogarithmic scale has the virtue, of course, of reducing all movements, regardless of price level, to a ratio or percentage basis. On a straight arithmetic scale, the trendline will ordinarily be steeper on a stock trading in the 50 range, for example, than on an issue selling around 15.

On weekly charts employing the same price scale, the angle of Intermediate Advance will, of course, be much steeper than on the daily plotting. Different scaling will produce different angles. It is pure happenstance that the TEKNIPLAT sheets tend to produce the 30-degree ascending line.

Validity of Penetration

We have these three criteria, then, for appraising the authority or accuracy of an Intermediate Up Trendline: (1) the number of times it has been "tested" or contacted without breaking, (2) its length or duration, and (3) its angle of ascent. Given a trendline which, by the application of one or more of these criteria (preferably by at least two of them), appears to be a reasonably accurate delimiter of the trend, our next problem is to determine when it has been finally and definitely broken.

Again, we can set up three tests or criteria, two of which are practically identical with the rules laid down in earlier chapters for determining decisive breakouts from Reversal or Consolidation Formations. The first is *extent of penetration*. To be decisive, prices must not only push through the line, but close beyond it by a margin equal to about 3% of the stock's price. This does not need to be accomplished in a single day, although it often is. The 3% penetration may come as a result of 2 or 3 days of gradual decline.

The second is *volume of trading*. We saw how activity should always be expected to rise notably on a genuine upside breakout from an Area Pattern, but need not increase to confirm a downside break. We have seen how, in many cases, volume does not show much increase on the first day of down-break from Descending Triangles, for example, but usually picks up rapidly as the decline proceeds. In our present discussion, we are dealing with *Up* Trendlines, and their penetration is, therefore, analogous to a downside breakout. We should expect the same rules to apply, and in general, they do. Given a close beyond the line by a price margin of 3%, it is not necessary for volume to have expanded much at that point to confirm the validity of the penetration.

The fact is, however, that the breaking of an Intermediate Up Trendline, much more often than not, is attended by some visible intensification of trading activity. To that extent, then, an increase in volume may be regarded as confirmation of a decisive penetration. It is a particularly useful adjunct in borderline cases. If, for example, prices start to decline from a point somewhat above the trendline, move down through it on *conspicuously expanding* turnover, and close beyond it, say, only 2% of the price but at or near the bottom of the day's range, our 3% margin rule has not been satisfied, but the lesser margin *plus* the volume action may be construed as decisive.

Beware, however, and do not be stampeded into a hasty commitment by the shakeout move which cracks down through a trendline with a great flurry of activity — perhaps several minutes of late tape — and then turns up again to close the day back above the trend or at least very close to it. This may very well be — in fact, usually is — a false move so far as that particular moment is concerned. But watch the next few days' performance very closely; the technical situation is evidently critical, else a shakeout could not have been easily staged.

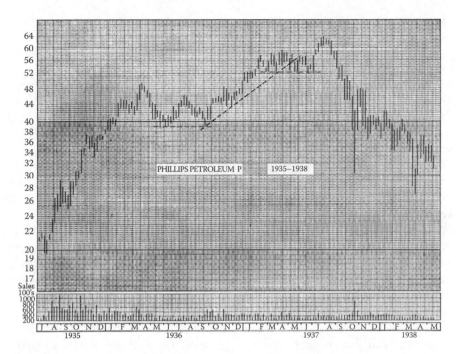

FIGURE 151. Valid trendline penetration and its normal consequences — Reaction or Consolidation — is illustrated on nearly every chart in this chapter and on many others throughout the book. The above weekly chart of Phillips Petroleum, however, is reproduced here to show an outstanding exception. The Intermediate Up Trendline projected from "P's" September 1936 low up across its early October and late November Bottoms was penetrated downside decisively the third week of May 1937. Moreover, a Multiple Head-and-Shoulders Top Reversal Pattern had been forming since February, with a critical neckline at 52. And the then current Bull Market had already run for 4 years; "P" had come all the way up from 2! Cover up the chart from July 1, 1937 on, and you will agree that there was plenty of reason for any technician to sell at once without waiting for the 52 neckline to be broken. But this, as we have said, was one of the exceptions which occur to all technical patterns and rules. "P" turned right around and shot up to 64 before it was finished. Nevertheless, developments such as this carry a valuable warning. They very seldom appear unless the Major Trend has almost run out; any further rise is dangerous to follow.

The third test is also one that applies particularly to breaks which are borderline so far as margin of penetration is concerned. Suppose a stock which is quoted in the neighborhood of 40 declines through a well-established Intermediate Up Trendline and closes 1 or 1⅛ points below it — a margin which is only slightly less than our specified 3% — without much, if any, enlargement in trading volume. Suppose it fluctuates there for a day or two in a dull and narrow market, and then starts to rally. If there is no pickup in activity on this recovery move — if prices simply edge up feebly to the underside of the trendline and tend to "round over" there without being able to close clearly above it — then the situation is indeed critical, and the slightest sign of renewed selling pressure may be taken as a signal that the uptrend has been decisively broken.

Such a return move as we have described in the preceding paragraph is known as a Throwback or Pullback. We have previously described analogous developments which follow breakouts from Head-and-Shoulders and other patterns, and will have more to say about them in connection with trendlines later on.

The three tests we have been discussing, which help to establish the validity of a trendline penetration, cannot, unfortunately, be applied inflexibly and without a modicum of judgment. The majority of Intermediate Trendlines can hardly be said to possess the precision of pattern boundary lines, and even in the latter, some leeway must be allowed. There are exceptions, as we have taken occasion to remark several times before, to every technical rule of price action. But judgment in the establishing of significant trendlines and in interpreting their penetrations does come with experience.

Amendment of Trendlines

When a trendline is broken by a margin less than decisive, and prices subsequently rally back up through it again, doubt naturally arises as to the continued authority of the original line. Should it be discarded, revised, or allowed to stand as is?

Here again, judgment and experience must be called into play, but a few general principles are helpful in deciding. If the original trendlines depended on only two points, i.e., on the first two Bottoms across which it was projected, and the indecisive penetration occurred when prices returned to it for the third time, the line had better be redrawn across the original first and the new third Bottoms. (Of course, you will not do this until prices have moved up from the third Bottom point and it has become clearly established as a Minor Bottom.) Or, you may find in such cases that a new line drawn across the *second* and third Bottoms works better; if the first Bottom was a Reversal Day with its *closing* level well above the low of its range, you may find that this new line, when extended back, strikes just about at that closing level.

If, on the other hand, the original trendline has been "tested" one or more times after it was drawn — if, that is, a third and perhaps a fourth Bottom have formed on it without penetrating it and have thus "confirmed" it — then the subsequent indecisive penetration may be disregarded and the original line considered to be still in effect.

An intraday break through an established trendline that, however, does not result in prices closing beyond the line may be disregarded and the line left as is. In fact, as has already been suggested, the closing prices frequently make a better trendline than the extreme intraday lows of successive

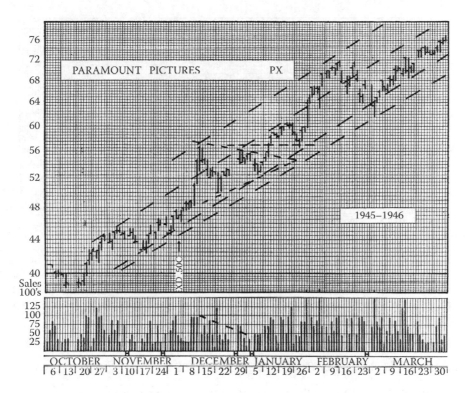

FIGURE 152. Double Trendlines (see next page) usually are not evident until after a trend has run for several months. In Paramount's accelerated phase of Intermediate Uptrend which began in October 1945, the double nature of the basic trendline was not detectable until January 1946. The inner (upper) line was broken again in April, but the outer (lower) line was not decisively penetrated downside until May, at the Bull Market Top.

Bottoms, and this is most apt to be true with "thin" stocks subject to erratic swings. A bit of experimenting with different lines often pays. A thin, transparent ruler is especially useful for trendline study.

There is another type of price action that may require redrawing a trendline. Sometimes, after a line has been projected up across the first two Minor Bottoms in an advancing trend, a third Minor Bottom will form, not on that line, but well above it. In such cases, let the original line stand, but draw in a new one across the second and third Bottom points, and watch developments. If the rally from the third Bottom peters out quickly, and the new trendline, as a consequence, is soon broken, then the original trendline is probably the correct one. But, if the third Bottom turns out to be a "strong" one, and the new line stands up well for several weeks (and if it was not, patently, too steep to begin with), then the old line may be abandoned and the new one regarded as the better trend definer.

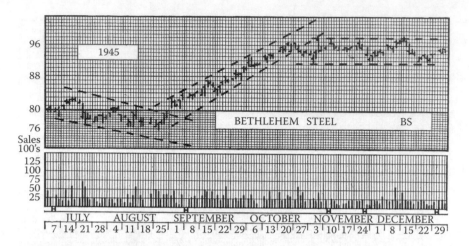

FIGURE 153. Trend Channels in Bethlehem Steel in 1945. Prices burst out of the 92–98 Horizontal Channel (Rectangle) on the upside in January 1946, and went on to 114. A short-term trader might have sold around 94–96 in early November (because of the uptrend break) and rebought at 99 in January on the Rectangle breakout. See discussion of Channels.

Double Trendlines and Trend Ranges

In the course of your "cutting and trying" in an effort to fit a good line to an Intermediate Uptrend, you may find that *two parallel lines*, perhaps a point or so apart in a stock selling in the thirties, will define the true trend pattern much better than any single line that can be drawn. Sharp Bottoms and shakeout thrusts in such cases will often fall along the outer or lower line, while the duller, more rounded reactions will stop at or near the upper or inner line. Or the two lines will mark off a *range* somewhere within which successive Minor Down Waves tend to halt and reverse.

Such Double Trendlines are really plentiful, although the majority of chart technicians seem to be quite unaware of them. It pays to develop an eye for them — to watch constantly for trends to which they can be applied. They will clear up many situations in which attempts to find a single critical line lead only to frustration and in finally giving up in disgust.

Trends that you find are best defined by Double Trendlines (or by a very Broad Trendline, if you prefer) cannot be regarded as ended until the outer, lower line has been decisively penetrated. In that connection, note what we said at the beginning of this topic: sharp, shakeout Bottoms tend to fall on the outer line. The recoveries from such Bottoms are usually just as sharp, and prices, therefore, rally back above the upper, inner line quickly. Warning of an impending break in the trend is given when prices come down to the outer line steadily, rather than by the quick "shake" type of reaction, and

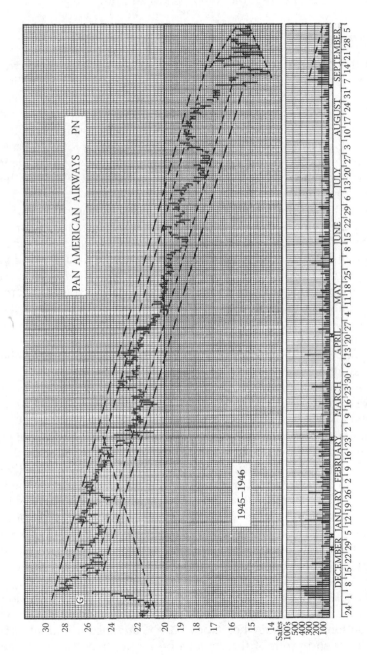

FIGURE 154. A 10-month downtrend, extraordinarily long and straight, which was nicely defined by Double Basic Trendlines above the Price Channel, and also by a double set of Return Lines below it. The Major Top started with a strong One-Day Reversal on December 3, 1945, and worked out into a Descending Triangle which broke February 19, 1946. The Symmetrical Triangle beginning to appear in September 1946 also broke out downside.

then have difficulty rallying back through the inner line. Watch such developments closely. A break down may not follow; the situation may still be "saved," but the chances are that the trend is near its end.

Trend Channels

At the start of this trend study, we applied the term Basic Trendline to the line which slopes up across the Wave Bottoms in an advance, and to the line which slopes down across the Wave *Tops* in a decline. And we noted that the opposite Reversal Points, i.e., the wave crests in an advance and the wave troughs in a decline, were, as a rule, less clearly delimited. That is one of the reasons why all of our discussion up to this point has been devoted to Basic Trendlines. Another reason is, of course, that the technician's most urgent task is to determine when a trend has run out, and for that purpose, the Basic Line is all important.

In a fair share of normal trends, however, the Minor Waves are sufficiently regular to be defined at their other extremes by another line. That is, the *Tops* of the rallies composing an Intermediate Advance sometimes develop along a line which is approximately parallel to the Basic Trendline projected along their Bottoms. This parallel might be called the *Return Line*, since it marks the zone where reactions (return moves against the prevailing trend) originate. The area between Basic Trendline and Return Line is the *Trend Channel*.

Nicely defined Trend Channels appear most often in actively traded stocks of large outstanding issue — least often in the less popular and the relatively thin equities which receive only sporadic attention from investors. The value of the Trend Channel concept for the technical trader would hardly seem to require extended comment here; its tactical utilization is discussed in the second half of this book.

Its greatest utility, however, is not what usually appeals to the beginner when he first makes its acquaintance, viz., the determination of good profit-taking levels. Experienced technicians find it more helpful in a negative sense. Thus, once a Trend Channel appears to have become well established, any failure of a rally to reach the Return Line (top parallel of the channel in an Intermediate Advance) is taken as a sign of deterioration in the trend. Further, the margin by which a rally fails to reach the Return Line (before turning down) frequently equals the margin by which the Basic Trendline is penetrated by the ensuing decline before a halt or Throwback in the latter occurs.

By the same token, given an established Trend Channel, when a reaction from the Return Line fails to carry prices all the way back to the Basic Trendline but bottoms out somewhere above it, the advance from that Bottom will usually push up out of the channel on the top side (through the Return Line) by a margin approximately equal to the margin by which the reaction failed to reach the bottom of the channel (Basic Trendline).

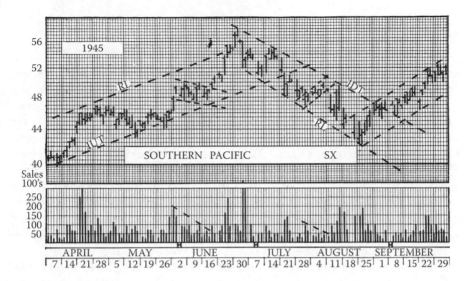

FIGURE 155. Well-marked Intermediate Basic Trendline and Return Lines in Southern Pacific, 1945. Note Flags within Trend Channels — an up Flag in June and a down Flag in August. The Uptrend Channel, which began August 22, ran until February 1946.

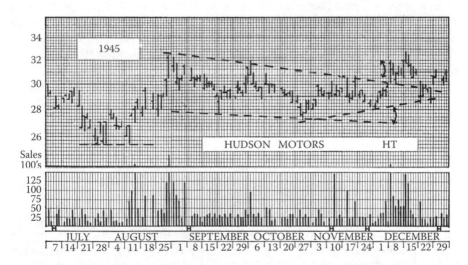

FIGURE 156. Note that the extent by which prices failed to come down to their Return Line in late November measured the distance by which they advanced through and above the Basic Down Trendline in early December. This rule is stated on the preceding page.

Experimental Lines

Your experienced technician, in fact, is constantly drawing trendlines of all sorts — Minor, Intermediate, and Major — on his charts. He will put them in at first very lightly penciled wherever he can find an excuse to draw one. Many will quickly prove to be of no significance, and those he may erase. Others will "stand up" — will show evidence of technical authority — and those he will make heavier, or color as suggested later on. He will be constantly on the watch for Double Trendlines and will draw tentative Return Lines to mark off possible channels at every opportunity. As soon as he has what appears to be a Basic Up Trendline projected from two Bottoms, for example, he will go back to the Top of the rally between those two Bottoms and draw from that parallel to the Bottom Trendline. If the next rally comes up to that parallel, stops there and turns down, he has a probable Return Line and channel established.

This practice of drawing in and experimenting with every trendline, which the price action permits or suggests, is earnestly recommended to the reader of this book, particularly if the technical approach is new to him. It is the quickest way — in fact, the only way — of acquiring the experience we have stressed as essential to recognition, judgment, and utilization of trendline implications in trading.

Perhaps we should add here one "don't" for the beginner. You will have noted that nowhere have we mentioned a line projected from a Bottom to a Top, or vice versa. Trendlines are *always* drawn across two or more Bottoms, or two or more Tops. They should never be drawn to cross through the price track. (Prices may cross their extensions later, but this should not have happened at the time the lines are first drawn.) If you did not know better, you might, for example, put in a line from the Top of the left shoulder to the Top of the right shoulder of a Head-and-Shoulders Formation, thus cutting through the head, but such a line would have no technical validity.

Consequences of Trendline Penetration — Throwbacks

At the beginning of this chapter, we mentioned the probable consequences of a break down through an Intermediate Up Trendline. To repeat, if an Intermediate Up Trendline has been constructed, has qualified as technically significant by the tests previously discussed, and has then been decisively broken, the inference is that uptrend is finished. And the consequences to be expected are either a full Intermediate Recession or a period of Consolidation (usually becoming a recognizable Area Formation). Technical indications of other sorts may be seen on the chart, which will suggest to you which of these two consequences is the more likely. In either event, the Intermediate Trend trader will certainly look twice before attempting to find further profit in that particular situation at that time.

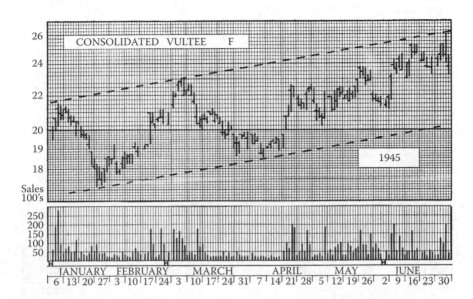

FIGURE 157. Six months of an Uptrend Channel which actually started to form in December 1943! It was broken downside in August 1945.

A more immediate but less important probable consequence of trendline penetration has also been mentioned — the "Pullback." This deserves further discussion. Pullbacks that follow breakouts from Reversal and Consolidation Formations have been described in our earlier studies of those price patterns. It is easy to understand why a rally which develops after prices break out through the lower boundary of a Rectangle, for example, will be stopped when it gets back to that boundary by the Resistance (supply) now residing there. Support–Resistance Theory enables us to rationalize most of the Throwback moves which occur after prices have broken out of other types of Reversal or Consolidation Areas. The Pullbacks which follow trendline penetrations cannot be thus rationalized; yet they occur much more frequently, and they appear to be stopped much more exactly at the old trendline level than is the case with Area Formations. Why should prices, after they have thrust down through a rising trendline, perhaps for several points, turn back up and ascend to or very near the old trendline, stop there and then go off in renewed decline? The Top of that Pullback Rally may be 2 or 3 points above the original penetration level, since the trendline is sloping up all the time; nevertheless, there it stops, falters, gives up. No one knows why supply should overcome demand, why Resistance should be so plainly evident at that particular point whose level is determined by *two* variants, the *slope* of the line and the *time* it is reached.

Of course, you cannot reasonably expect a Pullback Rally to climb all the way back to a trendline that is ascending at a very steep angle, which may mean the attainment of a new high price for the entire Intermediate

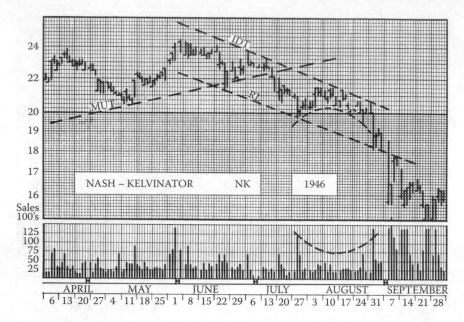

FIGURE 158. The downtrend which started in June 1946 in Nash–Kelvinator, signaled by the break of both its Intermediate and Major Up Trendlines (MUT) on July 15, made a nice channel until September. An Intermediate Down Trendline, drawn across the June 17 and July 1 highs, held for the August rally. The Return Line, drawn parallel to it across the June 20 low, held in late July but remained intact for only a few days at the end of August. The August rally in both price and volume pattern showed Bear Market characteristics. Compare this chart with Figure 68 and you will see that a Major Double Top was signaled on July 23.

Uptrend; yet even that happens in more than just a few cases. What can be counted on in the great majority of typical Up Trendlines (those which slant up at a normal or fairly flat angle) is that after the line has been broken, a Pullback Rally will develop, either in a few days or in the usual Minor Wave tempo, and will carry prices back up to the projected trendline.

Throwbacks do not occur, it should be noted, when prices erupt through a *Return* Line, i.e., break out of the top side of an Uptrend Channel. Or, more correctly stated, the Return Line does not function as a Support against a Throwback after prices have gone through it. An unusually strong upswing in a Rising Trend Channel may carry beyond the top of the channel as defined by its Return Line, but the next reaction may go right back down through it without evidencing any hesitation at its level.

The Throwback is one of the mysteries in trendline price action to which we alluded at the outset. The technical analyst who studies trends and trendlines over any considerable period will discover many other even more mysterious phenomena which cannot find space in this treatise, because no way has yet been found to put them to practical use in trading and investing.

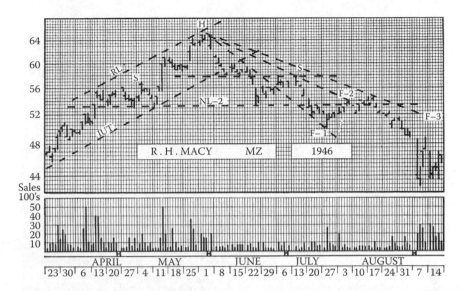

FIGURE 159. The decline that took Macy down through an Intermediate Up Trendline (IUT) in June 1946 turned out to be also the drop from the head of a "Flat-Shouldered" Head-and-Shoulders Top, which was, in turn, part of a larger Complex. The upper neckline was broken June 19 and the lower on July 16. Note Pullbacks to each. F1, F2, and F3 are tentative Fan Lines. Prices were finally able to clear F3 in December, but by that time a Primary Bear Market had been signaled; so, the Fan Rule no longer applied. Fans call the turn only on Secondary (Corrective) Moves.

They are extraordinarily interesting in retrospect, but are not subject to forecast.

Intermediate Downtrends

In all of the foregoing discussion of trends and trendlines we have concentrated on *uptrends*; we have, in fact, had in mind specifically Intermediate Advances in the direction of the Primary Trend, i.e., within a Major Bull Market. Those particular trends are most apt to develop "normally," are most amenable to trendline definition. Intermediate *Down* Moves in a Major Bear Market may well be taken up next. Before we discuss the respects in which they differ from Primary Advances, we should recall that the *Basic Trendline* on a down-move is the line projected across the *Tops* of the rallies within it. The Trend Channel will be to the left of that trendline and below it on the chart. The *Return* Line (if any) will define the *Bottom* of the channel.

Intermediate (Bear Market) Downtrends are far less regular and uniform in their development than Bull Market Advances. Their angles of decline are characteristically steeper, and this is particularly true, of course, of the Panic Moves which are typical of the second phase of a Bear Market, as we saw

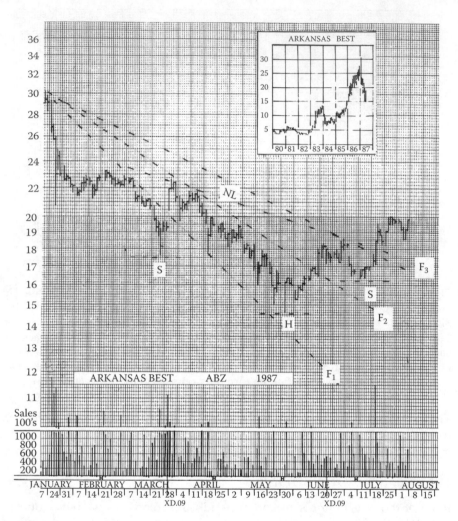

FIGURE 160. "ABZ" dropped sharply following its late January high, capped off a nearly uninterrupted 2-year rally. But despite the rapidity and severity of the Pullback, it was, in fact, a picture-perfect reaction, which stopped just above excellent long-term Support at the 1983 high after retracing almost exactly 50% from its January peak. Not only is the reaction a classic, but so, too, is the Fan Line development which, when coupled with the recently completed Head-and-Shoulders Bottom, suggests "ABZ" has reversed its short-term downtrend.

in our discussion of Major Trends in Chapter 3. Moreover, prices have a tendency to drop away from any trendline which is drawn across the first two Rally Tops; in other words, to curve down or accelerate as the move proceeds. This shows plainly on an arithmetically scaled chart and, even more conspicuously on a semilogarithmic sheet.

The *practical* results of this down-curving tendency are not so important, insofar as it delays the penetration of the original trendline and, hence, the giving of a signal of trend change. The fact is that prices tend to thrash around for some time, making a base at the Bottom of one of these precipitous declines. In so doing, they work out sideways on the chart, and the trend frequently does not turn up visibly until after the trendline has finally been reached and broken through on the upside after all. Thus, there is justification for drawing down trendlines and keeping them in view even though they may seem, for some time, simply to travel off into space with no apparent relevance to the actual trend of prices.

It naturally follows from the above that Return Lines on most Bear Market Declines have little practical utility; they are, more often than not, very quickly broken downside. Good channels are hard to find.

However, and this is of considerable practical importance, the very last Intermediate Downswing in a Major Bear Market, i.e., the last Primary Move which leads to the final, long-term Bottom, is usually cleaner, more regular, less precipitous — in other words, a more nearly normal trend of the sort we expect to find in most Intermediate Advances in a Bull Market (except, of course, that it slants down instead of up). This interesting habit is, as we said, of practical importance. Knowing it, we have an additional and very useful clue to the end of a Bear Market.

When, after a Major Bear Trend has proceeded for some time and distance, and has experienced at least one Panic Sell-Off, it then goes off in another but less active and more orderly decline, and this decline develops and follows a good trendline. Watch it closely. If this Intermediate holds to its steady and not-too-steep downward course — if its trendline is contacted several times by Minor Rallies — if it produces a fairly consistent channel, and prices do not "fall out of bed" down through its parallel Return Line, then the eventual upside penetration of this trendline may well signal a *Major* Turn, the inception of a new Bull Market.

Corrective Trends — The Fan Principle

In this study of Intermediate Trendlines, we have left to be taken up last the subject of Secondary or Corrective Trends. These are the Intermediate Declines which interrupt the Primary Advances in a Bull Market, and the Intermediate Recoveries which alternate with Primary Declines in Bear Markets.

Intermediate Reactions against the Major Direction of the market take a variety of forms. Sometimes, as we have seen in our earlier study of chart patterns, they run out into Consolidation Formations — Triangles, Rectangles, etc. — in which the net price reaction is of minor consequence, but time is consumed in backing and filling before the Primary Trend can be resumed. In such cases, of course, there is no basis for drawing an Intermediate Trendline, nor is one needed for any practical purpose.

At the other extreme, so to speak, we find Corrective Swings which develop as a more or less orderly straight-line return of moderate slope to

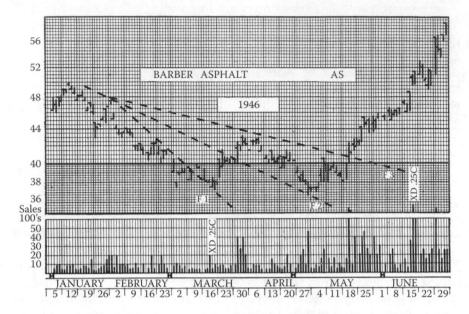

FIGURE 161. A valid application of the Three-Fan Principle. Note that prices, after they pushed up through F1 in March, fell back to it but did not repenetrate it. When F2 was broken in late March, prices came back to it at the end of April but did not go below it. F3 was surmounted in May. This was a Bull Market Reaction; "AS" made its final Top above 64 in August. The March–May pattern might be called a weak Double Bottom.

the nearest good Intermediate Support or Resistance Level, retracing perhaps a third to a half of the preceding Primary Swing. These reactions produce good trendlines, as a rule, and the eventual penetration of their trendlines is a good technical signal of Reversal. Intermediate Corrections clearly of this type, it may be added, are relatively rare.

A third form taken by Intermediate Corrections is nearly as common as the first named above (Consolidation Pattern) and much more common on the charts than the second. In a Bull Market, it starts with a sharp reaction which proceeds for several days — perhaps for as much as 2 weeks — producing a steep Minor Trendline. This line is broken upside by a quick Minor Rally, after which prices slide off again in a duller and less precipitate trend. A second Minor Trendline may now be drawn from the original high point across the Top of the upthrust that broke the first trend. This second trendline is broken by another partial recovery thrust, and a third and still duller and flatter sell-off ensues. A third trendline can now be drawn from the original high across the Top of the second upthrust. The whole move, by this time, has taken roughly and irregularly a "Saucering-out" form. The three trendlines drawn from the original Reversal points from which the

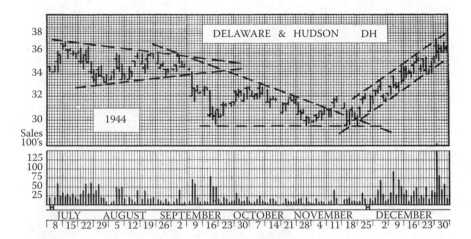

FIGURE 162. Try the Three-Fan Principle on this chart of the late 1944 Bull Market Reaction out of a Symmetrical Triangle in "DH." F1 should be drawn from the August 30 high down across the September 12 closing. F2 is already marked on the chart but not labeled. F3 would extend from August 30 across the Rally Top of November 9. It was surmounted on increased volume November 21. The mid-September to November price pattern looked at first like a Descending Triangle but volume began to rise in October.

Corrective Decline started, each at a flatter angle than its predecessor, are known as *Fan Lines*. And the rule is that when the *third* Fan Line is broken upside, the low of the Intermediate Correction has been seen.

There are exceptions to this rule — as there are to every so-called rule of technical chart analysis. Rarely, a correction of this type will go on to make another dip to a new low for the whole corrective move before prices really start to round up again. But the Three-Fan Principle works in the great majority of cases. Moreover, it offers the trader an opportunity to take a position at a point where he can logically employ a very near stop order and, thus, limit his loss to a controlled amount if the rule does not work out.

It is interesting to note that prices consistently Throwback in these movements to the preceding Fan Line after each upthrust. The new Primary Swing, once the low has been passed, usually starts slowly and carries out for a time the Saucer picture.

The Three-Fan Rule works just as well in calling the turn on Intermediate Recoveries in a Bear Market, the majority of which take the rounding form which is adapted to its use.

Note, however, that the Fan Principle is normally applied only to corrective moves, i.e., to determine the end of Intermediate Reactions in a Bull Market and of Intermediate Recoveries in a Bear Market.

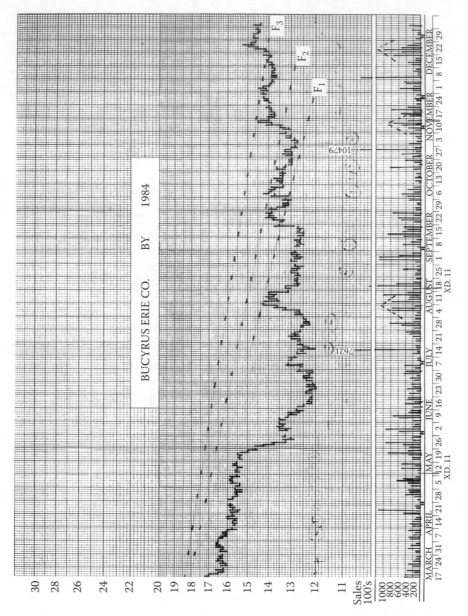

FIGURE 163. In a downtrend throughout the first half, "BY" gave back a large part of its 1983 rally by mid-summer. But the 1982 low held the Bears in check and over the following several months, this issue etched out an excellent Fan Pattern. Fan Line 1 gave way in mid-September on a high-volume penetration. The advance quickly lost its momentum, but old Resistance/new Support contained the Pullback perfectly, setting the stage for a rally through Fan Line 2. This occurred in mid-November on good volume. Following a 5-week correction, "BY" charged through Fan Line 3 on the best volume of the 3 breakouts.

We shall take up Major Trendlines in the following chapter, but, before we leave this study of Intermediate Trends, it will be well to state again that the practical application of trendlines in actual trading requires experience, and the good judgment to be attained only therefrom. Some technical analysts depend largely on trendline studies; a few attempt to use trendlines almost exclusively; but the majority have found that they are best employed as an adjunct to other technical data.

Technical analysis of a stock chart is something like putting together a jigsaw puzzle. There are many items to be considered, among them volume, pattern, and the measurements derived therefrom, Support and Resistance Levels, trendlines, general market prospects — and all fitted into place to get the complete picture.

chapter fifteen

Major Trendlines

In the preceding chapter on Intermediate Trendlines, mention was made of the distinctive effects produced by arithmetic and semilogarithmic plotting, but it was noted that these differences were unimportant in connection with Minor Trends or Intermediate Trends of average duration. When we come to Major Trends, however, we find the difference does become important.

If you will examine a large collection of arithmetically scaled monthly charts covering 10 years or more of market history, you will quickly see that Bull Trends, in the great majority of actively traded, more or less speculative common stocks, tend to *accelerate*. They start slowly and push up at a steeper and steeper angle as they approach a Major Top. This up-curving path takes them farther and farther away from any straight trendline drawn from two Bottom points in the first, slow-moving stage of advance. As a consequence, they top out and have gone down a long way in a recession which may be of Major consequence before their straight trendline is again touched.

Many of the stocks that show such typical *accelerating* curves in their advance (Major) Trends on arithmetic paper produce *straight* trends on a logarithmic scale. As a consequence, their logarithmic Major Trendlines are broken more quickly, and usually at a higher price level, when at last their trends do top out and turn down. In the case of such stocks, then, the logarithmic scale gives a better trend signal.

But there are other stocks — mostly of the more substantial investment or semi-investment type — which tend to advance in straight arithmetic trends. Consolidated Edison, General Motors, and Libbey–Owens–Ford Glass are examples. (The trends of these on a logarithmic scale show a decelerating curve, of course.) Still a third class, made up largely of high-grade preferred stocks, produces a rounding over or decelerating Bull Trendline even on the arithmetic scale. And, finally, there are a number of issues whose normal Bull Market Trendlines fall somewhere between our first two types; that is, they curve up away from a straight path on the arithmetic scale, but curve over to the right (breaking through a straight line) on the logarithmic scale. *EN: Fortunately, in this age of computers and easily processed data, there is analytical software which allows the analyst to instantaneously switch between the scales. Desktop packages are available (see Appendix D, Resources) and a number of Internet sites have these capabilities.*

All of which, the reader, at this point, no doubt finds most discouraging. Some stocks do this and some stocks do that, and what help is there for us in such a mix-up? The answer lies in studying the history of each issue in which you may be interested. Stocks — most of them, at least — do not change their habits and their technical characteristics much from one Bull and Bear cycle to the next. An issue which, like General Motors, produces a straight-line Bull Trend on an arithmetic chart in one Primary Upswing is likely to repeat that performance in the next.

As a matter of interest, stocks do sometimes change, of course, over a long period of years. Companies which were regarded as extremely speculative when their shares were first listed may attain a more and more important and stable position in the general economy, with the result that, eventually, their stock acquires a solid investment rating. Their Bull Market Trends will then gradually change from an up-curve to a straight-line and, finally, to a decelerating curve. Other old, established corporations may lose position and rating, shift from the investment type of trendline to the speculative. But, it is true in general, nevertheless, that Major Patterns do repeat.

If you are keeping your own set of manual monthly charts, you can choose whichever scale you please. But most technical chart followers prefer to buy their long-range pictures ready made, thereby getting a much more extensive history of many more issues than they could hope to chart themselves. Since the only comprehensive portfolios of monthly charts that are available at reasonable cost are arithmetically scaled, you will possibly have to make these serve all purposes. *EN: No longer necessary because of availability of good software and also Internet chart sites. See Appendix D, Resources.* You will find with a little experimentation that an architect's French curve can be used to plot good Major Uptrend Lines on many of the issues whose normal Bull Trends accelerate away from a straight line.

The tests for the technical significance of a Major Trendline are substantially the same as those specified for Intermediate Lines in the preceding chapter. A little more leeway must be allowed on penetrations — again, a matter of judgment — but you are dealing with coarse data and long swings here, and what you want from your monthly charts, primarily, is perspective on the broad picture.

One more point regarding the construction of Major Bull Trendlines: the best lines — the most useful — are drawn, as a rule, not from the absolute low of the preceding Bear Market, but starting, rather, from the next Intermediate Bottom. The accumulation area at the beginning of a Bull Market is usually long and drawn out in time, and relatively flat. The first trendline that can be drawn from the extreme low point may, therefore, be too nearly horizontal to express the genuine Bull Trend which starts with the markup phase. The several charts showing Major Trendlines which illustrate this chapter will demonstrate this point. *EN: Especially Figure 177.* It applies as well, we might add, to many Intermediate Moves which start from Area Formations. Take the Head-and-Shoulders Pattern for example: the true Intermediate Trendline usually starts from the right shoulder rather than from the head.

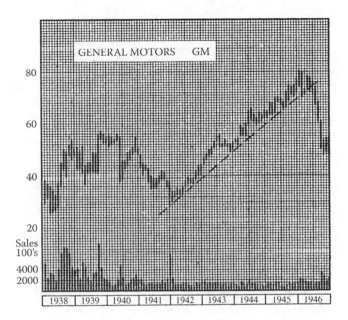

FIGURE 164. The straight-line Bull Market Trend of General Motors on an arithmetic monthly chart. 1941 low, 28⅝; 1946 high, 80⅜.

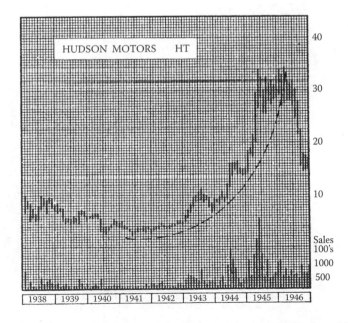

FIGURE 165. The up-curving trend of a speculative motors stock, Hudson Motors. Compare this with "GM." 1941 low, 2⅝; 1946 high, 34½.

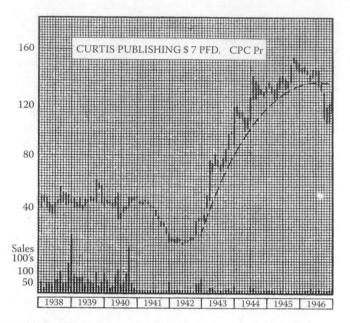

FIGURE 166. Typical decurving Major Bull Trend of a high-grade preferred stock. This is Curtis Publishing $7 Preferred. 1942 low, 12; 1945 high, 154.

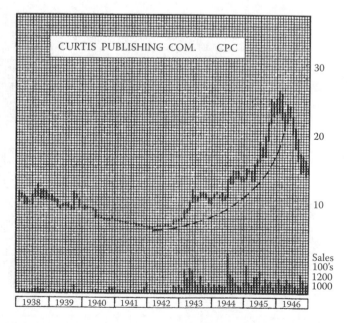

FIGURE 167. The accelerating uptrend of the common stock of the same publishing company. 1942 low, ⅜; 1946 high, 26.

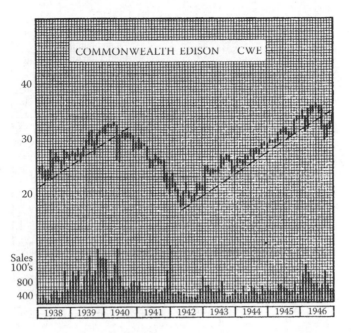

FIGURE 168. A conservative investment-type utility stock makes a straight-line Major Bull Trend. This is Commonwealth Edison. 1942 low, 17⅜; 1946 high, 36⅛. Leverage is an important factor in trends.

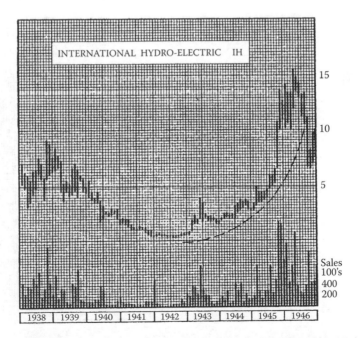

FIGURE 169. The up-curving trend of a low-priced "junior" utility, International Hydro-Electric. 1942 low, ¼; 1946 high, 15½.

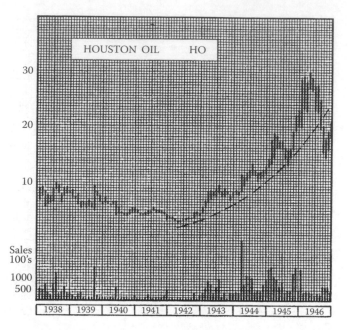

FIGURE 170.   A speculative oil stock, Houston Oil. 1942 low, 2¼; 1946 high, 30. Compare this picture with "SOH" in Figure 171.

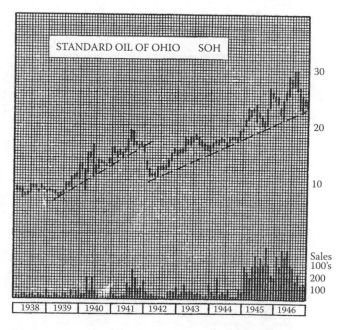

FIGURE 171.   Straight-line uptrends in an investment oil, Standard Oil of Ohio. 1942 low, 10⅛; 1946 high, 30. Note: trendline unbroken until 1948.

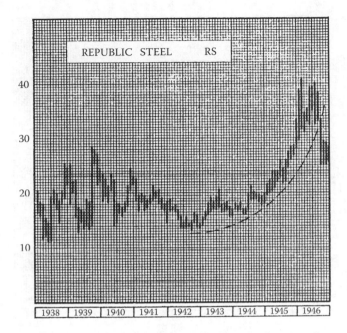

FIGURE 172. Steel stocks have the speculative or accelerating type of Primary Uptrend. Republic Steel. 1942 low, 13⅜; 1946 high, 40⅞.

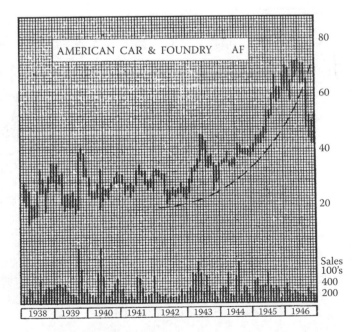

FIGURE 173. The normal Major Bull Trend of heavy industrial issues is up-curving. American Car & Foundry. 1942 low, 20; 1946 high, 72⅜.

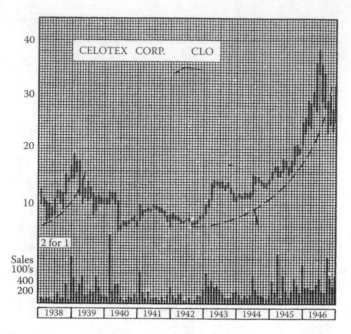

FIGURE 174.   A low-priced building stock, Celotex Corporation. 1942 low, 6⅛; 1946 high, 38⅛.

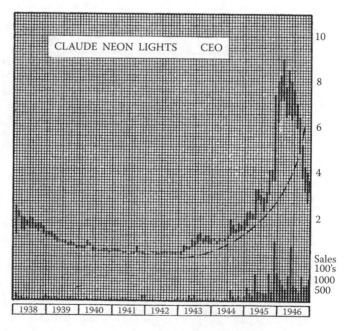

FIGURE 175.   A highly speculative, low-priced issue, traded on the Curb Exchange, Claude Neon Lights. 1942 low, ⅛; 1946 high, 9.

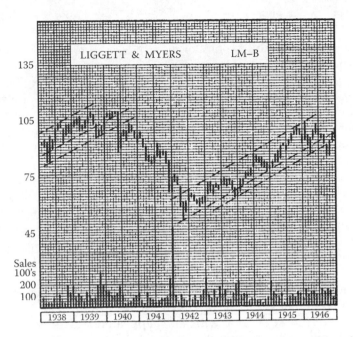

FIGURE 176. The tobacco stocks follow the investment type of trend. This is Liggett & Myers. Note Double Trendline. 1942 low, 50½; 1946 high, 103½.

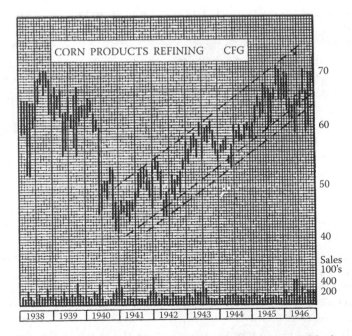

FIGURE 177. High-grade food issues (Corn Products Refining) resemble the tobaccos. 1940 low, 40¼; 1946 high, 75¾.

Major Downtrends

From the technical analyst's point of view, it is to be regretted that few Bear Markets have produced Major Trendlines of any practical significance on the charts of individual stocks. A notable exception was the long Bear Market of 1929–32 which produced magnificently straight trendlines on the arithmetic plotting of a host of issues (as well as in the Averages, to which we shall refer later). But it is almost impossible to find other instances where a Bear Trendline having any forecasting value can be drawn on either arithmetic or semilogarithmic scale.

The *normal* Major Bear Market Trend is not only steeper than the normal Bull Trend (because Bear Markets last, on the average, only about half as long as Bull Markets), but it is also accelerating or down-curving in its course. This feature is accentuated and, hence, particularly difficult to project effectively on the semilogarithmic scale.

The net of it is that the technician cannot expect to obtain much, if any, help from his *Major* Trendlines in determining the change from a Primary *Down* to a Primary *Upswing*. This should not be taken, however, as advice to draw no trendlines on a Major Down Move, or to disregard entirely any trendlines which may develop with some appearance of authority. If you do not expect too much of them, they may, nevertheless, afford some useful clue as to the way in which conditions are tending to change.

The student of stock market action who is not altogether concerned with dollars and cents results from his researches will find Bear Market Trendlines a fascinating field of inquiry. They do some strange things. Even though they fail in the practical function of calling the actual Major Turn, and go shooting off into space, they sometimes produce curious reactions (or, at least, appear to produce what would be otherwise inexplicable market action) when the real price trend catches up with them months or years later. But such effects, interesting as they may be, are, in our present state of knowledge, uncertain and unpredictable. *EN: This fact may persist into the mists of the future and be thought of like Fermat's Last Theorem. Our present state of knowledge in the 21st century is no further advanced than it was in Magee's time.*

We must dismiss this rather unfruitful topic with the reminder that one clue to the end of a Primary Bear Market is afforded by the Intermediate Trendline of its final phase, which we cited in the preceding chapter.

Major Trend Channels

We run into another difficulty when we try to draw Return Lines and construct channels for Major Trends on an arithmetic chart. Owing to the marked tendency for prices to fluctuate in ever wider swings (both Intermediate and Minor) as they work upward in a Primary Bull Market, their channel grows progressively broader. The Return Line does not run parallel to the Basic Trendline (assuming that we have a good Basic Trendline to begin with) but diverges from it. Occasionally, a stock produces a clear-cut Major Channel Pattern, but the majority do not.

Semilogarithmic scaling will, in many cases, correct for the Widening Channel effect in Bull Trends, but then we run into the opposite tendency in Primary Bear Markets, and for that, neither type of scaling will compensate.

Trendlines in the Averages

Practically everything stated in the preceding chapter regarding Intermediate Trendline development in individual stocks applies, as well, to the various Averages. The broad Averages or Indexes, in fact, produce more regular trends and, in consequence, more exactly applicable trendlines. This may be due, in part, to the fact that most Averages are composed of active, well-publicized, and widely owned issues whose market action individually is "normal" in the technical sense. Another reason is that the process of averaging smooths out vagaries of component stocks, and the result, thus, more truly reflects the deep and relatively steady economic trends and tides.

In any event, it is a fact that such averages as the Dow–Jones Rails, Industrials and 65-Stock Composite, *The New York Times* 50, and Standard & Poor's Average of 90 stocks (the last two named being probably the most scientifically composed to typify the entire broad market) *(EN: As the reader will note most of these are obsolete. In the modern age, the S&P 500 probably best fulfills this function)* do propagate excellent trendlines on their charts.

The very accuracy of their trends, particularly their Intermediate Moves, permits us to construe their trendlines more tightly. Less leeway need be allowed for doubtful penetrations. Thus, while we ask for a 3% penetration in the case of an individual stock of medium range, 2% is ample in the Averages to give a dependable break signal.

Experienced traders know that it pays to heed the Broad Market Trend. It is still easier to swim with the tide than against it.

EN: Trendlines in the Averages, and Trading in the Averages

Numerous averages and indexes have come online since the 5th edition: S&P 100, S&P 500, Russell 2000, and so on. It would be an exercise in daily journalism to attempt to list all the indexes now available. New ones spring up like weeds after the spring rain. This is because the invention of a widely adopted index can be very lucrative for its creator. S&P and Dow–Jones collect licensing fees from the "use" of their indexes by the exchanges. The constant addition of new trading instruments requires that current lists be kept in Resources, and the reader may also consult The Wall Street Journal, Barron's, *and* The Investor's Business Daily *where prices of indexes and averages are reported. Online brokerages and financial news sites*

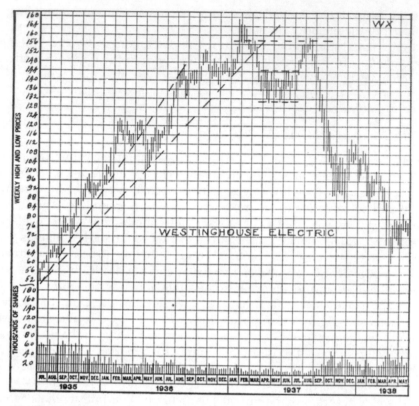

FIGURE 178.   In the process of "pulling back" to a very steep Up Trendline, prices may easily go to a new high. Note the Pullback of August 1936 in this weekly chart of Westinghouse Electric. The second, less steep line turned out to be the true Major Bull Trend. Note that the February–April price pattern in 1936 could not be considered a true Double Top Reversal of Primary import because the recession between the two highs was only about 10% of the Top's value (around 122). Figure 64 on page 119 shows on a daily chart the final Top Reversal Formation which "WX" made in 1937.

A large Rectangle base was made on this weekly chart in April, May, and June 1937, but observe the poor volume which accompanied the breakout and rise from that formation — an extremely Bearish indication for the Major Trend. The "measurement" of the Rectangle was carried out by August, but that was all.

As is usually the case, it was impossible to draw a Major Down Trendline which had any forecasting value on this chart. The beautiful straight trendlines which appeared in the 1929–32 Primary Bear Market led many chart students to expect similar developments in every Bear Market, but the fact is that 1929–32 was unique in that respect.

also offer up-to-the-minute lists and quotes on virtually all trading instruments. A list and links to these sites may also be found in Resources (Appendix D) and at edwards-magee.com.

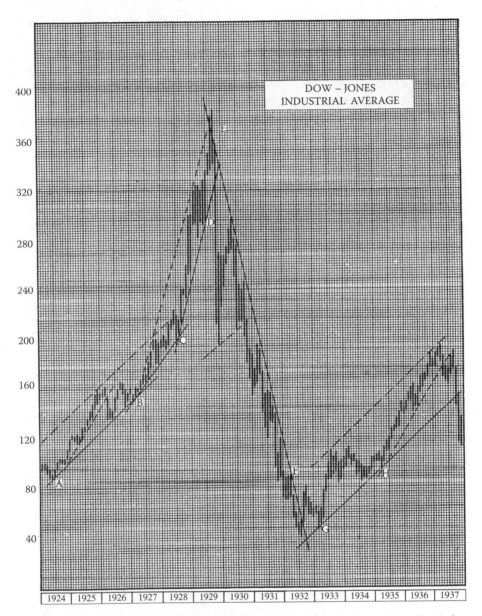

FIGURE 179. The 1929–32 Primary Bear Market was the only one in all stock market records which produced a Straight-Line Major Downtrend. Trace also the Support and Resistance Levels throughout this 14-year history of the Dow Industrials. Each rally in the great Bear Move stopped at or near a previous Bottom level. Each decline stopped near the level of a Congestion in the 1924–29 Bull Market. See also level of 1937 Top. Chart courtesy of Market Research, Inc. (Internet: barchart.com).

As of the turn of the century, the most important of these indexes, joining the Dow, are probably the S&P 500, the S&P 100, and the NASDAQ. In fact these are probably sufficient for economic analysis and forecasting purposes, and certainly good trading vehicles by means of surrogate instruments, options, and futures. Some would include the Russell 2000 in this list. These indexes and averages have been created to fill needs not filled adequately by the Dow–Jones Averages.

With this proliferation of measures of the market and various parts of it a different question arises. That is, the value of the Dow alone in indicating the Broad Market Trend is now questionable. Limited research has been done on this question. It is, however, my opinion that the Broad Market Trend must now be determined by examining the Dow Industrials, the S&P 500, and the NASDAQ Composite.

chapter 15.1

Trading the Averages
in the 21st Century

As I have pointed out in other new chapters and notes in the eighth edition, the ability to trade the Averages instead of individual stocks is a powerful choice offered by modern markets. Magee was of the opinion that the Averages offered technical smoothness often lacking in individual issues. This would seem to be true intuitively. After all, just as a moving average smooths data, the average of a basket of stocks should dampen price volatility. Of course, as Mandelbrot pointed out, in a 10-sigma market storm everything sinks.

Illustrated in this chapter are several detailed cases following Magee's suggestion of Average trading. I attempt to demonstrate here two perspectives: one, the horror of the immediate, that is, what the crash and panic look like as they occur, and two, what the crash and panic look like in retrospect. Of course we all live in the present, except for the great billionaires, who can afford to doze through horrific Bear Markets. Bill Gates' net worth varied by $16B (billion) or $17B in early 2000. This, of course, would put the ordinary investor out of business.

So the ordinary investor, you and I, have to respect the great yawning Bear Market. We must step to the sidelines and let the bear eat the foolish virgins, to borrow a Biblical metaphor.

You will remember that Magee opined that a trendline break of 2% was sufficient to cause liquidation of longs when analyzing the Averages. In the accompanying figures, this hypothesis is examined.

EN9: In respect to the breaking of trendlines (by 2% or 5%) I should note that the breaking of a trendline is as much a warning as a signal to act. The break, instead of a change of trend to the reverse, may indicate a change of trend to the sideways – into a reversal or continuation pattern.

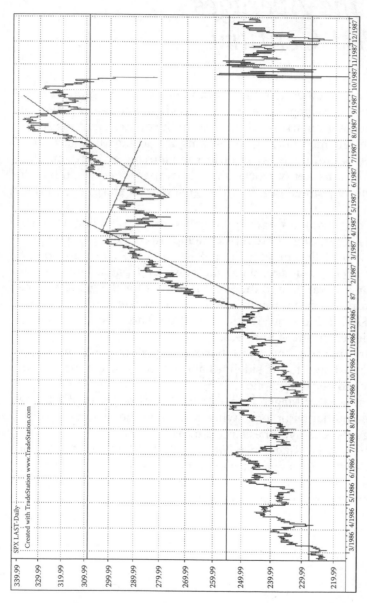

FIGURE 179.1. S&P Reagan Crash. As can be clearly seen this crash sent numerous signals, starting with the breaking of a major trendline by more than 2% in late August. Once this occurs extreme caution and watchfulness must be exercised. The darker and darker complexion of things is brought out by the "smart selling," which shows many "downthrust days" toward the end (October 10–20). The April trendline breaks (by more than 2%) would have ejected the trend trader also to be put back long in June. Observance of the 2–3% trendline-break rule and/or use of Basing Points and progressive stops (Chapters 27 and 28) would have avoided much needless grief. **NOTE: Figures 180–197 have been moved to Appendix C.**

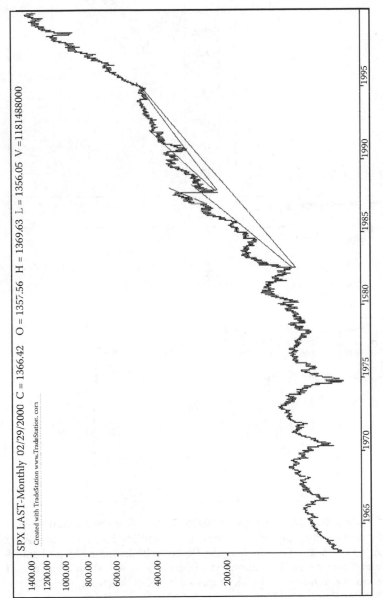

FIGURE 179.2. S&P Long-Term Perspective. Viewed from afar it seems an exercise in futility to attempt to "time the market." One must keep in perspective the crashes in market prices which are timed to coincide with personal and business needs for short-term liquidity; or, in a word, cash. One must also remember the market behavior from 1965–82, as well as the chart of Dow Theory Performance in Chapter 5.1.

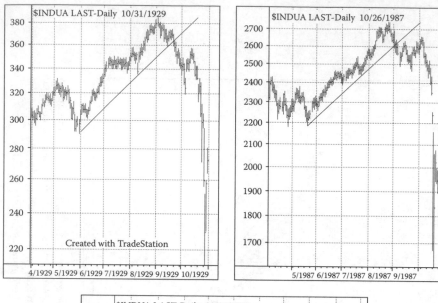

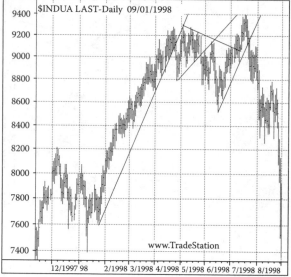

FIGURE 179.3. Three Bull Market Tops, 1929, 1987, 1998. Notice here that in each case the crash occurred after the nearest important trendline had been decisively broken — usually trendlines of approximately 3 months by 2% or more, and sometimes accompanied by reversal formations. All historic tops will show evidence of attempts to resume the trend after a break of this kind. Belief dies hard. Nonetheless, hedging or exiting on these trend breaks proves to be the best strategy over and over again.

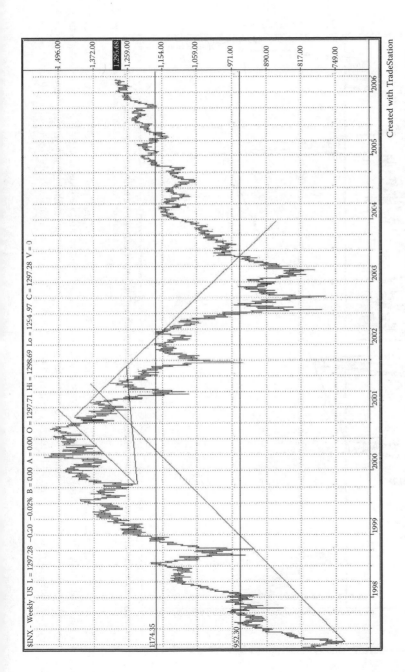

Created with TradeStation

FIGURE 179.3.1. The bull '90s top in the S&P gave much clearer readings than the Dow top, the broken trendlines being paramount. But while the Dow flirted with the emotions of bulls who *wanted to believe* in Dow 36,000 the S&P broke its trendlines and went south for the winter. Potentially a very long winter. This might have started off as a rounding top and then became a complex-complex top, and you can even see traces of Head-and-Shoulders top in it. It is the editor's opinion that we may never see such unruly tops again in this generation. The pent up greed and lust and naiveté as even the bootblacks (they still have those don't they?) rushed to get the latest tulip bulbs. Tulips are like century plants. They only bloom once each hundred years. A little old lady with a ruler could have saved her portfolio here. All it takes is not believing the hype (Dow 36,000 indeed!) and making an unemotional analysis and honoring the stops.

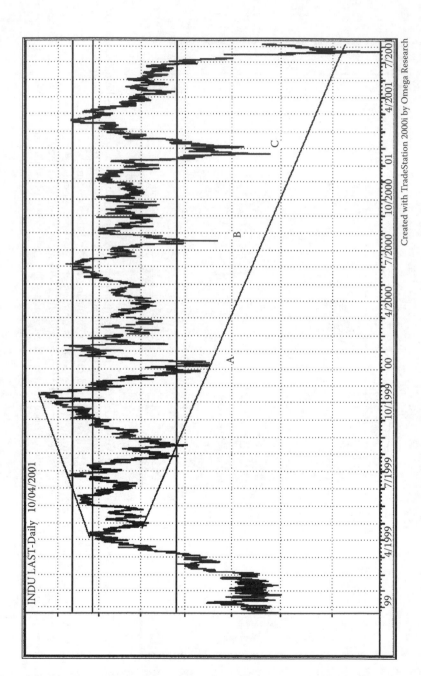

Created with TradeStation 2000i by Omega Research

FIGURE 179.3.2. Dow Jones Industrials 1999-2000. Illustrating that patterns can be found within patterns, the Dow made a broadening top which resolved into a diamond, then a couple of triangles. (Not drawn here.) All of which could be looked at as a gnarly messy rectangle. It is not so important to identify triangles in this situation as to recognize the general nature of the market — sideways to down. In general one of the more unruly situations in market history, as befitted the incredible (truly incredible, as in unbelievable) bull market it ended.

chapter sixteen

Technical Analysis of Commodity Charts

(EN9: Following the practice of allowing the reader to discriminate between the work of Edwards and Magee and that of the Editor, a chapter on commodity trading, Chapter 16.1, has been added to the 9th Edition. See same.)

A little thought suggests that the variously interesting and significant patterns which we have examined in the foregoing chapters on stock charts should logically appear as well in the charts of any other equities and commodities that are freely, constantly, and actively bought and sold on organized public exchanges. And this, in general, is true. The price trends of anything where market value is determined solely (or for all practical purposes within very wide limits) by the free interplay of supply and demand will, when graphically projected, show the same pictorial phenomena of rise and fall, accumulation and distribution, congestion, consolidation, and reversal that we have seen in stock market trends. Speculative aims and speculators' psychology are the same whether the goods dealt in be corporate shares or contracts for the future delivery of cotton bales.

It should be possible in theory, therefore, to apply our principles of technical analysis to any of the active commodity futures (wheat, corn, oats, cotton, cocoa, hides, eggs, etc.) for which accurate daily price and volume data are published. It should be, that is, if proper allowance is made for the intrinsic differences between commodity futures contracts and stocks and bonds.

In previous editions of this book *(EN9: Up to the 8th)*, traders who cast longing eyes on the big, quick profits apparently available in wheat, for example, were warned that commodity charts were "of very little help," as of 1947.

It was pointed out that successful technical analysis of commodity futures charts had been possible up to about 1941 or 1942. But that the domination of these markets thereafter by government regulations, loans, and purchases completely subject to the changing (and often conflicting) policies and acts of the several governmental agencies concerned with grains and other commodities had seriously distorted the normal evaluative machinery of the market. At that time, radical reversals of trend could and did happen overnight without any warning so far as the action of the market could show. The ordinary and orderly fluctuations in supply–demand balance, which create significant definite patterns for the technician to read, did not exist. And while fortunes were made (and lost) in wheat, corn, and cotton futures during the World War II period, it is safe to say they were not made from the charts.

However, during the past 5 or 6 years the application of technical methods to commodity trading has been reexamined. Under 1956 conditions, it appears that charts can be a most valuable tool for the commodity trader. The effects of present government regulation have apparently resulted in "more orderly" markets without destroying their evaluative function. And allowing for the various essential differences between commodities and stocks, the basic technical methods can be applied.

It may be in order here to discuss briefly some of the intrinsic differences between commodity futures and stocks referred to above, and some of the special traits of commodity charts. To begin with, the most important difference is that the contracts for future delivery, which are the stock-in-trade of the commodity exchange, have a limited life. For example, the October cotton contract for any given year has a trading life of about 18 months. It comes "on the board" as a "new issue," is traded with volume increasing more or less steadily during that period, and then vanishes. Theoretically, it is a distinct and separate commodity from all other cotton deliveries. Practically, of course, it seldom gets far out of line with such other deliveries as are being bought and sold during the same period, or with the "cash" price of the physical cotton in warehouses. Nevertheless, it has this special quality of a limited independent life, as a consequence of which long-term Support and Resistance Levels have no meaning whatever.

Second, a very large share of the transactions in commodity futures — as much as 80% certainly in normal times — represents commercial hedging rather than speculation. (It is, in fact, entered into to obviate risk, to avoid speculation.) Hence, even near-term Support and Resistance Levels have relatively less potency than with stocks. Also, since hedging is to a considerable degree subject to seasonal factors, there are definite seasonal influences on the commodity price trends which the commodity speculator must keep in mind, even if only to weigh the meaning of their apparent absence at any given period.

A third difference is in the matter of volume. The interpretation of volume with respect to trading in stocks is relatively simple. But it is greatly complicated in commodities by the fact that there is, in theory, no limit to the number of contracts for a certain future delivery which may be sold in advance of the delivery date. In the case of any given stock, the number of shares outstanding is always known. As this is written, there are in the hands of stockholders 13,700,203 common shares of Consolidated Edison, and that quantity has not varied for many years nor is it likely to change for several years to come. Every transaction in Consolidated Edison involves an actual transfer of one or more of those existing shares. In the case of commodity future contracts, however — say, September wheat — trading begins long before anyone knows how many bushels of wheat will exist to be delivered that coming September, and the open interest at some time during the life of the contract may exceed the potential supply many times over — and all quite legitimately. *EN9: Appendix C contains some material on the interpretation of futures volume data. As always volume data is a supplementary indicator to price. No one makes a profit on it.*

One more important difference may be mentioned. Certain kinds of news — news about weather, drought, floods, etc., that affect the growing crop, if we are dealing with an agricultural commodity — can change the trend of the futures market immediately and drastically and are not foreseeable given the present stage of our weather knowledge. Analogous developments in the stock market are extremely rare. *EN: Except for acts of God and Alan Greenspan.*

Under what might be called normal market conditions, those chart patterns which reflect trend changes in most simple and logical fashion work just as well with commodities as with stocks. Among these we would list Head-and-Shoulders formations, Rounding Tops and Bottoms, and basic trendlines. Trendlines, in fact, are somewhat better defined and more useful in commodities than in stocks. Other types of chart formations which are associated with stocks with short-term trading or with group distribution and accumulation, such as the Triangles, Rectangles, Flags, etc., appear less frequently in commodities and are far less reliable as to either direction or extent of the ensuing move. Support and Resistance Levels, as we have already noted, are less potent in commodities than in stocks; sometimes they seem to work to perfection, but just as often they don't. For similar reasons, gaps have relatively less technical significance.

It is not the purpose of this book to explain the operation of commodity futures markets, nor to offer instruction to those who wish to trade therein. This brief chapter is included only as a starter for readers who may want to pursue the study further. They should be advised that successful speculation in commodities requires far more specialized knowledge, demands more constant daily and hourly attention. The ordinary individual can hope to attain a fair degree of success in investing in securities by devoting only his spare moments to his charts, but he might better shun commodity speculation entirely unless he is prepared to make a career of it.

EN: The Editor has been, during his checkered career, a registered Commodity Trading Advisor. At the beginning of that career, I discussed these subjects with Magee and received essentially the above comments which are here reproduced from the fifth edition. Subsequently, I observed among my associates and partners, and on my own, that futures are eminently tradable with the adaptation of techniques and methods described in this book. It is also true, as Magee says, that futures trading is so different in tempo, leverage, and character that the novice risks life, limb, and capital in entering the area unescorted. Resource references are essential reading but the beginner is urged to educate himself before beginning trading with extensive study and paper trading.

Note that Figures 180-197 as well as Chapter 16 from the 7th edition are now found in Appendix C.

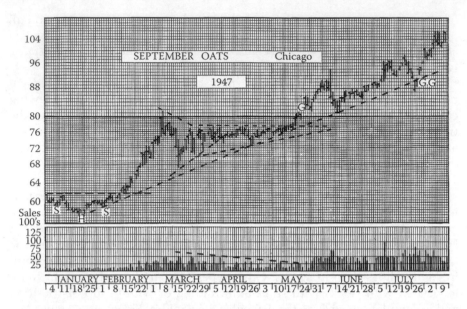

FIGURE 179.4. (Fig. 180, 5th edition). Oats. Oats, for obvious reasons, traced more "normal" patterns than Wheat during the 1940s. This chart contains an H & S bottom, a Symmetrical Triangle which merged into the Ascending form, a gap through a former top level, and an interesting trendline. The Island shake-out through the trendline was an extremely deceptive development.

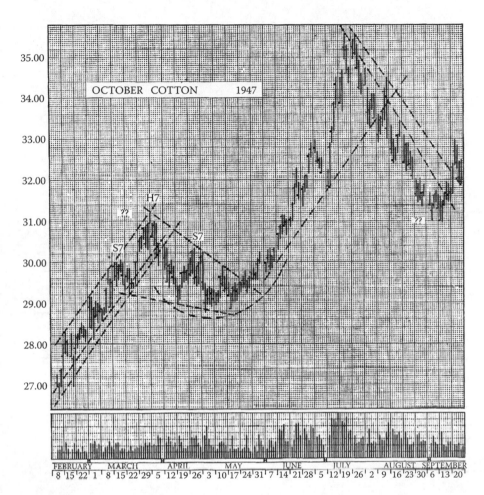

FIGURE 179.5. (Fig. 181, 5th edition). Cotton. In contrast with the grains, the technical action of the Cotton futures markets has been fairly consistent with normal supply–demand functioning ever since prices rose well above government support levels. In this daily chart of the 1947 October delivery (New York Cotton Exchange), the reader will find a variety of familiar technical formations, including critical trendlines, a Head-and-Shoulders top that was never completed (no breakout), and Support–Resistance phenomena much the same as appear in stock charts. Double trendlines are not at all unusual in Cotton charts.

chapter 16.1

Technical Analysis of Commodity Charts, Part 2

A 21st Century Perspective

In the search for the Philosopher's Stone more sweat and money have been put into the area of commodities and futures than were ever expended in the securities arena. There is a simple reason for this. Great fortunes are made and lost with much greater rapidity in the futures area than in securities. Of all the great dramatic moments in stock market history few are so memorable as the great Hunt silver market, or Soros facing off against the Bank of England, or of gold soaring to $1000 an ounce. And the saga continues in 2005. $50 oil? $60? $70? $100? And the effects, economic and psychological! In dimly lit garrets and brightly lit computer rooms thousands of researchers concoct systems to trade these markets — corn, soybeans, silver, copper...

Rocket Scientists

At times individual traders and groups of traders have plundered (harvested?) these markets for fairy tale profits. I know whereof I speak, having been a principal in California's first licensed commodity trading advisor which was founded by the NASA rocket scientist R.T. Wieckowicz. During the 1970s as the stock markets ground futilely around the 1000 level on the Dow the futures markets returned yearly gains in the 100% range. Consistently. For years. Those were the years of the California systems traders and the beginning of computerized trading. From the primeval slime of NASA the rocket scientists emerged to create a renaissance in market technology. At the time it seemed clear that science and genius had at last conquered the markets and that clients would come buzzing from the world over like bees to a honey pot and that the rivers of profits would last forever. They did last for some time, and then the markets changed. Mechanical systems which cut through the markets like a reaper in a wheat field in bull markets grind up capital like sausage in sideways markets. Science and genius were revealed as the happy combination of man, moment, system, and market.

Turtles?

During the 1980s from the sea came crawling the Turtles. Progeny of the protean trading wizard, Richard Dennis, the Turtles again harvested outsize profits from the markets, running it is said in the 80% yearly range. The so-called Turtles got their name from a comment that Dennis is reported to have made that traders were made not born and he was going to raise traders like turtles. Additional reading about the Turtles is available in Jack Schwager's fascinating book and books, *Market Wizards*, et al. Schwager's books are required reading for aspiring traders. And, the trading manual of the Turtles will be found in Appendix E of this ninth edition. This workbook, written by Curtis Faith, an original Turtle, contains virtually all of the elements necessary in a trader's systems and procedures manual. The manual was prepared according to the training Dennis gave his Turtles. Serious traders do not operate without some such document. Certainly all of the serious traders I have known (a considerable number) have had fully developed manuals like the Turtle workbook. I have attached the Turtle workbook as an appendix rather than others in my possession because it is publicly available at originalturtles.org and because it is beautifully articulated.

In the late '90s the Turtles were made into turtle soup in the futures markets as the majority of systems traders wound up as hamburger meat. *Is there a moral? Yes. The markets giveth and the markets taketh away. Science and genius are again revealed to be the happy combination of man, method, moment, and market.*

The Turtle system is basically an adaptation of Richard Donchian's channel breakout system. In the Donchian system the trader goes long when the 20 day high is broken and sells and goes short when the 20 day low is broken. In the 1970s Dunn and Hargitt evaluated a number of mechanical trading systems and found that Donchian's system was superior to the others evaluated at that time. Will Donchian's system still work? Yes, in broadly trending markets. Will the Turtle system still work? Yes, in broadly trending markets. And, like virtually all mechanical systems they don't know whether they are in a broadly trending market or not. They are blind. All they see are ones and zeros. The addition to these systems of prudently applied chart analysis will immeasurably improve their performance and risk characteristics.

The Application of Edwards and Magee's Methods to 21st Century Futures Markets

During my career as a Commodity Trading Advisor I have known a number of successful traders and advisors who used what I would describe as Magee type chart analysis to make their trades. Often there were other elements input into their decision making process, but manual charting was a key factor in their operations. Some of these traders used simple trendline analysis with price or volume filters and some used a combination of trendlines and support and resistance. *All were trend followers.*

Having looked at the futures markets with some attention over the past several years it seems to me that there is no reason why chart analysis should not work as well now as it has always worked. Essentially the questions raised by securities trading are the same as those presented by futures trading in the analysis of a chart. Is there a trend? Where are support and resistance? Is there a breakout? Are there waves and wavelets? How do you enter and how do you exit?

The great bug-a-boo of securities traders coming to the futures trading is the speed of the game. Like college football players stepping up to the NFL there is a brutal learning curve and rookies are the most likely to get killed. I am not going to make any effort here to present a primer for new futures traders. Rather I will look at some futures charts at the end of this chapter in order to show the journeyman that chart analysis can be used as a decision making method in these dramatic markets. Again, chart analysis has the weakness (or strength) of being a qualitative process. It will not make decisions for the average trader, as a mechanical system will.

On the other hand a breakout is a breakout. A gap is a gap, leaving aside the question of limit move gaps for the moment. A trend is a trend. And here is the great advantage that a firm grasp of charting methods can give the practitioner. *It can give him the perspective to recognize the essential nature of the market at hand and choose to wait or to enter.* Mechanical methods not having the qualitative discrimination of an experienced chartist will blindly take every trade until they are out of money. The experienced chart analyst can sit back and say, this market has not yet made a bottom and the time to begin trading it long has not yet come. Or, he can recognize the essential differences between a trading and a trending market and adjust his tactics accordingly.

As Magee noted in Chapter 16:

> Under what might be called normal market conditions, those chart patterns which reflect trend changes in most simple and logical fashion work just as well with commodities as with stocks. Among these we would list Head-and-Shoulders formations, Rounding Tops and Bottoms, and basic trendlines. Trendlines, in fact, are somewhat better defined and more useful in commodities than in stocks. Other types of chart formations which are associated with stocks with short-term trading or with group distribution and accumulation, such as the Triangles, Rectangles, Flags, etc., appear less frequently in commodities and are far less reliable as to either direction or extent of the ensuing move. Support and Resistance Levels, as we have already noted, are less potent in commodities than in stocks; sometimes they seem to work to perfection, but just as often they don't. For similar reasons, gaps have relatively less technical significance.

These words remain true today, as do virtually all the principles enunciated in this book by Edwards and Magee and myself. In fact most futures charts if given to an analyst without issue identification and dates would not be identifiable as commodity charts. Of course when limit moves appear the difference slaps one in the face. And on this point I might differ from Magee slightly as regards gaps. Obviously limit move gaps have breath taking significance. But all in all it seems to me that gaps often say the same thing to futures analysts that they say to stock analysts.

Another mathematical reason might be adduced for the practicality of using simple chart analysis to trade futures. That is the tautalogical nature of the method. A trend is a trend, and a trendline is a trendline. If you enter a suspected trend (setting a protective stop at a technically analyzed place) and follow the trend using Basing Points or observing the trendline and exiting on a break and reversal there will be no difference from doing the same with a stock. Well, some difference. Due to the leverage you will be required to be hyper aware of risk. In futures the penalty for holding a position through "a normal reaction" can be extremely harsh. That is why stops are so important.

Stops

Some traders set their stops using money management rules rather than technically identified points. I believe it is always better to find the technical point using a basing point, or support and resistance. To me it makes better sense to adjust position size to control risk as I described in Chapter 26. And the use of money management stops has been very successful for many traders. *If some logical and disciplined method of setting and observing stops is not installed the trader is assured of failure.*

A money management stop is, simply enough, a stop calculated by deciding to risk 2% (or 3 or 4 or x%) of capital on a trade. For example, William O'Neil says that when a stock trader enters a position he should set a stop 8% under his entry price. This is a little crude, and not strictly speaking a money management stop, but is better than no risk calculation at all. In a stricter sense, if we said that we wanted to limit the risk of the trade to 3% of capital we would use the 8% rule to set the stop and the Scott Procedure in Chapter 26 to determine the number of shares or contracts. The Turtle system in Appendix E contains similar procedures. Numerous studies have proven that the size of the risk per trade — 1%, 2%, 3% — is directly correlated to equity volatility.

A Variety of Methods

As noted above a competent chart analyst may, in my opinion (and in Magee's opinion), perform profitably in the futures markets. There are other questions, of course, namely of character, temperament, intelligence, judgment, etc…, Let us leave those questions to Dr. Elder and confine ourselves to the method question. Chart analysts proved their abilities in the futures markets long before computers existed. In fact long before in the case of Japanese rice traders, enlightening their efforts with candlesticks in the 18th century.

In the 1970s I saw point and figure chartists enjoy great success at Dean Witter and Merrill Lynch and other major firms in futures. I have seen least squares curve fitters, moving average calculators and abstruse statistical analysts all enjoy profitable outings in commodities. Not to speak of the Turtles who, using naturalistic high low systems, harvested good profits in the markets. As the saying goes, gateless is the gate and many are the ways to the great Dow. Although I have enjoyed great success myself using mechanical number-driven systems over the years I have become more and more attracted to "natural" systems. Chart analysis is essentially natural, as is the Turtle system. The Dow Theory is a natural system. In a natural system no mathematical algorithm comes between the analyst and the data. The essential, more, quintessential, weakness of all number-driven systems is their blindness. They do not have the ability to discriminate between the forest and the trees. The experienced human chartist can *see* (and hear) the changing rhythms of the market and respond to them, responding to factors too subtle (and even subconscious) to program. But even natural systems, like the Turtle systems, can fall into this trap. When the markets learn that a lot of capital is waiting just above the 20 day high they will set a trap for it. For "markets" you may read "they." If you apply the knowledge of this book to such situations you may avoid the trap.

Everything You Need to Know as a Chart Analyst Trading Futures

Jack be nimble. Jack be quick. Jack jump over the Candlestick. Yes, it is true, as the leverage is 10 times greater the speed is 10 times faster. I have illustrated in Figure 179.5.3 the combination of a very tight trendline with a run day which it seems to me is a good current (21st century) combination. Otherwise the same qualities which make a good security trader make a good futures trader once the great leap to leveraged quick-fire markets is made. If you have been successful trading stocks you will probably be successful trading futures. And you probably should practice on stocks while studying futures. A sobering fact which I often recount to my graduate students is that Richard Wyckoff worked in the securities business for 8 years before making his first investment. He studied the markets an additional 6 years before *trading*.

The Magee methodology will serve as a valuable cornerstone of your futures operations, and you must never cease studying. Mechanical systems have their attractions, especially when seasoned with experienced chart analysis. And no method will survive unless practiced with diligence, persistence, judgment, and patience. Time and again you will hear famous traders say, when asked the secret of their success, "discipline." What they mean by discipline is their ability to measure and contain the risk, set a stop based on technical or money management procedures and *then honor the stop*.

The most important lesson the futures trader has to learn from Edwards and Magee is the ability to see the character of the market, trading or trending, and then *to adjust his tactics accordingly*.

The Return of the Great Markets of the '70s

In the next great bull market in commodities, which may be about to occur as this book goes to press in 2006 (cf. following charts this chapter), these methods and systems derived from them will once again reap windfall profits.

I have attempted in this ninth edition of this classic book to show the book's usefulness to the intelligent futures trader. Simple classical chart analysis alone can be successful in the futures markets in the hands of an experienced competent analyst. Natural mechanical systems such as the Turtle system have been effective and will be again, perhaps with some tweaking (such as imposing a chart analysis super-structure). Wave analysis methods such as the Basing Points procedure of Chapter 28 can be used. Even number driven systems, such as moving averages, can be successful especially if combined with chart analysis.

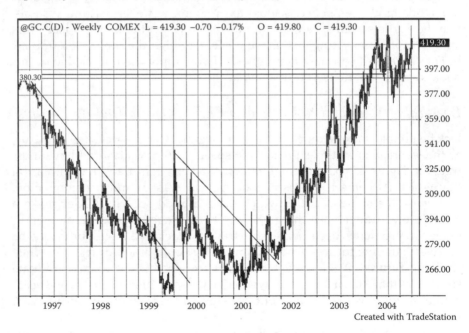

FIGURE 179.5.1. A Rounding Bottom in Gold 1997-2004. "These patterns, when they occur *after an extensive decline*, are of outstanding importance, for they nearly always denote a change in Primary Trend and an extensive advance yet to come. That advance, however, seldom carries in a "skyrocket" effect which completes the entire Major Move in a few weeks. On the contrary, the uptrend that follows the completion of the pattern itself is apt to be slow and subject to frequent interruptions, tiring out the impatient trader, but yielding eventually a substantial profit." So said Robert Edwards in remarking on Rounding Bottoms in stock charts. As may be seen here this Rounding Bottom consists of a downtrend, a false signal off the Double Bottom (upon which a pretty penny might have been made by the agile trader), and a handsome uptrend. And it all looks like a huge Rounding Bottom.

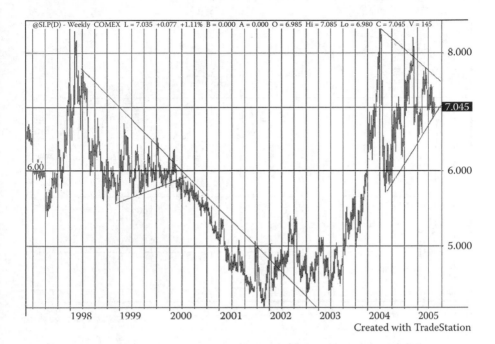

@SI.P(D) - Weekly COMEX L = 7.035 +0.077 +1.11% B = 0.000 A = 0.000 O = 6.985 Hi = 7.085 Lo = 6.980 C = 7.045 V = 145

Created with TradeStation

FIGURE 179.5.2.   A Rounding Bottom in Silver 1998-2005. The apparent Rounding Bottom in silver, combined with the same pattern in gold, would seem to cast a pall over the economic situation for some time to come in 2005. This coincides with the apparent long-term patterns setting up in the securities markets. If the best which can be hoped for in securities is a 1965-1982 kind of widely whipping market commodities may react as they did in the 1970s. With tidal wave markets. These markets can be traded by the well capitalized chart analyst who is well seasoned. Tyros of course will lose money learning the game whatever markets they trade. Their chances will be immeasurably improved by applying the techniques taught in this book. In addition to the technical pattern pictured here there is every reason to suspect that a large fundamental shortage of silver bullion exists and will worsen. Ted Butler, at doomgloom.com, is a long-term silver analyst (and associate of the editor) who anticipates that a new silver blow off is coming. One wonders what Nelson and Bunker Hunt are doing at present. A very cautious investor (like Warren Buffet who is reported to be long $1B (billion) silver bullion) may defeat futures silver volatility by buying the bullion.

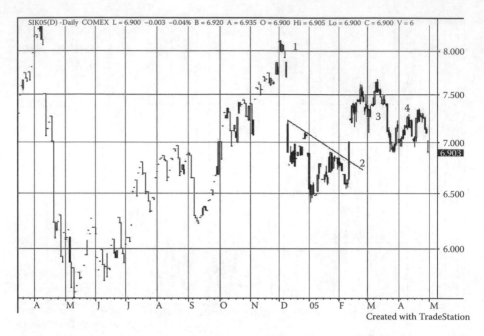

SIK05(D) -Daily COMEX L = 6.900 −0.003 −0.04% B = 6.920 A = 6.935 O = 6.900 Hi = 6.905 Lo = 6.900 C = 6.900 V = 6

Created with TradeStation

FIGURE 179.5.3.   Silver May 2005. While the long-term silver outlook may be bullish, the short term will be very volatile, especially for the thinly capitalized trader. Then short-term tactics must be adopted. The island top here at 1 is a gentle invitation to the trader to take his profits and be gone. Even to short, with a stop just above the high. The run day after 1 adds a note of urgency to the invitation. The gap is punishment for the hard of hearing and a bonus for the quick witted (everybody who survives in futures is either quick witted or extremely well financed). The stop moves down to the top of the gap day, then to the top of the next gap day and for the very apt profits are taken on the next run day down. On the principle of sell weakness, buy weakness. The tight trendline at 2 crossed by the heavy run day is a buy signal with the stop moving to the bottom of the gap at 3 where it is taken out a few days later by the long range day down. The run day at 4 is a short signal with the stop being at the day's high. Is it necessary to say that short-term futures trading can be quite rapid? Or, there is always bullion. Or associated stock plays.

FIGURE 179.5.4. Treasury Bonds. The double pump triple nod head fake is a specialty of futures markets. The fear and greed factor is multiplied by 10, like the leverage. But here in September 2004 Bonds we can see how simple chart analysis can serve the trader. The downtrend from March (1) is completely manageable with a simple trendline and trend analysis. The end of the downtrend in May is marked by two strong run days. At any rate the stop would have been at May 1st, using a Basing Point kind of analysis. If we were going to trade it long here this would have been traded for a scalp (because we don't know whether there is a bottom or not). The break of the trendline at 2 is an engraved invitation to get long and the trendline at 3 keeps us long until broken by the signal day at the end of July. Which would put us short again, a two-day trade as the signal day on the trendline at 4 puts us long again. Obviously we are using very tight, very short trendlines and long range days (or run days) as signals. The use of the run day as a signal, combined with other indicators, is common in my experience among traders.

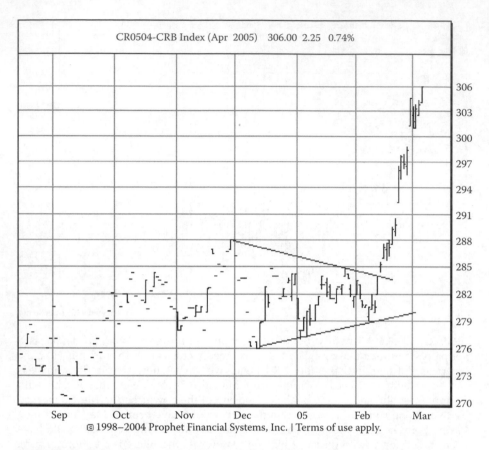

FIGURE 179.5.5. Commodity Research Bureau Index. April 2005 Futures. Just as triangles often work in securities they often work in futures. Breakaway gap. Second breakaway gap. Runaway gap. Second runaway gap. The formation before the second runaway gap is somewhat quizzical — it might be considered a flag, but it has the same effect, and depending on the trader's operating methods the stop would be just under the gap/runday anyway. It will not take much study for the reader to see that the principles of chart analysis used in this entire book are validated here. The main difference is in the setting of stops, and in fact, the same stop methods may be used if the trader is sufficiently well financed.

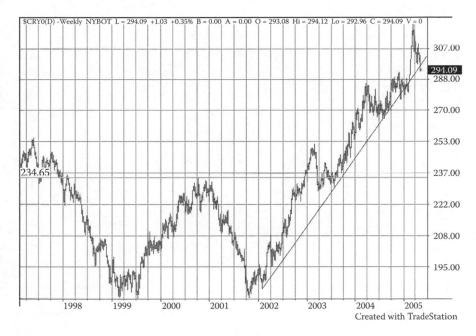

FIGURE 179.5.6.   Commodity Research Bureau. Long-term view. It does not take much analysis of this 10 year CRB chart to see a huge double bottom, and to consider its implications. If China and India are going to compete with us for natural resources we could see an entirely new economic paradigm, if the reader will excuse the term. Clearly there is a bull market in commodities. In Chapter 42, Pragmatic Portfolio Management, it is suggested that capital should flow to markets that are moving, rather than remaining committed to markets which are mired in mulish trends. Furthermore it is suggested in that chapter that a good natural hedge is to go long the uptrend of an index and short the components of it which are in downtrends. The CRB is somewhat thin but might lend itself to this strategy.

chapter seventeen

A Summary and Some Concluding Comments

We began our study of technical stock chart analysis in Chapter 1 with a discussion of the *philosophy* underlying the technical approach to the problems of trading and investing. We could ask that the reader turn back now and review those few pages to recapture a perspective on the subject which must have been dimmed by the many pages of more or less arduous reading that have intervened.

It is easy, in a detailed study of the many and fascinating phenomena which stock charts exhibit, to lose sight of the fact that they are only the rather imperfect instruments by which we hope to gauge the relative strength of supply and demand, which, in turn, exclusively determines what way, how fast, and how far a stock will go.

Remember that, in this work, it doesn't matter what creates the supply and the demand. The fact of their existence and the balance between them are all that count. No man, no organization (and we mean this *verbatim et literatim*) can hope to know and accurately appraise the infinity of factual data, mass moods, individual necessities, hopes, fears, estimates, and guesses which, with the subtle alterations ever proceeding in the general economic framework, combine to generate supply and demand. But the summation of all these factors is reflected virtually instantaneously in the market.

The technical analyst's task, then, is to interpret the action of the market itself — to read the flux in supply and demand mirrored therein. For this task, charts are the most satisfactory tools thus far devised. Lest you become enrapt, however, with the mechanics of the chart — the minutiae of daily fluctuations — ask yourself constantly, "What does this action really mean in terms of supply and demand?"

Judgment is required, and perspective, and a constant reversion to first principles. A chart, as we have said and should never forget, is not a perfect tool; it is not a robot; it does not give all the answers quickly, easily, and positively, in terms that anyone can read and translate at once into certain profit.

We have examined and tested exhaustively many technical theories, systems, indexes, and devices which have not been discussed in this book, chiefly because they tend to short-circuit judgment, to see the impossible by a purely mechanical approach to what is far from a purely mechanical problem. The methods of chart analysis that have been presented are those which have proved most useful, because they are relatively simple and, for the most part, easily rationalized; because they stick closely to first principles; because they are of a nature that does not lead us to expect too much of them; because they supplement each other and work well together.

Let us review these methods briefly. They fall roughly into four categories.

1. The Area Patterns or formations of price fluctuation which, with their concomitant volume, indicate an important change in the supply–demand balance. They can signify Consolidation, a recuperation or gathering of strength for renewed drive in the *same direction* as the trend which preceded them. Or they can indicate Reversal, the playing out of the force formerly prevailing, and the victory of the opposing force, resulting in a new drive in the *reverse direction*. In either case, they may be described as periods during which energy is brewed or pressure built up to propel prices in a move (up or down) which can be turned to profit. Some of them provide an indication as to how far their pressure will push prices. These chart formations, together with volume, furnish the technician with most of his "get in" and many of his "get out" signals.

    Volume, which has not been discussed in this book as a feature apart from price action, and which cannot, in fact, be utilized as a technical guide by itself, deserves some further comment. Remember that it is *relative*, that it tends to naturally run higher near the top of a Bull Market than near the bottom of a Bear Market. Volume "follows the trend," i.e., it increases on rallies and decreases on reactions in an overall uptrend, and vice versa. But use this rule judiciously; do not place too much dependence on the showing of a few days, and bear in mind that even in a Bear Market (except during Panic Moves), there is always a slight tendency for activity to pick up on rises. ("Prices can fall of their own weight, but it takes buying to put them up.")

    A notable increase in activity, as compared with previous days or weeks, may signify either the beginning (breakout) or the end (climax) of a move, temporary or final. (More rarely, it may signify a "shakeout.") Its meaning, in any given case, can be determined by its relation to the price pattern.

2. Trend and trendline studies supplement Area Patterns as a means of determining the general direction in which prices are moving and of detecting changes in direction. Although lacking, in many cases, the nice definition of Area Formations, they may frequently be used for "get in" and "get out" purposes in short-term trading, and they provide a defense against premature relinquishment of profitable long-term positions.

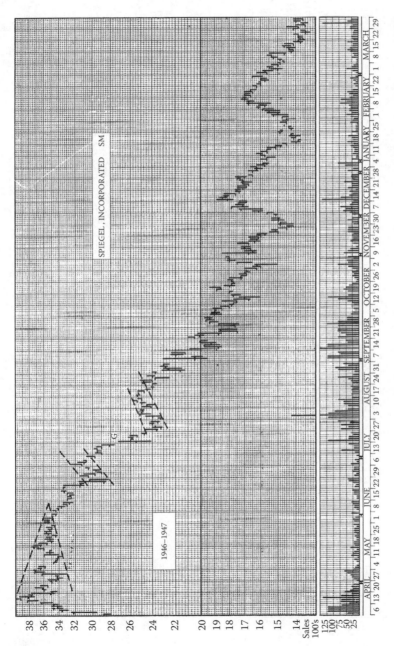

FIGURE 198. Spiegel's Bear Market started in April 1946 from a Symmetrical Triangle which changed into a Descending Triangle. Note the Pullback in June, and two Flags. This history is carried on in Figure 199.

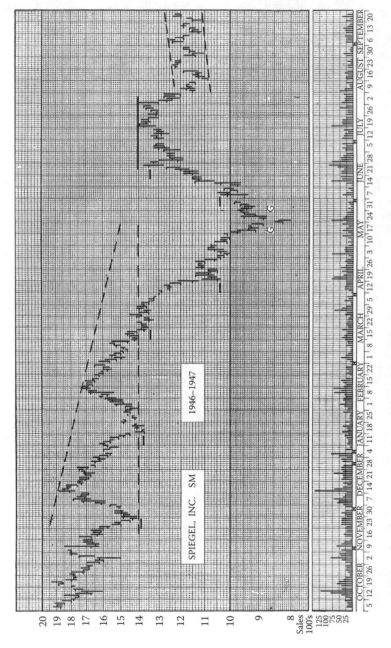

FIGURE 199. Overlapping Figure 198, this chart shows the move which ensued from the wide Descending Triangle of early 1947, culminating in a Reversal Day on May 19. Note various Minor and Intermediate Resistance Levels.

3. Support and Resistance Levels are created by the previous trading and investment commitments of others. They may serve to indicate where it should pay to take a position, but their more important technical function is to show where a move is likely to slow down or end, and at what level it should encounter a sudden and important increase in supply or demand.

   Before entering a trade, look both to the pattern of origin for an indication of the power behind the move, and to the history of Support–Resistance for an indication as to whether it can proceed without difficulty for a profitable distance. Support–Resistance studies are especially useful in providing "cash-in" or "switch" signals.

4. Broad market background, including the Dow Theory, should not be scorned. This time-tested device designates the (presumed) prevailing Major Trend of the market. Its signals are "late," but, with all its faults (and one of these is the greatly augmented following it has acquired in recent years, resulting in a considerable artificial stimulation of activity at certain periods), it is still an invaluable adjunct to the technical trader's Toolkit.

The general characteristics of the various stages in the stock market's great Primary Bull and Bear cycles, which were discussed in our Dow Theory chapters, should never be lost to view. This brings us back to the idea of *perspective*, which we emphasized as essential to successful technical analysis at the beginning of our summary. That stock which does not, to some degree, follow the Major Trend of the market as a whole is an extraordinary exception. More money has been lost by buying perfectly good stocks in the later and most exciting phases of a Bull Market, and then selling them, perhaps from necessity, in the discouraging conditions prevailing in a Bear Market, than from all other causes combined!

So keep your perspective on the broad market picture. The basic economic tide is one of the most important elements in the supply–demand equation for each individual stock. It may pay to buck "the public," but it does not ever pay to buck the real underlying trend.

Major Bull and Bear Markets have recurred in fairly regular patterns throughout all recorded economic history, and there is no reason to suppose that they will not continue to recur for as long as our present system exists. It is well to keep in mind that caution is in order whenever stock prices are at historically high levels, and that purchases will usually work out well eventually when they are at historically low levels.

If you make known your interest in your charts, you will be told that the chart analyst (like the Dow theorist) is always late — that he buys after prices have already started up, maybe not until long after the "smart money" has completed its accumulation, and that he sells after the trend has unmistakably turned down. Partly true, as you have no doubt already discovered for yourself. But the secret of success lies not in buying at the very lowest possible price and selling at the absolute top. It is in the *avoidance of large losses*. (Small losses you will have to take, and as quickly as possible as warranted by the situation.)

One of the most successful "operators" Wall Street has ever seen, a multimillionaire and a nationally respected citizen today, is reputed to have said that never in his entire career had he succeeded in buying within 5 points of the bottom or selling within 5 points of the top! *EN: Bernard Baruch, if I am not mistaken. And for perspective, the 5 points mentioned constituted roughly 10% of the market at that time.*

Before we leave this treatise on theory and proceed to the more practical matters of application and market tactics which are the province of the second part of this book, the reader will, we hope, forgive one more admonition. There is nothing in the science of technical analysis that requires one always to have a position in the market. There is nothing that dictates that something must happen every day. There are periods — sometimes long months — when the conservative trader's best policy is to stay out entirely. And there is nothing in technical analysis to compel the market to go ahead and complete (in a few days) a move that the charts have foretold; it will take its own good time. Patience is as much a virtue in stock trading as in any other human activity.

chapter 17.1

Technical Analysis and Technology in the 21st Century: The Computer and the Internet, Tools of the Investment/ Information Revolution

The purpose of this chapter is to put computer and information technology into proper context and perspective for chart-oriented technical analysts.

In John Magee's time, in his office in Springfield, MA, there was a chart room — a room filled with all-age chartists from teenagers to senior citizens. These people spent all their time keeping charts and assisting Magee in interpretation. These were wonderful and intelligent people who developed marvelous insights into the stocks they charted. They created the manual charts which adorn this book.

Today that room and all those technicians have been replaced by a beige (sometimes lime) box which sits crowded on our desktops and which is often worshipped as a fount of insight and wisdom: "Computer, analyze my stocks."

Unfortunately the computer does not have the discrimination and pattern recognition ability of the people in that chart room. Undeterred by this weakness in computer technology, traders and investors have poured incalculable money and effort into computer-aided research attempting to discover the keys to market success. More money has been spent in this effort than was ever put into the search for the philosopher's stone. Much of it was wasted, but it has not all been spent in vain. In some areas it has been quite productive. But no fail-safe algorithm has, in spite of all this effort, been found for investment success, and certainly not for stock trading. The research *has* demonstrated that even the algorithm of "buy low sell high" has fatal flaws in it.

In order to fully understand the importance of the computer, the reader should appreciate some basic differences in participants' approach to the markets. Or, we might say, schools of analysts/investors. We will not bother with fundamental analysts here, as they are of a different religious persuasion. Chart analysts, or we could say, Magee-type technical analysts, pretty much confine their analysis of the market to the interpretation of bar charts. (This does not mean that their minds must be closed to other inputs. On the contrary — anything which works.) Another chart analyst school uses point and figure charts, and another candlestick charts. Another breed of technical analysts takes basic market data, price and volume, and uses them as the input to statistical routines which calculate everything from moving averages to mystically designated indicators like %R or Bollinger Bands (cf. Appendix C). These are called statistical or number-driven technical analysts. All these analysts, or what have you, attempt to invest or trade stocks and other financial instruments (not including options) using some form of what is called technical analysis — that is they all take, as input to their analysis, hard data, data which people cannot lie about, misrepresent, and manipulate, unlike the data which are input to fundamental analysis (earnings, cash flow, sales, etc.).

Using number-driven or, if you will, statistical technical analysis, these latter schools attempt, just as chart analysts do, to predict market trends and trading opportunities. This can be more than a little difficult since the stock and bond markets are behavioral markets. That is, the stock markets are driven by human emotion, as perhaps the most important of many variables influencing price. And human emotion and behavior, its manic and its depressive elements, have not yet been quantified. But some chart analysts believe that they can recognize it when they see it on the charts.

In another area, the computer has yielded much more dramatic and profitable results. But that is in a model-driven market, namely the options markets. Quantitative analysts, those who investigate and trade the options markets, are a breed apart from technical analysts. In an interesting irony, emotion-driven markets, the stock markets, are used as the basis for derivatives, or options whose price is determined largely by the operation of algorithms called models. Quantitative analysts believe, as does this editor, that the options markets can be successfully gamed through quantitative analysis. Results of skilled practitioners indicate this belief is accurate.

Alas, life is not so simple for the simple stock trader. Stock prices having nothing to do with mathematics, except for being expressed as natural numbers, are not susceptible to easy prediction as to their future direction. Not even with Magee chart analysis or any other form of analysis — technical, fundamental, or psychic. (From a theoretical point of view each trade made based on a chart analysis should be looked at as an experiment made to confirm a probability. The experiment is ended quickly if the trend does not develop.) The fact that chart analysis is not mechanizable is important. It is one reason chart analysis continues to be effective in the hands of a skilled practitioner. Not being susceptible to mechanization, counter-strategies cannot be brought against it, except in situations whose meaning is obvious to everyone, for instance, a large important Support or Resistance Level or a glaringly obvious chart formation. These days everyone looks at charts to trade even if they don't believe in their use. In these obvious cases some market participants will attempt to push prices through these levels in order to profit from volatility and confusion. Indeed, human nature has not changed much since Jay Gould and Big Jim Fisk.

When these manipulations of price occur, they create false signals — bull and bear traps. Interestingly, the failure of these signals may constitute a reliable signal in itself — but in the direction opposite to the original signal.

The Importance of Computer Technology

Of what use and importance then is this marvelous tool — the most interesting tool man (*homo*) has acquired since papyrus? (Numerous computer software packages are available which are capable of executing the functions described in the following discussion.) If the computer can't definitively identify profitable opportunities, what good is it?

Probably the most important function the computer has for the Magee Analyst is the automation of rote detail work. Data can be gathered by downloading from database servers. Charts can be called up in an instant. Portfolio accounting and maintenance and tax preparation can be disposed of with one hand while drinking coffee with the other. All in all this might make it sound as though the computer is a great tool, but with a pretty dull edge. Not strictly true. There is at least one great leap forward for Magee Analysts with this tool, leaving aside the rote drudgery it saves. This great advantage is portfolio analysis. In *Resources (Appendix D)*, a complex portfolio analysis of the kind used by professional traders (Blair Hull and Options Research Inc.) is illustrated. Even simpler portfolios of the average investor can benefit from the facilities afforded by most portfolio programs, either on the net or in commercial software packages (locations and software identified in *Resources*).

Another advantage is the ability to see basic data displayed in many different forms: point and figure charts, candlestick charts, close-only charts — these are prepared in the flick of an eyelash, and may indeed contribute to understanding the particular situation under the magnifying glass. The effortless quantification of some aspects of analysis may be useful — volume studies, for instance, and given the popularity of moving averages, seeing the 50- and 200-day moving averages can be interesting. These moving averages are considered significant by many market participants — even fundamental analysts. The analysis of any of these should be considered in relation to the current state of the market as understood by the careful chart analyst.

But what about (the strangely named) stochastics, Bollinger Bands, %R, MACD, Moving Averages (plain vanilla, exponential, crossover, etc.), price/volume divergence, RSI (plain vanilla and Wilder), VP Trend, TCI, OBV, Upper/Lower Trading Bands, ESA Trading Bands, and AcmDis? Well, there is a certain whiff of alchemy to some of them, and some have some usefulness sometimes. And, all systems work beautifully at least twice in their lives: in research, and in huge monumental Bull Markets. These number driven indicators are also the times when trading genius is most likely to be discovered. These are briefly explored by a former editor in Appendix C. *EN9: It is also true, as I have said, that you can drive a nail with a screwdriver. And the inventor of a tool may be fabulously successful with it while its adopters lose their assets.*

It is also possible that the excess of technical information created by these indicators may be like the excess of fundamental information — another shell to hide the pea under, another magician's trick to keep the investor from seeing what is truly important, and what is necessary and sufficient to know to trade well. Perhaps the investor would be better off with a behavioral model, since the markets are behavioral. Number-driven technical analysis can do many things, some like Dr. Johnson's dog which walked on its hind legs, but they cannot put the market in perspective. Only the human mind can do that. Number-driven models after all do not consider skirt lengths, moon cycles, sun spots, the length of the economic cycle, the bullish or bearish state of the market (if Bear Markets still exist) *EN9: A wry ironical comment written before the market crash of the 2000s.* In the end, the human brain is still the only organ capable of synthesizing all this quantitative and qualitative information and assessing those elements which cannot be reduced to ones and zeros. The educated mind is still the best discriminator of patterns and their contexts.

Summary 1

The computer is a tool, a powerful tool, but a tool nonetheless. It is not an intelligent problem solver or decision maker. We use a mechanical ditch digger to dig a ditch, but not to figure out where the ditch should be.

The multitude of indicators and systems should be viewed with a skeptical eye and evaluated within the context of informed chart analysis. Sometimes an indicator or technique will work for one user or its inventor but strangely mislead the chart analyst who tries to use it — or buys it, even based on a verified track record.

So the experienced investor keeps his methods and analysis simple until he has definitive knowledge of any technique, method, or indicator he would like to add to his repertoire. And, most of all, he depends on his own observations and experience to evaluate his own and others trading techniques.

Other Technological Developments of Importance to the Technical Magee Analyst and All Investors

The computer is not the only technological development of interest to the technical investor. A number of information revolution technologies need to be put in perspective. These are, in broad categories, the Internet and all its facilities, developments in electronic markets, and advances in finance and investment theory and practice. This last is treated in Chapter 17.2.

Due to the enormous body of material on these subjects, no attempt will be made to explore these subjects exhaustively, but the general investor will be given the information he needs to know to put these subjects in their proper perspective. Resources will point the analyst to avenues for further investigation if the need is felt.

But first of all, are there any technological developments of whatever sort which have made charting obsolete? No. Are there any developments which have made trading a guaranteed success? No. The only sure thing is that some huckster will claim to have a sure thing. Those who believe such claims are the victims of their own naivete.

The Internet — the Eighth Wonder of the Modern World (EN9: Resources Appendix for the 9th Edition has been enormously expanded and is of paramount importance to modern investors.)

The Internet has been called the most complex project ever built by man. And that is probably true. Complex, sprawling, idiosyncratic, it has something for everyone, especially the investor. Every form of investment creature known to man has set up a site on the Internet, and waits like the hungry arachnid for the casual surfer. Brokers. Advisors — technical and fundamental. Newspapers. News magazines. Newsgroups. Touts. Mutual funds. Mutual fund advisories. Critics and evaluators of all the above. Database vendors. Chat rooms. Electronic marketplaces and exchanges. ECNs. The only unfilled niche that seems to exist is investment pornography. Perhaps naked options will be able to satisfy this need.

This is a bewildering array of resources. How does one sort them out? The implications of all this for the electronic or cyberinvestor may be further expanded to indicate the services and facilities available: quotes and data; portfolio management and accounting; online interactive charting; automatic alerts to PBDAs (personal body digital assistants or gizmos carried on the body, e.g., cell phone and handheld computer, etc.); analysis and advice; electronic boardrooms; electronic exchanges where trading takes place without intermediaries. *Resources (Appendix D)* supplies specifics on these categories. This chapter supplies perspective. It is one thing to contemplate this cornucopia of facilities and another thing to appreciate the importance and priority of its elements. What good are real time quotes if you are only interested in reviewing your portfolio once a week, except for special occasions? What good are satellite alerts and virtual reality glasses to a long-term investor? It is easy for the investor with no philosophy or method to be drawn into the maelstrom of electronic wonders and stagger out of it little wiser and much poorer.

Observe then the goods and services of all this which are of importance to the level-headed investor with his feet on the ground and his head out of the clouds. This hopefully not abstract investor, object of our attention here, needs what? He needs *data, charts,* and *a connection to a trading place.* Data are available at the click of a mouse. A chart occupies the screen in another click. Another click and a trade is placed. In the Internet Age it would be tautological to attempt to describe this process in prose when live demonstrations are as close as the desktop computer and an Internet connection. A demonstration of this rather simple process (easy to say when one does it without thinking) may be seen at locations linked in *Resources (Appendix D).* The trade will be made, of necessity, through a broker of some sort. Perhaps an electronic broker, or even a nonvirtual broker who communicates via telephone. And shortly, if not already, an electronic pit where one matches wits with a computer instead of a market maker or specialist.

How long brokers will be necessary is a question that is up in the air in the new century. (The broker who earns his keep will always be with us, and welcome, too.) Electronic marketplaces where investors meet without the necessity of a broker or specialist are already proliferating (see *Resources*), and will continue to gain the advantage for the investor over the trading pit, which is one of the last remaining edges the professionals hold over off-floor traders. Suffice it to say that their initial phases will undoubtedly be periods of dislocation, of risk and opportunity as their glitches are ironed out.

Placing electronic orders, whether to an electronic exchange or to the NYSE, has certain inherent advantages over oral orders. No one can quarrel about a trade registered electronically as opposed to orally where the potential for disagreement exists. In addition, the trader has only handled the data once — rather than making an analysis, calling a broker, recording the trade, passing it to the portfolio. If he just hits the trade button and the transaction is routed through his software package, no one will have any doubt as to where an error might lie. The manual method presents an opportunity for error at each step. And rest assured, errors occur and can be disastrous to trading.

The efficiency and ease of the process with a computer has much to recommend it — automation of trade processing, elimination of confusion and ambiguities, audit tracks, automation of portfolio maintenance, and, perhaps most important of all, automatic mark-to-market of the portfolio. (Marking-to-market is the practice of valuing a portfolio at its present market value whether trades are open or closed.)

Marking-to-Market

This book might have been entitled *Zen and the Art of Technical Analysis* if that title were not so hackneyed and threadbare. It conveys, nonetheless, the message of Zen in the art of archery, that of direct attachment to reality and the importance of the present moment. In his seminal book *The General Semantics of Wall Street* (now *Winning the Mental Game on Wall Street*) John Magee inveighed at some length against the very human tendency to keep two sets of books in the head — one recording profits, open and closed, and another recording losses, but only closed losses. Open losses were not losses until booked. Having an electronic portfolio accountant which refuses to participate in such self-deception has much to recommend it. If the portfolio is always marked to the market when the computer communicates with the data vendor, or the trade broker, it is difficult not to see red ink, and to see that the equity of the account reflects all trades, open and closed.

Separating the Wheat from the Chaff

It requires a gimlet-eyed investor to pick his way through the minefield of temptations in electronic investing and number-driven technical analysis. Playing with the toys, seeing what the pundits have to say, and fiddling with "research" can subtly replace profitable trading as the activity. Actually, almost all the research the Magee Analyst *must* do is addressed in this book.

Chaff

Chat rooms. Touts. News. Predictions. Punditry. Brokerage House buy, sell, hold, strong hold, weak buy, strong buy, and any other species of Brokerage House recommendation taken at face value. Remember brokerage firms survive by selling securities and make their money in general on activity. Actually, much of their money is made servicing their institutional clients and distributing their clients' shares to their retail cleintele – a blatant conflict of interest which blew up in their faces in the early 2000s resulting in many fines and some jail terms (*plus ça change...*). In the surging Clinton–Gore Bull Markets of the 1990s, all of these worked. In a serious Bear Market none of them will work. *(EN9: A serious bear market started in earnest in 2000 and was correctly identified with Magee chart analysis as may be seen from the John Magee Letters at the edwards-magee.com web site.*

Summary 2

Never in the history of the markets have so many facilities for private investors been available. The computer is necessary to take advantage of those facilities.

Data may be acquired automatically via Internet or dial-up sites at little or no cost.

A (as they say) plethora of web sites offer cyberinvestors everything from portfolio accounting to alerts sent to their personal body-carried devices (pagers, handheld PDAs, etc.).

Some of these even offer real-time data, which is a way for the unsophisticated trader to go broke in real time.

Many of these sites offer every kind of analysis from respectable technical analysis (usually too complicated) to extraterrestrial channeling.

Internet chat rooms will provide real-time touting and numerous rumors to send the lemmings and impressionable scurrying hither and yon. But, one expects, not the readers of this book.

Of more importance, the info-revolution and the computer will:

1. Relieve the analyst of manual drudgery, accelerate all the steps of analysis: data gathering, chart preparation, portfolio accounting, and analysis and tax preparation.
2. Give the analyst virtually effortless portfolio accounting and mark-to-market prices — a valuable device to have to keep the investor from mixing his cash and accrual accounting, as Magee says.
3. Enable processing of a hitherto unimaginable degree. An unlimited number of stocks may be analyzed. Choosing those to trade with a computer will be dealt with in Chapter 21, *Selection of Stocks to Chart*.
4. Allow the investor to trade on ECNs or in electronic marketplaces where there are no pit traders or locals to fiddle with prices.

chapter 17.2

Advancements in Investment Technology

Part 1. Developments in Finance Theory and Practice

Numerous pernicious and useless inventions, services, and products litter the Internet and the financial industry marketplace; but modern finance theory and technology is important and must be taken into consideration by the general investor. This chapter will explore the minimum the moderately advanced investor needs to know about advances in theory and practice. And it will point the reader to further resources if he desires to continue more advanced study.

Instruments of limited (or non-) availability during the time of Edwards and Magee included exchange traded options on stocks, futures on averages and indices, options on futures and indices, securitized indices and averages, as the most important and as a partial list only. Undoubtedly one of the most important developments of the modern era is the creation of trading instruments which allow the investor to trade and hedge the major indexes. Of these, the instruments created by the Chicago Board of Trade are of singular importance. These are the CBOT® DJIA^SM Futures and the CBOT® DJIA^SM Futures Options, which are discussed in greater detail in Part 2 of this chapter. (EN9: Not so singular, perhaps. Probably of greater importance to readers of this book are the AMEX ishares, particularly DIA, SPY and QQQQ, instruments which offer the investor direct participation in the major indices as though they were stocks.)

General developments of great importance in finance theory and practice are found in the following sections.

Options

From the pivotal moment in 1973 when Fischer Black and his partner, Myron Scholes, published their — excuse the usage — paradigm-setting Model to the third millennium, the options/derivatives markets have grown from negligible to trillions of dollars a year. The investor who is not informed about options is playing with half a deck. The subject, however, is beyond the scope of this book, which hopes only to offer some perspective on the subject and guides to the further study necessary for most traders and many investors.

Something in the neighborhood of 30% or more of options expire worthless. This is probably the most important fact to know about options. (There is a rule of thumb about options called the 60–30–10 rule: 60% are closed out before expiration, 10% are exercised, and 30% are "long at expiration," meaning they are worthless.) Another fact to know about options is: in the Reagan Crash of 1987, out of the money puts bought at $.625 on October 16 were worth hundreds of dollars on October 19 — if you could get the broker to pick up the telephone and trade them. (The editor had a client at Options Research, Inc. during that time who lost $57MM in 3 days and almost brought down a major Chicago bank. He had sold too many naked puts.)

The most sophisticated and skilled traders in the world make their livings (quite sumptuous livings, thank you) trading options. Educated estimates have been made that as many as 90% of retail options traders lose money. That combined with the fact that by far it is the general public which buys (rather than sells) options should suggest some syllogistic reasoning to the reader.

With these facts firmly fixed in mind, let us put options in their proper perspective for the general investor. Options have a number of useful functions. They offer the trader powerful leverage. With an option he can control much more stock than by the direct purchase of stock — his capital stretches much further. So options are an ideal speculative instrument. (Exaggerated leverage is almost always a characteristic of speculative instruments.) But they can also be used in a most conservative way — that is, as an insurance policy. For example, a position on the long security side may be hedged by the purchase of a put on the option side. (This is not a specific recommendation to do this. Every specific situation should be evaluated by the prudent investor as to its monetary consequences.)

The experienced investor may also use options to increase yield on his portfolio of securities. He may write covered calls, or write naked puts on a stock in order to acquire it at a lower cost (e.g., he sells out of the money options. This is a way of being long with the stock. If the stock comes back to the exercise price, he acquires the stock. If not, he pockets the premium.)

There are numerous tactics of this sort which may be played with options. Note, *played*. Played because, for the general investor, the options game can be disastrous, as professionals are not playing. They are seriously practicing skills the amateur can never hope to master. Many floor traders, indeed, would qualify as idiot savants — they can compute the "fair value" of options in their heads and make money on price anomalies of $.625, or, as they call it, a "teenie." For perspective, the reader may contemplate a conversation the editor had with one of the most important options traders in the world. This market maker remarked casually that his fortune was built on teenies. The reader may imagine at some length what would be necessary for the general investor to make a profit on $.625.

This does not mean the general investor should never touch options. It just means he should be thoroughly prepared before he goes down to play that game. In options trading traders speak of bull spreads, bear spreads, and alligator spreads. The alligator spread is an options strategy which eats the customer's capital *in toto*.

Among these strategies is covered call writing. This is a strategy which is touted as being an income producer on a stock portfolio. There is no purpose in writing a call on a stock in which the investor is long — unless that stock is stuck in a clear congestion phase which is not due to expire before the option expires. And if the stock is in a downtrend it should be liquidated. But to write a call on a stock in a clear uptrend is to make oneself beloved of the broker, whose good humor improves markedly with account activity and commission income. The outcome of a covered call on an ascending stock, of course, is that the writer (you, dear reader) has the stock called at the exercise price, losing his position and future appreciation, not to mention costs. The income is actually small consolation, a sort of booby prize — a way of cutting your profits while increasing your costs.

Quantitative Analysis

The investor should be aware of another area of computer and investment technology that has yielded much more dramatic and profitable results, but that is in a model-driven market — namely the options markets. Quantitative analysts, those who investigate and trade the options markets, are a breed apart from technical analysts. In an interesting irony, behavioral markets, the stock markets, are used as the basis for derivatives, or options whose price is determined largely by the operation of algorithms called models. The original model which for all intents and purposes created the modern world of options trading was the Black–Scholes options analysis model, which assumed that the "fair value" of an option could be determined by entering five parameters into the formula: the strike price of the option; the price of the stock; the "risk free" interest rate; the time to expiration; and the volatility of the stock.

The eventual universal acceptance of this model resulted in the derivatives industry we have today. To list all the forms of derivatives available for trading today would be to expand this book by many pages, and it is not the purpose of this book anyway. The purpose of this paragraph of the book is to sternly warn general investors who are thinking of "beating the derivatives markets" that they should undergo rigorous training first. The alternative could be extremely expensive.

At first the traders who saw the importance of this model and used it to price options virtually skinned older options traders and the public, who traded pretty much by the seat of the pants or the strength of their convictions, meaning human emotion. But professional losers learn fast, and now all competent options traders use some sort of model or antimodel, or anti-antimodel to trade. And true to form, options sellers, who are largely professionals, take most of the public's (who are buyers) money. This is the way of the world.

Options Pricing Models and Their Importance

After the introduction of the Black–Scholes Model numerous other models followed, among them the Cox–Ross–Rubinstein, the Black Futures, etc. For the general investor, the message is this: he must be acquainted with these models and what their functions are if he intends to use options. Remember that the model computes the "fair value" of the option. One way professionals make money off amateurs is by selling overpriced options and buying underpriced options to create a relatively lower risk spread (for themselves). Not knowing what these values are for the private investor is like not knowing where the present price is for a stock. It is a piece of ignorance for which the professional will charge him a premium to be educated about. Unfortunately, many private options traders never get educated in spite of paying tuition over and over again. But ignorance is not bliss. It is expensive.

Technology and knowledge works its way from innovators and creative geniuses through the ranks of professionals and sooner or later is disseminated to the general public. Of course by that time the innovators have developed new technology. Nonetheless, even assuming that professionals have superior tools and technology, the general investor must thoroughly educate himself before using options. As it is not the province of this book to dissect options trading, the reader may find references in *Resources (Appendix D)*.

Here it would not be untoward to mention one of the better books on options as a starting point for the moderately advanced and motivated trader. Lawrence McMillan's *Options as a Strategic Investment* is necessary reading. In addition the newcomer may contact the Chicago Board Options Exchange, the CBOE, at www.cboe.com, which has tutorial software.

Futures on Indexes

Futures, like options, offer the speculator intense leverage — the ability to control a comparatively large position with much less capital than the purchase of the underlying commodity or index. Futures salesmen are fond of pointing out the fact that, if you are margined at 5% or 10% of the contract value, a similar move in the price of the index will double your money. They are often not so conscientious about pointing out that a similar move against your position will wipe out your margin (actually earnest money). Unlike (long) options, a mishap in the market can result in more than the loss of margin. It can result in a deficit account and debts to the broker — in other words, losses of more than 100%. For this among other reasons, it is wise not to plunge into futures without considerable preparation.

This preparation might well begin, for the adroit investor, with the reading of Schwager's *Technical Analysis, Schwager on Futures*, currently one of the better books on the subject.

But let us say that instead of using futures to speculate that we want to use them as a hedge for our portfolio of Dow–Jones DIAMONDS or portfolio of Dow–Jones stocks. Now we are purchasing insurance, rather than speculating. As an oversimplified example, the investor might see the failure of the DJIA to break through a top as the beginning of a congestion zone (a consolidation or reversal pattern). He could then hedge his position by shorting the Dow–Jones futures. Now he is both long and short — long the cash, short the futures. He would place a stop on the futures above his purchase price to close the trade if the market continued rising. If the market fell, he would maintain the futures position until he calculated that the reaction had passed its worst point, or until it were definitely analyzed to have reversed. He would then take his profits on the futures position (taxable) but his cash position would be intact, and presumably the greater capital gains on those positions would be safe from taxation, and also safe from the costs and slippage and difficulties of reestablishing the stock position.

Options on Futures and Indexes

Conservative as well as speculative use may be made of options. For example, the investor might, after a vigorous spike upwards, feel that the S&P 500, or the SPDRs which he is long, were overbought. He might then buy an index put on the S&P as a hedge against the expected decline. If it occurs, he collects his profit on the option and his cash position in the S&P is undisturbed. If the Index continues to climb he loses the option premium — an insurance policy he took out to protect his stock portfolio.

Note well: The tactics described here are for the reader's conceptual education. Before executing tactics of this kind, or any other unfamiliar procedure, the investor should thoroughly inform himself and rehearse the procedure, testing outcomes through paper trading before committing real capital. *He must, in short, figure out how you lose.* A number of web sites offer facilities of this kind, and the investor may also build on his own computer a research or paper trading portfolio segregated from his actual transactions.

The trader might also choose to buy an option on a future. At the CBOT, the trader can trade both options and futures on the DJIA. These can be used as the above examples for speculating or hedging, except in this case the successful option buyer might wind up owning a futures contract instead of the cash position. This could be disconcerting to one not accustomed to the futures market, especially if large price anomalies between futures and cash occurred, as happened in 1987 and 1989 when futures prices went to huge discounts to cash. A primary reason for employing the futures would be for leverage. And the reason for using the options on futures would be the analysis that uncertainty was in store and the wish to only risk the amount of the options premium.

Obviously, a speculator can choose to forget the stock or futures part of the portfolio and trade only options. Before taking such a step the trader should pass a postgraduate course. The proportion of successful amateur option traders to successful professional traders is extremely skewed. In fact one might say that all successful options traders are professionals.

Modern Portfolio Theory (MPT)

MPT is a procedure and process whereby a portfolio manager may classify and analyze the components of his portfolio in such a way as to, hopefully, be aware of and control risk and return. It attempts to quantify the relationship between risk and return. Rather than analyzing only the individual instruments within a portfolio, MPT attempts to determine the statistical relationships among the members of the portfolio and their relationships to the market.

The processes involved in MPT analysis are (1) portfolio valuation, or describing the portfolio in terms of expected risk and expected return; (2) asset allocation, determining how capital is to be allocated among the classes of instruments (bonds, stocks, etc.); (3) optimization, or finding the trade-offs between risk and return in selecting the components of the portfolio; and (4) performance measurement, or the division of each stock's risk into systematic and security-related classes.

How important is this for the general investor? Not very. And there is a large question among pragmatic analysts, such as the editor, as to its pragmatic usefulness for professionals, although they cling to it as to a life ring in a shipwreck. Mandelbrot observed in articles ("A Multifractal Walk Down Wall Street") and letters in the *Scientific American* (February 1999 and June 1999) that MPT discards about 5% of statistical experience as if it didn't exist. (Although it [the experience] does.) And he observed that the ignored experience includes "10 sigma" market storms which are blamed for portfolio failures as though it is the fault of the data instead of the fault of the process.

The Wonders and Joys of Investment Technology

Are there any other innovations in finance and investment theory of which the general investor should be aware? (See Chapter 42 for discussion of VAR.) Well, it never hurts to know everything, and the very best professionals not only are aware of everything, but are in the constant process of finding new wrinkles and glitches and anomalies. But, as Magee would say, what is necessary and sufficient to know (see *Winning the Mental Game on Wall Street*)? Absolute certainty is the hallmark of religious extremists and the naive, who do not know what they do not know. So I will remark that *probably* this book contains either what is necessary and sufficient for the investor to know about these matters, and/or guides the reader to further study.

And, *nota bene*, any number of little old ladies with a chart, a pencil, and previous editions of this book have beaten the pants off professional stock pickers with supercomputers and MPT and Nobel Laureates and who knows what other resources. I personally know investment groups which have thrown enormous resources into the development of real-time systems which were in research 100% successful in beating the market. The only reality glitch was that the systems required so much computer power they could not be run quickly enough in real time to actually trade in the markets. Philosopher's stone *redux*.

Part 2. Futures and Options on Futures on the Dow–Jones Industrial Index at the Chicago Board of Trade

(EN9: The general investor MUST be aware that the methods and techniques described in this chapter are for advanced practitioners. Careless use of the described instruments can be extremely damaging to a portfolio.)

Investment and Hedging Strategies Using the Chicago Board of Trade DJIA^{SM} Futures Contract

A futures contract is the obligation to buy or sell a specific commodity on or by some specified date in the future. For example, if one went long corn futures he would be obligated to accept delivery of corn on the delivery date, unless he sold the contract prior to the settlement date. Shorting the contract would obligate the seller to deliver corn unless he offset (by repurchase) the contract. The "commodity" in our present case is the basket of stocks represented by the DJIA Futures index. All futures contracts specify the date by which the transaction must conclude, known as the "settlement date," and how the transaction will be implemented, known as "delivery." The DJIA futures contract price closely tracks the price of the Dow Jones Industrials as computed from stock market values.

The value of the future is found by multiplying the index price of the futures contract by $10. For example, if the futures index price is 10000, the value of the contract is $10000 \cdot \$10 = \$100,000$. So the buyer or seller of the futures contract is trading approximately $100,000 worth of stocks at that Dow Futures level. The value may be higher or lower owing to several factors, for example, cost of carry, which I will discuss below.

Settlement of Futures Contracts

All futures contracts must be "settled." Some futures are settled by delivery. This is the famous nightmare of finding 5000 bushels of soybeans delivered on your front lawn. Dow Index futures "settle" (are delivered) in cash. The short does not dump a basket of Dow stocks on the yard of the long. Thus on the settlement date of the contract the settlement price is $10 times a figure called the "Special Opening Quotation," a value calculated from the opening prices of the member stocks of the Dow Future following the last day of trading in the futures contract. This value is compared to the price paid for the contract when the trade initiated. For example, if the Dow Future is 10000 at expiration, a long who bought the contract at 9000 receives $10,000 ($10 \cdot 1000$) from the short.

Marking to Market

This $10,000, however, is paid daily over the life of the contract, rather than in one payment upon expiration of the contract. It is paid as successive daily "margin" payments. These payments are not really margin, but are in effect "earnest money" or a performance bond. And the practice of squaring up accounts at the end of every day's trading is called "marking to market." These daily payments are determined based on the difference between the previous day's settlement price and the contract settlement price at the close of trading each day.

As a practical example, if the settlement price of June Dow Index futures increases from 9800 to 9840 from May 17 to May 18, the short pays $400 ($10 · 40) and the long's account is credited $400. If the futures settlement price decreases 10 points the following day, the long pays $100 to the short's account — and so on each day until expiration of the contract, when the futures price and the index price achieve parity.

At any time the trader can close his position by offsetting the contract, that is, by selling to close an open long, or buying to close an open short. At the expiration date open contracts are settled in cash at the final settlement price.

Fungibility

One of the great contributions of the great established exchanges like the Chicago Board of Trade and the Chicago Mercantile Exchange is their institutionalization of contract terms and relationships. This, of course, is "fungibility." Any one futures contract for corn, or an Index, or any other commodity is substitutable for another of the same commodity. Similarly, the Exchange has negated counterparty risk by placing a Clearing Corporation between all parties to trades. So even if the other party to a trade went broke, the Clearing Corporation would assume his liability. And, using the mechanism of daily settlement, whereby losers pay winners daily, the danger of major default is avoided.

Futures "margins" (or "earnest money") are deposited with the broker on opening a trade. The leverage obtainable is quite extreme for a stock trader. Initial margin is usually 3–5% of the total value of the contract. Each day thereafter margins vary according to the process described above of marking to market.

As the reader can easily see, the purchase or sale of a Dow Future is the equivalent of a fairly large portfolio transaction, with the understanding that it is a transaction which must be closed in the future, unlike a stock purchase which may be held indefinitely.

Differences between Cash and Futures

The main two differences between the cash and the futures transactions are

1. In cash, the value of the portfolio must be paid up front, or financed in a stock margin account.
2. The owner of the cash portfolio receives cash dividends.

These are not the only differences of course. The leverage employed in the futures transaction is a two-edged sword. If the trader has no reserves, a minor move in the index wipes him out. Such a minor move would be barely noticed by the owner of a cash portfolio.

Dow Index Future

The price of the future and the price of the index are closely linked (cf. Figure 199.1). Any price anomaly is quickly corrected by arbitragers. On any significant price difference, arbitragers will buy the underpriced and sell the overpriced, bringing the relationship back in line. Their prices are not exactly the same because the futures contract value must reflect the costs of short-term financing of stocks and the dividends paid by index stocks until futures expiration. This is known as the "cost of carry." The "theoretical value" of the future should equal the price of the index plus the carrying cost. This is what is called the "fair" or "theoretical" value.

Using Stock Index Futures to Control Exposure to the Market

The owner of a cash portfolio in the Dow, or of DIAMONDS, can control his exposure, his risk, by using futures to hedge. If, for example, he is pessimistic about the market, or more to the point, a lot of uptrend lines have been broken and the technical situation seems to be deteriorating, he can sell a futures contract equivalent to his portfolio and be flat the market.

Readers will immediately recognize the advantages of this strategy. Tax consequences on the cash portfolio are avoided, as are the other negative consequences of trading — slippage, errors, etc. Long-term positions are better left alone. By flattening his position the investor has now insured the future value of his portfolio *and* the capital involved is now earning the money market rate of return.

What happens if the forecast market decline occurs? The portfolio is protected from loss, and the capital earns the market rate of return. *And* the investor should monitor his hedge closely, lifting it when he calculates that the correction has run its course. Taxes will, of course, then be due on the profits on the hedge.

In monitoring the hedge, the possibility must be considered that the market rises instead of falling. In planning the hedge in the first place, the investor must plan for this eventuality and determine where he will lift the hedge on the losing side. At worst, of course, the investor has surrendered portfolio appreciation. Not considering cash flow implications, of course.

It is worth emphasizing, in fact *strongly* emphasizing, that these techniques require knowledge, expertise, and study. Careless use of techniques

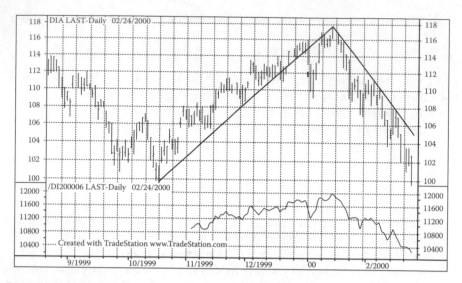

FIGURE 199.1.   Diamonds and Futures. The 2% plus break at the arrow of an 11-month trendline is an unmistakable invitation to hedge the DIAMONDS by shorting the futures. Profits on the short would have offset losses in the DIAMONDS. This convenient drill would have preserved liquidity, postponed capital gains taxes and avoided loss of equity. Notice the return to the trendline after the break. More of the foolish virgin syndrome?

of this nature can bloody the amateur investor. So it is probably best to have a professional guide for the first several of these expeditions, and to execute a number of paper transactions first.

The canny investor can increase his exposure to the market and the risk to his capital by buying index futures. But the canny investor must be careful not to turn into a burned speculator. Futures trading, because of the extreme leverage, is an area for dedicated and experienced speculators.

A Dow Futures transaction costs less than if you had to buy or sell a whole basket of stocks. Professional fund managers — as well as other professionals — regularly use futures for asset allocation and reallocation. In all likelihood, they are not using the extreme leverage afforded by futures. In other words, if they have a million dollar cash portfolio, they don't buy 10 million dollars worth of futures. It is not the leverage they are interested in, but the extreme convenience and agility offered by doing short-term allocations in futures. The ability to almost instantaneously move in and out of the market without disturbing the underlying portfolio is a powerful feature of these "proxy markets."

Investment Uses of Dow Index Futures

In the following examples, I describe the basic mechanics of using Dow Futures contracts. These can be used to adjust equity exposure in anticipation of volatile market cycles and to rebalance portfolios among different asset classes. The futures may also be used for other purposes not illustrated here. The following examples are not intended to be absolutely precise, but only to illustrate the mechanics involved. For the sake of simplicity, mark-to-market payments and cost of carry have been eliminated from the examples.

Situation 1: Portfolio Protection

You are a long-term Magee-type investor and you have old and profitable positions with which you are satisfied. But you have seen the broadening top of the Dow Jones (*circa anno* 2000) and it is almost October and you would not be surprised to see a little bloodshed. You have $400,000 in the Dow and $100,000 in money market instruments. You decide to reverse this ratio. But you don't want to liquidate the Dow portfolio, as there is no sign of a confirmed downtrend, only that of consolidation. So you sell $300,000 of index futures, leaving yourself with a $100,000 kicker in case you are wrong about the market's declining. At the time, the market is 10000 and the futures are 10500, meaning the cost of carry is approximately 0.5% $(10,500/10,000 - 1)$.

You sell three futures contracts ($300,000/($10 \cdot 10,000$)). You now have reversed your position and are long $100,000 Dow stocks and long $400,000 money market equivalents.

Validating your technical analysis, the market has begun to swing in broad undulations and, at the expiration of the futures, the Dow is at 10000. On your stocks you have a return of –0.5%, and the money market position has a rate of return of 0.5%.

What would have been the situation had you not hedged?

Stock Portfolio: $400,000 · 0.95	$380,000
Money Market + 100,000 · 1.005	$100,500
Total	$480,500

How the futures position affects the portfolio:

Short 3 futures 3 · $10 · (10,000 – 9500)	+$15,000
Total	$495,000

Value of portfolio with reallocation of assets in cash market:

Stocks $100,000 · 0.95	$95,000
Money market + $400,000 · 1.005	$402,000
Total	$497,000

By hedging in the futures market, you now have the equivalent of a $100,000 investment in Dow Future stocks and a $400,000 investment in the money market instrument. The stock market decline now affects only $100,000 of your stock portfolio rather than $400,000; in addition, you earn a money market rate of return of 0.5% on the $300,000 difference.

Without the futures transaction, the portfolio is worth $480,500. The $15,000 profit on the short futures position offsets the loss on the $300,000 of the portfolio that was moved out of equities by the short futures position. In brief, by selling futures, you are able to protect $300,000 of your initial portfolio value from a stock price decline, nearly breaking even, an achievement given these market conditions. Of course, had you been more confident of the market decline, you might have completely neutralized the equity risk on the portfolio by selling more futures contracts. This would have converted the entire stock position to a $400,000 investment in the money market. The amount of protection you should obtain depends on your assessment of the market and your tolerance for risk.

Situation 2: Increasing Exposure with Futures

Now let us look at the other side of the coin. The market has come off its highs in a predictable and controlled secondary reaction and your technical analysis is that the Bull Market will continue. At 10000, it appears headed for 11000 and you want to increase your commitment. Your portfolio is as previously described, split 80/20 between Dow stocks and money markets. It is time to go whole hog, you decide. You are acutely aware of the market maxim that bulls make money and bears make money and hogs wind up slaughtered, but there is also a market maxim that no market maxim is true 100% of the time, which is also true of this maxim.

Rather than liquidate your money market holdings, you buy one futures contract, which puts you long another $100,000 of stocks. The rate of return on the money markets in your portfolio is 0.5%. To get a $500,000 exposure in blue chips, you buy the following number of contracts: $100,000/($10 · 10000) = 1 contract.

Results: Your technical analysis of the direction of the market is correct, and the Dow Future rises to 11000 at the September expiration, or by 10%.

Value of portfolio with passive management:

Stocks	$400,000 × 1.10	$440,000
Money market +	$100,000 × 1.005	$100,500
Total		$540,500

Value of portfolio with futures position:

Long DJIA futures 1 · $10 × (11000 − 10000)	$10,000
Total	$550,500

Value of portfolio with reallocation of assets in cash market:

Stocks $500,000 × 1.10	$550,000
Money market	$0
Total	$550,000

In buying Dow Index futures, you are able to "equitize" $100,000 of your money market investment, effectively increasing your return from the money market rate of 0.5% to 10%. If you had not bought futures, the total value of your portfolio at the September expiration would have been $540,500 instead of $550,500. Not only do you have a $10,000 extra gain in your portfolio, but you have taken advantage of the market's continuing upward climb without having to adjust your portfolio.

Situation 3: Using Bond and Index Futures for Asset Allocation

Speculation in bonds can be quite profitable notwithstanding David Dreman's assertion that long-term investments in bonds are net losers. (*EN9: An oversimplification of a sophisticated thesis by an important figure.*) So it is not unusual for an investor to have both bonds and stocks in his portfolio. In this event, the portfolio can be managed with facility by using both Index futures and Treasury bond futures.

Many investors consider it prudent to reallocate their capital commitments based on inflation rates, interest rates, and the reported expression on Alan Greenspan's face before Congressional testimony.

An efficient and inexpensive way to reallocate assets between stocks and bonds is to put on spreads of Treasury bond futures and Dow Index futures.

Analysis of recent long- and medium-term trends in the market, however, has led you to consider increasing your equity portfolio and decreasing your bond portfolio. You have $200,000 invested in Dow stocks and $200,000 invested in Treasury bonds. You would like to take advantage of the sustained market rally by increasing your equities exposure to 75% and decreasing your bond holdings to 25%.

As for tactics, you can reallocate both sides of your portfolio — buying $100,000 of stocks and selling $100,000 of bonds — with the sale of Treasury bond futures and the purchase of Dow Index futures.

The Treasury bonds in your portfolio have a market price of 103 20. The price of September Treasury bond futures is 102-20 per $100 of face value, and $100,000 of face value must be delivered against each contract. The value of the Dow Future is 10000, and the price of the Dow Index futures contract is 10000 (ignoring the cost of carry, of course).

The number of T-bond futures to sell is: short T-bond futures: $100,000/(102-20 · $1,000) − 1 (number of futures is rounded to the nearest whole number). The number of stock index futures to buy is: long stock index futures: $100,000/($10 · 10000) = 1 (number of futures is rounded to the nearest whole number).

Results: at the September futures expiration, the value of the Dow Future is 11000, a rate of return of 10%, and the market value of the bonds is 101-08, a rate of return of −1%.

Portfolio value with no market action taken:

Stocks	$200,000 × 1.10	$220,000
Money market	$200,000 × 0.99	$198,000
Total		$418,000

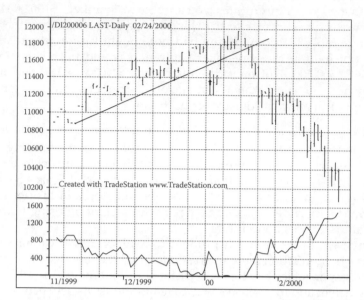

FIGURE 199.2. Dow Jones Futures and Options. A put purchased at the arrow on the break would have protected patiently won gains over the previous 11 months. Increase in value of put can be seen as futures track declining Dow cash. A theoretical drill, but theoretical drills precede actual tactics in the market.

Value of futures positions:

Long Dow futures	$10 × 1 × (11000 − 10000)	$10,000
Short bond futures	+$1000 × 1 × (102-20 − 101-08)	$1375
Total		$11,375
Grand total		$429,375

Value of portfolio had transaction been done in cash market:

Stocks	$300,000 × 1.10	$330,000
Bonds	+ $100,000 × 0.99	$99,000
Total		$429,000

By this simple maneuver you have quickly and easily changed your market posture to add an additional $100,000 exposure to stocks and subtract $100,000 exposure to bonds. Having correctly analyzed market trends, your action results in an increase in portfolio value from $418,000 to $429,375. You could have accomplished the same result by buying and selling bonds and stocks, but not without tax consequences and the attendant transaction headaches. The use of futures to accomplish your goals allowed you to implement your trading plan without disturbing your existing portfolio.

Perspective

While there can be no argument about the importance of CBOT® DJIA^{SM} Index futures — they are markets of enormous usefulness and importance — there can also be no doubt that the futures novice should thoroughly prepare himself before venturing into these pits. In such a highly leveraged environment, mistakes will be punished much more severely than an error in the stock market. By the same token, ignorance of this vital tool is the mark of an investor who is not serious about his portfolio, or who is less intense in his investment goals. "They" (the infamous "they") use all the weapons at their disposal. So should "we."

Options on Dow Index Futures

The buyer of this instrument has the choice, or the right, to assume a position. It is his *option* to do so — unlike a futures contract in which he has an *obligation* once entered. There are two kinds of options: calls (the right to buy the underlying instrument) and puts (the right to sell). And options can be bought (long) or sold (short) like futures contracts.

A long call option on Dow Index futures gives the buyer the right to buy one futures contract at a specified price which is called the "exercise," or "strike" price. A long put option on Dow Index futures gives the buyer the right to sell one futures contract at the strike price. For example, a call at a strike price of 10000 entitles the buyer to be long one futures contract at a price of 10000 when he exercises the option. A put at the same strike price entitles the buyer to be short one futures contract at 10000. The strike prices of Dow Index futures options are listed in increments of 100 index points, giving the trader the flexibility to express his opinions about upward or downward movement of the market.

The seller, or writer, of a call or put is short the option. Effectively selling a call makes the writer short the market, just as selling a put makes the writer long the market. As in a futures contract, the seller is obligated to fulfill the terms of the option if the buyer exercises. If you are short a call, and the long exercises, you become short one futures contract at 10000. If you are short one put and the long exercises, you become long one futures contract at 10000.

Buyers of options enjoy fixed risk. They can lose no more than the premium they pay to go long an option. On the other hand, sellers of options have potentially unlimited risk. Catastrophic moves in the markets often bankrupt imprudent option sellers.

Option Premiums

The purchase price of the option is called the option premium. The option premium is quoted in points, each point being worth $100. The premium for a Dow Index option is paid by the buyer at initiation of the transaction.

The underlying instrument for one CBOT futures option is one CBOT DJIA^{SM} futures contract; so the option contract and the futures contract are essentially different expressions of the same instrument, and both are based on the Dow–Jones Index.

Options premiums consist of two elements: intrinsic value and time value. The difference between the futures price and strike price is the intrinsic value of the option. If the futures price is greater than the strike price of a call, the call is said to be "in-the-money." In fact, you can be long the futures contract at less than its current price. For example, if the futures price is 10020 and the strike price is 10000, the call is in-the-money and immediate exercise of the call pays $10 times the difference between the futures and strike price, or $10 · 20 = $200. If the futures price is smaller than the strike price, the call is "out-of-the-money." If the two are equal, the call is "at-the-money." A put is in-the-money if the futures price is less than the strike price and out-of-the-money if the futures price is greater than the strike price. It is at-the-money when these two prices are equal.

Because a Dow Index futures option can be exercised at any date until expiration, and exercise results in a cash payment equal to the intrinsic value, the value of the option must be at least as great as its intrinsic value. The difference between the option price and the intrinsic value represents the time value of the option. The time value reflects the possibility that exercise will become more profitable if the futures price moves farther away from the strike price. Generally, the more time until expiration, the greater the time value of the option, because the likelihood of the option becoming profitable to exercise is greater. At expiration, the time value is zero and the option price equals the intrinsic value.

Volatility

The degree of fluctuation in the price of the underlying futures contract is known as "volatility" (cf. *Resources*, Appendix D, for formula). The greater the volatility of the futures, the higher the option premium. The price of a futures option is a function of the *futures price, the strike price, the time left to expiration, the money market rate, and the volatility of the futures price*. Of these variables, volatility is the only one that cannot be observed directly. Since all the other variables are known, however, it is possible to infer from option prices an estimate of how the market is gauging volatility. This estimate is called the "implied volatility" of the option. It measures the market's average expectation of what the volatility of the underlying futures return will be until the expiration of the option. Implied volatility is usually expressed in annualized terms. Implied volatility is suggested as an input to stop calculation in Chapter 27. The significance and use of implied volatility is potentially complex and confusing for the general investor, professionals having a decided edge in this area. Their edge can be removed by serious study.

Exercising the Option

At expiration, the rules of optimal exercise are clear. The call owner should exercise the option if the strike price is less than the underlying futures price.

The value of the exercised call is the difference between the futures price and the strike price. Conversely, the put owner should exercise the option if the strike price is greater than the futures price. The value of the exercised put is the difference between the strike price and the futures price.

To illustrate, if the price of the expiring futures contract is 7600, a call struck at 7500 should be exercised, but a put at the same or lower strike price should not. The value of the exercised call is $1000. The value of the unexercised put is $0. If the price of the expiring futures contract is 7500, a 7600 put should be exercised but not a call at 7600 or a higher strike. The value of the exercised put is $1000 and that of the unexercised call is $0.

The profit on long options is the difference between the expiration value and the option premium. The profit on short options is the expiration value plus the option premium. The expiration values and profits on call and put options can often be an important tool in an investment strategy. Their payoff patterns and risk parameters make options quite different from futures. Their versatility makes them good instruments to adjust a portfolio to changing expectations about stock market conditions. Moreover, these expectations can range from very general to very specific predictions about the future direction and volatility of stock prices. Effectively, there is an option strategy suited to virtually every set of market conditions.

Using Futures Options to Participate in Market Movements

Traders must often react to rapid and surprising events in the market. The transaction costs and price impact of buying or selling a portfolio's stocks on short notice inhibit many investors from reacting to short-term market developments. Shorting stocks is an even less palatable option for average investors because of the margin and risks involved and semantical prejudices.

The flexibility that options provide can allow one to take advantage of the profits from market cycles quickly and conveniently. A long call option on Dow Index futures profits at all levels above its strike price. A long put option similarly profits at all levels below its strike price. Let us examine both strategies.

Profits in Rising Markets

In August, the Dow Index is 10000 and the Dow Index September future is 10050. You expect the current Bull Market to continue, and you would like to take advantage of the trend without tying up too much capital and also undertake only limited risk.

You buy a September call option on Dow Index futures. These options will expire simultaneously with September futures, and the futures price will be the same as the cash index at expiration.

Your analysis is bullish, so the 10500 call (out-of-the-money strike price) is a reasonable alternative at a quoted premium of 10.10. You pay $1,010 for the call ($100 · 10.10).

The payoff: at the September expiration, the value of the Dow Future is 10610. Now, your call is in-the-money, and you exercise it and garner the exercise value less the premium, or $90 = $10 · (10610 − 10500) − $100 · (10.10) = $1,100 − $1,010. If the Dow Future stays at or below 10500, you let the call expire worthless and simply lose the premium. This is the maximum possible loss on the call. If the Dow Future increases by 101 points above the strike price, you break even.

Instead of buying the call option, the trader could have invested $100,500 directly in the Dow stocks. Given a value of the Dow Future of 10110 in September, he would have had a gain of $3,030. If he had invested directly in the stocks, however, an unexpected market decline would have led to a loss.

Exploiting Market Reversals

The trader expects a reversal of the Bull Market now at 7800 and would like some downside protection.

He buys a put with a strike price of 7700 (out-of-the-money). The put premium is 9.80, for a total cost of $980 = $100 · 9.80. If the Index decreases to 7600, with a corresponding decrease in the futures contract in September, the put is worth $1,000. The maximum loss is the premium cost, which is lost if the Dow Future is above 7700 at expiration. The trader breaks even if the Dow Future decreases by 98 points below the strike price.

Using Puts to Protect Profits in an Appreciated Portfolio

During a sustained Bull Market, investors often search for ways of protecting their paper profits from a possible market break. Even when fundamental economic factors tend to support a continued market upside, investors have to guard against unpredictable "technical market corrections" and market over-reactions to news.

Selling stocks to reduce downside risk is costly in fees and taxwise and sacrifices potential price gains. What is desirable in a sideways market environment is an instrument that protects the value of a portfolio against a market drop but does not constrain upside participation. This is precisely what put options are designed to do.

Situation 1

The market is in an uptrend in August. And the market lives in anxiety that the Federal Reserve will tighten short-term interest rates further in the coming months. The trader has $78,000 invested in the Dow portfolio, and the Dow Future is at 7800.

In order to hedge his portfolio, he purchases a put option on September futures against a possible market downturn. He buys a 7600 put at a premium of 6.60, cost $100 · 6.60 = $660.

Buying the put places a floor on the value of the portfolio at the strike price. Buying a put with a strike price of 7600 effectively locks in the value of the portfolio at $76,000. Above its strike price, a put is not exercised and the portfolio value is unconstrained. If the trader is wrong, and the market goes up, he loses the premium paid for the put. Depending on which strike price he chooses, he increases or decreases downside risk. He breaks even when the Dow Future reaches a value of 7534 = 7600 – 66, the strike price less the put premium. At this level, the unprotected and put-protected portfolio are equally profitable.

The similarity to life insurance is striking. If you don't die, the premium is wasted. But if you do....

Improving Portfolio Yields

Situation 2

All markets, as the reader is perhaps aware, are not trending. Days, weeks, months (sometimes years) can pass while the markets grind up and down in what are euphemistically known as trading range markets. When the astute technician identifies one of these market doldrums and judges that it will continue so he can reap other returns on his portfolio by selling puts and calls on Dow Index futures.

For example, when the Dow Index is 10000 and the trader calculates that it will not break out for the next month above 10200, he sells calls at a strike price of 10200. The quoted premium of the 10200 call is, say, 10.10; selling a 10200 call generates $1010 income.

The trader pockets the entire premium as a profit if the index remains below 10200 at the September expiration. The downside of this trade is that the trader gives up price appreciation above 10200. Above 10200, the combined value of the portfolio and short call premium is $101,010. The break-even point is 10301, where the Dow Future is equal to the sum of the strike price and call premium. Above this point the covered call portfolio becomes less profitable than the original portfolio. Since the short call is covered by the portfolio, this strategy is not exposed to the risk represented by a naked call. The main risk is that the trader gives up the profit potential above the strike price of the call. As is obvious to the technician, this is a bad strategy in trending markets. Only in clearly range-bound markets would an enlightened trader want to write covered calls. The call premium collected is some compensation for this risk, but cold comfort when the trader has misanalyzed the market. The best strike price of the call depends on the probabilities you have assigned to future increases and behavior of the Dow.

Using Option Spreads in High- or Low-Volatility Markets

Long and short stock positions reflect definite market opinions or analyses. The market will go up or the market will go down and the moderately competent technician should be right about this more often than the unwashed general public. In markets of coiling volatility (i.e., lower than average volatility and declining), it is sometimes possible to exploit uncertainty by putting on a long straddle. The long straddle combines a long put and a long call at the same strike price. This spread generates a return over two ranges of market values: values below the strike price of the put and values above the strike price of the call. It is a profitable strategy given sufficient volatility. The Editor's company used such a strategy immediately before the crash of 1987 for managed accounts and collected disproportionate profits on a very low risk position. Experienced speculators and traders generally sell high-volatility markets and try to backspread (go long) in chosen less volatile markets, expecting volatility to return to the mean. Sometimes they do this by writing a short straddle, a position with a short put and a short call at the same strike price.

Situation 3

In August, a technical analysis predicts that volatility will increase, and the market is in a coiling process. The direction of prices is uncertain but potentially explosive. The trader buys a straddle of a long put at 7800 and a long call at 7800. The quoted call premium is 18.90 and the quoted put premium is 13.90. The total cost of the straddle is $3280 = $100 · 32.80. This is the maximum loss if the Dow Future stalls at 7800.

The straddle makes a profit when the Dow Future moves enough to recover the cost of the straddle, either below 7472 = 7800 − 328 or above 8128 = 7800 + 328. The potential upside profit is unlimited. The maximum profit on the downside is $10 · (7800 − 328), or $74,720, if the Dow Future goes to zero (somewhat unlikely, but one never knows what Chicken Little the investor will do if he thinks the sky is falling).

Situation 4

In August, the investor calculates that options are overvalued and that volatility will be lower than implied volatility. He expects a dormant market to continue through the end of the summer. He decides to sell the September put and call at 7800, collecting $3280. The return on this short straddle will turn negative if the Dow Future in September goes below 7472 or above 8128. The maximum loss on the downside is $10 · (7800 − 328), or $74,720, and the loss on the upside is unlimited. The investor, however, perceives the risk as limited, because he believes that the Dow Future will neither increase nor decrease to these levels within the next month when the options expire. Of course, in these cases, the trader must also consider catastrophic risk — as, for example, the Editor's client who was short puts in the crash of 1987 and lost $57MM.

Perspective (EN9: Once again, do not practice the methods and techniques described in this chapter without complete confidence in their use. A course in futures and options is recommended, or professional consultation.)

I like to tell these stories so that prospective options traders and general investors are made dramatically aware of the potential dangers, as well as the potential profits. As I have said elsewhere in this book, the novice should work to achieve competence and experience before attempting advanced tricks in futures and options. On the other hand, the investment use of these instruments for prudent hedging and insurance is recommended to the investor willing to do his homework, acquire competence, and grow in investment skills.

Dow Index futures and futures options present new techniques of portfolio protection and profit-making for the general investor. Numerous strategies can be practiced by the moderately competent investor using these instruments. Keep in mind always that all the methods of analytical investing espoused in this book are the base discipline: that is, knowledge of the instruments and their use; prudent trade management; and stop loss discipline; and close attention to the dynamics of the situation.

Above all, the existence of these instruments allows the most conservative of investors insurance and hedging techniques not previously available.

In sum, knowledge of the DJIA Futures and Options on Futures is absolutely essential for the competent technical investor and trader.

Recommended Further Study

In view of the importance of this chapter, I note here references to advanced material, which will also be found in *Resources* (Appendix D). For more information:

> *Options as a Strategic Investment* by Lawrence Macmillan.
>   (www.optionstrategist.com)
> Chicago Board Options Exchange: www.cboe.com
> Chicago Board of Trade, 312-435-3558 or 800-THE-CBOT.
>   Fax: 312-341-3168; http://www.cbot.com

part two

Trading Tactics

Midword

As a kind of foreword to the second part of this book, we might mention a commentary, "On Understanding Science: An Historical Approach," by James Bryant Conant, president emeritus of Harvard.

Dr. Conant points out that, in school, we learn that science is a systematic collection of facts, which are then classified in orderly array, broken down, analyzed, examined, synthesized, and pondered; and then lo! a Great Principle emerges, pat, perfect, and ready for use in industry, medicine, or what-have-you.

He further points out that all of this is a mistaken point of view which is held by most laymen. Discovery takes form little by little, shrouded in questioning, and only gradually assumes the substance of a clear, precise, well-supported theory. The neat tabulation of basic data, forming a series of proofs and checks, does not come at the start, but much later. In fact, it may be the work of other men entirely, men who, being furnished with the conclusions, are then able to construct a complete, integrated body of evidence. Theories of market action are not conceived in a flash of inspiration; they are built, step by step, out of the experience of traders and students, to explain the typical phenomena that appear over and over again through the years.

In market operations, the practical trader is not concerned with theory as such. The neophyte's question, "What is the method?" probably means, actually, "What can I buy to make a lot of money easily and quickly?" If such a trader reads this book, he may feel that there is "something in it." He may feel "It's worth a try" (a statement, incidentally, that reflects little credit on his own previous tries). And he may start out quite optimistically, without any understanding of theory, without any experience in these methods, and without any basis for real confidence in the method.

In such cases, the chances are great that he will not immediately enjoy the easy success he hopes for. His very inexperience in a new approach will result in mistakes and failures. But even with the most careful application of these methods, in correctly entered commitments, he may encounter a series of difficult market moves which may give him a succession of losses. Whereupon, having no solid confidence in what he is doing, he may sigh, put the book back on the shelf, and say, "Just as I thought. It's no damn good."

Now if you were about to go into farming for the first time, you might be told (and it would be true) that the shade tobacco business offers spectacular profits. But you would not expect to gain these profits without investing capital, without studying how shade tobacco is grown, in what kinds of soils, in what localities, nor without some experience with the crop.

Furthermore, you would need confidence — faith in the opportunity and also in the methods you were using. If your first season's crop were blighted (and these things do happen), you would naturally be disappointed. If it should happen that your second year's crop were destroyed by a hailstorm, you would be hurt and understandably despondent. And if your third season's crop were to be a total loss due to drought, you would probably be very gloomy indeed (and who could blame you?). But you would not say, "There's nothing to it. It's no damn good."

You would know (if you had studied the industry and the approved cultivation methods) that you were right, regardless of any combination of unfavorable circumstances, and you would know that the ultimate rewards would justify your continuation no matter how hard the road, rather than turn to some easier but less potentially profitable crop.

So it is with technical methods in the stock market. Anyone may encounter bad seasons. The Major Turns inevitably will produce a succession of losses to Minor Trend operators using the methods suggested in this book. And there will be times when a man who has no understanding of basic theory will be tempted to give up the method entirely and look for a "system" that will fit into the pattern of recent market action nicely, so that he can say, "If I had only averaged my trades.... If I had followed the Dream Book.... If I had taken Charlie's tip on XYZ.... If I had done it this way or that way, I would have come out with a neat profit."

It would be better, and safer, to understand at the start that no method that has ever been devised will unfailingly protect you against a loss, or sometimes even a painful succession of losses. You should realize that what we are looking for is the probability inherent in any situation. And just as you would be justified in expecting to draw a white bean from a bag which you knew contained 700 white beans and 300 black beans (even though you had just drawn out 10 black beans in succession!), so you are justified in continuing to follow the methods which, over long periods, seem most surely and most frequently to coincide with the mechanism of the market.

So this book should not be given a quick "once-over" and adopted straightaway as a sure and easy road to riches. It should be read over and over, a number of times, and it should be consulted as a reference work. Furthermore, and most important, you will need the experience of your own successes and failures so that you will know that what you are doing is the only logical thing you can do under a given set of circumstances. In such a frame of mind, you will have your portion of successes; and your failures, which you can take in stride as part of the business, will not ruin either your pocketbook or your morale.

In short, the problem stated and analyzed through this whole volume is not so much a matter of "systems" as it is a matter of philosophy. The end result of your work in technical analysis is a deep understanding of what is going on in the competitive free auction, what is the mechanism of this auction, and what is the meaning of it all. And this philosophy does not grow on trees. It does not spring full-bodied from the sea foam. It comes gradually from experience and from sincere, intelligent, hard work.

The second section of this book, which follows, is concerned with tactics. Up to this point, we have been studying the technical formations and their consequences. We should have a good general understanding of what is likely to happen after certain manifestations on the charts. Knowing that, however, we will still need a more definite set of guides as to when and how it is best to execute this or that sale.

This section is based on one man's experience and his analysis of thousands of specific cases. It takes up questions of method, of detail, and of application, and should provide you with a workable basis for your actual market operations. As time goes on, you will very likely adopt refinements of your own, or modify some of the suggested methods according to your own experience. But the authors feel that the suggestions made here will enable you to use technical analysis in an intelligent and orderly way that should help to protect you from losses and increase your profits.

John Magee

chapter eighteen

The Tactical Problem

EN: Magee in this chapter addresses the question of tactics for the "speculator" who follows short- and medium-term trends. Chapter 18.1 addresses the question of strategy and tactics for the long-term investor. See Chapter 18.1 for a discussion of the term "speculator."

It is possible (as many traders have discovered) to lose money in a Bull Market — and, likewise, to lose money trading short in a Bear Market. You may be perfectly correct in judging the Major Trend; your long-term strategy, let us say, may be 100% right. But without tactics, without the ability to shape the details of the campaign on the field, it is not possible to put your knowledge to work to your best advantage.

There are several reasons why traders, especially inexperienced traders, so often do so poorly. At the time of buying a stock, if it should go up, they have no objectives and no idea of what policy to use in deciding when to sell and take a profit. If it should go down, they have no way of deciding when to sell and take a loss. Result: they often lose their profits; and their losses, instead of being nipped off quickly, run heavily against them. Also, there is this psychological handicap: the moment a stock is bought (or sold short), commissions and costs are charged against the transaction. The trader knows that the moment he closes the trade, there will be another set of charges. Also, since he is not likely to catch the extreme top of a rally or the extreme bottom of a reaction, he is bound, in most cases, to see the stock running perhaps several points against him after he has made his commitment. Even on a perfectly sound, wise trade, he may see a 10% or more paper loss, before the expected favorable move gets under way. Obviously, if he weakens and runs for cover without sufficient reason before the stock has made the profitable move he looked for, he is taking an unnecessary loss and forfeiting entirely his chance to register a gain.

The long-term investor who buys in near the bottom and remains in the market to a point near the top, and then liquidates and remains in cash or bonds until (perhaps several years later) there is another opportunity to buy in at the bottom, does not face the continual problem of when to buy and when to sell. This assumes that one can tell precisely when such a bottom has been reached, and that one can also tell when the trend has reached its ultimate top (and those are very broad assumptions indeed). The long-term investment problem for large gains over the Major Trends is by no means

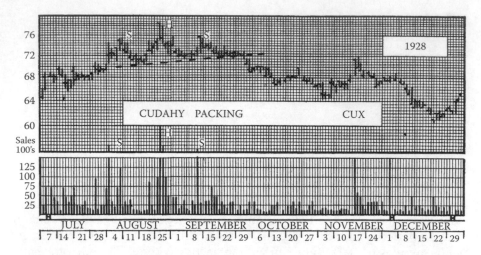

FIGURE 200.   It is possible to lose money owning stocks in a Bull Market. Notice that this Major Top Formation did not occur in 1929, but in the summer of 1928. For more than a year after this, a majority of stocks and the Averages continued the Bull Market Advance. But Cudahy declined steadily, reaching a price below 50 well before the 1929 Panic, and continued in its Bearish course for over 4 years, ultimately selling at 20. Except for the somewhat unusual volume on the head on August 21, this is a typical Head-and-Shoulders Pattern with a perfect Pullback Rally in mid-November. It underscores what we have mentioned before; that a Head-and-Shoulders Top in a stock, even when other stocks look strong, cannot safely be disregarded.

The Head-and-Shoulders Pattern, either in its simple form or with multiple heads or shoulders, is likely to occur at Major and Intermediate Tops, and in reverse position at Major and Intermediate Bottoms. It has the same general characteristics as to volume, duration, and breakout as the Rectangles, and the Ascending and Descending Triangles. In conservative stocks, it tends to resemble the Rounding Turns.

as simple as it sounds when you say, "Buy them when they're low, and sell them near the top." However, such large gains have been made over the long pull, and they are very impressive. *EN: Note the record of the Dow Theory in Chapters 5 and 5.1.*

This section of the book is concerned more particularly with the speculative purchase and sale of securities.

There are some basic differences between the "investment" point of view and the "speculative." It is a good thing to know these differences and make sure that you know exactly where you stand. Either viewpoint is tenable and workable, but you can create serious problems for yourself, and sustain heavy losses, if you confuse them.

One difference is that, as a speculator, you are dealing with stocks as such. A stock, to be sure, represents ownership in a company. But the stock is not the same thing as the company. The securities of a strong company are often weak; and sometimes the securities of a very weak concern are

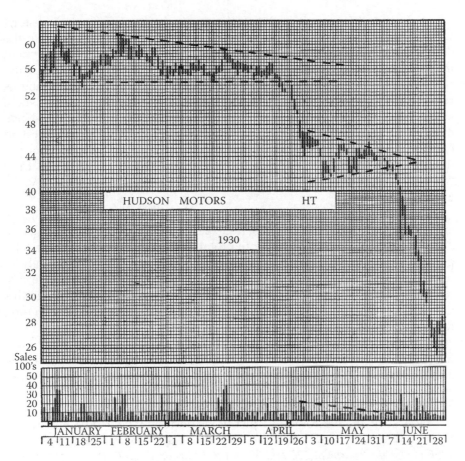

FIGURE 201. What would you have done with Hudson Motors? The great Panic Move of October–November 1929 carried the Dow–Jones Industrial Average down from its September all-time high of 386.10 to a November low of 198.69. A rally, bringing the Average back to 294.07 in April 1930, recovered 95 points or 51% of the ground lost, a perfectly normal correction.

Suppose you had bought HT after the decline from its 1929 high of 93½, say at 56, in the belief that the 37 point drop had brought it into a "bargain" range. On your daily chart, you would have seen the pattern shown above (which you will now recognize as a Descending Triangle) taking shape in the early months of 1930. Would you have had a protective stop at 51? Would you have sold at the market the day after HT broke and closed below 54? Or would you have hoped for a rally, perhaps even bought more "bargains" at 50, at 48, at 40? Would you still have been holding onto your "good long-term investment" when HT reached 25½ in June? Would you still have been holding HT when it reached its ultimate 1932 bottom at less than 3? (See Figure 65.) *EN: See Figure 201.1 for a recapitulation of the lesson from the 2000s.*

exceedingly strong. It is important to realize that the company and the stock are not precisely identical. The technical method is concerned only with the value of the stock as perceived by those who buy, sell, or own it.

A second difference is in the matter of dividends. The "pure investor," who, by the way, is a very rare person, is supposed to consider only the "income" or potential income from stocks — the return on his investment in cash dividends. *EN: This* rara avis *is largely extinct now.* But there are many cases of stocks which have maintained a steady dividend while losing as much as 75% or more of their capital value. There are other cases where stocks have made huge capital gains while paying only nominal dividends or none at all. If the dividend rate were as important as some investors consider it, the only research tool one would need would be a calculator to determine the percentage yields of the various issues, and hence their "value." And, on this basis, stocks paying no dividends would have no value at all.

From the technical standpoint, "income," as separate from capital gains and losses, ceases to have any meaning. The amount realized in the sale of a stock, less the price paid and plus total dividends received, is the total gain. Whether the gain is made entirely in capital increase, or entirely in dividends, or in some combination of these, makes no difference. In the case of short sales, the short seller must pay the dividends. But, here again, this is simply one factor to be lumped with the capital gain or loss in determining the net result of the transaction.

There is a third source of confusion. Very often, the "pure investor" will insist that he has no loss in the stock he paid $30 for, which is now selling at $22, because he has not sold it. Usually he will tell you that he has confidence in the company and that he will hold the stock until it recovers. Sometimes he will state emphatically that he never takes losses.

How such an investor would justify his position if he had bought Studebaker at over $40 in 1953 and still held Studebaker Packard at around $5 in 1956 *(EN: Or Osborne at $25 and $0 in the 1980s or Visacalc at similar prices in the same decade. EN9: Or Enron and WorldCom in the 2000s.)* is hard to say. But for him, the loss does not exist until it becomes a "realized" loss.

Actually, his faith that the stock will eventually be worth what he paid for it may be no more than a speculative hope; and a forlorn one at that.

Furthermore, one may question whether his reasoning is always consistent. For example, suppose another stock this investor had bought at $30 was now selling at $45. Would he tell you that he did not consider a profit or loss until the stock was sold? Or would he be tempted to speak of the "profit" he had in this purchase?

It is all right to consider gains or losses either on the basis of "realized" or completed transactions, or on the basis of the market values "accrued" at a particular time. But it is not being honest with yourself to use one method to conceal your mistakes and the other method to accentuate your successes. The confusion of these concepts is responsible for many financial tragedies. *EN: One might almost say, in the modern context, that such confusion amounts to willful or neurotic behavior. Given the easy availability of portfolio software which "marks to market" positions, avoidance of this knowledge can only be regarded as self-defeating.*

As a trader using technical methods, you will probably find the most realistic view is to consider your gains and losses "as accrued." In other words, your gain or loss at a given time will be measured with reference to the closing pricing of the stock on that day.

Recapitulating, it is important: (1) to avoid regarding a stock and the company it represents as identical or equivalent; (2) to avoid the conscious or unconscious attribution of "value" to a stock on the basis of dividend yield, without regard to market prices; and (3) to avoid confusing "realized" and "accrued" gains or losses.*

The technical trader is not committed to a "buy and hold" policy. There are times when it is clearly advantageous to retain a position for many months or for years. But there are also times when it will pay to get out of a stock, either with a profit or with a loss. The successful technician will never, for emotional causes, remain in a situation which, on the evidence at hand, is no longer tenable.

An experienced trader using technical methods can take advantage of the shorter Intermediate Trends, and it can be shown that the possible net gains are larger than the entire net gains on the Major Trend, even after allowing for the greater costs in commissions and allowing for the greater income tax liability on short-term operations.

But it should be understood that any such additional profits are not easily won. They can be obtained only by continual alertness and adherence to systematic tactical methods. For the market, regarded as a gambling machine, compares very poorly with stud poker or roulette, and it is not possible to "beat the market" by the application of any simple mathematical system. If you doubt this, it would be best to stop at this point and make a careful study of any such "system" that may appeal to you, checking it against a long record of actual market moves. Or ask yourself whether you have ever known anyone who followed such a system alone, as a guide to market operations, and was successful. *EN: After Magee wrote this, many successful traders, aided by computer technology and advances in finance theory, have created objective systems which have been successful in the financial markets. However, the markets usually become aware of the success of these systems and develop counterstrategies to defeat them. So there is a tendency for the performance of mechanical systems to degenerate or totally fail over time. In fine it is the happy combination of the system with markets hospitable to it which makes mechanical systems successful over defined periods of time.*

The practice of technical analysis, on the other hand, is not a mathematical process, although it does, of course, involve mathematics. It is intended to search out the significance of market moves in the light of past experience in similar cases, by means of charts, with a full recognition of the fact that

* Some of the most serious and dangerous "traps and pitfalls" of the market are tied up with difficulties of perception on the part of the investor, and consequent misevaluations and faulty identifications. For a particular study of these psychological problems, see *The General Semantics of Wall Street* by John Magee. *EN: Now in its second edition as* Winning the Mental Game on Wall Street, *a title chosen by a computer, as edited by the present Editor.*

the market is a sensitive mechanism by which all of the opinions of all interested persons are reduced by a competitive democratic auction to a single figure, representing the price of the security at any particular moment. The various formations and patterns we have studied are not meaningless or arbitrary. They signify changes in real values, the expectations, hopes, fears, developments in the industry, and all other factors that are known to anyone. It is not necessary that we know, in each case, what particular hopes, fears, or developments are represented by a certain pattern. It is important that we recognize the pattern and understand what results may be expected to emerge from it.

The shorter-term profits are, you might say, payment for service in the "smoothing out" of inequalities of trends, and for providing liquidity in the market. As compared to the long-term investor, you will be quicker to make commitments, and quicker to take either profits or (if necessary) losses. You will not concern yourself with maintaining "position" in a market on any particular stocks (although, as you will see, we will try to maintain a certain "total Composite Leverage" [or risk and profit exposure] according to the state of the market, which accomplishes the same result). You will have smaller gains on each transaction than the longer-term investor, but you will have the advantage of being able to frequently step aside and review the entire situation before making a new commitment.

Most particularly, you will be protected against Panic Markets. There are times (and 1929 was by no means the only time) *(EN: 1987 and 1989 also come to mind. EN9: Add 2001-2, if you please: 5/21/01, Dow 11350; 9/17/01, 8062; and 3/18/02, 10673; 7/22/02, 7532)*, when the long-term investor stands to see a large part of his slowly accumulated gains wiped out in a few days. The short-term trader, in such catastrophes, will be taken out by his stop–loss orders, or his market orders, with only moderate losses, and will still have his capital largely intact to use in the new trend as it develops. *EN: The best technical analysts' opinion in "modern times" is that even long-term investors should not grin and bear a Bear Market. This is a necessity only for bank trust departments and large Wall Street firms which cannot afford to offend their invest- ment banking clients by suggesting that their retail clients should sell their holdings.*

Finally, before we get on with the subject of tactics, the operations we are speaking of are those of the small- and medium-sized trader. The meth- ods suggested here, either for getting into a market or getting out of it, will apply to the purchase or sale of odd lots, 100 shares, 200 shares, and some- times up to lots of thousands of shares or more of a stock, depending on the activity and the market for the particular issue. The same methods would not work for the trader who was dealing in 10,000-share blocks (except in the largest issues), since in such cases, his own purchases or sales would seriously affect the price of the stock. Such large-scale operations are in a special field which is governed by the same basic trends and strategy, but which requires a different type of market tactics. *EN: Or, put another way, as Magee said to me one time, a mouse can go where an elephant can't.*

Created with TradeStation 2000i by Omega Research•1999

FIGURE 201.0. If an investor only learned one thing from this book, and it were this one thing, that one thing might be the salvation of his portfolio, or his retirement plan (if all his assets in the investment plan were shares of Enron). Instead, the employees of Enron made a major mistake in not having a diversified retirement portfolio – they had all their eggs in one basket, their income and savings came from one source. But diversification is not even the crucial lesson here. The lesson is get out of the stock when it reverses. The corollary of that lesson is, never buy a stock in a downtrend. And there is even a more important lesson: Never buy a stock when it is in a swan dive. So obvious you say. Not so obvious at the time for portfolio managers for the University of Miami who continued to accumulate Enron stock even as it neared earth at 100 miles an hour. Of course they had sophisticated (?) company. The Motley Fools had a death grip on the stock all the way to the bottom.

chapter 18.1

Strategy and Tactics
for the Long-Term Investor

What's a Speculator, What's an Investor?

In the years since Magee wrote Chapter 18, some different connotations have attached themselves to the terms "speculator" and "investor." A great cultural shift has also occurred. The days when the New Haven (New York, New Haven and Hartford Railroad) was a beacon of respectability (and lent luster to its investor) and paid good dividends are gone forever. And so is the New Haven. In fact, after the turn of the century, corporations saw a change in investor sentiment about dividends. Investors wanted capital appreciation and cared less for dividends. In fact it has lately been considered the mark of a "growth stock" not to pay dividends. Evidently, the days of the New Haven are gone forever, when an "investor" was one who bought, held, and collected dividends, and "speculators" were slightly suspect men like Magee who played the medium-term trends and bought "unchic," "speculative" stocks. It all has a sepia tone to it.

Yesterday's speculator might be called a medium-term investor today.

While the term "speculator" could still be applied to anyone who "trades" the market, today that old-time speculator and his kind would more likely be called traders than speculators. Commodity traders who have no business interest in the contracts they exchange are always referred to as *speculators*, as opposed to *commercials*, who are hedgers and users of the commodities they trade. Now "day traders" might be considered the equivalent of the old-time speculators. And only the passive, in the opinion of this editor, never trade at all and sit on their holdings during Bear Markets.

On the spectrum of investors, from investor to gambler, the old "New Haven Investor" who "wants his dividends" is pretty rare these days, and, again, may be one of those trust departments which doesn't want to get sued and so stays out of stocks which go up. After all, prudent men don't "trade in volatile stocks" but "invest in safe issues, like bonds," which only lose about 1.5–2.0% of their purchasing value per year, but preserve the illusion of having "preserved principal."

One Definition of the Long-Term Investor

Let us take as a long-term investor now one who expects to at least track market returns, for it has been demonstrated over a relatively long period of time that this can be done by passive indexing. At the turn of the century, as this is written, it would seem neither long-term nor medium-term nor short-term investors think about the risks involved in matching the market since, entering the third millennium, it has been so many years since we have had a really vicious Bear Market. Dow 36000? This is a passing phase. As each Bull Market reaches higher and higher, the odds are lower and lower that it will continue — historic Bull Markets of the 1990s notwithstanding.

What then are the strategy and tactics for the long-term investor to achieve a goal of matching the market? *(EN9: Is it necessary to remind the reader of Chapter 5.1 and the Dow Theory?)*

Let us remark immediately that the tactics Magee described for the speculator — or trader if you will — are not at all in conflict with the short-term tactics used occasionally by the long-term investor. As buying or selling time approaches the stops of the long-term investor, that investor becomes a trader. Then he can and should adopt the trader's tactics. Sooner or later the focus even narrows to real time at the moment of trade execution. Interestingly, the charting techniques we have described here work on tick-by-tick data in real time also. So if the trader wants to enter into the real-time environment, he can attempt to time his trade right down to the real-time chart formations. Of course, only the really active and skilled long-term investor will be concerned with squeezing the last half point or points out of his position. But this illustration of the time focus is addressed to any investor or trader or speculator to demonstrate the fractal nature of both price data and the applicability of Magee-type technical analysis to it.

The Strategy of the Long-Term Investor

The strategy of the long-term investor is to catch the long trends — to participate in trades which last months and years. But this strategy does not intend to be sucked into long Bear Markets. Rather, portfolios are liquidated or hedged when Bear Market signals are received. As has been previously seen in examples of the performance of (more or less) mechanical Dow Theory (Chapter 5), this kind of performance can be quite satisfactory — better indeed than buy-and-hold strategies which have come much into vogue because of the Clinton–Gore Bull Markets of the 1990s.

If the goal is to beat not only the markets but the mutual funds (only 20% of which outperform the market over the long term anyway), then passive indexing is the most likely strategy. This may be done in a number of ways — index funds, buying the basket, buying the futures, etc. But the most attractive method might be the use of the SPDRs and DIAMONDS and the like. The tactics may be calibrated to the risk tolerance and character of the investor. He might hedge or sell on Dow Theory signals, or on breaks of the 200-day moving average, or on breaks of the long-term or intermediate trends lines with a filter (Magee recommended 2%, and this might be calibrated to the character of the markets, and increased to 3% or a factor relevant to actual market volatility). Instruments we have previously discussed — SPDRs, DIAMONDS, index futures, and options — can be used to execute these tactics.

Suffice it to say that every strategy must provide for the plan gone wrong, in other words the dreaded Bear Market. Bear Markets would not be so fearsome if the average investor did not insist on seeing only the long side of the market. Long-term strategies go out the window quickly when blood runs on the floor of the NYSE. The well-prepared technical investor has a plan which provides for the liquidation of positions gone bad and presumably the discipline to execute it.

This involves the regular recomputation of stops as markets go in the planned direction, and ruthless liquidation of losers which do not perform. One may think of a portfolio as a fruit tree. Weak branches must be pruned to improve the yield. Stop computation is treated in a number of places in this book (cf. Chapter 27). For the investor trading long term, this may be, as an example only and not as a recommendation, the breaking of the 200-day moving average and/or the breaking of a long-term trendline. The 200-day moving average is widely believed to be the long-term trend indicator, and believing will sometimes make it come true. *EN9: Let me emphasize here that "200" is a parameter and an example. Personal research may fit a better parameter to the actual market.*

In reality, more than the 200-day or a manually drawn trendline should be looked at. The chart patterns comprising the portfolio should be considered also, as well as charts of major indexes and averages. Also consider the condition of the averages and their components — their technical state — whether they are topping, consolidating, trending as indicated by their charts.

Rhythmic Investing

In addition, if Chapter 31 on "Not All in One Basket" is weighed seriously, one might be rolling a portfolio from long to short gradually in natural rhythm with the markets and in harmony with the Magee Evaluative Index described there. That is the preferred strategy of the authors and editor of this book.

These things all depend on the goals, temperament, and character of the investor. If he is going to spend full time on the markets, he is probably not a long-term investor. Such men eat well and sleep soundly at night. The trader is lean and hungry — not necessarily for money, but for activity. It behooves one to know his type as a trader or investor. And knowing one's type or character is best established before finding it out in the markets, as the markets can be an expensive place to search for self-knowledge.

There is no inherent conflict in holding long-term positions and also attempting to profit from intermediate trends, depending on the amount of capital in hand. It depends on how much time and energy and capital the investor wants to put into trading. A long-term strategy can be implemented with a modicum of time and energy, as follows. Pay attention to the major indexes and averages and buy on breakouts, at the bottoms of consolidations and on pullbacks. Sell or hedge on the breaking of trendlines, calculated on basing points (see Chapter 28) and the penetration of support zones.

The long-term investor will accept greater swings against his position than the intermediate-term trader or speculator. As an example with the method of using basing points in Chapter 28, the speculator is using a "3-day-away rule," whereas a long-term investor might be using a 4-week basing point or some such analogy. And, if interested, when he suspects or analyzes that a long Bull Market is approaching a climax, he might adopt the 3-day rule also, or even begin following his stock with a daily stop just under the market. Beware though. Professionals look for stops just under the close of the previous day in situations such as these.

It would be wise not to confuse long term investing with "buy and hold" or as it was expressed in one investment fad in the 1970s, "one decision investing." As an example of this misguided thinking, in 1972, the "best and brightest" investment analysts (fundamental) on the Street picked a portfolio of stocks for the generation, or twenty years. The companies would be difficult to argue with as the crème de la crème of American business. After all who could qvetch at Avon, Eastman Kodak, IBM, Polaroid (unless he happened to look at Figure 253), Sears Roebuck, and Xerox? Even today if you didn't have a close eye on the market, you would immediately respond, "blue chips." Here is a table showing the stocks and the results achieved over the long term.

Stock	Price 4/14/72	Price 12/31/92	Percent Change
Avon Products	61.00	27.69	(54.6)%
Eastman Kodak	42.47	32.26	(24.0)%
IBM	39.50	25.19	(36.2)%
Polaroid	65.75	31.13	(52.7)%
Sears Roebuck	21.67	17.13	(21.0)%
Xerox	47.37	26.42	(44.2)%

Charts showing activity for IBM and Xerox appear on the following pages.

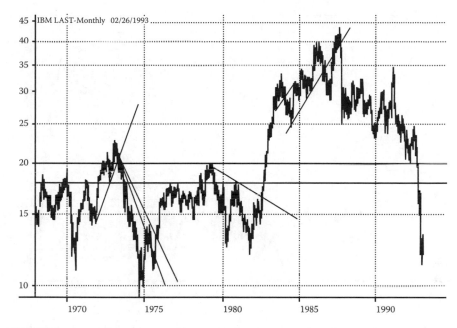

FIGURE 201.1.   The questionable—even bizarre—results of "one-decision invest-ing" are amply illustrated by this chart. First of all, the "best and brightest" recom-mended IBM at a decade high to see it decline by more than 50%. It subsequently recovered to double from their original recommendation. Ah, sweet justification! Only, unfortunately, at the end of 20 years to see it rest approximately 40% beneath the recommendation. The analytical lines give some hint of how a technician might have traded the issue. I like to say that there are bulls, bears, and ostriches, and anyone who followed this one-decision investment proves my case.

Figure 201.1.1 Like IBM in the previous figure, Xerox was recommended at a place where it should have been sold instead of bought. The comments there might apply to the chart here. The foolishness of "buy and hold" or "one decision investing" is amply illustrated by observing the long term swings of the stock and thus of the investor's equity. Technical analysis is intended to be an antidote to such foolishness.

Summary

The long-term investor attempts to catch major market moves — those lasting hundreds, if not thousands of Dow points and stay in trades for many months if not years.

Within this time frame he expects to take secondary trends against his position. Depending on his temperament and inclination, he may attempt to hedge his portfolio upon recognizing secondary market moves against his primary direction.

His preference for stocks and portfolio will be for market leaders, for baskets that reproduce the major indexes (or Index Shares) as the ballast for his portfolio, and he may choose some speculative stocks to add spice to his portfolio.

In spite of his penchant for long-lasting trades he will not tolerate weak, losing, or underperforming stocks. They are the shortest of his trades. He will cut losses and let profits run, the truest of the market maxims and the least understood by unsuccessful investors. The other maxim least understood by investors is "buy strength, sell weakness."

Truly sophisticated investors attempt to participate in Bear Market trends also. This is the greatest difference between professional and general investors — professionals have no bias against the short side.

For the convenience of day traders, the URL of Gamblers Anonymous is noted: www.gamblersanonymous.org.

chapter nineteen

The All-Important Details

In this chapter and the one following, we take up a number of elementary suggestions which are intended largely for the benefit of those who have never kept charts before. Much of this will seem obvious and repetitive to the advanced student, although even he may find some thoughts that will simplify his work. The beginner should read these chapters carefully and use them for later reference.

The details of how and when you keep the charts will not guarantee you profits. But if you fail to work out these details in such a way as to make your work easy, as part of a regular systematic routine, you cannot expect to keep up your charts properly, or to make any profits either.

Charting, and analyzing your charts, is not a difficult process, nor will it take too much of your time if you have determined on a reasonable number of charts, and if you have arranged for doing the work regularly, meaning every day without fail.

You will need a source of data — the day's market prices and volume. If you live in a big city, your evening paper will carry the complete list, and you can plan to set aside a certain period before dinner, or after dinner, or during the evening. If you cannot allot such a period and keep it sacred against all other social or business obligations, then plan to do the charting in the morning. But set a definite time and let nothing interfere, ever, or you are lost. *EN: Of course, this process is radically simplified by automated computer downloading procedures and access to data sources and Internet sites.* But the principle is the same.

You should have a suitable place to work and keep your charts. If it is at home, in the dining room or living room, other members of the family should understand that what you are doing is important. You should be able to shut the door and work without interruption. The light should be bright and as free from shadows as possible. (It makes a big difference, especially if you are keeping a large number of charts.) The ordinary desk lamp throws a reflected glare directly across the paper and into the eyes. It can be a strain if you are doing much of this close work. Better to have an overhead light, placed just a few inches in front of your head and a convenient distance above; and if this light can be a fluorescent fixture using two 40-watt lamps, you will get almost perfect shadowless lighting. These suggestions apply, of course, in case you are not working by daylight.

Have plenty of room. A big desk top, a dining room table, with a large clear space for chart books, extra sheets, pencils, scratch paper, ruler, calculator, computer equipment, and anything else you need. If your working surface is fairly low, say 28 or 29 inches from the floor, it will be less tiring than the usual 30-inch desk height.

Whether you are working in ink or in pencil, pick out the writing tool that is easiest for you to use. If you are using pencils, try several different makes and degrees of hardness. Find one that is hard enough not to smudge too easily, and yet is not so hard that you have to bear down to make a clean black mark. The wrong kind of pencil can tire you and irritate you more than you realize. Also, have plenty of pencils, a dozen at least, well-sharpened, so that as soon as one becomes a trifle dull and you are not getting a clean, fine line, you can simply lay it aside and continue at once with another fresh-sharpened pencil.

Keep your charts in loose-leaf books, with big enough rings to make turning the pages easy. Don't overcrowd the books. Get new books if a volume is too crowded. Finished charts may be kept in file folders. The only ones that need to be in the books are the current sheets and the sheets for the immediately preceding period. If possible, use a seven-ring binder. Pages are easily torn loose from two- and three-ring binders, but seven rings will hold the pages safely and you will seldom have one tear out.

The charts you keep will become increasingly valuable to you as the chart history builds up. The old chart sheets will be very helpful to you for reference. Provide a file or space where they can be indexed and kept in chronological order, and also file folders for brokers' slips, dividend notices, corporate reports, clippings and articles, notes on your own methods, and analyses and special studies of the work you are doing.

In this connection you will, of course, keep a simple but complete record of each purchase, sale, dividend, etc., on stocks you have bought or sold. This record will make your work much easier when the time comes to figure out income taxes. It will also give you all the statistical information you need to judge the results of your trading operations.

EN: At the beginning of my investment career, and often in the middle of it, I thought the above was cracker-barrel wisdom. The longer I last the more I think that homespun wisdom might be the best kind to have in investing — somewhat like Mark Twain, who was astounded at how much his father increased in wisdom the older Twain himself got.

We may restate the modest homilies above: Be serious. Be methodical. Be disciplined. Be business-like. Anyone who succeeds in investing without these qualities is the recipient of blind luck and will be fortunate not to fall into a hole before his career is over.

These thoughts occur when one is wondering how Magee would have viewed the advent of the microcomputer and its impact on technical analysis and investing. Might he have said, "What hath this tool wrought?! — Wonders and abominations!!"

Given the possibilities for complicating analysis and operations when confronted with all the bells and whistles of the average computer software package, the investor must maintain perspective. What, then, are the all-important details in practicing technical analysis with the aid of a computer?

The Simplest and Most Direct Way to Use a Computer for Charting Analysis

In reality, the computer can be used as a simple tool to do a simple job. There is nothing inherently complicated about keeping a chart on a computer. All computer software packages enable bar charting. And many, if not most, enable many other kinds of charting, from candlesticks to oscillator charting. The process, in almost all commercially available packages, is so simple that explaining it here would be superfluous (cf. Resources, Appendix D, for demonstrations), except to say, in general, it consists of retrieving data, updating the program's price database, and clicking an icon to run a chart. The software packages themselves explain their features better than can be done here. What is important here is to give perspective.

In this respect, charting can be done with quite expensive programs and also on publicly available free programs, or freeware. Charting can also be done with interactive charting programs on many Internet sites. The basic bar chart can be enhanced with an unending number of technical studies — moving averages, oscillators, etc., etc. Therein lies the danger. Chart analysis in itself is a qualitative process. Decorating graphic charts with number-driven information and studies can lead the general investor astray — and into confusion and indecision.

So the first preference of this analyst is to keep the process as simple as possible. Get the data. Draw a chart. Analyze the patterns. Consider the volume. Draw the appropriate analytical lines. This can usually be done by the program on the screen. Often a better graphic picture may be obtained by printing the chart and hand-drawing the analytical lines. And this brings to the fore one of the main problems of almost all the software packages — that screen graphics are poor and, at least to old chartists, disorienting. They are especially disorienting to analysts who are accustomed to working on Tekniplat chart paper. With passing editions of Resources, this problem will be dealt with. (EN9: In the intervening years since the 8th Edition two things have occurred: the Editor adjusted to modern technology and the technology achieved a level of excellence acceptable to a carping analyst. Internet technical analysis sites such as stockcharts.com and prophet.net improved to be surprisingly valuable resources at unbelievably low prices – even free.)

The question of graphic representation of the facts is worth noting as a persistent one. To a certain extent, the individual analyst will solve this conundrum by adapting his eye and mind to a graphic environment, using one graphic method consistently and seeing how it relates to the facts in the market. John Magee-oriented solutions to this problem will be available on the web site, www.edwards-magee.com.

In Resources, the reader may see some examples of very simple and inexpensive software packages and Internet sites which are quite adequate to the required tasks of charting technical analysis, as well as more complex number-driven analysis.

Summary

The computer is an invaluable tool for analysis. Use of it will enable the following:

- *Data may be acquired automatically via Internet or dial-up sites at little or no cost. Some of these even offer real-time data, which is a way for the unsophisticated trader to go broke in real time; but which the general investor may desire on the day of executing a trade. Many of these sites offer every kind of analysis from respectable technical analysis (usually too complicated) to extraterrestrial channeling.*
- *A computer package and Internet portfolio sites will give the analyst virtually effortless portfolio accounting and mark to the market prices — a valuable device to have to keep the investor from mixing his cash and accrual accounting, as Magee says.*
- *The computer will enable processing of a hitherto unimaginable degree. An unlimited number of stocks may be analyzed. Choosing those to trade with a computer will be dealt with in Chapters 20 and 21.*
- *Resources (Appendix D) contains information on software packages which the reader may try and purchase at quite reasonable prices. In all likelihood, the least expensive of these will be adequate to the needs of most general investors. In addition, I present a brief discussion of Internet sites and resources.*

chapter twenty

The Kind of Stocks We Want — The Speculator's Viewpoint

The specifications of the kind of stock we want to chart are fairly simple, and they are few. We want a stock which will enable us to make a profit through trading operations. That means a stock whose price will move over a wide enough range to make trading worthwhile. There are those who are concerned mainly with safety of principal and the assurance of income from a stock. For them, there are *(EN9: Or were.)* stocks which afford a very considerable degree of stability. You may (and probably will) want to keep a substantial part of your total capital in stocks of this type. They move in a narrow price range. They are extremely resistant to downside breaks in the market. They are also (and necessarily) unresponsive to fast upside moves in the market as a whole. These stocks are highly desirable for the conservative investor. However, they are not the most suitable issues for trading operations, since their swings are small, and commissions would tend to diminish the narrow trading profits that could be taken. Also, they do not make the sharp, clear chart patterns of the more speculative issues, but move in rounding, sluggish undulations. *(EN9: These remarks reflect a bygone time. The described stocks by and large went the way of the Dodo. When T can disappear from the market as a factor there is no place to hide, except in bonds, which, when stagnant, only lose real value at the rate of inflation and loss of purchasing power of the dollar. And even bonds should be subject to frequent reevaluation using the tools described in this book.)*

To amplify this comment and explain a bit about what underlies what we are doing, let us assume a certain company has two issues of stock, a preferred and a common. Since (we will assume) the concern has a certain steady minimum profit which it has earned for years, sufficient to pay the preferred dividend, the continuance of these dividends seems practically assured. But the dividends on the preferred are fixed at, let us say, 6%. Now the common stock gets all that is left. In one year, there may be 50 cents a share for the common stockholders. The next year, there may be $2.00 a share or four times as much. In a case like this, if there are no other factors, you would expect the preferred stock to sell at a fairly steady price without much change, whereas the common stock is subject to a "leverage" and might shoot up to four times its former value. The more speculative issues represent either a business which is, by its nature, uncertain as to net profit from year to year, where the volume of business or the profit margin fluctuates widely, or one in which the majority of the "sure" net profit has been sheared off for the benefit of senior obligations. There are also other factors that affect the speculative swing of a stock, and, as a result, one issue may be very sensitive and another extremely conservative; and between them there would be all shades and degrees of sensitivity or risk. It is enough here to note briefly that the nature of the business itself does not always account for the habits of the stock, since the other factors may be very important. But most stocks have a fairly well-defined "swing" power, and you can usually determine by past performance how a stock will behave in the future as to the extent of its swing. *(EN9: Or we might say, short-term volatility and long-term range.)*

Incidentally, for short-term trading *(EN9: Amusing in the modern context. By short-term trading Magee means trading of trends of shorter length than Dow Waves)*, we are thinking about the habits of the stock which are only partly determined by the business it represents. Purchase of stock in one company which has a somewhat uncertain or fluctuating profit record may be more conservative than purchase of a highly leveraged stock of another company whose basic business is steadier and more conservative. We will take up the matter of determining these risk constants a little later.

One should also understand that the short sale of a stock does not imply any feeling that the country is going to the dogs or even that the concern represented is going to the dogs. Such a sale merely indicates your belief that the stock may be temporarily overpriced; that earnings or dividends may have been abnormal in recent years and are likely to be reduced; or that for one reason or another, the stock of the company may be worth a bit less than it has been worth.

For technical trading, we want a fairly speculative stock, one which will make sizable swings up in a Bullish Trend, and down in a Bearish Trend. The very factors which tend to make a stock safe and desirable to the investor may make it entirely unsuitable for trading. And with certain reservations, which we will take up, the more speculative the stock the better it is for our purposes.

EN: Entering the third millennium (since we Anglo-Saxons started counting — the fourth or fifth by other measures) the distinctions between "speculative" stocks and every other kind of stock has grown increasingly blurry. Rather than apply a perhaps pejorative (in the minds of some readers) term like "speculative" to otherwise innocent stocks, we would do better to describe stocks as wide ranging or narrow ranging, as volatile or nonvolatile. Stocks may then be evaluated one against another by their betas and historical volatilities, statistical data easy to obtain. "Betas" and "volatilities" are dealt with in Chapters 24 and 42.

In line with this more current thinking, there is another question for readers of this book and that is the choice of trading (or investment) instruments for the long-term investor. That question is taken up by the editor in Chapter 20.1.

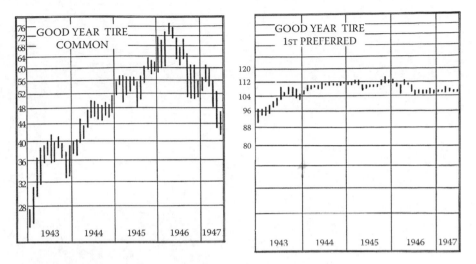

FIGURES 202 and 203.   Opportunity vs. security. Here (at left) is Goodyear Common, representing the residual interest in all profits after senior obligations have been met, compared (at right) with the Goodyear $5.00 Preferred, which carries a high degree of assurance that the $5.00 dividend will be met, but no promise of further participation in profits. Monthly range of each stock for the same 54-month period is shown on a ratio scale. As the Common makes an advance of over 300%, the Preferred advances about 25%, leveling off at a point which represents the maximum price investors are willing to pay for the sure $5.00 dividend.

The Kind of Stocks We Want — The Long-Term Investor's Viewpoint

Changing Opinions About Conservative Investing

Virtually no one invests like the conservative investor described above in Chapter 20 — except perhaps trust departments of antediluvian banks. There may be some investors still out there who are so risk averse that they still follow the method described. Bank trust departments may be still doing it. They used to do it so the trust beneficiaries couldn't sue them. Of course, they should be sued for incompetence. But that is the reason trust departments exist, in order to give legal cover (the so-called "prudent man rule") to trustees in case of suit by beneficiaries. Most enlightened trust departments and trustees now probably follow indexing or other more productive strategies in order to cater to new understandings of the prudent man rule. A beneficiary of a trust which has been mismanaged or has radically underperformed the market should certainly seek redress.

"Indexing" refers to the practice of constructing a portfolio so as to replicate or closely reproduce the behavior of a widely followed index such as the S&P 500 or the Dow–Jones Industrials. These portfolios never track the Indexes exactly because the advisors and funds who manage them take management fees and expenses. These fees are generally less than fees and expenses on actively managed funds, but in fact are not necessary for the private investor to pay. Unnecessary because even the tyro investor can now use "Index Shares" (e.g., DIA, SPY, QQQQ, etc....) or other proxy instruments to do what the funds and professionals do. Essentially what indexing does is track the Averages, a strategy which was impossible or difficult (expensive) when Magee examined it, as in Chapter 15. *(EN9: In the opinion of this editor hiring a management company to run an indexing strategy is imprudent and a waste of capital. Much better for the investor to invest directly AND to exit the market when uptrends end and reverse. This is a much better strategy than "passive indexing" which cleverly manages to capture both lossses and profits in the Averages.)*

The Kinds of Stocks Long-Term Investors Want

Perhaps one of the most important actualizations of this eighth edition is to bring current this book's treatment of the Averages, noting that it is now possible to trade the Averages in stock-like instruments. This fact deserves to be marked as an vitally important development in modern markets. The importance, if it is not obvious, was explained in detail in Strategies and Tactics for the Long-Term Investor, Chapter 18.1. This chapter will confine itself to describing facilities for trading and investing in the Averages and Indexes.

In 1993 the American Stock Exchange (AMEX) introduced trading in SPDRs™ or Standard & Poor's Depositary Receipts, an Exchange-traded unit investment trust based on the S&P 500 Composite Stock Price Index. The AMEX calls these securities Index Shares™, a name they also use for other similar instruments. As noted above, large investors and funds have long traded "baskets" of stocks representing the S&P 500, obviously an activity requiring large capital. And in fact a certain class of investment managers and funds have practiced "passive investing" meaning indexing, primarily for large clients.

The purchase and liquidation of these and other "baskets" is one form of "program trading."

Recognizing the utility of this investment practice, the AMEX created the SPDR as a proxy instrument to allow the smaller investor to practice the same strategy. The effectiveness of this product introduction may be measured by public participation in the trading of the SPDR (SPY). By 2000, almost $15 billion was invested in SPDRs with more than 100,000,000 shares outstanding. These units allow the investor to buy or sell the entire portfolio or basket of the S&P 500 stocks just as he would an individual stock. But the capital required to do so is radically reduced.

In 1998, the AMEX introduced DIAMONDS™ (DIA), Index Shares on the Dow–Jones Industrial Average™, which is analogous in every way to the SPDRs. Thus an investor may "buy the Dow–Jones Industrial Average." So in current financial markets, it is possible to "buy the market," unlike those conditions under which Edwards and Magee operated.

Construction of the Index Shares and Similar Instruments

The AMEX unit investment trusts are constructed to replicate the composition of their base instrument. The SPDR, for example, is an instrument which represents $1/_{10}$ of the full value of a basket of the S&P stocks and trades on the AMEX, just like a stock. Other characteristics of stocks are also reproduced. Long life: the SPDR Trust lasts into the 22nd century. Quarterly dividends: quarterly cash dividends are paid on the SPDRs reproducing dividends accumulated on the stocks of the S&P 500. Even dividend reinvestment is possible, and the units may be traded on the AMEX during regular trading hours. Under normal conditions, there should be little variance in the price of the SPDR relative to the S&P 500.

These elements, as discussed for SPDRs, are common to all the Index Shares — DIAMONDS, WEBs, etc. There are, of course, some expenses and costs to using the Index Shares — a small price to pay for the use of the instrument, and generally less than the costs of a fund. Index Shares are also much more flexible for the independent investor. Among other advantages the private investor can control the tax consequences of his investment, which is not possible in funds.

Other Exchanges have created similar security instruments or derivatives or futures to replicate or track the well-known averages and indexes. Among these are tracking shares or index shares or futures (let us call them "instruments") on other indexes (Russell, Nikkei, etc.) or options on the futures or indexes until there is a bewildering array of instruments available for trading, investing, and hedging. Among the more important exchanges and instruments traded are the Chicago Board of Trade (futures and options on futures on the Dow); the Chicago Mercantile Exchange (futures on the S&P, Nikkei 225, Mini S&P 500, S&P Midcap 400, Russell 2000, and NASDAQ 100); Chicago Board Options Exchange (S&P 100 and 500 options).... This, by no means, is an exhaustive list. All the futures and options which matter will be found listed in *The Wall Street Journal* under Futures Prices, or Futures Options Prices.

This book does not deal in comprehensive detail with futures and options. But it is worth mentioning these exchanges and their futures and options products because of the facility that they offer the investor and trader for hedging portfolios in Index shares and Average trading, not to mention opportunities for speculating.

Briefly, hedging is the practice of being neutral in the market. That is, one might be long the DIAMONDS and buy a put option on the DJIA at the Chicago Board of Trade, meaning that advances in the DJIA would result in profits in the DIAMONDS, and a loss of premium in the put. Conversely, a decline in the Dow would result in profits in the put and losses in the DIAMONDS. As this area is not the province of this book, this is a highly simplified description of a hedge. Nevertheless, the reader should see and understand that hedging can be a very important strategy. Hedging can take the place of liquidation of a portfolio when the analyst recognizes a change of trend or unstable conditions but does not wish to incur taxes, or wishes to defer them.

An Outline of Instruments Available for Trading and Investing

It would be herculean to attempt to list the entire panoply of averages, indexes, futures and options available for trading — herculean due to the fact that new trading instruments are constantly in creation, and due to the fact that, now operating at Internet speed, we may expect the rate of change to accelerate. In addition to those listed above, there are WEBS (World Equity Benchmarks — meaning that exposure to world markets may be arranged).

In all, approximately 30 or more Index Share units or instruments were available for trading on the AMEX at the turn of the century, in addition to DIAMONDS and SPDRs. Similar instruments exist on the Philadelphia and in Chicago, and others are being created daily. In order to reduce the confusion, the general investor will probably find the major indexes of the most importance. The more instruments one deals with the more complicated become the strategy and tactics. Therefore, the Dow, the S&P 500, and the NASDAQ composite (DIA, SPY, QQQQ) are probably sufficient for the purposes of the gentleman (or gentlelady) investor. The Mid-Caps, the Nikkei, etc., etc., begin to come into play when the trader begins to try to catch sector rotation, fads, short-term cycles, etc.

The Importance of These Instruments: Diversification, Dampened Risks, Tax, and, Most Important, Technical Regularity

It would be difficult to underestimate the importance of these new trading instruments. First of all, they afford the private investor what was previously reserved for the large capital trader — the ultimate in market diversification. The S&P 500 represents stocks comprising 69% of the value of stocks on the NYSE. Buying it is literally buying the American economy. The 30 Dow Industrial stocks represent the most important symbol in the American economy — and perhaps in the world. Investors are well advised to pay attention to both averages if they would fare well in the markets. Note the plural: *markets*. These two averages now have the influence or clout that once the Dow alone had to express the state of the markets and stocks in general.

Buying the SPDR or DIAMOND then represents the immediate acquisition of a diversified portfolio. And buying the NASDAQ or QQQQ gives one immediate exposure to the more speculative and volatile sector of the American economy. Given the long-term bullish bias of the averages and the American economy, it is difficult to argue with this as both strategy and tactics for the long-term investor. This does not mean that positions should be taken blindly without thought, or that positions should not be monitored. On the contrary, recall if you will the record of the Dow Theory. Even for the long-term investor, Bear Markets should not be allowed to destroy liquidity and equity value. These questions are discussed at greater length in Chapter 18.1.

While we believe these instruments are good vehicles, it is wise to remember Magee's frequent admonition (less important now than when spoken) that it is a market of stocks, not a stock market. Meaning that when the tide is flowing down with the Dow and S&P, prudence and care must be used in taking long positions in stocks which are in doubt as to direction. And it is worth noting that investments in these instruments will be less profitable than an astutely chosen individual stock. For example, Qualcomm appreciated approximately 240% (temporarily) in 1999–2000 compared to about 24% in the S&P over the same period. Those who bought Qualcomm at its top and sold it at the bottom of its reaction lost about 75% or about $148 a share. Traders in Qualcomm tended to obsess and pay hyperattention to the stock, while investors in the SPDRs reviewed it once a week or less, or told their computers or their brokers to give them a call if it broke the trendline, or entered stops. Then they slept at night and had eupeptic digestion.

Other advantages accrue to the trading of the SPDRs. Ownership of a fund can result in tax liabilities as managers adjust portfolios to reflect changing membership in the fund or withdrawals in capital by irate stock-holders. Since Index Shares last into the 22nd century the long-term investor has no need to realize gains and pay taxes. Bear markets may be dealt with by hedging with other instruments — futures, options, or proxy baskets of stock, or individual stocks, and accepting the tax consequences of these trades.

John Magee aptly observed before the direct trading of the averages was possible that the Dow–Jones Industrials were very regular and dependable from the technical point of view. This observation is annotated at some length in comments on Dow Theory in Chapters 5.1 and 36. So the investor in the Index Shares may have a smoother time technically than a trader of an individual stock.

Summary

The long-term investor and mid-term speculator attempt to capture long secular (as well as cyclical) trends in the markets. They shun frequent trading and capital-eroding transactions.

They recognize that risk fluctuates with time and trend and they know that frequent turnover benefits mainly the broker. The strategy of the long-term investor may be to match the market by using funds or SPDRs or baskets. But he does not like to participate in bear trends. He hedges or liquidates his positions on major trend shifts. And in fact he may even short the indices if his analysis indicates major bear markets.

If he desires to outperform the market (which will happen automatically if he follows the methods of this work), he finds some individual speculative stocks to trade in addition to his foundation portfolio. Depending on his risk tolerance, he may always be somewhat hedged. When long the indices, he finds some stocks in downtrends to short. When he is short the indices he finds some strong stocks to hold long. There is no excuse for a moderately skilled and reasonably capitalized investor to lose money over the long term in the market.

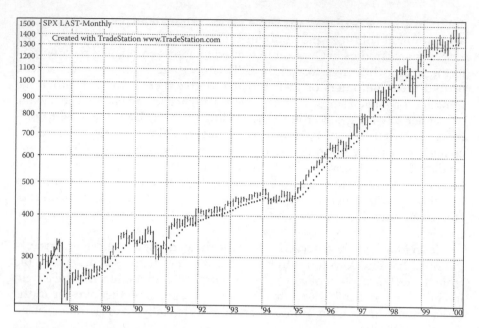

FIGURE 203.1.   S&P. Here the benefits of relaxed long-term investing may be seen, buttressed, of course, by the longest and handsomest Bull Market in American history in the Clinton–Gore years. At the end of this record, the effects of public enthusiasm (or as Chairman Greenspan of the Fed said, "irrational exuberance" *vide tulipomania)* can be seen in the wide undisciplined swings (best seen in Figure 203.2). Dotted line represents 150-day (approximately) Moving Average.

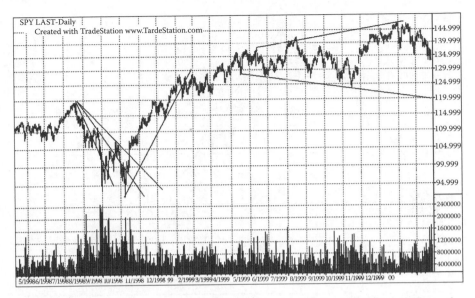

FIGURE 203.2.   SPDR. For illustration, here is a chart of the AMEX Index Share, the SPYDR, or share based on the S&P 500. The costs and benefits of this instrument as an investment vehicle are explored in the text of Chapter 20.1. After the, what shall we call it, crash?, of 1998 (the Asian Economic Flu crash), the fan lines tell a story, as does the last phase of the chart where the market whips in what appears a Broadening Top. *EN9: Note that this Broadening Top was identified in 1999–2000, before the crash. See Figure 203.3.*

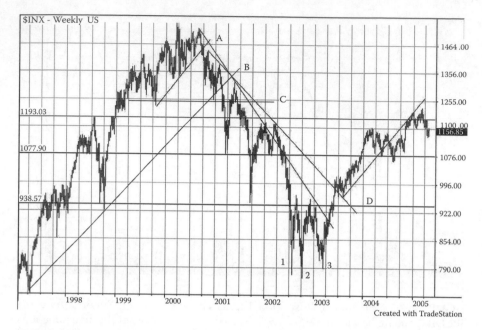

FIGURE 203.3.   The S&P 500 in all its glory and tragedy. An especially good portrait by Holbein, the younger. The Broadening Top pointed out in Figure 203.2 in 2000 foretold the decline of the S&P to below 790 – not quite 50% but close enough to catch the eye. Especially fine lessons here, besides the Broadening Top lesson. All of them *screaming* for action. The broken trendline at A, the broken trendline at B, the broken "neckline" or horizontal line at C. Notice the close correspondence of the break at B and C. The next lesson is not to buy down trends until a clear bottom is made in a major bear market. And clearly no bottom is made until the Kilroy Bottom at 1 – 2 – 3. Even then the least risky trade for the long term investor is when the Kilroy Fenceline (Neckline) is broken at D. All of this was knowable at the time.

chapter twenty-one

Selection of Stocks to Chart

The trader who operates on the "fundamental" basis, making his commitments on his analysis of earnings, dividends, corporate management, prospects for the industry, etc., will usually (of necessity) confine himself to a few stocks or a single group of stocks in the same field.

To the contrary, the technical trader, using daily charts, should have a large portfolio of issues. Since he is primarily interested in the technical chart patterns, he will not try to make an exhaustive study of the background of each company. In fact, the characteristics of the stocks themselves, as they act in the market, are more important to him than what these companies make or what they are earning. This is because, although the stocks represent ownership in the company, the capital structure, "leverage," and floating supply of the stock may (and very often does) mean fluctuations in the stock price that are not directly in proportion to changes in the affairs of the business.

You will also find many cases where the stock of a well-regarded, well-managed, long-established concern, whose latest earnings report shows increased profits, and with a long record of dividends paid, would not be a good buy at the market price. It may be overpriced and due for a serious depreciation. You will find other cases where a stock, which apparently represents no great promise of either earnings or dividends, suddenly starts a series of spectacular moves upward, and is indicated clearly as a buy. Of course, the answer, in each case, is that the records available apply to the past, not the future; and very often, chart action will indicate the inside knowledge of those who are in possession of facts the public has not yet received.

To change our example to something more easily visualized: there are two houses for sale. One is a fine, well-built, modern home in an attractive part of town at, say, $200,000 — and the other property, a somewhat shabby six-family tenement in a less attractive section, at the same price of $200,000. There is no question which is the "better" house. But in a case like this, the market for well-built single homes at this price may be poor, while the demand for apartments may be good. The six-family house may be the better investment.

And then again, we have the question of what is conservative and what is highly speculative. It is not always enough to judge from the type of business of the company itself. You may have a highly conservative concern, carrying on a stable volume of business, with a long record of successful operation. And yet, if there are bonds, debentures, preferred stocks, and other senior obligations, the common stock may be subject to wide fluctuations. Also, if the issue is small, or if a large part of it is closely held, you will have a "leverage" effect which results in wide swings in the stock.

Therefore, in choosing your stock to chart, you will want to consider the kind of stock and its character and habits in the market, rather than the business of the concern it represents. We will come back to this point and show you how you can shape up a list that will give you the kind of stocks you want for trading.

Meanwhile, the question "How Many Charts?" has been left hanging. One answer to this is that the more stocks you chart, the more good opportunities you will have. Many stocks, even of active issues, will go through long periods when the chart tells nothing — when, indeed, there is nothing much to tell. In a period of stability, the chart simply indicates that it is a period of stability, and the only possible trading activity would be purchases and sales at the Bottoms and Tops of its undulations. The charts are more informative when a change in the situation occurs; they will signal a change of trend as soon as (and usually before) the news of the changed conditions has come out. If you have enough charts, you will always have some stocks making decisive and clear-cut moves either up or down, at any time.

You should, therefore, keep as many charts as you can. Don't bite off more than you can chew, however. A man with only 15 minutes to half an hour a day for this work might have to confine himself to 20 or 30 charts. It would be much better if he could have 100. And if he is in a position to give a major part of his time to the work, he could very well run as many as 300 charts. A most important word of caution is indicated here. Don't start anything you can't finish. It is better to have too few at the beginning than too many. Then, if you find that you can add others, you will be in a better position, from your experience, to pick out the ones you want to include. But if you start with too many charts, begin to run behind with your analyses, you will not be getting the best use from your portfolio, and it would be better to cut down at once. *EN: Magee's admonitions are still in effect for the manual chartist. The modern computer-equipped investor has a different problem. He can chart every issue in the market every day. The question becomes, how many can he effectively study and analyze? There is even a computer answer to this question. Namely, the cybertrader can program the computer to report stocks on an exception basis. For example, "Computer, show me all the stocks which are above their 50-day moving average and which have unusual volume."*

From what we have already been over, you know that it is possible to chart anything that is sold in identical units in a free competitive market. This includes, of course, all kinds of commodities, bonds, debentures, when-issued contracts, etc., as well as stocks. You may have some special interest which will call for charting something outside the field of stocks. Well and good.

In general, however, you will want to chart active, listed stocks of well-established corporations. There is no reason an unlisted stock cannot be charted, but ordinarily, the only figures you can obtain on it are the bid and offer prices. On these stocks, you do not have a published statement of the volume of sales each day or any record of prices at which sales actually took place, and those are essential to the charting of daily technical action. Therefore, you will usually be charting stocks which are listed on some exchange. This is also an advantage, since concerns listed on the larger exchanges are required to meet certain conditions, publish certain information, and comply with definite rules and practices. In this book, most of the examples have been taken from stocks listed on the New York Stock Exchange. There are thousands of issues traded on the NYSE, and these stocks represent every type of security, from the most conservative to the most speculative, from the cheapest to the most expensive, and they include every principal type of industry and business. However, there is no reason that stocks should not be chosen from the American Stock Exchange, the NASDAQ, or from any other exchange in this country, or for that matter, in some other country. *So far as the chart action is concerned, the patterns and their meanings will be the same. (Editor's italics.)*

EN9: In general the stocks to watch, or chart, will tend to leap out of the haystack of stocks. For stock pickers Investors Business Daily *is in the constant process of sifting the markets for nuggets with its CANSLIM system. (Not a recommendation to use that system, only a recommendation to examine every tool that might be of use.) Stocks which appear suddenly on the most active lists of prophet.net and stockcharts.com might bear examination by the chart analyst. Optionable stocks which suddenly show a radical change in implied volatility. Stocks which pop up with suspicious volume spikes compared to average volume. And with Internet and software packages one might construct a filter to be informed by the computer of stocks breaking their 14, 44, 150, and 200 day moving averages. 14 because some professionals think the public thinks in this time frame; 44 because some think funds think in 44 day time frames. The others because everyone thinks they are important.*

chapter twenty-two

Selection of Stocks to
Chart — Continued

In choosing your stocks, you will probably look for the greatest diversity in the *kind* of industry. Since you are not specializing in the detailed study of a single group, you will try to get stocks from as many different groups as possible. You will want to include mines and oils, rails and chemicals, liquors and amusements, airlines, utilities, techs, Internets, biotechs, *ad infinitum*.... The reason for this is simply that, very often, many stocks in a particular industrial group will show the same or similar patterns, as the entire industry is affected by certain Major conditions. You will often find, for instance, that when Allis-Chalmers *(EN: or Dell)* makes a Triangle or other Area Pattern, followed by a sharp upward move, Deere *(EN: or Compaq)*, Minneapolis-Moline, Harvester, and Case will make similar Triangles, or possibly Rectangles or some other Consolidation Pattern, followed by a similar upward move. When Schenley is moving in a long downtrend, you will very likely find that Distillers — Seagrams, National Distillers, Publicker, and American Distilling — are also moving in a long downtrend. *EN: Metaphorical names, like the names of Greek gods. Or Ulysses and Leopold Bloom. The present-day reader may read Intel, Fairchild, and National Semiconductor or 3COM. The idea is the same.*

Therefore, unless you plan to keep enough charts to include several stocks of *each* important group, it is best to pick your stocks to make up as widely diversified a list as possible. In this way, during times when certain groups are moving indecisively, or are inactive, you will have some representation in other groups which may be active. (Do not infer from this that all stocks of a group move together at all times. Individual concerns will frequently move according to special influences that bear on a single company. But where the Major influence is some industry-wide condition, the group will move more or less as a unit.)

We, therefore, choose stocks representing a wide variety of groups or basic industries. But, suppose we are limited as to the number of charts, and we must choose one stock from a group; which stock to choose? Suppose, for instance, we must choose one stock from the transportation group. *EN: Or Biotech, or Internets.* As a matter of fact, you would probably want more than one because this particular group is so important and so large. But for the moment, let us choose just one. *EN9: Or, even better, why not one of the indexes for the desired group. An example of betting on all the horses rather than trying to pick the winner, and there is no conflict between making both bets.*

Should it be a high-priced stock or a low-priced stock? Let us examine that point first.

If you examine the past records of stocks you will find that, in general, the lower-priced issues make much larger *percentage* moves than the higher-priced stocks. It is not unusual for a stock selling around 5 to make a rise of 100%, moving up to 10 sometimes within a few weeks. On the other hand, you do not find 100% moves in days or weeks among the stocks selling at 100 or 200. The same industry-wide move which carries your $5 stock from 5 to 10 might carry your $100 stock from 100 to 140. Obviously, if you had put $1000 into outright purchase of the stock at 5, the move would have increased the value of your stock 100% or $1000. In the other case, if you had put the same amount into a stock at 100, the move to 140 (although many more points) would have increased your capital to only $1400. The gain in the lower-priced stock would be about two- and one-half times as great.

The authors have worked out and tabulated the percentage moves of large groups of stocks over long periods of time (cf. Appendix A), and have set up a table which shows the *relative* average sensitivity of stocks at different price levels. This table pertains only to the price level of stocks; thus, the same stock which today sells at 5 and makes wide percentage swings will not swing so widely when it has moved up to a price level of 20 to 30.

Several questions may come to your mind at this point. Do not the costs of trading low-priced stocks relative to higher-priced issues have to be taken into account? *EN: Yes, they do. Given the extreme changeability in these costs in the Internet economy, calculation of those costs here would be tantamount to wasting trees. This cost question may be researched quickly and easily given availability of google.com and the Internet.*

In selecting the price level of the stocks you prefer to trade in, you cannot set too arbitrary a limit, since there are other factors to consider, and you may have to make some compromises on one score in order to get what you want in some other direction. Stocks from 20 to 30 are in a good trading price range. Very often, you will find stocks in the 10 to 20 range which are so interesting you will want to chart them, and trade in them. You will find good situations in stocks selling at 30 to 40. Furthermore, you will understand, of course, that the stocks which are now selling at 10 may be selling next year at 40, or vice versa. And since you cannot be changing your portfolio of charts all the time, you must not be too "choosy" in picking the price range of your stocks. However, you would not ordinarily pick out a stock that was selling far above the price range of most stocks of its group, say at 150, when several others in the same industry were selling at 15, 28, or 37. For the high-priced stock, as we have said, is likely to be sluggish as

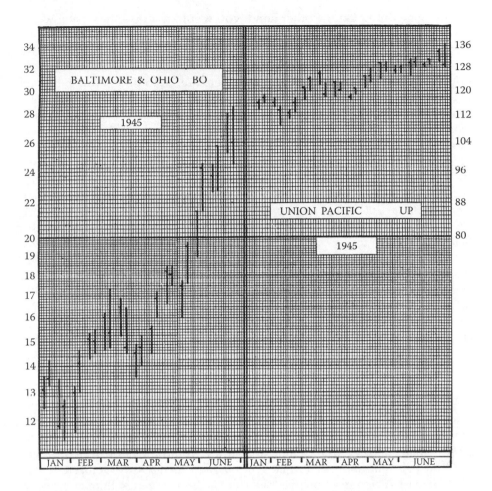

FIGURES 204 and 205. Low-priced stocks move faster than high-priced stocks.

Here are weekly charts of two rail stocks, charted on ratio scale over the same 6-month period. Baltimore and Ohio during this time advanced from 12⅜ to 28⅞, a gain of 16½ points, while Union Pacific moved up from 109 to 137, a gain of 28 points. The advance in "UP," however, compared to its price, is much less than the advance in "BO." A thousand dollars used for outright purchase of "UP" would show you a capital increase of 25%. On the other hand, if you had put a thousand dollars into outright purchase of "BO," your increase would have been 133%, or more than five times as much.

Bear in mind that low-priced stocks not only go *up* much faster, but also come *down* much faster than high-priced stocks. When you own a low-priced stock, you cannot safely "put it away in the box and forget it." For security and stability, you would do better to buy a few shares of a high-priced, gilt-edge security. But, for trading purposes, you will want to strike a compromise between the rather sluggish "blue chips" and the extremely erratic "cats and dogs" in the lowest price bracket.

a trading medium. On the other hand, you would not take the very lowest-priced issues of the group, selling at, say, 4 or 2 when others were in the 10 to 30 bracket. You would not only be faced with erratic and tricky chart action, and much higher percentage costs for commissions; but you might not be able to operate on margin at all. There are, from time to time, limitations on the amount of margin on stocks at all levels. In the lower-priced issues, these limits are often more stringent. And in the lowest-priced stocks, you are sometimes not permitted to trade on margin. *EN: Because these requirements are subject to the vagaries of the Federal Reserve Board, the investor must inform himself at his personal broker or ECN. For quite some years the general margin requirement has been 50%. The Fed came in for some sharp criticism for not dampening speculation in the* fin de siècle *bubble by raising margin rates to 100%, and its lack of action exacerbated the blow off of 2000. A change in margin rates should get the immediate attention of the tecnical analyst. Something will be up.*

Ordinarily, you will get the greatest effective leverage at some point in the 20s, considering all these factors. And your trading can run down through the teens and up through the 40s. Above 40 and below 10, you will have to have strong reasons for trading, which might be, of course, ample capital. It would therefore be best for the moderately financed investor to choose a majority of his stocks from the middle price range (10 to 40), plus only those special situations you are particularly interested in watching among the very low and very high brackets.

However, if you will go back to the long-time past record of any group of stocks, you will find that even among stocks moving at nearly the same price levels today, there are widely different behavior patterns. You will find that some stocks respond to a severe market setback by reacting, let us say, 20% — that is, if they were selling at 30, they would move down to around 24. And you will find others that will respond to the same setback in the general market by a reaction of 50% — that is, if they were selling at 30, they would end up at around 15. And you will notice, if you examine the records, that the same stocks which make these relatively different reactions in one setback will make about the same moves, relative to each other, in other setbacks. Furthermore, the same ones which make only moderate corrections on declines will make only moderate advances on rises. And the ones that go down sharply on setbacks will also skyrocket in a Bullish Market. This has nothing to do with the phenomenon we discussed earlier, by which we saw that cheap stocks move faster than expensive stocks. This is due to the habits of particular stocks, and these habits seem to be quite stable over periods of many years.

We will find, for instance, volatile and speculative issues which make larger percentage swings than most other stocks at their price level. And, on the other hand, we will find a stock, selling for much less, that has smaller percentage swings than most stocks at its price level. This fact may be obscured, as the comparatively low-priced stock may actually make larger swings than the higher priced. It is only when we have taken the price level into account that we can see what the individual habit of the stock really is. Knowing this, we can project that habit to other price levels.

We are not too interested, as we have said before, in stocks which do not ordinarily make substantial moves. We are very much interested in those which make the wider moves. We can compute the basic swing power of a stock, which we call the Sensitivity Index, and will outline the method for doing this in Appendix A. *EN: The procedure Magee speaks of here, of computing a "Sensitivity Index," may be regarded as the historical predecessor of what are now called "betas." The beta of a stock compares its relative volatility to that of the market as a whole, so that if the beta of the market is 1.00 and the beta of the stock in question is 1.50 a move of $1 in the market will probably be matched by a move of $1.50 in the higher beta stock. The formula for beta will be found in Resources, and calculated betas at* finance.yahoo.com.

So, you will have eliminated from your list stocks at the wrong price level and stocks without enough swing power (for you want to chart only those stocks in which you can trade profitably). Of the ones that are left, you will eliminate others. You will find that some stocks, which make wide price moves and apparently offer large opportunities for profit, may be very "thin." The charts will be spotty, filled with gaps, days of "no sale," and moves of several points on only a few hundred shares of business. These stocks are thin because of a small issue, because of ownership of a large block of shares by some corporation or by insiders, or for other reasons. They are difficult to trade in because they are hard to buy and hard to sell; you stand to lose heavily on the "spread" between bid and offer. It might be hard to liquidate even 500 shares without driving the price down badly, to your loss, and sometimes you will see changes of 1 or 2 full points between sales of single hundreds. These you will want to eliminate, and if you do not know the habits before you choose your portfolio, you will probably find it worthwhile to drop any stocks that prove too thin, substituting new and more dependable choices.

After you have culled the list from all these angles you will find you have left a choice of a number of stocks, all of them selling in a price range that is attractive, all of them sufficiently active and responsive to market trends, and all of them available in sufficient supply to provide a good trading medium. The final choice of any one (or several) of these stocks is then a matter of personal preference.

After you pick out your stocks from one group, study the other groups — the motors group, the amusements, the computers *(EN: the Internets)* and so forth, until you have finally made up your selection of stocks to follow. Try to get as complete and balanced a representation of groups as the number of your charts will allow. *EN: In this context, the process described here is made infinitely simpler by available software and by the proliferation of group indexes and indicators. In fact, if the investor desires, rather than trading an individual stock in an industry group, he may often choose to trade the average or index itself and cushion his risks. This will almost never be as profitable as a well-chosen individual issue, but will always be better than a badly chosen individual issue.*

In this connection, if you are not planning to represent all groups, there are some groups that are more likely to provide good trading stocks than others. The foods and tobaccos, for example, are generally less responsive to market swings than the rails, liquors, and airlines, which are very responsive. Do not worry too much, however, about exactly which stocks to choose. For even if you took the first 50 or 100 stocks in the listed issues, you would have among them at least 25 good trading stocks. You can start with almost any list, and, as time goes on, you will drop some and add others, improving your portfolio and tailoring it to your own needs.

EN: As additional commentary here it is worth noting that "techs," "biotechs" (or whatever the mania of the moment is — probably space hotels and intergalactic travel in this millennium) will present areas of risk and reward sufficient to excite the 17th century tulip trader. The centered investor and trader will consider vogues and manias as he chooses his active portfolio and choose to participate (or not) depending on his appetite for risk and excitement. Or as the popular maxim has it, one man's champagne is another man's poison. This question is pursued in greater detail in Chapter 23.

By way of further simplification, the investor may choose to follow only one or two issues — the SPDRs (SPY) or DIAMONDS (DIA). If it were not only bought, but also sold, or hedged, the market would be outperformed. This would be a simple investor's life indeed.

chapter twenty-three

Choosing and Managing High-Risk Stocks: Tulip Stocks, Internet Sector, and Speculative Frenzies

Nothing could more vividly illustrate the timeless nature of chart patterns and situations than the Internet stocks which bloomed at the turn of the century. These stocks repeated that eternal pattern — the tulipomania, the gold rush, the can't-fail-opportunity-to-get-rich-quick.

It is almost impossible to resist comparing the speculative frenzy which took place in the Internets and technology issues to the famous 17th century mania which Holland experienced in the famous tulipomania. In MacKay's undying classic account (*Extraordinary Popular Delusions and the Madness of Crowds*), the trading of tulip bulbs replaced sober commerce and business as the occupation of the country, and enormous fortunes were made trading the tubers. Blocks of real estate, breweries, assets of real and large value were traded for one tulip bulb. And MacKay produced my favorite paragraph in the literature of finance: "A golden bait hung temptingly out before the people, and one after the other, they rushed to tulip-marts, like flies around a honey pot. Every one imagined that the passion for tulips would last forever, and that the wealthy from every part of the world would send to Holland, and pay whatever prices were asked for them."

That mania ended in ruin. A better long-term prospect may be in store for the Internets as there is a basis of technology and economic substance to the sector. You could not, after all, use your tulip to check the market for prices. And, in fact there were those, admittedly a small number, who struck it rich in the California gold rush of 1849. It's an ill wind, etc....

But as an exercise in rueful perspective, the seventh edition of this book remarked, in the words of Richard McDermott, "Companies like Lotus or Microsoft went public and grew into business giants in a short period of time.... A significant theme stock for the 1990s has been Internet stocks. Names like America Online, CompuServe, and Netscape have provided important products and services that allow individuals to 'surf the net' for information around the world." Young students of the market will search in vain for Lotus, CompuServe, and Netscape in the lists of stock symbols. The giant Lotus was swallowed by IBM, in part because Microsoft, a ruthless competitor, disemboweled it. CompuServe and Netscape disappeared into the belly of a larger fish, AOL, with some of the same factors involved. Later Microsoft got its comeuppance — halving in value as the U.S. Justice Department brought successful antitrust action against it.

There are those who fault the great Wall Street investment banks for having brought half-baked potatoes (or unblooming tulips) to market. The Street firms, cashing in on the mania, were willing to sell the public every immature profitless idea and company named "dot.com inc" that venture capitalists floated on a sea of seed money. Mining engineers will recognize the phenomenon of "salting the mine." It was the finest moment for the great old firms of the Street since the investment trusts of the 1920s. The reader is most recommended to look into *The Great Crash 1929* by John Kenneth Galbraith to compare the Street firms' behavior from one mania to the next. It will be found most edifying. At the pinnacle of great manias, no one can be trusted.

Managing Tulipomanias and Internet Frenzies

In a time of excess, the centered investor maintains his composure and focus. Probably easier said than done. Nonetheless, many investors and traders profited from the Internet boom or were not severely damaged. Many managers and traders watched with envy from the sidelines, and with *schadenfreude* when the bubble burst.

For technical analysts speculating and trading according to the principles of this book, important opportunities arise in speculative frenzies and buying panics — namely important profits may be made by remaining calm and methodical while the uninformed and naive cause speculative blow-offs. And, speculative blow-offs have some things in common with the ends of great bull trends in substantive issues.

So the question becomes that of realizing some of the profits to be made in these exciting times. Of course, the first thing to do is not get excited. These manias come and go — sometimes they are called biotechs, sometimes computers, sometimes Internets, and probably, at some point, human genome miracle drugs or Martian real estate. It should be emphasized that these profits are to made on both sides, long and short. The crowd will only think of the riches to be made long. Professionals and skilled technicians, professional or not, will take the profits on the short side.

Here is the most important concept in trading these runaway issues: *all of the techniques and methods described in this book remain valid for dealing with these kinds of stocks.* In addition, here are some other points which should be taken into consideration. The sector in question, tech-tech, web-tech, biotech, Internet, space travel, whatever, will be a market unto itself, and special technical factors will apply to it. The phases of market lives, accumulation, attraction, mark up, mania, blow-off will occur in compressed time spans — much shorter than the cyclical life of an issue with fundamental data to attach it to reality (cf. Figure 205.2 of Palm Computing).

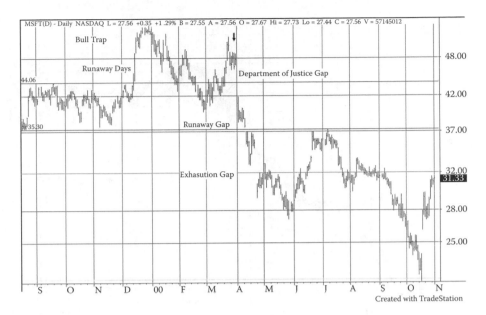

FIGURE 205.1. Multitudinous lessons in Microsoft. But short-lived joy. The top rounds over, price makes another attempt, and then the momentum is clearly, if puzzlingly down. The cancellation of the runaway day in January definitely marked this move as a bull trap, and the short-term trendline from October would also have taken the trader out of the trap. Use of basing points technique (Chapter 28) would also have allowed escape from the trap. Failed signals, as this one, often are excellent signals for a trade in the other direction.

By the time the IPO occurs, the insiders are already prepared to begin the distribution phase. For example, when Palm Computing was spun off from 3Com in 2000, only 3% of the shares were sold — creating an artificial scarcity and propelling it to absurd heights — so that Palm attained an instant market value greater than that of 3Com which owned most of its stock. *EN9: We have, since The Fall, learned of "laddering." In order to let their inside clients in on the IPO some of the underwriters required the clients to buy more of the stock in the open market after the IPO at higher prices. A clever way to throw gasoline on a raging bonfire. Whether Palm was laddered or not is not known.*

These issues must be traded with the utmost care and attention. For example, it is the height of foolishness to enter a market order to buy on the issue of the IPO. An issue going public at 12 might trade on the opening at 50 in these frenzies — a sign to the savvy technician that the sheep are headed for the shearing shed.

Certain factors must be kept in mind. Some IPOs collapse shortly after going public. Others rocket off before distribution is complete. So stops must be carefully computed. Once it is clear that the rocket is taking off, as indicated by price and volume, some discreet pyramiding might be possible for the experienced and skilled speculator.

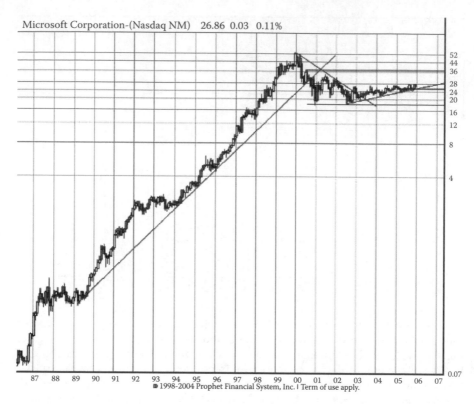

FIGURE 205.1.1. MSFT Monthly. It is easy to lose perspective when looking at a daily chart of a bull trap in which one has lost a leg. A monthly long-term look at Microsoft can help restore perspective. Unfortunately, the Dow–Jones Company was looking at this chart, not the nearby, when they added Microsoft to the Dow 30 in 2000. Expert timing? At the time the John Magee Newsletter observed that it was a negative indicator of a major top in the Industrials.

Detailed Techniques for Management of the Runaway Issues

The technique described in Chapter 28 for progressive stops is certainly one way of dealing with these stocks. There the method for finding basing points and raising stops based on the 3-days-away rule is detailed. Also, especially in the case of these rocket stocks, the practice of raising stops based on new percentage highs should be implemented. Since these are "game" situations, and irrational, one may employ tactics that he might not ordinarily use with his serious capital — some light pyramiding and some scaling out of the position based on continuous new highs. Additionally in the blow-off phase when close monitoring is necessary, one might want to exit on a long reversal day, or on a key reversal pattern (see Chapter 10.1), and then go to the beach. Or, if from Texas, one might want to short the issue.

MSFT(D) - Weekly NASDAQ L = 25.27 +0.82 +3.35% B = 24.27 A = 26.28 O = 24.88 Hi = 25.30 Lo = 24.79 C = 25.30 V = 98849923

Created with TradeStation

FIGURE 205.1.2.   The editor learns a lesson. Never leave a chart unanalyzed, even if the implications are obvious. And never be afraid to belabor the obvious. Obviously Figure 205.1.1 should have had a long-term trendline drawn on it. No monumental bull market should be ignored. Why give the market its money back? It should have been obvious from Figure 205.1 that the Microsoft party was over and not just the fat lady but the entire chorus was beating on anvils. And. The protective line must be drawn. Here the broken line at A is the most important and saves a bit of capital rather than waiting for the plaintive signal at C. Given the robust bull market in Microsoft the long-term investor might have been justified in waiting until the C trendline was broken. A matter of investing style and philosophy. There appears to be some long-term support at 18. And the 5 year sideways market appears to be resolving itself into a macro triangle which might breakout one way or the other in 2005. This is a case in which an investor might make a fundamental analysis to guide his position (always confirming with the chart analysis). Microsoft is beset with howling wolves on all sides. Linux, Unix, sales of only one copy of Windows in China, hackers playing hob with security holes in its software. Can it rise again? Only the chart knows for sure, and it is silent at this recording.

Essentially, I view these stocks as interesting aberrations in the early part of their lives. So I would not look for long-term investment type trades. Take the money and run. In all likelihood, these stocks will explode like fireworks and then expire. There will, of course, be the Microsoft and — it remains to be seen — the Yahoo. After the fireworks show, the patient technician may return to the scene of the crime to see if there are any burning embers. Once they have blown off, crashed, and made reasonable bottoms, then one begins to look for investment possibilities, which there will definitely be. The technology of the

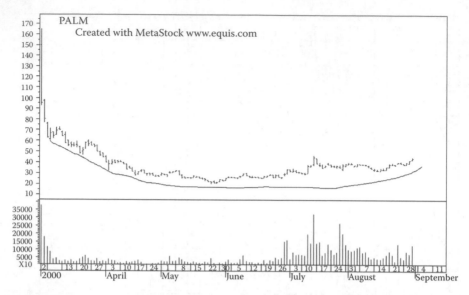

FIGURE 205.2. PALM. Fool's gold. Fool's gold with naivete writ large on it. Here is a spike reversal day on the initial day of trading. The accumulation, markup, and most of the distribution occurred behind closed doors before this trick was perpetrated. After the *matanza*, the continuation takes on the shape of a rounding bottom. Perhaps there is some real gold there — but only over the long term.

Internet — and biotech, and the human genome — there is too much potential in all of them for some phoenix not to rise from the ashes.

And, in the beginning it behooves the trader to regard them as speculative instruments of exceptional risk and opportunity.

Several caveats are in order.

> One, that the prudent speculator does not commit too much of his capital to such enterprises. Probably no more than 5–10%.
>
> Two, when selling them short, one should not be early. A definite top should be seen, because there might be a second stage of the rocket.
>
> Three, emotional involvement with tulips and Internet stocks — or stocks of any kind actually — can lead to a broken heart. In the charts, note the success in a number of cases of trading the key reversal day.
>
> *EN9: Reviewing charts from the apocalypse is a sobering experience. So many rash and mad adventures. So much capital sucked into the black hole of underwriters and 21-year-old huckster CEO wallets. Better than the South Seas Bubble. And, as definite proof that man is directly descended from geese and sees no farther ahead than the next feeding bowl the ghost of the mania oozes from the closet in 2005, reborn as Google mania. Man (or goose if you will) never learns. That's why he's so much fun to watch. Honk.*

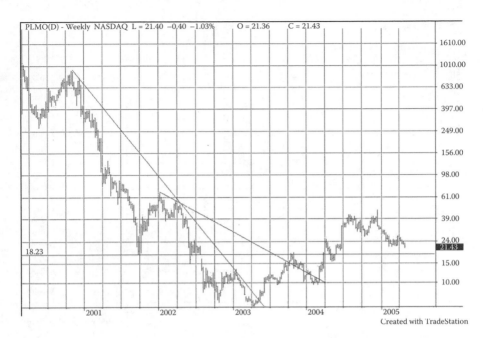

FIGURE 205.2.1.   Dealers palmed all the missing capital in PALM? Somebody made the money disappear up a shirt sleeve. What makes you think the deck was stacked? Or that the IPO was laddered? Maybe it was just fools chasing tulips. Those investors (gamblers) playing the shell game with PALM found themselves playing with 6 shells instead of three as like an insidious amoeba PALM divided into two tulips PLMO and PSRC. Keep you eye on the magician closely. For the analyst all the smoke and mirrors could not hide the fact that gravity took PALM in all its manifestations down. The downtrend lines are broken in 2003 and 2004 and a respectable Kilroy Bottom is made. But. The implications of the bottom may have already been carried out. A continuing story for speculators or astute (very astute) investors who know something fundamental and have very long-term vision.

Google. What a creature is man! What a game is the market! Google, a wonderful company, and a great concept goes public in 2004 after world class (World class? Intergalactic class!) hype. Floated as a red herring at 135 it eventually goes IPO at 85 in an innovative public offering. Then the fun starts. Future readers of this book may observe the mark up made as of the date of writing (November 2004) and judge whether the method worked. A company on roller blades, impossible to dislike as a company. Remember, unless you are Warren Buffet you are buying the stock, not the company.

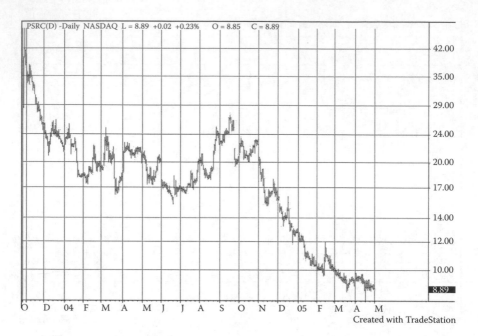

FIGURE 205.2.2. PSRC in its amoeba-like glory. The failure of what might have been a rounding bottom, especially with the breakdown gap in October and the failure to rally back to the neckline left no doubt as to the fate of PALM by any other symbol. Broken trendlines are also indicative. Remember that any large pattern can be broken down into smaller patterns susceptible to short trend line analysis, as in this case. Sooner or later a palm-size computer, PDA, widget device is going to be the wave of the future. The canny investor will not mistake the company for the stock, and will also not venture capital until there is a better chart story.

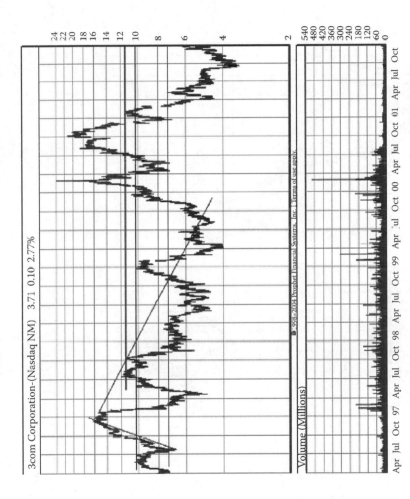

FIGURE 205.3. COMS. Underwriters cleverly only three 3% of 3Com-owned Palm stock onto the market at the IPO. Palm wound up "worth" more than 3Com for a short time. Here the lesson of tulipomania is vivid. The contrast in before and after volume. The necessity of analysis to deal with tulips in bloom. The fatal lesson of heeding (or not heeding) gaps across horizontal trendlines. Impossible to manage for the buy and hold investor.

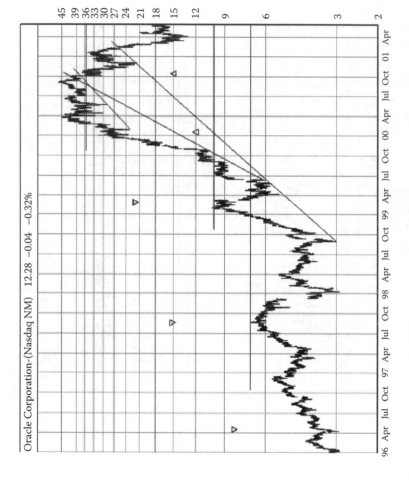

FIGURE 205.4. ORCL. True to the character of stocks during the tulipomania, Oracle was difficult to handle without careful analysis. Stock splits preceded a number of the sell offs (note gaps post splits). Bullish gaps are also frequent here, and the tulip top is obvious, and was at the time. An excellent trading vehicle. A wreck for the casual investor.

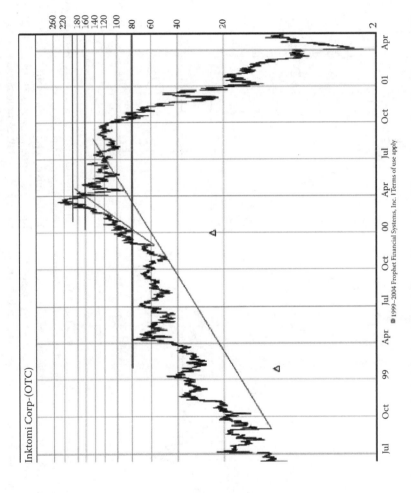

FIGURE 205.5. INKT. The pleasures and delights (and disappointments) of Internet stocks. The last trendline, in conjunction with the second horizontal trendline, clearly marks the end of the party (AND WILL FOR ANY STOCK WHATSOEVER). The break of the long term trendline is the last exit signal, as if the previous signals weren't clear enough. Is it not obvious that this issue was (and is) manageable with technical analysis?

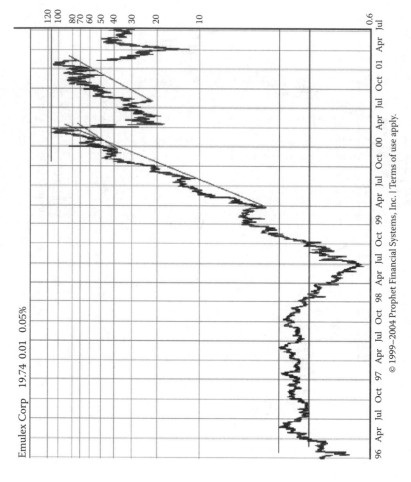

Emulex Corp 19.74 0.01 0.05%

© 1999–2004 Prophet Financial Systems, Inc. | Terms of use apply.

FIGURE 205.6. EMULEX. (ELX) The message of 2000, a severe drubbing, and precipitous at that, would have been lost on the non-technician. Those who continued to ride the roller coaster relearned a lesson technicians know, that stocks often repeat the same behavior (or misbehavior). The lesson of monster breakaway gaps (or air gaps) may have needed relearning also. Oh well, after such a gap the damage is done, the unenlightened investor says, only to see the damage continue down to 10 (from 110!). These are signals of such magnitude that disaster awaits him who denies its significance. The air gap here nicely complements those of Figure 130 and Figure 269.

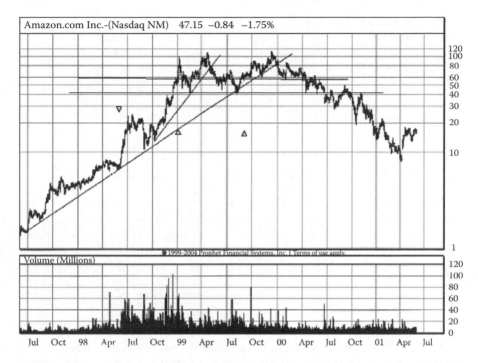

FIGURE 205.7.   Amazon weekly. Amazing Amazon dances in the Internet follies. The breathtaking plunges are the direct result of the breathtaking speculative excess. See the daily chart (Figure 205.7.1) for a closer look at the details of the blow-off.

AMZN (Amazon.com, Inc.)
08/26/2006 5:51 PM EDT

FIGURE 205.7.1.   Amazon daily. In cases of speculative blow-off, trendlines are of little use. A dozing trader (presumably it was obvious that this was not an investment issue) would have been mauled in the plunge. An alert trader, knowing that in blow-offs the procedure is to sell strength, might have avoided it. Other techniques include recognition of the second exhaustion gap and exit. Also a trader using the techniques described in Chapter 28, setting progressively tight stops, might have avoided the fall.

FIGURE 205.7.2. The wild frontier of the Internet and of the gunslinger speculators (gamblers?). Amazon bucks on. Give us a slug of rotgut whiskey and get out the ruler. A clear top for the rational analyst with clear broken trendlines and broken horizontal lines and then a clear bear market with a clear bottom resembling a Kilroy Bottom and then a clear breakout and another bull market and then another downtrend. Talk about your fearless bull riders down at the rodeo. But this bull/bear is ridable with a little technical analysis. Without technical analysis it's like being the target in a shooting gallery. A sitting duck.

FIGURE 205.8 CISCO. (CSCO) While the first long term trendline beautifully intercepts the downtrend in progress at a gap (a coincidence of indicators which occurs too often to be a coincidence), the trendlines drawn later are of such strength that even the novice analyst should know how to exit. And, in fact, one of my students, an employee of Cisco, did just that, saving himself thousands of paper dollars in this very case.

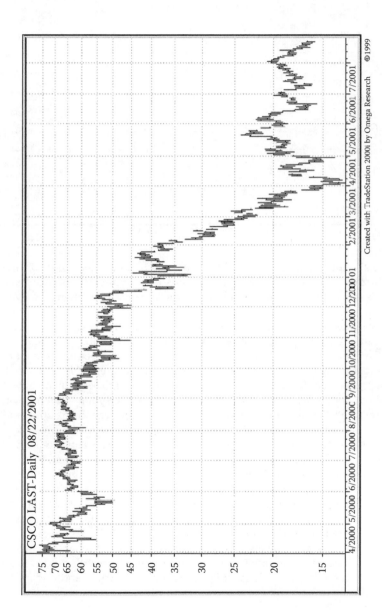

FIGURE 205.8.1 Is there any way the trader (investors keep away) could avoid stepping off this cliff? Extreme paranoia is one way. Another way is by being acutely conscious of the pattern of behavior manifested by Cisco in Figure 205.8.

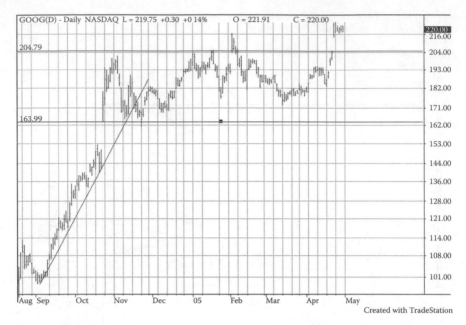

FIGURE 205.8.2. You thought all the tulips and bulls had been exhausted in the tulipomania in 2000? Silly you. There is an inexhaustible supply. All you need is a company and a story and an underwriter to peddle it. Sometimes there are even earnings. Sometimes the earnings are even real. Sometimes the earnings are skating uphill on roller blades. And sometimes the characters are so appealing that you are almost willing to buy the IPO at face value. But not if you are a cynic as all technical analysts are. Google was rumored at $200 or more on the IPO. The editor offered to sell all of it at that price and throw in the Brooklyn Bridge for free. This offer (well, there may have been other factors also) knocked the IPO down to $85 (still an arrant speculation), but only insane, not unreasonable. The oversubscription in an innovative offering revealed that the tulip virus was not dead, but very much alive and infecting not just the same old suspects, but many new ones. We love a horse race and this is a great one. Notice the obvious defensive lines and support and resistance. How long Google can defy gravity (a galactic P/E ratio) remains to be seen. Prudent gamblers will have a stop identified. On this chart, for the long-term gambler it might be in the 182 area. For the more agile gambler it might be failure of the support around 204, or closing of the breakaway gap there. No opprobrium is attached to the-term gambler. In fact bolder investors (competent readers of this book) should take a flyer from time to time with about 5% of their capital. This, of course, is the flyer which should have been taken. The breakaway gaps in October and April, operating against disbelief, were signals of enormous technical strength. And Google went to 475!! The lesson here, which must be learned and relearned and...*ad infini-tum*... is: Trust the chart. Ignore the story.

chapter twenty-four

The Probable Moves of Your Stocks

At first glance, all stocks appear to move helter-skelter without rhyme or reason, all over the lot. All stocks go up at times, and all go down at times — not always at the same time. But we already have seen that in these rises and falls stocks do follow trends, make various typical patterns, and behave in a not completely disorderly manner.

It is also true that each stock has its own habits and characteristics, which are more or less stable from year to year. Certain stocks normally respond to a Bullish Phase of the market with a very large upsurge, while others, perhaps in the same price class, will make only moderate moves. You will find that the same stocks which make wide upward swings are also the ones which make large declines in Bear Markets, whereas the ones that make less spectacular up-moves are more resistant to downside breaks in the market. In Appendix A you will find in a discussion of Composite Leverage that there are stocks which ordinarily move many, many times as fast as others. We do not know, for example, whether a year from now Glenn Martin *(EN: Read, Microsoft, Ebay)* will be moving up or down, but we do know, and it is one of the most dependable things we know, that whichever way it is going, it will be covering ground much faster than American Telephone and Telegraph. *(EN9: Even T accelerated into hyperspace after its ill-advised divestment of local Bells. And, unlike the leopard, completely changed its spots.)* These differences of habit, of course, are due to the size of issue, floating supply, nature of business, and leverage in the capital structure, matters we have touched on briefly before. As a matter of fact, we are not especially concerned with why the differences exist. We are interested mainly in what the differences are, and how we can determine them.

This is important: stocks which habitually move in a narrow range, although excellent for investment purposes where stability and income are the chief desiderata, are not good trading stocks. A fairly high degree of sensitivity *(EN: volatility)*, with wide percentage moves, is necessary in order to make possible profitable commitments that will cover costs and leave a net gain. In order to be in a position to make a profit, you should see the probability of at least a 15% move in your stock.

How then are you going to tell which stocks are most sensitive and potentially most profitable?

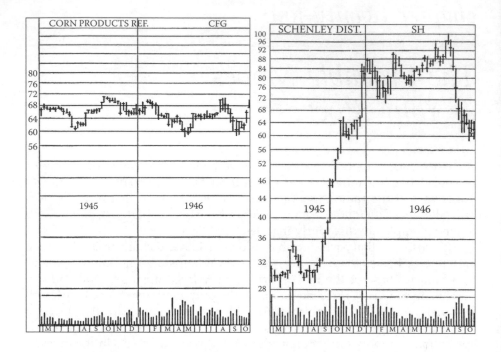

FIGURES 206 and 207. Some stocks move faster than others. We have already noticed that low-priced stocks have much larger percentage moves than high-priced issues. But even between two stocks, which may, at a particular time, be selling at the same price, there are enormous differences in their habits. Furthermore, these habits change very little from year to year.

Here we have a weekly chart of Corn Products Refining Company (left), covering an 18-month period in the years 1945 and 1946. Also a chart of Schenley Distillers (right) for the same period. The average price between the high and low on these charts is about 64½, the same for both stocks.

However, during this period, we see "CFG" moving between a low of 58½ and a high of 71, a range of 12½ points, while at the same time, "SH" has moved between 28½ and 100, a range of 71½. A thousand dollars put into outright purchase of "CFG" at its extreme low would have grown to $1210 at its extreme high, whereas the same amount used for outright purchase of "SH" at its low would have grown to $3510. Your gain of $2510 in "SH" would be more than 10 times the gain of $210 in "CFG," and this without using margin.

It is not likely, of course, that you would actually purchase either stock at the extreme low, nor sell at the extreme high. The point we are bringing out here is that there are enormous differences in the swing habits of stocks.

Individual stocks have their characteristic habits, and so do some entire industries. In general, the food stocks, of which "CFG" is one, are stable and slow-moving. On the other hand, liquor stocks make wide moves on any general advance or decline of the market. At this time "CFG" had a Sensitivity Index *(EN9: Or beta equivalent)* of 0.58, whereas Schenley's was 2.05.

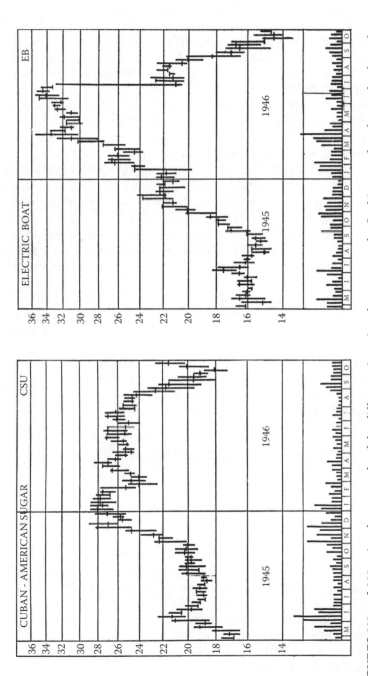

FIGURES 208 and 209. Another example of the difference in swings between stocks. In this case also, the stocks show the same average price between the high and low of the period, and both stocks are plotted for the same 18 months in 1945 and 1946. Although in a lower price range and even though the disparity in their Sensitivity Indexes is less, there is a considerable difference in their actions. Cuban–American Sugar (left), a food stock, shows a range of 76% from its low of 16½ to its high of 29, whereas Electric Boat (right), a shipbuilding concern, advances more than 140%.

By examining the record of a certain stock for a number of years back, and comparing the percentage moves it has made with the percentage moves of the market as a whole, you can obtain a fair picture of that stock's habits. You will not be able to say, at any particular moment, "This stock is now going to move up 25%," but you can say, with a good deal of confidence, "If the market as a whole makes an advance of 10%, this stock will probably advance about 25%." Or, conversely, of course, "If the market goes down 10%, this stock will very likely go down at least 25%."

Many methods have been used for measuring and checking these percentage-move habits, differing only in detail. Indexes on several hundred important stocks listed on the New York Stock Exchange have been computed by the authors and are presented in Appendix A.

EN: Current day betas may be compared with these and/or substituted for them in other computations suggested in this book, for example in Composite Leverage formulas. The reader may read in the following text "beta" for "Sensitivity Index" and avoid the annoyance of excessive notation by the editor.

The Indexes are relative. They show that stocks with a high Sensitivity Index *(EN: beta)* will move much faster in either Bull Markets or Bear Markets than stocks with low Indexes, and about how much faster, relative to the other stocks.

EN: As is obvious to the experienced reader, and new to the inexperienced, Magee's method predates the compilation of betas. Beta measures the systematic risk of a stock, or for those who are not into financial industry jargon, the sensitivity of a stock to the market. Thus, if the market moves one point, a stock with beta of 1.5 will move 1.5 points. And a stock with a beta of .5 will move a half a point. Approximately. Or more or less. For readers who like to roll their own, I offer here the formula for computing the beta of a stock, which is somewhat more sophisticated than Magee's method:

$$\left((N)(Sum\ of\ XY)\right) - \left((Sum\ of\ X)(Sum\ of\ Y)\right)$$

where
N = *the number of observations*
X = *rate of return for the S&P 500 Index*
Y = *Rate of return for stock or fund.*

The general investor may not be avidly interested in this calculation, especially when the beta is readily available at Value Line and is published regularly by Merrill Lynch.

Of equal or greater importance is the individual risk of a stock which professionals like to determine by computing its volatility. Somewhat akin to Magee's "normal range for price," volatility measures the variability of a stock's returns (price movement). The general investor should be informed that the study of volatility is an extremely sophisticated subject, and that professionals expend enormous *resources dealing with the question. Numerous methods are used to derive volatil-ities, but these mainly come into play in options arbitrage and professional trading on exchange floors.*

For the private investor it is sufficient to know of the dangers of this arcane area. Before venturing into "volatility plays," the newcomer should take a postgrad-uate course. For the general investor who wants to know enough to calculate his own volatilities (not recommended or necessary), I note the formula here:

To calculate the volatility of a portfolio, first find the difference between each return and the average. Then square each difference and add them together. Divide the sum by the number of returns minus one. This result is known as the variance. Finally, take the square root of the variance to get the volatility. Combining these steps into a formula:

- *Step 1: Calculate the average return.*
- *Step 2: Calculate the deviation of each return.*
- *Step 3: Square each period's deviation.*
- *Step 4: Add them together.*
- *Step 5: Divide the sum by the number of periods − 1. This is the variance.*
- *Step 6: Take the square root.*

$$\sigma = \sqrt{\frac{\sum_{i=1}^{n}\left(R_i - \mu\right)^2}{n-1}}$$

The less punctilious investor may find volatilities at optionstrategist.com, cboe.com, as well as other locations findable at google.com.

chapter twenty-five

Two Touchy Questions

This chapter is directed largely to the new trader, to the investor who has followed other analytical methods, and to the investor type who is now, for the first time, taking up the technical trading of stocks for the shorter term.

The first question here is the use of margin. There are many people who, knowing of the disastrous margin calls of 1929 and the staggering way losses can be multiplied against one in a margined account during a sharp break in the market, take the attitude that the use of margin is intrinsically bad, dangerous, foolish, and unsound. They will tell you that they are willing to risk their own money, but they never speculate on borrowed funds. They will tell you that by buying securities outright, they are safe against any kind of break in the market.

There is something to this line of argument, although very often you will find that the arguer has not really thought the case through all the way. If he had, he might realize that, in buying outright stocks which are sensitive or highly leveraged, he is accomplishing almost exactly the same thing as someone else who buys more conservative stocks on a margin basis. Very often, despite his feeling that outright purchase is more conservative than margin buying, he is a speculator at heart. He is not really interested in dividends and a stable investment. Rather, he is looking for "something with appreciation opportunity." And because he is not facing the issue squarely, he may fall into expensive errors.

To be thoroughly consistent here, a man who shuns the risks inherent in margin trading should shun the risks of leverage and volatility. He should avoid risk, forget "opportunity for appreciation," and confine himself to sound, income-producing stocks of a sort that will not fluctuate widely.

If we are looking for stability, we do not want excessive fluctuation. And there are securities that provide stability. In this work, however, we are looking for "swing power." We want the highest degree of fluctuation we can handle safely. We can secure this by buying outright a stock that is normally subject to fairly broad swings; that is, a stock with a high Sensitivity Index *(EN: beta)*. We can get the same effect by trading in a stock of more conservative habits, but increasing the Composite Leverage *(EN: or simple leverage)* by using margin. (The method of computing and comparing Composite Leverages in various situations is covered in Appendix A.)

Let us assume, for example, that we will buy 100 shares of a rather speculative stock, which we will call UVW, on an outright basis. It has a

Sensitivity Index of 1.50, and now sells (let us say) at 20. At the same time, we buy a somewhat less speculative stock, XYZ, also selling at 20; but in this case, we buy on 70% margin, putting up only three quarters of the value of the stock. In a general advance affecting both of these stocks, the probabilities would favor a somewhat greater percentage move in UVW than in XYZ. If such a general rise should bring UVW to 30, we might expect XYZ to rise to a lesser degree, say to 28. Now the advance of 10 points on the $2000 invested in outright purchase of LVW will represent a gain of $1000 or 50%. The advance of XYZ to 28 on the $1400 invested at 70% margin will mean a gain of $800 or 57%. In other words, we have, by the use of margin, increased the effective leverage of XYZ; made it, in fact, slightly more speculative than UVW.

The effect of margin use is simply to accentuate or increase the sensitivity of a situation. It is a mechanism for assuming more risks and, therefore, more opportunities for faster gains. Assuming you are willing to assume risk (as you must be if you intend to make speculative commitments), it is simply a matter of knowing approximately what risks you are taking and whether you can afford to take them. The danger in margin lies in cases where the customer grossly overextends himself, taking on a risk far beyond his ability to protect himself. This will not happen if he sets a reasonable limit to his total leverage (*EN: put another way, his portfolio risk*).

The margin transaction is simply a matter of buying (or selling short) more stock than you have money to pay for in full. The purchase of a home on a mortgage is essentially a margin transaction. The financing of business operations, using borrowed money for part of the capital, is the same. The buying of anything where the purchaser puts up part of the capital and borrows the rest, using the value of the purchased property as security for the loan, is exactly similar to the trading of stocks on margin. In each case, any change in the value of the property will cause a larger net change in the value of the *margin* capital. Thus, if a man buys a home for $100,000, paying $50,000 cash, and later sells it for $150,000 (an increase of 50% in the value of his property), he will benefit to the extent of $50,000 profit, or 100% on his invested capital.

The question of margin calls, being "wiped out" on margin transactions, will seldom, if ever, come up if you protect yourself properly by maintaining stops at all times or by closing out the transaction when it has violated certain predetermined danger points. Needless to say, if you have allowed a trade to go so bad that it has reached the minimum margin maintenance range, the best thing is to take your loss and forget it; not try to meet the margin call. But again — this need not ever happen.

As we will see in discussions of sensitivity and leverage, stop levels, etc., there are certain limits which can be fairly well defined, beyond which you cannot safely venture. If you could buy stock on a 10% margin, as you could at one time, you might have visions of highballing a thousand dollars up to a million in one Bull Market. But that is not a reasonable hope, and it is not safe to risk your capital on a 10% margin, since, in many cases, your perfectly logical purchase would sag enough to wipe you out entirely before going ahead to the normal advance you expected. *EN: In a nutshell, the risk of trading commodities and futures.* In judging how much margin you can or should use, within the limits of margin trading laid down by law, you must take into account the method of trading you are using, the amount of adverse fluctuation you must expect in the normal operation of your method, the nature of the stock you are dealing with, that is, its Sensitivity Index and Normal Range-for-Price *(EN: at the risk of being repetitive, beta and volatility)* at the time you make the original commitment.

Short Selling

The other touchy question is that of short sales. A majority of traders avoid the short side of the market. Six out of seven you meet, who have bought or sold stocks, will tell you that they would never sell a stock short under any conditions, at any time. In fact, short selling is limited, very largely, to skilled professionals. *EN: The private investor, because of his fears and prejudices, voluntarily grants this "edge" or advantage to professionals. Magee dealt with this subject at length in* Winning the Mental Game on Wall Street, *which I wholeheartedly recommend to the reader. EN9: The widespread proliferation of hedge funds in the new century attests to the frustration of professional managers with mutual fund rules requiring them to maintain only long positions. Even with this development short selling by the general investor remains a limited technique — to the disadvantage of the nonprofessional.*

Now, if you have studied long-term charts (weekly and monthly), and the daily charts in this book, you will recognize several facts about the action of markets. Most stocks go up most of the time. There are almost always more advances than declines in the list of most active stocks published each day. Stocks, in general, advance about two thirds of the time, and go down only about one third of the time. *(EN9: Probably a truth over the long term, but in the modern context ample short opportunities exist.)*

Furthermore, most of the news releases, rumors, and comments in the press related to stocks and corporate affairs have to do with the brighter side of industry. It is only natural that executives, public relations people, and the reporters themselves should be interested in forward-looking developments, new processes, expansion of facilities, increased earnings, and the like; and that such items should prove more newsworthy than less optimistic reports.

These various factors may explain why "the public" is always Bullish. The public is always hoping and expecting stocks to go up *all the time*. If stocks are rising and in a Bullish Phase, the public expects them to go still higher. If stocks have declined sharply, the public will argue that they are now better buys than before and must surely go up soon. But it is *up, up UP*, always up, in the mind of the public.

And, yet, examination of the long-term charts, covering the action of the Averages over many years, will show you that through these long periods, the levels rise and fall about the same amount.*

This being the case, it must follow that stocks come down as far as they go up, and since they go up about two thirds of the time, they must come down much faster than they go up. This you will find is true. The angles of decline in the Averages and also in individual stocks are usually steeper in Bear Market Moves than the advances are in Bull Market Moves. A corollary to that is that profits *can be made faster on the downside* of the market than on the upside.

Such profits are made by *selling short*. It is important if you are a trader that you understand the meaning of a short sale. When you sell a stock short, you borrow that stock from someone who owns it, and then you turn around and sell it to someone else, agreeing with the original owner to replace his shares at some unspecified time in the future. All of the detail of this transaction is, of course, handled by your broker. Shares of most stocks of large outstanding issue are available for loan at all times in the hands of brokers, and your own broker has access to them. The mechanics of this borrowing and sale are interesting; you may wish to get from your broker the whole story of how these operations are carried out. For all practical purposes, however, all you need to do is tell your broker what you wish to sell and leave the rest to him.

He will advise you if, by any chance, the stock you have selected for short sale is not available for loan. Another practical point, although of minor consequence, is that a slight additional tax is assessed against short sales. *EN: In that gains on short sales are not eligible for long-term capital gains tax.*

It is important also, if you are a trader, that you accept opportunities to sell short as readily as you go long stock. Unfortunately, there are psychological barriers to short selling. There are, for example, the unintelligent and entirely irrelevant slogans about "selling America short." There is the feeling on the part of many who are poorly informed that short selling is the somewhat unethical trick of the manipulator. Others have the impression that, in selling short, one is hoping to profit by the misfortunes of others at times of disaster and Panic. It is not the purpose of this book to persuade anyone to sell stocks short, any more than it is our purpose to advise anyone who shouldn't to speculate on the long side of the market. But so many questions are constantly raised, even by fairly sophisticated investors, about

---

* This principle probably still holds even after the extension of the Dow Industrial Average into new all-time high ground since late in 1954. *EN: And into the economic stratosphere at the turn of the millennium with predictions — we will not assess their credibility — being made that the Dow will in good time reach 36000.* In spite of the long-term "secular trend" and the history of these recent years (*EN: 1950s and 1960s*) in the Average, it seems safe to assume that there will continue to be major general declines in the future as there have been in the past. As a matter of fact, a number of important stocks have been in Major Downtrends throughout the past few years of the mid-20th century Bull Market: Celanese, for example, Kresge, Lorillard, Schenley, and Studebaker–Packard. *EN: Compare the historic Bull Markets of the 1990s and Kodak, Avon, Xerox, General Motors, and IBM, all of which were under their 1990 benchmarks in 2000.*

the ethics, as well as the practical procedure of short selling, that we may perhaps be pardoned for saying a few more words in its defense.

All of the popular ideas about short selling mentioned in the preceding paragraph may be branded as so much nonsense. There is nothing more reprehensible about selling short than buying long. Each is a speculation in relative values. The truth is that money is a commodity, just as much as a share of stock. There is no moral or practical difference between borrowing money to buy stock because you believe that the latter will go up in value in terms of the former, and borrowing stock in order to "buy" money because you believe the latter is going to go up in value in terms of the former. In each case, you are obligated eventually to repay the loan whether it be money or stock. In each case, you are taking a risk on the basis of your considered forecast as to the future trend of *relative* values.

There are, in fact, many common business practices which are more or less analogous to selling stocks short. For example, every time the publisher of a magazine accepts cash in advance for a subscription he is making something like a short sale. His ultimate profit or loss will depend on what the magazines he will eventually supply have cost him by the time the subscription runs out.

When you sell stocks short, you (or rather your broker) receives the proceeds of the sale at once but you are obligated to turn back an equal number of the same shares at some future date to the man from whom the stock certificates were borrowed. *EN: One of the advantages or edges that professionals enjoy over private investors is the credit of short sales to their accounts and the payment of interest thereon. While the proceeds are credited to the private investor, no interest is generally paid on it, unless the investor has influence with the broker. A favorable situation is created, however, in that, if a short sale of $100,000 were made on, say, 50% margin, a credit of $150,000 would be made to his account, and no interest would be charged. Any dividends the trader paid on the transaction would be expensible.* Consequently, sooner or later, you have to go into the market again and buy those shares. When you buy them, you (or rather your broker) returns the shares to the original lender, thus discharging your obligation. If the cost of your purchase was less than the proceeds of the earlier sale, the difference is your profit. If it costs you more to buy in the shares   or as it is termed, cover your short   then the difference represents a loss. Of course, you do not enter into a short-side transaction unless you expect the price of the stock to go down and, hence, show you a profit.

One of the little-appreciated results of a large volume of short selling is actually to strengthen the market. Every short seller is a potential buyer. Most short sellers are glad to cover and take their profits on a relatively Minor Decline. Consequently, if there is a big short interest at any given time in a particular issue, that means that there are many people waiting to buy that stock when it goes down. This situation tends to "cushion" bad breaks. Some astute operators will actually buy a stock when they learn that there is a very large short interest in it (that is, that a great many shares of it have been sold short and not yet covered) because they realize that competition among the short sellers to buy the stock whenever it has a small decline may result in a very fast and profitable Short-Covering Rally. Any stock is stronger, technically, if there is a good-sized short interest in it.

There is one further objection raised against short selling. It will be pointed out that when you buy stock, your loss, if worse comes to worst, can be no more than the total amount you paid for it. But in the case of a short sale, the price of your stock could, theoretically, rise against you to $50, $100, $1000, $10,000 a share; in other words, could rise without limit. This argument sounds much more alarming than it really is. Certainly there is no occasion to lose sleep over it. Stocks do not go up without limit all of a sudden. It is just as easy to set a stop on the loss you are willing to take on a short-side transaction as it is on a long purchase. Such situations as the famous 1901 corner in Northern Pacific are not likely ever to occur again under present regulations. *EN: The famous "short squeeze." Short squeezes still occur but extremely rarely in big liquid issues. A famous short squeeze occurred in the silver markets of the 1980s when the Hunt brothers trapped Exchange members and almost bankrupted them. The Members, of course, being in control, retaliated by quintupling margin requirements and bankrupted the Hunts.* The authors realize that nothing they can say, and probably no amount of cold-blooded analysis on the part of the reader himself, will remove entirely the trepidation which most nonprofessional traders experience when they sell short. The mental hazards will always be slightly greater than in buying long. Nevertheless, from every practical angle, a short sale is exactly the same thing (although in a reverse direction) as a long purchase, with no greater risk, with actually somewhat greater chance of quick profit, and differing only in details of execution.

A commitment in commodity futures contracts, whether long or short, though quite different in theory, has some similarities to a short sale of stock. In making a contract, no actual sale takes place, and no loan of either cash or the commodity is involved. Such a contract is simply a binding legal agreement to accept delivery or to deliver a certain commodity at a certain price at a certain time. In this respect, it is *different* from a short sale of stock. It is also different in that it must be closed out on or before a definite date. But the purchase or sale of a commodity contract is similar to a stock short sale in that: (1) it is necessarily a margin transaction, and (2) it creates an "open" or incomplete transaction which must eventually be liquidated.

A short sale of stock must always and necessarily be a margin transaction. Thus, if you buy 100 shares of stock outright at 20, it can sink to 15 and you cannot be called for more margin. You have lost $500, but the stock is still yours. If you sell, you get back $1500, disregarding commissions. On the other hand, if you sell a stock short at 20, putting up a margin of 100%, and the stock rises to 25, you will also have lost $500. The broker, under certain conditions, such as the 100% margin requirements in effect at one time, might call on you for $500 additional margin. Or, if the transaction were to be closed out at that point, you would receive back $1500 less commissions, the same as in the long transaction. In the case of this short sale, had the price dropped to 15, your profit would have been $500.

On short-term moves, the effect of short selling is exactly the same as the buying of long stock, but in the opposite direction. You simply apply the same methods here in reverse, during a Bear Market, that you would use in a Bull Market. As we have already seen, the various technical indications that point to upward moves in a Bullish Phase have their counterparts in downside signals during a Bearish Phase.

Execution of short sales cannot be made at any time and at any price you wish. A short sale must be made in a rising market. You are not permitted to sell a stock short on the New York Stock Exchange during a market break when each regular sale is at a lower price than the one before it *(EN9: the uptick rule)*. However, this need not bother you much since, ordinarily, you would make such a sale on the rally as it reached your price, and this would naturally fill the requirement of a rising market. Your broker can give you, in detail, the special rules and regulations that apply to short sales. It will pay you to study these so that you can place your orders correctly when the proper time comes to make such sales. *EN9: At the AMEX short sales on ETFs and some HOLDRS are exempt from the uptick rule as are futures contracts on the futures exchanges.*

chapter twenty-six

Round Lots or Odd Lots?
(EN: Or, Put Another Way, Size?)

One of the minor tactical questions bound to plague you is whether to trade in round lots of 100 shares or odd lots (less than 100 shares in active stocks).

EN: In Internet Age markets this question has virtually lost its relevancy. In Magee's time, there was a distinct disadvantage to trading odd lots, and one only traded odd lots if hampered by limited capital. Now that an investor can achieve full diversification in an odd lot position by buying odd lots of SPDRs and DIAMONDs there seems little point in discussing it. There is, of course, always the question of broker commission — if the broker has a fixed commission rate regardless of the size of the trade, then the small investor gets nicked. It would seem that this follows the old adage that the rich get richer. But now the small investor can strike back by finding a broker who does not charge commissions. At first I thought that commission-free brokers were making up their profit on volume. But there are in fact other ways to make a profit on trades than charging a commission — for example, directing the execution of the orders to a trader who needs "order flow."

In the Internet Age, the question of what size a trade or investment should be is different from the question which confronted traders of, as it were, ancient times. Now it is not so much a matter of cost disadvantage in trading odd lots as it is a much deeper question — that of risk and portfolio management. So how does the aware investor determine the size of any individual trade?

I am indebted to a longtime friend, colleague and broker, and fellow trader, William Scott, for articulating the common sense procedure here for calculating trade size and controlling risk.

First, we determine the percentage of our capital we want to risk on any given trade. Among many professional traders of our acquaintance, this figure is often 2 or 3%. For the sake of illustration, using round numbers, if we have $100,000 capital this means we will be risking $3000 on a trade. Let us say that we are going to buy a $20 stock and defend our position with a stop-loss order $5 away. Our formula for computing position size is

$$3000/5 = n \text{ number of shares, or } 600 \text{ shares}$$

If we were going to accept a $10 risk, our trade size would be 3000/10 = 300 shares. Thus we adjust our trade size to fit our risk parameters.

This is a simple, practical, elegant way to implement risk control at the individual trade level.

chapter twenty-seven

Stop Orders

We are going to take up two kinds of stop orders, or, rather, two entirely different uses of the mechanism of stop orders.

First, let us look at the protective stop order. At best, it is not a happy subject. Stop orders of this type are like fire extinguishers. The occasions when they are put into operation are not times of rejoicing. Stop orders are used for emergency rescue when things get so bad that there seems no reasonable hope for a situation.

Wherever you set your protective stop, it is likely to be touched off at what seems to be the worst possible moment. You will set it at a safe distance under a certain bottom. The stock will break through, catch your stop, and then proceed to build a new bottom at this level for the next rise, or to rally at once and make new highs. No matter. You had your reasons for setting the stop. The stock did not act the way it should have. The situation is not working out according to Hoyle, and certainly not the way you hoped it would. Better to be out of it, even at a loss, rather than face a period of uncertainty and worry. If the stock has started to act badly, you cannot tell how much worse it is going to behave. If you fail to set a stop, you may go on day after day hoping for a rally that never comes, while your stock sinks lower and lower, and eventually you may find (as millions have found) that what started to be a small reaction, and an annoying but trivial loss, has turned out to be a ruinous catastrophe. Stop orders cannot always be placed. In certain cases in active stocks, the exchanges may even restrict the use of stop orders.

The question is where and when to set the stop, realizing that there is no perfect and absolutely satisfactory rule. If the stop is too close, you will, of course, take unnecessary losses; you will lose your holdings of stocks that eventually forge ahead and complete the profitable rise you hoped for. If stops are too wide (too far away), you will take larger losses than necessary in those cases where your stock definitely has broken out of pattern.

Now it will be obvious that the setting of stop orders depends on the price of the stock and its habits. You would not place your stop level at the same percentage distance under a Bottom in a conservative, high-priced stock when it is selling at 80 that you would to protect a speculative issue at a time when it is selling at 8.

The higher-priced stocks, as we already have seen, make smaller percentage moves. Conversely, the lower-priced stocks make wider percentage moves. Therefore, the lower-priced stocks should have more leeway for their gyrations. We will need a wider stop for them than we will for the less volatile "blue chips."

Similarly, we can take our Sensitivity Indexes *(EN: Betas in considering a stock relative to the market, and Volatilities for absolute measure of one stock against another)* to give us a picture of the individual habits of the stock. Although two stocks may be selling at the same price at a given moment, you would expect a high-beta, high-volatility stock to make wider swings than a low-beta, low-volatility stock; therefore, you will set your stops wider on the higher-volatility stock.

We must take these factors into account and work out some sort of simple rule of thumb that we can follow. Let us arbitrarily assume an imaginary stock of "average" habits and a price of 25. Let us further assume that we will be satisfied, in this particular case, with stop protection 5% below the last established Minor Bottom.

For a stock of the same sensitivity selling at 5, we would need about half again as much stop leeway (on a percentage basis). That is, the stop would be placed 7.5% below the last Bottom *(EN9: Significant low)*. We arrive at this by taking the normal expected range of an average stock at price 25, which is represented by the Index Figure 15.5, and comparing it with the normal range of a stock selling at 5, which is 24. These are merely relative indexes and mean only that the stock selling at 5 will normally move about 24%, while the stock selling at 25 is making a move of about 15.5%. We multiply the basic stop distance of 5% by the fraction 24/15.5, and we get approximately 7.5%.

In exactly the same way, we introduce the relative sensitivity of the stock, using the Sensitivity Index. If this Index should be 1.33, we multiply the stop distance again by this figure and get 10%. In the case of a stock having a sensitivity of 2.00 at this same price, our stop distance would be 15%. If the sensitivity of the stock were only 0.66, we would get 5%.

In any case, the stop distance, expressed as a percentage, is obtained by dividing the Normal Range-for-Price by 15.5, then multiplying by the Sensitivity Index, and multiplying this result by 5%. (This operation can be done most easily and quickly with a calculator or computer routine.)

All of the foregoing may seem needlessly complicated to the average reader. We realize that many will not care to take the time and trouble to work out an exact, scientific stop level for each of their occasional commitments. However, the method of determining where stops should be placed in a systematic and consistent way has been given in some detail here, so that the principles involved will be perfectly clear, and so that you can change or adapt the various factors if you feel your experience justifies changes.

For most ordinary purposes, a simplified table of stop distances will be sufficient. This table, which follows, gives you the approximate stop distance you would get by the method outlined above, for stocks in various price classifications and of various degrees of sensitivity.

Table of Stop Distances
(Expressed in Percent of the Price of the Stock)

Price	Conservative Sensitivity under 0.75 Implied Volatility under 0.40	Median Sensitivity 0.75 to 1.25 Implied Volatility 0.41–0.79	Speculative Sensitivity over 1.25 Implied Volatility over 0.79
Over 100	5%	5%	5%
40 to 100	5%	5%	6%
20 to 40	5%	5%	8%
10 to 20	5%	6%	10%
5 to 10	5%[a]	7%	12%
Under 5	5%[a]	10%	15%

[a] *Note:* Ordinarily, stocks in these price ranges would not be in the conservative group.

EN: The informed reader may consider an alternative to Magee's Sensitivity Index which I have conjectured here — that is, basing the stop distance on implied volatility, which would present a dynamic method of adjustment. Implied volatility is produced from, for instance, the Black–Scholes Model when the model is solved for volatility rather than price, taking the market price as the given.

The stop level should be marked on your chart as a horizontal line as soon as an actual or theoretical transaction has been entered into, and it should be maintained until the transaction is closed, or until progressive stops (which we will explain in a moment) have been started in order to close it out. In the case of purchases, the stop level ordinarily will be at the indicated distance below the last previous Minor Bottom. In the case of short sales, it ordinarily would be at the indicated distance above the last Minor Top.

To determine the position of this stop level, simply figure what the percentage distance would amount to at the price of the stock. If you are dealing with a stock selling at 30 and the stop distance comes out 10%, then allow 3 points under your last Minor Bottom.

To make this even easier, if you are using the TEKNIPLAT paper, you will see that it is possible to divide each of the two cycles making up a chart sheet into five spaces. If the center of the paper were numbered 10, then these spaces would be from 10 to 12, 12 to 14, 14 to 16, 16 to 18, and 18 to 20. Each of these "jumps" is made up of 16 of the smallest vertical spaces. In the lowest section, it will take about four of these small spaces to make 5%. It will take five in the second position, six in the third position, seven in the fourth, and eight in the top position. You will soon learn to count out an approximate stop interval of 15% or 8% or 12% at any price level, without a moment's hesitation.

In no case would we ever set a protective stop level at less than a 5% interval, even for the most conservative, high-priced stocks.

These questions remain: "What constitutes a Minor Bottom? What makes an established Minor Top? How do we know how to choose the *basing point* (EN9: cf. Chapter 28) from which to measure off our stop level interval?" What constitutes a Bottom or a Top will be taken up in the next chapter. For the present, let us accept the proposition that we will determine the correct basing point and that we will always, always set our stop level at the moment we make the commitment.

It is understood, of course, that protective stops under long stock are never moved down, nor are protective stops over shorts ever moved up. As soon as the stock has moved in the right direction far enough to establish a new basing point, the stop level is moved up (on longs) or down (on shorts), using the same rules for determining the new stop level as were used in fixing the original level.

The Progressive Stop

There is another use of the stop which is properly considered here. This is the progressive stop, used to close out a stock that has made a profitable move, or in some cases where a stock has given a danger signal before either completing a profitable move or violating a previous Minor Bottom.

You will find that on many moves, the stock will progress in the primary direction for several days, and then may develop exceptional volume. Often, this occurs just as the stock reaches an important trendline or pattern border or Resistance Area. This heavy volume means one of two things. Usually it means that the Minor Move has come to an end, that this is the top of the rise for the moment. Occasionally, however, the volume may signal the start of a breakaway move that may run up several (and perhaps many) points, almost vertically. (The reverse situation, of course, may develop on downside moves.)

If, noticing the heavy volume following a good rise, and assuming that this day marks the end of the move, you sell the stock at the market or at a limit, you are going to be dreadfully disappointed if this should be one of those rare cases where the stock opens next day on an upside gap and continues 3, 5, or 20 points up in the following days. On the other hand, experience will have shown you that it will not pay to expect that sort of move very often. You will know that, nine times out of ten, you will be better off out of the stock.

Very well. After such a day when volume is exceptionally high (provided this is not the first day of breakout into new high ground beyond the last previous Minor Top), cancel your protective stop and set a stop order for the day only, just ⅛ point under the closing price. For example, you have bought a stock at 21. It goes up on moderate volume, smashes through the old Minor Top one day at 23 on very heavy volume, the next day continues to 23¾ on moderate volume, the third day advances on moderate volume to 24¼, and, finally, the fourth day makes a rise to 25 on much heavier volume than it has shown on any day of the rise except the day it broke through 23. The morning after this close at 25, you will notice the volume signal. You will cancel your protective stop, which may be at 18, and you will place a stop order, for the day only, to sell on stop at 24⅞. In most cases, this will mean that your stock will be stopped out on the first sale of the day. And you may get a slightly lower price than you would get with a straight market order. On the other hand, after a day of high volume activity, you are not likely to be left in a thin market; there should be bids enough, near the top, to get you out at or near your stop price.

Meanwhile, you are protected against losing the stock if there should be a continued move in the right direction. Suppose the opening the morning after you set your stop at 24⅞ should be a gap at 25¼, and that prices then move up further, closing at 26. (On "runaway" moves of this sort, the closing for the day during the move is likely to be at the top.) You will then set your stop, again for a single day only, at 25⅞. If the stock then opens at 26⅜ and moves up to 28, you will set another day stop at 27⅞, which, let us assume, is caught at the opening the following day at 27⅝. In this example, you risked only ⅛ point on the first day, and eventually netted an extra gain of 2⅝ points. This, it should be pointed out, is all net gain, since your commissions are approximately the same in either case.

A progressive stop of this sort can be indicated on the chart by any mark you choose to use; for example, a band of short diagonal lines. When a stock moves for several days in a runaway move, you may repeat this mark each day, indicating a tight stop ⅛ point under the close for each successive day, until finally, one of these stops is caught. In the case of short sales, a buy stop is used in precisely the same way as the selling stop we have discussed, to follow the stock down on a sharp runaway dive.*

This use of stop orders is indicated wherever a stock has reached its reasonable objective on high volume, or where it has exceeded its objective and is moving out of the Trend Channel in free air, so to speak, and in some cases, where the stock has failed to reach its objective.

If your stock, for instance, is rising in a Trend Channel, and, about halfway between the lower and upper trendlines, suddenly develops great volume, then a progressive tight stop will protect you against the threatened failure of the move. Extreme volume in such a case, before there has been a breakout to a new high above the last Minor High, is definitely a warning and a threat. This would be especially true if there were also a gap or a One-Day Reversal at this point.

---

* In the case of a stock which has presumably completed its profitable move and has given a Minor Top signal by volume, you may place a near *(EN: or "Hair-trigger" Stop)* (⅛ point) stop the first day. If the stock moves up the next day, without abnormal volume, you may leave the stop at this same point each day until another "blowoff" or Top signal appears; that is, until you see another day of heavy volume, a gap, or a One-Day Reversal, and then move the stop up to ⅛ point below the close of that day. This method often works out somewhat better than the continuously progressive near stop.

The one day on which a tight stop would not be applied after heavy volume had appeared would be the day the stock made a new high, running entirely through the previous Minor Top and closing above it. This action generally means the move is not yet completed. However, should the move continue higher and again show heavy volume, even if it is the very next day, we would then protect with a progressive stop.

In this chapter, as throughout the book, the expression "heavy volume" means heavy only with respect to the recent volume of sale in the stock you are watching. A thousand shares may be significantly heavy volume in some thin issues, whereas 10,000 shares would be no more than a normal turnover in more actively traded stocks. The volume chart itself will show, by a market peak, when a day of abnormally heavy volume occurs.

It should be understood that the progressive stops we have been discussing are intended to take short-term gains, or to close out an exceptionally profitable runaway move terminating in an Intermediate Climax. While the extreme conditions that call for this type of operation are by no means rare, they are not the usual, everyday action of the market. In the case of ordinary Minor Tops, even when they are fairly apparent on the basis of Trend Channels, volume peak, and other indications, many traders and investors will prefer to wait out the expected reaction rather than pay additional commissions and lose a position that is still presumably in a favorable Major Trend.

In short, the progressive stop is a device which may be very useful on occasion, but it is intended to cope with a special and somewhat unusual move.

The protective stops, on the other hand, offer the average trader, the man who is not able to spend his entire time studying the market, or who has not had long experience, a device by which he can limit his possible loss. He will be protected from his own unwillingness to close out the bad holding, and so, he will avoid the ruinous condition of becoming frozen into a hopeless situation. Since he will be taken out automatically, regardless of whether he has an ultimate gain or loss, he will have the capital to use in better-looking issues and will not have to worry about the prospects of recovery in his stock after it has gone many points against him.

However, if one has sufficient knowledge and sufficient determination to get out as soon as the trend has shown convincing evidence on a turn, there is less need for the stop orders. *EN: This editor believes that only the proven trader-investor should trade without a stop in the market. The reader may determine if he meets this criterion by examining his portfolio to see if he has ever let a loss run, or allowed a significant profit to slip away. If so he, or she, or they, or it, is not proven.* It is possible for such a person to operate successfully without them; and there are some advantages in doing this, since a stop order will occasionally be caught by a false move or an extended dull reaction. There are also advantages in not using stop orders for the experienced technician who is looking toward a possible long-term gain and who is willing to wait out a Secondary reaction. But it is a thousand times better for the person who is not sure of his methods to be stopped out early, then to be left holding a stock bought at, say 60, when it has declined to 29 — or to 5!

chapter twenty-eight

What Is a Bottom — What Is a Top?

EN9: In this extremely important chapter I have left intact Magee's usage of "'Tops and Bottoms." It will be less potentially confusing for the reader to think of "highs and lows" as that terminology is commonly used in the business in the modern era. Also, thinking in terms of highs and lows is an important concept in itself. Thus, for a bull trend, higher highs, higher lows. And when this pattern is broken in an important way the trader should be alert for a trend change. And, as the use of eighths is of the essence in Figure 210, I have left the discussion in eighths while the reader knows that decimals are now used in the markets.

In this chapter, we are not talking about what makes a Major Top or Bottom, nor what makes an *Intermediate* Top or Bottom. We are speaking of the Minor Tops and Bottoms that give us important hooks on which to hang our technical operations. Stop-order levels, trendlines, objectives, Supports and Resistances are determined by these *Minor* Tops and Bottoms. They are of prime importance to us as traders.

Usually, these Minor Tops and Bottoms are well marked and perfectly clear. Often they are not. Sometimes, it is not possible to say definitely that this or that place is or is not a Top or Bottom. But it is possible to set certain standards, practical working rules, that will help us in making these points; and these rules will not fail us too often.

A good rule for setting stop levels is to consider that a Bottom has been made when the stock has moved "three days away" from the day marking the suspected low of the Bottom. If a stock reacts for some days and finally makes a low at 24, with a high for that day at 25, then we will not have an established Bottom until we have had 3 *days* in which the stock sells at no lower than 25⅛. The entire price range for 3 full days must be entirely above the top price for the day making the low. This is the "three days away" rule, and it would apply in reverse in declining markets, where the range for 3 days must be entirely below the entire range of the day making the high.

This gives a rule for setting an original stop order. It also gives a rule for changing the stop order. As soon as the stock has moved 3 days away from a new Bottom, we move the stop order to a position below that Bottom. (We have already explained in Chapter 27 how we determine the distance this stop level should be below the Bottom.)

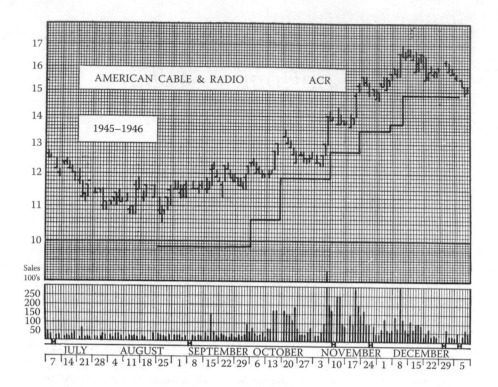

FIGURE 210. Advance of a protective stop order in a long commitment. The daily chart of American Cable and Radio in the summer of 1945 made a Rounded Bottom, part of a long period of Consolidation following the advance which ended in July 1944. A breakout on heavy volume occurred September 12, and purchases were then possible on any Minor Reactions.

The first protective stop would immediately be placed 6% below the previous Minor Bottom of August 21, using the table given in Chapter 27. This would put the stop level at 9⅞. On September 19 and 20, we would have 2 days of market action entirely "away" from the September 17 Minor Bottom, and, on September 28, a third day. We would then move the stop up to 6% under the September 17 Bottom, or to 10⅝. The next move would come after the new high closing of October 11, which is more than 3% higher than the October 1 Minor Peak. The stop would now be placed at 11⅞. On November 2, a new high close was registered more than 3% over the October 15 Minor Peak; the stop would be raised to 12¾. On November 15, another high closing topped by over 3% the Minor Peak made on November 7. The stop would be moved up again, this time to 13½. November 29 made the third day the entire range was "three days away" from the November 26 Bottom, and the stop was upped to 13¾. The closing on December 5 gave us a 3% advance over the November 17 high, and again we moved the stop, raising it to 14⅞. Finally, on January 3, 1946, this stop was caught as shown on the chart. In a Bear Market, protective stops would be moved down in exactly the same manner to protect a short sale. *EN9: A number of inconsistencies exist in this figure and caption which are clarified later in the text.*

Protective stops for *long* stocks can move only up. A stop level, once established, is never to be moved down except when the stock goes ex-dividend or ex-rights; then the stop may be dropped the amount of the dividend or rights. Similarly, protective stops for short sales are to be moved only down, and may not be raised. (In the case of ex-dividends and ex-rights, the short-sale stop would be dropped the amount of the dividend or rights.)

There are certain situations where it is difficult to determine Bottoms and Tops; where, indeed, it seems as though a Consolidation or Correction had been made without any significant move in the Secondary Direction. In such cases (as contrasted to the obvious situation where the stock moves up or down in series of well-marked steps and reactions, like a staircase), you will need all your judgment and experience to determine where the Minor Basing Points actually occur.

Basing Points

Let us call the levels which determine where stops should be placed *Basing Points*. In a Bull Market Move, we will consider the Bottom of each Minor Reaction as a Basing Point, from which we will figure our stop-order level as soon as the stock has moved up to "three days away." We will also use each Minor Top as a Basing Point in a Bull Move. In a Bear Market, we will consider the Tops of each rally and also each Minor Bottom as Basing Points for the protective stops, in the same way.

Where a stock makes a substantial move in the Primary Direction, say a move of 15% or more, and then moves back at least 40% of the distance covered from the previous Basing Point to the end of the Primary Move, that surely gives us a Basing Point as soon as the stock again starts off in the Primary Direction. However, if the stock reacts less than 40%, perhaps even marks time at the same level for a week or more, that should also be considered a Basing Point as soon as the move in the Primary Direction is continued (provided the volume indications are right).

The daily volume, as we have seen, is like the trained nurse's clinical thermometer; it tells a great deal about what is happening in a stock, more than the superficial symptoms of price alone. There are three times at which you may look for exceptionally heavy volume: (1) on the day of breakout from a pattern or a period of inaction, especially if the breakout is on the upside; (2) on the day on which the stock goes into new ground in the Primary or Intermediate Direction, that is, goes above the last Minor Top in a Bull Market, or below the last Minor Bottom in a Bear Market; and (3) the day on which the Minor Move is completed or nearly completed, that is, the new Minor Top in a Bull Market and the Minor Bottom in a Bear Market. To this we might add that extra heavy volume on any *other* day during a move in the Primary Direction is likely to indicate that the move is at an end and will not complete the hoped-for advance or decline.

Now, after a Minor Top has occurred, the stock now being in new high ground, and the Top having been made on very heavy volume, we may look for the corrective move. Ordinarily, that would be a decline of several days, a week, sometimes longer. Occasionally, the correction, as we said a few paragraphs back, will take the form of a horizontal hesitation lasting a week or more without any particular corrective move in the downward direction. Where there is a downward correction, it is likely to come down to or near the Top of the last previous Minor High (support). Also, and often at the same time, the corrective move will carry down to the Basic Trendline drawn through two or more previous Minor Bottoms; or to the "parallel"; or to a trendline drawn through the last two or more previous Minor Tops. If the corrective move is horizontal, it is likely to run out until it meets one of these lines.

In any case, the thing to watch for is the decline of volume. If the trading shrinks, perhaps irregularly, but on the whole, steadily, for some days after a new Top has been made, during which time the stock either reacts or, at any rate, makes no progress in the Primary Direction, then you are justified in considering this as a Minor Correction. If the stock now continues the Primary Move and gets to a point that is "three days away," you can consider the Bottom (that is, the point you draw your trendline through, not necessarily the extreme low point in the case of horizontal moves) as a new Basing Point.

Where a stock is starting what appears to be a new move, a breakout from a period of vacillating moves, it is sometimes hard to say precisely what point should be considered the Bottom. There may be several small and indecisive moves on low volume preceding the real breakout. In such a case, we would consider the appearance of high volume as the breakout signal, and set our Basing Point at the low point immediately preceding this signal. There will usually be such a point on one of the low-volume days in the 3 or 4 days just before the breakout.

All that has been said about Basing Points in a Bull Market would also be true, in reverse, in a Bear Market, except that heavy volume does not always accompany a downside breakout.

Now there comes the difficult and distressing situation where the stock, having made a long runaway move (let us assume it is an upward move), starts out, apparently, to make a Flag, and is bought after a sufficient correction of 40% with a decline of volume, and then continues to go down steadily, without any rallies and without any clear volume indications. This is an unusual situation, but it does happen on both the upside and the downside, from time to time. In the case we have just mentioned, we would look for Support Levels (Consolidation Patterns, Multiple Tops, etc.) formed on the way *down* in the previous trend, and lying below the level at which we purchased the stock. We would use these supports as Basing Points rather than hold a stop under the extreme Bottom of the vertical move.

In many cases of this type, you will not be able to find adequate Basing Points. Therefore, it seems unwise to try to get in on corrections after long runaway moves except: (1) where the stock has risen well above good Support that can serve as a Basing Point, or (2) where the stock is completely above all prices for several years and is moving "in the clear." (The reverse, of course: in Bear Markets, the stock should have fallen below a strong Resistance Area, or must be in new low ground for the past several months before you consider a short sale.) And in any case of this sort where you are thinking of a trade in a stock that appears to be making a Consolidation after a fast, long, vertical move, you *must* have pronounced and conspicuous drying up of volume throughout the formation of the Flag or Pennant Correction.

There is one more word of caution needed here regarding trading in an Intermediate Trend. A series of moves in a trend will often take place in very regular form. There may be a good trendline, and the reactions may be about 40% to 50% and may come back to the previous Minor Tops. The volume on the Corrections may shrink, with increasing volume on the new Tops. It is easy to start trading on such a "staircase" in the expectation that the moves will continue to be regular and consistent. But trends do not go on forever. Any Minor Top may be the last. The importance of finding your Basing Points is to enable you to get out, at best, on any closing violation of one of these points, and at worst, on your protective stop order. The volume may again come to your aid in this question of when to stop trading on a trend. Although you look for high volume on the Tops, you will be exceedingly suspicious of volume that is *much* higher than that on any of the preceding Minor Tops (or Bottoms in a Bear Market). The final, or the next-to-final, "blow-off" of a trend will usually show more volume than any of the Minor blow-offs along the way; and when you see such climactic volume, you should prepare to retire into your shell and wait for a full Correction of the entire series of moves making up your Intermediate Trend. Later, weeks later, or perhaps months later, you may find the stock has corrected 40% or more of the whole Intermediate Move and is resting quietly with very little activity. Then is the time to watch it for new opportunities and a new trend in the Primary Direction.

EN9: In a book composed of nothing but important chapters this Chapter 28 might not get the emphasis it deserves from the unwary reader. In fact the procedure outlined here is of absolutely basic importance in analyzing and trading trends. In Chapter 28.1 I have added to it material which has been of great importance to my trading and to the trading of my students.

Basing Points – A Case Analyzed

The longer one thinks about the chart so casually tossed off in Figure 210 the more he realizes that it embodies a profound and natural understanding of trends and the market. Consider — wave up, wave recedes; wave up, wave recedes, and so on. As long as the trader or investor is not chased from his position by the corrective wave he will under normal circumstances ride the trend to its natural end. But locals and hedge funds and those who profit from volatility know that the previous low is where investors and traders set their stops. So in the ordinary flow of trading if they see an opportunity to take out an important low they will do it. If possible. And it is sometimes possible. And the low sometimes falls from the natural flow of trading.

Bruce Kovner, on being interviewed by Jack Schwager (*Market Wizards*), was asked where he set his stops. "Where they're hard to get to," he said. A stop set on a basing point with a prudently calculated filter is hard to get to, unless the market has truly reversed direction. In fact, what is a long-term moving average but a lagging stop with a filter built in?

And what are Basing Points but the marking of highs and lows in full realization that a pattern of higher highs and higher lows is a bull trend, and when that pattern changes to one of lower highs and lower lows the trend is changing, or has changed. This is the principle behind Dow Theory, and it is the principle behind trading trends of lesser duration than Dow trends. And, as is quickly realized, a pattern of lower highs and lower lows means inevitably *that the trendline has been broken.*

As for Figure 210, Mark Twain had some cogent comments on it. He said that anyone trying to make sense of it would go crazy, and anyone trying to justify the prices with the chart would be shot. Figure 210 preserves unexplainable conundrums and conflicts carefully preserved since the earliest editions. The reader is urged to take it as a concept rather than using it as a lesson. And see Figure 210.1. Therefore let me codify the rules implicitly presented in the Figure:

1. A high is made, being recognized by no higher prices occurring for the moment.
2. Prices recede and a low is made. This low is found by watching each day after the previous high until no lower prices are made. As prices begin to rise again we note each day on which prices are completely outside the range of our low day candidate.

3. When three such days are observed before a new low is made we
    mark the candidate day as a Basing Point and raise our stop to 6%
    (or x%) under the low of the basing point day. (See Chapter 27).
4. If a new high is 3% greater than the previous high a new Basing Point
    is found at the low of the new high day.

The Basing Points Paradigm

By no means will every issue be amenable to this kind of analysis. But the
method is so paradigmatic that it is worth examining at greater length. And
like virtually every other method of classical chart analysis it must be used
with caution and good and thoughtful judgement. Sometimes on some
stocks it will seem to work as smooth as silicon lubricant and on other issues
it will appear to be useless. However, even on recalcitrant issues the principles underlying the method will be of use, if not the actual method itself.
With this in mind Figure 210.1 is presented. The careful reader will see that
the chart in this example uses only bottoms or lows in stop setting and does
not advance stops on the making of new highs as in Figure 210. This is done
for instructional purposes and to keep the example simple for the general
investor. More advanced traders will want to study and perhaps utilize the
techniques in Figure 210.

Figure 210.1 actually serves more than one instructional purpose. It
illustrates a picture perfect case of the use of Basing Points, and it also
illustrates a complete analysis of a bull market from entry to exit with keys
marking events in the life of the market. Thus, the observation of Basing
Points, the setting of the stops, the tracking of potentially false turns are all
noted. The chart is accompanied by the keys. Originally the marked and
keyed chart was used in graduate seminars at Golden Gate University for
instructional purposes. Shortly it became obvious that marking the chart in
this manner was extremely useful in trading. So it is suggested to the reader
as a way of making his charts more communicative and more useful.

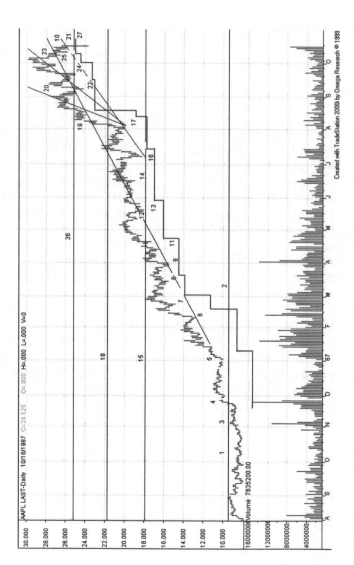

FIGURE 210.1 Apple Computer, bull market of 1987. A near perfect example of the use of Basing Points for trading of a reasonably regular and smooth bull market. Only low wave Basing Points are illustrated.

KEY TO FIGURE 210.1 ANALYSIS

1. A rounding bottom, or perhaps a scallop.
2. Resistance or breakout line.
3. Wake up call on volume.
4. Run Day, big volume. Breakout through line 2. Sure entry signal.
5. First Basing Point (BP) Notice prior volume fall off in consolidation, and surge on run-day. A stop was entered before this BP using the low of the formation before the entry.
6. BP
7. A weak BP (because of shallowness of retracement)
8. BP
9. Test of BP at 8.
10. A trendline drawn after point 9.
11. BP
12. BP candidate which fails 3 day rule.
13. BP
14. A potential BP but not a very good one because new high has not been made from 13.
15. A support/resistance line.
16. BP.
17. BP
18. A resistance/support line.
19. Flag which becomes BP.
20. TL, but too steep to last.
21. Trendline.
22. BP
23. Trendline.
24. BP
25. BP
26. Horizontal trendline.
27. BP at 26.75 (stop 25.41). Stopped out at 25.41.

A Narrative of the events in the Chart

1,2,3. Had we been asleep the event at number 3 should have awakened us. A volume day like this should catch the attention, and we begin paying attention to the stock and note the pattern that has been developing—the rounding bottom, or scallop.

4. And at number 4 we see a 'run day' on heavy volume. A good signal for entry with the breaking of the horizontal line at 2. When we enter we set our stop 5% under the recent low. After entering on strength there is every possibility that some profit taking will occur as well as probing by locals to chase out *arrivistes*.

5. We watch with interest for the first reaction. Each day we observe as a candidate for a possible 'Basing Point.' This occurs at 5 and we now begin to count 'days away' from the Basing Point, that is, days whose range is entirely outside the range of the candidate day, and which occur before a lower low is made. When the Basing Point at 5 is confirmed we raise our stop to 5% under the low of 5.

6. A higher high is made after 5 with a subsequent reaction to 6, which proves to be another Basing Point. So we raise our stop to 5% under 6.

7. Prices continue to climb and another Basing Point is made at 7. The procedure is becoming clear: Find a Basing Point and establish a stop a prudent distance under it. If a new Basing Point is made raise the stop. Watch with interest the reactions against the trend. Either they allow you to establish a new higher Basing Point, or they end your trade.

8,9. We find a new Basing Point at 9, raise our stop and draw the trendline at 10. At 9 we have a lower low than 8, but our 'filter,' our 5% padding keeps our position intact. We do not lower our stops using 9 as a new Basing Point. One of the inviolable rules is that stops are never lowered. The filter is important, since traders try to take out nearby lows and exacerbate volatility. It is called the running of the sheep.

11. At 11 we find a new, if tenuous Basing Point. An advance with a thin higher high.

12. At 12 we have a candidate for a Basing Point which fails the 3 day rule.

13. At 13 we find the Basing Point that is good and raise our stop.

14. And at 14 we are confronted with a marginal situation. It is potential Basing Point. But a marginal one because a higher high was not made after 13.

15. At 15 we are able to draw a line defining resistance — a line which will become a support line.

16. At 16 a new Basing Point which would have tested a point at 14.

17. At 17 we find a new Basing Point and at 18 we can identify a resistance line. The spurt across this line is both gratifying and a warning. Because it becomes a flagpole from which the flag at 19 flies. Flags and flagpoles are messages that the market has heated up and now wants close watching. A flag can serve as a Basing Point, so we move our stop again, fully aware that the end may be approaching. The trendline at 20 is further confirmation of this environment due to its steepness. But we see two good anchor points in 16 and 17 and draw trendline 21 — a better line to defend.

22. A good reaction finally occurs at 22 giving a strong Basing Point and good rationale for raising the stop. Notice the interesting fact that points 22 and 24 have come back to rest on the trendline we drew at 10.

24. As the tempo has increased and the volatility 24 furnishes us another valid Basing Point.

25. Even 25 is a valid point and we can now see the clear support line at 26.

27. When this line is pierced at 27 upon extraordinary volume, and in the process takes out our Basing Point stop from 25, it is clearly time to exit the train.

The Basing Point concept is even more thoroughly explored in the paper titled "Stair Stops" on the John Magee Technical Analysis website: www.edwards-magee.com

chapter twenty-nine

Trendlines in Action

From what has already been said in Part One of this book, you will be familiar with the characteristic single-line trends of stocks, and the numerous exceptions and deviations that come into the picture from time to time. We know that stocks often move in parallel trends, sometimes for months, occasionally even for years. We also know that they may, and do, break out of trend or change the direction of their trends without notice.

Most of the pattern formations we have studied can be considered as manifestations of trend action, that is, as Continuations or Reversals of a trend.

Thus, a Symmetrical Triangle is simply the meeting of two trends. During the formation of the Triangle, the stock is following both trends in a narrowing pattern, until finally, the dominant trend asserts itself. An Ascending Triangle is following an upward trend, but has encountered a Resistance Level at the Top. A Head-and-Shoulders shows the end of an upward trend and the beginning of a downward trend. A Rectangle is a Parallel Trend Channel running in a horizontal direction. And so on.

We can project a Parallel Trend, and, in the case of stocks which happen to continue moving in that trend, we can buy and sell at almost the precise points of contact with the trendline. Unfortunately, long and perfect straight-line trends of this sort are the exception rather than the rule. For actual trading purposes we will project our trends more or less continuously on the basis of the most *recently established data*.

From the standpoint of tactics, let's consider the trends as they are indicated by the successive Minor Tops and Minor Bottoms. For illustration of this, and as a guide to what we are leading up to, we will consider simplified, ideal situations (see diagram examples on the next page).

To avoid confusion, mark the top trendline in blue and the bottom trendline in red. This can be done on daily charts easily by using colored pencils. We will refer to the upper trendline as the Blue Trend, and the lower trendline as the Red Trend. From time to time, we will also want to draw a line parallel to a Blue Trend across the Bottom of the trend so as to include a segment of the Trend Channel between two Tops within parallel lines. This we will call the Blue Parallel, and we will mark it with a dotted or broken blue line. Conversely, we may wish to draw a parallel to the Red Trend so as to include the segment of the Trend Channel between two Bottoms; and this dotted red line we will call the Red Parallel.

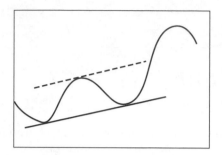
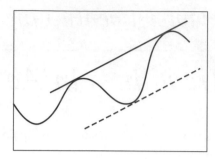

DIAGRAM 3 (Left, above). Here is a rising trend showing the Basic Trendline across two Bottoms, which we call the Red Trendline, and its parallel (indicated by a broken line) through the Top of the intervening peak. The parallel suggests the approximate objective of the next move if the stock continues in trend.

DIAGRAM 4 (Right, above). The same rising trend with the Return Line, which we call the Blue Trendline, drawn through two Tops. Broken line represents its parallel through the intervening Bottom. This Blue Parallel is useful in determining a buying point, especially in trends of rapidly changing form when the stock may not react to its Basic Trendline.

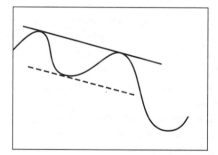
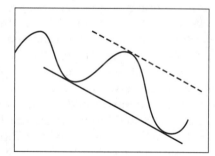

DIAGRAM 5 (Left, above). This is a declining trend showing the Basic Trendline across two Tops, which we call the Blue Trendline, and its parallel (indicated by a broken line) through the Bottom of the intervening decline. The parallel suggests the approximate objective of the next move if the stock continues in trend.

DIAGRAM 6 (Right, above). The same declining trend with the Return Line, which we call the Red Trendline, drawn through two Bottoms. Broken line represents its parallel through the intervening Top. This Red Parallel is useful in determining a point at which to make short sales, especially in trends of rapidly changing form when the stock may not rally to its Basic Trendline.

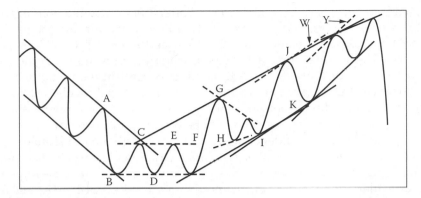

DIAGRAM 7. Simplified diagram of a stock chart showing trend action. Basic Trendlines are marked with heavy lines; Return Lines are marked lightly.

At the start, the stock declines in a Parallel Trend Channel. Blue Trendline is basic here. A short sale on a rally to the Red Parallel at point A will find its objective on the Blue Parallel at B. Another short sale on the Red Parallel at C would be followed by failure to reach the objective. Chances are good, however, that increased volume would develop at the Double Bottom and give warning to get out of short commitments. The upside penetration of the basic Blue Trendline at E, alone, is not sufficient reason to reverse position and go long. Trendlines set up during formation of the Rectangle would be marked in the regular way, but are indicated here by broken lines to emphasize the pattern. Another short sale, if tried on the sixth point of contact with the Rectangle at F, would be stopped out on the breakout.

The trend is now rising, although we cannot yet draw a Basic (Red) Trendline. The first buy would be made on a 40–50% correction of the breakout move from the Rectangle, or on a return to the Top (Support) level at H.

A trendline would be drawn to the first Bottom established in the Triangle. This is not shown, as it would ultimately be replaced by the line shown through the outermost point in the Triangle. We have indicated by broken lines the trendlines set up during the formation of the pattern.

The objective of the breakout move from the Triangle would be the Red Parallel to our now rising Basic Trendline. This objective is reached at J. A Return Line (Blue) would be drawn from the first Reversal Top of the Triangle at G through the Top of the breakout move at J, and the parallel to this through point I would indicate about where to make the next purchase. As a matter of fact, the stock does not actually get back to that point; in practice, the purchase would probably be made at K on the basis of a 40–50% correction, or on a reaction to the Support Level G.

The subsequent upward move would not carry through to the Red Parallel marked W. However, the alarm would probably be sounded clearly by a day of heavy volume, a One-Day Reversal, or a gap. Since the trend is now obviously convergent, no further purchases would be considered. The next move fails to make such headway and falls far short of the objective set by the Red Parallel marked Y. Soon after, the Wedge breaks out downside.

Since, ordinarily, a Top will be formed after a Bottom and a Bottom after a Top, we will expect to draw, alternately, a Blue Trendline and then a Red Trendline, these lines being drawn as soon as the new Top or Bottom is established. (In some cases, a light pencil line may be drawn to indicate suspected Tops or Bottoms, until developments confirm their validity.)

We have already taken up the important and rather difficult question of determining the Minor Tops and Bottoms. Very often, these points will be clear and obvious. Sometimes they will be obscure, and you will be able to draw trendlines with confidence, in such cases, only after considerable experience covering many types of action. The most difficult times to determine Minor Trends are during Reversals, especially where these are of the rounded and irregular types. However, in these cases (of Reversal), we will not depend so much on the trendlines to determine buying and selling points.

So long as a stock persists in a Parallel Trend Channel, it is perfectly clear that you should buy near the Bottom of the channel and sell near the Top. From the geometry of the situation (see examples), you will see at a glance that it is not likely to be profitable to sell short in an upward-moving trend (since the reactions are necessarily smaller than the advances), nor to buy stock in a downward-moving trend.

Therefore, a trend must show that it is presumably an uptrend before you are justified in buying stock. And you must have what is presumably a downtrend to justify a short sale.

You will notice from the simplified examples shown here that pattern formations indicate trends. The breaking of a Rectangle on the upside results in an upward slope of the Blue Trend. The move up out of an Ascending Triangle confirms the rising Red Trend and creates a rising Blue Trend. The downside breaking of a Head-and-Shoulders neckline confirms a descending Blue Trend and sets up a descending Red Trend. And so on.

From studies of these patterns and various trend actions, we arrive at a compact set of trading rules based on these Red and Blue trendlines. These rules are summarized below.

Buying Stock, "Going Long"

- **Preparatory Buying Signals** (indicating that a buying opportunity may be in the making). Penetration of Blue Trend to a new high closing (in most cases). (The simple breaking of a descending Blue Trendline, where no other pattern or indication is present, is not sufficiently conclusive evidence of Reversal to justify commitments.)
  - Contact with the ascending Blue Trend if Red Trend is also ascending, provided the trends do not converge (Parallel or Divergent Trend Channel).

- Contact with horizontal Blue Trend if Red Trend is also horizontal or ascending (Rectangle, Ascending Triangle).
- Penetration of descending Blue Trend on volume if Red Trend is ascending (Symmetrical Triangle).
- **Execution of Buys** (after preparatory buying signal).
  - In case the previous Blue Trend has been ascending, draw the Blue Parallel and buy at or near this line.
  - In case the previous Blue Trend has been horizontal or descending (that is to say, emerging from Rectangles, Triangles, and various Reversal Patterns), buy on a reaction of 40 to 45% of the distance from the last previous Minor Bottom to the extreme Top of the most recent move.

Liquidating, or Selling a Long Position

Immediately on execution of the buy order, determine the stop level (see Chapter 27 on Stop Orders), and place your protective stop. Penetration of this stop level will automatically close out your transaction. The stop level may be moved up according to the "three days away" rule, but may never be moved down (except to adjust for ex-dividend or ex-rights). If the stock closes below a previous Minor Bottom (thus setting up a descending Red Trend), sell on tight *(EN: or hair-trigger)* progressive stops.

If the stock advances on moderate volume and then develops unusually high volume on any day during the advance before either the Blue Trend is broken (with a close above that trendline) or before the stock has made a new high closing over the last Minor Top, close out the transaction on tight progressive stops.

If the stock develops high volume on the day on which it either tops and closes above the Blue Trend or makes a new high closing over the previous Minor Top, hold it. If heavy volume again occurs on the following day or any subsequent day, however, sell on tight progressive stops.

You will find that, in many cases, the heavy volume signal will develop (sometimes with also a One-Day Reversal or an Exhaustion Gap) on or near the Red Parallel. You will watch especially for this volume indication as a sign of a good profit-taking point. If the volume signal does not show up, your selling objective is this Red Parallel, at a limit or on tight progressive stops. In case there is no such volume signal at the top of the move and the move does not reach the Blue Trend nor make a new high, you are very likely running into a Triangle situation. In that case, you will have to wait for a breakout one way or the other. Meanwhile, maintain your stop protection underneath.

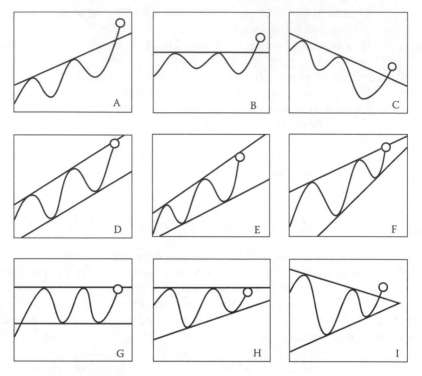

DIAGRAM 8. Preparatory buying signals shown by trend action.

(A) Penetration of an ascending Blue Trendline.

(B) Penetration of a horizontal Blue Trendline.

(C) The penetration of a descending Blue Trendline without other technical indications is not conclusive evidence of a change in trend, and does not justify long commitments.

(D) Contact with the Blue Trendline of an Ascending Parallel Trend Pattern.

(E) Contact with the Blue Trendline of an Ascending Divergent Trend Pattern.

(F) In this case, contact with the Blue Trendline does not suggest a buy on the next reaction, since the trend appears to be converging; a possible Wedge in the making, with Bearish implications.

(G) Contact with the Blue Trendline of a Rectangle at its fifth point of Reversal.

(H) Contact with the Blue Trendline of an Ascending Triangle.

(I) Penetration on volume of descending Blue Trendline when Red Trendline is ascending (Symmetrical Triangle).

In rising trends, the Blue Trendline is a Return Line, and purchases will be made on reactions to a line parallel to the new Blue Trendline established at the Top of the signal move, and drawn through the intervening Bottom. Note that in the case of decisive breakouts from patterns such as Rectangles and Triangles, a purchase may also be made on the basis of a computed 40–50% correction of the breakout move, or on a return to Support.

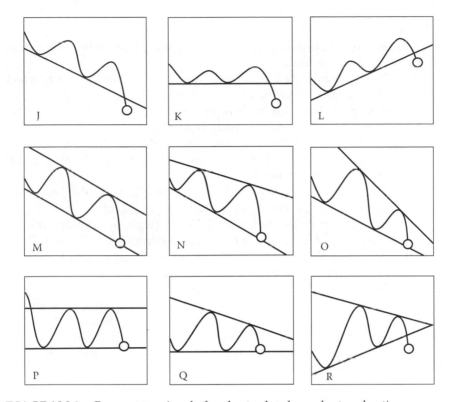

DIAGRAM 9. Preparatory signals for short sales shown by trend action.

(J) Penetration of a descending Red Trendline.

(K) Penetration of a horizontal Red Trendline.

(L) The penetration of an ascending Red Trendline without other technical indications is not conclusive evidence of a change in trend, and does not justify short commitments.

(M) Line of a Descending Parallel Trend Channel.

(N) Contact with the Red Trendline of a Descending Divergent Trend Pattern.

(O) In this case, contact with the Red Trendline does not suggest a short sale on the next rally, since the trend appears to be converging; a possible Wedge in the making, with Bullish implications.

(P) Contact with the Red Trendline of a Rectangle at its fifth point of Reversal.

(Q) Contact with the Red Trendline of a Descending Triangle.

(R) Penetration of ascending Red Trendline (with or without volume) when Blue Trendline is descending (Symmetrical Triangle).

In descending trends, the Red Trendline is a return Line, and short sales will be made on rallies to a line parallel to the new Red Trendline established at the Bottom of the signal move and drawn through the intervening peak. Note that in the case of decisive breakouts from patterns such as Rectangles and Triangles, a short sale might also be made on the basis of a computed 40–50% correction of the breakout move, or on a return to Resistance.

Selling Stock Short

- **Preparatory Selling Signals** (indicating that an opportunity for short sales may be in the making).
  - Penetration of Red Trend to a new low closing (in most cases). (The simple breaking of an ascending Red Trendline where *no other* pattern or indication is present is not sufficiently conclusive evidence of Reversal to justify commitments.)
  - Contact with descending Red Trend if Blue Trend is also descending, provided the trends do not converge (Parallel or Divergent Trend Channel).
  - Contact with horizontal Red Trend if Blue Trend is also horizontal or descending (Rectangle, Descending Triangle).
  - Penetration of ascending Red Trend (with or without volume increase) if Blue Trend is descending (Symmetrical Triangle).
- **Execution of Short Sales** (after preparatory selling signal).
  - In case the previous Red Trend has been descending, draw the Red Parallel and sell at or near this line.
  - In case the previous Red Trend has been horizontal or ascending (that is to say, emerging from Rectangles, Triangles, and various Reversal Patterns), sell on a rally of 40 to 45% of the distance from the last previous Minor Top to the extreme Bottom of the most recent move.

Covering Short Sales

Immediately on execution of the short sale, determine the stop level (see Chapter 27 on Stop Orders), and place your protective stop. Penetration of this stop level will automatically close out your transaction. The stop level may be moved down according to the "three days away" rule, but may never be moved up.

If the stock closes above a previous Minor Top (thus setting up an ascending Blue Trend), buy to cover on tight progressive stops.

If the stock declines on moderate volume and then develops unusually high volume on any day during the decline before either the Red Trend is broken (with a close below that trendline), or before the stock has made a new low closing under the last Minor Bottom, close out the transaction on tight progressive stops.

If the stock develops high volume on the day on which it either breaks and closes below the Red Trend or makes a new low closing under the previous Minor Bottom, hold it short. If heavy volume again occurs on the following day or any subsequent day, however, buy to cover on tight progressive stops.

You will find that in many cases the heavy volume signal will develop (sometimes with also a One-Day Reversal or an Exhaustion Gap) on or near the Blue Parallel. You will watch especially for this volume indication as a sign of a good profit-taking point. If the volume signal does not show up, your buying objective is the Blue Parallel, at a limit or on tight progressive stops. In case there is no such volume signal at the bottom of the move and the move does not reach the Red Trend nor make a new low, you are very likely running into a Triangle situation. In that case, you will have to wait for a breakout one way or the other, meanwhile maintaining your stop protection overhead.

Additional Suggestions

When a level is reached which appears to be either a Minor Bottom on a reaction or a Minor Top on a rally, and when the stock continues to stall and remain at this point, moving in a very narrow range for 3 weeks or more without giving any signal either by way of price change or volume action as to its next move, it is wise to assume that this congestion is definitely a key area, should be considered a Minor Top or Bottom, and protective stops adjusted to it as a Basing Point, instead of the previously established Top or Bottom, as against the possibility that the move out of this area, when it comes, *may* be in the wrong direction.

After a series of moves in a trend, with each move in the Primary Direction marked by heavier volume than the retreats or Corrective Moves against the trend, you are likely to have a move in the Primary Direction, which is marked by *extraordinary* volume; that is to say, by much larger volume than the normal increase for a Primary Move. On such a move, after taking your profits on previous commitments, you would ordinarily begin to plan the next commitment on the Correction. But in this particular case, noting the extreme volume, you would cancel any immediate plans for further commitments in the Primary Direction.

The reason for this is that such *climactic* volume normally indicates the final "blow-off" of the Intermediate Trend, to be followed either by a Reversal, or at least by a period of stagnation, or formation of Consolidation Patterns, or Intermediate Correction. In such a case, it is not safe to make any further commitments on this trend pending further developments and the positive reassertion of the trend.

If you examine daily charts of various stocks, covering long and important trends, you will find that the series of Minor Moves making up the Intermediate Trend is likely to culminate in a Minor Move marked by tremendous volume. This is more true of Tops than Bottoms, although at the end of the Panic Phase of a Bear Market, we very often see climactic volume. The climax indicates, on the other hand, the sale of large amounts of stock by strong investors to weak traders, near the top; on the other hand, the liquidation of holdings by weak traders occurs near the bottom, into the hands of strong investors who will hold them for the next Major Move.

One of the most common errors, and one of the easiest to fall into, is to mistake a Climactic Top or Bottom for a normal confirmation or preparatory signal for a new commitment in line with the preceding trend.

It is similar in nature to the error often made by novices in the market of buying on the Minor Tops (becoming dazzled with the rapid price advance and the great volume of activity). However, in the case of these final "blow-off" moves, the volume is greater and the adverse portent far more serious.

General Outline of Policy for Trading in the Major Trend

A. Always trade in the direction of the Major or Primary Dow Trend *(EN: See the editor's comments in Chapter 3)* as it is indicated at the time.
B. If the two component Averages of the Dow Theory (Industrials and Rails *EN9: Transportations*) are not in agreement, trade in the direction of the last established Primary Trend but only in the component which is still following that trend.
C. Examine charts of group Averages covering groups of businesses in the same or related lines; trade in the Primary Direction when the trend of the group corresponds.
D. Trade in any particular stock when its own individual chart indicates a trend in the same direction as the Primary Trend, and when the technical picture has indicated a probable move in that direction.

Make all new commitments on the reactions or rallies following the signaling move in the Primary direction, except in the case of Primary Reversals from Bull Market to Bear Market, when short sales may be made at the market immediately following the Reversal.

Exception: after an extended move or a series of moves in the Primary Direction, when signs of exhaustion and Reversal appear in individual charts, commitments in the opposite direction may be made with objectives limited to a correction of the preceding Intermediate Move in the Primary Direction.

EN9: Now the reader's head is spinning and the color blind are completely confused. As this book is unfortunately printed in black and white the reader without colored pencils will be at sea. But the principles articulated here by Magee are of great value to a Trader and are worth study. Technology rides to the rescue. A color PDF of this chapter will be found in the distant future on the John Magee Techical Analysis website at www.edwards-magee.com.

chapter thirty

Use of Support and Resistance

We know that after many breakouts from well-defined Reversal and Consolidation Patterns, we get a short countermove back to the edge of the pattern, and that the checking of this move at that point is an example of Support or Resistance, as the case may be. Also, we should be familiar by now with the tendency of stocks to move up or down in a series of zigzag steps. If the move is upward, the reaction after each advance tends to stop at the level of the preceding peak. If the move is downward, the rally after each decline tends to stop at the level of the preceding bottom. This is again a matter of Support and Resistance, and provides the basis for buying on reactions or selling on rallies.

It has also been pointed out that Intermediate Secondary Moves will frequently stop at or close to the previous Intermediate Top or Bottom.

It is necessary to evaluate the importance of these phenomena of Support and Resistance, and apply them in market practice, for they are among the most important tools we have. Unfortunately it is not easy to reduce this particular subject to a neat formula or body of rules. *(EN9: And the effort will be made. See endnote of this chapter for an interesting effort to do just that.)* Here you will depend very largely on experience and observation. You will have to be alert in spotting the levels where Resistance or Support is likely to be encountered, and some judgment is needed in balancing the various factors that will affect the situation.

For example, there is a stock which has broken up out of a well-defined Rectangle of considerable duration. Should the heavy volume of the breakout move give way to a dull reaction, you will look for an opportunity to buy this stock at a point a little above the top level of the Rectangle. It will probably not penetrate very far below that level and, indeed, will often fail to react all the way to the Support. If the stock should then advance to a new high, and once more decline on low volume, you may look for another buying point at about the level of the peak reached on the original breakout. Another advance may be followed by reaction to the second peak, and this process may be repeated a number of times, each reaction carrying back to the level of the preceding high.

Now we all know that this sort of thing does not continue indefinitely. When the stock first breaks out, moving from, say, 15 to 19, we may buy rather confidently on the reaction to 17, if that is the Support Level. If we did not buy on this move, we may buy with considerable assurance on the reaction to Support after the next advance. This advance might have carried the price to 21 and our buying point would, of course, be at the previous peak of 19. However, as the stock moves up to 25, 30, 40, it must be clear that we are approaching a real Top; that although we cannot say where that Top will be reached, we can be sure that it is becoming increasingly tempting to long-time holders of this stock to sell and take their substantial gains. The series of steps is bound to come to an end. To be sure, the Major course of the stock and of the market may continue up for months or years, but after a series of sharp rises, we may reasonably expect a Reversal and a rather substantial Intermediate Decline before the upward move is continued.

Therefore, we must regard each successive step of advance with increasing suspicion, and it is a fair rule that after a stock has made three such moves in the Primary Direction, it is time to look for an Intermediate Correction, or at least an important period of Consolidation.

Thus, we have the rough shape of a rule. Buy on the reaction to Support after the first breakout. Buy on the reaction to the first Minor Peak after the next move. But do not buy on the reaction to the second Minor Peak.

Let us say, then, that we have been successful in two short-term moves, buying on the reaction to Support and selling on the climax after a new Top has been made. But we have decided not to attempt a third such trade. What, then, may we expect next? We may see a period of Consolidation, we may see the beginning of an Intermediate Decline, or we may see the stock actually go right on moving up. No matter. We will wait for the Intermediate Reaction. We will wait until the stock makes a very substantial decline, and this may take many weeks. Then, if the Major Trend has not reversed itself, we will again look for a buying opportunity at (or somewhat above) the Intermediate Support, which will usually be the top level of the advance preceding the one just completed, for this is the level from which the next Primary Advance is likely to proceed and is a good buying point.

Of course, we find the same situation in Bear Markets. A breakout is likely to be followed by one, two, three, or more steps of decline, with intervening rallies to Minor Resistance. Sooner or later (and we would count on no more than three such steps in a series), we will get a turn and an Intermediate Recovery. We will then wait for this rally, which may itself be made up of several Minor steps, to reach or approach closely the preceding Intermediate Bottom, at which point we may look for substantial Resistance. Here is the place again to put out shorts.

Questions will come to your mind. One of them, and one of the most important is: how do we decide when an expected Support or Resistance has failed us, and at what point do we then abandon our position?

It will be clear that this question can be a very painful one. Let us suppose you have seen a stock rise to 25 and have placed an order to buy it at 23½ on the basis of expected Support at 23, the level of a previous Minor Peak. The order is executed during a dull reaction. The next day, the stock slips down to 22½, on perhaps only two or three sales. The next day, it continues down to 21½, still on low volume. And during the next week, it goes down steadily, without much volume, nearly every sale being at a lower price, as though no new bids were being received, and as though no substantial number of bids were standing on the book at any point. A decline of this sort can eventually assume the magnitude of an Intermediate Reaction. The move may carry down to 15 before it turns. Obviously this was not what you expected, and you should be out of the stock.

The painful part of these drifting moves is that you do not want to sell your stock (which you bought at 23½) on just a slight move down, say to 22¾, since the probability is strong that it will shoot up at any moment to new high levels. And yet, at some point during a continued decline, you must decide, "This has gone through the Support; I should sell and take a small loss now, rather than risk a more serious loss." And the most painful part of all is that sometimes, the moment you have sold and taken your loss, the stock will come to life and complete what would have been an extremely profitable move.

You might just as well prepare yourself for this sort of disappointment; for it will happen to you. But to avoid nights of pacing the floor and days of worry, you should decide, *at the time you make the original commitment*, just how much leeway you are prepared to give the stock. Then you will not be tempted to put off a decision from day to day if things are not going the way you hoped.

In the case of purchases or short sales made against Minor Peaks or Bottoms, as the case may be, you might set up the following rule. Measuring from the extreme high of the previous (Supporting) Minor Top, or the extreme low of the previous (resisting) Minor Bottom, set a stop using the method we have outlined in Chapter 27. *(EN9: See also Chapter 28. And consider the risk limitation procedures in Chapter 42.)* This would often be the intraday high or low, not necessarily the closing price. Penetration to that extent should be presumptive evidence that your expected Support or Resistance is not going to function.

Where you are buying against Major or Intermediate Support, or selling short against Major or Intermediate Resistance, you can allow a little more leeway for penetration. In such cases, examine the Support or Resistance Area, and estimate visually its core or axis; in other words, try to gauge the "center of gravity" of this area, the point which is most nearly the mean price of sales occurring there, taking into account the volume, since the important thing is to determine the approximate price level at which a great many shares changed hands. Having determined this point, set your stop beyond it, according to the methods specified in Chapter 27.

Up to this point we have concerned ourselves (reversing the usual order) with how to get out of situations which have gone bad. We have said nothing about where, precisely, to get in, nor where, precisely, to take profits.

In the matter of getting in, i.e., making the original commitment, you will feel, perhaps, that there is a conflict between acting on Support or Resistance, and acting on either trendline action or a computed reaction of 40% to 50% after a previous move. At times there is such conflict, and it is not possible to state any exact rule which will reconcile these three different trading indications. However, in a great number of cases, you will be delighted to observe that a reaction of about 45% will bring your stock to the trendline, and will also bring it near to the Support or Resistance Level. After a move to a new Minor Top, a stock may be expected to react: (1) about 40% to 50% of that move, (2) to the Basic Trendline, and (3) to the previous supporting Minor Top. Your purchase, then, will be based on a consideration of all three factors. If you have bought "early," on the basis of one factor alone, you may expect the stock to react a bit further without spoiling the triple indications to the extent of catching your stop. It would be best to make your purchases on the basis of whichever factor indicates the smallest reaction, and to place your stop beyond the greatest reaction indicated by any of the three. Ordinarily, there will not be too much difference between these three points. As usual, the method applies in reverse to short sales.

Where you are buying after an Intermediate Decline, or selling after an Intermediate Rally, you will lean somewhat more heavily on Support and Resistance than on either a computed percentage for the Secondary Move or a trendline. You will, of course, examine the history of the stock, preferably on weekly or monthly charts first, to see its Major Trend, to locate important Support or Resistance Areas, and to estimate roughly the extent of the Corrective Move, the termination of which you are trying to gauge. You will then check these data in the more detailed picture you can get from your daily charts. As the Intermediate Corrective Move approaches within 4% or 5% of the Support or Resistance Level, you may come to a day of extremely heavy volume; and this day may also be a One-Day Reversal. If so, your commitment should be made at once, protected, of course, by a stop. Otherwise, you may make your commitment whenever the chart begins to hesitate or flatten out, or, lacking other indications, when it has come to within 3% of the Support or Resistance.

Now in this case, your problem in taking profits is a bit more difficult than in the case of Minor Moves. You are expecting a Reversal of the Intermediate Corrective Move and the establishment of a new Intermediate Trend in the Primary Direction. You are at a point where the course of the market is uncertain. You must realize that prices may stay at the Support (or Resistance) Level, forming a Line or Rectangle, and finally penetrate that level, establishing Reversal of the Major Trend. Or they may be stopped and turned at the Support or Resistance Level, only to make a small move away and then return for another, and possibly successful, attempt at penetration. Or (and this is what you hope, of course) a continuation of the Major Trend may develop, with a sharp move on increased volume in the favorable direction, to be followed, perhaps, by a Minor Corrective Move and another thrust in the Primary direction; perhaps a new series of Minor Moves carrying the entire Primary Trend into new ground.

Taking these cases one by one, if the stock remains at the Support or Resistance Level for many days or several weeks, and then penetrates that level, closing at a price that is clearly through it, get out at once. If the stock makes a small move in the right direction and returns to the Support or Resistance, prepare to get out if there is a definite penetration. If, however, the move is in the right direction, watch for volume indications, and prepare to set tight stops to take your profits as soon as heavy volume appears (except on a day of breakout). Of course, once such a signal has appeared, you are then justified in continuing to make new commitments on the following Minor Correction, and the one following that, for you are again moving in the Major Trend.

There is one other situation that should be mentioned here. Up to this point, we have assumed that all of your commitments have been made to take advantage of a move in the direction of the Major Trend. Let us suppose, however, that a move which has carried a stock up to new high levels in a series of Minor steps proceeds to form and then breaks out of a Reversal Pattern. We must now look for a Secondary Move of Intermediate extent. We may sell short on the rally to the Minor Resistance, and, if the move continues down, we may make a second and even (more cautiously) a third commitment against successive Minor Bottoms. But, in this case, we will be looking for the decline to end somewhere in the vicinity of the last previous Intermediate Top, which is now a Support Level. Similarly, following a recognized Reversal Pattern and upward breakout on volume during a Bear Market, we may expect an Intermediate Rally which can be used for trading up to the previous Intermediate Bottom where strong Resistance is likely to show up. A skillful trader can turn these Secondary Moves into profits during periods when it is not possible to trade along the indicated Primary Trend; but it should be remembered that, ordinarily, such moves cannot be expected to go as far as will those in the Primary Direction.

We might close this chapter by reminding you again that, while Support and Resistance action in the Minor Trend is shown clearly in daily charts, the Intermediate and Major Supports and Resistances are most easily recognized on weekly or monthly charts.

EN9: It seems to this editor that Magee's discussion here of the use of Support and Resistance is really most pertinent to position building and pyramiding. Alternatively the method applies to an issue which has just caught the analyst's attention, and he has missed the breakout, which is usually obvious (at least in hindsight). I feel strongly that the serious trader should not miss the original breakout. Chasing moving trains is never a helathy activity. Does this appear an impossible occupation, watch thousands of stocks? Impossible for your average analyst, but not for your average computer. For example the computer may be programmed to alert you when a stock is gapping on volume or trading at volumes which are suspiciously large. And given the plethora of services and user groups the trader stands a good chance of spotting an issue to put on his watch list before it takes off.

Investors should, in theory, never miss a breakout, because they should be watching a much more limited group of issues. In my opinion these are primarily indices and ishares. Of course an investor's portfolio might include a few well chosen individual issues, but these would be of obvious visibility to the individual, e.g., biotechs for an investor with some knowledge of the area, or Internets for an engineer, etc.

The unending effort to remove ambiguity from market interpretation extends to identifying areas of support and resistance. Metastock (metastock.com), an excellent software package, has a number of value added packages. One of the more interesting of these, Powerstrike™ by John Slauson of Adaptick, Inc. (adaptick.com) attempts to mathematically define support and resistance zones. Slauson's package is interesting, and the reasoning and observation behind it are interesting. Market analysis is rooted in one thing: the intelligent observation of the operation of the market. Dow watched the markets for years and came to the understanding of waves which led to Dow Theory. Schabacker and Edwards, equipped with these observations and comments, collated and observed more data and recognized the persistent patterns which occurred over and over in the markets, and added Magee for his practical engineer's approach to solving the tactical and strategic questions. In the 1980s one of my friends, a Chicago market maker in the options pit, noticed that there was a 90 second delay on data coming out of the futures pits to the options pit. He set up a "human ticker" with a direct phone connection to his pit and enjoyed a 90 second advantage over other market makers until the glitch was noticed and corrected.

Slauson (among others) noticed that important trading and support and resistance in optionable stocks tended to cluster around important option strike price levels. In fact these levels influence stock prices and may be said to determine where "important" buying and selling occur. Obviously support and resistance levels are set by concentrated face offs between buyers and sellers. A battleground metaphor is appropriate: Since the time of the Greeks battles have occurred time and again in the same physical locations. The reason is obvious. You need physical space to deploy an army. So commanders will be attracted to the plain or open ground for face offs, and to the high ground for defensive purposes. Option strike prices have the same attractiveness for traders that a good battleground has for a military commander. A good place to test the enemy.

Powerstrike™ analyzes the instrument price and volume around the nearby option strike prices and determines whether support or resistance is stronger. All in all a clever application of number-driven analysis to the support and resistance question. The chart analyst may supplement his analysis with a routine like this.

chapter thirty-one

Not All in One Basket

EN: As diversification for the small investor is nowadays infinitely easier, an interesting endnote follows Magee's text.

Diversification is important because technical patterns do not always carry out their original promise. If all your capital is tied up in one stock, or in a few stocks of the same group or line of business, you may be hurt by a false move affecting only your holdings, even though the rest of the market may continue to hold firm or even to move farther along the Primary Trend. By diversifying, you are protected by the law of averages against all of your holdings going the wrong way, except of course, in the case of some Reversal that affects the entire market or a large segment of it.

Intelligent diversification calls for study of the costs of buying and selling stocks, especially in small quantities. You might wish to have a portfolio of stocks representing the entire Dow–Jones Averages, or a selection that includes at least one stock of every major group. But if your capital is limited, this might mean buying only a half-dozen shares of each stock, and the minimum commission charges would make this an expensive operation, entirely too costly for short-term trading. The short-term trader must always think of these costs. They are more important to him than to the long-term investor who may intend to hold the same stock for many months or years. To you as a trader, a quarter point or a half point may mount up to serious proportions when it is multiplied through a number of transactions.

Your broker can give you a schedule showing commission and tax costs, and in case there are any important changes in the rates, you should study them to see what effect they will have on your costs of trading in stocks at various prices. *EN: You may also evaluate these charges at gomez.com and by checking websites of scottrade.com, etrade.com and tdameritrade.com. google.com is as ever an important price checking resource, and Barron's publishes a yearly edition evaluating brokerage houses. In general this editor believes that the investor who does it the "old-fashioned way," i.e., by phone and human broker operates at a disadvantage unless the broker's value added can be quantified and proven.*

You will find that your round-trip costs are a higher percentage of the capital invested in low-priced stocks than in high-priced stocks. Also, that the percentage costs will be higher on a smaller number of shares than on a round lot, and increasing as the number of shares decreases. Also, that the percentage costs rise as the total amount of capital used is less.

If your capital is, say $1000 or $2000, you might do well to divide it into units of about $500 each and confine your trading to odd lots of stocks selling at 40 or higher. With larger capital, you could use larger trading units and extend the range of trading into somewhat lower-priced stock. In any case, it is important to diversify your holdings. By dividing your capital and using it in such a way as to avoid unnecessary penalties in high costs, you will have greater protection against freak moves and sudden changes that might affect a single stock very seriously.

On the other hand, if you have sufficient capital to secure plenty of diversification (8 or 10 stocks should be a maximum for an active trading account), you can increase the size of the trading units. The whole question here is as to the minimum amounts to be invested in a single commitment, and if these amounts were doubled or tripled, it would not increase costs, but would, in many cases, reduce them.

EN: Diversification and Costs

In this original chapter, Magee discussed the necessity for considering costs while striving for diversification. In present-day markets, diversification may be achieved through the use of SPDRs and DIAMONDS and similar instruments at compara- tively reasonable costs. Index funds and mutual funds also represent diversification and cost control for the general investor. Mutual funds will not control costs and expenses as efficiently as the Index Shares. This is because mutual funds create costs that the Index Shares do not: management fees and expenses, slippage, the spread, turnover, and taxes resulting from realized gains. These costs may be avoided by the careful independent investor.

An internationally prominent trader has told me, on more than one occasion, that his respectable trading fortune amounts to what brokers and specialists would have made off him if he had been a member of the general public. The most important weapon in his *quiver was seats in Chicago, New York, and San Francisco.*

The message is extremely clear. The general investor must control his costs. The more frequently he trades the greater his chances of having his capital ground to hamburger meat by brokers, specialists, floor traders, market makers, tax authorities, Exchanges, etc. Etcetera, because there is undoubtedly another party out there taking a chunk as the capital changes hands. The phone company maybe.

Trading costs are the last item brokerage firms want to focus on (see the book Where are the Customer's Yachts?*). For years the Street firms and Exchanges controlled commission costs, but entering the Internet Age a different ethos rules — Cutthroat (and cutfees) competition, reluctantly brought to the old-line exchanges by upstart competitors, and not suppressed by the SEC and CFTC.*

It would be misleading to attempt to analyze costs in this book because of the mercurial nature of cost figures as firms compete in the Internet Age.

The SEC, runs a mutual fund calculator for computing costs of mutual funds. Mutual funds are among those that manage somehow to not be overly punctilious in estimating (read, disclosing) their costs to investors. (See Resources, Appendix D.) morningstar.com is also a good resource for researching mutual funds.

But let me emphasize once again that ishares and etfs have really made mutual funds obsolete if the investor uses the simple procedures outlined in this book.

chapter thirty-two

Measuring Implications
in Technical Chart Patterns

If you show one of your charts to a friend and tell him it looks Bullish, he will reply immediately, "How far do you think it will go?" This is an automatic response; you can count on it.

The question is a good one. How far is this expected move likely to go? You don't know. Nobody knows. Very often you can say, with a fair degree of assurance, "This stock, which has just made such-and-such an advance, is likely to react to around such-and-such a price." *That* you can estimate fairly closely seven or eight times out of ten, by referring to the Basic Trendline, the parallel projection of the top trendline, or the Support Level.

These rules work out fairly well as applied to reactions in the Bull Trend, and similarly, we can estimate rallies in a Bear Trend. Not so with the move in the direction of the trend itself. A Bullish Move may, and often does, overrun the upper trendline by running up as far again as the move to the trendline. A Bearish Move may exceed the downtrend, dropping apparently without limit. (That is one reason we have protective stops — to prevent disaster in case the trend suddenly reverses itself.) And that is why we prefer the use of nearby progressive stops as a method of taking profits, rather than using limit orders placed at a trendline, Resistance Level, or at some other definite point. Very often, to be sure, a stock *will* check its advance at one of these indicated points, but the cases where a move carries beyond its objectives are fairly common, and in such cases, no one can make even a reasonable guess as to what limit the stock will reach on the move.

This follows because the move itself is an unreasonable one. It is an example of public participation, the surge of uncontrolled speculation (and very often, it is the final surge of that particular trend).

In exactly the same way, and often more violently, the uncontrolled falling out of trend in a downward move is an example of Panic, and being completely beyond reason, it follows no rule and knows no predetermined limits.

There are, however, certain patterns and certain situations where we can make some estimate of the probable extent of a move in the Primary Direction — usually an estimate of its minimum extent. In these cases, we have a guide to help us in making the decision as to whether the situation offers enough potential gain to be worth the risks involved. Also, the indicated measurement gives us *at least* a hint of about where we might reasonably begin to look for the volume which will indicate the Top.

For example, a decisive breakout from a Symmetrical Triangle is likely to carry *at least* as far as the height of the Triangle measured along its first reaction. This is a conservative measurement. The move may go much farther. In fact, the trend implications of the Triangle would suggest a continuation equal to the move preceding the Triangle and leading into it, for if the trend continues valid, the move should run up to the upper limit of the channel. In the case of a Reversal, we would also use the height of the first reaction as a minimum measure. With Right-Angle Triangles, we also can take the long side (formed by the first reaction) as a rough measure of the minimum expected move.

And with Rectangles, the minimum we may reasonably expect after a breakout is a distance equal to the height of the Rectangle. The Head-and-Shoulders Pattern carries a good measuring stick. The height of the formation from the extreme Top of the head down to the point directly beneath where the neckline crosses represents the minimum probable move from the neckline down. Again, this is a matter of Trend Channels, and most emphatically this is only a minimum move. Some Head-and-Shoulders Patterns, representing an implied move of no more than three or four points, have marked the start of a decline eventually running to hundreds of points.

The rather unusual breakout which takes the form of an almost vertical "mast" running up (or down) many points before arriving at a stopping point, where some Consolidation Pattern is made, carries with it a most explicit measuring rule, and one which works out with amazing accuracy. The Flag or Pennant Consolidation will occur at the halfway point — "the Flag flies at half mast." The speculation move leading up to the Flag very likely will be duplicated by another rise, at least equal to the first, in the near future. Following this rise, there may be another Consolidation and other rises, or there may not. After two surges of this sort, it is best to stand back and let someone else carry the ball. If you keep enough charts, and for a long enough time, you will see many perfect examples of this beautiful formation. You will also see some imperfect examples, some failures. And because the move is so spectacularly profitable when it works out, you will be tempted to buy on every Consolidation Pattern formed after a sharp rise. It would be best to wait until the example is clear — a nearly vertical, almost unbelievable rise, followed by several days of congestion with practically no volume. If the congestion continues or sags off for more than about 3 weeks, sell the stock; it is probably not the real thing.

Needless to say, this same pattern appears in reverse in downtrends and can be traded on accordingly.

The questions relating to the measuring attributes of gaps have been reviewed in detail in Chapter 12. The only type of gap which carries substantial implications as to the extent of the move to follow is the Runaway or Continuation Gap. The appearance of such a gap during a rapid price move is likely to mark approximately the halfway point; and two or more such gaps can be weighed, in connection with volume and total extent of the move, to estimate the probable mid-point of the move, and thus to predict a probable ultimate objective.

Measuring properties have been ascribed to other patterns and occasionally work out according to plan. In general, however, the best measuring devices are your trendlines, Support-and-Resistance Levels, and the all-important signals of increased volume.

EN9: I have always been extremely chary of measuring moves. If the measurement does not lead the trader to indulge in expectations which distract him from the crucial nature of the moment at hand *it might be quite all right. So as an off hand casual tool it might serve some use. Always better to observe closely what the situation is when the price arrives at the measured point. Decisions should always be made in the here and now, not in the I measured it then.*

chapter thirty-three

Tactical Review
of Chart Action

The Dow Theory

The record shows that an investor who had bought a representative group of stocks on every Major Bull Market signal according to the Dow Theory as outlined in Chapters 3, 4, and 5, and had sold all his stocks on every Major Bear Market signal, since the start of the Dow Averages, would have come out very well indeed over the years *(EN: See tables, Chapters 5 and 5.1)*. Although this tabulation does not take short sales into account, *(EN9: Now taken into account in the 9th Edition)* it would be perfectly consistent to add that a representative group of stocks might be sold short on every Major Bear Market signal and covered at the next Bull Market signal. And if the figures for such short sales, based on the level of the Industrial Average, were included, the total profits on these theoretical transactions, both long and short, would be enormous. *(EN9: Buy and Hold to 2004: $39,685.03. Dow Theory, long only: $347,895.51. Dow Theory, long and short: $1,914,490.)*

We believe that this record carries some weighty implications which have a bearing on the operations of every trader and investor. We will comment on these shortly.

But before doing so, it should be pointed out that few, if any, investors have actually followed the long-time Dow signals, buying or selling 100% on every Major signal.

In the first place, to do so would require a long market lifetime, and would presuppose that the investor had accepted the Dow Theory in its classic form *in toto* from the start, and that he had never wavered, never altered the definitions nor his method of trading, and that he had never withdrawn any of his capital during the entire period.

In the second place, we would have to assume that our ideal investor had an extraordinary degree of courage in order to stand firm in periods during which the Major Trend appeared to be making dangerous threats against his position, and an extraordinary degree of patience in order to wait out the many months of stagnation when the trend seemed to be getting nowhere at all.

And in the third place, we would have to make the assumption that the group of stocks actually bought or sold really represented a fair cross-section

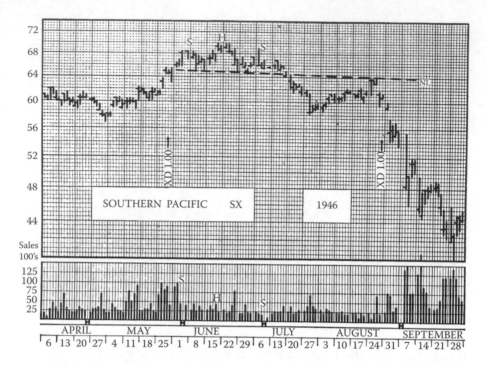

FIGURE 211. Head-and-Shoulders Top. The Bull Market that carried Southern Pacific from 8 to 70 in the years 1941 through 1946 culminated in June 1946 with this formation. Notice the heavy volume on the left shoulder, lower volume on the head, and small volume on the right shoulder. The breakout signal, which was decisive on July 15, served notice on holders of long commitments to sell at the market the next day (at about 63) instead of waiting for the protective stop, which would have been set at 61, to be caught. Volume eventually developed at the Bottom of the breakout move at about 58½, which move, incidentally, carried out the minimum measure of the Head-and-Shoulders prediction.

From this point, however, a weak rally on low volume started, and continued up for 4 weeks. The weakness of this picture would justify a short sale on a rally of 40 to 50% of the move from the left shoulder to the bottom, or on a return to the neckline, say, at 63. The rally actually extended to the neckline at 64, broke away on a gap with volume, and continued down in a move that led, in the next 3 months, to prices below 40, and later even lower.

An extraordinary feature of Head-and-Shoulders Tops is the frequency with which a comparatively small formation, such as the one shown here, will herald a Major Move, changing the course of the stock for months or even years to come. Not all patterns of this type will lead to such big moves as this, but no Head-and-Shoulders should be regarded lightly, ever.

of the Averages in that they would make about the same moves as the Average itself. As a matter of fact, if the group were well diversified, the chances are good that its moves might approximate those of the Averages.

But it is taking a lot for granted to suppose that an investor could meet all these conditions over a period of years, which he would have to do in order to operate strictly as a "Dow Theory" trader. It is not seriously suggested that anybody try to follow any such plan literally. *EN: Well, in retrospect, why not? Given, in the Internet Age, the availability of trading instruments and markets, (DIA, SPY) it might not be such a bad idea. The implementation of such a plan in Magee's time would have been extremely cumbersome and expensive, but it is eminently practicable in modern markets.*

The important implications of which we spoke are these: if the record of the Averages shows that on these Major Signals it is possible to take substantial theoretical profits over the long term, and if the Averages are composed of the prices of individual stocks, then the probabilities favor buying or selling a majority of stocks in line with the Major Trend of the Averages. The evidence shows that Major Trends normally continue for months or years. The line of "most probable gain," therefore, is the line of the Major Trend.

On this basis, we would be on safe ground to say that when a trend of sufficient importance gives a Major Signal that the Averages are under way, there will be a greater likelihood of finding profitable situations among individual stocks moving in that trend than among those moving in the reverse trend.

It is suggested that you read this preceding paragraph again, carefully. It means that we do not try to sell stocks "at the Top" in a Bull Market. We do not try to "pick up bargains at the Bottom" in a Bear Market. We do not deliberately buck the kind of trend that history shows is likely to continue for an undetermined and possibly long time.

What we have said here is stated with a little different emphasis than in previous editions of this book. You will notice we have not said that you will never sell a stock short during a Major Bull Market, nor buy a stock in a Bear Market. There will be, and often are, cases of stocks which are moving against the Major Trend, and which, on the basis of their individual technical behavior, may justify a commitment against the trend of the Averages.

But we feel such trades should be made cautiously and with a full realization that the majority of stocks are moving in a contrary manner. Such trades might be made, for example, in particular cases as indicated by the charts of the stocks involved, as partial hedges to reduce overall risk. For example, if a Bull Market had persisted for several years and was still presumably in effect, but certain stocks had broken badly and showed individual weakness, a trader might continue to hold three quarters of his capital in good long positions, but might make a limited number of short sales in the weaker stocks. If, then, the Bull Market continued, he might eventually have to close out the shorts for losses, which could be regarded as the reasonable cost of "insurance." On the other hand, if the general weakness became greater and eventually reversed the Major Trend, then the short sales would cushion the depreciation of the longs up to the time of the Reversal signal. *(EN9: An extremely wise observation which the present Editor has developed at greater length in the theory of "natural hedging." And, given the complexity of modern markets profits may be made on both sides of the hedge, and this should be the objective.)*

By using an Evaluative Index (see Chapter 38) instead of, or in addition to, the Averages, it is possible to say, "The market appears to be about 60% Bullish," or "55% Bullish," instead of merely Bullish or Bearish. This takes account of the fact that some markets are more Bullish or more Bearish than others; and it enables the investor to "roll with the punch" instead of having to take an all-out position one way or the other. *(EN9: I have called this "Rhythmic Trading.")*

It should be noted, however, that while he may take such a partial position against the (presumed) Major Trend, he will continue to use the bulk of his capital in situations which accord with the main trend. He will never risk the larger part of his assets in opposition to the trend, and he will make any countermoves with a clear understanding that they are of the nature of insurance and serve this purpose even though they ultimately may be closed out as small losses.

Summarizing all these implications of the Dow Theory: do not make a majority of your commitments against the Major Trend. During periods of potential Reversal, gradually reduce your long holdings, and make short sales to a limited amount in weak stocks; but do not attempt to anticipate either a Major Top or Major Bottom in the Averages by making an all-out commitment counter to the main trend.

EN: Regarding specific formations, the following suggestions are made:

Head-and-Shoulders Top

A. If you are long a stock, should a breakout down through the neckline occur, with a closing at least 3% below the neckline, next morning place a stop ⅛ point below the last close. Continue to place such "tight stops" if not caught the first day, ⅛ point under each day's close until one is caught.

B. Short sales may be made after a breakout, on a recovery of 40% of the distance from the top of the right shoulder to the bottom of the breakout move, or on a recovery to a line drawn down across the top of the head and right shoulder, or on a Pullback to the neckline, whichever point is reached first. If the breakout move continues down another day, or for several days, the 40% recovery would be based on the entire move from the top of the right shoulder to the lowest point reached.

Head-and-Shoulders Bottom

EN: The editor, long distressed by the paradox of the term "Head-and-Shoulders Bottom," proposes that this formation be renamed in technician's nomenclature to "the Kilroy Bottom." See Figure 23.1.

A. If you are short a stock, should a breakout on increased volume occur, penetrating the neckline and closing at least 3% above it, place a stop next morning to cover at ⅛ point higher than the close. If such a stop is not caught, continue each day to place a stop ⅛ point higher than the previous day's close until one is caught.

B. New purchases may be made after a breakout, on a reaction of 40% of the distance from the bottom of the right shoulder to the top of the breakout move (which reaction must be on decreasing volume), or on a reaction to a line drawn across the bottom of the head and the right shoulder, or on a Throwback to the neckline, whichever is reached first. As in the case of the Top Formation, this 40% reaction is figured on the entire distance of the breakout move if it should continue up for several days.

Complex or Multiple Head-and-Shoulders

The same tactical suggestions apply to these as to the simple Head-and-Shoulders. Definitions and special features of these formations are covered in Chapter 7.

Rounding Tops and Bottoms

It is difficult to set precise rules for trading on these gradual changes of trend. In the case of Rounding Tops, if one is long the stock, the general appearance of a Rounding Formation, extending over a period of several weeks, leveling off from the rise and then turning down, very likely with a tapering off of volume nearing the top of the rise and a pick-up of volume as the turn starts down, would suggest getting out of the stock at the market as soon as the picture looks more or less definite. A short sale of a Rounding Top could be very profitable; but no exact rule could be stated except that, in the absence of fixed Basing Points, one would want to be very certain that the formation was unmistakably a Rounding Top. It would need to be well formed and following a long rise, and extending over a period of some weeks in its formation. It would also need to be protected with a stop above the Top of the curve, as explained in the chapter on stops.

You would not be likely to be short a stock on a Rounding Bottom. The long and gradual rounding appearance with dull volume, followed by a sudden revival on greatly increased volume, would be signal enough to cover if you should find yourself in this uncomfortable position. Purchases would be justified in a stock whose chart showed a Rounded Bottom or Saucer, after the first spasm of activity following a long, dull period of dormancy. You would buy, according to the rules we have given for purchases on reactions, not on the breakout, but on the reaction following it, which would almost surely come.

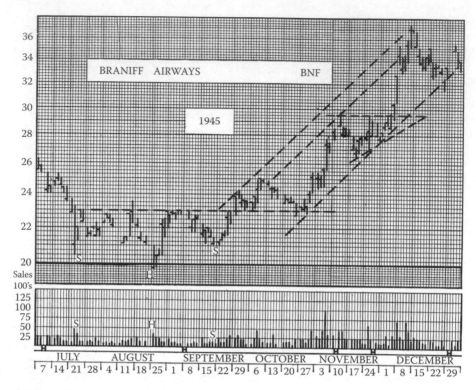

FIGURE 212. Head-and-Shoulders *(or Kilroy)* Bottom in Braniff Airways, 1945. Strictly speaking, a Continuation Head-and-Shoulders after a Secondary Correction in the Bull Market. A Major Bottom, reversing a long Bear Market, would normally take much longer to form.

Here we see heavy volume on the left shoulder, somewhat less on the head, and very little on the right shoulder, with a sharp increase, as required, on the breakout move of September 21. The breakout was followed by a Throwback to the neckline on diminishing volume, providing a good opportunity for purchases at 23. The upward move was resumed, and again there was a reaction to the neckline Support. A second reaction of this sort is not unusual. The closing at 22¾ on October 19, below the previous Minor Bottom, and on increased volume, was mildly disturbing. But in view of the strength of the pattern and breakout, we would not have sold the stock, and the protective stop at 21⅞ was not even threatened. On October 25, the advance was resumed with a Breakaway Gap and continued up to 29½, where the move was signed off with a One-Day Reversal and Exhaustion Gap.

Notice that on reaching 29½, "BNF" went into a Consolidation Pattern for over 3 weeks, making an Ascending Triangle, before leaping to 37½. Notice also (we might as well get all we can out of these examples) that the Ascending Triangle takes shape at approximately the halfway point of the whole advance. We are already familiar with this tendency of stocks in fast moves to form "halfway" patterns.

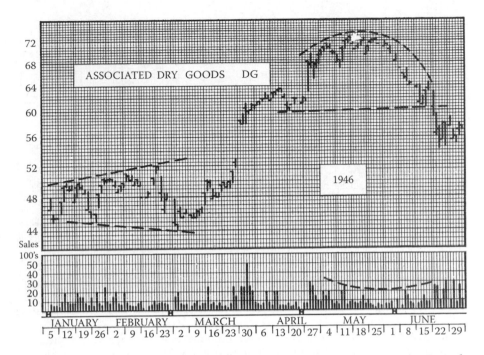

FIGURE 213.   Associated Dry Goods winds up its Bull Market Trend with a Rounding Top. This is a daily chart for the first 6 months of 1946.

The advance in "DG" from 4 to above 72 in just 3½ years, when seen on monthly charts, is a smooth, accelerating curve which emerged from a long Bottom Formation that had lasted 5 years from 1938 through 1942.

As we enter the final 6 months leading up to the ultimate peak, note first the action during January and February. "DG" had just completed a fast run-up in the last quarter of 1945, and was about due for a Consolidation or a Secondary Correction. On reaching 48, it turned back to 45, advanced to 50½, to 51, and finally to 52, and then reacted to 44 at the end of February. Had the move on January 22 gone a little lower and closed below the January 3 low, and then been followed by an even lower closing on February 26, we would have had to consider this January–February pattern a completed Broadening Top, a definite Reversal signal. However, the pattern was not perfect, and, therefore, not valid, but the erratic price action shows incipient weakness.

It is not unusual in these last stages, when public participation is running high, for the climactic advances to be spectacular and fast. And that is what we see here. A 5-point Breakaway Gap occurred on March 25, followed by an advance which petered off at 63½, reacted, and then ran up to over 68.

From here on, the move advanced slowly, with suggestions of a Convergent Trend and a succession of "heads" and "shoulders," and volume dropped off as the Top was reached. The drop on June 4 to below the May 7 Minor Bottom on increased volume would complete the Rounding Top and call for immediate sale if we were still long; and the penetration of the "neckline" on June 18 was a conclusive break.

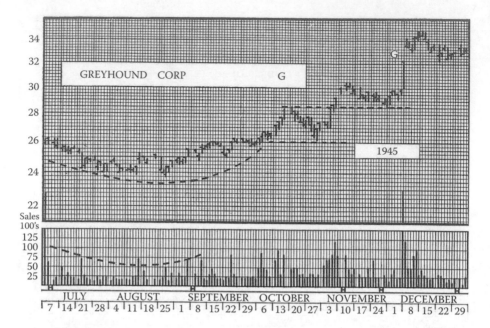

FIGURE 214.   Greyhound: a Rounding Bottom in 1945. A Continuation Pattern after the May run-up to over 29 and reaction to Support at 24, the 1944 high.

In July, volume ran fairly high on downside days, drying up as we entered August. August 10 showed a spurt of volume on the upside, then more dullness.

The various small moves through August and September would not give us any basis for trading operations. The move to a new high in the pattern on August 31 suggested an upturn, and again on September 19–20, we see another little push up to the 26 level. Still not conclusive, however.

The move which got under way in the week ending October 13 is more definite. This decisive move with good volume carries right out of the "Bowl" in an almost vertical ascent. Not a big move, but a clear indication of the probable trend. We would look for a point to buy "G" on a correction of 40–50% of the entire move up from the Bottom, or on a return to near the Support Level around 26. The purchase would probably be made around 26½. Notice the drying up of volume on this reaction.

The advance from here to 30, marking an entirely new Bull Market high, came almost immediately. On November 3, with very heavy volume for a Saturday, "G" closed at 30, and since this volume was not on the day of breakout, we would have closed out the transaction on a tight stop at 29⅞ on Monday (unless we had elected to wait out the next Minor Reaction for a further advance).

Two weeks later, on the basis of the reaction to good Support, we would have bought "G" again at about 29 (you cannot figure on getting the extreme low price on any reaction). The following advance carried up to 34¼ in 2 days. At that point, profits could have been taken or the stock held for the longer term. "G," it might be noted, continued up eventually to 54.

Symmetrical Triangles

A. *If you already have a position in the stock.* During the formation of a Symmetrical Triangle, you may be unable to make any change in your holdings. Let us say you have bought the stock on a reaction after a Bullish Move. The next upsurge fails to make a new high and gives no sufficient volume signal to cause you to sell out. The next reaction fails to carry below the previous one. You are "locked" into the Triangle, and you cannot safely sell, since the Triangle that has formed may eventually break out in the original direction and show you a good profit (in fact, the odds favor that it will break out in that direction). In case of a breakout move (which, of course, must be on increased volume on the upside), you can close it out for a profit (according to rules for trading we have already given), and immediately mark it as a rebuy on the next reaction. If the breakout is down (whether or not on increased volume), with a closing outside the Triangle, you should protect yourself with a tight (⅛ point) stop the next day, and continue to set such tight progressive stops under each day's close until it is sold.

   If you are short the stock, the same rules in reverse would apply, except that the breakout in the right direction (down) would require no volume confirmation, and the adverse breakout (up) would need such increased volume.

B. *If you do not have a position in the stock.* Stay away from any stocks making Symmetrical Triangles until a clear and definite breakout close has been made. After such a breakout, if on the upside, buy on the next reaction if the Major Trend is up, or if on the downside, sell short on the next rally if the Major Trend is down. Rules for making such commitments have already been given.

Note: avoid breakouts from Symmetrical Triangles of the type which have continued to narrow until the breakout point comes far out toward the apex. The most reliable breakouts occur about two thirds along the Triangle.

Right-Angle Triangles

The same rules would apply to Right-Angle Triangles as to Symmetrical Triangles (see Chapter 8 on Triangles). Early breakouts are more dependable here, as in the case of Symmetrical Triangles. Volume confirmation is more important on upside breakouts from Ascending Triangles and is not strictly required on downside breakouts from Descending Triangles. Commitments already made are retained until the breakout and then closed out in the same way as any transaction that shows a gain.

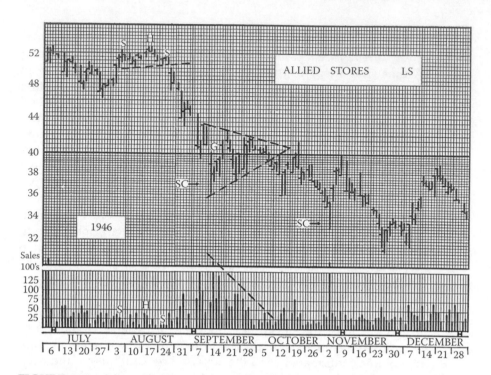

FIGURE 215. Symmetrical Triangle in Allied Stores, a Consolidation in the 1946 decline. Notice heavy volume as "LS" crashed to the first Reversal point of the pattern on September 10, and the drying up of volume during the successive swings of the Triangle. In Point-and-Figure charts, this type of pattern is known as a Pendulum Swing, since it does seem to come to rest like a pendulum. Often, volume will pick up somewhat at each Reversal point, but a valid Triangle must show some overall decrease of volume.

If, by some unhappy chance, you were then long "LS," you should have had your protective stop at 33⅛, 8% below the Bottom reached at 36. However, the move down out of the Triangle on Friday and Saturday, October 4 and 5, although on slight volume, was a true breakout (remember that *downside* breakouts do not require volume confirmation), and you would have been justified in selling your long commitment at the market on Monday. You would have received about 38½. To justify a *short sale*, however, the breakout would have had to close at least 3% outside the Triangle. The return to the border of the pattern at 40 was interesting, and you will notice that volume increased characteristically as the decline really got under way on October 9 and 10.

No question about the validity of this breakout. Short sales were in order on a return to the border of the Triangle, or a 40–50% Correction of the breakout move, say at 38½ to 39. The rally carried to the apex of the Triangle, then broke away fast for the decline to 33 where, on October 30, a Selling Climax and One-Day Reversal occurred — a signal to take profits.

Notice the small Head-and-Shoulders in August. This was a Continuation Pattern marking the top of the rally before the September–November crack-up.

Since the Ascending and Descending Triangles carry a directional forecasting implication that the Symmetrical Triangles do not have, it is possible to make new commitments on reactions within an Ascending Triangle or rallies within a Descending one. However, since the flat horizontal side of one of these Triangles represents a supply or demand area of unknown magnitude, and since, therefore, such a Triangle can be (and sometimes is) turned back before the horizontal line has been decisively penetrated, it might be better policy to note such formations in the making, and wait until the decisive breakout before making the new commitment.

Broadening Tops

Presumably, you would not be long a Broadening Top. The early Reversals in the pattern would have taken you out of the stock, if you follow the tactical rules based on trendlines, as previously outlined, long before completion of the pattern. Neither would you be tempted to buy into such a pattern, since the trend indications would be clearly against a move.

On the other hand, a Broadening Top, after its completion, offers excellent opportunities for a short sale. After downside penetration and close below the fourth point of Reversal in the pattern, you are justified in selling short on a rally of about 40% of the distance covered from the extreme top (fifth point of Reversal), and the lowest point reached on the breakout move. The stop, of course, would be placed at the proper distance above the fifth Reversal, that is, the extreme top of the pattern.

Rectangles

A. *If you already have a commitment in the stock.* The early moves of a Rectangle may provide no volume signals to permit you to get out. And there will, of course, be no "breakout" moves during the formation of a Rectangle that will allow you to take a profit. However, as soon as the character of the Rectangle is well established (and that will require at least four Reversals to set up a clear Top and Bottom), you may trade on the Tops and Bottoms, that is, sell at or near the Top; or buy at or near the bottom. Since, as in the case of Symmetrical Triangles, there is a definite presumption in such formations that they are more likely to lead to continuous moves than to Reversals, this would mean that you would probably pass up your first opportunity to get out (on the fifth Reversal), and would indeed probably decide to "ride along" in the expectation of a continuation of the original move, which will be in the "right" direction for your commitment. In the case of a breakout in the right direction, you would dispose of your commitment according to the rules for trading already stated. If in the wrong direction, use the tight (⅛ point) progressive stops, the same as with the Triangles.

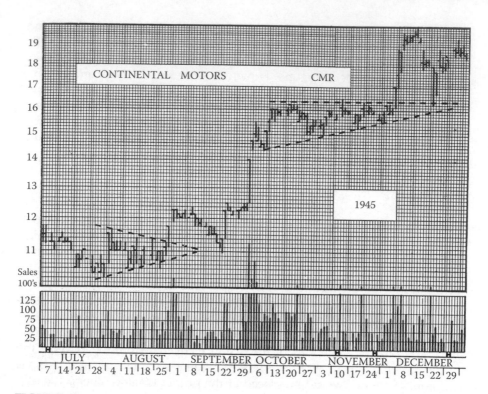

FIGURE 216. An Ascending Triangle. "CMR," after emerging from the doldrums in 1943, forged up to about 12 early in 1945. The first 8 months of the year on a monthly chart showed an Ascending Triangle with Top at 12¼. On daily charts, however, we see the more detailed aspects of this large pattern. For instance, the final reaction of the whole (monthly) formation in August became here a Symmetrical Triangle. The breakout from this pattern carried out the minimum measuring requirements, bringing the price again to the 12¼ Top, from which point there was a reaction which was stopped cold at 11, the apex of the Triangle. A purchase on the reaction after the powerful breakout from the Triangle, say around 11½, would have been closed out on progressive stops, starting September 28 when "CMR" reached 14, the sale being consummated October 2 at 14⅞, a highly profitable move.

Profit-taking of this sort would largely explain the stopping of the rise and the formation of a Consolidation Pattern which turned out to be the Ascending Triangle with Top at 16¼, lasting 8 weeks. Notice the November 7 volume when price went through the 16¼ level, but failed to close outside the pattern; and the volume on November 30 when a clean, decisive breakout move closed at 17. This move ran to 20, and purchases would have been made at 18 or less on the reaction. The next wave took "CMR" to its ultimate Bull Market Top at 24 in January. On the ratio scale, the Top of the Ascending Triangle was exactly halfway between the September Bottom at 11, and the extreme high of 24. This type of halfway consolidation is typical of Flags and Pennants, and this is a very similar case.

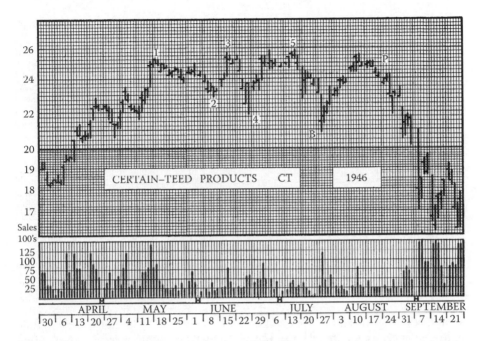

FIGURE 217.   A Broadening Top. This somewhat rare but beautiful and highly dependable formation developed as CertainTeed made its Bull Market Peak in 1946. A quick glance at the volume scale in this daily chart shows the high volume on the final stages of the advance, the dullness during the development of the Top Pattern, and the increased volume after the breakout.

As we all know by now (or go back to Chapter 10 and review the specifications), a Broadening Top is a Five-Point Reversal, differing from the Head-and-Shoulders, Triangles, Rectangles, etc., in that each Reversal must be at a new high or low for the pattern. It is, if you wish, a sort of reversed Triangle with its apex to the left, the swings becoming continually wider.

In the second week of May, "CT" (the symbol has since been changed to "CRT") made a new Bull Market high at 25¼ (marked "1"). The reaction carried back to Support at the previous Minor Peak (point "2") and the following week, "CT" advanced to another new high at 3, closing ⅛ point above the previous Top.

Another week had brought "CT" down to point "4" with a closing at 22½, three quarters of a point below point "2." This, in itself, is not sufficient reason for making short commitments. Three weeks later, "CT" closed at 25⅝, another new high, at point "5." Finally, the stock dropped to 21½ on July 23, and at this point (marked "B"), the pattern was completed. Notice the tendency of volume to rise at each Reversal point of the pattern.

Long holdings would be sold at the market the day after the breakout. But short sellers should wait for a correction of 40–50% of the move from point "5" to point "B." If shorts were put out at 23, we would not worry if the stock advanced for a time, as it did, without making a new high. The downside move in "CT" went quickly to 15½, and within 12 months to 11½.

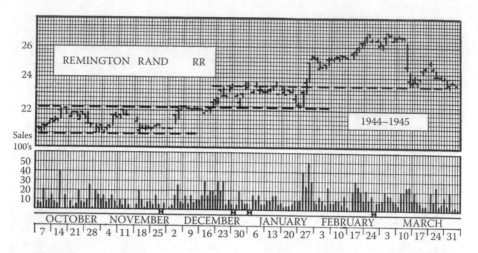

FIGURE 218.   Rectangles in Remington Rand. This is part of a long Bull Market rise that carried "RR" from under 10 to above 50 in the period from 1942 to 1946. The last 3 years of this advance were almost continuous, as seen on monthly charts, without any extensive reactions. When we put the chart on a daily basis, such as this section covering the end of 1944 and the early months of 1945, right in the middle of the advance, we see that the rise was not actually continuous but was built up of steps in an ascending "staircase" of Accumulation Patterns. Each sharp advance on increased volume is followed by a period of dullness and slight recession.

A picture of this type suggests the methodical campaign of buyers who intended to purchase large blocks of the stock for large long-term advances without creating a "skyrocket" market by their own buying operations. Presumably each advance was checked by the temporary distribution of part of the stock held by such buyers, and reaccumulation started on reactions.

In October and November, there is a well-marked Rectangle between 20¾ and 22. A purchase could have been made at or near the bottom limit, say at 21, on the fifth Reversal on November 14. The move out of pattern in the week of December 2 did not carry 3% out of pattern, but about 2 weeks later a move got under way that qualified as a valid breakout, with volume confirmation as required on upside moves. Notice the volume increase and One-Day Reversal on December 20 as this move neared its Top. Purchases would have been made at about 22½ on the basis of a normal correction, and you would have expected Support at the 22 level. This Support was respected, but the move did not advance beyond 23¾, made this same Top 3 times in a period of 2 weeks, and returned again to 22¼.

There was no question about the breakout on January 25. Extent and volume were decisive. Notice the gap and One-Day Reversal on the following day as this Minor Move reached its end.

In mid-March, as you will see, "RR" plunged down from its high of 27, but the decline was stopped in its tracks at the top level of the January Rectangle, a good Support shelf. Never again during the Bull Market did "RR" even threaten this level, since it moved up in April and continued its long march to the 1946 Top.

B. *If you are not committed in the stock.* Trades can be made within the Rectangle on the fifth and subsequent Reversals. Since there is the slight probability that the move will eventually continue in the same direction as the preceding move leading up or down to the Rectangle, it might be best to wait until the sixth Reversal for new commitments, which would set your interests in the same direction as a continuation. And, of course, short sales can be made after any downside breakout close from a Rectangle, or purchases after an upside breakout close with increased volume. Both the short sales and the long purchases would be made on the Corrective Move following the breakout.

Double Tops and Bottoms

Double and Multiple Tops or Bottoms are not valid unless they conform to the requirements for such formations. Chapter 9 on these patterns should be read carefully in this connection.

A. *If you are long a stock.* On penetration and close at a price lower than the extreme Bottom of the pattern between the Multiple Tops, dispose of the stock on tight (⅛ point) progressive stops.

B. *If you are short a stock.* On penetration of the highest point of the Inverted Bowl or rise between the Bottoms, with a close above that point, close out the short sale on tight stops.

C. *If you are not committed in the stock.* Consider a penetration and close beyond the limit of the correction between the Tops (or Bottoms) as a signal of Reversal, and make new commitments on rallies or reactions.

Right-Angled Broadening Formations

The handling of these on breakouts through the horizontal side would be similar to what has been said about Multiple Tops and Bottoms, and Right-Angle Triangles.

The Diamond

If you are sure that what you have is a valid Diamond Pattern, the rules for trading will be the same as those we have already covered in connection with breakouts from Symmetrical Triangles. As in the case of such Triangles, new commitments should wait for a definite breakout; and commitments already in force would have to remain until such a breakout had occurred, either declaring a Reversal, or indicating a probable continuation of the original trend.

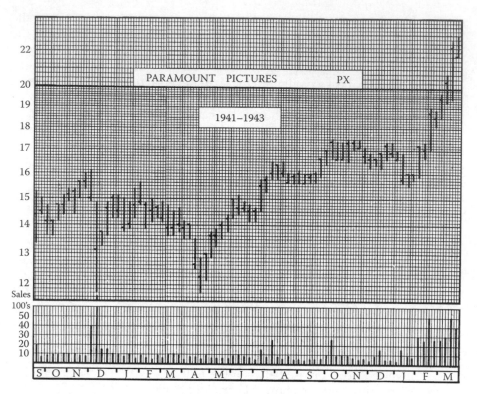

FIGURE 219. A Double Bottom in Paramount Pictures. Double Tops and Double Bottoms are not as common as many traders like to think. They require considerable time to develop and must conform to specifications as to price range and time, and also (on upside breakouts from Double Bottoms) as to volume. They are easier to spot on weekly charts than on dailies.

This is a weekly chart of "PX" from September 1941 through March 1943. A Bottom was made on climactic volume at 11¾ during the "Pearl Harbor Panic" Move. Then came a rise lasting 8 weeks which brought "PX" back to 15⅝ — a rise, incidentally, on feeble volume, strongly suggesting the possibility of another crack-up to even lower levels. This rise, you will notice, was a considerable one, amounting to 35% of the price at the December low.

The downward move, however, which lasted to mid-April, was on low volume and ended precisely at the December low of 11¾. (**Note:** it is not necessary that moves of this sort end at exactly the same level; the second Bottom could have been a bit higher or lower without spoiling the pattern.)

The second week in July shows the first sign of a possible Reversal when the price advanced on increased volume, but it did not close above 15⅝, and was, therefore, not a breakout. Two weeks later, on heavy volume, "PX" had moved up to 16½, closing the week at 16. This is a true breakout, and purchases would have been in order on reactions from this point on.

The move continued up for 3 years to an ultimate Top at 85.

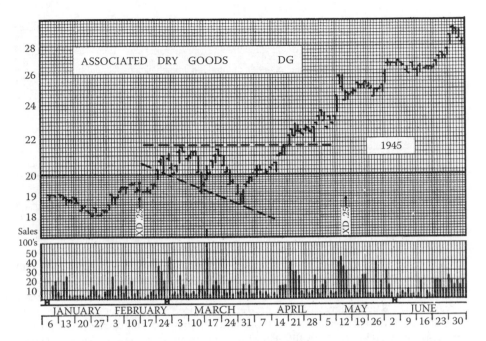

FIGURE 220. A Right-Angled Broadening Formation in Associated Dry Goods. A beautiful example of a breakout through Multiple Tops, followed by an important move. This is, however, a pattern that is more fun to observe in retrospect than to follow as an active trader. The stock had moved up from an important Bottom around 4, established in 1938, 1940, and 1942. At the time of this chart in 1945, "DG" was starting the accelerating climb that eventually ended with the 1946 Rounding Top at over 70. (See Figure 213.)

If you had been holding the stock, you would have been watching for a substantial corrective move after the advance from 12 to 20. In late February and the first week of March, "DG" went into new Bull Market high-ground, reacted to Support around 19 to 19½, and then advanced again in the week of March 17, failing in this move to make a new high. Ten days later, "DG" had reacted to 18½, closing below the previous Minor Bottom. An inexperienced observer might, at this point, have commented "Double Top" and planned to sell "DG" at once or even to make a short sale. However, the pattern was not large enough in duration nor extent of price movement to qualify as a Double Top, nor did it conform to any other recognizable pattern of Reversal. Nor was the volume as high as one would expect on an important Top.

The rally in early April carried through to a decisive breakout of more than 3% in the move which reached 22⅞ on April 18. This move was a near penetration of the middle Top, and confirmed the uptrend. If you still held your long stock, you would not rest easier, and in any case, you would have looked for a chance to buy on a reaction after the breakout. If you had tried to buy at the 21½ Support Level, you would have been left behind, but if you had put your order in a little higher, say at 22, you would have had a nice profit on the advance to 25⅞, where you would have sold on a tight stop at 25¾.

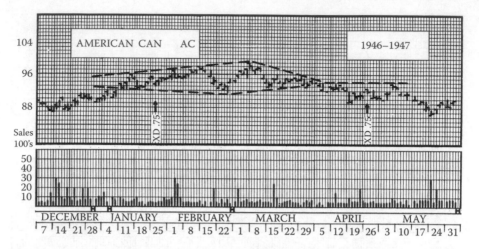

FIGURE 221. A Diamond Pattern in American Can. The daily chart covers the period from 3 December 1946, through May 1947, inclusive. For background on this situation, keep in mind that "AC" made its Bull Market Peak in October 1945 when it reached 112. The tendency of high-grade, high-priced stocks to top-out early at the end of a Bull Market has already been noted. The first decline carried nearly to 90 and was followed by a rally to 106. The stock then dropped to below 80 and a second rally brought us to the situation we see here.

You will notice at once that the moves have a gradual "rounding" appearance, due to the fact that, at this price, conservative stocks do not make large percentage moves. If charted on a scale having larger vertical intervals, the patterns would look very much like those in more speculative stocks.

The first part of the pattern is similar to a Broadening Top. The first Minor Peak at 96 is followed by a reaction to 92. The second peak carries even higher, to 98; and the reaction this time goes down to 91¼. A third rally takes "AC" to 99. So far, we have the five Reversal points of a Broadening Top, needing only a close below 91¼ to confirm the Bearish indications. However, the next decline fails to break out of the pattern, and for several weeks, we have a *narrowing* picture like a Symmetrical Triangle.

Eventually, the stock makes a clean breakout to 89, which is the signal to get out of longs and to consider short sales on the next rally. As a matter of fact, the 3-week rally which then started never made an upside penetration of the Resistance Level at 94, the level of the apex of the converging lines bounding the latter part of the Diamond.

American Can did not make a spectacular move down from this point, which is not surprising considering the markdown that had already taken place in "AC," and considering the habits and price of the stock, and the general condition of the market. It did not, however, again rise to the level shown here, and, in fact, retreated to the 80 level.

To review the nature of the Diamond — it is not a common pattern. It is somewhat like a Complex Head-and-Shoulders with a bent neckline. It resembles, at the start, a Broadening Top, and its latter phase narrows like a Symmetrical Triangle.

Wedges

There is no need to set forth detailed rules for policy within a Wedge and during its formation, since the general principles taken up in connection with trendlines and Support and Resistance, would take you out of such a situation at the first opportunity after the convergent nature of the pattern became clear. At the very worst, your stops (which we hope you maintain faithfully in all situations) will take you out before the consequences become serious.

Regarding new purchases (from a Falling Wedge breakout) or short sales (from a Rising Wedge), the same volume characteristics would be expected: notably increased volume on an upside breakout from a Falling Wedge; less pronounced volume action on the first stages of breakout from a Rising Wedge. New commitments, in line with the implications of the breakout, may be placed on rallies or reactions after a clear breakout closing occurs, carrying beyond the trendlines forming the Wedge.

One-Day Reversals

One-Day Reversals are not technical patterns suitable for trading in the same sense as the important Reversal and Consolidation pictures we have examined. They are mainly useful as a gauge in helping to find the precise Top or Bottom of a Minor Move in order to protect profits on commitments previously made. The One-Day Reversal, the Exhaustion Gap, and the day of exceptionally heavy volume following several days of movement in a Minor Trend are strong indications that the move may have run out. Any of these three signals is worth watching for; any two of them together carry more weight than one alone; and the appearance of all three carries very strong implications of a Minor *(EN: or even a Major)* Top or Bottom.

So far as trading on movements signaled by One-Day Reversals, this type of trading would lie almost in the field of gambling, or at least trading for quick, small profits on short moves. It would not be the same kind of trading at all that we have been studying in the greater part of this book. The indications and some suggestions for trading on those one-day moves are covered in the discussion of them in Chapter 10.

Flags and Pennants

In many cases, the total decline from a Flag in an uptrend will bring the price back to a point where the stock may be bought according to our regular trading tactics, that is, the decline may carry down to the Basic (Red) Trendline, to the Blue Parallel, or make a 40 to 50% correction of the rising "mast" preceding the Flag. If the "mast" move is the first such move out of a level or only moderately rising trend, and if the Major Trend of the market

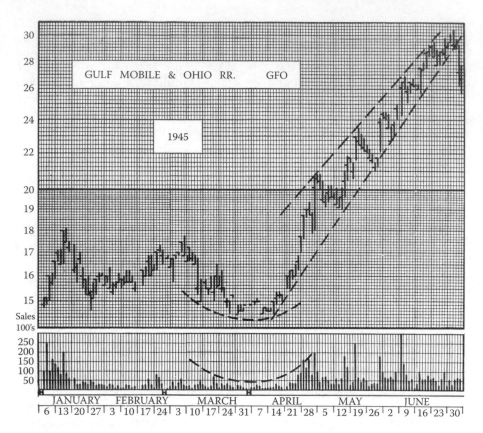

FIGURE 222.   Gulf, Mobile, and Ohio builds a beautiful Wedge, as shown on this daily chart for the first half of 1945. This was the move which terminated the spectacular rise of "GFO," its final Bull Market Top.

Immediately after the downside breakdown from the Wedge, "GFO" came down to 18¾, and from this Intermediate low, which was reached in August, rallied into a long Rectangle between 23¾ and 26¾ from which it eventually broke down in a series of crashes that found it, in May 1947, selling for 6⅛!

It is rather hard, with a formation of this sort, to say at what precise point the convergence of the trends is established. The breakout move late in April was, of course, normal; the stock was a buy on the next reaction. The following advance in May, which reached 23½, did not carry out a Parallel Trend Channel, and we saw a tendency to converge as prices retreated on the reaction. The next three advances all repeated and confirmed the Wedge picture, and at the top, we see a sort of "bunching up" as prices make little or no headway. The chances are that at 11 an alert trader would have taken profits on long commitments after the high volume appeared at the top of the Minor Move ending June 4 and 5. In any case, he would have maintained a protective stop at all times to take him out if and when a downside breakout occurred.

is Bullish, we would be justified in buying at the first opportunity, which would be on the Blue Parallel. In such a case we would expect, and ordinarily get, some further reaction, but it is important to get in early because sometimes the reaction is very brief, and does not meet either of the other requirements for the correction. It is most important in a situation like this that the volume drop off sharply. Volume must decrease and remain slight. Any increase of volume during the formation of the Flag should be reviewed as casting suspicion on the entire pattern, except, of course, the increasing volume that characteristically attends the start of the breakout drive. This drive is usually so virile that we would be safe in placing a tight (⅛ point) stop under the close of any day during formation of a Flag or Pennant that showed notably increased volume. So that if the volume indicated failure of the pattern, we would be taken out at once; but if the breakout was under way, we would probably be left in, since the stock would ordinarily move up then without a reaction, very often making a Breakaway Gap.

In downward movements, when the Major Trend of the market is Bearish, the same suggestions would apply, with one difference. The final high day of the Flag-type of rally may be on high volume, and, of course, may also show the Exhaustion Gap or One-Day Reversal. If a short sale has been made into such a day showing high volume, gap, or One-Day Reversal, a stop order placed above the peak of the Flag will protect you should the advance be resumed unexpectedly.

In either the up-moving or down-moving manifestations of this type of action, there may be Flags having horizontal Tops and Bottoms, which are, of course, Rectangles. If the drying-up of volume and other aspects of the picture, including the sharp upward or downward move preceding it, suggest a Flag-type Consolidation, you would be justified in making a commitment on the sixth Reversal point, or for that matter, at almost any point in the pattern (since you cannot expect this pattern to continue very long).

Flags and Pennants which do continue too long (over 3 weeks) are open to question. Stops should then be set at the usual computed distance above or below their extreme Tops or Bottoms (as the case may be). The fairly frequent appearance of Flag-like Formations which eventually fail is unfortunate, since it is particularly hard to give up hoping with this kind of pattern, and it is necessary to set the 3-week time limit to prevent the stock from drifting all the way back to previously established stop levels. On the other hand, breakout moves from these patterns, when completed normally, are among the fastest and most profitable forms of market action.

The question remains what to do in the case of stocks you may be holding as they go into Flag or Pennant Formation. Obviously, they should be held if you are long and the move leading to the Flag is up; or short positions should be retained if the move is down. However, this would not happen

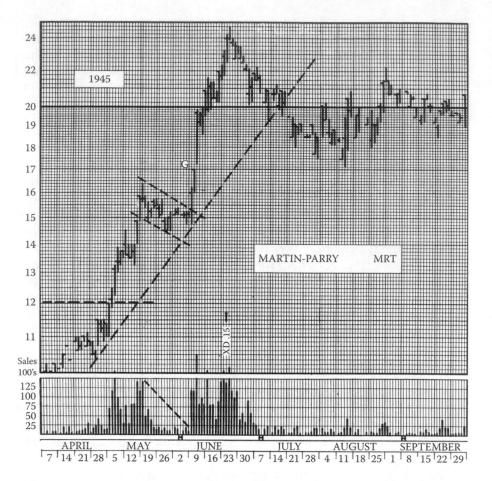

FIGURE 223. A Pennant in Martin–Parry. This type of pattern is fairly common in fast-moving markets. The extraordinary point about Flags and Pennants (and sometimes other Consolidation Patterns in fast moves) is their tendency to form almost exactly halfway between Bottom and Top.

Just before this move, "MRT" had built a Rectangle between 10 and 12 lasting 7 months, which followed the 1944 rise from around 4 to 12. The May breakout on heavy volume carried "MRT" right to the top of the Pennant without any adequate reaction. Note the increase of volume at the top of that rise. For 3 weeks prices drifted off with a drying up of volume that is clearly shown in the chart. The pattern did not correct the entire first phase, but found Support at the Minor Peak at 14½.

Suddenly, on high volume, the move was resumed, and this time went right up to 24¾. The chances are that traders who were still long their original stock or who had bought in around 15 on the Pennant would have sold after the high volume of June 6 when "MRT" reached 19⅞.

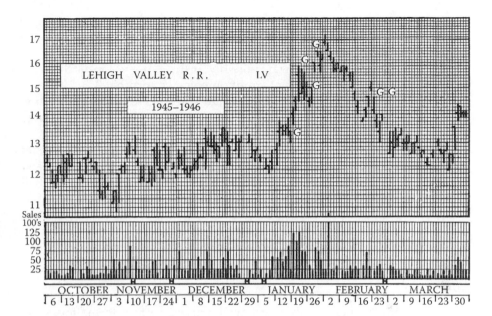

FIGURE 224.   This daily chart of Lehigh Valley R.R. through late 1945 and early 1946 shows a variety of gaps. At this particular time, "LV" was completing a Secondary Corrective Move before making one more (and as it turned out, final) effort to exceed the 1945 Top just above 17. This long-term situation could be used for a discussion of Double Tops, since the Bottom of the intervening move was violated in the summer of 1946 and the stock continued a downward course to below the 5 level.

Not all gaps are significant; for example, the first gap shown, on October 3, when the stock was moving in a narrow range on low volume. The gap on Saturday, November 3, however, is important, since the Saturday volume (when doubled) is high. The move failed to quality by a 3% new high closing as a true breakout, but the implications of the move were Bullish and might well have justified purchases on Minor Reactions. The low-volume gaps on these reactions were of no particular interest.

It is not until the third week of January that we see another gap that looks like a real breakaway. On January 14, with high volume, "LV" moved up and out in a rush that took it to 15⅞ on January 16, closing at 15½. The second appearance of volume here would have suggested application of progressive stops, and long trades would have been closed out at 15⅜.

New purchases could have been made on the reaction at 14½. A second advance accompanied by a Breakaway Gap developed on January 23. If we consider the second gap (of January 24) a Runaway or Measuring Gap, we would estimate the probable top of this move at around 17¾. However, when a third gap appeared on January 28 with a One-Day Reversal and climactic volume, it would be clear that this move was about finished, and progressive stops would be used to clear out longs at 16¾.

Note the attempt to rally after the sharp drop, and the One-Day Island formed by two gaps as "LV" fails to hold at the 15 level.

ordinarily if you had followed the trading rules strictly. In most cases, your signals calling for tight (⅛ point) progressive stops would have appeared during the formation of the "mast." You would have been taken out of the picture somewhere along the way, possibly at the extreme top of the mast (though ordinarily, you could not count on being so fortunate).

If, however, no signal should appear, and you still are holding a position as the Flag starts to make its appearance, by all means hold your position. The odds favor a continuation of the original move.

Now if you have been holding the stock long (in a Bull Market), and have seen it break out and start leaping to new highs, say from 20 to 32, and you have been stopped out at 30, and then you see the price advance, halt and during the next several days retreat, with the rather high previous volume drying up to practically nothing (it must be a drastic drying-up, and no mistake about it), then you are justified in buying right back in again, even at a higher price than you received only a few days before.

Gaps

If you are long a stock which is in a well-marked pattern formation, or in an area of dull movement within fairly narrow limits, and the stock suddenly breaks out on the upside with high volume and a gap, that is a Bullish indication. You will hold the stock until signs of exhaustion appear as the rise continues, or reappearance of high volume, or another gap or One-Day Reversal. Then, particularly if two or all three of these indications show up at the same time, you can protect your commitment with tight progressive stops. You will have to consider whether a second gap should be considered an exhaustion gap or a continuation gap, depending on the volume and the speed of the rise, as discussed in the chapters on gaps and their measuring implications.

Ordinarily, after a Breakaway Gap, regardless of whether you sell on the next Minor Top, you would consider the move Bullish, and would prepare to make a purchase on the next reaction.

Now if you are long a stock, and during the course of a sharp rise it develops a gap after several days of the move, you must make your decision as to whether or not it is a Continuation (Runaway) Gap. If so, you would prepare to hold the stock for a further rise approximately equal to the rise up to the gap; and you would watch the approach to the ultimate objective indicated very closely, so that, on the appearance then of Reversal signals, you could protect your holding with tight stops.

If you are satisfied that a gap following a good rise is actually an Exhaustion Gap, then you should protect your stock with a tight progressive stop at once.

In Bear Markets, you would apply these same rules in reverse to your short sales, remembering that a downside breakaway is not necessarily accompanied by the high volume you expect on an upside breakaway.

Where you are long or short a stock which is moving in a Pattern Formation, and the stock then makes a Breakaway Gap in the adverse direction, the commitment should be closed out immediately at the market, or on tight progressive stops.

Support and Resistance

When you are long a stock, you do not want to see it violate any Minor Bottoms previously made. Neither do you want to see it violate any of the preceding Minor Tops which it has surpassed. Therefore, your stop orders will be placed at a computed distance, as explained in Chapter 27 on stop orders, using both the Minor Bottoms and the Minor Tops as Basing Points. Normally, the Minor Bottom most recently formed will be at the approximate level of the preceding Minor Top, so that often these Basing Points will coincide. Ordinarily, therefore, in a rising trend, we look to the most recently formed Minor Bottom. When the stock has, for 3 days, made a price range which is entirely above the entire range of the day marking this Bottom, you may move up your stop protection to a place indicated by this new Basing Point.

The same procedure will apply in Bear Markets; the "three-day" rule being used to confirm Basing Points established by Minor Peaks and also by the preceding Minor Bottoms. But, ordinarily, it will be sufficient to use the Minor Peaks as Basing Points.

Intermediate Tops and Bottoms are used in determining the probable objectives of Intermediate Moves, since previous Tops constitute Support under Intermediate Reactions, and previous Bottoms indicate Resistance over Intermediate Rallies.

Multiple Tops are Support Levels. Multiple Bottoms are Resistance Levels. The neckline of a Head-and-Shoulders Pattern is a Support or Resistance Level, as the case may be. The apex of a Symmetrical Triangle is a strong Support and Resistance point which may show its effect again on a subsequent move. Any congestion or area at a certain price level or within narrow price limits may provide Support or Resistance when a stock moves again to that price or range.

Trendlines

We have already gone into the methods of following trends in stocks, and the use of the Top and Bottom Trendlines (Basic and Return Lines) as indicators of Bullish and Bearish opportunities, and as price determinants for executing purchases or short sales.

There remains the tactical problem of the stock in which you are committed, which is acting badly, but which has neither broken out of a recognized pattern nor violated an established Minor Peak. This is not a common situation, but it can present a very difficult problem when it does come up.

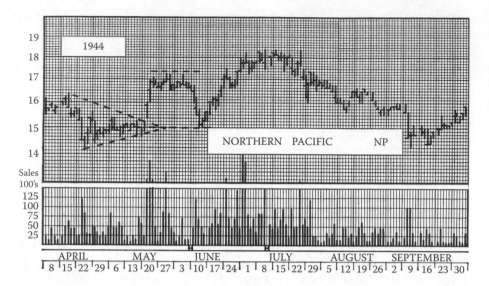

FIGURE 225. This daily chart in Northern Pacific, covering 6 months during 1944, shows several examples of Support and Resistance. The entire chart covers only part of the series of Consolidations that took place in 1943 and 1944 preceding the 1945–46 advance that carried beyond 38.

Support and Resistance phenomena appear, of course, on many, in fact on most of the charts in this book, and you will find them on the charts you set up for yourself. There is nothing unique or even unusual about the Support–Resistance action in "NP."

Starting at the left in April, after the downside move on volume to 14¼, notice the recovery to 15⅝ where the move stops at the Resistance Level of the preceding 2 weeks. After the formation of the Symmetrical Triangle, there is a breakaway move with a gap which runs right on up to above 17, where a small Rectangle is built during the next 3 weeks. The stock ultimately breaks down from this pattern on considerable volume. It is doubtful whether one would want to trade on this as a normal reaction after the breakout from the Triangle, because of the downside volume and the implications of the Rectangle.

However, note how the reaction stops cold at the 15 line, the apex level of the Triangle, and then moves right on up. Rather surprisingly, there is only a 3-day hesitation at the Bottom of the Rectangle, but a little setback occurs at the Top of that pattern.

The July Top might be classed as a Head-and-Shoulders or Complex or Rounding Top; in fact, it is almost a Rectangle, and after the downside breakout, prices hesitate at the level of the Top of the May Rectangle, continue down, find temporary Support again at the April Support Shelf around 16, and ultimately wind up a bit under 15. Although "NP" actually did penetrate and close slightly below the apex of the Triangle, the violation was barely 3%, and it is interesting to note that this September Bottom was the lowest point reached. From here, the stock started its climb to the 38 level, which was reached in December 1945.

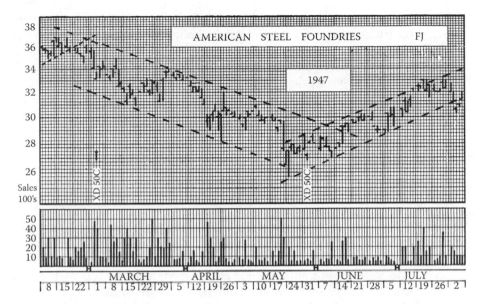

FIGURE 226. Trendlines in American Steel Foundries. This daily chart shows the tendency of trendlines to develop along straight channels. We have already pointed out that these channels are frequently easier to see in retrospect than during their formation, that stocks move in perfect channels only occasionally, and that all channels come to an end, frequently without warning. In this case, the long trend channel does give a warning of Reversal.

In 1946, "FJ" had declined from 48 to a Support Level of 30. From here it rallied for 3 months in a Trend Channel that brought us to the February Top at 37. The next decline broke the previous trend, and volume developed at the bottom of this break. If you will follow the entire chart, you will notice that volume nearly always shows an increase at the points of Reversal, which are also usually points of contact with the Trend Channel. Notice also the way the Corrective Rallies tend to stop at or near the previous Minor Bottoms in the downward trend, and how reactions tend to stop at the previous Minor Tops in the upward trend.

Trading on this situation would have been profitable. The Secondary Intermediate Rally up to February approached the Resistance Level marked by a 1946 Bottom around 40, and a correction of the drop from 48 to 30 would indicate short sales around 37 (which objective was just barely reached). Such sales, if made, would have been covered after the first drop (week of March 1) around 33¼. New shorts at 34½ would have been closed in the week of March 15 at about 31½. Shorts made on the rally of the March 22 week around 33 would be covered in the week of April 19 at 30. If shorted again, the same week at 31, the sale would have been covered after the Climactic Bottom in the week of May 24; and the combination, here, of great volume and a One-Day Reversal would have warned against further shorts.

The Rising Channel, being a Secondary, presumably of limited extent, would not offer any great inducement to long-side trading in the absence of other good reasons.

Let us say the Major Trend is Bullish, and a certain stock which has been moving up irregularly in a Parallel Trend Channel confirms its uptrend by a long, more or less continuous advance and calls for repurchase on the next reaction. You buy on the reaction, and the stock continues down; that is, the reaction continues with prices sagging for days and weeks, without any rallies, Consolidations, or Corrections that are sufficiently well-defined to serve as Basing Points for stop orders.

In the absence of clear indications during the reaction, and also during the preceding large upward move, your stop would be placed at a computed distance *below the top of the preceding rise*. And if the reaction continues down until that level is reached, you will have sustained an abnormally large loss.

In a case like this, you should examine the trendlines making up the long advance in the Trend Channel. The points of contact with the Basic Trendline can serve as a fair emergency substitute for Minor Bottoms. Your stop level should, therefore (in the absence of more definite Basing Points), be placed at the computed distance below the last point at which the stock made contact with the bottom trendline and moved decisively up away from it. If penetration and close below this point occurs without catching the stop, sell on tight progressive stops. *EN: The editor feels that such situations should occur only in position building or pyramiding cases. Every effort should be made to join trends on breakout or origination, whatever the source. There is no excuse for "chasing stocks" in the modern environment where literally monitoring all stocks is possible with a computer, and instructing the system to alert one to the conditions attending breakouts. EN9: On the other hand, human frailty being what it is we will all find ourselves chasing a train at some time or other.*

The reverse of this rule would apply to the same type of situation in a Bear Market, where stops for short sales would be placed at the computed distance above the point at which the stock made contact with and fell away from the upper trendline.

The changes of angularity and direction in Intermediate trendlines are helpful in showing the gradual turning of a Major Trend.

chapter thirty-four

A Quick Summation of Tactical Methods

There are three types of tactical operations: (1) Getting into new commitments; (2) getting out of commitments which have moved as expected and show a profit; and (3) getting out of commitments which have not moved as expected, whether the transaction shows a profit or a loss.

The principles of taking profits based on trends, Resistance and Support Levels, measuring implications of patterns, and most especially, on the daily technical and volume action of the stock, already have been covered. These profit-taking operations seldom present very difficult problems, since the picture has developed normally and in the way you hoped and expected it would. The "stepping off" point is usually easy to determine.

The more difficult problems arise in making new commitments correctly, and in the very important defensive operations of getting out of losing commitments with the least possible loss.

It should be emphasized that a stock which has ceased to act in a Bullish manner and which should, therefore, be sold is not necessarily a short sale on the next rally. In other words, the signal that shows weakness or failure of a move in one trend is not always a signal to make new commitments on the opposite side of the market. More often than not, in fact, it is nothing of the kind.

We know that certain moves, such as adverse breakouts from Symmetrical Triangles or Rectangles, advise us simultaneously to get out of commitments in what is now clearly the "wrong" direction and to make new commitments in the "right" direction. The simple failure of a trendline, however, where the stock merely penetrates an old Minor Bottom without completing a Head-and-Shoulders or other Reversal Pattern, although reason enough to get out of commitments which are showing losses, is not sufficiently conclusive, by itself, to justify reversing policy and making new commitments in the opposite direction. Therefore we separate the two types of signals as follows:

Get out of present commitments
- On adverse breakout from Head-and-Shoulders Formation.
- On adverse breakout from Symmetrical Triangle.

- On adverse breakout from Rectangle.
- On establishment of new Minor low or new Minor high in adverse direction.
- On adverse breakout from Diamond.
- On adverse breakout from Wedge.
- On One-Day Reversal if marked by heavy volume or a gap.
- On adverse breakout from Flag or Pennant.
- On clear penetration of any Resistance or Support Level in the adverse direction.
- On an adverse Breakaway Gap.
- On the appearance of an Island after a move in the favorable direction.
- On penetration of basic trendline in the absence of pattern or other favorable criteria.

Note: It is understood that all breakouts must close in the breakout area. A closing 3% beyond the Support, trend, or pattern is sufficient to give the danger signal. All takeouts are performed by the use of ⅛-point progressive stops.

Make new commitments
- In line with the Major Dow Trend, or to a limited extent in countertrend moves as insurance to reduce overall risk.
- On breakout from Head-and-Shoulders Pattern.
- On breakout from Symmetrical Triangle, provided it is not working into the final third of its length toward the apex.
- On breakout from Right-Angle Triangle.
- On breakout from Rectangle, or (possibly) on points of contact, beginning with the sixth Reversal.
- On breakout from a Broadening Top.
- On breakout from Double or Multiple Top or Bottom. (By this is meant breakout through the Bottom of the valley between Tops, or upside penetration of the "dome" between Bottoms.)
- On breakout from Wedge, or (possibly) commitments within the Wedge in the last third of its length as it approaches its apex.
- On Flags and Pennants, after sufficient Secondary or Corrective Move by the pattern, or (possibly) within the pattern, provided that volume and all other indications tend strongly to confirm the pattern.
- On clear penetration of a well-defined Support or Resistance Area.
- On Breakaway Gap (possibly).
- After formation of an important and well-defined Island following a considerable move.
- On contact with, or penetration of, the "favorable" trendline if both trendlines are moving in the Major Trend direction. (Blue Top Trendline in a Bull Market, Red Bottom Trendline in a Bear Market.)

Note: Breakouts and penetrations must show a closing in the breakout area and must conform to volume requirements. Breakout closings should conform to the 3% rule.

New commitments (marked "possibly") may be made in certain cases within some patterns: Rectangles, Wedges, Flags, and Pennants. Exceptional care should be used in such cases.

It is extremely difficult to catch Breakaway Gaps, and we would not recommend this as a general practice. *EN: This is not so difficult as it was in Magee's time due to modern communications, computers, and the Internet.*

All commitments, except those just noted, are made on the next following reaction or rally, to rules previously stated.

All commitments are protected by stops from the moment they are made. Stops are moved, as conditions justify moving them, but always in the favorable direction, never in the adverse direction.

chapter thirty-five

Effect of Technical Trading on Market Action

The question often is asked whether the very fact that traders are studying methods and patterns tends to create those very patterns and trends — in other words, whether the technical method sets up, to some extent, an artificial market in which the market action is merely the reflection of chart action instead of the reverse.

This does not seem to be true. The charts we make today seem to follow the old patterns; the presumption is very strong that markets have followed these patterns long before there were any technicians to chart them. The differences mentioned briefly in Part One, due to changed margin requirements, restraining of manipulative practices, etc., seem to have changed these habits, if at all, only in degree and not in their fundamental nature.

The market is big, too big for any person, corporation, or combine to control as a speculative unit. *(EN9: And even beyond big in the 21st century. Gargantuan.)* Its operation is extremely free, and extremely democratic in the sense that it represents the integration of the hopes and fears of many kinds of buyers and sellers. Not all are short-term traders. There are investors, industrialists, employees of corporations, those who buy to keep, those who buy to sell years later — all grades and types of buyers and sellers.

And not all short-term traders are technicians by any manner of means. There are those who trade on fundamentals for the short term; those who rely on tips, hunches, on reading the stars, on personal knowledge of the company. They are all part of the competitive market, they are all using methods different from yours — and sometimes they will be right and you will be wrong.

The technician using the various tools of technical analysis, Dow Theory, Point-and-Figure charts, oscillators, scale order systems, and monthly, weekly, and daily charts is in the minority. The cold attempt to analyze a situation on the basis of the market record alone does not appeal to many people. Technical analysis leaves out the warmth and human interest of the board-room, the trading room, the fascinating rumors of fat extra dividends to come, the whispered information on new patents, and the thrilling study of the quarterly earnings reports. *(EN9: Unless I am mistaken the only appearance of irony in Magee's work.)*

It is the influence of all these rumors, facts, and statistics that causes people to buy and sell their stocks. It is their actions that build the familiar chart patterns. You are not interested in why they are doing what they are doing. So far as your trading is concerned, you are interested only in the results of their actions.

The habits and evaluative methods of people are deeply ingrained. The same kinds of events produce the same kinds of emotional responses, and hence, the same kinds of market action. These characteristic approaches are extremely durable. It is not quite true that "you can't change human nature," but it is true that it is very difficult to change the perceptive habits of a lifetime. And since the "orthodox" investors greatly outnumber the technicians, we may confidently assume that technical trading will have little or no effect on the typical behavior of free markets.

EN: This statement by Magee is still true in principle. And, it should be noted that in modern markets professional investors attempt to learn (or perhaps it is "the mysterious and anomalous market*") what makes systems and other investors successful. They then take action to frustrate those methods which are inimical to their self-interest. For example, locals and professionals will search for stops above a congestion zone in an attempt to cause the market to break away. This might be in an attempt to create a trend, or it might be in an attempt to create a bull trap.*

The proliferation of systems trend traders in the futures markets has, some of those traders feel, created conditions hostile to systems traders as a group. The moral of the story is that the trader/investor must be ever alert for the false move and the changing rhythm of the markets.

No one has been able to quantify chart analysis, nor to disguise his own activities from the x-ray of the charts. Nor has anyone changed human nature to eliminate treachery and perfidy and truculent defense of self-interest.

EN9: And – dramatic drum roll – in 2005 Smith-Barney fires its entire technical analysis staff. What to make of this is left to the imagination of the reader. Some commentators attribute it to the bearish outlook of the technical staff as opposed to the need of the firm to sell long positions to its customers. In my view an unintended validation of the craft. When you have to shoot the messenger it says something about the state of the market, as well as something about the industry.

Also, in conversation at a meeting of the Technical Securities Analysts Association of San Francisco (tsaasf.org), Larry Williams: "I hate technical analysis." I am reasonably certain that the "technical analysis" referred to is number driven analysis.

chapter thirty-six

Automated Trendline: The Moving Average

There was a time back in 1941 when we were still filled with starry-eyed ignorance, and we felt that if only we worked hard enough and looked shrewdly enough, we would discover the sure, unbeatable formula or system that would solve all our problems in the stock market, and all we would have to do for the rest of life was apply the magic and telegraph our broker periodically from Nassau, or Tahiti, or Switzerland, or wherever we happened to be enjoying life at the time.

We have learned (we hope) quite a bit since then. We have learned most particularly a number of things not to do; and by not repeating the same errors over and over, we have been able to improve our performance substantially. We have also learned that (to date) *(EN: still true in the 21st century)* there are no sure, unbeatable formulas or systems in the market, that even the most useful and generally dependable forecasting methods must be regarded as statements of probability only, subject to revision and vulnerable to failure at times.

One of the useful tools, and one of the first many students of market action adopt, is the trendline. Whether a stock is moving generally up, or generally down, or generally sideways, there seems to be a tendency for the Major Trend to continue, to persist. It is true that every trend is broken sooner or later, and the fact that it has been broken is often significant. But given a well-established trend, the probabilities certainly appear to favor its continuance rather than its Reversal.

However, as with all other market studies, there are times and conditions in which the simple trendline action seems "not quite good enough." One feels that there should be some mechanical or mathematical way of determining the trend that might avoid some of the perplexities of choosing the right point through which to draw a trendline. And, it was back in 1941 that we delightedly made the discovery (though many others had made it before) that by averaging the data for a stated number of days, or weeks, or months, one could derive a sort of Automated Trendline which would definitely interpret the changes of trend over the past 30 days, or 200 days, or 12 months, or whatever period was chosen. It seemed almost too good to be true. As a matter of fact, it was too good to be true.

The Moving Average is a fascinating tool, and it has real value in showing the trend of an irregular series of figures (like a fluctuating market) more
clearly. It also has value in that it can be used to cancel out the effect of any
regular cyclical variation, such as a normal seasonal range of temperatures
in order to get a better picture of the true secular trend.

The trouble with a Moving Average (and which we discovered long
since, but keep bumping into from time to time) is that it cannot entirely
escape from its past. The smoother the curve (longer cycle) one has, the more
"inhibited" it is in responding to recent important changes of trend. And
there is a very bad fault of Moving Averages in that "the tail tends to wag
the dog"; the figures back to the first date of the current tabulation, perhaps
6 months ago, or a year ago, if they are large, may unduly affect the present
average, and may conceal or mask some important feature by distorting the
curve.

We feel the Moving Averages trendlines are useful. But they should be
understood and used with discretion, and with a full perception of their
limitations.

Now that we have gone through some of the caveats of Moving Averages, let us give you some of the ways to construct them. Moving Averages
can be classified as Simple Moving Averages, Weighted or Exponential Moving Averages, and Linear Moving Averages. We prefer, and have found over
the years, that the simple methods work just as well and sometimes better
than the more complicated Moving Averages, and the others are more useful
when using computers.

For this reason, we will concentrate on Simple Moving Averages. The
most common are the 50-day and the 200-day Moving Averages. If you want
to increase the sensitivity of a Moving Average, shorten the Moving Average
by using 10 or 20 days. Another way is to increase the lead time by starting
on the third day for the 10-day Moving Average, or on the 20th day for a
50-day Moving Average, etc.

To construct a Simple Moving Average, whether it is 5 days, 10 days,
50 days or 200 days, you add the price of 5 days, and divide by 5, or the
10 days and divide by 10, or the 50 days by 50, or 200 days by 200. A simple
way of doing the 5-day Moving Average, instead of adding all 5 prices each
time, is to drop day 1 and add day 6. A similar method can be used in doing
the 50-day Moving Average or the 200-day Moving Average. Instead of
adding the 50-day Moving Average each time, just drop the first day of the
previous average and add the 51st day. The same with the 200-day Moving
Average; drop the first day of the previous 200 and add the 201st day.
Another way of doing the 200-day Moving Average is to take one day of the
week of 30 weeks, such as Wednesday or Thursday, add them and divide
by 30. This will give you the same Moving Averages as you would have
doing 200. Another way to put it is, on the second day, take the total, add
the new day's price, and subtract the oldest day's price from your 5-day
Moving Average, 10-day Moving Average, 50-day, or 200-day, whichever
way you are doing it. Repeat the process on a daily basis and divide by the

representative day — for the 5-day, you would divide by 5; for the 10-day, you would divide by 10; for the 50-day, divide by 50; and for the 200-day, you would divide by 200.

Sensitizing Moving Averages

The shorter the time period, the greater the sensitivity you will develop in your Moving Average. The 5-day Moving Average will be much more sensitive than a 10-day. The problem with short-term Moving Averages is that you can have a greater number of false moves. Shorter Moving Averages are more suitable for commodities. On commodities, we would even advise using a 30-hour, a 3-day, and a 6-day Moving Average.

It is often better to use two Moving Averages, one of shorter duration and one of longer duration. In addition, you can use channels, a Moving Average of lows, and a Moving Average of highs.

Crossovers and Penetrations

As a general rule, consider the crossing of two lines by the price line as a sell or buy signal in the direction of the crossover or penetration.

1. Uptrends — Long positions are retained as long as the price trend remains above the Moving Average Line.
   a. When the price line intersects or penetrates the Moving Average Line on the upside, it activates a buy signal.
   b. When the price line goes above the 200-day Moving Average, but falls sharply toward it without penetration, it is a buy signal.
   c. When the price line falls below the Moving Average Line while the line is still rising, it could be a buy signal.
   d. When the price line spikes down too fast and far below a declining Moving Average Line, a short-term rebound toward the line may be expected: a possible whipsaw trap.
2. Downtrends — Short positions are held as long as the price trend remains below the Moving Average. When the price trend reaches a bottom and turns upward, a penetration of the Moving Average is a buy signal.
   a. When the price line moves above the average line while the average line is still falling, it is a sell signal.
   b. When the stock price line moves below the average line and rises toward it, but fails to penetrate and breaks down again, it is a sell signal.
   c. If the price line rises too fast above the rising average line, a short-term reaction may be expected: could be a whipsaw.
   d. Occasionally, penetration of the Moving Average Line will occur in close conjunction with the penetration of a trendline, then according to its direction, it is a buy or sell signal.

3. Horizontal, Diagonal or Sideways Movements — If the fluctuations are broad in comparison to the length of the Moving Averages being used, the price trend will fluctuate back and forth as the Moving Average, true to its character or purpose, moves horizontally.
4. Gaps — Moving Averages, depending on their length, may have a tendency to be penetrated in close proximity to a Breakaway Cap, particularly at the beginning of a Major Phase of an Intermediate cycle, and also in such cases where Breakaway Gaps occur at the beginning of correction phases.

Area Patterns can be a pitfall for the Moving Averages. Normally, the Moving Average oscillates through the center of these areas producing buy and sell signals in rapid succession. In Area Patterns, the Moving Average is a headache to the trader because he never knows which penetration is the one preceding either the renewal of the trend or Confirmation of a Reversal.

When trading areas develop in the form of Triangles — Descending, Declining, or Symmetrical — the Moving Average will trend through the center of the Triangle. The technician has some small advantage in judging which of the series of penetrations of a Moving Average is the important one. When the Triangle reaches its apex, and the stock breaks out in one direction or another and penetrates the Moving Average, the penetration is likely to be the most important one during the sideways movement of the Triangle's development. Penetrations occur many times in close conjunction with the penetration of a trendline.

As a price derivative product, the Moving Average can be a trend indicator by the way it fits a trendline. But, nevertheless, it should be considered an adjunctive tool to everything else you have learned in relation to technical analysis.

A 150-day Moving Average is charted on the following page.

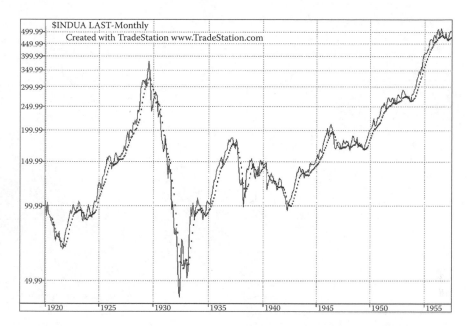

FIGURE 227. 150-day moving average (dotted line). Up to the 1980s (the period during which Ronald Reagan tripled the national debt) trading the 150-day moving average (buying on an up crossover and selling on a down crossover) gave a trader somewhat the same advantage that trading the Dow Theory afforded. In the 1980s, the system stopped working. But here in 1929 it would have been a life saver as can be seen.

chapter thirty-seven

"The Same Old Patterns"

To the newcomer, the market appears filled with wonders and mysteries as the landscape of Mars will appear to the first space travelers to land there. There are strange rumblings, apparently unexplainable upheavals, weird growths. An unknown stock will suddenly emerge from a morass of debt and deficit, and proceed to soar to great heights. An old and trusted issue will paradoxically sag and droop, although apparently rooted in the soil of economic stability. All will seem peaceful and secure; and suddenly, the ground opens up and swallows values in a sensational market break.

Such a newcomer, perhaps not realizing what appears unusual and alarming is only the normal fluctuation and adjustment that goes on continually in the market according to the changing evaluations of millions of investors, will feel frightened, insecure, and indecisive. He may scurry from boardroom to boardroom, personally or on the telephone, scan the financial pages, talk with friends, accumulate a mass of conflicting information, and end up shutting his eyes and making a blind stab in the hope that he may come up with the right answer.

Some never, even after years of contact with the market, achieve a tranquil and assured approach.

But it is possible to learn something about the basic nature of stock trends. It is possible to know, within reasonable limits, about what might be expected in certain situations. And it is also possible to find ways of coping with these situations, including the exceptional cases that persist in doing the unexpected. To repeat: It is possible to deal successfully with the unexpected and with that which cannot be precisely predicted.

To put it another way, it is possible to be wrong part of the time, and still to be successful on the balance. And to do this, it is only necessary to have a background of experience sufficient to know what will usually happen under particular conditions, about how often the unexpected will occur, and how to deal with the unexpected when it does happen. These are the same general problems that would confront the space traveler, the chemist, the physician, or almost anyone else in his daily affairs.

There are men who have observed the market long enough and carefully enough to discover that there are not quite so many unexpected events as the newcomer might be led to believe.

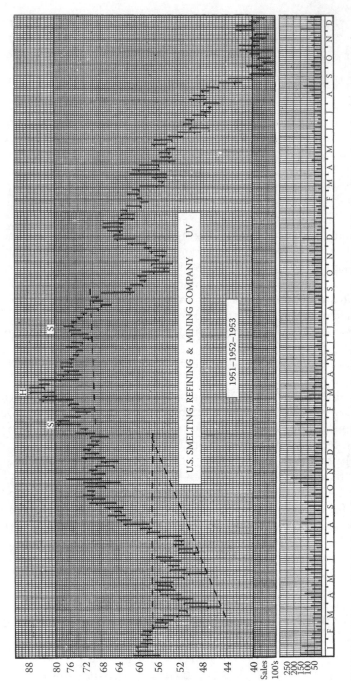

FIGURE 228. A 1952 Major Head-and-Shoulders Top in U.S. Smelting, Refining & Mining. This stock had moved up from a bottom at 33 in 1950 to the peak at nearly 88 shown here. The decline carried down to 37. This chart shows the typical high volume on the left shoulder. The volume at the head is a little higher than in the "ideal" pattern. Light volume on the right shoulder is a definite warning. Notice the Pullback Rally to the neckline in the last week of August. Also the Secondary Recovery in November and December. There also appears at the left side of this chart in 1951 a beautiful example of an Ascending Triangle, indicating the resumption of the previous interrupted advance.

The charts in this book are, in the main, the same as used for examples in the first edition in 1947. Some of them show situations from 1928 and 1929, others from the 1930s and 1940s. *EN: And still others from the 1990s and the 2000s.* The reader can hardly overlook the similarities that occur in various stocks at different times during corresponding phases of their trends or turning points.

We have said that these same patterns, trends, and Support Resistance phenomena repeat themselves over and over again, and that they may be observed by anyone in his own current charts for any period of time, in any normally active stocks, and on any exchange or market.

By way of demonstration, there were included in this chapter of the fifth edition a number of typical technical examples, similar to those already discussed, but taken from the period 1947 to 1966. *EN: The eighth edition includes examples taken up through the turn of the millennium.* It would be possible to include ten times the number of good examples, for almost every situation that has been previously illustrated has appeared again and again in recent years.

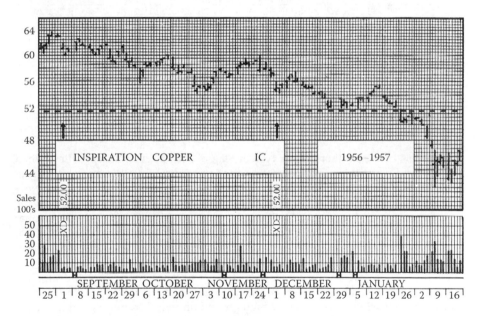

FIGURE 229. Downtrends seldom show the perfect and regular trendlines we often see in uptrends. But in spite of the irregular, ragged rallies and spotty volume action, the basic principles are about the same as for advances. Notice that in this 6-month period Inspiration Copper had no rally which carried above the Top of a preceding rally. A well-marked downtrend of this sort must be presumed to continue until there is a marked change in the pattern and volume action. Notice the volume on the day "IC" broke the historically important 52 level; and subsequent action.

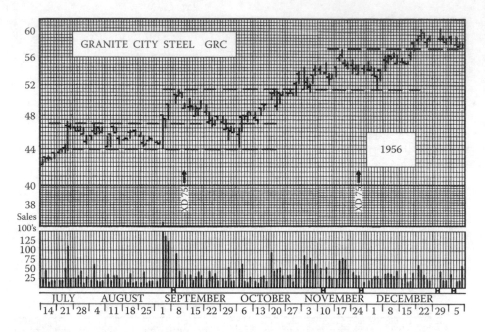

FIGURE 230. Part of the Major Advance in Granite City Steel. Here we see the familiar phenomenon of Support and Resistance in almost every move through the period shown.

The August–September Rectangle held for 6 weeks between the top limit of 47, which was reached on three occasions, and the bottom at 44. Like most Rectangles, it was marked by heavy volume at the start on July 19, and gradually declining volume as the pattern progressed. The breakout move on August 29 was on enormous volume.

After this breakout, there was a typical Flag-like reaction on sharply diminished volume; and while this move penetrated the top border of the Rectangle, the penetration was not decisive or significant, and the lower border was never violated. Now see how volume appears on October 15 as the old high is reached, and again at the top of the move on November 14. The decline returns to the level of the September high on a low-volume reaction. It is interesting how, on five occasions in this chart, the 52 level served as a Support or Resistance point: twice as Resistance on the way up, and three times after the new October high, as Support.

On the next rise, we see almost the same type of advance. In this case, the Support-Resistance Level is about 57. Notice the approach to the critical level, the backing away, the aggressive move into new high ground (in mid-December), and the recession to the Support at 57.

Advances of this sort seem to represent the ebb and flow of the Minor Moves during a Major Trend when there are no great "news developments" to change the normal progress of the trend. Where there are frequent and important changes in the market or in news affecting the industry, we may see long Consolidations or Secondary Reactions. But the Major Trend is durable. We must not assume a Major Reversal prematurely.

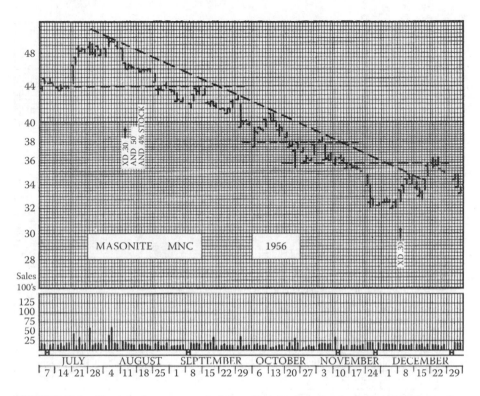

FIGURE 231. During the same period that Granite City Steel was making the series of steps upward, as shown in Figure 230, Masonite was doing almost the same thing in reverse.

To have continued to hope for a change in trend with a stock which was acting as "MNC" did through the latter part of 1956 would have required an unusual amount of optimism or innocence about the habits of stocks. Actually, of course, there would be good reason for optimism if the stock had been sold short early in the trend.

This is almost a perfect counterpart to the "GRC" chart. We have not only a series of declines with rallies which fail to establish even Minor highs above the previous Tops, but we are also able to draw a trendline which has a number of points of contact on the way down, which is somewhat unusual in a down-trending situation.

Notice the tendency of the rallies to stop short at the level of previous bottoms in a series of Support–Resistance Levels. We see such action at 44, at 41, at 38, and at 36. We would certainly not consider the breaking of the trendline on the upside in late December as evidence of a Reversal. Such a break after a trend of this sort probably means no more than a Secondary Recovery. To be of greater significance, it would certainly call for some volume showing, which was utterly lacking here; and before we would consider the stock again strong enough to buy there would have to be some sort of Reversal Pattern. A faltering rally back to around 40 would, in fact, suggest the advisability of further short sales.

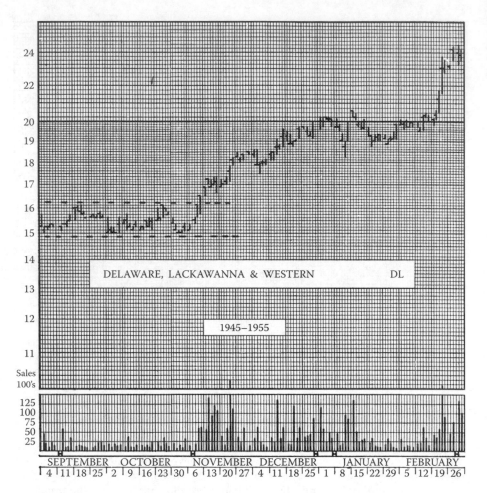

FIGURE 232. Very often you will hear the question, "But how can you tell whether a technical formation or a breakout is valid?" In many cases, and in a great majority of upside patterns, the volume gives such a decisive answer that all doubts are removed. Not always is the volume confirmation as clear as in this chart of Delaware, Lackawanna & Western, but this is typical of a good many breakouts in uptrends. You will see that the volume was generally light during the Rectangle, in which we see five plainly marked Tops and Bottoms.

On Thursday, November 4, the volume increased sharply as the price moved up to the top of the Rectangle and closed at that point. The following day, Friday, we see good volume again with a close beyond the top border. From this point on, the move is obviously upward.

There was no indication of Reversal at any time after the breakout. A Top was reached in March at 25½.

This was an especially vigorous move as it came out of the Rectangle. Normally, we would look for Minor Setbacks such as the series of reactions in "GRC," Figure 230. And if these had occurred, it would in no way have weakened the Bullish Pattern.

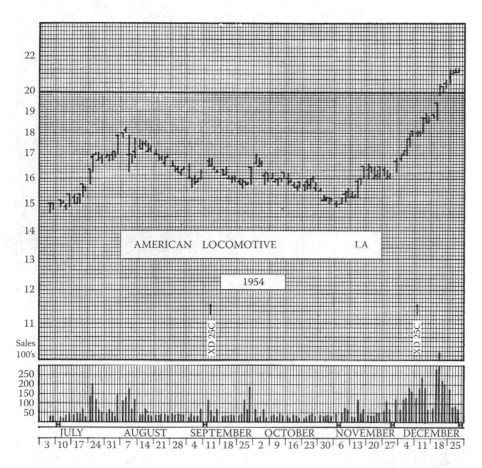

FIGURE 233. The situation, somewhat similar to "DL" in Figure 232, presents a little complication. The problem would have been whether to sell or continue to hold "LA" after the late October break down through the Bottom of the Rectangle. There was no important volume on this drift move, and on only one day did the price close barely 3% below the bottom of the pattern. A holder of the stock might well have sold it, might even have executed a short sale.

Suppose now, that you had actually sold the stock short. Observe the volume and the price action on Thursday, November 4 and Friday, November 5. Notice the volume and the price on the following Monday and Tuesday as it reacted slightly. Then see the quick pickup in volume as the price advanced on Wednesday, the week and a half of dull Consolidation, and the larger volume on the move up on Friday. Surely by the middle of the first week of December, if not before, you would have seen the danger signals and closed out your short.

Such a turnabout does not need to be a tragedy nor even a discouragement. Some easily discouraged traders would be so concerned about the small loss realized on their unsuccessful short sale that they would not be ready to seize the opportunity to reverse position and buy the stock after the strong up signals. This move carried to 26¾ in March 1955.

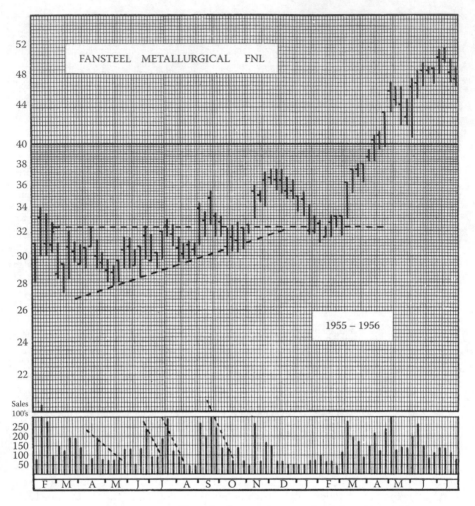

FIGURE 234. Bottoms normally take longer to complete than Tops. That is one reason we have this chart of Fansteel on a weekly basis, so that a year and a half of the action can be shown. The pattern shown at the left is a Consolidation formed after a rise from the 1953–54 Multiple Bottoms around 21. The top of the Ascending Triangle corresponds roughly with the April 1953 peak.

Of course, at the time this Triangle started, in early 1955, it was not possible to identify it as such — particularly since the February high ran a little higher than the horizontal Tops that eventually formed. However, during the 7 months that preceded the first breakout move, it became increasingly clear that each rally to the neighborhood of 32½ was followed by a reaction on low volume, and that these reactions were forming a series of Rising Bottoms.

In the first week of September we see a clean penetration upside, and from here on, the advances and declines fit into the typical pattern of a Major Advance. Notice the Breakaway Gap in November, and the low volume throughout the December–January–February reaction.

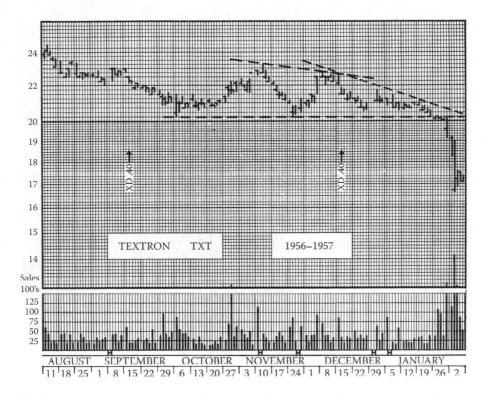

FIGURE 235. Here, in a daily chart, we see once again the dramatic sequel to a Descending Triangle. Here is the typical series of declining Tops on rather low volume, with retreats between the rallies to a horizontal line.

Notice that the important Support here was violated with heavy volume on Friday, January 25. Although the degree of penetration was not great, in view of the generally Bearish reaction to this point we would sell at once. A Descending Triangle has Bearish implications even before the breakout. There was no substantial Pullback after the breakout. Since it is not possible to count on such a recovery after a break through Support, it is safest to sell long holdings immediately or to place a very near stop on them as soon as a close outside pattern occurs (in this case, outside the pattern as adjusted for ex-dividend).

Notice the pickup of volume as the price drops into a tailspin at the end of January. Heavy volume is not necessarily a feature of important downside moves, but it may, and often does, accompany them, and when it does, it simply underscores the significance of the move.

Question: Does Textron look like a "bargain" to you at the end of January on this chart? Would you be tempted to buy this stock because "it can't go down any more," or because it is "due for a rally," or because it is "selling below its true value"?

Suppose that "TXT" did have a technical rally, which seems quite likely after the move shown. How far would you look for it to go? Would you expect it to penetrate the 20 level in the near future? Would you call this a Bullish Situation at the end of January 1957?

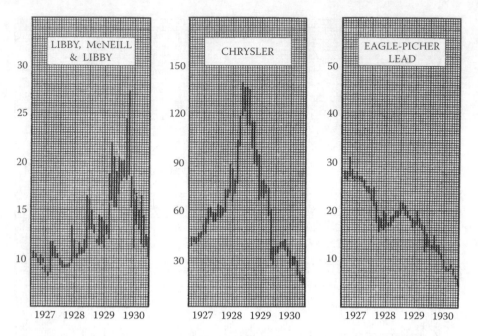

FIGURE 236 (Left, above).   Libby, McNeill & Libby showed no serious effects at the time of the October 1929 panic, and went on to new highs in March and April 1930.
FIGURE 237 (Middle, above).   Chrysler, one of the great market leaders, made its Bull Market Top in 1928, more than a year before the Panic, and had already lost 60% of its value before October 1929.
FIGURE 238 (Right, above).   Eagle–Picher Lead never enjoyed any Bull Market at all. Aside from an unimpressive rally in 1928 it was in a downtrend all the way.

The examples given are not rare exceptions. There are many others involving important stocks which did not follow the pattern set by the Averages. This variety of behavior is typical of the market. It is to be seen today. They are *not* "all the same," and each stock must be studied individually. In Figures 239, 240, and 241 are a few examples showing disparate action during the years 1953–56. There are hundreds of others that would illustrate the point equally well.

Not All the Same

Although a majority of stocks will participate in a big market trend, they will not all move at the same time nor to the same degree. Some will move quite independently and contrary to the Averages. There was a "boom" in the 1920s. And there was a Panic in October 1929. But these are inadequate statements, half-truths if you will, and can be very misleading if they are swallowed whole. A technician, following the individual behavior of stocks, would have been able, through a balanced and diversified portfolio, to protect himself against irreparable loss.

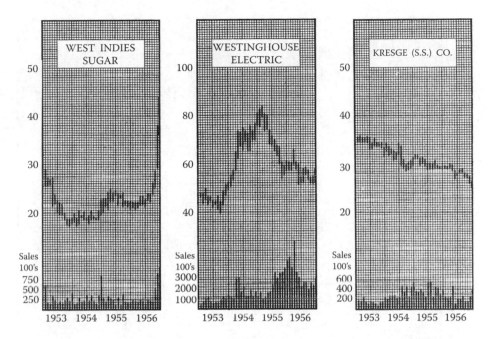

FIGURE 239 (Left, above). West Indies Sugar broke out of its "Scalloping" Pattern in late 1956 to make its own Bull Market at a time when action in the Averages was apathetic and generally weak.

FIGURE 240 (Middle, above). Although the Averages continued to make new highs through the spring of 1956, Westinghouse Electric made its top and went into a Major Decline more than a year earlier.

FIGURE 241 (Right, above). Here is a companion piece to Eagle–Picher's chart of more than 25 years ago, shown above it. Kresge, like a number of other "blue chips," did not participate in the Bull Market Moves of 1953–56.

These six charts were adapted from "Graphic Stocks" (F.W. Stephens, New York). The 1927–30 charts are from a Special Edition covering nearly 700 stocks through the period 1924–35. The 1953–56 charts are from a later edition of "Graphic Stocks."

The facts are that of 676 stocks we have studied through the period 1924–35, only 184 made a Bull Market Top in August–September–October 1929 and suffered Major Declines in October and November of that year. There were 262 stocks actually in Major Downtrends before the year 1929. Another 181 stocks made their Bull Market Tops in the first 9 months of the year and were already moving down before the end of the summer. Five stocks did not start their decline until after 1929. And 44 stocks continued to make new highs after 1929. In Figures 236, 237, and 238 are three stocks showing very different trends during the years 1927–30.

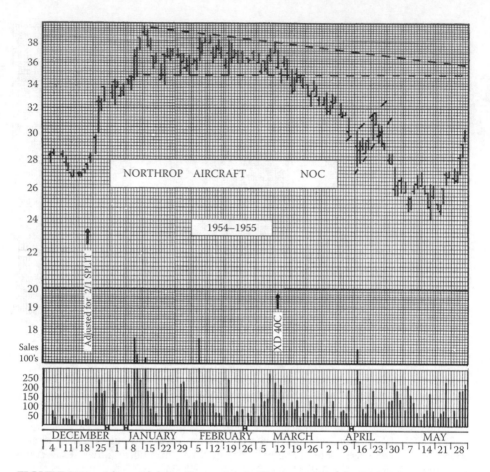

FIGURE 242.   A beautiful Top Formation in Northrop Aircraft, 1954-1955. The move which ended here at 39¾ in January 1955 emerged from a Bottom in 1953 at 6¼.

The Descending Triangle is marked by rather unusual volume at the peaks of rallies in February and March. Otherwise it is typical of this sort of Reversal Pattern. As so frequently happens, there was a Pullback effort after the March 14 breakout; but this rally lasted only 2 days.

You will notice that the volume on the breakout and throughout the downside move was not so spectacularly heavy, not nearly as heavy, in fact, as that on the Minor Rallies within the Triangle. However, as pointed out previously, we do not need nor expect so much volume on a decline as we look for in an advance.

Volume did not develop until the end of the first stage of the decline. It is quite usual for heavy volume to show up at the end of a Minor Move whether on the upside or the downside.

Notice the Flag formed on the subsequent rally in mid-April. The measuring implications of this Flag were approximately carried out a month later.

During the following year and a half "NOC" never reached 31 again.

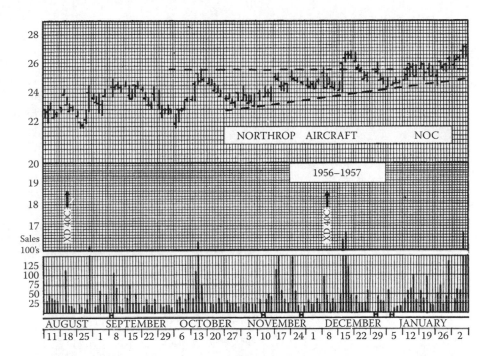

FIGURE 243. Bearing in mind the 1954–55 chart of Northrop in Figure 242, we now turn to the action in this same stock in the latter part of 1956 and the beginning of 1957. The question, of course, is whether the Major Downtrend is still in effect or whether an important upturn has taken place.

As usual, it is the volume that must be watched and studied. Notice the Minor Peak on August 14, then the very heavy volume on August 24. See how the activity dries up during September, but resumes briskly as a new Minor Top is established in October. Observe the drying-up of volume on declines and the activity on rallies to the 25½ level, which, by the middle of December, has become the horizontal Top of an Ascending Triangle.

There was no question about the validity of the breakout move on December 10; and the subsequent reaction in the next 2 weeks confirmed this by the lack of activity on the decline. And again, in early February, we see volume pick up notably as a new high is registered.

At the time this is written *(FN: 1957)*, it is not possible to say whether or not "NOC" will continue this upward course and eventually smash the "31 barrier." But we feel there will be no doubt in the reader's mind that at the beginning of February, Northrop was presumably moving in an uptrend, and must be presumed to be in that trend until a definite change in its market action has taken place. It seems quite probable that if "NOC" should advance to the 30–31 level, there is likely to be a period of Consolidation with the formation of an Area Pattern before a successful advance above 31 is accomplished.

As a sidelight on this chart, it might be mentioned here that during the period of advance shown above many aircraft stocks were moving lower.

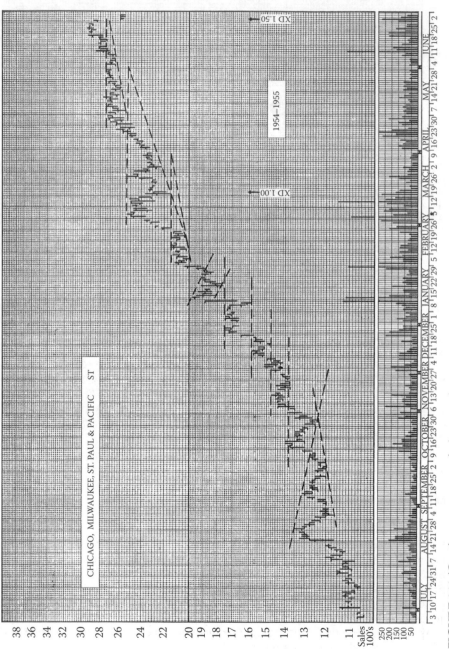

FIGURE 244 (Caption appears on facing page)

FIGURE 244. The 1954–55 advance in Chicago, Milwaukee, St. Paul & Pacific is an object lesson in Bull Market technics. Where would such a trend (of which there are many similar cases) leave the man who sells just "because he has a good profit," say at 15, or who feels "17 is too high a price"?

Here is a chart that is worth considerable study, since it exemplifies a great many features of the "ideal" uptrend. In this full year of advance, there is no point at which even a tyro technician could find reasonable cause for anxiety or justification for selling the stock. And we should not overlook the tax advantages of long-term gains.

Here, in August and September, we have a perfect example of the Symmetrical Triangle as a Consolidation. The volume is typically heavy at the start of the pattern and shrinks to almost nothing as it progresses. The breakout volume is decisive. The reaction after the breakout, also on lower volume, as it should be, runs right back to the apex, the "cradle point" which is nearly always a strong Support on such a reaction.

Now follow the action from here. The two days of higher volume in the early November rally represent the penetration of the previous Minor Top, and the end of the rally, respectively. The reaction comes back to the previous top.

The December rally is marked by heavier volume when the November top is exceeded, and again, to a lesser degree, at the end of the move. Once more there is a reaction, this time to the November top.

A fast move near the end of December repeats the same price and volume action, and is followed by a typical low-volume reaction to the early December top. (This is becoming monotonous. But it is important. You are seeing here a long-term demonstration of Bullish technical action.)

Next we have the January breakout. How far would you expect its Minor Reaction to go? Would you be surprised if it found Support at the level of the three little Tops formed early in the month at 17½?

The following advance drives through the 20 level, and, in a series of small fluctuations, forms an Ascending Triangle. By the end of February, another new high has been established. Can you estimate where to look for support on the reaction? And now we see the formation of the second Ascending Triangle (notice the relatively low volume), which is broken on the upside in a burst of trading activity toward the end of April. The next reaction comes back to the support of the former Tops as you would expect.

Once again, an Ascending Triangle is formed, and you will see how the volume dries up throughout this pattern, coming to life emphatically on the breakout on Wednesday, June 8.

Many students, on first seeing this chart, remark, "Well, the trend wasn't broken until Tuesday, June 21." Actually, of course, no break occurred on that day. The stock simply went ex-dividend $1.50, which, as you will see if you adjust the price by that amount, merely brings it back to the Support at the top level of the April–May Ascending Triangle.

It is inconceivable that any such regular series of Bullish Patterns could appear throughout a full year of trading in a stock "by accident." This is part of the normal mechanism of the market, representing the judgments, opinions, fears, hopes, and trading tactics of thousands of traders and investors. However, it should be added that it is not often that one sees such a long and "perfect" Major Advance as this. Normally, there are interruptions, distortions, or Secondary Reactions from time to time.

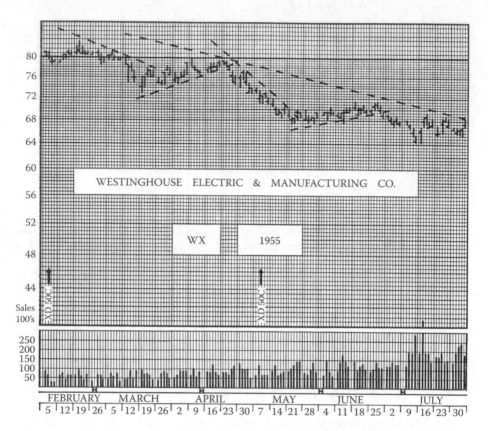

FIGURE 245. Does it require second sight to perceive that this is a Bearish stock? If you were keeping a chart on Westinghouse Electric & Manufacturing, wouldn't you have recognized, long before the end of the period shown above, that the trend was down, not up?

It is one of the great delusions of the market that the stock we own must be "good." As prices decline, the price–dividend ratio, based, of course, on past history, will improve. And the price–earnings ratio likewise will look continually better. Investors will begin to speak of "averaging their cost" by putting more money into a tumbling stock (instead of looking for something that is going their way). They will talk endlessly about improved outlook, new products, a forward-looking management. They will prove to you that it is selling "below its true value," whatever that may mean. They will bend every effort to establishing that what is going on before their eyes is not true; that the very weak-looking stock is actually strong; that the American public is making a great mistake and is misjudging this stock; that the tape is wrong because they must be right.

But values in the market are determined democratically and, by and large, probably represent the best composite appraisal you can find. A move like this is not meaningless, nor is it possible today to attribute it to the machinations of a few manipulators. In the chart we are seeing the reflection of a collective evaluation which cannot be lightly disregarded. Westinghouse reached 50⅞ in November 1956.

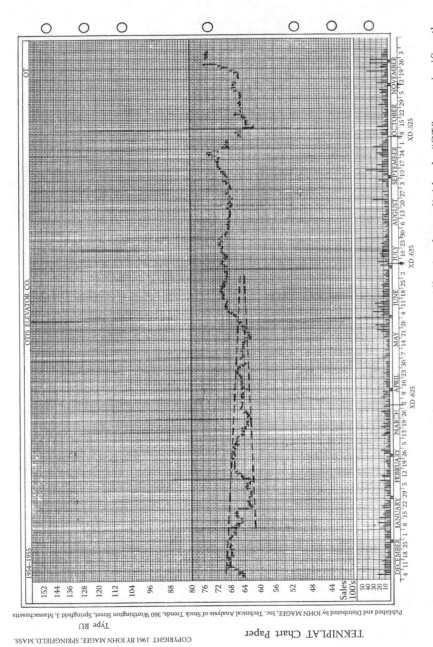

FIGURE 246. A typical stock chart on TEKNIPLAT charting paper. Allowing for ex-dividends, "OT" never significantly violated the apex of the Triangle. The advance ultimately added 60% to the value of the stock. (Continued on page 530.)

(Continued on page 530.)

FIGURE 246 (Continued from previous page).   This chart, in its long, mostly side-ways movement, is a good example of the importance of making allowance for the ex-dividend drop in the price. During the first 5 months shown, we see an almost perfect Symmetrical Triangle. The first critical point would be on the slight break-down in the middle of May. The lower border of the Triangle was violated just a trifle, even if we had allowed for the 62½¢ March dividend. If one had sold the stock here, who could blame him? And no great or immediate harm would have been done. However, an experienced technician might have taken into account the insig-nificant volume at this point and waited a bit, with a stop at, say, 60. (See the somewhat similar situation in the chart of "LA," Figure 233.) If "OT" had been held, the volume pickup on the rally would have shown that the trend had not yet reversed itself. The second critical point came in late September and early October at the time of President Eisenhower's illness. However, if we allow for the two dividends which went ex in July and October, the break did not violate the May Bottom. Furthermore, it was on relatively light volume. If the stock was still held, there was no valid reason for selling on this decline. From here on, breaking upward sharply from the Octo-ber–November Island, "OT" resumed the Major Advance interrupted by this long period of Consolidation, and advanced to the equivalent of over 100 (adjusted for two-for-one split) in 1956.

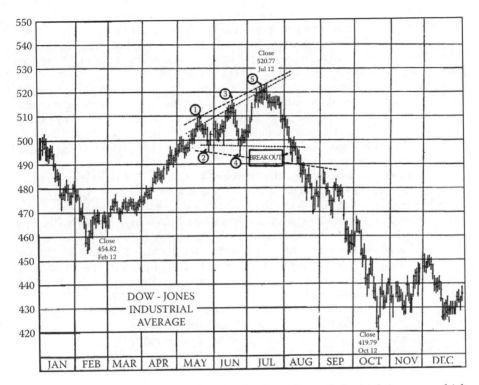

FIGURE 247. The Broadening Top in the Dow–Jones Industrial Average which formed in May, June, July, and August 1957. Although Broadening Tops have appeared many times in individual stocks, and, as a rule, have carried out their Bearish implications, such a chart pattern has never before been completed in the Industrial Average. (Continued on the following page).

FIGURE 247 (Continued from previous page). In 1929, on two occasions, there were patterns which began to show Broadening tendencies, but since these were interrupted by continuation moves, about all one can say of them is that they may have indicated a growing technical weakness in the market.

The 1957 situation, on the other hand, was very definite and was fully completed. During the early stages of the pattern, several of our friends wrote, calling attention to the possible Broadening Top, among them Charles E. Carden of Fort Worth, TX, who has handled Dow Theory comment and analysis for the *Fort Worth Star Telegram*. The chart shown in Figure 247 is adapted from one of Mr. Carden's charts and is reproduced with his permission.

The first significant point after the February 12 Bottom was the Minor Peak of Tuesday May 21, marked (1). The Minor Decline from this point on Tuesday, May 28 (2) was quite normal, as was the renewed advance to Monday, June 17 (3).

The first sign of a broadening tendency was when the Average closed on Monday, June 24 (4), below the May 28 bottom. However, this by itself did not indicate a Reversal. The advance was resumed, and surmounted the May 21 and June 17 Minor Tops, reaching a high closing figure of 520.77 on Friday, July 12 (5). The Broadening picture was now quite evident, and the completion of a Broadening Top required only a close below the June 24 Bottom.

On Tuesday, August 6, the Industrial Average closed decisively below the June 24 Bottom, signaling the completion of the Broadening Top. This, of course, was an indication of Major weakness, a warning not to be taken lightly.

The Broadening Top, as we have pointed out previously, is an indication of a wildly gyrating market, a market without leadership or definite trend. The presumption is that heavy distribution is going on under cover of the rallies, and the breakout move is seldom a false one.

Since we are dealing, here, with an Average, rather than a single stock, we would consider that *any* closing below point (4) after the peak at (5), regardless of how slight the margin might be, would constitute a valid breakout, since Averages are less sensitive than individual stocks, and it is customary to consider even slight penetrations at signal points (as in Dow Theory) as perfectly satisfactory. You will notice also that, although it would be possible to draw the Broadening Top through the extreme ranges of the price, as we have done with the wide-dashed line, we have used the closing prices as marked by the narrow-dashed line. This, too, is in line with Dow Theory practice, where only closing prices are considered.

The implication of the pattern here was Bearish for the "market-as-a-whole." As might be expected, a majority of stocks showed weak patterns of trends at this time. However, as always, it was necessary to examine each stock separately on its merits, since, as we will show in the following pages, not all stocks behaved alike even in this extremely weak market situation.

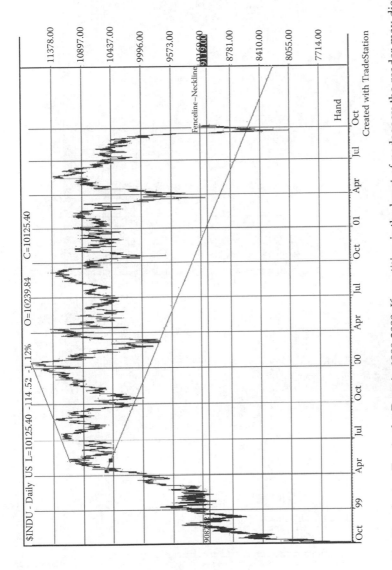

FIGURE 247.1. The Broadening Top in the Dow in 1999-2000. If repetition is the heart of pedagogy the reader may die of heart disease with looking at the Dow Broadening Top. Especially if he was long at the time and either disregarded the signs, or was not educated as to their significance. And the lesson is always the same: Bad news is on the way. The numerous technical aspects of this historic market top are discussed at length in other views of the Dow taken at this time. Remember. This time it's different. The market paradigm has changed, etc. etc., etc....Those who listen to fools will be fooled.

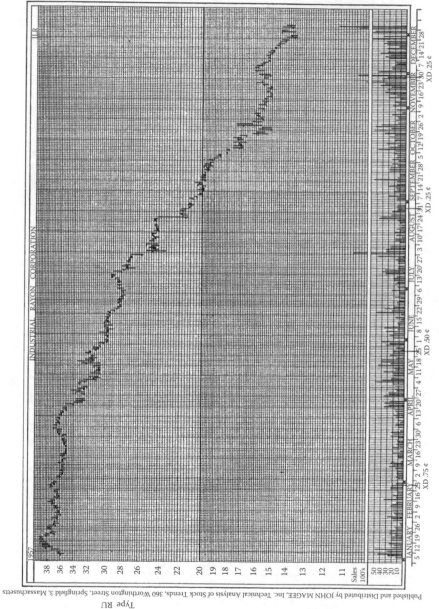

FIGURE 248 (Caption appears on facing page.)

FIGURE 248. 1957 Bearish Trend in Industrial Rayon. At no time did this stock show significant strength.

Averages do not tell the whole story. Each stock has to be considered on its own merits. Long before the formation of the 1957 Broadening Top in the Industrial Average, Industrial Rayon was moving down in a Major Decline. You will find many cases where it is difficult to "see" what a stock is doing, or to determine its Major Trend. But in such a situation as this (and this is not a rare case), it is perfectly obvious that the trend is down. Although there were a number of Minor Rallies and Consolidations during the decline, the entire pattern was so obviously part and parcel of the same big decline that no one who was even slightly familiar with typical stock behavior would have been tempted to buy the stock, even to cover shorts.

On Monday, July 29, there was a sharp downward break with a gap on climactic volume. This would have suggested the probability of a Minor Bottom, and for three and a half weeks, the stock did stabilize at around 24. But even during this Consolidation, the continuing weakness showed up on the small Descending Triangle that was formed, and ultimately on Wednesday, August 21, the price broke sharply to continue the Major Decline.

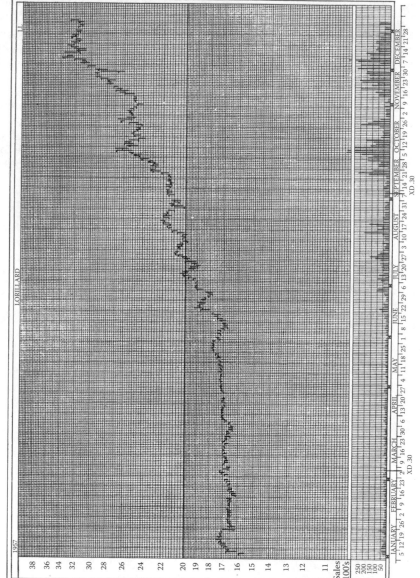

FIGURE 249 (Caption appears on facing page.)

FIGURE 249. 1957 Bullish Trend in Lorillard. Although most stocks declined in 1957, there were a number of strong issues like this one which appeared to be totally unaffected by the general pessimism.

Averages do not tell the whole story. It will come as a shock to many readers, who rightly regard the latter half of 1957 as a Major Bear Market, to see Lorillard making a typical Bull Market Advance. Lorillard moved up from 15⅝ to 34 during the year — and reached 54⅛ during the first 3 months of 1958. It is hard to believe that this chart and the Industrial Rayon chart we just looked at cover the same period, that is, the year 1957.

The majority of stocks did suffer severe depreciation. But there were a good many issues which, like Lorillard, enjoyed a generally Bullish Trend all year. Among the important stocks that moved up consistently in 1957 were American Chicle, Anchor Hocking Glass, Colgate-Palmolive, General Foods, General Cigar, Grand Union, National Biscuit, Parke Davis, Penick & Ford, Plough, Inc., Proctor & Gamble, Ruberoid, Vick Chemical, Winn-Dixie Stores, and Zenith Radio.

Whatever theories we may have as to the condition of the "market-as-a-whole," we must always realize that we are buying and selling individual stocks. *(EN: Unless we are trading Index Shares.)* We may get a picture of extreme Bullishness or extreme Bearishness in the "general market," but if this picture conflicts with the clear evidence in a particular stock, we must recognize that it is the stock, not the Average, that we have to deal with. We cannot assume that a stock "must" follow the Average. And it is often possible to obtain greater stability and safety by buying a few strong stocks in a Bear Market or by selling short a few weak stocks in a Bull Market, than by attempting to maximize profits with an "all-out" position one way or the other.

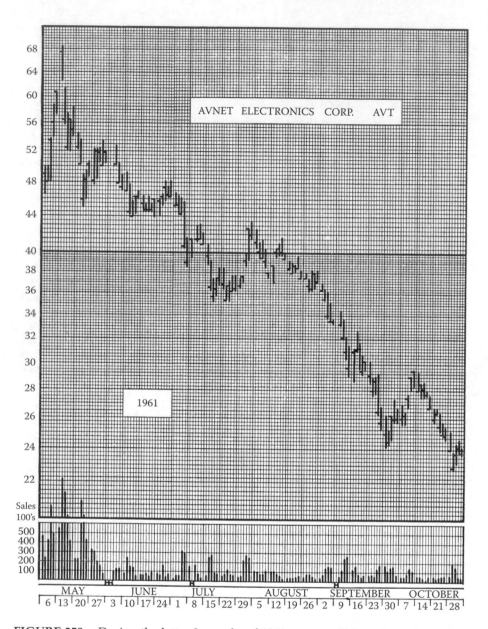

FIGURE 250. During the latter 9 months of 1961, some well-known market Averages continued to show new all-time highs. However, the Evaluative Index (see Chapter 38), in this period did not indicate any such overall strength; many stocks were in almost continuous decline for the 9 months. These included such important issues as Air Reduction, Allied Chemical, Allis-Chalmers, Aluminum, Ltd., Fansteel Metallurgical, Flintkote, Heyden Newport Chemical, Sperry Rand, Texas Instruments, Trans World Airlines, Universal Match, and many others. At such times it is best to choose stocks selectively and maintain adequate liquid reserves.

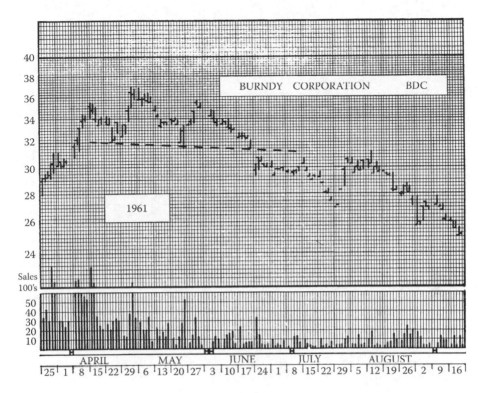

FIGURE 251. A familiar Top Pattern. From the end of 1957 to the spring of 1961, Burndy Corporation moved from below 10 to 37 in a generally Bullish Trend. The advance accelerated sharply on the post-election rally of late 1960 and early 1961. But with Burndy, as with many other stocks, the rally ended in the early months of 1961. Here, we have not only a perfect example of the Head-and-Shoulders Top in the price action, but we have the typical volume confirmation. The early April rally was on heavy volume. The rally in the last week of April was on somewhat disappointing volume, although a new high was made at that time. We have a definite increase of volume on the retreat from this peak, and practically no enthusiasm in the final rally of the first week of June. The breakdown on Monday, June 19, accompanied by heavier volume and a definite gap in the price track, confirmed the Top Formation. Although Burndy held around the 30 level for a time, and after a further drop recovered to 31, the Major Trend had definitely been reversed. By June 1962 Burndy was selling at 11¾.

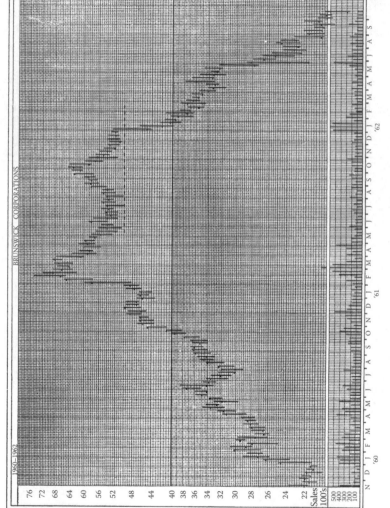

FIGURE 252 (Caption appears on facing page.)

FIGURE 252. Weekly chart of Brunswick Corporation showing the final stages of the long Bull Market in "BC," the Climactic Top in March 1961, the distributive phase through December 1961, and the ultimate breakdown.

For 5 years, from 1956 into early 1961, Brunswick advanced in a great Bull Market surge. During this period, the stock was split four times. In the first week of March 1961, terminating the post-election rally, "BC" made a new high on extraordinary volume, but closed the week nearly at the bottom of the weekly range. The One-Week Reversal might well have served as a warning to the market trader.

However, assuming that the owner of shares in Brunswick was not a trader, and was interested in the stock from a long-term point of view, he might have held the stock through the breakdown from the Symmetrical Triangle formed in March and early April. He might have continued to keep his shares through the summer and fall of 1961 and the rally of September and October. If so, and if he had been watching the action of the stock, he would realize that the 50–52 level was a critical area. That a break through this previous Bottom would represent a serious failure of Support. And certainly, the decisive violation of the 50 level in the first week of January 1962 (with heavy volume) could be recognized as a very dangerous Reversal Signal, calling for immediate sale of the stock regardless of capital gains tax or anything else. Although this move preceded the general collapse of the market by several months, it was a clear technical indication of extreme weakness and extreme danger in Brunswick, regardless of the action of other stocks at that time. If an investor had noted the break but decided to "wait for a rally" to sell his stock, he would have had no chance to get out. Brunswick never recovered, never rallied, and by October 1962 it was selling at 17.

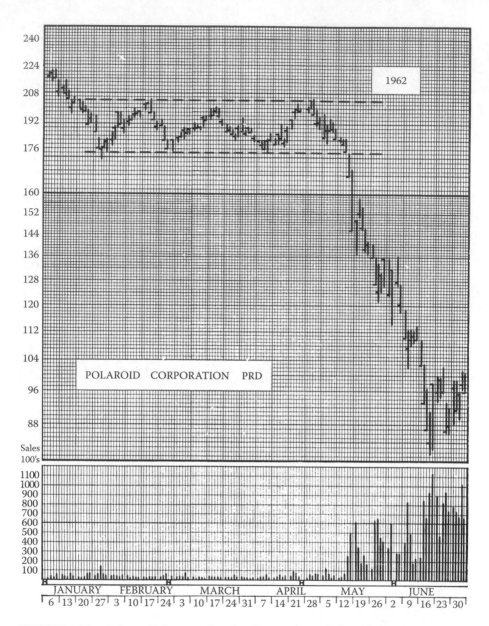

FIGURE 253. A beautiful example of a Rectangle in Polaroid. Notice the low-volume fluctuations between (approximately) 178 and 202. On Thursday, May 10, on the highest volume of that year to date, Polaroid broke Support and plunged to 168. This was a clearly Bearish Move. It would have been fatal to "hold for a rally," for there was no rally. It can be very expensive to hold onto a stock wishfully when the situation has changed radically, no matter how good it may have looked previously. Note that this break came more than 2 weeks before the "near-panic" of May 28. By that time, "PRD" had dropped 50 points and was headed for still lower levels.

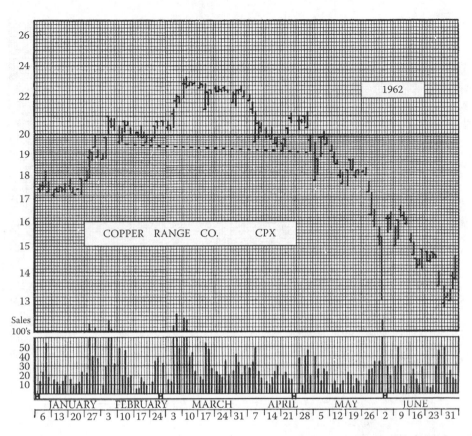

FIGURE 254. At a time when a majority of stocks were already showing signs of serious weakness, early in 1962, Copper Range was making vigorous new highs. Actually, the move did not get far; it never substantially broke above the 1961 Top. The evidence of weakness in "CPX" did not become apparent until, after the relatively weak April rally, the stock broke through 19 on Monday, April 30, and closed at 17¾. This was, of course, the completion of a well-marked Head-and- Shoulders Top. In this case, there were 3 days of rally before the downward move really got under way, but it might have been dangerous to count on a rally after the clearly Bearish signal.

Incidentally, this Top Formation was completed well before the precipitous drop of May and June.

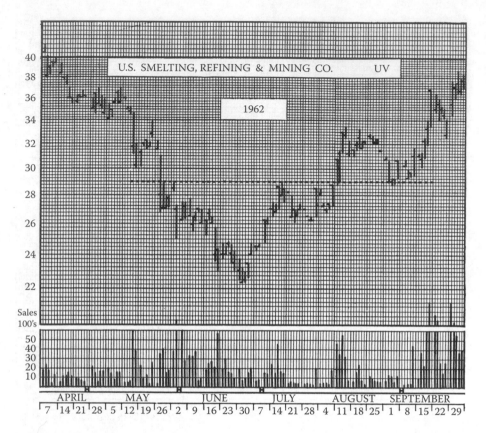

FIGURE 255.   Like practically all stocks, "W" went into a tailspin in the spring of 1962. After the "bad day," May 28, it continued to slide throughout the month of June. At this point, there started what could be considered no more than a technical rally in a Bear Market. This rally stopped at 29 and was followed by a dull decline lasting about 2 weeks.

The next move, in the second week of August, was marked by considerable volume, and while there was no obvious, clear-cut pattern, it seemed significant that the 29 level, briefly touched on May 23, May 28, and July 12, was penetrated on August 6. Whether to regard this August 6 closing as an immediate buy signal, or to wait for the completion of the breakout move and look for an opportunity to buy on a reaction, would be a problem. In this case, it would have paid to wait. Notice that the late August reaction came back to the 29 level where it found Support, and then continued its upward move.

Considering the weakness of most stocks in this period, the action of "W" is remarkable. The important thing to recognize here is that individual stocks do not necessarily follow "the main trend" of the Averages.

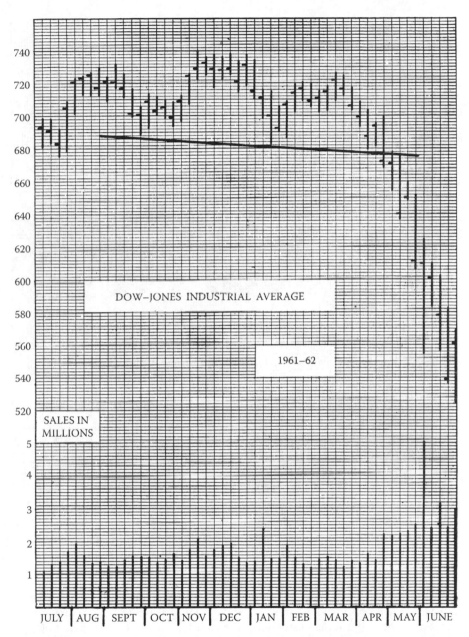

FIGURE 256. Weekly, July 1961 through June 1962. This chart shows the Head-and-Shoulders Top Formation in the Industrial Average which preceded the collapse of April, May, and June 1962. Normally, and especially in the charts of individual stocks, there would tend to be heavier volume on the left shoulder. However, the price pattern alone is sufficient to mark the pattern as a dangerously toppy situation. During the entire period in which this formation took shape, many individual stocks representing important companies were showing Top Reversal symptoms, as might be expected. Note that so far as this Head-and-Shoulders Pattern is concerned, the Reversal Signal is not definite until the neckline has been penetrated.

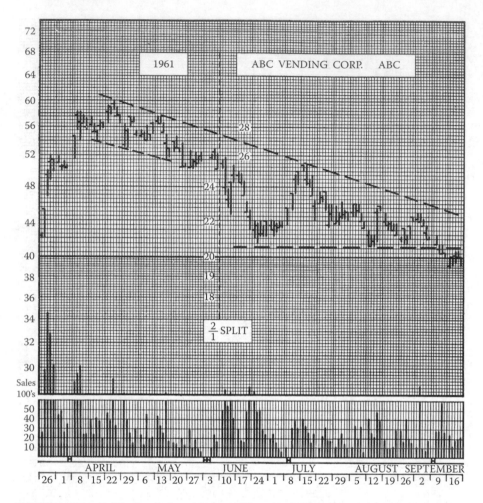

FIGURE 257. Daily, April through September 1961. Here is a rather confusing and complicated chart, but one which contains several points of interest worth a bit of analysis. Notice the beautiful little Head-and-Shoulders Top in April and May, especially the volume weakness on the final rally before the downside breakout. Notice also that this stock was split 2-for-1 in June, but that such a split does not materially affect the technical action of the stock, except that since there are now two shares of stock (at half the market value) for each share of old stock, there may be some increase in the average number of shares traded per day. Notice also that once the downtrend was established, the rallies (especially the mid-July rally) do not penetrate the trendline drawn through the April and May peaks. This trend continued down for over a year after this, reaching a low of 11¼ in October 1962.

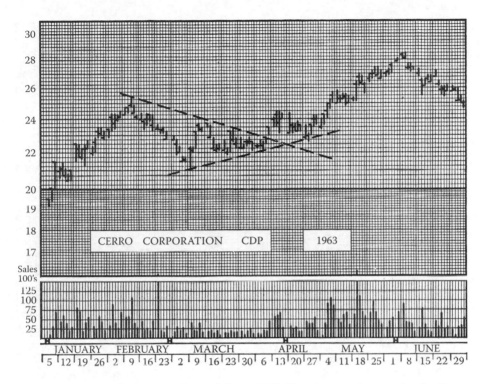

FIGURE 258. Daily, January through June 1963. Here is a good example of a Symmetrical Triangle as a Continuation Pattern. Triangles of this (Symmetrical) type may mark Consolidations in a Major Trend, or may constitute a Reversal Formation. The characteristics in either case are an active move to the first turning point of the Triangle, and then, generally diminishing volume as the price fluctuates in a narrowing pattern. During this period, it could be said that the stock was in *both* an uptrend, marked by the lower boundary of the formation, and a downtrend, indicated by the upper boundary. Notice the increase of volume on the breakout, which, in this case, was on the upside. Also notice the reaction to the "cradle point" defined by the intersection of the two boundary trends of the Triangle. The advance of the stock from April to June measures just a little more than the height of the open side of the Triangle. The attainment of this "objective" does not necessarily mean the termination of the Major Trend, however, and by August 1963 Cerro had reached 33¼.

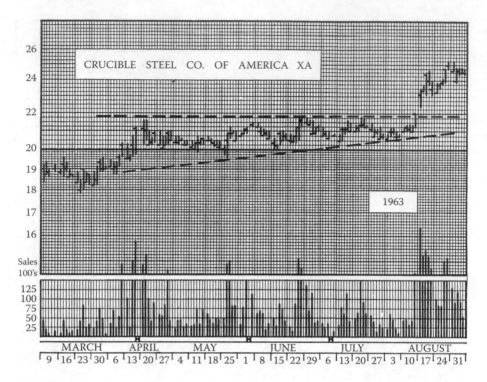

FIGURE 259. Daily, March through August 1963. Here is a good example of an Ascending Triangle, in which the rallies advance repeatedly to a given level, and the reactions find Support at gradually higher points. Such a pattern normally indicates a potentially Bullish situation in the making, just as the reverse (Descending Triangle) implies a Bearish tendency. Notice the higher volume on the various peaks near 22, and the very high volume on the breakout move in August. If any further evidence of the strength of this move was needed, the Breakaway Gap at the opening, Monday, August 12, would supply it. After a breakout of this sort, it would be quite normal for the stock to suffer some profit-taking reaction, usually on light volume, and such a reaction might run back to 22 or even a little below this without altering the essentially Bullish nature of this picture.

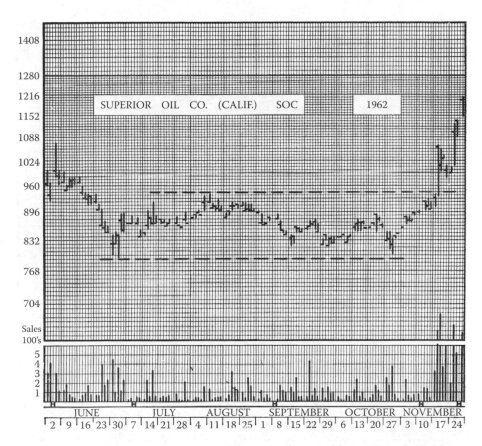

FIGURE 260. Daily, June through November 1962. Before commenting on the November breakout here, we should call attention to the fact that "SOC" was one of the stocks that held up fairly well during the Cuban crisis in October 1961, and did not make a new low under the June bottoms. This chart picture is an excellent example of a Double Bottom. It is not necessary that the two Bottoms be at exactly the same level if they are reasonably close. The important thing is that the stock has found Support once, has rallied, then declined again, and has found Support at nearly the same point. The Bottoms should be some distance apart; there should be at least 6 weeks between them, preferably more. Also, the rally between them should be definite and should amount to at least a 15% gain at its peak. The formation does not acquire significance as a Major Bottom Pattern until the level of the top of the rally is penetrated on substantial volume. This penetration took place on Tuesday, November 13, and from that time continued in a Major Bullish Trend, reaching 1559 in May 1963, an advance of over 500 points from the close on the day of breakout.

Double Tops have an opposite significance; they are similar to the Double Bottoms, but consist of two tops at approximately the same level, separated by some weeks or months, and with a decline between them, which must be penetrated to validate the Top Formation.

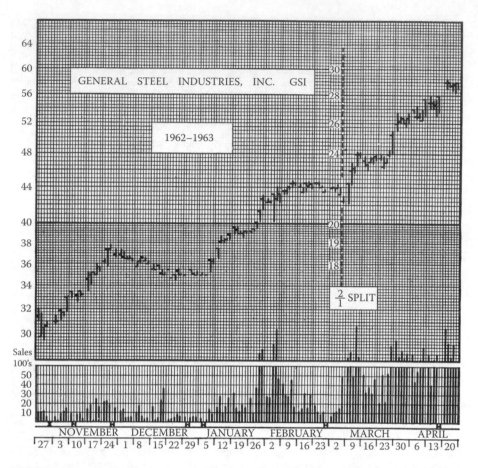

FIGURE 261. Daily, November 1962 to April 1963. To the average person, unfamiliar with the usual behavior of stocks in the market, the price fluctuations appear meaningless and entirely fortuitous. If they are aware of general trends lasting months or years, they are often inclined to consider only the trend of "the Averages," and are not conscious of the fact that many stocks may be making large advances at the very same time that others are sliding lower and lower. It is not always possible to lay a straight edge ruler along the trend and show that it makes a perfect straight line (though this does sometimes happen) but, as in the case of General Steel Industries, there is no question but that the advance is fairly consistent over a long period of time, barring the relatively unimportant reactions, Consolidations, etc., along the way. You will notice, too, that the two-for-one split in early March did not materially affect the upward trend except to show somewhat more volume, as might be expected with a greater number of (new) shares. For a contrasting (downside) trend, see the chart of Avnet Electronics, Figure 250.

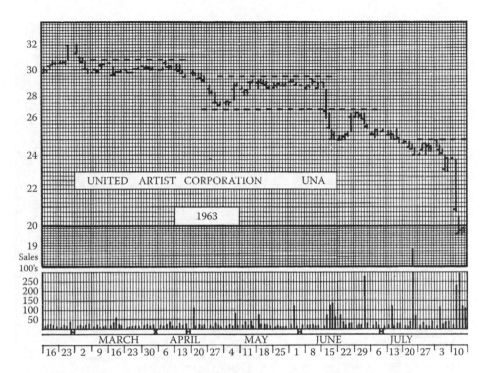

FIGURE 262. Daily, February to August 1963. This is an interesting study of Support and Resistance phenomena. Incidentally, it is also an example of a Bearish Stock (and not the only one by any means) in what was generally considered a Bullish Market, during the spring and summer of 1963. We would point out several rallies to 31 in March and April, and the breakdown in early May. In May and June, the stock rallied, but stalled at about the level of the March low. Then there was another drop, and in the rally this time came back to the late April low. The next drop, in July, was followed by a little rally to the June Bottom at 25. This is fairly typical Support–Resistance behavior. The price level which has been a support tends to become a resistance once the support has been substantially broken. Vice versa, as regards overhead Resistance; after it has been broken, it tends to serve as a support level.

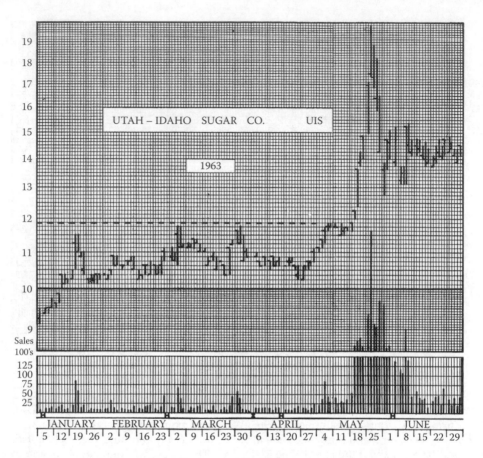

FIGURE 263. January through June 1963. Sometimes a move happens all of a sudden and does not result in a continuing long trend. In this case, it is not possible to say whether the long-term trend will be up or not. The purpose of showing this chart is to point up the remarkable action that can follow a break through an important Support or Resistance Level. You will notice that the entire period from mid-January to Tuesday, May 14, can be regarded as a Rectangle on the chart, with Bottoms at about 10⅛ or 10¼, and Tops at about 11¾. Notice the increase of activity on the several rallies during the formation. The move, which was a "situational" thing in sugars, affected all sugars in May, and turned out to be somewhat of a flash in the pan. Nevertheless, it was a spectacular one, and a trader with courage and acuity might have picked up this stock as a speculation after the close of Tuesday, May 14. The next 5 trading days advanced the price from Wednesday's opening at 12 to Tuesday, May 21, close at 17½, an advance of 46%. This is a type of market trading we would not recommend generally; it calls for courage, experience, and the willingness to take a number of small losses in order to secure one substantial gain. However, the in-and-out trader, who observed the action on May 21 and noticed the One-Day Reversal with abnormal volume and a gap, could have secured maximum quick profits either by selling his stock at the opening of the next day, or by placing a stop-loss order just under the close, say at 17⅜.

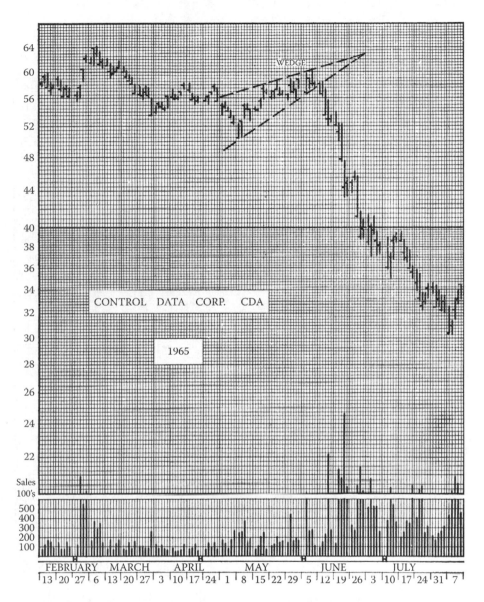

FIGURE 264. There are some warning signs in "CDA" in the Minor Breakdowns of late March and early May. What seems especially significant, though, is the nature of the recovery move in May and early June 1965. The two convergent boundaries of the Recovery Trend form an up-sloping Wedge, which has rather definite Bearish implications. If the Wedge had been pointed down, it would strongly suggest the possibility of a decisive upward breakout. Notice that on the 2 days when the highest prices were attained during this Wedge Pattern, the stock closed near the Bottom of the day's range. The subsequent history here, the collapse on heavy volume, shows clearly how dramatic a break from this not-too-common formation can be.

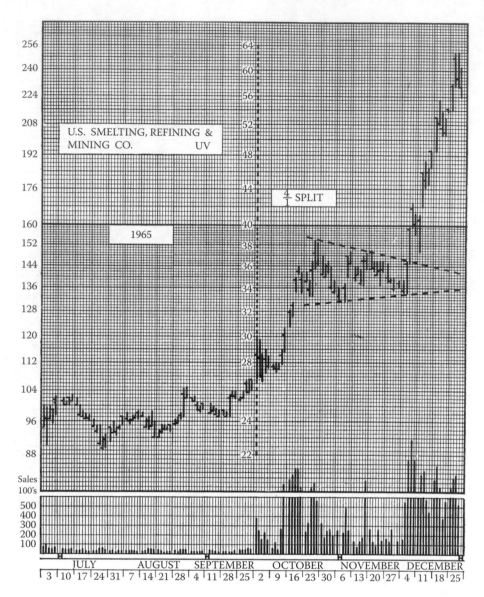

FIGURE 265. Here is a chart that shows several interesting technical features. In July, August, and most of September, "W" was in a period of dormancy. The breakout of September 27 was followed by a week of inaction, and then a strong continuation of the move on big volume. Notice the October–November Consolidation, which took the form of a large Symmetrical Triangle. If we draw the upper boundary of this Triangle, and the lower, we see that the breakout signaling a continuation of the move, on Wednesday, December 1, was decisive both in price and volume action. At no time during the advance from 28½ to over 62 was there any indication of potential weakness.

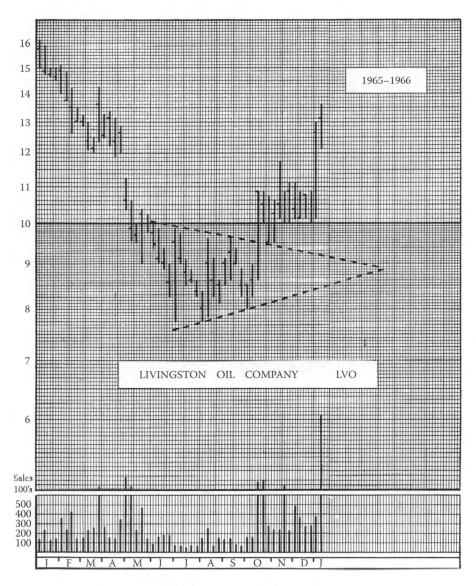

FIGURE 266. The weekly chart of Livingston Oil from January 1965 into January 1966 is a good example of a Major Bottom. Just how weak the stock was during the early months of 1965 can be judged by the clear Downside Gap during the month of May. Also, you will notice that the volume on this whole headlong collapse was rather heavy. However, from July to the middle of October, the trading activity "dried up," and the stock fluctuated in narrower and narrower swings, forming a Symmetrical Triangle. The pickup of volume on the October breakout was spectacular, and an observant investor would have had a "second chance" to buy on the reaction in the first week of November, when the stock drifted back to the top of the Triangle.

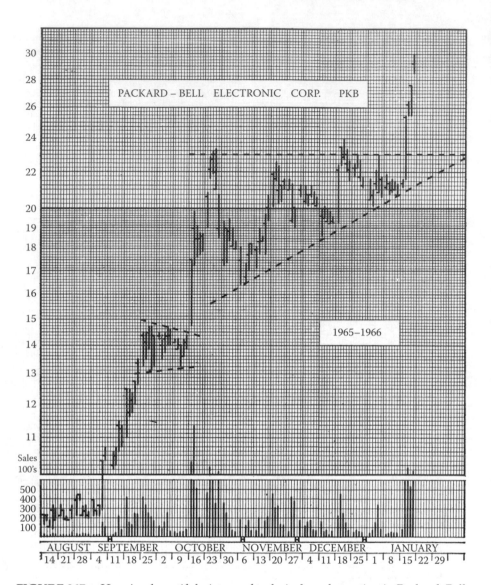

FIGURE 267.   Here is a beautiful picture of technical market action in Packard–Bell Electronics from August 1965 into January 1966. The first point of interest is the Flag Consolidation in September and October, a classic example ("The Flag flies at half-mast") and on the resumption of the up-move, the stock did duplicate the earlier move, and a bit more. (Compare with the 1945 chart of Martin–Parry, Figure 223.) Notice the nearly flat Tops and the rising Bottoms from October to January, with generally declining volume (Ascending Triangle), and the magnificent breakout move in the second week of January 1966. In this case, we can see no evidence calling for selling the stock all the way from September into January.

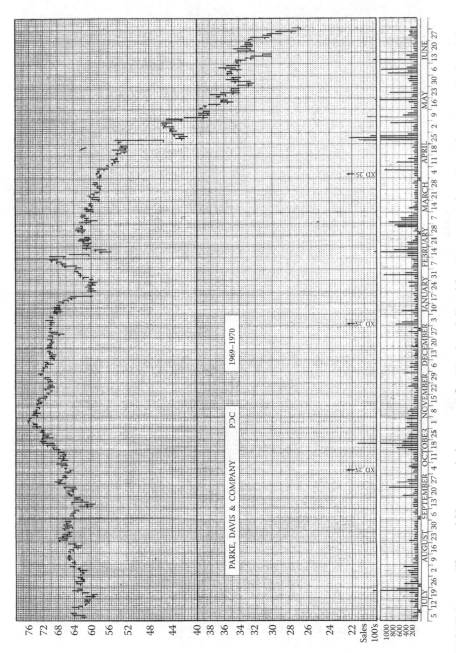

FIGURE 268. This could be regarded as a very flat Head-and-Shoulders Top or as a long Rounding Top. The breakdown through 66 was a warning, and certainly the sharp break below 60 in February was a definitely Bearish signal.

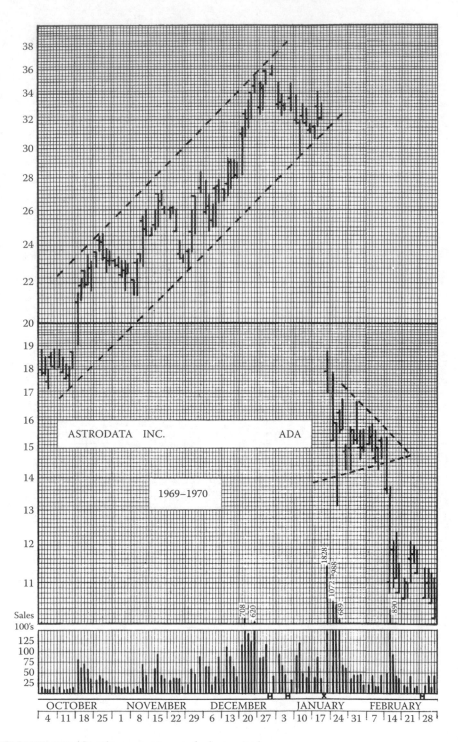

FIGURE 269 (Caption appears on facing page.)

FIGURE 269. A complete collapse in one day, Astrodata in January 1970. Not the sort of action you see every day, or every month. But it is "normal" in the sense that it is a phenomenon we have seen many times in the past and which will undoubtedly be seen many times in years to come. When it does happen, it should be heeded. It means trouble. "ADA" was doing well in what appeared to be a typical and perfectly healthy uptrend. After a one-day suspension on January 15, it reopened many points lower and never recovered. Trading was halted in late September. Some readers may remember other downside moves of this nature in the past. In Mack Trucks, in Fifth Avenue Coach, and some may even recall, many years ago, a break like this in American Woolen. Such a break is, of course, due to some sudden development or change in company affairs; but it is not necessary "to know the reasons"; the chart speaks for itself. As Lady Macbeth put it (in another connection), "Stand not upon the order of your going, but go at once." There was a good example of this type of a "Gap Move" in Villager Industries on April 30, 1971, when the stock dropped 42%, from 7⅜ to 4¼ in one day. Such moves as we are discussing here are nearly always on the downside; we do not often see comparable upside gap moves. And after this type of break, although there may be brief rallies, the stock nearly always resumes the downtrend, and in many cases, is delisted from the Exchange. Anyone caught holding such a stock should not feel that he had made a mistake in buying it, nor should he look for evidence of weakness before the big breakdown, for ordinarily, there is none. But he should get out immediately to avoid further loss. And by way of reassurance, it can be repeated that this kind of collapse is a rather rare occurrence.

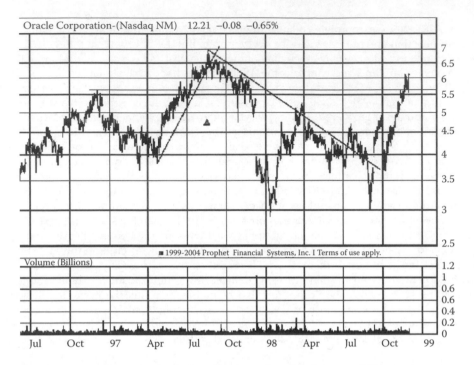

Oracle Corporation-(Nasdaq NM)   12.21 −0.08 −0.65%

■ 1999-2004 Prophet Financial Systems, Inc. I Terms of use apply.

Volume (Billions)

Jul   Oct   97   Apr   Jul   Oct   98   Apr   Jul   Oct   99

FIGURE 269.1.   Lest one think that the air pocket gap does not still exist, here is an example from the turn of the century (third millennium). These gaps, caused by disappointing earnings, were so prevalent at the end of the century at the top of that Bull Market, that one could short vulnerable stocks before earnings reports with little upside risk and often collect nice scalps like this one.

FIGURE 270 (Figure appears on facing page).   A typical electric and gas utility stock. There are a great many stocks in this group, serving various municipalities or regions. They tend to show similar market behavior because they are basically similar in nature.

There is, of course, a relation between the earnings of a company and the dividends paid, and the market price of the shares. However, neither earnings nor dividends alone are sufficient to constitute a complete determination of "value," since there are many other factors that can affect the "value" considered from different angles, such as dependability of earnings, future prospects, taxability, research and development investment by the company, and so forth.

The electric and gas companies, enjoying a regulated monopoly position in most communities, have a sure and steady income; and they are also in a definite "growth" situation because of the constantly increasing demands for power by users. Most utilities will show a record and pattern of trading over a period of years very similar to that of "PEG." You will notice that reported earnings have been larger each year from 1959 through 1970. Also, the dividend rate has been increased each year except in 1970, when it was unchanged from the year before. Anyone basing his estimate of "value" on a simple index such as "price–earnings ratio" would conclude that the stock was 2½ times as good a buy in 1970 as it had been in early 1965.

Obviously, there is more to it than that. The big funds and other large holders of stock are not giving up "bargains" of that sort lightly and for no reason. The depressed chart is undoubtedly reflecting the whole thorny outlook facing the utility industry, including costly new facilities, antipollution devices, and other problems including deregulation.

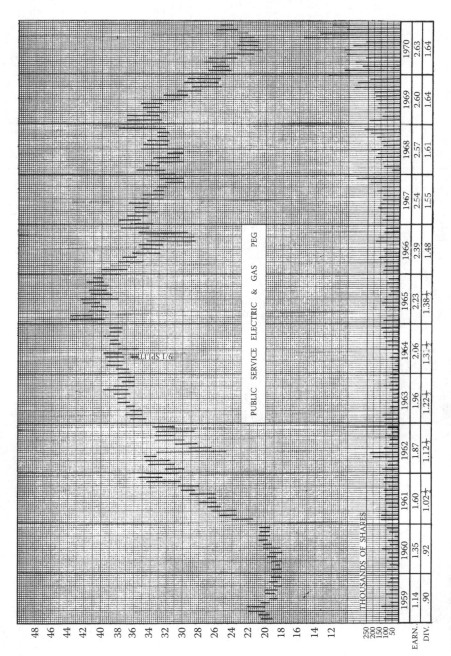

FIGURE 270 (Caption appears on facing page.)

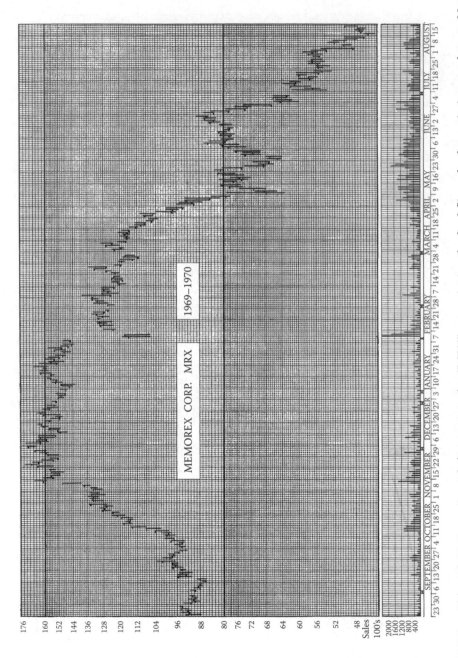

FIGURE 271. Although 1969 was Bearish for most stocks, "MRX" was enjoying the final fling of a dramatic 4-year advance. Notice the Island-like Top in November, December, and January, and the low volume all through this period. The Breakaway Gap in early February speaks for itself. See also Figure 269.

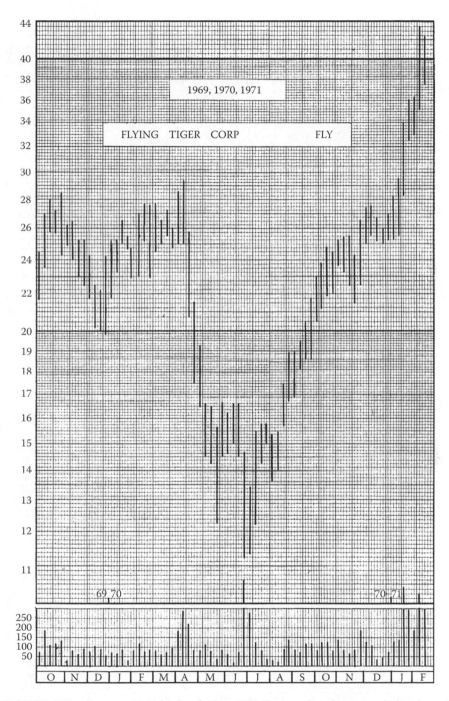

FIGURE 272. From a 1967 high of 48½, "FLY" started a downtrend that lasted 2 years and took the stock down to 11¼. But during the spring and summer of 1970, the stock found bottom, made a Head-and-Shoulders Reversal, and took off in a skyrocket move that, by February 1971, had recovered nearly all of the 2-year drop.

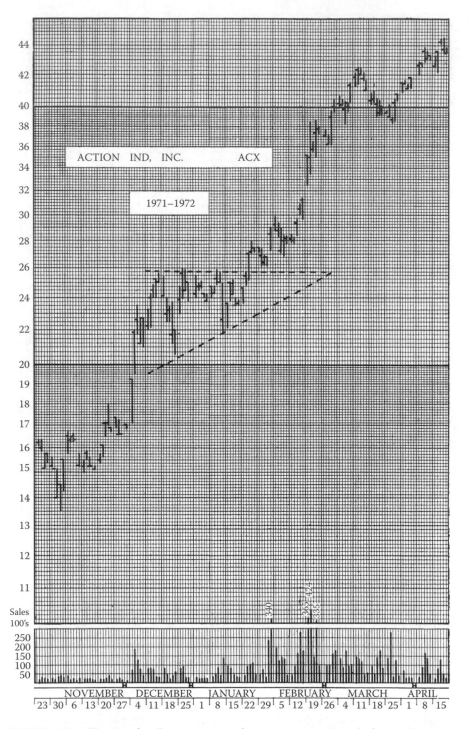

FIGURE 273. Here is a familiar pattern you have seen many times before in the pages of this book or in your own charts. Here we see a large Ascending Triangle in the daily chart of Action Industries, formed in December of 1971 and January of 1972. Notice the typical breakout and reaction moves and the continued uptrend into April of 1972.

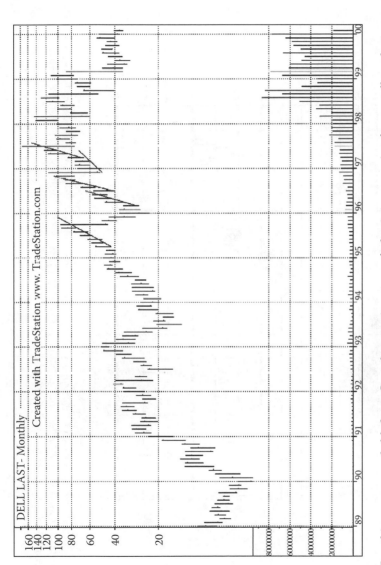

FIGURE 273.1. Two things are remarkable here. One, the amazing story of a business emerging from a college dorm room — a computer business, of course — and two, the regular occurrence of air pockets, which will be seen better on the next chart. Not a stock for those who dislike carnival rides and surprises. One should fit his portfolio to his digestion. Dell broke its long term trendline, which the reader may easily draw here with a ruler, and after setting a bull trap, went to 20, displaying several major warning downside gaps (see next chart). The out of proportion volume at the chart end is a prewarning.

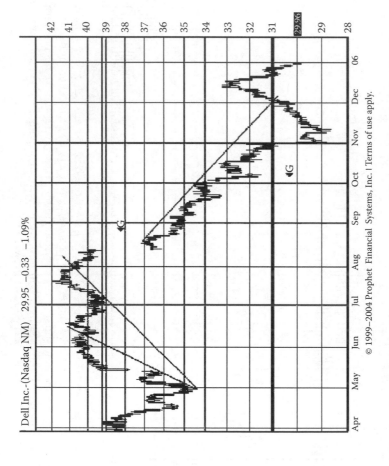

FIGURE 273.1.1.   DELL. The breakaway or air pocket gap continues to astound, so frequently choosing to occur at horizontal lines. An exceptionally alert trader might have avoided the air pocket, observing the broken trendlines. The average technician would have got out and shorted the breakaway gap. Seen one tulip, seen them all.

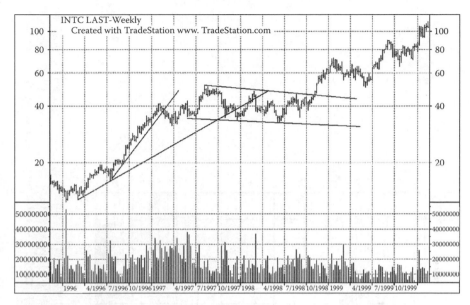

FIGURE 273.2. The benefits of the "Wintel" partnership are reflected in Intel's chart. The trader might have been in and out of Intel several times based on tightening trendlines, while the long-term investor would have patiently waited out the — call it a "rectangular wedge" — which never was violated on the downside. The steeper the trendline the more likely — even the more certainly — it will be broken.

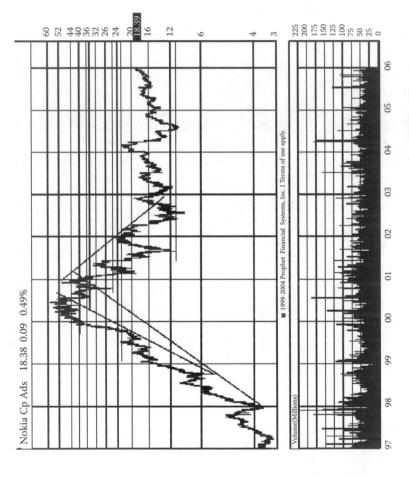

FIGURE 273.3.   NOKIA. (NOK) Not enough is made of the marking of zones of support and resistance (highs and lows) with horizontal trendlines. These benchmarks help the technician to mark the running of the tide, just like Dow's stakes on the beach. Notice how the high of '99 influences the high of '04. The breaking of horizontal lines here after the breaking of the steepest trendline once again tells the tale for the technician.

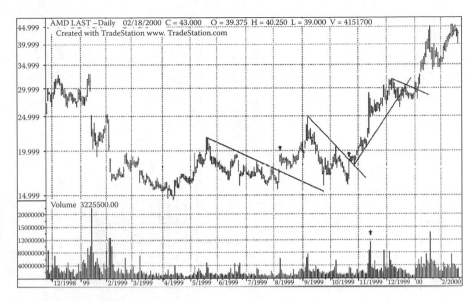

FIGURE 273.4. AMD. Reflecting the vagaries of the semiconductor business, including the felicity of being a competitor of Intel, AMD shows trading opportunities both up and down. Here the intermediate-term trader would respond to the vigorous breaking of short term downtrend lines to get long.

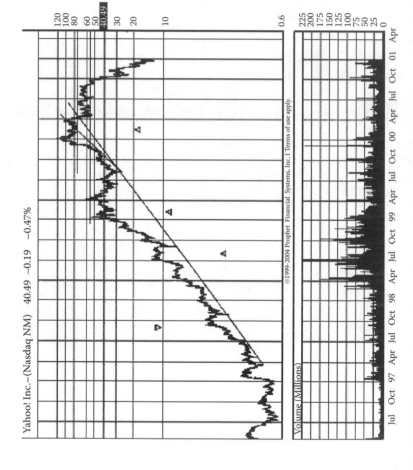

FIGURE 273.5. YAHOO. (YHOO). A superb trendline which should have kept the technician long until April of 2000 — and then got him out. Especially when combined with the top horizontal trendline. The extravagant volume at the very top is the exclamation point on the warning.

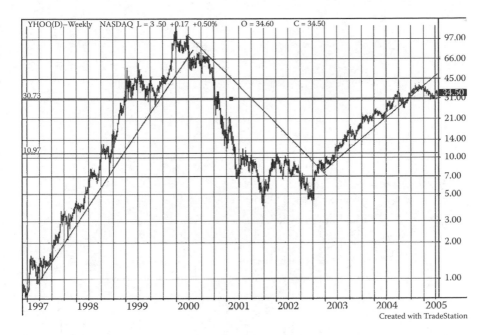

FIGURE 273.5.1. Any resemblance between this chart and Amazon, (Figure 205.7.2) is not strictly coincidental. Readers will remember Magee's principle that birds of a feather flock together. Internet goony birds certainly do, or did. Yahoo looks in this guise somewhat stronger than Amazon, but then selling books and mortar is a harder row to hoe than selling electronic images (best business in the world). And again such an attractive fundamental story. Gooks (or geeks) on skates helping revolutionize the wild frontier. We love these stories. But not enough to stop drawing lines on the chart and selling them when the violate our lines. Even love must obey the rule of the ruler.

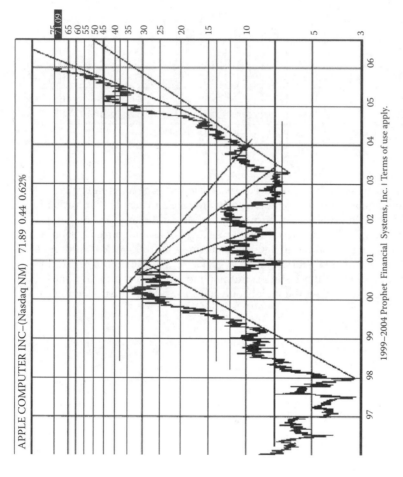

FIGURE 273.6.   APPLE. (APPL). Apple is an especial delight because it illustrates vividly one of the central principles of technical analysis: Ignore (or take with a cellar of salt) the news. Anytime the media swarms on a company, be skeptical. If we believed the media, Apple would have more lives than a cat, considering how many times the media has written it off as dead. It is also a chartist's design as illustrated in my Basing Point studies (Chapter 28), and here, by trendlines (horizontal and sloped) and a large fan. Readers years from now will want to observe how the trendlines here forecast Apple's future. Figure 274 vividly illustrates the technical signal that kicked off Apple's run, complete with triangle and run day, and wake up volume.

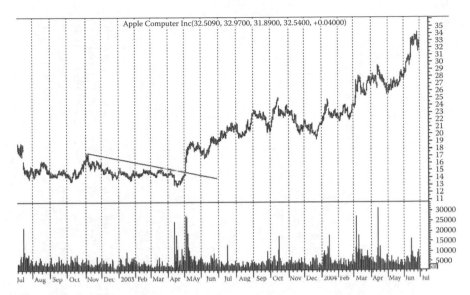

FIGURE 274. The file of press clippings predicting the death of Apple weighs as much as the daily output of the Augean Stables. And is worth as much. One wonders why the press likes to beat on Apple so. Especially when the wizard is up to his never ending tricks. And when the wizard, (Steve Jobs) has millions of fanatics ready to support his next trick. And, although the Beatles are mad at Jobs and Apple, Apple is now a music company as well as a computer company. The smooth as silicon lubricant iPod made music to investor's ears and Apple took off on another run. The start of the latest trick is pictured here. The volume in April is the wake up call. And of course, what is that volume? A shakeout. The breakout across the descending triangle line after the false signal (Remember? Those false signals are often followed by valid signals) the volume and the surging run days — all good grist for the analyst's mill. Furthermore the surge across the downtrend line on big volume should be recognized as an important technical pattern regardless of what proceeds it.

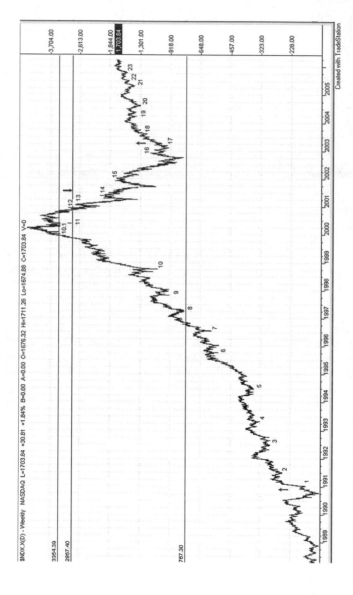

FIGURE 275. $NDX, THE NASDAQ 100. Following the Basing Point Procedure in Chapters 28 and 28.1, an almost completely objective procedure may be devised for the very long term investor to replace or augment Dow Theory. In this chart, the Basing Point Procedure is applied to weekly bars. Thus, instead of three-days-away we look for three-bars-away. The result is a trade which lasts around 10 years! The method gets long in 1991 at the arrow, holds the trade till about 2001 and reverses. Observes the bottom of 2002 and reverses again and is long into the bull markets of 2006. Arrows show the signals. Numbers mark the Basing Points. Stops, which would be about 5% under the Basing Points, are not illustrated.

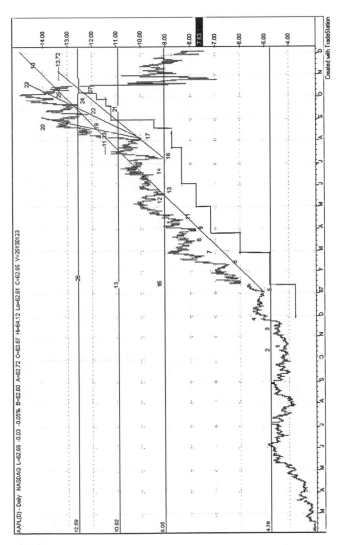

FIGURE 276. BASING POINTS PROCEDURE. In Figure 210.1 the use of Basing Points calculated on wave lows was documented. For the great majority of investors that will be sufficient. In Figure 210 Magee laid out the entire procedure, including advancing stops based on a new high 3% above the previous wave high. This chart shows stops so generated at 11.33 and 13.72. These stops would have stopped out the trader in this case sooner than the wave low Basing Points. There are pluses and minuses to this part of the procedure. A mid-trend blowoff might cause an premature exit from the position leaving the trader to grasp for a new entry point, unless the position were constructed with scale-in scale-out units as recommended in Chapter 42. We also see in this chart the result of not honoring stops, as Apple falls off the table in the Reagan Crash of 1987.

chapter thirty-eight

Balanced and Diversified

The average investor wants a clear-cut, simple, easy answer to his question, "What do you think of the market?" To him, it must be at all times either a Bull Market or a Bear Market. If, in answer to his insistent demand, you reply with the question, "What particular stocks are you interested in?," he will avoid that issue and say, Oh, I mean in *general*.

And if you will examine the pages of any magazine or newspaper carrying a great deal of financial advertising, you will find that many advisers and advisory services make a great point of giving unhedged opinions as to the future course of the market, and these opinions are most frequently couched in terms of what the market as a whole is going to do.

Now, there is just enough truth in the common belief that they all move together, to make this an exceedingly dangerous assumption. It is true, for example, that we can set up *definitions* of what we feel constitutes a Bull Market or a Bear Market, such as the Dow Theory, and if a given set of conditions meets the rules we have laid down (our definitions, that is), then we can say accurately, "according to my premises this is now a Bull Market" (or a Bear Market, as the case may be). It is also true that over the years, if we had treated the Dow Industrial Average *as if* it were a stock, and had theoretically bought it and sold it according to classic Dow Theory, we would have done very well. *EN: As is vividly illustrated in Chapter 5.1, where buying and selling by the Theory netted one $362,212.97 as opposed to $39,685.03 (EN9: $347,895.10 December 31, 2004) through buying and holding. Of course now it is a stock, DIA.*

It is also true that in the great inflationary and deflationary movements, which reflect the changes in the relative values of dollars to equities, there is a tendency for the majority of stocks to move with the tide.

And it is furthermore true that in the day-to-day movement of stock prices, it appears that most stocks move up or move down together.

But we should never lose sight of the fact that the Averages themselves are abstractions, not railroads, manufacturing companies, airlines, etc. If the Averages move, it is because the individual stocks making up the Averages have moved. And while it is true that during a time when the Averages are advancing, a majority of stocks are also advancing, it is not quite possible to reverse this and make it absolute by saying that *because* the Averages are advancing, therefore *all* stocks *must* advance. If we carried this to its logical conclusion, we would arrive at the point (which some have arrived at) where the fact that a stock has not advanced, but has declined in a Bull Market, is considered sufficient to make the stock attractive for purchase on the basis that it must catch up with the others.

If we examine the facts, that is, the long-term records of what stocks have actually done, we find that there are periods when most stocks go up in value and other times when most of them go down. We find, sometimes, that laggard stocks will eventually join the procession in an upward trend.

But this does not always happen. And it can be extremely uncomfortable to have bought stocks in a presumably Bullish Market, because they are behind the market, or because they are all going to go up, and then wait for months as we watch other stocks climbing to new highs while our own securities continue to languish or decline further.

From what you already know of the market you will surely agree that it is not a wise policy to put all your capital into buying stocks in what is clearly a Bear Market in the Averages and in most stocks. And you will agree, too, that it is not a safe thing to sell stocks short to the limit of your resources in a skyrocketing Bull Market.

If you have to be 100% on one side or the other, it is much better to go with the trend. In that way, you will be in line with the probabilities as shown by a majority of stocks, and by the Averages.

But you should realize that going with the trend is not always as easy as it sounds. We can set up definitions, as we have, of what constitutes the Major Trend. Then the question is whether you have the patience and the courage to maintain a position in line with these definitions through months of uncertainty and possible adverse moves. During turning periods it is often hard to make the decision to buy or sell.

And most especially, there is the difficulty of knowing what to buy or what to sell, and when.

The simple patterns and signals of the Averages do not tell the whole story. There is a certain usefulness in regarding the market as a whole in studying Dow Theory, just so long as we keep in mind that the Averages we are studying are generalities (high-order abstractions), and the rules for determining their trend apply to these generalities and not necessarily to each and every stock listed on the Stock Exchange.

In many cases, for example, a group of stocks will top out and start an important Bearish Trend while other groups of stocks are continuing to make new highs. This occurred in 1946, when we saw a large number of stocks topping out in January and February, and others continuing strong until the end of May.

We think of 1929 as the year the market made its great peak, and crashed in October to start the series of breaks that continued into 1932. There is some truth in this; but it is not the whole truth. There were some important stocks that made their highs long before the 1929 Top. Chrysler, for example, made its high in October 1928, and had dropped from 140 to 60 *before* the Panic of 1929. There were stocks which never enjoyed a Bull Market at all in the whole period from 1924 to 1929. By actual count of nearly 700 listed stocks, 262 issues made their Bull Market highs before 1929, 181 topped in 1929, but before August of that year. There were several stocks which did not have their first downside break until after 1929. Forty-four stocks went into new Bull Market high ground after 1929 and before mid-1932. Only 184 of the 676 stocks studied made their Bull Market highs in August, September, or October of 1929 and crashed in October and November.

In other words, only 27% of the stocks acted the way everybody knows *all* stocks acted. *EN: As the Dow and S&P 500 made all-time highs in 1999 and were near those highs in 2000, the same condition held true again. Many stocks had topped and were in long downtrends. EN9: And as stocks crashed after the top of March 2000 Dow stocks held up well compared to NASDAQ stocks and the S&P 500, which saw declines of around 50%. See Figure 203.3.*

It is all right to accept the general trend as a useful device, so long as we know it is a device only, and not a picture of the detailed reality. We have to face the problem which continually confronts every student of the market: How to protect ourselves from uncertainties in interpretation of the Averages, and how to protect ourselves against stocks which are not moving with the majority.

The problem can be met, first of all, by not taking an unreasonable amount of risk at any time (see Chapter 41).

It can also be met by using an Evaluative Index instead of switching from all out Bullish to all-out Bearish. By this we mean using an indicator that will show not merely whether it is a Bull Market or a Bear Market, but how Bullish or how Bearish it seems at a given time.

At first glance, this may seem not too different a conception from that of classic Dow Theory. The same technical methods apply. Also, during a strongly Bullish Market, an Evaluative Index will also indicate approximately the *degree* of strength. As the market begins to develop weak spots, as did the market in 1928 and 1929, the *degree of Bullishness* will gradually decline.

Before considering the use of this Index, let us outline what it is and how it may be constructed. You will understand it is not a precise tool; it gives only an approximate picture of the state of the market; it gives no positive signals; and, in the final analysis, it is a reflection of the judgment and opinion of the person who is maintaining it.

Suppose you are keeping daily charts of 100 stocks. At the end of each week, you can mark these along the bottom of the chart with a small plus or minus, indicating your opinion as to whether each particular stock is moving in a Bullish Major Trend, or is Bearish. In some cases, you will find it hard to make a decision. This is not too important, however, since these cases will not be numerous, and in the majority of stocks, you will normally be able to mark them plus or minus on the basis of their obvious action. If you now total the plus stocks and also the minus stocks, including those in which you have had to make a tentative decision, you will have two figures totaling the number of your charts. If 75 of these are plus, you can say that the market looks 75% Bullish to you. If next week the percentage is higher,

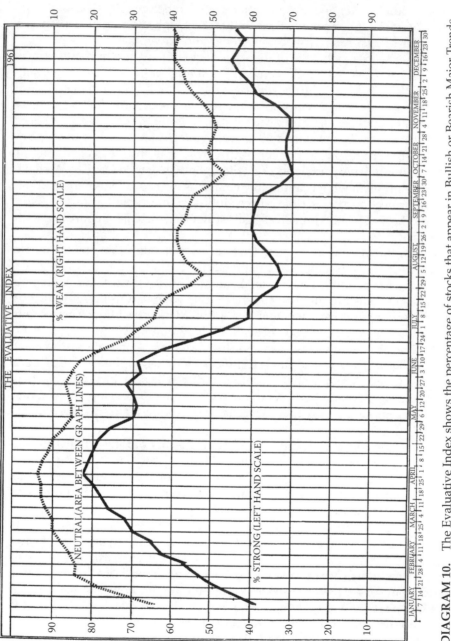

DIAGRAM 10. The Evaluative Index shows the percentage of stocks that appear in Bullish or Bearish Major Trends. In 1961, this Index conflicted with "stock Averages," suggesting a possible Major Turn.

say 80%, it indicates a stronger or more Bullish condition. If it is lower, say 70%, it shows that, on balance, there are fewer of your stocks that look strong, hence the market is presumably weaker.

As we have said before, if the Averages are making new highs, you will expect (and find) that the Evaluative Index will range well above 50%. In an obvious Bear Market, the Index will stand considerably lower than 50%.

But notice that we do not speak, here, of signals. There is no point at which we need to say, "Sell everything." Neither is there a point at which we can say, "Buy now," in an all-out sense. The Index will float and adjust itself continually to the shifting conditions.

It must be clear that a market in which only 53% of a large group of representative stocks are moving Bullishly is not as strong as one in which 80% of these stocks are acting Bullish.

Therefore, you would be justified in making larger commitments on the long side in this second case.

You would still have the problem of *selection* of the individual stocks to buy. But you would be justified in making larger total commitments, or in assuming total greater risk (see again Chapter 41), than in a market that was barely qualifying as a Bull Market.

By bringing the total of one's investment program into line with this Index, it is possible to roll with the punch; and one would almost automatically be withdrawn from a deteriorating market before things became too dangerous. Furthermore, this would be accomplished without the need for torturing decisions as to whether to sell now or wait a while.

There is a further extension of this method. If an investor were to follow the Evaluative Index only by increasing or decreasing his long commitments with the rise and fall of the Index, he might be better off than if he had only the two alternatives of complete optimism or complete pessimism. But in this case, he would still be pointed always in one direction, and would stand to lose to some degree on his long commitments if the market did eventually reverse and go into a Panic Move.

The extension of the method is to proportion capital, or a certain portion of capital, between the long side and the short side of the market. Assuming that your interpretation of your own charts is reasonably correct in a majority of cases, you can, at any particular time, select several stronger-than-average stocks, and similarly, several weaker-than-average issues.

With the Index standing in the vicinity of 50% (as it did for a number of months in mid-1956), you can then select several strong stocks to buy, and several candidates for short sale, making commitments that will approximately balance your total risk. In the case of an upward surge that sweeps all before it, you will, of course, accrue losses on the short sales, and may eventually have to reverse your classification of them from minus to plus, closing them out for a loss. But in such a case, the gains on your good long positions will more than offset the loss, assuming your choices were well made; and the loss realized can be absorbed as insurance, the price you have paid to be in a protected position.

On the other hand, should the market collapse suddenly (as it did, for example, at the time of President Eisenhower's illness in 1955) *(EN: and as it did on rumors of Reagan's incompetence in October 1987, and the Aisian Flu of 1998, etc., etc....)*, the accrual of loss in the long positions will be offset by accrual of gains in the short positions. And if the decline should continue to a point calling for sale of the long stock, the losses here could be considered the price of the insurance protection to the shorts provided by the longs. *EN: In the tradition of the Texas Hedge, I take a somewhat different view of shorts. While they would be viewed in Pragmatic Portfolio Theory as reducing risk, I like to view shorts as another profit opportunity with the added benefit of reducing total risk. Of course, being short a stock in a confirmed Uptrend is simply feckless. And vice versa.*

It is also quite possible, in a more normal market, that both the long positions and the short positions will show gains.

What we are proposing is a systematic and continuous arbitrage or hedge. As the Evaluative Index advances, the proportion of short positions would gradually be reduced, and the long positions increased. As the Index declines, the reverse would happen. *(EN9: I have suggested that the method outlined here be called a "Natural Hedge," and the implementation of the hedge be called Rhythmic Trading. A Natural Hedge of the Dow would consist of a long commitment to, for example, the DIA in a bull market and short positions in bear stocks within the Dow. Or, even better, short positions in stocks positively correlated to the weak Dow stocks. This last because even weak members of the Dow will tend to be cushioned by the large holdings of passive indexers.)*

This method is essentially conservative. Those who have always feared the short sale as a purely speculative gamble might well reexamine short selling from the standpoint of using the short sale as a regular part of their investment program as counterbalance to the long holdings.

The result to be looked for in this conservative balanced and diversified program is primarily protection of capital. By its very nature, it eliminates the possibility of plunging for spectacular profits.

But it also provides the mechanism by which the technical method can stand on its merits, largely independent of the changes and chances of the market. It makes it possible to eliminate a large part of the anxiety and uncertainty that so many traders and investors carry every day and often late into the night.

EN: Many modern readers are probably unaware that John Magee wrote a weekly advisory letter for four decades. These wise and practical letters comprise the John Magee Market Letter Archive. From this Archive I append here the letter of September 28, 1985, relative to the Magee Evaluative Index. It speaks very strongly for itself:

September 28, 1985: An Oversold Market

This week, the Magee Evaluative Index fell to 9% Strong, its deepest penetration into the oversold quadrant this year. Not since June of 1984 has this

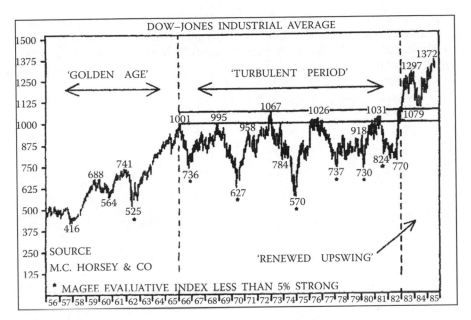

DIAGRAM 10.1. From Collected Market Letters, September 28, 1985. Magee Evaluative Index computed on the Dow–Jones Industrials illustrating the use of the Index to identify tops and bottoms in the market. A sort of "oversold/overbought" indicator.

index been lower (see Figure 14; *EN: Now Diagram 10.1.*). Shortly after its June low of 8% Strong, the MEI headed steadily higher, giving an Aggressive Buy signal throughout late June and July.

The June 1984 MEI low of 8% Strong, together with the 8% level reached on February 25, 1984, constituted a Double Bottom oversold reading for this index. It corresponded to the 1079 Bottom recorded by the Dow–Jones Industrial Average on June 18, 1984, after which that index advanced steadily to its recent July peak of 1372.

For over 20 years, all major stock market Bottoms have corresponded with extremely low MEI readings. During the "turbulent period" when the stock market oscillated violently but showed no gain at all, MEI readings of 5% Strong or less corresponded with all Major DJIA Bottoms until the June 1982 low of 9% Strong, which immediately preceded the stock market's upward explosion.

That slightly higher than "5% Strong or less" Bottom was an important clue that a reinvigorated stock market was at hand; the straight-line DJIA advance from 770 to nearly 1300 ended a 17-year "do-nothing" period for stock prices and ushered in the "renewed upswing" period shown on the chart.

In this context, the "8% Strong Bottom" of June 1984, and the current MEI reading of 9% Strong, take on added meaning. If, in fact, we are in a period of Renewed (or major secular) Upswing, stock market Bottoms will tend to be less severe and Tops more extremely overbought than would otherwise be the case. Both the June 1982 DJIA low and that of June 1984 fit this model. Because secular stock market waves tend to last for many years, even decades, the likelihood is that the current MEI reading of 9% Strong will also define a Major DJIA low.

chapter thirty-nine

Trial and Error

You will not expect to turn in a perfect record from the start. You may indeed do poorly. That is one of the reasons we have suggested using only a safe amount of your capital, allowing enough leeway so that if you should misread and misdirect your campaigns, or if you should encounter an Intermediate Setback in the trend of a Major Turn, you will be able to get back on course, undismayed, and richer in experience.

Your records of actual transactions (and notes on theoretical transactions) will help you. As time goes on, you will discover new trading refinements. Try these methods against your previous chart records. See whether your improvements work out consistently to your advantage. In that way, you can test new details of method without risking actual capital until you have checked the operation thoroughly.

In one actual case, a trader who had shown a rather poor record of performance through a fast-moving Bear Phase of the market, rechecked 30 of his actual trades made during that period in the light of new methods he had subsequently developed. Where the original record showed a loss at the rate of about 40% per year on the capital for the time it was tied up, the changes he introduced, applied to the same situations, would have resulted in a profit at the annual rate of 156%. Such a result, while not conclusive, would strongly suggest trying out the new method in all similar situations in the future, and if the performance continued to show this advantage, to adopt it as a permanent policy. It is only by continual checking and testing that you can learn to pick up more of the profitable opportunities and protect yourself better against the unexpected Reversals.

If you follow the suggestions of this book, those already given, and those in the following chapters, you will proceed slowly and cautiously, not risking all your capital on a single move in a single stock. Errors and plain bad luck, when they hurt you, will not hurt you too seriously. You will be prepared for false moves, wrong interpretations, and complete Reversals of expected developments.

If you have worked thoughtfully and serenely, without permitting your emotions to rule your judgment, the law of averages will bring you continually greater success. You are not gambling blindly in this work; you are intelligently using past experience as a guide — and it is a dependable guide. Your operations are part of the competitive workings of a free market; your purchases and sales are part of the process of interpreting the trend, checking runaway inflation and crashes, and determining the value of the American industrial plant.

The market will continue to go up and down in the future as it has in the past. Your technical knowledge will save you from "buying at the top" in the final Climactic Blow-off, and it will save you from selling everything in a fit of depression and disgust when the Bottom is being established. In your studies of past market action, you have a strong shield against the sudden thrusts that surprise and often defeat the novice trader.

EN9: I have often told my students that if their knowledge of this material does nothing more than keep them from making stupid mistakes *like buying a top or buying a downtrend or buying before a bottom has completed forming, then their time will have been well spent. The elimination of amateur blunders such as these can immeasurably improve investment performance.*

chapter forty

How Much Capital to Use in Trading

Up to this point, we have been talking mostly in terms of points and percentages. Little has been said about dollars. From here on we are going to turn the spotlight on the questions revolving around money, capital, the dollars you will actually be using in your operations. For, just as an understanding of the technical signals and patterns alone will not guarantee your profits without a tactical method of applications, so your tactics alone will not insure you profits until you have tailored your method to fit your pocketbook, and until you have a systematic control of your trading in terms of dollars and cents.

At the start of your charting operations, you will be using no capital. You will be making no trades either actual or theoretical. Any commitment you might make during the first 4 or 5 weeks on a new chart would be no more than gambling on a hunch. It will take about 2 months of thankless charting before you have any clear picture of how any of your stocks are acting technically. From then on, your chart history will become more valuable each week. Your first trades probably will be theoretical ones. You will want to get the feel of the charts and learn to apply the methods you have studied. Eventually, you will want to make an actual transaction.

EN: The prudence of this approach can hardly be disputed. And, just as markets have changed, stock market mentality and awareness have changed. The mere existence of this book and of the general atmosphere enable the modern investor to progress more rapidly than the old pencil and paper and slide rule chap. The availability of computers and databases and tutorial tools, not to mention online and offline courses in the subject, are unparalleled resources.

Then the question will come up, "How much of my capital shall I use for trading purposes?" *EN: In a certain sense, this question begs the question. It presupposes that the reader has capital. If the reader does not have capital, but is gambling with the milk money or the mortgage payment, his failure is virtually assured. Do not speculate with money whose loss will occasion you more than passing discomfort.*

That will depend on your circumstances and how much of your time and effort you plan to put into stock trading, and also on your experience in the market. If you have been buying and selling stocks for a number of years, you will naturally continue along the same lines, simply applying the new techniques to your operations.

On the other hand, if stock trading is entirely a new field for you, or if it is only a minor hobby or sideline, it would pay to make haste slowly. Some writers have pointed out that it usually takes about 2 years to gain enough practical experience to operate safely in the market, that during the 2-year apprenticeship period, many traders come in, gradually lose their capital, and retire permanently from the field, leaving their money behind them. Therefore, no matter how confident you may be or how anxious to get in and start pitching, it would be safest to do most of your experimenting on the theoretical basis, and to use only a small amount of your actual capital, so that after, say, 2 years, if you have shown some actual profits, consistently and regularly, even though small, you will be much better prepared to use more of your capital wisely and safely. And conversely, if during that time you have made repeated mistakes and have registered many unnecessary losses, you will be able to correct your methods and continue on a sounder basis, without having lost your main capital reserve.

In no case do you want to risk everything you can scrape together on the theory that here is the quick way to make easy money. That simply is not true, and the chances are overwhelmingly against you if you go ahead under any such plan.

Better to figure out how much you can spare, how much you could afford to spend for experience, considering that the amount you start with is in the same category as money you might use for taking a special course of instruction, or for improving property you hope to sell. Or, to take another example, it would be similar to the salary you might lose in accepting a lower-paid position in a new kind of work that eventually should be worth more than your present job.

In other words, you will not depend, from the start, on any returns from the capital you use in trading. You will plan your own budget outside of these funds, even if that calls for trimming your budget to make that possible. Then you can go ahead and follow your trading method free from any pressure to take unnecessary risks, free from the need to sell stock prematurely to meet obligations, and free from heckling fears and worries.

You can start operations with as little as $500. *EN: This is especially true in the Internet Age. Free commissions in many sites and the availability of low cost diversified trading instruments like indexes and AMEX trusts offer the small investor more opportunity than ever before in financial market history.* Better to have $1000 or several thousand. It makes little difference, so long as you have worked out what you can afford to use during the apprenticeship period, and as long as you are sure you will have capital to continue your operation as you develop ability. The important thing at the start is not how many dollars you can make, but what percentage of increase per year you can average with the capital you are using.

If you approach the serious business of trading in this frame of mind, you will not be afraid to take losses when it is necessary (and there are times when that is the only wise course to adopt). You will not be straining to make an unreasonable or impossible profit (with the usual disastrous results). And you will be able calmly to build your trading policy in the sure conviction that the market will still be there next year, that opportunities will still be waiting for you, and that the basic procedures you are developing are more valuable than any "lucky break" you might pull out of thin air or a boardroom rumor.

chapter forty-one

Application of Capital in Practice

EN: Today we would refer to this question as "asset allocation," about which many learned books and articles have been written (see Resources, Appendix D). The modest suggestions in this chapter are, like Magee, very pragmatic and simple — and quite possibly more effective for the general investor than those complicated procedures spun out by super computers for complicated Street portfolios.

Let us now restate a number of ideas we have already investigated and on which (let's hope) we are thoroughly agreed. *EN: If the reader is not in agreement, he should reread the book up to this point carefully.*

1. Major Trends ordinarily run for long periods of time, covering a tremendous number of points in total advance or decline.
2. Almost unbelievable profits could be made by one who could buy stocks at the extreme Bottom of a Bear Market and sell at the extreme Top of the following Bull Market; or sell short at the extreme peak of a Bull Market and cover at the extreme Bottom of the following Bear Market.
3. It is not possible to accomplish either of these desirable results.
4. It is possible to avoid becoming trapped in purchases made at or near the extreme Bull Market Top so that losses become dangerous or ruinous in a Major Reversal. It is also possible, of course, to avoid such losses through ill-advised short sales near the extreme Bottom of a Bear Market.
5. It is possible to make profits by trading in line with the Major Trend, and in some cases, by trading on the Intermediate Corrections to the Major Trend, or, occasionally on the individual behavior of a stock which is moving contrary to the Major Trend.
6. The greatest and most dependable profits may be made along the Major Trend during the principal period of advance (or decline, in the case of short sales), but not during the earliest phases when the movement first gets under way, nor during the rounding off or Reversal phenomena near the end of the movement.

Therefore, in order to get the greatest benefits from following the Major Trends, one would want to have a relatively small equity in the market at the very start of the move and very little at or near the termination of the move, but a very substantial interest during the mid-portion when the advance or decline was making the greatest headway.

The writers have felt it should be possible to express this relation between the amount of capital tied up and the state of the Major Trend in a neat and definite equation. But inasmuch as the idea of a Major Trend is, itself, a matter of definition, and since, as we have already pointed out, the trend is an abstraction from the individual movements of many stocks, it does not seem possible to arrive at any such easy solution to the problem of how much capital to use at a given time.

Nor is it necessary to have a definite and exact answer. As we have already seen, it is possible to set up an Evaluative Index which will give an approximate answer good enough for all practical purposes so far as weighing the "strength" of the trend at a particular time. *EN: To clarify and make more explicit the concept here, I would point out the Asset Allocation implications of the Magee Evaluative Index. If the analyst's analysis of the market indicated that 30% of stocks were bullish, 30% bearish, and 40% neutral he might so commit his capital — 30% long, 30% short, and 40% cash. This would also assume that his assessment of risk also indicated that the risks of the long and short positions were balanced, or approximately equal — approximately equal, since infinite precision is only achievable by the writers of academic treatises working with excellent hindsight.*

There are, however, some other questions. Most importantly, there is the question of how much total "risk" you are assuming. Since some stocks are very conservative and others are very speculative, it is not enough to determine what part of your capital should be applied in a market trend. The proportion of your total capital used is not necessarily the whole measure of your participation. The price level of a stock will affect its habits (low-priced stocks make bigger percentage moves than high-priced stocks). The amount of margin you are using will have an effect on the degree of risk.

There is some substance to this plan (otherwise we would not be taking the time to discuss it here at all), but there is a serious question whether the decision as to the amount of capital to be used at any specified time can ever be reduced to a simple mathematical operation. *EN: Still true although there are those who attempt it.*

Let us suppose you are convinced that this is a Bull Market, in a phase of such potency that you would be justified in using 80% of your capital. But you will immediately realize, from what has been said in earlier chapters, that if this money is put into a high-priced *(EN: and low-beta)* stock it will not give you as much likelihood of either profit (if you are right) or loss (if you are wrong), as it would if put into a lower-priced *(EN: and high-beta)* stock. In the same way, your money put into a stock having a low Sensitivity Index, that is, a conservative stock like a Utility stock, will not give you as much likelihood for either profit or loss as a stock of high Sensitivity Index *(EN: volatility)*, that is, a speculative stock such as an Internet issue. These factors, quite as much as the amount of actual dollars, affect your status, and are factors in answering the question, "Am I out on a limb and, if so, how far out?"

To make this perfectly clear, we could take 80% of our capital, say $8000 out of $10,000, and put this amount into the market by purchasing a conservative preferred stock, outright. A great rise in the general market might bring us an increase in value of a few points, perhaps 4% or 5%. And conversely, a great decline might depress the issue by about the same amount. An example of going to the other extreme might be to purchase $8000 worth of options on a low-priced, extremely speculative stock, in which the probable result within 90 days would be either a profit of several hundred percent, or a total loss of $8000.

Obviously, we could vary our status during the progress of the market either by increasing or decreasing the amount of the total commitment, or by changing the nature of the account, switching part of the total into more or less speculative stocks, higher- or lower-priced stocks, and also by varying the amount of margin used.

In Appendix A we will show how the principal factors affecting a given sum of capital used (namely: sensitivity, price, and margin) can be combined into one figure, which we are going to call the Composite Leverage Index. *EN: Once again Magee demonstrates a practical vision and intuitive understanding both of the markets and of the basic character of investing far ahead of investment theory and understanding of his time. What we have in this concept is nothing less than the original glimmerings of VAR, or Value at Risk. The concepts and practices of VAR are succinctly summarized in Chapter 42.*

It is perfectly true that you must vary your Composite Leverage *(EN: risk exposure)* so as to take advantage of the fast-moving central portions of important moves, using a lower Composite Leverage at the beginning of such moves, and during the tapering-off or turning periods near the end.

However, it is one thing to express the Composite Leverage accurately, and another thing to write a formula for applying specific degrees of leverage at particular times. The method suggested at the very beginning of this chapter has some value, but owing to the Secondary Reactions and the difficulty of determining Major Trends in individual stocks, it is not possible to make this into the neat, pat rule we are looking for.

It must be a matter of experience, or intuition based on experience. You will not permit your Composite Leverage factor to run out to a dangerous point on the limb. Neither will you allow it to become so low during times of good market opportunity that you are not getting full benefits from the move.

We can keep the general shape of a Major Swing in our minds as we consider this. Bull Markets normally rise through a series of irregular advances and declines, starting with a moderate upward trend, and gradually accelerating as the market approaches its ultimate top. Bear Markets are likely to move fastest at the start, and taper off gradually toward the end. Bear Markets are steeper than Bull Markets. These considerations will help us to judge the times when the market will offer the best opportunities, the times when our Composite Leverage should be increased.

There are other factors, even harder to pin down in simple figures. We would, at times, make switches of our holdings for reasons that had no direct relation to the factors making up the Composite Leverage Index of the stocks. We know, for example, that high-grade issues, the active market leaders, and perhaps some stocks of a more conservative nature will tend to start their moves in a Bull Market fairly early, and to continue their advance at a fairly steady pace. Eventually, they will reach their tops and make a Reversal Pattern. They will decline from this point, probably at a steeper average angle than the ascent. Low-priced and low-grade issues, on the other hand, tend to be slow in getting started, will remain dormant during the early phases of a Bull Market, and will then suddenly and spectacularly skyrocket in a series of moves that brings them to their ultimate Top. However, this Top is likely to be reached at a later point (perhaps months later) than the point at which many of the more conservative stocks topped out. The speculative group will then drop very fast and will return to the dead levels of inaction before the conservative group has finished its more leisurely Major Decline.

This means that you will do well to concentrate your Bull Market trading in the early stages, in the higher-grade stocks, and in the later stages, in the lower-grade stocks. In a Bear Market, you would perhaps be able to make short sales unsuccessfully in high-grade stocks even while some of the "cats and dogs" were still completing their final run-up; but you would be watching for the opportunity to cover those shorts and go short the low-grade stocks as soon as their Reversal was signaled.

Appendix A will go into the Composite Leverage Index. It should be a useful gauge for you in your market operations, and a protection against overtrading. But do not expect that you can use it mechanically as an index against the market to answer all your questions involving the nature and size of your commitments. For in gauging the condition of the Major Trend at any time, your own experience and judgment must be the final arbiters.

Put and Call Options

Options of various sorts have a long history in commercial markets. Nearly 2000 years ago, the merchants who operated in the Mediterranean region used "to arrive" agreements which amounted to option contracts, as insurance to reduce the risks of storm and piracy. Modern commodity futures contracts resemble stock options in their dual nature of serving either as trading media or as insurance devices. Options are also widely used in real estate transactions and in various other applications.

For many years, stock options were traded only on the basis of individual agreement between a buyer or a writer, and an opposite number, directly or through a broker or dealer. The customer and the writer were free to decide what stock (any stock) would be optioned, at what exercise or striking price, for what period of time, and at what premium.

In 1973, a new method of handling option contracts was inaugurated by the Chicago Board Options Exchange and later the American Stock Exchange, and then to other Exchanges around the country in which call options on a selected list of actively traded stocks are offered with standard expiration dates (like commodity contracts) and at definite exercise prices, the premium depending on the bids and offers of buyers and writers. An excellent guide to this rapidly expanding market is *(EN) Options as a Strategic Investment* by Lawrence G. McMillan.

EN: In the Internet Age options and derivatives markets have attained an astounding economic importance. One amusing way of measuring this importance is by listing some of the great debacles which have occurred to major traders of derivatives. Bank Negara, Malaysia's central bank, lost $5B (billion) in 1992–93 through bad bets on exchange rates. Showa Shell Seikiyu, Japan, lost $1.58B in 1993. Metallgesellschaft, Germany, lost $1.34B in the same period. Barings Bank lost $1.33B on stock index futures. From 1987–1995 known losses like this totaled $16.7B. And, as Magee would say, etc., etc. Of course, compared to the estimated total market in 1995 of $25T (trillion), this is a mere bagatelle. Perhaps this is sufficient to warn the general investor that the field is strewn with financial mines for even the sophisticated.

EN9: If the investor considers stocks a complex or difficult area (though it is hoped this book will make it less so for him) options are exponentially more difficult. Professionals beat amateurs at that game so thoroughly and so often as to consider it easy money. So the general investor should be sternly warned that much training and study should be undertaken before becoming fodder for the pros.

EN9: Tradestation, the superlatively fine trading system and brokerage operation, distributed with Tradestation 2000i, its standalone software package, an intelligent little book by Charlie Wright, Trading for a Living *which among its other fine points offered a plan for the ongoing allocation of capital to trading.*

chapter forty-two

Portfolio Risk Management*

As we suggested in the preceding chapter, there is some relation between the state or stage of a Major Market and its potentialities for profit. There are many mechanical plans and systems for coping with the problem, but we do not believe it can be fully solved by mechanical means alone. We mentioned one plan by which the commitments were governed according to the consensus of trends in an entire portfolio of charts. *EN: The Magee Evaluative Index, or MEI.* There are other plans which depend on pyramiding the commitment as the trend proceeds; and still others which are based on averaging costs by increasing the commitment working against the trend, that is, by buying on a scale-down at progressively lower levels in a Bear Market, and selling on a scale-up in Bull Markets. *(EN9: Invitations to disaster, both techniques. Avoid such methods.)*

None of the plans, taken by themselves, are adequate to answer the questions of when to buy and when to sell. The primary purpose of this book is to study the technical phenomena of individual stocks. If we can learn from the charts at what points to buy and under what conditions to sell, we have acquired the basic machinery for successful trading. On the other hand, obviously, if your buying and selling are at points which more often than not result in net losses, then it makes no difference how you divide up your capital or apply it in the market, for it will be bound to shrink until, eventually, it has all disappeared. *EN: An investor who finds himself in this situation should set a benchmark. He should decide that if he loses 50% of his capital he will quit trading and put his money in mutual funds or in the hands of an advisor. Generally speaking, an advisor is preferable to a mutual fund. And both are preferable to an investor with two left feet. They can certainly do no worse than a consistently losing performer.*

The first problem, then, is to learn to use the technical tools, patterns, trends, Supports, Resistances, etc. Then we can consider how much money we will risk and in what way.

We have already seen that it makes a difference, sometimes a great difference, how we apply our capital. The various factors of price level, sensitivity, and margin enter into the concept we are going to call the Composite Leverage Index. In Appendix A, we will give a definition of this.

---

* "A Discussion of Composite Leverage" in the seventh edition has been moved to Appendix A.

Meanwhile, we have said enough so you will understand what we are driving at if we use the term in connection with your market commitments.

You realize, of course, that you do not want to be so conservative that you will rule out practically all opportunities for making gains. If you decide never to oppose the Primary Trend, you will have to be inactive during long Secondary Trends, and may be left waiting, sometimes for weeks on end, for a continuation of the Primary Move. Naturally, you will pass up all weak signals and convergent trends, and shun new commitments after very active blow-offs or Panic Climaxes. You could, no doubt, carry your refinement of caution so far that your percentage of success, instead of being a mere 60, 70, or 80%, might approach 90%; you might actually be right 95% of the time in your decisions. But this extreme conservatism would also mean that you would trade only in the very finest possible situations, when every factor was clean-cut and favorable. You would not have such opportunities very often. The result might be a profit, but too small a profit to justify all the work and study you would be putting into your charts, for you can obtain nominally respectable returns on your capital without very much study and without much risk, and you must expect a much higher rate of return if your efforts are to be worthwhile.

EN: These "nominally respectable returns" are obtained by investing in T Bonds and similar instruments. Bond traders and investors traditionally consider these investments "risk free," which is, of course, another form of the denial of reality. In reality as David Dreman has demonstrated (Contrarian Investment Strategy, Simon & Schuster) *bonds are a kind of deteriorating asset due to the unarrestable depreciation in the commodity-denominated value of currency.*

In order to put your charts to work, you have to avail yourself of the higher-leveraged stocks, stocks which carry more opportunity for gain and, hence, more risk of loss. You have to accept, deliberately, a greater risk than the man who is content to buy a "safe" security, put it in the box, and forget it.

By maintaining your Composite Leverage *(EN: Portfolio Risk)* at or near some constant level which your experience and judgment tells you is safe for the particular state of the market, you will be protected against overcaution. More important, if you maintain this Composite Leverage in your operations, you will be protected against unconsciously overtrading. This is a fault more common than extreme caution, and can be a dangerous enemy even when your percentage of theoretical trading gains is high. When you select a definite Composite Leverage *(EN: i.e., Portfolio Risk Strategy)* and adhere to it in your trading commitments, changing it as necessary to meet changed conditions, you will be forced to restrain your enthusiasm within safe limits, and you will be continually aware of the risks you are taking.

Overtrading — and a Paradox

This leads to another point. A series of identical percentage gains and losses on your capital does not give you a series of equal gains and losses in dollars and cents. This is a serious problem, worth understanding, for a trader who is greatly overextended is intensifying this problem (which exists in any case, but which does not need to cause him too much worry if he has planned his program).

You can understand the paradoxical statement that percentage gains and losses are not equal if you take the extreme case, first, of a man, who, in every business venture he enters, risks his entire capital with the expectation of either a 100% gain or a 100% loss. If this first venture is a loss, he loses 100%. He is finished, because he cannot gain by making 100% on nothing. However, if the first venture is successful and he then uses his entire capital, including the new profits, again on the same terms, and the second venture is a failure, he will be wiped out completely. No matter how many successes he may have, he stands to lose everything on his first failure. *FN: This is, of course, the problem of "gambler's ruin," which has been admirably analyzed by a number of writers, including Niederhoffer with the most delightful illustration. See Resources (Appendix D) for the formula and discussion.*

In a lesser degree, this is the situation we are speaking of. You would not risk all of your capital on a basis of doubling your money or losing all. But suppose you were extended, continually, to a point where you were taking the risk of a 40% net loss on each transaction, with the hope of a 40% net gain. Should you start with $1000 and have a succession of 10 losses, you would wind up with about $6. Now suppose the very next 10 transactions were all successful. You would finally come out, after 10 losses and 10 gains, each of 40%, with capital of less than $100. It would not be necessary either that these 10 losses and 10 gains come in the order given. You might have the 10 gains first, or three gains, four losses, seven gains, and then six losses. The result would be the same. After 10 gains and losses, in any order, you would have lost more than 90% of your capital.

On the other hand, if you risked your entire capital each time on 20 ventures, in 10 of which you took an 8% net gain and in 10 an 8% net loss, your $1000 after the 10 gains and losses would be reduced only to $937. You would still have about 94% of your original capital. Therefore, in this case (and 8% is a fair average figure for short-term transactions resulting in a loss, in fact, a rather liberal figure according to extensive tabulations of actual transactions), you would have a handicap due to this paradox of only about 1/3 of 1% on each trade.

Now it is conceivable that 10 successive trades *might* go wrong, though that would be an unusual condition. There was one period of 10 months between the actual turn of the market and the Dow Signal for a Reversal of the Primary Trend. True, the resulting new trend, once established, ran far and long, and would have made up all losses and produced fine profits. But during the 10 hard months, allowing the fair average time of 30 days per transaction, it is possible that 10 successive wrong-way trades might have been stopped out for losses, reducing the original $1000 to $434.

The important thing here is that the next 10 successful trades would have brought this $434 back to $937; in other words, you could have righted the boat and sailed right on if you were working on the 8% basis, whereas if you had been following the 40% basis we gave previously as an example, you would have been sunk without a trace, a victim of overtrading.

Therefore, by maintaining a sane Composite Leverage Index *(EN: Portfolio Risk Exposure)* and letting the law of averages work for you and with you, you will be on solid mathematical ground. Your technical studies will have every opportunity to make you a profit. Otherwise you can, simply by unwise overextension of your trading, prevent even the best technical analysis from producing a net profit.

EN: John Magee could easily be called the father of modern investment theory but modern investment theory is so unenlightened as to technical analysis that academics largely have not recognized his contributions — and many probably have not read his work. If they had, he would be recognized as having identified what theorists now call systematic risk, or what is now called the beta *(Greek letter β) with his concept of the Sensitivity Index. Similarly, his work on Composite Leverage precedes (and may be more practical than) modern portfolio risk analysis, if cumbersome in the modern context.*

In his original exposition of Composite Leverage in this chapter Magee made use of some cumbersome manual procedures which I have relegated to Appendix A. There is nothing invalid about them, but there might be more simple and convenient ways for the present-day trader to assess his leverage, his risk, and profit exposure. One of these is certainly utilizing VAR technology. But — or, and — there might be simpler more pragmatic (and even more effective) ways of extracting this information from our trading portfolios.

Volatility, for example, tells us something about the risk of a stock. Portfolio volatility gives us a way of measuring the riskiness of a group of stocks. In researching our systems and methods we should be able to get some handle on "drawdown," or the largest negative swing against our equity in an account. Simple conclusions follow: if we are willing to accept larger risks, we pick a portfolio of volatile stocks — a portfolio of Internet (or whatever the current frenzy is) stocks rather than a portfolio of utility stocks.

It is indispensable to maintain a regular periodic review of portfolio statistics to assure oneself that excessive risks are not being undertaken heedlessly. These important numbers include:

- *Original risk per trade*
- *Actual realized loss*
- *Average loss and profit per trade and their relationship (average profit divided by average loss)*
- *Number of winning and losing trades and their ratio*
- *Time in winning and losing trades (long-time trades combined with oversize losses is an ominous sign)*
- *Equity swings: average drawdown, maximum drawdown*
- *Costs and expenses, summation, and per trade*
- *Daily risk, yearly risk, and catastrophic risk, as computed by Pragmatic Portfolio Theory (as discussed below)*

Risk of a Single Stock

The beginning of conventional, or academic, analysis of risk is the examination of volatility.

The formula for calculating the volatility of a stock (or downloading it) was discussed in Chapter 24. As a theoretical exercise, the formula and the theory make certain assumptions which are not necessarily of interest to the pragmatic practitioner. One of the assumptions is that the holder chooses to accept the inherent volatility of the stock at hand. But the point of technical analysis is to limit the risk accepted while attempting to realize profit opportunities. Thus the volatility of a stock, its risk, is 0.30 or 30%, but when we trade it, we put a stop loss on it and only risk a move of (say arbitrarily) 5–8% against our position. (Where the 5-8% sums to 2-3%, or x of total capital.) So our method of risk control is basically more dynamic than the theory. Nonetheless, volatility will give us a measure of the stocks which make interesting trading vehicles.

It is perfectly possible to take our own experience with a stock, or our system's experience with a stock and calculate its volatility to ourselves, using the method described in Chapter 24. If the dispersion of its returns was greater than our appetite, we could then eliminate it from our watch list. To my knowledge the literature does not mention this method for customizing our analysis of risk. Use of a customizing procedure like this would give us an idea of the reliability of our methods in a particular case. Stocks which didn't behave would be banished to the portfolios of mutual fund managers.

Risk of a Portfolio

If you have sufficient experience with a portfolio, you can calculate its volatility the same way you calculate the volatility of a stock. And the method in Chapter 24 can be used. You may also dramatize the volatility of your portfolio by preparing a frequency distribution. The dispersion of the returns would certainly highlight characteristics of your trading system or style.

Academicians and investment managers use a measure called the Sharpe Ratio to compare the performance of two systems or competing money managers. It is discussed in Resources (Appendix D), and has severe deficiencies in analyzing portfolio risk. I will address this question later in this chapter after looking at some of the ways professionals treat risk.

The reader may judge for himself in the use of Composite Leverage as presented in Appendix A by Magee, or he may consider the following brief presentation of modern portfolio management and risk analysis. The purpose of Composite Leverage is to measure and control risk and profit exposure in a more or less quantitative manner. Present-day portfolio managers might use VAR technology, or do this as follows. The Editor offers this exposition only for perspective. His own preferred method, Pragmatic Portfolio Theory, follows thereafter.

EN9: Risk and Trend

Risk of a Portfolio and risk of a stock are affected by being the right way in the trend. It seems intuitive and it is observable that losses (thus risk) expand in an Enron case where the trader remains long while the stock dies. The converse is also true. Risk is diminished to a portfolio and a stock when it is with the trend. In a paper submitted to the Market Technicians Association (mta.org), *Dissecting Dow Theory*, Bassetti and Brooker argue (with some success in the opinion of this editor) that risk can be proved to diminish in the Industrials when the portfolio (of Industrials) is with the trend as identified by Dow Theory. Charts 9.1 and 9.2 present other material from this paper which is available at the Magee website, www.edwards-magee.com.

VAR Procedure

Returns of the individual securities are determined and, from these, returns of the portfolio are calculated. This is done based upon some time period for which the portfolio is held. Thus, from day to day the returns, or changes in value, of the portfolio will vary — some positive and some negative. Taking a totality of returns, an average return will be determined. A frequency distribution of returns may be constructed. The width of this frequency distribution measures the riskiness of the portfolio. Thus, a portfolio which has a minimum return of 1% and a maximum return of 8% is inherently less risky (according to investment theory) than one with returns varying from −1% to 20%. And while a frequency distribution is illustrative, it does not give us a common measure for two different portfolios. That is done by determining the volatility of the portfolio.

Volatility measures the deviation of returns from the mean. This is known as the standard deviation and is indicated by the Greek letter sigma (σ). The higher the volatility of a portfolio the greater its risk, according to the academic theory. This would seem to be intuitive, in that a commodity portfolio might range from −30% to 100% returns because of leverage, whereas a bond portfolio would vary only by the market price of the bonds and would return face value at maturity. Of course in calculating bond risks, managers ignore the deterioration of money — but that is a little secret among us pragmatic analysts and we needn't bother academicians and bond traders with that information, as they wouldn't want to know it anyway.

As pointed out above, portfolio volatility can be easily obtained if we have sufficient experience with the portfolio. If we have to calculate the volatility, the procedure gets quite complicated and the entire procedure for determining our VAR requires some statistical sophistication as well as a gamut of data. We must weight the components of our portfolio, determine their correlations, compute correlation coefficients, and on and on. And, as Mandelbrot notes in Scientific American, *at the end of all this, we would still be wondering what to do in the* Perfect Storm. *A crystal-clear procedure for computing VAR is presented in Philippe Jorion's* Value At Risk.

Pragmatic Portfolio Theory (and Practice)

Perhaps, rather than giving ourselves headaches trying to remember college statistics, we should look for something simpler and more pragmatic — something just as serviceable for the general investor: Pragmatic Portfolio Theory. The academic world, and the world of rarefied Wall Street, strives madly to quantify everything in the world except the risks and liabilities that they themselves create for their customers.

Let us seek simpler methods to quantify the risks of individual stocks and the portfolios they reside in, knowing all the time that absolute precision is impossible. (Viz., Professional portfolio managers' performance in The Great Panics — 1929, 1957, 1987, 1989. Viz., Long-Term Capital Management which almost brought down the world financial system in 1998, and Leland O'Brien Rubinstein Portfolio Insurance which contributed mightily to the Reagan Crash in 1987.)

Pragmatic Portfolio Risk Measurement

Determining the Risk of One Stock

The theoretical risk of a stock is commonly agreed to be its volatility, which is determined as detailed in Chapter 24. So we might say that the theoretical risk of our stock, Microsoft, for example, equals on 100 shares, our position, at the market price of 120 and annualized volatility of .44:

$$Theoretical\ Risk = Volatility \times Position \times Price$$

$$V \times Po \times Pr = T\$Risk$$

$$.44 \times 100 \times 120 = \$5200$$

where
$T\$Risk$ = Theoretical $Risk
V = Volatility
Po = Position (number of shares)
Pr = Price

Theoretically speaking then, the annual risk for Microsoft should be volatility × Price or (in 2000) 0.44 × 120 or $52. In fact, those non-chart analysts who bought Microsoft at 120 (there were some) and who did not have the technician's ability to set a stop and discipline to stick to it saw a risk of 50% from its top of 120 in February 2000 to its (presumed) bottom of 60 in June 2000.

There is another measurement which might be more meaningful to us, Operational Risk. Operational Risk refers to the specific instance of the particular trade. For example, we have taken an initial position in Microsoft of 100 shares. Our analysis has identified a stop point where we put our stop, which is 5% away from the market price. Our Operational Risk is:

$$Operational\ Risk = Market\ Price - Stop\ Price \times Position$$

$$(MP - S) \times Po = O\$Risk$$

$$(120 - 114) \times 100 = 600$$

where
$O\$Risk$ = Operational Risk
MP = Market Price
Po = Position
S = Stop Price

Determining the Risk for a Portfolio

Computing the theoretical risk for a portfolio is quite a complex process. It involves, in essence, finding the volatility for the portfolio as a whole, and multiplying the portfolio market value by the portfolio volatility. This does not sound so complex, but volatility is not determined by simply adding together volatilities of individual securities. Rather, correlations between instrument returns must be computed, and variance and covariance of securities must be determined as steps along the way. This by no means presumes to be a complete description of the process, further study of which may be guided by entries in Resources (Appendix D).

The theoretical risk for a portfolio is, for a simple case:

$$Volatility \times Market\ Value$$

$$TP\$Risk = MV \times V$$

where
$TP\$Risk$ = Portfolio Theoretical Risk
MV = Market Value
V = Volatility

Under normal market conditions, the Operational Risk of a simple Portfolio, PO\$Risk, may be calculated by first taking the sum of the Operational Risk figures, O\$Risk, for each stock held long. Then the sum of O\$Risk for short positions is subtracted from the first figure.

$$PO\$Risk = (sum\ of\ O\$Risk\ longs) - (sum\ of\ O\$Risk\ shorts)$$

In the situation of perfect negative correlation, the two factors would be summed.

Measuring Maximum Drawdown, or Maximum Retracement

In the designing and testing of a system, or in actual trading experience, we care little about standard deviations and cold statistics. What bothers us is the flow of blood, that is to say, the worst run of "luck" or experience we have. What is the greatest sustained loss we suffer before our system or trading method rights itself, stanches the flow of blood, and begins to accumulate profits again? Constructing a wave chart is one way to look at this experience. (A wave chart is illustrated in Figure 2.)

Measuring from the top of the wave to the bottom gives us our maximum drawdown, and an idea of what amount of capital we need and how much reserves to maintain. It also gives us a vivid depiction of our results. A chart with many tsunamis (in the wrong direction) probably means that we need to modify our methods — unless we genuinely enjoy riding roller coasters (with the full understanding that dreadful accidents do sometimes happen on thrill rides). If constructing a system without actual market experience, one should multiply maximum drawdown by 3 or 4 to get a reasonable amount of capital to back the system with.

Pragmatic Portfolio Analysis: Measuring the Risk

In analyzing a portfolio, we must first know what is important to measure. In order to be able to control risk, we must be able to measure it. Theoreticians identify risk with volatility. There are some real-life problems with this concept but we will use it for the moment anyway. In a portfolio, we want to be able to separate our various types and weights of risk. In terms of volatility, bonds are obviously less volatile than stocks, and unleveraged commitments are less volatile than, say, futures. Similarly, if the portfolio is not risk balanced, that is, if one issue represents a large proportion of the whole, then it represents a larger portion of the risk. But, if a portfolio consisted of only the S&P 500, that would obviously be a different case, since a commitment like this would be by definition diversified. So we must know what is important to measure. (Cf. Philippe Jorion's Value At Risk. *In addition there is a piece of tutorial software called Risk Management 101, which is excellent in presenting these concepts.)*

In operational or pragmatic terms, a trader wants to know what his operational risk is, rather than his theoretical risk. And he doesn't consider upside equity volatility a negative. A trader may choose to measure risk by the pragmatic method outlined here. In doing so, he will want to know for his Portfolio Ordinary or Normal Risk, POR, his Risk Over Time, PRT, and his Extraordinary or Catastrophic Risk, PCR.

Portfolio Ordinary, or Operational, Risk

First consider that we want to measure our risk today. Our Ordinary Risk today is easily computed by taking the stop price from the market price on each position and summing the differences, as above. Dividing this figure by the allocated capital (Total Capital, TC) will give us a Portfolio Risk Factor, PRF. And that is the risk factor the trader is willing to assume for one day.

$$POR = sum\ of\ Differences$$

$$PRF = PO\$Risk/TC$$

Portfolio Risk Over Time

The number can be annualized to give us a number for risk over time — or it can be computed for a week or a month, etc. Or, this factor may be collected from operations. It may be collected by taking each day's Ordinary Risk, summing and dividing for the desired time period (and plotted). It may also be computed by taking the average return and the variances therefrom and calculating the standard deviation. This is Risk Over Time. *Annualized risk, for example:* $DR \times \sqrt{365}$ *where* $DR = Daily\ Risk.$

Portfolio Extraordinary or Catastrophic Risk

Extraordinary Risk *is the risk of market collapse or panic on any given day. The way to look at this risk is, first of all, to assume normal behavior of the markets, or your everyday panic. In this case, if all of one's positions cratered, one would take his worst-case, one-day loss and be out of the market. To extend this analysis, assume that the market makes a two, then four, then six standard deviation move. What will be the effect on your position in this event, when stops will not be honored by specialists and market makers and the market will be stampeding like spooked cattle for the exits? That is, meltdown. This is* Extraordinary *or* Catastrophic Risk.

Controlling the Risk

The most danger in these meltdown events is in the greatest leverage — so the greatest risk is in short options — and usually short puts. You will remember my story of my customer who lost $57MM during the Reagan Crash of 1987. He was short puts. Some market makers have been destroyed by shorting calls, but the case is rare and specifically results in the case of takeovers and unwise concentration of commitments in one issue only.

The least risk lies in being hedged. To oversimplify, long the stock, long the put. The profit of one makes up for the loss on the other. Also, if one were long some stocks and short others, that also is a kind of hedge. Or long the Dow and short futures on the Dow, or some of its components.

Now let us be pragmatic. If we have during the management of our portfolios consistently measured the market with the Magee Evaluative Index and balanced our portfolio accordingly, we will be at less risk, both from the Ordinary and the Extraordinary viewpoint. In fact, we may profit from an event which disemploys many professional money managers.

If you have been religiously raising your stops, following the market with progressive stops, and in fact raising them based on new highs as described in Chapter 28 (3-days-away procedure), it is quite possible that while the market is storming you will be sailing to Byzantium in your customer yacht.

Summary of Risk and Money Management Procedures

The procedures described above are easily reducible to simple formulas, even for the mathophobic.

Trade size is the basic unit for controlling risk. Regardless of volatility, 500 shares of anything is riskier than 100 shares.

To determine trade size, take the difference between the entry price and the stop price, giving Dollar Risk 1 ($R1). Take the Risk Control Factor, the percentage of total capital to be ventured on the trade, and multiply times Total Capital — e.g., 3% times TC of $100,000, giving Risk-per-Trade. Divide Dollar Risk 1 by Risk-per-trade to determine Trade Size.

$$EP - SP = \$R1$$

$$RCF \times TC = RpT$$

$$\$R1/RpT = TS$$

where
TS   = Trade Size
EP   = Entry Price
SP   = Stop Price
$R1 = Dollar Risk 1
RCF = Risk Control Factor
TC   = Total Capital
RpT = Risk-per Trade

Daily, measure Operational Risk as described above. Divide Operational Risk by Total Capital to determine Portfolio Operational Risk Factor. If this factor is too high, look for hedges or positions to eliminate, starting, of course, with those which are underwater.

Recompute stops frequently (daily for a trader) raising them according to the Basing Points Procedure. Or Support and Resistance, or Trendlines. Or a money management stop may be employed, where the trader says, for instance, that no more than 8% from the market price will be risked. And this 8% must represent no more than x% of total capital. Money management stops, it should be noted, are inherently less dynamic than technically placed stops.

As the markets proceed inevitably through their phases, track their internal composition with the Magee Evaluative Index, and as positions are naturally terminated, put on new positions in accord with the general long/short strength readings of the MEI. Remember that exceptionally high MEI readings coincide with broad market tops, and exceptionally low MEI readings coincide with broad market bottoms.

Professional risk managers compute daily the Extraordinary Risk potential in the markets using the procedure described above to constrain traders under their authority from overexposure. In fact, panics and crashes rarely occur out of the blue. There is almost always a prepanic phase which the truly alert trader can identify, especially with the aid of a computer. These are marked by insider and professional selling which creates increasing volume with Reversal Days occurring in many stocks and Gaps and Runaway down days. Almost always these conditions will be preceded by many top formations among key stocks — double and triple tops and heads and shoulders and v-tops.

Eternal vigilance is the cost of freedom. It is also the cost of investing success.

chapter forty-three

Stick to Your Guns

It has often been pointed out that any of several different plans of operation, if followed consistently over a period of years, would have produced consistently a net gain on market operations. The methods we have discussed in this book (representing the technical approach) are a case in point.

The fact is, however, that many traders, not having set up a basic strategy and having no sound philosophy of what the market is doing and why, are at the mercy of every Panic, boom, rumor, tip, in fact, of every wind that blows. And since the market, by its very nature, is a meeting place of conflicting and competing forces, they are constantly torn by worry, uncertainty, and doubt. As a result, they often drop their good holdings for a loss on a sudden dip or shakeout; they can be scared out of their short commitments by a wave of optimistic news; they spend their days picking up gossip, passing on rumors, trying to confirm their beliefs or alleviate their fears; and they spend their nights weighing and balancing, checking and questioning, in a welter of bright hopes and dark fears.

Furthermore, a trader of this type is in continual danger of getting caught in a situation that might be truly ruinous. Since he has no fixed guides or danger points to tell him when a commitment has gone bad and it is time to get out with a small loss, he is prone to let stocks run entirely past the red light, hoping that the adverse move will soon be over, and that there will be a "chance to get out even," a chance that often never comes. And, even should stocks be moving in the right direction and showing him a profit, he is not in a much happier position, since he has no guide as to the point at which to take these profits. The result is he is likely to get out too soon and lose most of his possible gain, or overstay the market and lose part or all of the expected profits.

If you have followed the preceding chapters carefully, you will have realized that none of the technical formations and signals is certain and unfailing. The chart action of a stock discounts and records *all presently known* information about that stock (which *includes* all matters of dividends declared or expected, split-ups, and mergers that are known to be planned, political angles as they affect the market, world affairs, management, earning records, etc.). The chart does not and cannot forecast unforeseeable events, matters that are completely unknown to anybody. In a majority of cases, the charts are dependable. If you are not satisfied that this is true, you should study further, or else plan not to use charts at all.

On the other hand, if you have satisfied yourself that the charts are, for you, the most dependable indication of the probable future course of stock prices, then you should follow explicitly the signals given on your charts, either according to the rules we suggest here, or according to such other rules and modifications as your experience dictates. But while you are following any set of rules and policies, follow them to the letter. It is the only way they can help you.

If you do this, you will have certain large advantages, right at the start: (1) you will never be caught in a situation where a single stock commitment can wipe out your entire capital and ruin you; (2) you will not find yourself frozen in a market that has turned against you badly, with a large accumulated loss and your capital tied up, so that you cannot use it in the reversed trend to make new and potentially profitable commitments; and (3) you can make your decisions calmly, knowing exactly what you will be looking for as a signal to take profits, and knowing also that your losses, at the very worst, will be limited to a certain definite amount.

All of this means that you will have peace of mind. You will take losses and you will make gains. In neither case will you have to take your notebooks home and lie awake worrying. You will have made certain decisions. If developments prove you were right, you will, at the proper point, take your profit. And if it turns out that you were wrong, then you can take your comparatively small loss, and start looking for a better situation, with your capital still largely intact, liquid, and available.

Your job, as a speculator, is to provide liquidity in the market, and to counteract the irrational excesses of market-in-motion. Part of that job is to keep yourself free to become liquid whenever it is necessary, in order to reverse your position. And to keep yourself free from irrational and excessive emotional actions. If you do this intelligently and consistently, you will be performing a useful and necessary service to the general economic welfare, and you will find that the market offers as good or better returns for your efforts as any other line of endeavor.

EN9: With the 9th Edition I expect the reader will have some powerful new guns to stick to: the Turtle trading manual (which has applications to stocks, as Robert Colby has shown); new lessons in Basing Points which show what a powerful procedure it can be; new analyses of Dow Theory which refresh and reinforce the validity and persuasiveness not just of the Theory but of long-term investing as such. Good trading and stick to all your guns!

appendix A

Chapter A
(Magee's Original Chapter 24 from the Seventh Edition)

The Probable Moves of Your Stocks

At first glance, all stocks appear to move helter-skelter without rhyme or reason, all over the lot. All stocks go up at times, and all go down at times — not always at the same time. But we already have seen that in these rises and falls, stocks do follow trends, make various typical patterns, and behave in a not completely disorderly manner.

It is also true that each stock has its own habits and characteristics, which are more or less stable from year to year. Certain stocks normally respond to a Bullish Phase of the market with a very large upsurge, while others, perhaps in the same price class, will make only moderate moves. You will find that the same stocks which make wide *upward* swings are also the ones which make large *declines* in Bear Markets, whereas the ones that make less spectacular up-moves are more resistant to downside breaks in the market. In Appendix A, Chapter B you will find in a discussion of Composite Leverage that there are stocks which ordinarily move many, many times as fast as others. We do not know, for example, whether a year from now Glenn Martin *(EN: Read, Microsoft)* will be moving up or down, but we *do* know, and it is one of the most dependable things we know, that whichever way it is going, it will be covering ground much faster than American Telephone and Telegraph. These differences of habit, of course, are due to the size of issue, floating supply, nature of business, and leverage in the capital structure, matters we have touched on briefly before. As a matter of fact, we are not especially concerned with *why* the differences exist. We are interested mainly in what the differences are, and how we can determine them.

This is important: stocks which habitually move in a narrow range, although excellent for investment purposes where stability and income are the chief *desiderata*, are not good trading stocks. A fairly high degree of sensitivity *(EN: volatility)*, with wide percentage moves, is necessary in order to make possible profitable commitments that will cover costs and leave a net gain. In order to be in a position to make a profit, you should see the probability of at least a 15% move in your stock.

How then are you going to tell which stocks are most sensitive and potentially most profitable?

By examining the record of a certain stock for a number of years back, and comparing the percentage moves it has made with the percentage moves of the market as a whole, you can obtain a fair picture of that stock's habits. You will not be able to say, at any particular moment, "This stock is now going to move up 25%," but you can say, with a good deal of confidence, "If the market as a whole makes an advance of 10%, this stock will probably advance about 25%." Or, conversely, of course, "If the market goes down 10%, this stock will very likely go down at least 25%."

Many methods have been used for measuring and checking these percentage-move habits, differing only in detail. Indexes on several hundred important stocks listed on the New York Stock Exchange have been computed by the authors and are presented in Appendix A, Chapter D, Sensitivity Indexes.

EN: Current day betas may be compared with these and/or substituted for them in other computations suggested in this book, for example in Composite Leverage formulas. The reader may read in the following text "beta" for "Sensitivity Index" and avoid the annoyance of excessive notation by the editor.

The Indexes are relative. They show that stocks with a high Sensitivity Index *(EN: beta)* will move much faster in either Bull Markets or Bear Markets than stocks with low Indexes, and about how much faster, relative to the other stocks.

(EN9: The general investor who in the 21st century operates with a computer and the Internet will not find the following necessary reading.) In order to compute the Sensitivity Indexes, the range of each stock from high closing to low closing, each sheet of the chart is marked with a dotted blue (top) and red (bottom) line in the left-hand margin of the next chart sheet for that particular stock. At the end of each series of chart sheets, this price range for each stock in the period covered by the chart sheet just finished is measured from top (blue) line to red (bottom) line, and these ranges, expressed in eighths of an inch, are added together and divided by the total number of stocks charted. This gives you an *average range* for the period, representing the composite or average movement of the entire group of stocks. An arbitrary "normal" average range is permanently selected (on the basis of the average range for a number of series of charts for several years),* and as each series of new charts is completed, this "normal" average range is divided by the average range for the new series, to arrive at a decimal fraction which represents the reciprocal of that market movement for the period. (Thus, a period of wide market activity would show a small decimal less than 1, such as 0.65, whereas a period of dull and inactive markets would result in a larger figure, such as 1.49.) We will call this (just to give it a handy name for future reference) the Market Reciprocal for this period or series of charts.

---

* Theoretically, the "normal" average range should be adjusted continuously at the close of each period. Practically, there is no need for such refinement.

Now the price range, expressed in eighths of an inch, for each stock in turn, is divided by the range corresponding to the "normal" or average range for a stock at that price (see Range-for-Price table, Appendix A, Chapter C), and this fraction is multiplied by the Market Reciprocal. The resulting figure is the fractional Sensitivity Index covering the action of this particular stock for this particular market period. In order to obtain the overall or long-term Sensitivity Index for a stock, we simply add the fractional indexes for each period together and divide by the number of periods. As new chart sheets are completed, we add the new fractions and compute the new index. A single fractional index is, as you might expect, unreliable and rather meaningless as regards the future. The second, third, and fourth series fractions will revise and "smooth" the Index. As time goes on and new series are added, these Sensitivity Indexes will settle down to fairly constant figures; corrections, if any, will be slight as new series are added. And these Indexes are very reliable in forecasting the probable future sensitivity of each stock.

The measuring of price ranges in eighths of an inch, in order to get figures representing percentage moves, implies of course that you are using a ratio chart paper. With other types of paper, you would have to compute the percentage price range for each period from the high and low closing prices on your charts.

We have outlined this method in some detail so that you can, if you wish, compute your own Sensitivity Indexes. *EN: As previously mentioned, the modern reader will probably wish to obtain betas, if interested, from sources documented in Resources (Appendix D). It is not necessary that your stocks all be* from the New York Stock Exchange. Using this method, you can include others from other exchanges, averaging them all together and treating your entire portfolio as a group in determining your Market Reciprocals.

You will find that sensitivity runs from over 2.00 (which we would speak of as 200%) in the case of highly speculative issues, down to 0.20 (20%, that is) or less on ultraconservative investment stocks. Roughly, you may consider that stocks with a Sensitivity Index of 50% or less are extremely conservative, 50% to 100% moderately conservative, 100% to 150% speculative, and anything over 150% highly speculative.

Chapter B
(Magee's original Chapter 42 in the Seventh Edition)
A Discussion of Composite Leverage

EN: The general reader may expect more than a little difficulty in comprehending this chapter. The editor has kindly supplied some comments as an endnote, which will aid those interested in Magee's thinking. As the chapter predates much work in risk analysis and portfolio management theory, I have left it "as is." In concept, it certainly has more than historical value and can in fact be used by the manual chart-keeping investor. The concern of the chapter, namely measuring portfolio risk, is addressed for the computerized investor in Chapter 42.

As we suggested in the preceding chapter, there is some relation between the state or stage of a Major Market and its potentialities for profit. There are many mechanical plans and systems for coping with the problem, but we do not believe it can be fully solved by mechanical means alone. We mentioned one plan by which the commitments were governed according to the consensus of trends in an entire portfolio of charts. *(EN: The Magee Evaluative Index.)* There are other plans which depend on pyramiding the commitment as the trend proceeds; and still others which are based on averaging costs by increasing the commitment working against the trend, that is, by buying on a scale-down at progressively lower levels in a Bear Market, and selling on a scale-up in Bull Markets.

None of the plans, taken by themselves, are adequate to answer the questions of when to buy and when to sell. The primary purpose of this book is to study the technical phenomena of individual stocks. If we can learn from the charts at what points to buy and under what conditions to sell, we have acquired the basic machinery for successful trading. On the other hand, obviously, if your buying and selling are at points which more often than not result in net losses, then it makes no difference how you divide up your capital or apply it in the market, for it will be bound to shrink until, eventually, it has all disappeared. *EN: An investor who finds himself in this situation should set a benchmark. He should decide that if he loses 50% of his capital, he will quit trading and put his money in mutual funds. They can certainly do no worse than that.*

The first problem, then, is to learn to use the technical tools, patterns, trends, Supports, Resistances, etc. Then we can consider how much money we will risk and in what way.

We have already seen that it makes a difference, sometimes a great difference, how we apply our capital. The various factors of price level, sensitivity, and margin enter into the concept we are going to call the Composite Leverage Index. In the latter part of this chapter, we will give a definition of this. Meanwhile, we have said enough so you will understand what we are driving at if we use the term in connection with your market commitments.

You realize, of course, that you do not want to be so conservative that you will rule out practically all opportunities for making gains. If you decide never to oppose the Primary Trend, you will have to be inactive during long Secondary Trends, and may be left waiting, sometimes for weeks on end, for a continuation of the Primary Move. Naturally, you will pass up all weak signals and convergent trends, and shun new commitments after very active blow-offs or Panic Climaxes. You could, no doubt, carry your refinement of caution so far that your percentage of success, instead of being a mere 60, 70, or 80%, might approach 90%; you might actually be right 95% of the time in your decisions. But this extreme conservatism would also mean that you would trade only in the very finest possible situations, when every factor was clean-cut and favorable. You would not have such opportunities very often. The result might be a profit, but too small a profit to justify all the work and study you would be putting into your charts — for you can obtain nominally respectable returns on your capital without very much study and without much risk, and you must expect a much higher rate of return if your efforts are to be worthwhile.

EN: These "nominally respectable" returns are obtained by investing in T Bonds and similar instruments. Bond traders and investors traditionally consider these investments "risk free," which is, of course, another form of the denial of reality. In reality as David Dreman has demonstrated, bonds are a wasting asset due to the unarrestable deterioration in the commodity denominated value of currency.

In order to put your charts to work, you have to avail yourself of the higher-leveraged stocks, stocks which carry more opportunity for gain and, hence, more risk of loss. You have to accept, deliberately, a greater risk than the man who is content to buy a "safe" security, put it in the box, and forget it.

By maintaining your Composite Leverage *(EN: Portfolio Risk)* at or near some constant level which your experience and judgment tells you is safe for the particular state of the market, you will be protected against overcaution. More important, if you maintain this Composite Leverage in your operations, you will be protected against unconsciously overtrading. This is a fault more common than extreme caution, and can be a dangerous enemy even when your percentage of theoretical trading gains is high. When you select a definite Composite Leverage and adhere to it in your trading commitments, changing it as necessary to meet changed conditions, you will be forced to restrain your enthusiasm within safe limits, and you will be continually aware of the risks you are taking.

Overtrading — and a Paradox

This leads to another point. A series of identical percentage gains and losses on your capital does not give you a series of equal gains and losses in dollars and cents. This is a serious problem, worth understanding — for a trader who is greatly overextended is intensifying this problem (which exists in any case, but which does not need to cause him too much worry if he has planned his program).

You can understand the paradoxical statement that percentage gains and losses are not equal if you take the extreme case, first, of a man, who, in every business venture he enters, risks his entire capital with the expectation of either a 100% gain or a 100% loss. If this first venture is a loss, he loses 100%. He is finished, because he cannot gain by making 100% on nothing. However, if the first venture is successful and he then uses his entire capital, including the new profits, again on the same terms, and the second venture is a failure, he will be wiped out completely. No matter how many successes he may have, he stands to lose everything on his first failure. *EN: This is, of course, the problem of "gambler's ruin," which has been admirably analyzed by a number of writers, including Niederhoffer with the most delightful illustration. See Resources (Appendix D) for the formula.*

In a lesser degree, this is the situation we are speaking of. You would not risk all of your capital on a basis of doubling your money or losing all. But suppose you were extended, continually, to a point where you were taking the risk of a 40% net loss on each transaction, with the hope of a 40% net gain. Should you start with $1000 and have a succession of 10 losses, you would wind up with about $6. Now suppose the very next 10 transactions were all successful. You would finally come out, after 10 losses and 10 gains, each of 40%, with capital of less than $100. It would not be necessary either that these 10 losses and 10 gains come in the order given. You might have the 10 gains first, or three gains, four losses, seven gains, and then six losses. The result would be the same. After 10 gains and losses, in any order, you would have lost more than 90% of your capital.

On the other hand, if you risked your entire capital each time on 20 ventures, in 10 of which you took an 8% net gain and in 10 an 8% net loss, your $1000 after the 10 gains and losses would be reduced only to $937. You would still have about 94% of your original capital. Therefore, in this case (and 8% is a fair average figure for short-term transactions resulting in a loss, in fact, a rather liberal figure according to extensive tabulations of actual transactions), you would have a handicap due to this paradox of only about ⅓ of 1% on each trade.

Now it is conceivable that 10 successive trades *might go wrong*, though that would be an unusual *(EN: but perfectly predictable)* condition. There was one period of 10 months between the actual turn of the market and the Dow Signal for a Reversal of the Primary Trend. True, the resulting new trend, once established, ran far and long, and would have made up all losses and produced fine profits. But during the 10 hard months, allowing the fair average time of 30 days per transaction, it is possible that 10 successive wrong-way trades might have been stopped out for losses, reducing the original $1000 to $434.

The important thing here is that the next 10 successful trades would have brought this $434 back to $937; in other words, you could have righted the boat and sailed right on if you were working on the 8% basis, whereas if you had been following the 40% basis we gave previously as an example, you would have been sunk without a trace, a victim of overtrading.

Therefore, by maintaining a sane Composite Leverage Index and letting the law of averages work for you and with you, you will be on solid mathematical ground. Your technical studies will have every opportunity to make you a profit. Otherwise you can, simply by unwise overextension of your trading, prevent even the best technical analysis from producing a net profit.

Composite Leverage Index of a Single Stock

If you keep a record of sensitivity as outlined in (*EN: original Chapter 24, Chapter A of this Appendix*) and have computed the Sensitivity Indexes for your stocks, then you can set down the Composite Leverage of any purchase or short sale as follows:

- Let **S** represent the Sensitivity Index of the stock.
- Let **N** represent the Normal Range-for-Price, based on the price at the time of the original commitment.
- Let **T** represent the Total Net Paid or received on the original transaction.
- Let **C** represent the Capital reserved to finance this commitment. In the case of outright cash purchases or 100% margin short transactions, this figure cancels out against **T** in the numerator.

Then

$$\text{Composite Leverage} = \frac{\text{SNT}}{15.5 \times \text{C}}$$

(15.5 is the Normal Range for a stock selling at a price of 25, and is simply an arbitrary selection to serve as a fixed point of reference in determining ratios.)

Composite Leverage on an Entire Portfolio

The Composite Leverage on the entire account is a summation of the risks of the component stocks, and can be figured in this way:

$$\text{Total Composite Leverage} = \frac{\text{Sum of SNT*}}{15.5 \times \text{Total Capital or Net Worth}}$$

Let us add one more striking example of the importance of Composite Leverage. At a time when stocks could be bought on a 30% margin, it would have been possible to buy, with $1000, $3300 worth of a highly speculative stock, Standard Gas and Electric $4 Preferred, then listed on the New York Stock Exchange. Let us assume that the price at that time was $25 a share. The Composite Leverage, then, on your $1000 capital would be 693% using

* Sum of SNT means that you figure S × N × T for each stock in the portfolio separately, and add all these figures together.

the methods we have just outlined in determining this Composite Leverage. At this same time, using the same methods of figuring, an outright purchase of $1000 worth of Celanese 4¾% 1st Preferred at 106 would give a Composite Leverage of only 11.8%. Comparing these two transactions, your purchase of "SG Pr" provided a leverage of 693 to 11.8 as compared to the purchase of "CZ 1st Pr" or approximately 60 to 1 (58.7 to 1). Presumably, and based on the past history of the stocks, your chances of capital gain or loss were about 60 times as great in the "SG Pr" as in the "CZ 1st Pr."

The method proposed here gives you a means of knowing at least approximately how much risk you are assuming in a stock or in a group of stocks. It can help you to avoid exposing yourself unwittingly to an inordinate degree of risk or, on the other hand, restricting unduly your opportunities for gain.

Investment Account Policy

Ordinarily, investment account management is based largely on considerations of the "fundamentals," and not to any great extent on technical indications. Furthermore, such accounts would normally be set up on a more conservative basis, and would not try to use Bear Markets for short sales. *EN: Magee refers here to what he considered "the long-term investor" or, one who moved only when major fault lines shook — i.e., major changes in the Dow or some such. As strikingly illustrated by the long-term record of the Dow in Chapter 5 and 5.1, this can be a successful strategy but this editor feels strongly that short sales and Bear strategies fit well with even the most conservative of investment portfolios. MPT (implicitly) encourages it and any investor who had some shorts in his portfolio on October 19, 1987 (or September 11, 2001), felt a lot better on following mornings.*

Nevertheless, the matter of Composite Leverage figured on the entire account is a help in determining the overall nature of the investment. It would be a help in determining whether the account should be placed in a more conservative position, or whether it could stand a change in the direction of somewhat more speculative holdings. These decisions would, naturally, depend on the size of the account, the condition and requirements of the owner, and on the general condition of business and the market itself. However the Composite Leverage Index will provide a useful gauge for appraising the character of the account as a whole at any particular time. *(EN9: Cf. Portfolio Operating Risk computations in Chapter 42.)*

Negative Composite Leverage

From what we have said about the "insurance" function of short sales in a Bull Market (and purchases in a Bear Market), where these "contrary" transactions are used to achieve balance by means of the Evaluative Index, it must be clear that such short sales or protective purchases must tend to reduce the Composite Leverage or total risk of the account, which is exactly why they would be used.

It might seem that by considering the contrary transactions as negative, and those in line with the presumed Major Trend as positive, this sum could be reduced to zero, or at least to a point where there was no substantial total risk at all. This is not quite possible, since we are dealing, at best, with rough approximations, and also because we are dealing with more or less independent variables which may, and will, at times, make erratic moves.

EN: In fact, after the development of the Black–Scholes formula for calculating options values, some very astute traders developed the "Delta Neutral" method of arbitraging options. Among the most sophisticated of these was Blair Hull, the editor's boss at Options Research, Inc. Delta Neutral means that over very short time periods market price movement, up or down, should not, theoretically, affect the value of options arbitrage portfolios. Large fortunes have been made by marketmakers practicing this method. See Schwager's books on the Market Wizards.

However, it is true that we can greatly reduce the total risk and that the contrary moves do, in a real sense, "subtract" risk from the total account.

This "subtraction" of risk appears in commodity accounts, where it is customary for brokers to reduce the margin required on total commitments if some of these commitments are "contrary," that is, if there are some shorts along with a majority of long positions, or vice versa.

EN: Modern Portfolio Theorists have sagaciously adopted some of these concepts, probably like the Russians, discovering them for themselves or at least not crediting Magee if they learned of the concepts from his work. Chapter 42 explores the idea which Magee is concerned with here — that of measuring portfolio risk and profit opportunity. He is concerned not just with risk but also with opportunity, and maintaining a balance between them. He also wants to maintain a consistent stance to the market, exposing his capital to most risk and opportunity when he analyzes the market to present most promise, and keeping a lower profile at times of uncertainty and at turning points.

The procedures presented here are still workable by the dedicated manual technician and, if I am not mistaken, are still effective, if cumbersome in the age of computers. All of the data, tables, and Indexes necessary are included in this Appendix. Computer-oriented analysts will probably find the procedures outlined in the main sections of the book to be somewhat more convenient and also sufficient.

Chapter C

Normal Range-for-Price Indexes

The figures in this table represent that particular component of the Composite Leverage of a stock which is a function of its price level. They are based on actual tabulations from 3800 stock charts. They state the *relative* proportion or percentage range of movement of a stock in each price range through an average 6-month period.

Price	Normal Range	Price	Normal Range	Price	Normal Range
1¼	38.0	32	14.5	68	11.7
1½	35.0	33	14.4	69	11.6
1¾	33.0	34	14.3	70	11.6
2	31.5	35	14.2	71	11.5
2¼	30.0	36	14.1	72	11.5
2½	29.2	37	14.0	73	11.4
3	27.6	38	13.9	74	11.4
3½	26.5	39	13.8	75	11.3
4	25.3	40	13.7	76	11.3
5	24.0	41	13.6	77	11.2
6	22.8	42	13.5	78	11.2
7	22.0	43	13.4	79	11.1
8	21.2	44	13.3	80	11.1
9	20.4	45	13.2	81	11.1
10	19.8	46	13.1	82	11.0
11	19.2	47	13.0	83	11.0
12	18.7	48	12.9	84	11.0
13	18.4	49	12.8	85	10.9
14	18.0	50	12.7	86	10.9
15	17.6	51	12.7	87	10.9
16	17.3	52	12.6	88	10.8
17	17.0	53	12.6	89	10.8
18	16.8	54	12.5	90	10.8
19	16.6	55	12.5	91	10.7
20	16.5	56	12.4	92	10.7
21	16.3	57	12.4	93	10.7
22	16.1	58	12.3	94	10.6
23	15.9	59	12.2	95	10.6
24	15.7	60	12.1	96	10.6
25	15.5	61	12.0	97	10.5
26	15.3	62	12.0	98	10.5
27	15.2	63	11.9	99	10.5
28	15.1	64	11.9	100	10.4
29	14.9	65	11.8	150	9.0
30	14.7	66	11.8	200	8.0
31	14.6	67	11.7	250	7.0

Chapter D

Sensitivity Indexes of Stocks*

Although it is not possible to predict the advance or decline of a stock over the years in the future, it is possible to make a reasonable estimate of the most likely "degree" of advance or decline, based on its long-term market history. Barring major changes in corporate structure or in the nature of the company's product, we can assume that the relatively conservative stock will usually continue to move conservatively, and that the relatively specu-lative stock will continue to be subject to wide swings of advance or decline.

This new table of Sensitivity Indexes shows the approximate relative sensitivity of stocks, based on the percentage price range of each stock for each year over the period from 1964 to 1973 inclusive, and the median price of each stock in each year. The values are adjusted for major split-ups and price level, and also for the overall range of the market in each year. For this correction, we have used a Market Reciprocal which is inversely proportional to the total price range of all the stocks considered, and this makes it possible to set up the annual Sensitivity Indexes from which the 10-year figures used in the table are obtained.

Since some students may want to work out their own relative sensitivity figures or use this data in other ways, we are giving here the Market Recip-rocals used for each of the years in these computations:

1964	1.544	**1969**	0.953
1965	1.320	**1970**	0.861
1966	1.089	**1971**	1.075
1967	1.027	**1972**	1.238
1968	1.122	**1973**	0.786

Abbott Laboratories	.948	Allegheny Ludlum Industries	1.192
ACF Industries, Inc.	1.095	Allied Chemical Corp.	.916
Adams Express Co.	.535	Allied Stores Corp.	1.045
Addressograph-Multigraph	1.593	Allis-Chalmers Corp.	1.195
Aetna Life & Casualty Co.	.967	Alpha Portland Industries	.922
Air Producers & Chemicals	.844	Aluminum Co. of America	1.069
Airco, Inc.	.842	AMAX Inc.	.830
Akzona, Inc.	1.031	AMBAC Industries	1.184
Alcan Aluminum Ltd.	.889	Amerada Hess Corp.	1.332
Allegheny Corp.	1.084	American Air Filter	1.365

* Prepared by Cynthia Magee and Paul B. Coombs of the Technical Staff of John Magee Inc.

American Airlines Inc.	1.440	Briggs & Stratton Corp.	.975
American Brands Inc.	.724	Bristol-Myers Company	.961
American Broadcasting Cos.	1.401	British Petroleum	.878
American Can Company	.834	Brunswick Corp.	1.315
American Chain & Cable	.746	Bucyrus-Erie Co.	1.170
American Cyanamid Company	.874	Budd Company	1.047
American District Telegraph	1.238	Bulova Watch Co., Inc.	1.172
American Home Products	.888	Burlington Industries	1.076
American Hospital Supply	1.050	Burlington Northern, Inc.	1.033
American Motors Corp.	.972	Burroughs Corporation	1.683
American Standard Inc.	1.112	Campbell Soup Co.	.677
American Sterilizer Co.	1.056	Canadian Pacific Limited	.502
American Stores Co.	.956	Capital Cities Commun. Inc.	1.195
Ametek, Inc.	1.087	Carborundum Company	1.044
AMF, Inc.	1.429	Carnation Company	1.090
AMP Inc.	1.011	Carpenter Technology	.916
Amstar Corp.	.958	Carrier Corporation	1.284
Amsted Industries	.886	Caterpillar Tractor Co.	1.078
Anaconda Company	1.260	CBS Inc.	1.724
Anchor Hocking Corp.	1.078	Celanese Corporation	1.20]
Anderson Clayton & Co.	.860	Cenco Instruments	1.221
ARA Services, Inc.	1.418	Central Soya Co.	.710
Archer-Daniels-Midland	.928	Cerro Corporation	1.221
Armco Steel Corp.	.736	Champion International	1.062
Armstrong Cork Co.	.939	Champion Spark Plug Co.	.789
ASA Ltd.	1.509	Chase Manhattan Corp.	.735
ASARCO Inc.	1.090	Chemetron Corporation	1.034
Ashland Oil Inc.	1.022	Chesebrough-Ponds, Inc.	.986
Associated Dry Goods	1.094	Chessie System Inc.	.869
Atlantic Richfield Co.	1.399	Chicago Milwaukee Corp.	1.938
Automatic Data Processing	1.473	Chicago Pneumatic Tool Co.	1.047
Avco Corporation	1.154	Chicago Rock Island & Pacific RR	1.406
Avery Products Corp.	1.087	Chrysler Corporation	1.393
Avnet Inc.	1.409	Cincinnati Milacron Inc.	1.195
Avon Products, Inc.	1.278	CIT Financial Corp.	.819
Babcock & Wilcox Co.	1.172	CITICORP	.856
Baker Oil Tools, Inc.	1.192	Cities Service Company	.947
Barber Oil Corp.	1.299	Clark Equipment Company	.961
Bath Industries, Inc.	1.538	Clorox Company	1.530
Bausch & Lomb, Inc.	2.287	Cluett, Peabody & Co., Inc.	1.069
Baxter Laboratories	1.197	Coastal States Gas Corp.	1.312
Beatrice Foods Co.	.788	Coca-Cola Bot. Co. of N.Y.	1.253
Beckman Instruments Inc.	1.362	Coca-Cola Co.	.983
Becton Dickinson & Co.	1.148	Colgate-Palmolive Co.	.867
Bell & Howell Co.	1.501	Colt Industries, Inc.	1.724
Bendix Corporation	1.143	Combustion Engineering Inc.	1.218
Beneficial Corp.	1.092	Commonwealth Oil	1.140
Bethlehem Steel Corp.	.768	Communications Satellite	1.577
Black & Decker Mfg.	1.145	Conrac Corp.	1.633
Boeing Company	1.705	Consolidated Foods Corp.	.952
Boise Cascade Corp.	1.563	Consolidated Freightways, Inc.	1.198
Bond Industries	1.006	Continental Air Lines, Inc.	1.557
Borden, Inc.	.766	Continental Can Company	.880
Borg Warner	.833	Continental Corp.	.727
Braniff Int'l	1.649	Continental Oil Co.	.787

Control Data Corp.	1.847	Freeport Minerals Co.	1.388
Cooper Industries	1.451	Fruehauf Corporation	.872
Corning Glass Works	1.353	Gamble-Skogmo, Inc.	1.143
CPC International, Inc.	.956	Gardner-Denver Co.	.908
Crane Company	1.037	Gen. Am. Investors Co., Inc.	.919
Creole Petroleum	.841	Gen. Am. Transportation Corp.	.878
Crown Cork & Seal Co. Inc.	.931	General Cable Corp.	1.195
Crown Zellerbach Corp.	1.050	General Dynamics Corp.	1.362
CTS Corporation	1.022	General Electric Co.	.914
Cummins Engine Company	.911	General Foods Corp.	.757
Curtiss Wright Corp.	1.373	General Instrument Corp.	1.393
Cutler Hammer Inc.	1.245	General Mills, Inc.	.874
Cyprus Mines Corp.	1.000	General Motors Corp.	1.020
Damon Corporation	1.644	General Portland Inc.	.939
Dana Corporation	.796	General Signal Corp.	1.106
Dayco Corporation	.905	General Tire & Rubber Co.	.994
Deere & Company	1.056	Genesco Inc.	1.270
Delta Air Lines, Inc.	1.373	Genuine Parts Co.	1.050
Diamond International	.783	Georgia-Pacific Corp.	1.086
Diamond Shamrock Corp.	.860	Getty Oil Co.	1.427
Digital Equipment Corp.	1.566	Gillette Company, (The)	1.127
Disney (Walt) Productions	1.867	Goodrich (B.F.) Company	.948
Distillers Corp.-Seagrams Ltd.	.753	Goodyear Tire & Rubber Co.	.810
Dome Mines Ltd.	1.376	Gould, Inc.	1.147
Dow Chemical Company	1.012	Grace (W.R.) & Co.	.955
Dow–Jones Rail Averages	1.434	Graniteville Co.	.931
Dr. Pepper Company	.919	Grant (W.T.) Co.	1.343
Dresser Industries, Inc.	1.072	Great A & P Tea Co., Inc.	.875
du Pond (E.I.) Inc.	1.050	Great Northern Iron Ore	.566
Eastern Air Lines, Inc.	1.669	Great Northern Nekoosa Corp.	.867
Eastern Gas & Fuel Associates	1.396	Great Western Financial Corp.	1.253
Eastman Kodak Company	1.098	Greyhound Corp.	.777
Echlin Manufacturing	1.353	Grumman Corp.	1.376
Eckerd (Jack) Corp.	1.170	Gulf & Western Industries Inc.	1.523
Eltra Corporation	1.209	Gulf Oil Corporation	.774
Emerson Electric Company	.872	Halliburton Co.	1.379
Emery Air Freight Corp.	.989	Hammermill Paper Co.	.942
Englehard Minerals & Chem.	1.253	Harris Corporation	1.176
Esmark Inc.	1.014	Helca Mining Co.	1.104
Ex-Cell-O Corp.	1.019	Helmerich & Payne, Inc.	1.267
Exxon Corp.	.772	Hercules Inc.	.927
Faberge, Inc.	1.303	Hershey Foods Corp.	.735
Fairchild Camera & Instruments	2.640	Hewlett-Packard Co.	1.420
Fansteel Inc.	1.453	High Voltage Engineering	1.488
Federal National Mortgage	1.055	Hilton Hotels Corp.	1.613
Federated Department Stores	.961	Holiday Inns, Inc.	1.610
Fibreboard Corp.	1.187	Homestake Mining Co.	1.349
Firestone Tire & Rubber Co.	.830	Honeywell Inc.	1.532
First Charter Financial	1.103	Houdaille Industries, Inc.	.903
Flintkote Co.	.956	Household Finance Corp.	.872
Fluor Corporation	1.276	Howard Johnson Co.	1.399
FMC Corporation	.835	Howmet Corp.	1.315
Ford Motor Company	.903	Hudson Bay Min. & Smelt. Co.	.875
Foremost-McKesson, Inc.	1.067	Ideal Basic Industries, Inc.	.718
Foster Wheeler Corp.	1.236	Illinois Central Industries, Inc.	1.271

Imperial Oil Ltd.	.866	Marriott Corp.	1.221
INA Corporation	1.268	Marshall Field & Co.	.942
Ingersoll-Rand Co.	.947	Martin-Marietta Corp.	.835
Inland Steel Company	.677	Masco Corp.	1.151
Inspiration Consol. Copper	.869	Masonite Corp.	1.041
Interco Inc.	1.062	Massey-Ferguson Ltd.	.917
Internat. Flavors & Frag. Inc.	.864	Matsushita Electric ADR	1.098
Internat. Minerals & Chem.	.900	May Department Stores Co.	1.229
International Bus. Machines	1.811	McDermott (J.R.) & Co., Inc.	1.697
International Harvester Co.	.903	McDonald's Corp.	1.533
International Nickel Co. of Canada	.813	McDonnell-Douglas Corp.	1.374
International Paper Company	.846	McGraw-Edison Co.	.981
International Tel & Tel. Corp.	1.033	McGraw-Hill Inc.	1.165
Jefferson-Pilot Corp.	.934	McIntyre Mines Ltd.	1.407
Jewel Companies, Inc.	.931	Mead Corp.	.880
Johns-Manville Corporation	.919	Melville Shoe Corp.	1.108
Johnson & Johnson	1.299	Merck & Co., Inc.	.944
Jones & Laughlin Steel Corp.	1.070	Mesta Machine Co.	1.160
Joy Manufacturing Co.	1.321	Metro-Goldwyn-Mayer, Inc.	1.279
Kaiser Aluminum & Chemical	1.154	Metromedia, Inc.	1.580
Kansas City Southern Ind.	1.002	MGIC Investment Corp.	1.984
Kaufman & Broad, Inc.	1.688	Microdot Inc.	1.435
Kawecki Berylco Inc.	1.097	Microwave Associates, Inc.	1.668
Kellogg Company	.613	Midland-Ross Corp.	1.025
Kennecott Copper Corp.	1.065	Minnesota Mining & Mfg.	.914
Kerr McGee Corp.	1.287	Missouri Pacific R.R. Co.	.846
Kimberly-Clark Corporation	.908	Mobil Oil Corp.	.991
KLM Royal Dutch Airlines	1.906	Molycorp Inc.	1.538
Koppers Co., Inc.	.963	Monroe Auto Equipment Co.	1.363
Kraftco Corp.	.672	Monsanto Co.	1.131
Kresge (S.S.) Co.	1.315	Morgan (J.P.) & Co.	.891
Kroger Company	1.017	Morton-Norwich Products, Inc.	1.037
Lehigh Portland Cement Co.	.888	Motorola Inc.	1.889
Libbey-Owens-Ford Co.	.897	Murphy Oil Corp.	1.056
Libby McNeil & Libby	.816	N.L. Industries, Inc.	.792
Liggett & Myers Inc.	.894	Nabisco, Inc.	.629
Lilly (Eli) & Co.	.799	Nalco Chemical Co.	.914
Litton Industries	1.512	National Airlines, Inc.	1.649
Lockheed Aircraft Corp.	1.320	National Aviation Corp.	.736
Loews Corp.	1.909	National Can Corp.	1.170
Lone Star Industries	.807	National Chemsearch Corp.	.972
Louisiana Land & Exploration Co.	.986	National Distillers & Chem.	.601
LTV Corporation	2.109	National Gypsum Company	.864
Lubrizol Corp.	1.045	National Semiconductor Corp.	1.591
Lukens Steel Co.	1.468	National Steel Corp.	.852
Macmillan Inc.	1.268	National Tea Company	.641
Macy (R.H.) & Co., Inc.	.987	Natomas Co.	2.368
Madison Fund, Inc.	.719	NCR Corp.	1.359
Magnavox Co.	1.226	Neptune International Corp.	.924
Mallory, (P. R.) & Co., Inc.	1.058	Newmont Mining Corp.	1.006
Marathon Oil Co.	1.329	Norfolk & Western Ry. Co.	.951
Marcor, Inc.	1.150	Northrop Corp.	1.139
Maremont Corp.	1.858	Northwest Airlines, Inc.	1.599
Marine Midland Banks, Inc.	.675	Northwest Industries	1.285
Marion Laboratories, Inc.	1.251	Norton Simon Inc.	1.256

Occidental Petroleum Corp.	.948	St. Joe Minerals Corp.	.888
Olin Corp.	1.067	St. Louis-San Francisco Bay Co.	.972
Otis Elevator Co.	1.011	St. Regis Paper Company	.763
Outboard Marine Corp.	1.312	Santa Fe Industries Inc.	.807
Owens-Corning Fiberglass Corp.	.936	Schering-Plough Corp.	1.034
Owens-Illinois Inc.	.992	Schlitz (Jos.) Brewing Co.	1.125
Pacific Petroleums Ltd.	1.058	Schlumberger N.V.	1.309
Pan American World Airways	1.510	SCM Corporation	1.275
Papercraft Corp.	1.218	Scott Paper Co.	.816
Pasco Int.	1.332	Scott, Foresman & Co.	.980
Peabody Galion Corp.	1.490	Seaboard Coast Line Industries	1.256
Penn-Dixie Industries	1.126	Searle (G.D.) & Co.	1.209
Penney (J.C.) Co.	1.027	Sears, Roebuck & Co.	.947
Pennwalt Corp.	1.016	Sedco, Inc.	1.298
Pennzoil Co.	1.326	Shell Oil Co.	.880
PepsiCo, Inc.	.980	Sheller-Globe Corp.	1.377
Perkin-Elmer Corp.	1.147	Sherwin-Williams Co.	.902
Pfizer, Inc.	.869	Signal Companies Inc.	.986
Phelps Dodge Corp.	.827	Simmons Company	1.006
Philip Morris, Inc.	1.023	Simplicity Pattern Co.	1.356
Phillips Petroleum Co.	.885	Singer Company	1.153
Pillsbury Company	1.008	Skelly Oil Co.	.978
Pitney-Bowes, Inc.	.961	Smith (A.O.) Corp.	1.058
Pittston Co.	1.100	Smith Kline Corp.	.884
Polaroid Corp.	1.588	Sony Corporation ADR	1.449
Ponderosa Systems, Inc.	2.588	Southern Pacific Co.	.973
PPG Industries, Inc.	.909	Southern Railway Co.	.905
Prentice-Hall Int.	1.137	Sperry Rand Corp.	1.379
Procter & Gamble Co	.870	Sprague Electric Co.	1.582
Pullman Inc.	1.045	Square D. Company	.905
Quaker Oats Co.	.148	Squibb Corp.	.989
Quaker State Oil	1.223	Standard Brands, Inc.	.887
Ralston Purina Co.	.704	Standard Oil Co. California	.860
Rapid American Corp.	1.176	Standard Oil Co. Indiana	.891
Raytheon Co.	1.416	Standard Oil Co. Ohio	1.098
RCA Corp.	1.047	Stauffer Chemical Co.	.852
Reed Tool Co.	1.323	Sterling Drug Inc.	.777
Republic Steel Corp.	.878	Stevens (O.P.) & Co., Inc.	1.301
Research-Cottrell	1.714	Stewart-Warner Corp.	.769
Revco D.S., Inc.	1.203	Stokely-Van Camp, Inc.	1.164
Revlon Inc.	.995	Stone & Webster, Inc.	.928
Reynolds (R.J.) Industries Inc.	.927	Stop & Shop Companies, Inc.	.973
Reynolds Metals Co.	1.126	Storer Broadcasting Co.	1.496
Richardson-Merrell Inc.	.945	Stovill Manufacturing Co.	1.137
Rio Grande Industries Inc.	.978	Studebaker-Worthington Inc.	1.512
Rite Aid Corp.	1.858	Sun Oil Company	.880
Robertshaw Controls Co.	1.062	Sunbeam Corp.	.963
Robins (A.H.) Co.	1.214	Sundstrand Corp.	1.608
Rockwell International Corp.	.775	Sunshine Mining Co.	1.543
Rohm & Haas Co.	1.215	Syntex Corporation	2.279
Rosario Resources Corp.	1.239	Taft Broadcasting Co.	1.523
Royal Crown Cola Co.	1.314	Technicolor Inc.	1.487
Royal Dutch Petroleum Co.	.878	Tektronix, Inc.	1.739
Ryder Systems Inc.	1.209	Teledyne Inc.	1.738
Safeway Stores, Inc.	.743	Tesoro Petroleum Corp.	1.416

Texaco Inc.	.858	Universal Oil Products	1.201
Texas Instruments, Inc.	1.557	Upjohn Company	1.122
Texasgulf Inc.	1.646	USLIFE Corp.	1.051
Textron Inc.	1.098	USM Corporation	1.184
Thiokol Corporation	1.216	Utah International, Inc.	.847
Tiger International, Inc.	1.501	UV Industries, Inc.	1.502
Time Inc.	1.474	Varian Associates	1.273
Timken Co.	.722	Vendo Company	1.265
Trane Co.	1.103	Victor Comptometer Corp.	1.708
Trans-Union Corp.	1.122	Walgreen Company	.973
Trans-World Airlines, Inc.	1.724	Walker (Hiram)	.782
Transamerica Corp.	1.223	Wallace-Murray Corp.	1.064
Transway International Corp.	1.072	Warner Communications Inc.	1.332
Tri-Continental Corp.	.630	Warner-Lambert Co.	.891
Tropicana Producers, Inc.	1.794	Warner & Swasey Co.	1.282
TRW Inc.	1.128	West Point-Pepperell	1.153
Twentieth Cent.-Fox Film	1.257	Western Air Lines, Inc.	1.406
U.S. Gypsum Co.	.931	Western Bancorporation	.747
U.S. Industries	1.260	Westinghouse Electric Corp.	1.081
U.S. Shoe Corporation	.945	Westvaco Corp.	.956
U.S. Steel Corporation	.774	Weyerhaeuser Co.	1.050
U.S. Tobacco Company	.789	Whirlpool Corp.	.886
UAL, Inc.	1.498	Williams Companies	1.284
UMC Industries, Inc.	1.221	Winn-Dixie Stores, Inc.	.700
Union Camp Corp.	.870	Woolworth (F.W.) Co.	1.030
Union Carbide Corp.	.755	Wrigley (Wm.) Jr. Co.	.791
Union Oil Corp.	1.078	Xerox Corp.	1.359
Union Pacific Corp.	.956	Xtra, Inc.	1.359
Uniroyal, Inc.	.886	Zale Corp.	1.259
United Brands Co.	1.334	Zapata Corp.	1.725
United Corp.	.479	Zenith Radio Corp.	1.264
United Merchants & Mfg.	.849	Zurn Industries	1.494
United Technologies	1.529		

UTILITY STOCKS

Allegheny Power System, Int.	.534	Detroit Edison Co.	.532
American Electric Power Co. Inc.	.607	D.J. Utility Average	.613
American Natural Gas Co.	.744	El Paso Natural Gas	.649
American Tel. & Tel Co.	.591	Florida Power Corp.	.933
Arizona Public Service Co.	.777	Florida Power & Light Co.	.732
Arkansas Louisiana Gas Co.	.707	General Public Utilities Corp.	.616
Baltimore Gas & Electric Co.	.580	General Tel. & Electronics Corp.	.725
Boston Edison Co.	.554	Gulf States Utilities Co.	.657
Brooklyn Union Gas Co.	.498	Houston Lighting & Power Co.	.713
Central & South West Corp.	.651	Idaho Power Co.	.619
Cincinnati Gas & Electric Co.	.565	Lone Star Gas Co.	.780
Cleveland Electric Illum. Co.	.557	Long Island Lighting Co.	.602
Columbia Gas System Inc.	.552	Middle South Utilities, Inc.	.683
Commonwealth Edison Co.	.630	Mississippi River Corp.	.866
Consolidated Edison New York	.538	New England Electric System	.544
Consolidated Natural Gas Co.	.529	Nevada Power Co.	1.041
Consumers Power Co.	.693	Niagara Mohawk Power Corp.	.465
Delmarva Power & Light Co.	.599	Northern Natural Gas Co.	.746

Northern States Power Co.	.557	Southern California Edison	.696
Ohio Edison Co.	.548	Southern Company	.599
Oklahoma Gas & Electric Co.	.693	Southern Natural Resources, Inc.	.977
Pacific Gas & Electric Co.	.635	Tenneco Inc.	.747
Pacific Lighting Corp.	.510	Texas Eastern Transmission Corp.	1.075
Panhandle Eastern Pipe Line Co.	.780	Texas Utilities Co.	.641
Pennsylvania Power & Light Co.	.597	UGI Corp.	.696
Peoples Gas Co.	.658	Unitel Inc.	.722
Philadelphia Electric Co.	.499	Virginia Electric Power Co.	.716
Public Service Electric & Gas Co.	.611	Western Union Corp.	1.317

appendix B

Section 1
Magee's Original Chapter 23
in the Fifth and Seventh Editions

The Mechanics of Building a Chart

You are now ready to start building your set of charts, which will in time, if faithfully kept, provide you with an invaluable working tool or "capital asset."

You have before you a supply of whatever type of chart paper you have decided to use, the binder or binders for the charts, pencils, triangle, ruler, and the stock page of the daily newspaper. You will have these things arranged on a large, cleared, well-lighted working area; and you will be left free to work undisturbed. You have already chosen the list of stocks you intend to chart.

Fill out a chart form for each stock. In the upper left-hand corner, put the dates covered by the 52 weeks or whatever period of time is to be covered by the chart sheet. It would be a good idea, right from the start, to divide your charts into four groups. All stocks from A to C inclusive might have chart sheets dated January through December 1957, for example (if you are using the full-year charting paper), followed on their completion by sheets dated January through December 1958. Then all stocks from D to I inclusive will be on charts dated April 1957 through March 1958, and these will be followed on their completion by sheets dated April 1958 through March 1959. Similarly, a third group will include stocks from J through R, dated July 1957 through June 1958, and a fourth group will include the remaining issues from S through Z, dated October 1957 through September 1958. Thus, each 3 months, a quarter of your charts will run out and call for new pages, and at no time will all your charts come to the ends of their sheets simultaneously. If the date on which you are starting a chart happens to fall in August, set up the sheet dated as for other stocks in its alphabetical group, leaving blank whatever months lie before the start of your chart. Then you will be on the right track from the beginning and will never have any confusion as to the dating of chart sheets.

Put the name of the company in the title space at the center of the top; put the dates covered by the sheet to the left, and the ticker symbol to the right. Then fill in the scale of prices on the vertical left margin. If you are using arithmetic paper, you can simply write the figures representing prices up and down from the center, letting the center come at or near the stock's market price at the time of starting the chart. With square-root paper or logarithmic (ratio) paper, place the scale, so that the center of the paper will be as near as possible to the present price. (**Note:** if you are using the TEKNIPLAT chart paper, which is a ratio paper, you will find a detailed outline of procedure in Appendix B, Section 2, though if you are familiar with ratio scale, you will have no difficulty in setting up the chart.)

From chart examples in this book, you will see how charts may be titled, dated, and scaled. You will also notice that on sheets especially printed for charting stock prices, each sixth vertical line is somewhat heavier than its neighbors; this represents a Saturday, on which you will have no entry since the market does not operate on Saturday. However, this slight break each week will not affect your trends and other technical indications materially, and serves to provide a space between the weeks, making it easier for the eye to pick out a particular day of the week quickly in charting. It is important to make your first entry on the correct vertical line for the day of the week, so that the ending of the first week will come on a "Saturday" line. If a month should start on Monday, start your chart on the first line immediately to the right of the left border. If the month should start on Thursday, begin three small spaces farther to the right, so that Saturday falls on the first heavier line.

Finally, you will have a volume scale near the bottom of the chart and a time scale along the very bottom showing the date of each Saturday over the period covered by the chart sheet.

There are four figures you must pick up for charting from the newspaper you are following. At first, you will find it necessary to look back and forth several times, taking the high, low, closing price, and day's volume separately. With practice, and by making a conscious effort to train your eyes and mind, you will find it possible to grasp the four figures in one single "grab," fixing them in your mind for the few seconds it takes to mark them in on the chart sheet. This knack, when you have mastered it, can cut down the time needed for charting 50% or more; it is well worth a bit of extra effort.

Holidays–Ex-Dividend Days

When a holiday occurs or when for any reason the market is closed, simply skip that day, leaving blank the space (vertical line) where you would have entered it. When there are no sales of a stock on a particular day, mark a small "0" in the volume scale. If you happen to be watching a particular situation in a stock closely, you might want to indicate by a dotted line the approximate level between the closing bid and the offer prices on the day no sale occurred. But there is no need to make this a regular procedure.

Ex-dividend dates can be indicated by an "x" along the bottom margin of the volume scale, and any data about dividends can then be written in on the extreme bottom margin; for example, "$.5D Unchanged Quarterly" or "Payable in American funds, $1.00." Or the amount of the dividend may be written in vertically right on the face of the chart on the line representing the ex-dividend date. Stock dividends and rights should be entered in the same way, and their market value indicated. When stocks go ex-dividend, especially if the dividend is a large one, there may be a price gap which can sometimes appear to change or spoil a technical chart pattern. An Ex-Dividend Gap is not a significant gap in the technical sense, and if it is no larger than the amount of the dividend (or rights or other benefit), it may be disregarded. The newspaper tabulation of stock prices takes this into account. For example, if a stock goes ex-dividend 50 cents and closes ⅜ of a point lower than the previous day, the paper will report the stock "plus ⅛" not "minus ⅜."

In the case of Ex-Dividend Caps, you may, if you wish, extend the price range of the stock by a dotted line equal to the amount of the dividend; and you should, on the day of ex-dividend or similar distribution, move down stop-order levels, limit orders, trendlines, etc. Very often the stock will continue in the (adjusted) pattern or trend even though its level has been changed on the ex-dividend day.

Stock split-ups or other changes in capitalization cause extra work in charting. Where the split is two-for-one or four-for-one, there is no problem because the entire scale from that point on is simply changed to the new price by halving or quartering each horizontal line's previous value. You rescale the chart and continue. The chart may, and probably will, become more active as to volume (because of the larger number of shares outstanding) and may develop "coarser texture" in its patterns from this point on, but it will respect the (adjusted) Resistance and Support Levels, trends, etc., previously established. Where a split-up is not 2-for-1 or 4-for-1, but some odd figure such as 3 for 1 or 1-for-7, you will usually have to start a new sheet, plotting the chart at the new prices, and then extending it back a few weeks by dividing the previous prices by 3 or by $4/7$, and plotting them on the new scale.

You may find it convenient to mark on your charts special information on certain companies — purchases of subsidiaries, reduction of bond issues, earnings or other important data — although, in this work, we do not concentrate on these "fundamental" matters, but on the chart itself.

When the Chart Goes Off the Paper

When one of your stocks which has been selling in the neighborhood of 20 moves up close to 40 and appears likely to rise through 40, it will be well to rescale the center of the chart at 40. For a time, you can chart the stock on both scales simultaneously, so that if it should proceed up through the 40 level, you will have a few weeks of the chart in centered position all ready to continue. If, on the other hand, the stock recedes to 35 or so, the new auxiliary chart may be dropped for the time being. Naturally, when such a situation exists, where you are carrying the same stock on two scales simultaneously, the next following chart sheet will be scaled to continue only the chart on which the price trend is nearer the center of the paper.

The Chart Record of Transactions

It would be possible to give a good deal of space to the interesting study of "paper accounts" in which theoretical trades are marked and recorded on the charts, without actually making commitments in real cash. Detailed suggestions for this work were outlined, and it was planned to include a chapter on the subject, but the authors decided that very few readers would be willing to carry out the detailed study, records, and analysis which, to be of any value, would require as much work as actual trading.

However, it should be pointed out that anyone who contemplates further research or original work in technical analysis, or who intends to make his career in the stock market, will need a great many more cases for tabulation than his own actual trades will supply. He will need hundreds of situations in order to strike an average, so that he can say, "This particular idea seems to work out in 75% of the cases," or, "That plan does not provide, on the average, enough gain to justify the risk and the costs of taxes, commissions, etc."

The important thing about theoretical trading is that the buying or selling points should be clearly marked on the chart before the expected move has occurred, and theoretical orders should be assumed to have been executed exactly as they would have been in a broker's office, with proper deduction made from the final gross gain (or additions to the loss) to cover broker's commissions, odd-lot fractions, dividends or rights received, and (in case of short sales) dividends or rights paid. It does not pay to cheat at solitaire, and the only possible value of such "paper trading" is a record of experience that represents exactly what would have happened in an actual account.

By recording every promising situation and the action to be taken as it unfolds, an analyst will maintain an alertness to possible opportunities for actual trading. He will be ready to seize opportunities as they appear, and he will acquire confidence as he sees his own predictions materializing. If he keeps a careful and honest record of his theoretical trades, and tabulates all of these on the completion of each series of charts, he will have a yardstick for studying his own improvement, and the comparison between his theoretical work and his actual results. Furthermore, he will have source material for almost any type of advanced research he may want to delve into.

For the beginner (although these words will fall mostly on deaf ears), it will pay to make all trades "on paper" for a number of months before venturing any actual capital in the market. If good opportunities for profit occur, there is no need to feel that this or that situation is the last good chance the market will offer. The market will be there next month and next year; there will be other opportunities just as good. Meanwhile, it is possible to appraise a situation, indicate what you would like to do, and study what subsequently happens. If only more novices had the patience to experiment in this way for a time before risking their money, they could avoid many of the pitfalls and traps that so often lead to losses and discouragement.

Supplementary Memoranda on the Chart

There are several special marks to go on the chart which should be mentioned. We have already spoken of keeping (on the chart itself) a record of possible buys and sells, and of theoretical trades — when bought, when sold, time of holding, net gain or loss after commissions and after dividends, etc. You should also record any actual purchases or sales, noting the number of shares, price, broker (if you carry more than one account), etc. This record can be kept near the top of the sheet, perhaps in blue if long and red if short, extending from the date of original commitment to the date of closing out.

On starting a new (continuation) chart sheet, transfer to its left margin any notes as to actual or theoretical commitments that are still open, stop orders, etc. Also, it would be a good idea to mark all sheets covering a certain 52-week period with an identifying series number or letter ("A," "B," etc.) in the upper left corner. This would make it easy to refile charts in their proper chronological folder after they have been taken out for study.

In the left-hand margin, at the proper price levels, mark the highest closing price of the previous sheet with a dotted blue line. Also mark the lowest closing price of the previous page with a dotted red line. These levels give you important high and low points, violation of which often means important further moves in the same direction. They also give you the "range" of the stock in the preceding 52-week period, which is essential in figuring its velocity, or what we call the sensitivity of the stock during that period. We will use this range in making the longer-term Sensitivity Index which is a factor in determining Composite Leverage ratios.

One last point on chart mechanics: the longer you keep a record of a stock, the more useful your chart will be. Do not make unnecessary changes in your chart portfolio, but add and drop stocks only gradually and when you feel certain the change will improve the group. When you first start a new chart, mark it "New," showing that it is an addition to your portfolio. Then you will not waste time later on looking for a previous sheet on that stock. Also, a new chart may well have to be carried along for a number of weeks or even months before you have enough definite chart information to enable you to trade in it. If it seems desirable to make a commitment in a stock you do not now chart, it would be best to run back a chart for at least 3 months from your files of the financial pages, which we hope you cherish and keep to meet just this need.

EN: *Alternatively you can get the data from the Internet, which saves all the space which used to be dedicated to years of* The Wall Street Journal *yellowing in the corner.*

Section 2
TEKNIPLAT Chart Paper

If you have never kept charts on this type of paper, known as semilogarithmic, ratio, or proportion, these instructions will help you to read and understand the charts more easily, and they will help you in getting started if you are setting up charts of your own.

There will be no problem here for the engineer or the experienced chartist, but many people who have not kept charts before, or who are familiar only with the arithmetic price scale where the intervals are uniform throughout, may be puzzled at first by the continually changing vertical spaces. As you will discover, however, this very feature makes for easier and faster charting, because the various prices always lie at the same point in one of the "banks," and the eye becomes adept in placing the point needed automatically, without reference to the index figures along the left margin.

On many simple charts, showing hours of work, temperature changes, depth of water, etc., it is perfectly satisfactory to use ordinary cross-section paper, so that each "hour," "degree," or "foot" is represented by the same vertical distance on the chart. The difference between 5 feet and 10 feet is the same as the distance between 105 feet and 110 feet.

But this is not a good way to represent the differences in stock prices. It is perfectly true that the difference in market value between a stock selling at $5 a share and one selling at $10 a share is $5, or $500 on a block of 100 shares. And that the difference between the value of a stock selling at 100 and one at 105 is also $5, or $500 on a block of 100 shares. But in this latter case, there is a great deal more of your capital involved.

For example, if you put $1000 into a stock at 5, you would get (disregarding commission) 200 shares. And if you sold these at 10, you would receive $2000. You would have a profit of $1000, or 100%. But if you put your $1000 into a stock selling at 105, you would be able to buy only 9 shares. And when you sold five points higher at 110, your profit would be only $45, or 4½%.

It will give you a better comparison of the percentages of profit in various stock transactions if the price scale of your chart is designed to show equal percentages of advance or decline of equal vertical distances, regardless of the price of the stock. This is exactly what the TEKNIPLAT charting paper does. A certain vertical distance on the paper will always indicate the same percentage change, and a trend moving at a certain angle will always indicate the same rate of percentage change, no matter what the price of the stock may be.

Obviously, one point of advance or decline is much more important to you in a stock selling at $5 or $6 a share than in one selling at $100. So it should not surprise you that the interval between 5 and 6 is much larger than that between 100 and 101. And since the stocks at lower prices make larger percentage moves for each point, or half point, or one-eighth point, these moves will show up more plainly on their charts. Actually, it is not possible on the TEKNIPLAT paper to show a single eighth of change for a stock selling as high as 100. But this is just another way of saying that a single eighth is not important at that price. You might well be concerned about the difference between 1¼ and 1⅜. But you would not care too much whether you sold at 103 or 103⅛.

Since all your stocks will be plotted on a proportion basis, you can compare directly the action of any one stock with any other as to pattern, trend, etc. Thus, a stock selling at 16 can be compared with a stock selling at 56. However, although the percentage moves will be strictly comparable, it should be pointed out that, typically, the very high-priced issues make smaller percentage moves than the low-priced ones.

The price scale on TEKNIPLAT paper consists of two "banks," occupying the upper and lower halves of the main chart space. These two banks are exactly alike. Each represents a doubling of prices from its bottom to its top, so that whatever value is assigned to the center line, the top line will be twice that figure and the bottom line will be half of it. Let us say the center point is marked 20; then the top will be 40, and the 9 Intermediate lines will be 22, 24, 26, 28, 30, 32, 34, 36, and 38, reading from center to top, with each of the smallest spaces representing ¼ point. In the lower half of the chart, the bottom line will be 10, the Intermediate heavy lines to the center will be 11, 12, 13, 14, 15, 16, 17, 18, and 19, and each of the smallest spaces will be ⅛ point. Since the spaces get smaller as one goes up the chart, one bank shades into the next, making a continuous scale. Obviously, you could have 20 at the top, 10 at the center, and 5 at the bottom; or 10 at the top, 5 at the center, and 2½ at the bottom.

At first you may have some trouble with the different values assigned to the small spaces at different price levels; you may wonder whether a single small space represents ¼ or ⅛ or perhaps a full point. Do not let this bother you. You can see from the scale where 19 is and where 20 is, and obviously 19½ is the midpoint, 19¼ is one quarter of the way up, and so on. Very quickly, you will find that your mind and your eye adjust almost instantly without any conscious thought or effort.

Where a stock goes off the top or bottom of the paper, it is a simple matter to rescale by moving the chart scale down one bank. If the chart runs off the top at 40, mark the center of the paper 40; from then on, the top becomes 80 and the bottom, 20.

For uniformity, and because the paper is ruled to divide either bank of the heavy Intermediate lines into 10 parts, with smaller spaces representing standard stock-trading fractions of these main divisions, you must use the figures 5, 10, 20, etc., as the values for the center lines, tops, and bottoms of

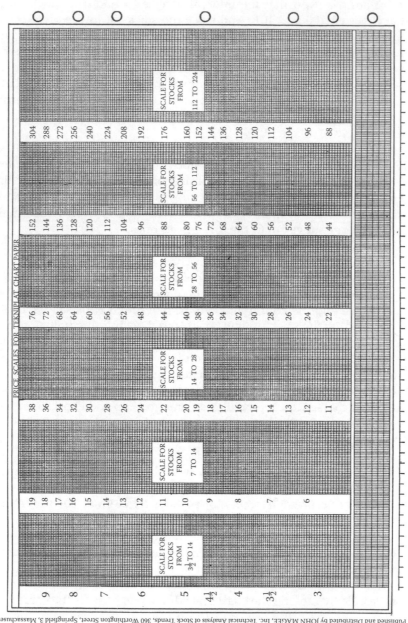

PRICE SCALES FOR TEKNIPLAT CHART PAPER

SCALE FOR STOCKS FROM 3½ TO 14	SCALE FOR STOCKS FROM 7 TO 14	SCALE FOR STOCKS FROM 14 TO 28	SCALE FOR STOCKS FROM 28 TO 56	SCALE FOR STOCKS FROM 56 TO 112	SCALE FOR STOCKS FROM 112 TO 224
9	19	38	76	152	304
8	18	36	72	144	288
7	17	34	68	136	272
	16	32	64	128	256
6	15	30	60	120	240
	14	28	56	112	224
5	13	26	52	104	208
	12	24	48	96	192
4½	11	22	44	88	176
	10	20	40	80	160
4		19	38	76	152
	9	18	36	72	144
3½		17	34	68	136
	8	16	32	64	128
		15	30	60	120
3	7	14	28	56	112
		13	26	52	104
	6	12	24	48	96
		11	22	44	88

TEKNIPLAT Chart Paper

Type RU

COPYRIGHT 1961 BY JOHN MAGEE, SPRINGFIELD, MASS.

Published and Distributed by JOHN MAGEE, Inc. Technical Analysis of Stock Trends, 360 Worthington Street, Springfield 3, Massachusetts

DIAGRAM 11.   A sheet of TEKNIPLAT chart paper cut away to show six price scales most frequently used.

charts. For selection of scales on stocks for which you are starting new charts, use this table.

If the stock now sells between	Center line will be	Top	Bottom
224 and 448	320	640	160
112 and 224	160	320	80
56 and 112	80	160	40
28 and 56	40	80	20
14 and 28	20	40	10
7 and 14	10	20	5
3½ and 7	5	10	2½
1¾ and 3½	2½	5	1¼

Note: This table can, of course, be continued up or down as far as necessary by multiplying or dividing the key figures by two.

The Time Scale

The paper provides for a full year of charting. The sheet is divided into 53 weeks, each consisting of 6 days in which the heavier line represents a Saturday, and this is ordinarily left blank since the major markets are not open on Saturday. However, the heavier line will serve to make it easier to locate a day within a week, quickly. The omission of the Saturday will not perceptibly affect the trend of the technical patterns.

Holidays, when they occur, are skipped. Usually, a small "H" is inserted at the bottom of the chart to note the holiday and explain the break in the chart.

Many technicians start their charts as of the first of a calendar year, filling in the dates of Saturdays marking the end of each week at the bottom of the paper in the spaces provided, and immediately above these dates, the months. There is no reason, however, that charts cannot be started at any time, and if you keep a large number of charts, it may be a help to start some of these in each calendar quarter. Thus, you might start all charts from A to F in January, from G to M in April, from N to S in July, and from T to Z in October.

The volume scale that has proved most satisfactory is arithmetic, that is, each unit measured vertically represents the same number of shares traded. Space for volume entries is provided in a special section above the dates. At one time, a logarithmic volume scale was used, but it was given up because the highly significant volumes on very active days tended to be compressed, while low volume in periods of dullness was given too much emphasis.

It is necessary to determine the proper figures for the volume scale. No rule for this can be suggested. It is simply a matter of trial and error. With a little experience, you will be able to estimate, from your knowledge of the stock you are about to chart, about how much volume is likely to appear on very active days, and you can set up a volume scale that will allow for the maximum expected peak. What you want to avoid is the situation where volume too frequently runs beyond the top of the volume section; it should do this only at times of unusual activity.

Where a stock is new to you, and you have no knowledge of its habits, it may be best to mark a tentative volume scale, lightly and in pencil, and keep the volume on this scale for a few weeks. Then if it is necessary to change the scale, you can do so without having to draw the entire chart over.

Ex-Dividends and Split-Ups

When a stock goes "ex-dividend," "ex-rights," etc., the price will usually drop approximately the amount of the benefit that was "ex." A note should be made on the chart on this day, and this can be entered conveniently at the very bottom, below the dates, showing the amount of the dividend, approximate value of the rights, or other benefits. If the amount involved was substantial and the price drop is large enough to require explanation, a dotted line may be drawn vertically on that date from the old price to the "ex" price, showing that this drop was not a market fluctuation, but merely the adjustment of price to the distribution.

In the case of a split-up, spin-off, or other capital change, a similar procedure is followed. If the stock is split three-shares-for one, for example, the price level will change, and the chart will be continued at a new level. A dotted vertical line plus an explanatory note will make clear what happened. In order to get continuity of the chart in such a case, the previous price pattern can be traced and then transferred with carbon paper in the correct position to give a continuous chart adjusted to the new basis for as far back as you need it.

However, if a stock is split two-shares-for-one or four-for-one, you will not have to make any change in the chart except to note the fact on the split, and to change the scale by dividing all figures by 2 or 4, as the case may be. In other words, if a stock has been selling at 80 and is split 2-for-1, we simply rescale the chart with the price at 40 and carry on. Very often it will help to rule a vertical red line through the date on which a split-up or other capital adjustment takes effect.

EN: As the reader is aware by now, most of the charts in this book are drawn on TEKNIPLAT paper. Figure 246 offers a full view of the form. Readers interested in manual charting may purchase TEKNIPLAT paper at www.edwards-magee.com.

appendix C

Technical Analysis of Futures Charts (Using Number Driven Methods)

EN: This Appendix is an edited version of Chapter 16 from the seventh edition by the redoubtable editor of that edition, Richard McDermott. It will serve as a handy brief introduction to some of the concepts of number-driven analysis. For an excellent (and highly recommended) work on the technical analysis of futures see Jack Schwager's On Futures, Technical Analysis.

EN9: The reader should understand clearly the purpose and intent of this Appendix and of all treatments of number-driven methods in this book. This Appendix is not intended to be a comprehensive treatment of number-driven technical analysis in the futures area. It is presented to give the reader a brief survey of some of the methods used by this breed of analysts. The original authors of this work (and the present editor) were and are chart analysts and practitioners of natural systems. AND I believe that the methods presented here can be better used when practiced by a competent chart analyst.

Commodities Futures

Futures (a standardized instrument allowing the investor to buy at current prices for future delivery) are traded on commodities such as agricultural products (e.g., corn, oats, wheat, soybeans, livestock); metals (e.g., gold, silver, platinum, palladium); forest, fiber, and food (e.g., lumber, cotton, orange juice, sugar, cocoa, coffee); energy, (e.g., crude oil, heating oil, gasoline, natural gas); financial and other derivative markets (e.g., debt instruments such as U.S. Treasury Bonds, stock indexes, currencies).

The futures industry began in the United States in the early 1800s as a way to stabilize crop producers' and buyers' incomes by locking in a current commodity price for delivery at a later date. As the futures market developed and became standardized, the primary investment strategies of hedging and speculation evolved. Trading of futures and options has expanded to numerous types of investment products and, in recent years, has become global.

Empirical experience demonstrates that chart patterns exist for equity shares of stock and also for other financial instruments traded on public exchanges. Commodities trading is another place to look for indicative chart patterns. Price trends of actively traded properties, limited only by the constraints of supply and demand, also illustrate meaningful patterns when plotted on a graph. Rising or Declining Trends, Congestion, Consolidation, and Reversals will be evident, similar to the pattern formation created by shares of common stock. Activities of the speculators and the underlying investor psychology are similar, whether the securities are stock shares or futures contracts.

Principles of technical analysis apply to any of the active commodity futures such as: corn, cotton, cocoa, coffee, wheat, and others. Some allowance must be made for the intrinsic differences between commodity futures contracts and equity stocks or bonds, of which four are noted here.

1. Limited Life — One of the most prominent differences is the fact that commodity futures have a limited life; they expire on a set date. Although each futures contract has a certain life of its own, it will tend to trade in a pattern similar to cash for delivery prices and similar to other comparable contracts. The limited independent life has consequences of long-term Support and Resistance Levels which have less value for analysis, although they have some value for the short term.

2. Hedging — Another important difference between commodity and stock analysis is the fact that many investors are using futures for hedging, a conservative strategy, rather than speculating. The result of this situation is the fact that near-term levels of Support or Resistance have less meaning than with equities. Futures with commodities grown as crops can also have seasonal influences which are observed and evaluated by both hedgers and speculators. Seasonal factors can have an effect on the reliability of signals in the technical analysis of commodities.

3. Volume — A third major difference is volume. Volume's relation to stock trading is not complex. A specific number of shares exist for trading. Changes in the total number of shares available must go through an approval process and be well publicized. Average daily volumes can be calculated and used as a benchmark to show sudden increases or declines. With futures, there is virtually no limit to the total number of contracts which can be bought or sold for future delivery on any one commodity, although there are limits on the number of contracts a single investor can buy or sell on a specific futures contract. It is possible for the open interest to exceed the amount of an underlying commodity actually delivered. In fact, most contracts are closed out before the delivery date.

4. Weather — A final major difference is the fact that weather news regarding such things as droughts, floods, etc., can impact the commodity crop and change the trend of the futures market immediately and dramatically. The stock market has few such influences. *EN: Except for Alan Greenspan and the Federal Reserve Board.*

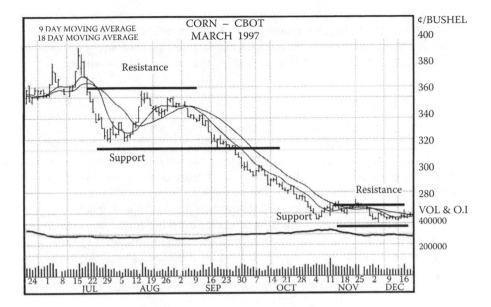

FIGURE 180. Corn Futures, March 1997. A declining market. A rally from Support (the Double Bottom in July–August). Resistance met at 360, and a reversal. As the price declines areas of Support become Resistance. Note the Support Line from early November, well into December. (See Chapters 13 and 30 for more on Support and Resistance.)

Observable Patterns

With the differences accounted for, under normal market conditions, chart patterns can still be observed and used for analysis of commodities, as they are used with common stocks, such as:

- Head-and-Shoulder Formations
- Rounding Tops and Bottoms

Basic Trendlines can be observed and plotted. Other patterns, common with equities, like Triangles, Rectangles, Flags, etc., appear less frequently in commodities and tend to be unreliable in forecasting many directional changes of some commodity futures prices. Support and Resistance Levels seem to be accurate at times and insignificant at other times (probably due to supply and demand factors outside the patterns established by hedge and speculative trading). Price gaps also seem to have less meaning.

Triangle patterns occur less frequently in commodities and aren't as reliable as with equities, but they do occur. Breaks tend to be stronger initially when they do not occur at the apex of the Triangle, which is the same tendency as with stock chart patterns.

Successful speculation in commodities futures requires an extensive background in understanding the influences on their prices. Although chart patterns can be observed, as shown here, reliability of signals due to inherent differences between stocks and commodities should be approached with caution.

Importance of Stop-Loss Orders

A stop-loss order is a closing transaction for an open order. It is an order to sell at the current market price, if the stop price is traded on or through, or if the opening transaction was a buy (long position). It is an order to buy at the current market price, if the stop price is traded on or through or if the opening transaction was a sell (short position).

Whereas stop orders are much debated in the equities market, any professional commodities trader will acknowledge their importance to avoid catastrophic losses. The 1990s served witness to incidents where public and private institutions lost billions of dollars in the futures and other derivatives. Where were their stop-loss orders? The essential stop-loss order is an insurance policy which should be considered part of the cost of doing business.

An ideal stop-loss is placed far enough away from the current trading range in order to not be activated by normal market fluctuations, yet be there for a Major Reversal. But, the market is not an ideal universe. Reality says the orders will be placed too close or too far away. Of those two alternatives, too far away is preferable for many. Too close leads to frustration and increased transaction costs. Left with only two alternatives, most investors would lean toward the least frustrating, that of being too far away. Multiple transactions can also cause confusion and thereby increase risk.

The too-far-away stop can be further honed and refined by mathematical analysis (e.g., standard deviation) or simple observation of the chart pattern, including levels of Support and Resistance. Placing the stop-loss away from current trading will cause the order to be activated only if trading violates the range. The too-far-away method can be improved with practice. These distant stops do avoid reentry problems as well as keep slippage and transaction fees under control; however, the overall portfolio risk is greater. Whichever system is used, the primary caution is to avoid switching back and forth between too close and too far away. In some markets, flip-flopping could easily lead to whipsawing by cutting profits both ways. (See Chapter 27, Stop Orders.)

Weekly Charts

The detail of the daily price chart is important, but it is also important to double-check the daily chart by comparing it to the weekly or monthly price chart. The longer-term charts give "the bigger picture" and help to explain the development of current trends. "The Trend Is Your Friend" can be as true in commodities trading as it is in equity trading.

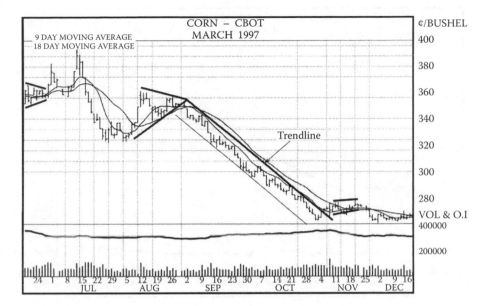

FIGURE 181. Corn Futures, March 1997. Although the patterns shown here are clear, there is a possibility that the downturn in July is the end of a Broad Head-and-Shoulders Pattern (including the head and right shoulder). Notice the decline in volume during August. The lower volume is possibly under a right shoulder. It is important to determine if this was from a Head-and-Shoulders Formation (see weekly chart Figure 183). Triangle formations here seem to be quite accurate. (See Chapter 8 for more on Triangles and Chapters 14, 15, and 40 for more on trendlines.) Notice how the Downtrend Line aligns itself with the apex of a Triangle. Chart courtesy of Market Research, Inc. (www.barchart.com).

Trends

Trends usually endure for comparatively long periods of time and a trading position that doesn't fight the trend ordinarily does better. As with equity chart patterns, Uptrend Lines are drawn under the lows and Downtrend Lines are drawn across the highs. Many chartists draw trendlines on both sides of the trend to indicate the Trading Channel. Trendlines can be drawn through highs and lows or through closing prices shown by the dots on the right side of each high–low bar (a dot to the left of a high–low bar indicates an opening price).

If a commodity trendline isn't broken, it remains, usually until at least two closing breaks occur. Many times a market will go sideways near the Bottom of a downtrend. The sideways trend gives traders time to believe the downtrend is over. For this reason they appear most often at the Bottom, and, the longer Consolidating sideways trends continue, the stronger the next rally will be. False turns happen most often at the Top where everyone gets nervous. Although the most reliable trendlines move at or near a 45-degree angle, any trendline running consistently for more than 4 weeks tends to continue.

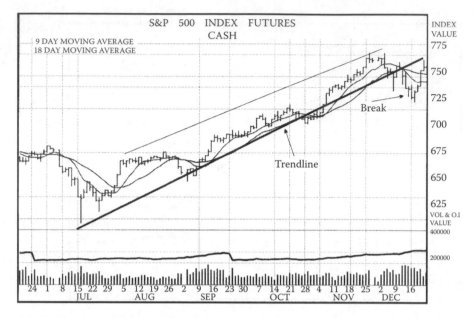

FIGURE 182. Standard & Poor's 500 Index (Cash). Although the weekly chart gives more history to a trend, it will look at cash prices instead of futures prices, simply because of the narrowly defined futures life which has a beginning and an end. The trend in the 1996 market was unmistakably Bullish. After the July correction Resistance was continually penetrated and Support held firm until December. The December break was significant, but, at this point, appears to be a correction and not necessarily a Reversal. (See Chapters 14, 15, and 40 for more on trendlines.) Chart courtesy of Market Research, Inc. (www.barchart.com).

Market Timing Indicators

The reliability of chart trend patterns can be enhanced and improved by observing other market timing indicators which have a track record for producing reliable signals in the commodities markets. Often times such indicators need confirmation of another system to enhance the timing of buys and sells. Chart patterns and other timing indicators fit together well.

Moving Averages

Moving Averages are some of the oldest technical indicators, and remain some of the most useful indicators for market analysts. A Moving Average is the average price of a security at a specific point in time. A Moving Average shows a trend. The purpose of the Moving Average is to show the trend in a "smoothed" manner, with less apparent volatility. Although a smoothed

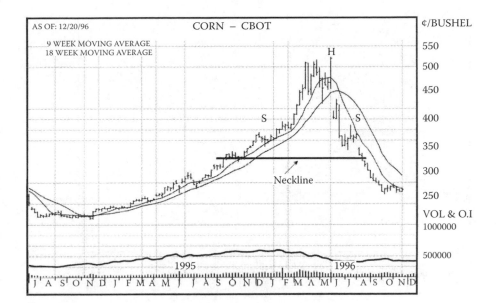

FIGURE 183. Weekly Corn Prices (Cash). As was suspected in the corn daily futures price chart (Figure 181), a broad, 9-month Head-and-Shoulders Topping/Pattern formed in the corn market. The left shoulder occurred in mid-December 1995, with the head in May–June of 1996, and finally the right shoulder (on lower volume) in August. Although the Consolidation could be the Bottom, it appears to be viewed with some caution in the November–December area. (See Chapters 6, 7, and 8 for more information on Head-and-Shoulders Formation and measuring.) Chart courtesy of Market Research, Inc. (www.barchart.com).

trend can be considered a chart pattern *(EN: i.e., trendline)*, Moving Averages give unique signals that can be used in conjunction with other traditional chart patterns.

Time Span

The user selects the time span. For stocks, the most common time periods are 10-day, 30-day, 50-day, 100-day, and 200-day Moving Averages. Most technicians, however, use variations of these numbers to suit their individual needs. There isn't just one "right" time frame. Moving Averages with different time spans show different stories. The shorter the time span, the more sensitive the Moving Average will be to price changes. The longer the time span, the less sensitive or the more smoothed the Moving Average will appear.

The other factor to define is the price used in computations. The most common price used is the close for a particular day. However, technicians

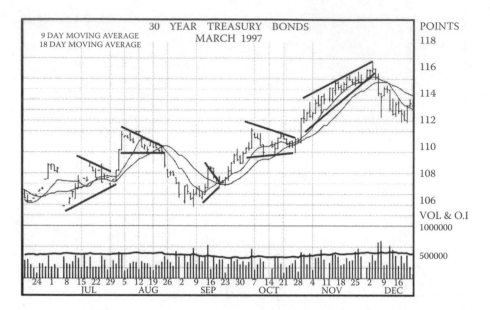

FIGURE 184. 30-Year Treasury Bond Futures (March 1997). Here again are Triangle patterns indicating approaching market breaks. The first in July broke significantly to the upside with an accompanying increase in volume. The second break in mid-August had a decline, as did the break in late November. Although the October break showed a slight increase in volume, September's break only had a Minor increase. Support held well in four instances: June, July, and two in September. Resistance from July–August held in early October, but when penetrated later in the month had a significant Rally. (See Chapter 7 for more on Triangle formations.) Chart courtesy of Market Research, Inc. (www.barchart.com).

use several other variations. They are (high + low)/2; (close + high + low)/3; (open + close + high + low)/4; and the weighted variation is (high + low + close + close)/4. Closing prices are significant because they represent positions that investors are willing to carry overnight.

Single Moving Average

Perhaps the best way to understand a Moving Average is with an example. Assume we have been tracking the closing price of IBM for the past 100 days and want to create a 50-day Moving Average. First, add the closing prices together for the first 50 days. Then divide this amount by 50. This is the first point plotted on the chart. Then add the closing prices together for Day 2 through Day 51. Next, divide this amount by 50, establishing the second point on the chart. Then add the closing prices for Days 3 through 52 together and divide the number by 50, etc. Connect all the points plotted together in a line and run it through the price bars.

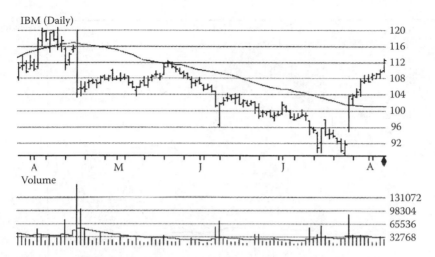

FIGURE 185. IBM 1996, 50-Day Moving Average (Exponentially Smoothed). The plotted Moving Average shows a smoothed price trend. A buy signal is given when price crosses above the Moving Average and the Moving Average is directed upward. A sell signal is given when price drops below the Moving Average and the Moving Average is directed downward. Buy and sell signals are not given when the Moving Average changes direction but price does not cross above or below the Moving Average. Chart courtesy of AIQ MarketExpert (www.aiqsystems.com).

Dual Moving Averages

Moving Averages can become more powerful when multiple Moving Averages are plotted. One combination is to plot a 9-day Moving Average and an 18-day Moving Average on the same chart. A buy signal is given when the 9-day Moving Average crosses above the 18-day Moving Average and both Moving Averages are in an upward direction. A sell signal is given when the 9-day Moving Average crosses below the 18-day Moving Average and both Moving Averages are declining.

Although any number of Moving Averages can be used, the use of three or four is not uncommon. Dual Moving Averages appeal to many technical analysts. Research shows using two averages tends to be the most effective. Like many other indicators, averages can be unreliable or difficult to trade in fast markets. They contain data not within the current range of volatility; the data never reach the present. The averages do call attention to the current movement in relation to the past.

False signals can be given when prices fluctuate in a Broad Sideways Pattern. To compensate, technicians use other indicators to confirm the direction of price. Looking to the chart patterns can be the indicator of choice for

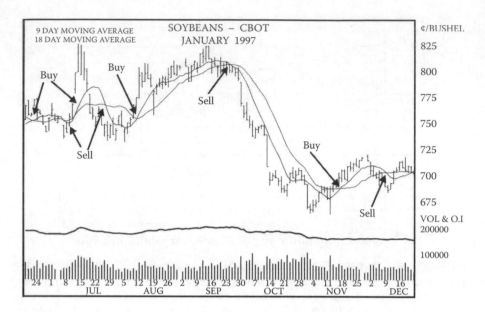

FIGURE 186.   Soybean Futures, January 1997. A chart with four buy signals and four sell signals, some with only minor gains. Watchers of Moving Averages need to establish which signals are significant enough for them to make a trade. (See Chapter 36, Automated Trendline: The Moving Average.) Chart courtesy of Market Research, Inc. (www.barchart.com).

these occasions. Pattern Formations will be Rectangles, Triangles, Pennants, or other Consolidations. Seeing them on a chart can clarify the Moving Average signals. (See Chapter 11 on Consolidation Formations.)

Weighted and Exponential Moving Averages

There are two other types of Moving Averages, the Weighted Moving Average and the Exponential Moving Average. If a simple Moving Average is centered, the signal is delayed. To overcome this, many technicians use a Weighted Moving Average where the data are weighted in favor of the more recent data. A Weighted Moving Average reverses direction more quickly than a simple Moving Average.

The most frequently used method to weight a Moving Average is, for a 5-day Moving Average, multiply the first observation by 1; the second observation by 2; the third observation by 3; the fourth observation by 4; the fifth observation by 5. Then divide this sum by the sum of the weights. In this case, the divisor is $1 + 2 + 3 + 4 + 5 = 15$. The sum in the first part of the equation is divided by 15. With a Weighted Moving Average, a buy or sell signal is given when the Weighted Moving Average changes direction.

An Exponential Moving Average is a form of a Weighted Moving Average. To construct a 20-day Exponential Moving Average, first construct a 20-day Simple Moving Average. The Simple Moving Average becomes the starting point. Assume the Simple Moving Average value for Day 20 is 42; the Simple Moving Average value for Day 21 is 43; and the Simple Moving Average value for Day 22 is 44. We then subtract the Day 20 Moving Average value from Day 21 Simple Moving Average value and get a difference of 1.00. This value (1.00) is multiplied by an exponent. In this case, the exponent is 0.1. Next, add 0.1 to the Simple Moving Average value of Day 20. The Exponential Moving Average value of Day 20 now becomes 42.100. And this goes on indefinitely. To calculate the exponent, divide 2 by the time period. In our case, we divided 2 by 20 to arrive at 0.1.

The average itself can act as an area of Support and Resistance. The more times a Moving Average is touched, the greater the significance of a violation. A penetration of a Moving Average is a signal that a change in trend may be taking place. Confirmations of trend changes should be confirmed from alternative sources. Generally, the longer the time frame of the Moving Average, the greater the significance of a crossover.

Moving Average Caveat

The largest difficulty with Moving Averages is their reliance on trending markets. Flat or Consolidating markets will create similar Moving Average Lines (see Chapter 11, Consolidation Formations). Another annoyance is for a quick-turning market to be well ahead of the turn in the Moving Averages, which are buoyed up by the numbers from previous dates. Although Weighted or Exponential Averages partly get around being buoyed, they tend to whipsaw with the market and the smoothing factor is lost. These are reasons for not being dependent on Moving Averages alone. Traditional chart patterns can be useful in combination with Moving Averages.

EN9: Without a doubt one of the most important contributions chart analysis can make to a mechanical system is to make the user aware of the state of the market. A competent analyst should recognize the difference between trading and trending markets and adjust his tactics accordingly. Unfortunately few traders seem to use this "hybrid" approach. They fear "discretionary trading," not trusting their own emotional strength to deal with the enormous stress of futures trading.

Moving Average Convergence Divergence (MACD)

MACD, an oscillator, is derived by dividing one Moving Average by another. Basically, it combines three Moving Averages into two lines. In today's computer programs, the Moving Averages are usually exponentially weighted, thus giving more weight to the more recent data. It is plotted on a chart with a horizontal equilibrium line.

The equilibrium line is important. When the two Moving Averages cross below the equilibrium line, it means that the shorter EMA is at a value less than the longer EMA. This is a Bearish signal. When the EMAs are above the equilibrium line, it means that the shorter EMA has a value greater than the longer EMA. This is a Bullish signal.

The first line is the difference between a 12-period Exponential Moving Average and a 26-period Exponential Moving Average. The second line (signal line) is an approximate exponential equivalent of a 9-period Moving Average of the first line. The exponential values being 0.15, 0.075, and 0.20. A MACD can be displayed as a line oscillator or a histogram.

Software allows a user to change values when calculating MACD. Some systems require the entering of exponential values, and others use the actual number of periods for the three Moving Averages. There is a caution on changing original values of MACD to curve fit the data. It is recommended that two differing sets of values be used, one for the buy-side and another for the sell-side. Both use a 9-period (0.20) signal line, but the 0.15, 0.075 combination is for the sell-side only. The buy-side values are 8-period (0.22) and 17-period (0.11). The sell-side formula is normally slower *(EN: with the intention of buying quickly and letting profits run).* It is probably best to stay with the standard sell-side formula in the commodities market; even though slower, it should be more reliable in most situations.

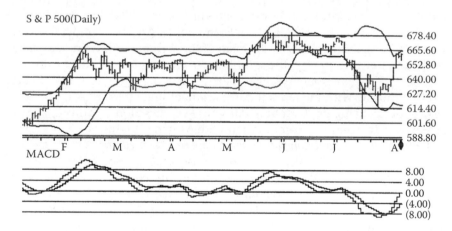

FIGURE 187. Standard & Poor's 500 Index 1996, MACD. Buy signals are generated when the faster line crosses the slower line from below. Sell signals come from the opposite, when the faster line crosses the slower line from above. It is easy to see some of the difficulties and risks involved with mechanically trading every buy and sell signal from MACD. Using different periods for buy and sell can help overcome some of the difficulties, but using other indicators, such as trendlines drawn on the MACD line, can also assist the trader in selecting entry and exit points. The use of trendlines here changes the number of trades from nine to three and they are all on the right side of the market. Chart Courtesy of AIQ MarketExpert (www.aiqsystems.com).

Buy and Sell Signals

Buy signals are generated when the faster line crosses the slower line from below. Sell signals come from the opposite, that is, when the faster line crosses the slower line from above. Beware of mechanically trading every MACD crossover, as it can lead to whipsaws and substantial drawdowns. The fact is, narrow trading ranges give many false signals which can be avoided with additional interpretation. *EN9: This additional interpretation being conscientious observance of the bar charts.*

MACD Overbought–Oversold

Gerald Appel, who originally developed MACD in 1979 (as a stock market timing device), sets the overbought and oversold signals for the S&P Index as a plus or minus 2.50 on the MACD scale. With the NYSE Index he recommends plus or minus 1.20. When the Differential Line crosses into these areas, a signal is generated for buy or sell. Similar levels can be observed and established for any market, thereby eliminating the whipsawing of short price swings. MACD is best used as a long-term analysis tool.

MACD Trendlines, Divergences, and Combinations

Drawing a trendline along the MACD and trading when the trendline is violated can often precede a change in the market. MACD crossovers have more significance when they are preceded by, or are in conjunction with, a violation of the trendline. Aggressive traders can use the trendline break as an action signal and cautious traders can wait for further confirmation. However, it is possible to have a trendline break and a delayed crossover, which can be frustrating.

Divergence is one of the most common and effective patterns in technical analysis. Patterns where the MACD shows Divergence from what the prices are doing can be an important signal, although the pattern needs time to develop and should not be anticipated.

Combining crossovers with other technical patterns can make the MACD system more reliable as a system for trading. Major Trends are identified by using a long-term MACD to confirm the short-term MACD. A monthly MACD can be used to confirm weekly patterns, the weekly pattern can confirm the daily, and the daily can be used for confirmation of intraday. Shorter-term signals can be traded in the direction of longer-term MACD; this helps avoid problems of whipsawing markets. As with other commodities trading systems, the use of stop-loss orders is recommended.

Reversals

Reversals in the direction of a Moving Average are usually more reliable than a Moving Average Crossover. In an uptrend, the following conditions apply:

- Long positions are maintained as long as price remains above the Moving Average.
- If price crosses above the Moving Average, a buy signal is generated.
- If price falls to the Moving Average but doesn't cross it and then moves back up, a buy signal is generated.

If a price drops sharply below the Moving Average Line a rebound toward the Moving Average Line may occur, resulting in a whipsaw action. In a downtrend, short positions are held as long as price remains below the Moving Average. A sell signal is generated when price moves above a declining Moving Average Line. If price moves up to the Moving Average Line but doesn't cross it and drops down again, a sell signal is generated.*

Bollinger Bands (BB)

Developed by John Bollinger (as the Financial News Network's Chief Technical Analyst), Bollinger Bands are Alpha–Beta bands positioned two standard deviations from a 20-day Moving Average. They were developed in an attempt to improve on the concept of fixed-width trading bands (trading bands drawn parallel, at a fixed distance to a Moving Average). Bollinger selected standard deviations because the calculation involves squaring from the average; it makes the system responsive to the short-term price changes.

Overbought or Oversold

The primary purpose of the developed Bollinger Bands is to indicate whether prices are relatively too high or too low. Once the determination is made, the trader can turn to other indicators for trading signals (such as a Relative Strength Indicator).

Customizing

The standard deviation value can be altered. Some traders increase the value of the standard deviation from two standard deviations to 2.5 standard

---

* "The Moving Average Convergence–Divergence Trading Method" from Technical Toolbox, a special monthly feature of *Technical Traders Bulletin,* January 1990.

deviations away from the Moving Average when using a 50-day Moving Average. Conversely, many technicians lower the value of the standard deviation from two to 1.5 standard deviations away from the Moving Average when using a 10-day Moving Average. Any alteration should have the bands containing most but not all of the data.

Bollinger Bands with Other Indicators

Since Bollinger Bands do not generate buy and sell signals alone, they are used with other indicators, such as a Relative Strength Index (RSI) or chart patterns. When price touches one of the bands, it can indicate a continuation of the trend; or it might indicate a Reversal. Bollinger Bands need buy and sell signals from other sources (see Chapter 30, Support and Resistance).

When combined with an indicator such as RSI and chart patterns, Bollinger Bands can become quite powerful. RSI is an excellent indicator with respect to overbought and oversold conditions. When price touches the upper Bollinger Band, and RSI is below 70, it is an indication that the trend will continue. Conversely, when price touches the lower Bollinger Band, and RSI is above 30, it indicates the trend should continue.

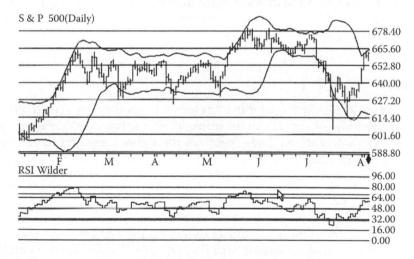

FIGURE 188. Standard & Poor's 500 Index 1996, Bollinger Bands. John Bollinger's "Bollinger Bands" have gained an excellent reputation as a reliable indicator for stock trading and commodities trading. Bollinger's intent was to create a system whereby the market would tell him what it was doing, rather than his trying to impose an external discipline on the market. The bands indicate overbought and oversold, but rely on other indicators for buy and sell signals. Here with RSI Wilder, as discussed in text. Chart Courtesy of AIQ MarketExpert (www.aiqsystems.com).

If a price touches the upper Bollinger Band and RSI is above 70 (possibly approaching 80) the trend may reverse and decline. On the other hand, if a price touches the lower Bollinger Band and RSI is below 30 (possibly approaching 20) it indicates the trend may reverse and move upward.

Driven by Market Variables

The logic behind Bollinger Bands was to create a system driven by market variables, rather than trying to impose an external discipline on the market. It asks the market what is happening, rather than trying to tell the market what it is doing. Charting follows the same line of reasoning and can be effectively used with the bands.*

Stochastics

The Stochastic Oscillator, developed by George Lane, compares a security's price closing level to its price range over a specific period of time. With this indicator, Lane theorized, in an upward-trending market, prices tend to close near their high; and during a downward-trending market, prices tend to close near their low. As an upward trend matures, prices tend to close further away from their high; as a downward trend matures, prices tend to close away from their low.

Clusters

The Stochastic Indicator attempts to determine when prices start to cluster around their low of the day in an uptrending market, and cluster around their high in a downtrend. Lane theorizes these conditions indicate a Trend Reversal is beginning to occur.

%D Line and %K Line

The Stochastic Indicator is plotted as two lines, the %D Line and %K Line. The %D Line is more important than the %K Line. The stochastic is plotted on a chart with values ranging from 0 to 100. The value can never fall below 0 or above 100. Readings above 80 are considered strong and indicate a price is closing near its high.

---

* "Bollinger Bands," TTB Interviews John Bollinger, from *Technical Traders Bulletin*, July 1990.

Readings below 20 are strong and indicate a price is closing near its low. Ordinarily, the %K Line will change direction before the %D Line. However, when the %D Line changes direction prior to the %K Line, a slow and steady Reversal is often indicated.

When both %K and %D Lines change direction, and the faster %K Line changes direction to retest a crossing of the %D Line, though doesn't cross it, the incident confirms stability of the prior Reversal. A powerful move is under way when the indicator reaches its extremes around 0 and 100. Following a Pullback in price, if the indicator retests extremes, a good entry point is indicated. Many times, when the %K or %D Lines begin to flatten out, the action becomes an indication the trend will reverse during the next trading range.

Periodicity of D

For commodities, the number of periods to use in stochastics is based on the cycle of the commodity being traded. First, determine the cycle of the commodity, then use the number of bars for stochastics corresponding to one half of the period of the cycle. If an 18-day cycle is observed, 9-day stochastics are used. Shorter-term stochastics should be used to fine-tune an entry or exit at the point of decision. However, the analyst should immediately revert back to the optimum stochastic and be certain to trade with the trend.*

Divergence

Quite often Divergence appears on the chart. The price may be making higher highs, but the Stochastic Oscillator is making lower lows. Or, conversely, price may be making lower highs, and the Stochastic Oscillator is making higher highs. In either case, the indicator is often demonstrating a change in price before price itself is changing.

The Stochastic Oscillator analysis system was originally developed by George Lane back in the mid-1950s. At first, he believed the only valid signal was the Divergence between %D and the securities price. Later, he recanted and stated this was not strictly true and, furthermore, adherence to the original could get a beginning analyst into trouble.

In an uptrending market, Lane has learned, many congested Tops, often Double Tops or Triple Tops (see Chapter 9, Important Reversal Patterns, for more information on Double and Triple Tops), can take several time periods to turn down and approach the bottom trendline. He refers to them as "Garbage Tops."

* "Stochastics Revisited" by George C. Lane, Technical Toolbox, a special monthly feature of *Technical Traders Bulletin*, December 1990.

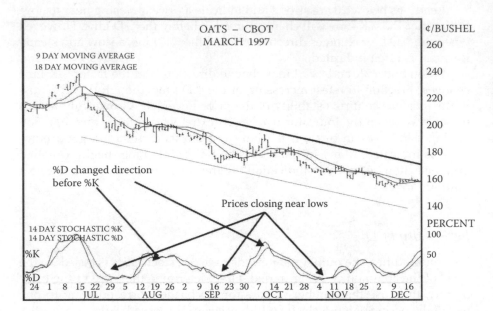

FIGURE 189.   Oats Futures (with stochastic chart), May 1997. Reversals were signaled when the %D changed direction prior to %K's change in late August and early October. Prices closed near their lows in mid-July, late September. Late October to early November prices also closed near their lows, as shown by both %K and %D Lines being at the bottom of their range. Chart courtesy of Market Research, Inc. (www.barchart.com).

When prices finally do turn down, they often bottom quickly and turn right back up again, creating "Spike Bottoms." These are to be expected in an uptrending market. Knowledge of them can be helpful in strong trending markets.

The 0% and 100% Misunderstandings

A misunderstanding some stochastic analysts have refers to the %K reaching the extremes of 100% or 0%. When the %K Line reaches 100%, it does not mean that the prices can't go higher. Conversely, even though the %K is at zero, prices can still go lower. Zero is not necessarily a Bottom; in fact, the opposite could be true. The extremes denote strength at the 100% level and extreme weakness at zero.* The misunderstanding comes from levels commonly believed to indicate "overbought" or "oversold." When the %K and %D Lines rise above 75%, it is considered an overbought situation.

---

* "Stochastics Revisited" by George C. Lane, Technical Toolbox, a special monthly feature of *Technical Traders Bulletin*, December 1990.

Conversely, if they drop below 25%, it is considered oversold (some traders use 80% and 20% for the indicator levels). When the move is a sustained move, the price decline can continue for an extended period, with the oscillator remaining near the bottom.

Check the Weekly/Monthly

Stochastics, as well as trend charting, should always look at the bigger picture as well as the tight focus. If a daily chart is followed, it should be compared to a weekly chart for a better understanding of what is happening in the longer term. The longer-term trend chart helps the analyst to understand developments leading up to the current market situation.

Stochastics, used in combination with conventional charting techniques and common sense, can work well. For example, if an unviolated trend is in force, with no Consolidations or Reversal Patterns forming, the stochastic signal is likely false. If, however, a Symmetrical Triangle is forming and a trend is being violated, the signal is confirmed.

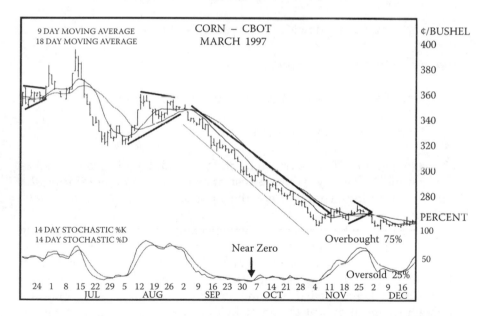

FIGURE 190. Corn Futures, March 1997. Even though the Stochastic Lines are nearly zero, many would consider this oversold. The price of the corn futures continues to decline. Some erroneously believe a Reversal is imminent when the lines are near zero. Near zero signifies extreme weakness. In a sustained move, the values can remain in the below 25% area for some time. In this example, the oscillator remained low from early September through early November. Chart courtesy of Market Research, Inc. (www.barchart.com).

Stochastics Formula

Stochastics charts begin with three value calculations:

- The Raw Value
- %K
- %D

The three values are plotted on a scale from 0 to 100. If the raw value and %K are plotted on the same chart, it results in "fast stochastics." Fast stochastics show several up and down swings in a short period of time. When the %K and %D are used, they create "slow stochastics." Slow stochastics have smoothed data lines.

$$\text{Stoachastics Raw Value} = 100 \times \frac{\text{last close} - \text{20-day low}}{\text{20-day high} - \text{20-day low}}$$

%K is a 3-day Moving Average of the raw value.

%D is a 3-day Moving Average of the %K.

Updating Stochastics Formula

New %K = ⅔ previous %K + ⅓ new stochastics raw value.

New %D = ⅔ previous %D + ⅓ %K.

Raw value requires 20 days of information; the 20-day high is the highest price and the 20-day low is the lowest price for a commodity during that 20-day time period. They are not the high and low price from 20 days previous.

Stochastics can be useful in analyzing changes in commodities trading. It has been around for more than 30 years and has a well-established track record. Even so, like most systems of analysis, it is best used in combination with conventional charting techniques and common sense. The price of the commodity is being traded, not the stochastic signal or other indicator. Although technical indicators can be helpful, they must always be viewed in the context of what is happening with the market trend.

Volume and Open Interest

Investors always like to see strong volume on market advances and light volume on declines. Volume is considered an important indicator of market sentiment in the stock market. It is also important, but different, in the futures markets.

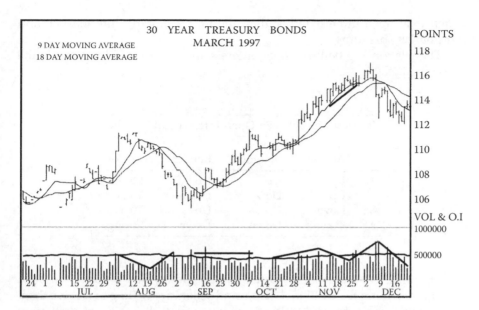

FIGURE 191. 30-Year Treasury Bonds, March 1997 Futures. With futures trading, volume cannot push the market because for every buyer there must be a seller. Although volume is part of the big picture, forecasting from volume can be unreliable. Notice the volume decline in November, even though prices were still advancing. (See Chapter 6, Important Reversal Patterns, for more information on volume.) Chart courtesy of Market Research, Inc. (www.barchart.com).

Volume as Confirmation

Volume patterns are considered normal on a day-to-day basis, and any sudden change represents a Divergence. Volume doesn't have the same significance as with equity trading and the information is comparatively delayed. Although volume is part of the picture, it is only somewhat useful as a confirmation (in hindsight) of what other indicators are signaling.

Money Flow

Open-interest figures are normally plotted on a line above the volume information. In a general sense, they measure the amount of money flowing into and out of the futures market. When both sides of a trade are new to the market, the open interest increases. If one side is new and the other is old, open interest is unchanged. When both sides close out, open interest declines.

Analysis of open interest is complicated by *(EN: the following factors:)* seasonal implications (e.g., hedging activities tend to be heaviest at harvest time); speculative interest; whether the futures are nearby (it is better to watch total open interest rather than month by month); intermarket; and intramarket spreading.

The relationship between open interest and volume is illustrated in the following table:

	Price Action	Open Volume	Interest	Market
Relationship Between Open Interest and Volume:				
1.	Up	Up	Up	Strong
2.	Up	Down	Down	Weak
3.	Down	Up	Up	Weak
4.	Down	Down	Down	Strong

Open interest and prices will rise as new money flows into the market. Buyers are willing to pay higher prices and sellers are willing to receive them (the number of buyers and sellers is always equal). It is a Bullish situation for the commodity.

When prices rise and open interest declines, there are few new buyers and money is leaving the market. Rallies can be caused by the covering of short positions exiting the market. Although the situation can obviously be Bullish for the short term, it will turn Bearish. Any rally will falter without new money coming into the market; however, short covering can take longer than expected.

When prices are falling and open interest is rising, and new money is coming into the market and there is selling pressure, it is considered Bearish.

Prices fall and open interest falls is the opposite of situation 2. Short sellers are staying in the market and long-position holders are closing. There is little new money coming into the market and the situation is initially Bearish, but can turn Bullish. As the declining momentum slows, short sellers will quickly begin to cover and new money often returns.

New Money

Futures are dependent on new money for price stability and growth because for every buyer there is a seller. With equity stocks, it is possible to have pressure situations with more buyers than sellers or the other way around. It is the new money in futures that creates the rising prices in an uptrend. New money coming in will cause the open interest and volume to rise, but to be a truly Bullish indicator, they must be accompanied by rising prices. The action might be over by the time all three are observed.

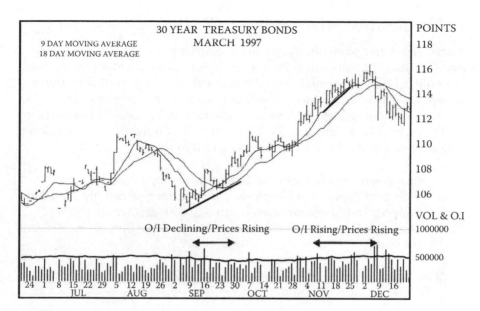

FIGURE 192. 30-Year Treasury Bonds, March 1997 Futures. When prices rise and open interest declines, there are few new buyers and money is leaving the market. Rallies can be caused by the covering of short positions exiting the market. Although the situation can obviously be Bullish for the short term, it will turn Bearish. In this example it didn't turn so Bearish, but rather sideways until the open interest began to increase with prices. The rising prices showed the entrance of new money. Rallies will falter without new money coming into the market; however, short covering can take longer than expected. Note the decline in open interest even though prices advanced. Open interest didn't show a significant increase until early November. Chart courtesy of Market Research, Inc. (www.barchart.com).

Even though volume and open interest data have value as far as the big picture is concerned, the data can be late and unreliable if used alone for forecasting short-term. Other indicators can be more reliable, with volume and open interest used in a more general sense or for confirmation.

Volume data with equities can have greater significance because of immediacy and the fact that an imbalance of buyers and sellers can exist. In futures trading there is a seller for every buyer. Open interest data can have some significance, but it is often not as reliable as other indicators for trading purposes.*

* "Volume and Open Interest" from the Technical Toolbox, a special monthly feature of the *Technical Traders Bulletin,* July 1990.

Wilder Relative Strength Index (RSI)

Although relative strength, comparing a security price to a benchmark index price (such as the Standard & Poor's 500 Index), has existed for many years, the Wilder Relative Strength Index was developed by J. Welles Wilder as a system for giving actual buy and sell signals in a changing market.

Relative Strength is often used to identify price tops and bottoms by keying on specific levels (usually "30" and "70") on the RSI chart, which is scaled from 0–100. The RSI can also be useful to show:

1. Movement which might not be as readily apparent on the bar chart.
2. Swing failures above 70 or below 30, warning of coming Reversals.
3. Support and Resistance Levels appear with greater clarity.
4. Divergence between the RSI and price can often be a useful Reversal indicator.

The Relative Strength Index requires a certain amount of lead time in order to operate successfully.

Swing Failures ("W" Formations)

When a Relative Strength Index Line spikes down and penetrates 30 on the Index Scale, then moves up, then is followed by another down spike (less than the first), a buy signal is generated as the index line rises to a level equal to the middle of the "W" Formation. A sell signal appears in a similar manner, but spiking up rather than down (an upside down "W"), above 70 on the index scale.

Divergence

Probably the most common and significant trend pattern in virtually all technical indicators is the pattern of Divergence. Divergence refers to instruments which normally follow the same general direction together moving apart and proceding in different directions, and indicates trend weakness in the current direction. It often signals a reliable Reversal. Divergences in trends are analyzed between the Dow Industrial Average as compared to the Dow Transportation Average, stock prices compared to indexes (e.g., Standard & Poor's 500 Index) or between futures prices and a 10- to 14-day Relative Strength Index. Traders will often wait for a confirmation of a Divergence before placing their transactions in order to not be taken in by false signals.

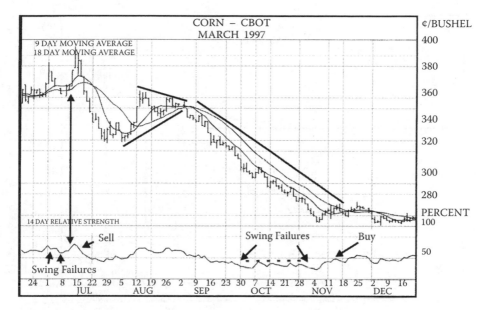

FIGURE 193. Corn Futures, March 1997. The sell signal in July had excellent timing for a trade. The buy signal appeared in the 14-day Relative Strength Index as the line penetrated the high point between the Swing Failures in early October and early November. Also, there is an important Divergence between the RSI moving sideways and the downtrend of prices. Divergence between prices and a Relative Strength Index is considered an important Reversal signal. The late July through August time period possibly has other Failure Swings followed by penetrations, but they are not as well defined as the others. Chart courtesy of Market Research, Inc. (www.bar-chart.com).

Time Periods

Although the most popular time period appears to be the 14-day Relative Strength Index, other time periods can be used. Shorter, 6-day RSIs are frequently used for intraday analysis to find profit-taking points after the RSI reaches 75 or higher and pulls back. The shorter RSI is more responsive in showing a pause in the current trend. Some go further and use a very sensitive 3-day RSI to determine reentry points as the indicator moves back to neither overbought nor oversold (between 70 and 30). A 10-week RSI Divergence is often used with financials. It frequently gives good signals in stock indices, bonds, and currencies. However, weekly signals appear to be somewhat less accurate and frequent in other markets.*

---

* "Relative Strength Index (RSI)" from the Technical Toolbox of the *Technical Traders Bulletin,* September 1989.

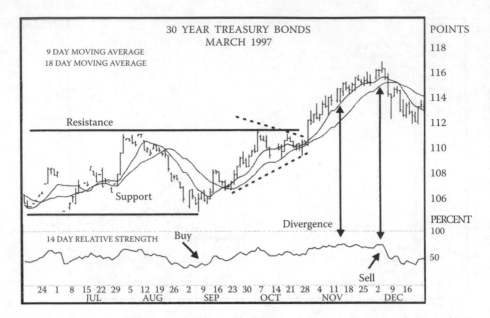

FIGURE 194. 30-Year Treasury Bond Futures, March 1997. Overbought is above 70 and oversold below 30. The RSI dropped to the 30 mark in late August, but didn't sharply penetrate, showing a weak buy signal for the sensitivity of this 14-day indicator. Although a sell signal was generated after the above 70 Failure Swings in November, an even stronger signal was given by the Divergence between the futures prices and the Relative Strength Index. (See Chapter 12, Support and Resistance.) Chart courtesy of Market Research, Inc. (www.barchart.com).

Relative Strength Formula

RSI is based on the difference between the average of the closing price on up days vs. the average closing price on the down days. A time period of 14 days is common, but other periods can also be used.

$$RSI = 100 - \left(100/I + U/D\right)$$

U = average of upward price closes (EMA of gains)
D = average of downward price closes (EMA of losses)

Relative Strength Indexes have become popular as countertrend oscillators. They give reliable overbought and oversold indications in most markets and can show long-term Divergence Patterns indicating Major Tops and Bottoms. The buy and sell signals given by an RSI are generally clear, but can be adjusted to greater sensitivity for short-term or long-term trading.

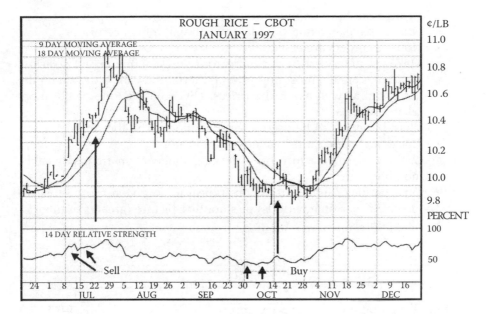

FIGURE 195. Rough Rice Futures, January 1997. The signals won't precisely hit the price bottom or top, but with Rough Rice they hit reasonable levels before the Reversals. The sell signal came in July, after the RSI (above the 70 level) showed two down spikes with an upturn rising above the middle between the spikes. The buy signal came after a similar situation (below the 30 level) in October. Chart courtesy of Market Research, Inc. (www.barchart.com).

Chart patterns offer commodities traders another visual perspective of where prices are likely to go and when they are likely to reverse. Although chart patterns have a history of success and need no validation, it is interesting to see how well they match the signals given by oscillators, bands, Moving Averages, and other indicators. Identical signals of trend and change between chart patterns and other indicators are common. In fact, if identical signals do not appear, the validity of those appearing should be questioned. One of the most frustrating tendencies of all indicators is to give false signals from time to time. The frustration can be partly moderated by using more than one signal-producing indicator. Confirmed signals and trends, with experience and understanding of the markets, produce profitable trading results.

Important Concepts in Commodities/Derivatives Trading

- Prices are influenced by external factors such as weather changes, supply, and demand.
- Futures trading is mostly made up of hedgers and speculators in for a shorter period of time than with stock trading.

- Futures can have an unlimited number of contracts open.
- Futures have an expiration date which will influence prices.
- Stop-loss orders are essential.
- Make use of more than one indicator to make a buy or sell decision.
- Trendlines are the most important patterns and can be drawn on the indicators as well as on the prices. Divergence is one of the more reliable signals.
- Chart patterns can be used in combination with other indicators.
- Trades are made on prices, not on indicators.
- Look at the big picture by observing longer-term trends (weekly, monthly).
- Time periods can be altered on indicators to give a more sensitive picture (fewer time periods) or smoother picture (greater number of time periods).

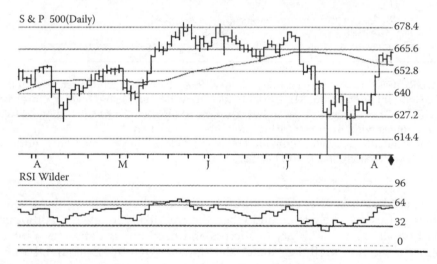

FIGURE 196. Standard & Poor's 500 Index Futures (SPX). Using a 3-day period for a Wilder RSI gives a clear buy signal, whereas the 14-day time period is indefinite. The shorter time period is more sensitive to recent moves and can give more definite buy signals. Charts Courtesy of AIQ MarketExpert (www.aiqsystems.com). (Figure 197 on the following page also illustrates this concept.)

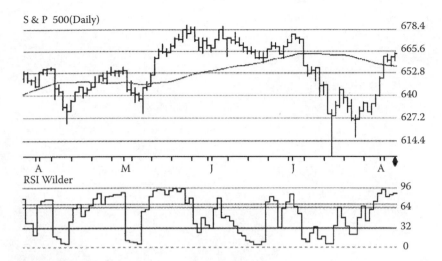

FIGURE 197. Standard & Poor's 500 Index Futures (SPX). Using a 3-day period for a Wilder RSI gives a clear buy signal, whereas the 14-day time period is indefinite. The shorter time period is more sensitive to recent moves and can give more definite buy signals. Charts Courtesy of AIQ MarketExpert (www.aiqsystems.com).

appendix D

Resources

- Section 1: Important and Indispensable Sites
- Section 2: References for Further Study
- Section 3: Investment-Oriented Sites
- Section 4: The Sharpe Ratio
- Section 5: Calculating Volatility and Examples of Professional Risk Analysis
- Section 6: Gambler's Ruin
- Section 7: The Essence of Fundamental Analysis
- Section 8: Software Packages and Internet Technical Analysis Sites

Section 1
Important and Indispensable Sites

Contact information for:

john magee technical analysis::delphic options research ltd (jmta::dor)

email	bassetti@edwards-magee.com
jmta::dor website	www.edwards-magee.com

SEC Enforcement	enforcement@sec.gov

(Whenever I receive touts or investment spam, I immediately forward it to this important branch of the SEC. All responsible investors should do the same.)

TEKNIPLAT chart paper	visit www.edwards-magee.com
Volatilities and Options:	www.optionstrategist.com
	www.cboe.com
Software reviews and info	www.traders.com
Software demos and packages	www.omegaresearch.com
	www.comstar.com
	www.aiqsystems.com
	www.tradestation.com
	www.equis.com
Web analysis site	www.prophet.net
Morningstar	www.morningstar.net
Industry Evaluations	www.gomez.com
Mutual Fund Cost Calculator	www.sec.gov/mfcc-int.htm
Internet Analysis	www.stockcharts.com

Section 2
References for Further Study

On Volatilities and Options:	www.optionstrategist.com
(and futures)	www.cboe.com
DOW Futures and Options	www.cbot.com
AMEX ishares (DIA, QQQ, ETC)	www.amex.com
On betas	www.finance.yahoo.com

On Risk:
Value at Risk, Jorion, Phillipe; New York, John Wiley & Sons, 1996.
Against the Gods, Bernstein, Peter; New York, John Wiley & Sons, 1996.
Risk Management 101 (software), Zoologic Inc.
See also Appendix E and Chapter 42

On Candlesticks:
Japanese Candlestick Charting Techniques, Nison, Steve; NYIF, New York, 1991.
Beyond Candlesticks, Nison, Steve; New York, John Wiley & Sons, 1994.

On Futures:
Schwager on Futures, Technical Analysis, Schwager, Jack; John Wiley & Sons, 1996
(and other titles by Schwager in References).

On Portfolio Management:
The Journal of Portfolio Management
Risk Management 101 (software), Zoologic Inc.

Section 3
Investment Oriented Sites

AARP Investment Program	www.aarp.scudder.com
Accutrade	www.accutrade.com
ADR.com	www.adr.com
American Association of Individual Investors	www.aaii.com
American Century	www.americancentury.com
American Express Financial Services	www.americanexpress.com/direct
(American Express now advertises free trades for some accounts)	
American Stock Exchange	www.amex.com
Ameritrade (has little-advertised free trade site)	www.ameritrade.com
Annual Report Gallery	www.reportgallery.com
Barron's	www.barrons.com
BigCharts	www.bigcharts.com
Bloomberg Financial	www.bloomberg.com
Bonds Online	www.bondsonline.com

Briefing.com	www.briefing.com
Brill's Mutual Funds Interactive	www.fundsinteractive.com
Business Week	www.businessweek.com
CBS MarketWatch	www.marketwatch.com
Chicago Board of Options Exchange	www.cboe.com
CNNFN	www.cnnfn.com
DailyStocks	www.dailystocks.com
Excite	www.excite.com
Federal Deposit Insurance Corp	www.fdic.gov
Federal Trade Commission	www.ftc.gov
Fidelity Investments	www.fidelity.com
Financial Times	www.ft.com
Forrester Research	www.forrester.com
FundFocus	www.fundfocus.com
Fund Spot	www.fundspot.com
Gomez Advisers	www.gomez.com
H&R Block	www.hrblock.com
Hoover's StockScreener	www.stockscreener.com
IPO Central	www.ipocentral.com
Lombard	www.lombard.com
Marketplayer	www.marketplayer.com
Market Technician's Assoc.	www.mta.org
Microsoft MoneyCentral	www.moneycentral.com
Morningstar	www.morningstar.net
National Assoc. of Securities Dealers	www.nasd.com
National Discount Brokers	www.ndb.com
Net Investor	www.netinvestor.com
New York Stock Exchange	www.nyse.com
Online Investor	www.onlineinvestor.com
Philadelphia Stock Exchange	www.phlx.com
Quick & Reilly	www.quickwaynet.com
Quicken	www.quicken.com
Quicken Financial Network	www.qfn.com
Realty Stocks	www.realtystocks.com
Reuters	www.reuters.com
Schwab, Charles	www.schwab.com
SEC Enforcement	enforcement@sec.gov
Securities and Exchange Commission	www.sec.gov
Securities Industry Association	www.sia.com
Securities Investor Protection Corporation	www.sipc.org
SmartMoney	www.smartmoney.com
Social Security Online	www.ssa.gov
Standard & Poor's Fund Analyst	www.micropal.com
Standard & Poor's Ratings Services	www.ratingsdirect.com
Stock Guide	www.stockguide.com
Stockpoint	www.stockpoint.com
Suretrade	www.suretrade.com
1040.com	www.1040.com
The Motley Fool	www.fool.com

TheStreet.com	www.thestreet.com
Technical Securities Analyst Association of San Francisco	www.tsaa.org
T. Rowe Price	www.troweprice.com
TreasuryDirect	www.publicdebt.treas.gov
VanguardBrokerage Services	www.vanguard.com
Wall Street Access	www.wsaccess.com
Wall Street Journal Interactive Ed	www.wsj.com
Yahoo! Finance	www.finance.yahoo.com
Zacks Investment Research	www.zacks.com
ZD Interactive Investor	www.zdii.com

Brokerage Houses

Waterhouse Securities	www.tdwaterhouse.com 800-934-4134
A. B. Watley	www.abwatley.com 888-229-2853
Web Street Securities	www.webstreetsecurities.com 800-932-0438
Jack White	www.jackwhiteco.com 800-753-1700
WitCapital	www.witcapital.com 888-494-8227
Net Investor	www.netinvestor.com 800-638-4250
Quick & Reilly	www.quickwaynet.com 800-672-7220
Charles Schwab	www.schwab.com 800-435-4000
Suretrade	www.suretrade.com 401-642-6900
Vanguard Brokerage Services	www.vanguard.com 800-992-8327
Wall Street Access	www.wsaccess.com 888-925-5782
Empire Financial Group, Inc.	www.lowfees.com 800-900-8101
E*TRADE	www.etrade.com 800-786-2575
Lombard	www.lombard.com
National Discount Brokers	www.ndb.com 800-888-3999
Accutrade	www.accutrade.com 800-494-8939
Ameritrade	www.tdameritrade.com 800-326-7507
See also	www.freetrade.com
Discover Brokerage	www.discoverbrokerage.com 800-688-3462
DLJ Direct	www.dljdirect.com 800-825-5723
Datek Online	www.datek.com
Discover Brokerage	www.discoverbrokerage.com
DLJ Direct	www.dljdirect.com
Dow Jones Markets	www.djmarkets.com
DRIP Central	www.dripcentral.com
Empire Financial Group	www.lowfees.com

Section 4
The Sharpe Ratio

Although this formula is flawed, it will not hinder the reader to know about it and understand it. Believing in it would be quite a different matter, however. The Sharpe Ratio itself is as follows:

$$SR = (E = 1)/sd$$

where
E   is the expected return
I   is the risk-free interest rate
sd is the standard deviation of returns.

The effect of this inflexible formula is to stick the trader with a measuring tool of little use to the practical trader. It assumes that volatility of returns as measured by sd equals risk (the common academic problem). In the inflexibility of the sd calculation, it fails to measure the most important fact in trading, the maximum drawdown, or, the inevitable fluctuations in gains and losses. Specifically, the greatest expected or experienced loss, the retracement from greatest high to greatest low, and the sequences of these experiences.

Section 5
Calculating Volatility

To calculate volatility of a portfolio, first find the difference between each return and the average. Then square each difference and add them together. Divide the sum by the number of returns minus one. This result is known as the variance. Finally, take the square root of the variance to get the volatility. Combining these steps into a formula:

Step 1: Calculate the average return.
Step 2: Calculate the deviation of each return.
Step 3: Square each period's deviation.
Step 4: Add them together.
Step 5: Divide the sum by the number of periods minus 1.
Step 6: Take the square root.

$$\sigma = \sqrt{\frac{\sum_{i=1}^{n}\left(R_i - \mu\right)^2}{n-1}}$$

DIAGRAM 12. Volatility formula. Illustrated is the formula for computing volatility. (1) Calculate the average return; (2) calculate the deviation of each return; (3) square each period's deviation; (4) add them together; (5) divide the sum by the number of periods minus 1 to get the variance; (6) take the square root.

Portfolio Analysis Screens

Diagrams 13 And 14 deal with portfolio risk and profit analysis. Illustrated are the sophisticated quantitative portfolio Profit and Risk reports of Delphic Options Research as implemented for Standard & Poor's trading systems and Prudential Securities to give the reader an appreciation of the depth and complexity of professional thinking about risk and portfolio analysis. The originals of these reports were designed by Blair Hull and Lester Loops for their own use in market making.

PORTFOLIO RISK ANALYSIS (.30 *Filename*)

OMS+	.30	PORTFOLIO RISK ANALYSIS								3/24/87	10:55:28	
--STOCK--		----DELTAS----										
SYM	POS	OPTION	TOTAL	PROFIT	BETA	$BETA	$DELTA	$GAMMA	$THETA	$RISK	%RISK	
FDX	2800	−3063	−263	16734	1.60	−32081	−7017	158136	−121	18075	7.3	
GE	3200	−3089	110	12632	.95	11374	2993	120104	−16	13000	5.3	
HWP	−6200	5682	−517	8270	1.20	−45959	−13404	−522208	734	56617	22.9	
LIT	−6700	0	−6700	0	1.40	−569834	−122107	0	0	122107	49.3	
NSM	3600	−4080	−480	10411	1.45	−21076	−7267	150464	−169	17436	7.0	
XRX	−3600	3991	391	−882	1.05	18132	4835	186506	−260	20232	8.2	
*TOT	−6900	−559	−7459	47165		−639444	−141969	93000	166	247470	100.0	

AVERAGE VOLATILITY:	.338
EQUIVALENT MARKET EQUITY:	−419613.40
PORTFOLIO PROFIT RATIO:	.191
PORTFOLIO PROFIT GAMMA RATIO:	4.815

DIAGRAM 13.   Risk analysis.

Key: portfolio risk report. The Portfolio Risk Analysis screen summarizes delta, profit, and several measures of risk for a portfolio of user-specified stocks and options.

The screen displays:

STOCK SYM = The stock symbol;
STOCK POS = The stock position, or number of shares owned;
DELTAS TOTAL = The sum of the stock deltas and option deltas;
BETA = The stock beta for each stock (implementation pending);
$BETA = $The dollar risk due to movement of the general market:
    $Beta = (Delta × Stock Price) × Beta;
$DELT = An annualized risk figure based on Position imbalance:
    $Delta = (Total Delta × Stock Price) × Volatility;
$GAM = An annualized risk figure based on curvature of the position. A positive $Gamma
    indicates a backspread, and a negative $Gamma indicates a vertical position: $Gamma =
    Total Gamma × (Stock Price × Volatility);
$THETA = Theoretical dollar amount a position will gain or lose in one day if the stock price
    remains unchanged;
$RISK = The annualized standard deviation of the position based upon a composite of $Delta
    and $Gamma;
%RISK = Percent of portfolio risk in each position;
TOT = Totals for each of the above categories;
AVERAGE VOLATILITY = Average volatility for the stocks;
EQUIVALENT MARKET EQUITY = Sum of each of the stock prices multiplied by their total deltas;
PORTFOLIO PROFIT RATIO = Total portfolio profit divided by the total portfolio risk;
PORTFOLIO PROFIT GAMMA RATIO = Total portfolio profit divided by the portfolio $Gamma
    squared.

PORTFOLIO PROFIT ANALYSIS (.31 *Filename*)

		STOCK	DELTAS		M TO M	PROFIT				$	$	%
SYM	POS	OPTION	TOTAL	M TO M	TOTAL	/DAY	/RISK	/DY/RISK	THETA	RISK	RISK
FDX	2800	−3063	−263	423162	16734	213	.93	4.31	−121	18075	7.3
GE	3200	−3089	110	704006	12632	107	.97	3.01	.16	13000	5.3
HWP	−6200	5682	−517	53787	8270	150	.15	.97	734	56617	22.9
LIT	−6700	0	−6700	−407025	0	0	.00	.00	0	122107	49.3
NSM	3600	−4080	−480	157293	10411	105	.60	2.21	−169	17436	7.0
XRX	−3600	3991	391	−4431	−882	−18	−.04	−.34	−260	20232	8.2
·				·							
·				·							
·											·
·											·
*TOT	−6900		−559	−7459	926792	47165	557	.19	.00	166	247470	100.0

The header row reads: `OMS+ .31 PORTFOLIO PROFIT ANALYSIS    3/24/87    10:55:28`

AVERAGE VOLATILITY:	.338
EQUIVALENT MARKET EQUITY:	−419613.40
PORTFOLIO PROFIT RATIO:	.191
PORTFOLIO PROFIT GAMMA RATIO:	4.815

DIAGRAM 14. Profit analysis.
Key: portfolio profit report. The Portfolio Profit Analysis screen summarizes delta, profit, and several measures of profit for a portfolio of user- specified stocks and options.

The screen displays:

STOCK SYM = The stock symbol;
STOCK POS − Stock position, or number of shares owned;
DELTAS OPTION = Total delta of the option position;
DELTAS TOTAL = Sum of the stock deltas and option deltas;
M TO M − Mark to market: Total value of stock and options positions based upon market prices;
PROFIT TOTAL = Total theoretical profit for each position;
PROFIT/DAY = Theoretical profit divided by the number of days to expiration;
PROFIT/RISK = Ratio of theoretical profit to risk;
PROFIT/DY/RISK = Ratio of theoretical profit per day to risk;
$THETA = Theoretical dollar amount a position will gain or lose in one day if the stock price remains unchanged;
$RISK = The annualized standard deviation of the position based upon a composite of $Delta and $Gamma;
%RISK = Percent of portfolio risk in each position;
TOT = Totals for each of the above categories;
AVERAGE VOLATILITY = Average volatility for the stocks;
EQUIVALENT MARKET EQUITY = Sum of each of the stock prices multiplied by their total deltas;
PORTFOLIO PROFIT RATIO = Total portfolio profit divided by the total portfolio risk;
PORTFOLIO PROFIT GAMMA RATIO = Total portfolio profit divided by the portfolio $Gamma squared.

Section 6
Gambler's Ruin

Reprinted from *The Education of a Speculator* by Victor Niederhoffer. With permission.

The classic gambler's ruin problem, which applies to all speculative situations, can be framed this way. A speculator with initial capital of C plays a game with a casino: he wins $1.00 each play with probability P, or loses $1.00

with probability Q, which is 1 − P. The speculator plans to stay in the game until his capital appreciates to A or depreciates to ruin at 0. It can be shown that, in such a game, the speculator's probability of ruin is:

$$\frac{(Q/P)^A - (Q/P)^C}{(Q/P)^A - 1}$$

Plugging numbers into the formula, a speculator who has a 60% chance of winning each play, and who starts with $1.00 and tries to run it to $10.00, will face a 66.1% chance of ruin for the session. Because he has a 33.9% chance (100% − 66.1%) of finishing the session with $10.00, his expected final bankroll is $3.39. He started with $1.00, so he expects to gain $2.39.

The table below summarizes the expected gains for a gambling session, given initial capital C and probability P of winning each day. With a 60% chance of winning, the size of the bankroll becomes critical. By starting with $4.00 rather than $1.00, the speculator increases his expected gain from $2.39 to $4.17 — an increase akin to the winning edge held by strong, well-funded players in a poker game. Above a $4.00 bankroll, the decreased risk of ruin is more than offset by the diminished benefit of achieving the $10.00 goal. For example, with capital of $9.00, ruin is very rare, but the upside is only $1.00 ($10.00 − $9.00).

A Gambler's Expected Gain

Capital Probability	$1.00	$2.00	$3.00	$4.00	$5.00	$6.00	$7.00	$8.00	$9.00
100%	$9.00	$8.00	$7.00	$6.00	$5.00	$4.00	$3.00	$2.00	$1.00
90%	7.89	7.88	6.99	6.00	5.00	4.00	3.00	2.00	1.00
80%	6.50	7.38	6.84	5.96	4.99	4.00	3.00	2.00	1.00
70%	4.72	6.16	6.21	5.66	4.86	3.94	2.98	1.99	1.00
60%	2.39	3.65	+.16	4.17	3.84	3.28	2.58	1.78	0.91

This idealized formulation of the gambler's ruin problem demonstrates the tradeoff that arises in practical trading. The speculator wants to bet lightly enough, relative to his capital, to fend off gambler's ruin, but heavily enough to make his desired rate of return. Unfortunately, the real-life speculator doesn't know his true odds of winning on each trade, so he can't look up the optimum betting levels in a table.

When the odds of success are less than 50%, the situation changes.

Whereas the player with an edge should bet small, trying to grind out a profit, the player with the worst of it is better advised to go for the home run, betting the maximum, because this is the only way he can end up a winner. This explains, in part, why casinos have limits on the stakes that players can use against them, and why the exchanges have established position limits on what the public can hold.

Section 7

From the *John Magee Market Letters* December 15, 1984
(by Richard McDermott)

The Elliott Wave Theory: Perspective and Comments

This week we had the pleasure of attending the December meeting of the Market Technicians Association of New York.

Long-term subscribers will remember the MTANY as the organization which honored John Magee with its "Man of the Year" award in 1978. The speaker was Robert Prechter, publisher of "The Elliott Wave Theorist," an investment advisory which bases its forecasts on interpretations of R.N. Elliott's work on the stock market.

Of primary interest to SAS subscribers are Prechter's comments on technical analysis itself. The Elliott Wave Theory, it must be remembered, is really no more than a "catalog" of stock market price movements, laid one on top of the other, so to speak, until a grand, underlying, and enduring pattern is observed; in short, pure *technical* analysis. Among Prechter's definitions and observations regarding fundamental analysis are the following:

1. "First let's define 'technical' versus 'fundamental' data ... technical data is that which is generated by the action of the market under study."
2. "The main problem with fundamental analysis is that its indicators are removed from the market itself. The analyst assumes causality between external events and market movements, a concept which is almost certainly false. But, just as important, and less recognized, is that fundamental analysis almost always requires a *forecast of the fundamental data itself* before conclusions about the market are drawn. The analyst is then forced to take a second step in coming to a conclusion about how those forecasted events will affect the markets! Technicians only have one step to take, which gives them an edge right off the bat. Their main advantage is that they don't have to forecast their indicators."
3. "What's worse, even the fundamentalists' second step is probably a process built on quicksand.... The most common application of fundamental analysis is estimating companies' earnings for both the current year and next year, and recommending stocks on that basis....And the record on that basis alone is very poor, as Barron's pointed out in a June 4 article, which showed that earnings estimates averaged 18% error in the thirty DJIA stocks for any year already completed and 54% error for the year ahead. The weakest link, however, is the assumption that correct earnings estimates are a basis for

choosing stock market winners. According to a table in the same Barron's article, a purchase of the ten DJIA stocks with the best earnings estimates would have produced a ten-year cumulative gain of 40.5%, while choosing the ten DJIA with the worst earnings estimates would have produced a whopping 142.5% gain."

We enjoyed Prechter's polished exposition of a technical approach different from our own. As for his observations about fundamental analysis, we simply couldn't agree more.

Section 8

The first cave men, fighting over resources used teeth and claws. The nature of warfare was changed forever when one of the smarter ones picked up a tree branch. Then another smart one discovered the principle of artillery and picked up a rock. Naïve and arrogant traders laughed at Wyckoff's charts. Market makers on the Pacfific Coast Options Exchange sniggered at Blair Hull when he started appearing on the floor with print outs. In the days of the wooden racquet squash players hated the *arrivistes* who appeared with metal and then composite racquets.

No longer. The last to adopt the new weapons is a dead man. Charts showed their power and so did Hull's wonky print outs made with the Black Scholes Model. The losers figured out pretty quickly they needed new weapons. With that dissertation on the epistemology of warfare I present some of my favorite weapons in the following software and Internet sites. No attempt whatsoever is made to be comprehensive or encyclopedic. On the contrary, idiosyncrasy is my operating method and no disfavor is implied to those not included here.

For myself, three desktop software packages are powerful and sufficient for all the needs of a technical analyst: AIQ Trading Expert Pro (aiqsystems.com); Metastock 9.0 (equis.com); and TradeStation 2000i (tradestation.com). The reader will find examples of charts sprinkled throughout this book, supplementing the beautiful hand drawn charts of Magee. All these packages have the basic requirements necessary for technical chart analysis, basic charting on readily available data and portfolio. I have said before that all the chart analyst really needs is the ability to draw lines on a chart ... and then perhaps to see the chart as a line chart, or a candlestick chart or.... And so on and so on. The analyst is soon seduced by the dazzling features, AND the analysis is enriched and made more powerful. And even if one says (as I do) when he looks at an oversold tool "What do I need that for? I saw it on the bar chart." The analyst finds himself wanting to know more about %R. If it worked for Larry Williams there must be something in it.

AIQ – TRADING EXPERT PRO

AIQ's package includes an on-screen control panel and scrolling indicator boxes which are color coded and this information is synthesized in an indicator barometer. Data management is smooth and easy and the user may use a system module to create and test his own trading ideas. A panoply of reports are available to aid the investor. For the trader real time alerts are a feature. A portfolio manager module aids the investor in managing not just the portfolio but his positions by making stop management facile. An Expert Guru lurks behind the curtain to aid the user in analyzing situations.

METASTOCK 9.0

Metastock 9.0 boasts an impressive array of tools and indicators. "System Experts" pop up on demand and can also guide the user through systems tests and explorations. The Experts can also suggest buys and sells. A point and figure toolbox is a valuable feature. The ability to create and test trading systems, with exhaustive and critical data analysis, is a powerful tool. Metastock adapts easily to add ons, of which Slauson's Powerstrike (the quantitative tool for finding critical support/resistance zones) is a good example.

Tradestation 2000i and Tradestation 8

Tradestation 2000i is the standalone version of Tradestation 8. Tradestation 8 is a real time on-line package which allows for trading through the Tradestation brokerage affiliate. The package is so powerful that on-line professional and semi-professional users probably benefit by combining their software arrangement with a brokerage arrangement. 2000i requires the user to maintain his local database, while Tradestation 8 always has the data on demand. For the creatively lazy (among them the editor) this is an attractive feature. Systems building and testing has always beeen and remains a powerful feature of Tradestation. With "EasyLanguage" the user may specify virtually any system he can think of. And then chat about it with the Tradestation community of traders. This community has contributed to a large data base of trading systems and ideas.

The Internet: prophet.net

And, for the even lazier and more casual investor there is prophet.net an Internet technical analysis site whose free features will fulfill the needs of the general charting investor. With powerful interactive charts and portfolio reporting the penurious investor will save many pennies at prophet.net. And, as Mark Twain said, a penny saved is a penny earned. Actually, what did Ben mean by that? A penny saved is capital when put to work. A user community and sharing are other attractions. And of course, no local data maintenance is necessary. And among its most valuable features prophet.net occasionally distributes market commentary and analysis by this editor. All in all prophet.net appears to deserve the continuing awards it has received from Barron's and Forbes, as well as *Technical Analysis* magazine.

The Internet: stockcharts.com

Of similar quality, and similarly honored by Forbes and *Technical Analysis* magazine, stockcharts.com has an additional valuable feature: point and figure charting. I have not remarked on P&F charting here, but it is an important technical method, especially for the patient investor. All the other features are available at stockcharts.com, candlesticks, bar charts, etc. And the distinguished analyst John Murphy makes his electronic home there with Greg Morris, a noted candlestick authority. There is also a "Voyeur" feature which allows the user to see what other traders are doing.

A Brief Summary

Knowledge is power. Knowing where to find knowledge is even more powerful. The inquiring investor can keep himself up to date on these sites through the yearly evaluations in Barron's and Forbes, and the financial press regularly updates its evaluations of Internet resources.

appendix E

*EN9: In a unique act of intellectual generosity Curtis Faith, one of Richard Dennis'
original Turtles, wrote a fully articulated account of the trading system used in the
futures markets by the Turtles. This document, which may be found in its entirety
at originalturtles.org is the very model of a modern major general's trading notebook.
(Occasionally Gilbert and Sullivan intrude into even the most disciplined account
of trading systems.) I have a number of systems and procedures manuals like this
in my files. For all intents and purposes they have very similar contents. Faith's
Turtle manual is probably the best written in my experience. And probably the one
with which I am most in agreement.*

My agreement with the document stems from my preference for "natural" systems, as opposed to "number driven" systems. Chart reading systems fit naturally over market facts, as a glove over a hand. High/low systems, like the Turtle system and *like Dow Theory* self-adjust to the rhythms of the markets. And like all mechanical systems it has its virtues and vices. The absolute worst vice of the mechanical trading system is, like a machine run amok, if the market rhythms get on the wrong harmonic the system will treat capital like a meat grinder treats beefsteak. A bloody sight to behold. Especially when it is your ox being ground.

It would be unspeakably rash of me to recommend the adoption out of the box of this system. But I strongly suspect that in broad trending markets some adaptation of it will be very productive.

And, I *require* all of my graduate students to produce such a workbook, and this is the model I give them to emulate.

Chapter 1
A Complete Trading System

> *The Turtle Trading System was a Complete Trading System, one that
> covered every aspect of trading, and left virtually no decision to the
> subjective whims of the trader.*

Most successful traders use a mechanical trading system. This is no coincidence. A good mechanical trading system automates the entire process of trading. The system provides answers for each of the decisions a trader must make while trading. The system makes it easier for a trader to trade consistently because there is a set of rules which specifically define exactly what should be done. The mechanics of trading are not left up to the judgment of the trader.

If you know that your system makes money over the long run, it is easier to take the signals and trade according to the system during periods of losses. If you are relying on your own judgment during trading, you may find that you are fearful just when you should be bold, and courageous when you should be cautious.

If you have a mechanical trading system that works, and you follow it consistently, your trading will be consistent despite the inner emotional struggles that might come from a long series of losses, or a large profit. The confidence, consistency, and discipline afforded by a thoroughly tested mechanical system are the key to many of the most profitable traders' success.

The Turtle Trading System was a Complete Trading System. Its rules covered every aspect of trading, and left no decisions to the subjective whims of the trader. It had every component of a Complete Trading System.

The Components of a Complete System

A Complete Trading System covers each of the decisions required for successful trading:

- Markets — What to buy or sell
- Position Sizing — How much to buy or sell
- Entries — When to buy or sell
- Stops — When to get out of a losing position
- Exits — When to get out of a winning position
- Tactics — How to buy or sell

Markets — What to buy or sell

The first decision is what to buy and sell, or essentially, what markets to trade. If you trade too few markets you greatly reduce your chances of getting aboard a trend. At the same time, you don't want to trade markets that have too low a trading volume, or that don't trend well.

Position Sizing — How much to buy or sell

The decision about how much to buy or sell is absolutely fundamental, and yet is often glossed over or handled improperly by most traders.

How much to buy or sell affects both diversification and money management. Diversification is an attempt to spread risk across many instruments, and to increase the opportunity for profit by increasing the opportunities for catching successful trades. Proper diversification requires making similar, if not identical bets on many different instruments. Money management is really about controlling risk by not betting so much that you run out of money before the good trends come.

How much to buy or sell is the single most important aspect of trading. Most beginning traders risk far too much on each trade, and greatly increase their chances of going bust, even if they have an otherwise valid trading style.

Entries — When to buy or sell

The decision of when to buy or sell is often called the entry decision. Automated systems generate entry signals which define the exact price and market conditions to enter the market, whether by buying or selling.

Stops — When to get out of a losing position

Traders who do not cut their losses will not be successful in the long term. The most important thing about cutting your losses is to predefine the point where you will get out *before* you enter a position.

Exits — When to get out of a winning position

Many "trading systems" that are sold as complete trading systems do not specifically address the exit of winning positions. Yet the question of when to get out of a winning position is crucial to the profitability of the system. Any trading system that does not address the exit of winning positions is not a Complete Trading System.

Tactics — How to buy or sell

Once a signal has been generated, tactical considerations regarding the mechanics of execution become important. This is especially true for larger accounts, where the entry and exit of positions can result in significant adverse price movement, or market impact.

Summary

Using a mechanical system is the best way to consistently make money trading. If you know that your system makes money over the long run, it is easier to take the signals and follow the system during periods of losses. If you rely on your own judgment, during trading you may find that you are fearful just when you should be courageous, or courageous when you should be fearful.

If you have a profitable mechanical trading system, and you follow it religiously, then your trading will be profitable, and the system will help you survive the emotional struggles that inevitably result from a long series of losses, or large profits.

The trading system that was used by the Turtles was a Complete Trading System. This was a major factor in our success. Our system made it easier to trade consistently, and successfully, because it did not leave important decisions to the discretion of the trader.

Chapter 2
Markets: What the Turtles Traded

*The Turtles traded liquid futures that traded on U.S. exchanges
in Chicago and New York.*

The Turtles were futures traders, at the time more popularly called commodities traders. We traded futures contracts on the most popular U.S. commodities exchanges.

Since we were trading millions of dollars, we could not trade markets that only traded a few hundred contracts per day because that would mean that the orders we generated would move the market so much that it would be too difficult to enter and exit positions without taking large losses. The Turtles traded only the most liquid markets.

In general, the Turtles traded all liquid U.S. markets except the grains and the meats. Since Richard Dennis was already trading the full position limits for his own account, he could not permit us to trade grains for him without exceeding the exchange's position limits.

We did not trade the meats because of a corruption problem with the floor traders in the meat pits. Some years after the Turtles disbanded, the FBI conducted a major sting operation in the Chicago meat pits and indicted many traders for price manipulation and other forms of corruption.

The following is a list of the futures markets traded by the Turtles:

Chicago Board of Trade
- ③ 30 Year U.S. Treasury Bond
- ③ 10 Year U.S. Treasury Note

New York Coffee Cocoa and Sugar Exchange
- ③ Coffee
- ③ Cocoa
- ③ Sugar
- ③ Cotton

Chicago Mercantile Exchange
- ③ Swiss Franc
- ③ Deutschmark
- ③ British Pound
- ③ French Franc
- ③ Japanese Yen
- ③ Canadian Dollar
- ③ S&P 500 Stock Index
- ③ Eurodollar
- ③ 90 Day U.S. Treasury Bill

Comex
- ③ Gold
- ③ Silver
- ③ Copper

New York Mercantile Exchange
- ③ Crude Oil
- ③ Heating Oil
- ③ Unleaded Gas

The Turtles were given the discretion of not trading any of the commodities on the list. However, if a trader chose not to trade a particular market, then he was not to trade that market at all. We were not supposed to trade markets inconsistently.

Chapter 3
Position Sizing

The Turtles used a volatility-based constant percentage risk position sizing algorithm.

Position sizing is one of the most important but least understood components of any trading system. The Turtles used a position sizing algorithm that was very advanced for its day, because it normalized the dollar volatility of a position by adjusting the position size based on the dollar volatility of the market. This meant that a given position would tend to move up or down in a given day about the same amount in dollar terms (when compared to positions in other markets), irrespective of the underlying volatility of the particular market.

This is true because positions in markets that moved up and down a large amount per contract would have an offsetting smaller number of contracts than positions in markets that had lower volatility.

This volatility normalization is very important because it means that different trades in different markets tend to have the same chance for a particular dollar loss or a particular dollar gain. This increased the effectiveness of the diversification of trading across many markets.

Even if the volatility of a given market was lower, any significant trend would result in a sizeable win because the Turtles would have held more contracts of that lower volatility commodity.

Volatility — The Meaning of N

The Turtles used a concept that Richard Dennis and Bill Eckhardt called N to represent the underlying volatility of a particular market. N is simply the 20-day exponential moving average of the True Range, which is now more commonly known as the ATR. Conceptually, N represents the average range in price movement that a particular market makes in a single day, accounting for opening gaps. N was measured in the same points as the underlying contract.

To compute the daily true range:

$$\text{True Range} = \textit{Maximum} \ (\text{H-L, H-PDC, PDC-L})$$

where:
H   = Current High
L   = Current Low
PDC = Previous Day's Close

To compute N use the following formula:

$$N = \frac{\left(19 \cdot \text{PDN} + \text{TR}\right)}{20}$$

where:
PDN = Previous Day's N
TR   = Current Day's True Range

Since this formula requires a previous day's N value, you must start with a 20-day simple average of the True Range for the initial calculation.

Dollar Volatility Adjustment

The first step in determining the position size was to determine the dollar volatility represented by the underlying market's price volatility (defined by its N).

This sounds more complicated than it is. It is determined using the simple formula:

$$\text{Dollar Volatility} = \text{N x Dollars per Point}$$

Volatility Adjusted Position Units

The Turtles built positions in pieces which we called Units. Units were sized so that 1 N represented 1% of the account equity.

Thus, a unit for a given market or commodity can be calculated using the following formula:

$$\text{Unit} = \frac{\text{Account of 1\%}}{\text{Market Dollar Volatility}}$$

or

$$\text{Unit} = \frac{\text{Account of 1\%}}{N \times \text{Dollars per Point}}$$

Examples

Heating Oil HO03H:

Consider the following prices, True Range, and N values for March 2003 Heating Oil:

Date	High	Low	Close	True Range	N
11/1/2002	0.7220	0.7124	0.7124	0.0096	0.0134
11/4/2002	0.7170	0.7073	0.7073	0.0097	0.0132
11/5/2002	0.7099	0.6923	0.6923	0.0176	0.0134
11/6/2002	0.6930	0.6800	0.6838	0.0130	0.0134
11/7/2002	0.6960	0.6736	0.6736	0.0224	0.0139
11/8/2002	0.6820	0.6706	0.6706	0.0114	0.0137
11/11/2002	0.6820	0.6710	0.6710	0.0114	0.0136
11/12/2002	0.6795	0.6720	0.6744	0.0085	0.0134
11/13/2002	0.6760	0.6550	0.6616	0.0210	0.0138
11/14/2002	0.6650	0.6585	0.6627	0.0065	0.0134
11/15/2002	0.6701	0.6620	0.6701	0.0081	0.0131
11/18/2002	0.6965	0.6750	0.6965	0.0264	0.0138
11/19/2002	0.7065	0.6944	0.6944	0.0121	0.0137
11/20/2002	0.7115	0.6944	0.7087	0.0171	0.0139
11/21/2002	0.7168	0.7100	0.7124	0.0081	0.0136
11/22/2002	0.7265	0.7120	0.7265	0.0145	0.0136
11/25/2002	0.7265	0.7098	0.7098	0.0167	0.0138
11/26/2002	0.7184	0.7110	0.7184	0.0086	0.0135
11/27/2002	0.7280	0.7200	0.7228	0.0096	0.0133
12/2/2002	0.7375	0.7227	0.7359	0.0148	0.0134
12/3/2002	0.7447	0.7310	0.7389	0.0137	0.0134
12/4/2002	0.7420	0.7140	0.7162	0.0280	0.0141

The unit size for the 6th of December, 2002 (using the N value of 0.0141 from the 4th of December), is as follows:

Heating Oil
N = 0.0141
Account Size = $1,000,000
Dollars per Point = 42,000
    (42,000 gallon contracts with price quoted in dollars)

$$\text{Size Unit} = \frac{0.01 \cdot \$1,000,000}{0.0141 \times 42,000} = 16.88$$

Since it isn't possible to trade partial contracts, this would be truncated to an even **16** contracts.

You might ask: "How often is it necessary to compute the values for N and the Unit Size?" The Turtles were provided with a Unit size sheet on Monday of each week that listed the N, and the Unit size in contracts for each of the futures that we traded.

The Importance of Position Sizing

Diversification is an attempt to spread risk across many instruments and to increase the opportunity for profit by increasing the opportunities for catching successful trades. To properly diversify requires making similar if not identical bets on many different instruments.

The Turtle System used market volatility to measure the risk involved in each market. We then used this risk measurement to build positions in increments that represented a constant amount of risk (or volatility). This enhanced the benefits of diversification, and increased the likelihood that winning trades would offset losing trades.

Note that this diversification is much harder to achieve when using insufficient trading capital. Consider the above example if a $100,000 account had been used. The unit size would have been a single contract, since 1.688 truncates to 1. For smaller accounts, the granularity of adjustment is too large, and this greatly reduces the effectiveness of diversification.

Units As a Measure of Risk

Since the Turtles used the Unit as the base measure for position size, and since those units were volatility risk adjusted, the Unit was a measure of both the risk of a position, and of the entire portfolio of positions.

The Turtles were given risk management rules that limited the number of Units that we could maintain at any given time, on four different levels. In essence, these rules controlled the total risk that a trader could carry, and these limits minimized losses during prolonged losing periods, as well as during extraordinary price movements.

An example of an extraordinary price movement was the day after the October 1987 stock market crash. The U.S. Federal Reserve lowered interest rates by several percentage points overnight to boost the confidence of the stock market and the country. The Turtles were loaded long in interest rate futures: Eurodollars, TBills and Bonds. The losses the following day were enormous. In some cases, 20% to 40% of account equity was lost in a single day. But these losses would have been correspondingly higher without the maximum position limits.

The limits were:

Level	Type	Maximum Units
1	Single Market	4 Units
2	Closely Correlated Markets	6 Units
3	Loosely Correlated Markets	10 Units
4	Single Direction – Long or Short	12 Units

Single Markets — A maximum of four Units per market.

Closely Correlated Markets — For markets that were closely correlated there could be a maximum of 6 Units in one particular direction (i.e. 6 long units or 6 short units). Closely correlated markets include: heating oil and crude oil; gold and silver; Swiss franc and Deutschmark; TBill and Eurodollar, etc.

Loosely Correlated Markets — For loosely correlated markets, there could be a maximum of 10 Units in one particular direction. Loosely correlated markets included: gold and copper; silver and copper, and many grain combinations that the Turtles did not trade because of positions limits.

Single Direction — The maximum number of total Units in one direction long or short was 12 Units. Thus, one could theoretically have had 12 Units long and 12 Units short at the same time.

The Turtles used the term **loaded** to represent having the maximum permitted number of Units for a given risk level. Thus, "loaded in yen" meant having the maximum 4 units of Japanese Yen contracts. Completely loaded meant having 12 Units, etc.

Adjusting Trading Size

There will be times when the market does not trend for many months. During these times, it is possible to lose a significant percentage of the equity of the account.

After large winning trades close out, one might want to increase the size of the equity used to compute position size.

The Turtles did not trade normal accounts with a running balance based on the initial equity. We were given notional accounts with a starting equity of zero and a specific account size. For example, many Turtles received a notional account size of $1,000,000 when we first started trading in February 1983. This account size was then adjusted each year at the beginning of the year. It was adjusted up or down depending on the success of the trader as measured subjectively by Rich. The increase/decrease typically represented something close to the addition of the gains or losses that were made in the account during the preceding year.

The Turtles were instructed to decrease the size of the notional account by 20% each time we went down 10% of the original account. So if a Turtle trading a $1,000,000 account was ever was down 10%, or $100,000, we would then begin trading as if we had a $800,000 account until such time as we reached the yearly starting equity. If we lost another 10% (10% of $800,000 or $80,000 for a total loss of $180,000) we were to reduce the account size by another 20% for a notional account size of $640,000.

There are other, perhaps better strategies for reducing or increasing equity as the account goes up or down. These are simply the rules that the Turtles used.

Chapter 4
Entries

> *The Turtles used two related system entries, each based on Donchian's channel breakout system.*

The typical trader thinks mostly in terms of the entry signals when thinking about a particular trading system. They believe that the entry is the most important aspect of any trading system.

They might be very surprised to find that the Turtles used a very simple entry system based on the Channel Breakout systems taught by Richard Donchian.

The Turtles were given rules for two different but related breakout systems we called System 1 and System 2. We were given full discretion to allocate as much of our equity to either system as we wanted. Some of us chose to trade all our equity using System 2, some chose to use a 50% System 1, 50% System 2 split, while others chose different mixes.

System 1 — A shorter-term system based on a 20-day breakout

System 2 — A simpler long-term system based on a 55-day breakout.

Breakouts

A breakout is defined as the price exceeding the high or low of a particular number of days. Thus a 20-day breakout would be defined as exceeding the high or low of the preceding 20 days.

Turtles always traded at the breakout when it was exceeded during the day, and did not wait until the daily close or the open of the following day. In the case of opening gaps, the Turtles would enter positions on the open if a market opened through the price of the breakout.

System 1 Entry — Turtles entered positions when the price exceeded by a single tick the high or low of the preceding 20 days. If the price exceeded the 20-day high, then the Turtles would buy one Unit to initiate a long position in the corresponding commodity. If the price dropped one tick below the low of the last 20 days, the Turtles would sell one Unit to initiate a short position.

System 1 breakout entry signals would be ignored if the last breakout would have resulted in a winning trade. **Note:** For the purposes of this test, the last breakout was considered the last breakout in the particular commodity irrespective of whether or not that particular breakout was actually taken, or was skipped because of this rule. This breakout would be considered a losing breakout if the price subsequent to the date of the breakout moved 2N against the position before a profitable 10-day exit occurred.

The direction of the last breakout was irrelevant to this rule. Thus, a losing long breakout or a losing short breakout would enable the subsequent new breakout to be taken as a valid entry, regardless of its direction (long or short).

However, in the event that a System 1 entry breakout was skipped because the previous trade had been a winner, an entry would be made at the 55-day breakout to avoid missing major moves. This 55-day breakout was considered the Failsafe Breakout point.

At any given point, if you were out of the market, there would always be some price which would trigger a short entry and another different and higher price which would trigger a long entry. If the last breakout was a loser, then the entry signal would be closer to the current price (i.e., the 20 day breakout), than if it had been a winner, in which case the entry signal would likely be farther away, at the 55-day breakout.

System 2 Entry — Entered when the price exceeded by a single tick the high or low of the preceding 55 days. If the price exceeded the 55-day high, then the Turtles would buy one Unit to initiate a long position in the corresponding commodity. If the price dropped one tick below the low of the last 55 days, the Turtles would sell one Unit to initiate a short position.

All breakouts for System 2 would be taken whether the previous breakout had been a winner or not.

Adding Units

Turtles entered single Unit long positions at the breakouts and added to those positions at ½ N intervals following their initial entry. This ½ N interval was based on the actual fill price of the previous order. So if an initial breakout order slipped by ½ N, then the new order would be 1 full N past the breakout to account for the ½ N slippage, plus the normal ½ N unit add interval.

This would continue right up to the maximum permitted number of units. If the market moved quickly enough it was possible to add the maximum four Units in a single day.

Example:

Gold
N = 2.50
55-day breakout = 310

First Unit added	310.00
Second Unit	310.00 + ½ 2.50 or 311.25
Third Unit	311.25 + ½ 2.50 or 312.50
Fourth Unit	312.50 + ½ 2.50 or 313.75
Crude Oil	
N = 1.20	

55-day breakout = 28.30

First Unit added	28.30
Second Unit	28.30 + ½ 1.20 or 28.90
Third Unit	28.90 + ½ 1.20 or 29.50
Fourth Unit	29.50 + ½ 1.20 or 30.10

Consistency

The Turtles were told to be very consistent in taking entry signals, because most of the profits in a given year might come from only two or three large winning trades. If a signal was skipped or missed, this could greatly affect the returns for the year.

The Turtles with the best trading records consistently applied the entry rules. The Turtles with the worst records, and all those who were dropped from the program, failed to consistently enter positions when the rules indicated.

Chapter 5
Stops

The Turtles used N-based stops to avoid large losses in equity.

There is an expression that, "There are old traders; and there are bold traders; but there are no old bold traders." Traders that don't use stops go broke. The Turtles always used stops.

For most people, it is far easier to cling to the hope that a losing trade will turn around than it is to simply get out of a losing position and admit that the trade did not work out.

Let us make one thing very clear. Getting out of a losing position is absolutely critical. Traders who do not cut their losses will not be successful in the long term. Almost all of the examples of trading that got out of control and jeopardized the health of the financial institution itself, such as Barings, Long-term Capital Management, and others, involved trades that were allowed to develop into large losses because they were not cut short when they were small losses.

The most important thing about cutting your losses is to have predefined the point where you will get out, *before* you enter a position. If the market moves to your price, you must get out, no exceptions, every single time. Wavering from this method will eventually result in disaster.

Turtle Stops

Having stops didn't mean that the Turtles always had actual stop orders placed with the broker.

Since the Turtles carried such large positions, we did not want to reveal our positions or our trading strategies by placing stop orders with brokers. Instead, we were encouraged to have a particular price, which when hit, would cause us to exit our positions using either limit orders, or market orders.

These stops were non-negotiable exits. If a particular commodity traded at the stop price, then the position was exited; each time, every time, without fail.

Stop Placement

The Turtles placed their stops based on position risk. No trade could incur more than 2% risk.

Since 1 N of price movement represented 1% of Account Equity, the maximum stop that would allow 2% risk would be 2 N of price movement. Turtle stops were set at 2 N below the entry for long positions, and 2 N above the entry for short positions.

In order to keep total position risk at a minimum, if additional units were added, the stops for earlier units were raised by ½ N. This generally meant that all the stops for the entire position would be placed at 2 N from the most recently added unit. However, in cases where later units were placed at larger spacing either because of fast markets causing skid, or because of opening gaps, there would be differences in the stops.

For example:

Crude Oil
N = 1.20
55-day breakout = 28.30

	Entry Price	Stop
First Unit	28.30	25.90

	Entry Price	Stop
First Unit	28.30	26.50
Second Unit	28.90	26.50

	Entry Price	Stop
First Unit	28.30	27.10
Second Unit	28.90	27.10
Third Unit	29.50	27.10

	Entry Price	Stop
First Unit	28.30	27.70
Second Unit	28.90	27.70
Third Unit	29.50	27.70
Fourth Unit	30.10	27.70

Case where fourth unit was added at a higher price because the market opened gapping

up to 30.80:

	Entry Price	Stop
First Unit	28.30	27.70
Second Unit	28.90	27.70
Third Unit	29.50	27.70
Fourth Unit	30.80	28.40

Alternate Stop Strategy — The Whipsaw

The Turtles were told of an alternate stop strategy that resulted in better profitability, but that was harder to execute because it incurred many more losses, which resulted in a lower win/loss ratio. This strategy was called the Whipsaw.

Instead of taking a 2% risk on each trade, the stops were placed at ½ N for ½% account risk. If a given Unit was stopped out, the Unit would be re-entered if the market reached the original entry price. A few Turtles traded this method with good success.

The Whipsaw also had the added benefit of not requiring the movement of stops for earlier Units as new Units were added, since the total risk would never exceed 2% at the maximum four Units.

For example, using Whipsaw stops, the Crude Oil entry stops would be:

Crude Oil
N = 1.20
55-day breakout = 28.30

	Entry Price	Stop
First Unit	28.30	27.70

	Entry Price	Stop
First Unit	28.30	27.70
Second Unit	28.90	28.30

	Entry Price	Stop
First Unit	28.30	27.70
Second Unit	28.90	28.30
Third Unit	29.50	28.90

	Entry Price	Stop
First Unit	28.30	27.70
Second Unit	28.90	28.30
Third Unit	29.50	28.90
Fourth Unit	30.10	29.50

Benefits of the Turtle System Stops

Since the Turtle's stops were based on N, they adjusted to the volatility of the markets. More volatile markets would have wider stops, but they would also have fewer contracts per Unit. This equalized the risk across all entries and resulted in better diversification and a more robust risk management.

Chapter 6
Exits

The Turtles used breakout based exits for profitable positions.

There is another old saying: "you can never go broke taking a profit." The Turtles would *not* agree with this statement. Getting out of winning positions too early, i.e., "taking a profit" too early, is one of the most common mistakes when trading trend following systems.

Prices never go straight up; therefore it is necessary to let the prices go against you if you are going to ride a trend. Early in a trend this can often mean watching decent profits of 10% to 30% fade to a small loss. In the middle of a trend, it might mean watching a profit of 80% to 100% drop by 30% to 40%. The temptation to lighten the position to "lock in profits" can be very great.

The Turtles knew that where you took a profit could make the difference between winning and losing.

The Turtle System enters on breakouts. Most breakouts do not result in trends. This means that most of the trades that the Turtles made resulted in losses. If the winning trades did not earn enough on average to offset these losses, the Turtles would have lost money. Every profitable trading system has a different optimal exit point.

Consider the Turtle System; if you exit winning positions at a 1 N profit while you exited losing positions at a 2 N loss you would need twice as many winners to offset the losses from the losing trades.

There is a complex relationship between the components of a trading system. This means that you can't consider the proper exit for a profitable position without considering the entry, money management and other factors.

The proper exit for winning positions is one of the most important aspects of trading, and the least appreciated. Yet it can make the difference between winning and losing.

Turtle Exits

The **System 1 exit** was a 10 day low for long positions and a 10 day high for short positions. All the Units in the position would be exited if the price went against the position for a 10 day breakout.

The **System 2 exit** was a 20 day low for long positions and a 20 day high for short positions. All the Units in the position would be exited if the price went against the position for a 20 day breakout.

As with entries, the Turtles did not typically place exit stop orders, but instead watched the price during the day, and started to phone in exit orders as soon as the price traded through the exit breakout price.

These Are Difficult Exits

For most traders, the Turtle System Exits were probably the single most difficult part of the Turtle System Rules. Waiting for a 10 or 20 day new low can often mean watching 20%, 40% even 100% of significant profits evaporate.

There is a very strong tendency to want to exit earlier. It requires great discipline to watch your profits evaporate in order to hold onto your positions for the really big move. The ability to maintain discipline and stick to the rules during large winning trades is the hallmark of the experienced successful trader.

Chapter 7
Tactics

Miscellaneous guidelines to cover the rest of trading the Turtle System Rules.

The famous architect Mies van der Rohe, when speaking about restraint in design, once said: "God is in the details." This is also true of trading systems. There are some important details which remain that can make a significant difference in the profitability of your trading when using the Turtle Trading Rules.

Entering Orders

As has been mentioned before, Richard Dennis and William Eckhardt advised the Turtles not to use stops when placing orders. We were advised to watch the market and enter orders when the price hit our stop price.

We were also told that, in general, it was better to place limit orders instead of market orders. This is because limit orders offer a chance for better fills and less slippage than do market orders.

Any market has at all times a bid and an ask. The bid is the price that buyers are willing to buy at, and the ask is the price that sellers are willing to sell at. If at any time the bid price becomes higher than the ask price, trading takes place. A market order will always fill at the bid or ask when there is sufficient volume, and sometimes at a worse price for larger orders.

Typically, there is a certain amount of relatively random price movement that occurs, which is sometimes known as the bounce. The idea behind using limit orders is to place your order at the lower end of the bounce, instead of simply placing a market order. A limit order will not move the market if it is a small order, and it will almost always move it less if it is a larger order.

It takes some skill to be able to determine the best price for a limit order, but with practice, you should be able to get better fills using limit orders placed near the market than with market orders.

Fast Markets

At times, the market moves very quickly through the order prices, and if you place a limit order it simply won't get filled. During fast market conditions, a market can move thousands of dollars per contract in just a few minutes.

During these times, the Turtles were advised not to panic, and to wait for the market to trade and stabilize before placing their orders.

Most beginning traders find this hard to do. They panic and place market orders. Invariably they do this at the worst possible time, and frequently end up trading on the high or low of the day, at the worst possible price.

In a fast market, liquidity temporarily dries up. In the case of a rising fast market, sellers stop selling and hold out for a higher price, and they will not re-commence selling until after the price stops moving up. In this scenario, the asks rise considerably, and the spread between bid and ask widens.

Buyers are now forced to pay much higher prices as sellers continue raising their asks, and the price eventually moves so far and so fast that new sellers come into the market, causing the price to stabilize, and often to quickly reverse and collapse partway back.

Market orders placed into a fast market usually end up getting filled at the highest price of the run-up, right at the point where the market begins to stabilize as new sellers come in.

As Turtles, we waited until some indication of at least a temporary price reversal before placing our orders, and this often resulted in much better fills than would have been achieved with a market order. If the market stabilized at a point which was past our stop price, then we would get out of the market, but we would do so without panicking.

Simultaneous Entry Signals

Many days as traders there was little market movement, and little for us to do besides monitor existing positions. We might go for days without placing a single order. Other days would be moderately busy, with signals occurring intermittently over the stretch of a few hours. In that case, we would simply take the trades as they came, until they reached the position limits for those markets.

Then there were days when it seemed like everything was happening at once, and we would go from no positions, to loaded, in a day or two. Often, this frantic pace was intensified by multiple signals in correlated markets.

This was especially true when the markets gapped open through the entry signals. You might have a gap opening entry signal in Crude Oil, Heating Oil and Unleaded Gas all on the same day. With futures contracts, it was also extremely common for many different months of the same market to signal at the same time.

Buy Strength — Sell Weakness

If the signals came all at once, we always bought the strongest markets and sold short the weakest markets in a group.

We would also only enter one unit in a single market at the same time. For instance, instead of buying February, March and April Heating Oil at the same time, we would pick the one contract month that was the strongest, and that had sufficient volume and liquidity.

This is very important! Within a correlated group, the best long positions are the strongest markets (which almost always outperform the weaker markets in the same group). Conversely, the biggest winning trades to the short side come from the weakest markets within a correlated group.

As Turtles, we used various measures to determine strength and weakness. The simplest and most common way was to simply look at the charts and figure out which one "looked" stronger (or weaker) by visual examination.

Some would determine how many N the price had advanced since the breakout, and buy the market that had moved the most (in terms of N).

Others would subtract the price 3 months ago from the current price and then divide by the current N to normalize across markets. The strongest markets had the highest values; the weakest markets the lowest.

Any of these approaches work well. The important thing is to have long positions in the strongest markets and short positions in the weakest markets.

Rolling Over Expiring Contracts

When futures contracts expire, there are two major factors that need to be considered before rolling over into a new contract.

First, there are many instances when the near months trend well, but the more distant contracts fail to display the same level of price movement. So don't roll into a new contract unless its price action would have resulted in an existing position.

Second, contracts should be rolled before the volume and open interest in the expiring contract decline too much. How much is too much depends on the unit size. As a general rule, the Turtles rolled existing positions into the new contract month a few weeks before expiration, unless the (currently held) near month was performing significantly better than farther out contract months.

Finally

That concludes the Complete Turtle Trading System rules. As you are probably thinking, they are not very complicated.

But knowing these rules is not enough to make you rich. You have to be able to follow them.

Remember what Richard Dennis said: "I always say that you could publish my trading rules in the newspaper and no one would follow them. The key is consistency and discipline. Almost anybody can make up a list of rules that are 80% as good as what we taught our people. What they couldn't do is give them the confidence to stick to those rules even when things are going bad." — From *Market Wizards,* by Jack D. Schwager.

Perhaps the best evidence that this is true is the performance of the Turtles themselves; many of them did not make money. This was not because the rules didn't work; it was because they could not and did not follow the rules. By virtue of this same fact, few who read this document will be successful trading the Turtle Trading Rules. Again; this is not because the rules don't work. It is because the reader simply won't have the confidence to follow them.

The Turtle rules are very difficult to follow because they depend on capturing relatively infrequent large trends. As a result, many months can pass between winning periods; at times even a year or two. During these periods it is easy to come up with reasons to doubt the system, and to stop following the rules:

What if the rules don't work anymore? What if the markets have changed?

What if there is something important missing from the rules?

How can I be really sure that this works?

One member of the first Turtles class, who was fired from the program before the end of the first year, suspected early on that information had been intentionally withheld from the group, and eventually became convinced that there were hidden secrets which Rich would not reveal. This particular trader could not face up to the simple fact that his poor performance was due to his own doubts and insecurities, which resulted in his inability to follow the rules.

Another problem is the tendency to want to change the rules. Many of the Turtles, in an effort to reduce the risk of trading the system, changed the rules in subtle ways which sometimes had the opposite of the desired effect.

An example: Failing to enter positions as quickly as the rules specify (1 unit every ½ N). While this may seem like a more conservative approach, the reality could be that, for the type of entry system the Turtles used, adding to positions slowly might increase the chance that a retracement would hit the exit stops — resulting in losses — whereas a faster approach might allow the position to weather the retracement without the stops being hit. This subtle change could have a major impact on the profitability of the system during certain market conditions.

In order to build the level of confidence you will need to follow a trading system's rules, whether it is the Turtle System, something similar, or a completely different system, it is imperative that you personally conduct research using historical trading data. It is not enough to hear from others that a system works; it is not enough to read the summary results from research conducted by others. You must do it yourself.

Get your hands dirty and get directly involved in the research. Dig into the trades, look at the daily equity logs, get very familiar with the way the system trades, and with the extent and frequency of the losses.

It is much easier to weather an 8-month losing period if you know that there have been many periods of equivalent length in the last 20 years. It will be much easier to add to positions quickly if you know that adding quickly is a key part of the profitability of the system.

Chapter 8
Further Study

Where do you go from here? There is no substitute for experience.

The humorist Barry Le Platner said: "Good judgment comes from experience, and experience comes from bad judgment." If you want to become a trader, you must start to trade. There is no substitute. You must also make mistakes.

Making mistakes is part of trading. If you don't start trading using actual money — and enough money that it affects you when you win or lose — you won't learn all the lessons of trading. Paper trading is not a substitute for trading with real money. If you aren't using real money, you won't learn how hope, fear, and greed affect you personally.

At the same time, it is important to get a thorough understanding of the fundamentals of trading. Armed with this knowledge you will make fewer mistakes, and you will learn much more quickly from the mistakes that you do make.

Here are some suggested areas for further study:

Trading Psychology

Trading psychology is the most important aspect of trading, and understanding yourself and your own personality as it relates to your trading is critical. This journey is much more about making a sincere and open-minded attempt to understand your own personal psychology than it is about finding the magic psychology book with all the answers.

Money Management

Money management is the most important aspect of a mechanical trading system. Controlling risk in a manner that will allow you to continue trading through the inevitable bad periods, and survive to realize the profit potential of good systems, is absolutely fundamental. Yet, the interplay between entry signals, exits and money management is often non-intuitive. Study and research into the state-of-the-art in money management will pay enormous dividends.

Trading Research

There is no substitute for statistically valid historical research when developing mechanical trading systems. In practice, this means learning how to program a computer to run simulations of trading system performance.

There is a lot of good information on curve-fitting, over-optimization, trading statistics and testing methodologies on the web and in books, but the information is a bit hard to find amongst the hype and bull. Be skeptical, but keep an open mind, and your research will pay off.

Final Warning

There are a lot of individuals who try to sell themselves and their advice as "expert." Don't blindly accept the advice of these self-proclaimed experts. The best advice comes from those who aren't selling it, and who make their money trading. There are many books and biographies that give insights into the habits of those who have been — or who are — successful traders.

Learning how to become a good trader — or even an excellent trader — is possible, but it requires a lot of hard work and a healthy dose of skepticism. For those of us who have chosen this path, the journey never ends. Those who continue to be successful will never reach their destination, but will learn to find joy in the journey itself.

List of Illustrations and Text Diagrams

Regarding the illustrations in this book, except for those which are marked as adapted from other sources, the charts listed as Figures below have been reproduced from the authors' own "working" charts. As such, they were made up originally for private use only and without a thought to their eventual reproduction, much less their publication. They are not and do not pretend to be works of art, but it is hoped that they will, despite their "homemade" appearance, serve the purpose of illustrating the various formations, patterns, market phenomena, and trading principles discussed in the text. That they do not show the clean line and expert lettering of a professional draftsman's work is regretted. The reader will, we trust, make allowances.

As for their selection, it should be stated most emphatically that it was not necessary to search through thousands of charts in order to find good examples of all these various technical formations. Many dozens, even hundreds, were available for practically every type of pattern. Anyone who has learned to recognize them can find for himself plenty of good technical pictures in a quick examination of even as small a portfolio as 50 or 100 charts. In other words, the illustrations in this book are in no sense unique. In selecting them, we have tried only to show as much variety as possible and samples from previous as well as more recent *(EN: up to the year 2005)* market history.

Perhaps it is not necessary, but it is at least in accord with custom, to add that the information as to specific market prices, volume of transactions, etc., used in preparing our illustrations (or cited in the text of this book) has been derived from sources believed to be reliable, but is not guaranteed.

EN: All graphics (except those after Figure 274) added by the editor for the eighth (and ninth) *editions are identified by a "x.1" number; thus, DIAGRAM 10.1 or FIGURE 10.1 is new and chosen by same.*

Part One

Part Two

Text Diagrams

The charts listed as Figures all represent actual market history. In contradistinction, the diagrams listed below do not depict real trading history, but have been specially drawn as simplified, hypothetical market situations to facilitate the explanation of certain trading principles. *EN: Certain of these rather than drawings are exhibits of other interest.*

Alphabetic Index of Stock Charts

Glossary

EN: The Glossary is the work of the distinguished editor of the seventh edition, Richard McDermott. Minor changes are so noted.

EN9: Some entries are written by other analysts, whose names are noted.

While it requires the use of the human brain and some discrimination and judgment the great virtue of Magee chart analysis is that it allows the practitioner to evaluate how well number driven indicators function. As, for example, use of a moving average to identify the trend works wonderfully well in a trending market. And, if used as a signal generator in a trading market results in whip-saws. Similarly, oscillators often are useful in trading markets, but can mislead the trader when the market begins to trend. The reasonably accomplished chart analyst can recognize the state of the market and view the performance of number driven indicators from a more informed perspective. Thus the reader should keep this in mind while reading about ADXs and suchlike.

ACCUMULATION — The first phase of a Bull Market. The period when farsighted investors begin to buy shares from discouraged or distressed sellers. Financial reports are usually at their worst and the public is completely disgusted with the stock market. Volume is only moderate, but beginning to increase on the rallies

ACTIVITY — See Volume.

ADX (Average Directional Movement Index) — The ADX is a trend-following indicator devised by Welles Wilder (RSI Wilder) and is based on the concept of directional movement. It is designed to evaluate the trending characteristics of a security. The ADX is frequently used to avoid trendless markets, and signals when a trend reaches a profitable trading level. In a trendless market, the ADX indicates avoidance.

Directional movement is a measure of the net total price movement during a set period of time. First, the positive and negative directional movements are determined by summing the daily up and down moves. The values obtained are next normalized by dividing them by the "True Range," the absolute value of the total move for the period; this difference between normalized values (expressed as a percentage) is the directional movement.

The ADX is then obtained from directional movement by the use of exponential average and ratios. The ADX is often charted with a second line, the ADXR Indicator. ADXR is a smoothed average of the ADX.

A rising ADX indicates significant directional movement and the beginning of a good trading period. The declining ADX is shown during a poor period for trend following. Normally, an ADX Indicator above 25 signals significant directional movement and good trading.

APEX — The highest point; the pointed end, tip, of a Triangle.

ARBITRAGE — The simultaneous buying and selling of two different, but closely related instruments to take advantage of a disparity in their prices in one market or different markets. *EN: Those who buy the acquirer and sell the acquired in takeover situations — sometimes called "arbs" or arbitrageurs — are ersatz or faux arbitrageurs. They are really spreaders. Arbitrageur is a solecism used in that sense. It is also a false cognate to the French.*

AREA GAP — See Common Gap.

AREA PATTERN — When a stock or commodity's upward or downward momentum has been temporarily exhausted, the ensuing sideways movement in the price usually traces out a design or arrangement of form called an Area Pattern. The shape of some of these Area Patterns, or Formations, have predictive value under certain conditions. (See also Ascending Triangle, Broadening Formations, Descending Triangle, Diamond, Flag, Head-and-Shoulders, Inverted Triangle, Pennant, Rectangle, Right-Angle Triangles, Symmetrical Triangles, and Wedges.)

ARITHMETIC SCALE — Price or volume scale where the distance on the vertical axis (i.e., space between horizontal lines) represents equal amounts of dollars or number of shares.

ASCENDING (PARALLEL) TREND CHANNEL — When the tops of the rallies composing an advance develop along a line (sometimes called a Return Line), which is also parallel to the basic up trendline (i.e., the line which slopes up across the wave bottoms in an advance); the area between the two lines is called an Ascending or Up Channel.

ASCENDING (UP) TRENDLINE — The advancing wave in a stock or commodity is composed of a series of ripples. When the bottoms of these ripples form on, or very close to, an upward slanting straight line, a basic Ascending or Up Trendline is formed.

ASCENDING TRIANGLE — One of a class of Area Patterns called Right-Angle Triangles. The class is distinguished by the fact that one of the two boundary lines is practically horizontal, while the other slants toward it. If the top line is horizontal and the lower slants upward to an intersection point to the right, the resulting Area Pattern is called Ascending Triangle. The implication is bullish, with the expectant breakout through the horizontal line. Measuring Formula: add the broadest part of triangle to the breakout point.

AT-THE-MONEY — An option, the strike price of which is equal to the market price of the underlying instrument.

AVERAGES — See Dow–Jones Industrial Averages, Moving Averages, Dow–Jones Transportation Averages, and Dow–Jones Utility Averages.

AVERAGING COST — An investing technique where the investor buys a stock or commodity at successively lower prices, thereby "averaging down" his average cost of each stock share or commodity contract. Purchases at successively higher prices would "average up" the price of stock shares or commodity contracts. *EN: A very foolish technique for the amateur.*

AXIS — In the graphic sense, an axis is a straight line for measurement or reference. It is also the line, real or imagined, on which a formation is regarded as rotating.

BALANCED PROGRAM — Proportioning capital, or a certain part of capital, equally between the long side and the short side of the market.

BAR CHART — Also called a Line Chart. A graphic representation of prices using a vertical bar to connect the highest price in the time period to the lowest price. Opening prices are noted with a small horizontal line to the left. Closing prices are shown with a small horizontal line to the right. Bar charts can be constructed for any time period in which prices are available. The most common time periods found in bar charts are hourly, daily, weekly, and monthly. However, with the growing number of personal computers and the availability of "real-time" quotes, it is not unusual for traders to use some period of minutes to construct a bar chart.

BASIC TRENDLINES — See Trendlines.

BASING POINT — The price level in the chart which determines where a stop-loss point is placed. As technical conditions change, the Basing Point, and stops, can be advanced (in a rising market), or lowered (in a falling market). (See Progressive Stops.)

BASIS POINTS — The measure of yields on bonds and notes. One Basis Point equals 0.01% of yield.

BASKET TRADES — Large transactions made up of a number of various stocks.

BEAR MARKET — In its simplest form, a Bear Market is a period when prices are primarily declining, usually for a long period of time. Bear Markets generally consist of three phases. The first phase is distribution, the second is panic, and the third is akin to a washout, where those investors who have held through the first two phases finally give up and liquidate.

BENT NECKLINE — See Neckline.

BETA — A measurement of an individual stock's sensitivity to market swings.

BETA (COEFFICIENT) — A measure of the market or nondiversifiable risk associated with any given security in the market.

BLOCK TRADES — Large transactions of a particular stock sold as a unit.

BLOW-OFF — See Climactic Top.

BLUE CHIPS — The nickname given to high-priced companies with good records of earnings and price stability. Also called gilt-edged securities. Examples: IBM, AT&T, General Motors, and General Electric.

BLUE PARALLEL — A line drawn parallel to the trendline (Blue Trendline) which connects at least two highs. The Blue Parallel is started off a low and used to estimate the next low point.

BLUE TRENDLINE — A straight line connecting two or more Tops together. To avoid confusion, Edwards and Magee use a blue line for Top Trendlines and a red line for Bottom Trendlines.

BOLLINGER BANDS (BB) — An envelope, in the form of two lines, which surrounds the price bars on a chart. Bollinger Bands are plotted two standard deviations away from a Simple Moving Average. This is the primary difference between Bollinger Bands and other envelopes. Envelopes are plotted a fixed percentage above and below a Moving Average. As standard deviation is a measure of volatility, Bollinger Bands adjust themselves to differing market conditions. The bands grow wider during volatile market periods and narrower during less volatile periods.

Bollinger's premise is to ask the market what it is doing, rather than tell it what to do. He focused on volatility with the use of standard deviation to set the band width. The bands are normally plotted two deviations away from the standard deviation, which is effectively a 20-day Moving Average Line. The plot is valid if an average acts as a Support Line on market corrections. If the average is penetrated on corrections, it is too short. Bollinger recommends 10-day Moving Averages for short-term trading, 20-day for intermediate-term trading, and 50-day for longer-term trading. Deviations also need to be adjusted: 10 days can use 1.5 deviations, 20 days use two deviations, and 50 days use 2.5 deviations. The nature of the time periods does not matter; the bands can be used on monthly, weekly, daily, and even intraday figures.

Bollinger Bands do not usually generate buy and sell signals alone. Most often they provide a framework within which price may be related to other indicators. Bollinger recommends using the bands in relation to other buy and sell signals. However, the bands can be an integral part of the signal. If a price touches an upper band and indicator action confirms it, no sell signal is generated (it is a continuation signal if a buy signal was in effect). If a price touches an upper band and an indicator does not confirm (diverges), it is a sell signal. If a Top Price Chart Formation is formed outside the bands and is followed by a second Top inside the bands, a sell signal is generated. The exact opposite is true on the buy side.

When combined with other indicators, such as the RSI, the Bollinger Bands become quite powerful. RSI is an excellent indicator with respect to overbought and oversold conditions. Generally, when price touches the upper Bollinger Band and RSI is below 70, it is an indication that the trend will continue. Conversely, when price touches the lower Bollinger Band, and RSI is above 30, it is an indication the trend should continue. If a situation occurs where price touches the upper Bollinger Band and RSI is above 70 (possibly approaching 80), it is an indication that the trend may reverse itself and move downward. On the other hand, if price touches the lower Bollinger Band and RSI is below 30 (possibly approaching 20), the trend may reverse itself and move upward. (See also Multicolincarity, Percent B, Wilder RSI.)

BOOK VALUE — The conventional accounting measure of what a stock is worth based on the value of the company's assets less the company's debt. Eminently manipulable.

BOTTOM — See Ascending Triangle, Dormant Bottom, Double Bottom, Head-and-Shoulders Bottom, Rounding Bottom, and Selling Climax.

BOUNDARY — The edges of a pattern.

BOWL — See Rounding Bottom.

BRACKETING — A trading range market or a price area that is nontrending.

BREAKAWAY GAP — The hole or gap in the chart created when a stock or commodity breaks out of an Area Pattern.

BREAKOUT — When a stock or commodity exits an area pattern.

BROADENING FORMATION — Sometimes called Inverted Triangles, these are formations which start with narrow fluctuations that widen out between diverging, rather than converging, boundary lines. (See also Right-Angled Broadening Formations, Broadening Top, Head-and-Shoulders, and Diamond Patterns.)

BROADENING TOP — An Area Reversal Pattern which may evolve in any one of three forms, comparable in shape, respectively, to inverted Symmetrical, Ascending, or Descending Triangles. Unlike Triangles, however, the Tops and Bottoms of these patterns do not necessarily stop at clearly marked diverging boundary lines. Volume, rather than diminishing in triangles, tends to be unusually high and irregular throughout pattern construction. No Measuring Formula is available.

BULL MARKET — A period when prices are primarily rising, normally for an extended period. Usually, but not always, divisible into three phases. The first phase is accumulation. The second phase is one of fairly steady advance with increasing volume. The third phase is marked by considerable activity as the public begins to recognize and attempt to profit from the rising market.

CALL OPTION — An option that gives the buyer the right to buy the underlying contract at a specific price within a certain period, and that obligates the seller to sell the contract for the premium received before expiration of the designated time period.

CANDLESTICKS — A Japanese graphical representation of price action using the same data as bar charts, but which adds color to the candlestick (or data) to indicate the direction of prices from the opening. Cf. Nison, Bibliography.

CATS AND DOGS — Low-priced stocks of no investment value.

CHANNEL — If the Tops of the rallies and Bottoms of the reactions develop lines which are approximately parallel to one another, the area between these lines is called a Channel. (See also Ascending Trend Channel, Descending Trend Channel, and Horizontal Trend Channel.)

CHART — A graphic representation of a stock or commodity in terms of price and/or volume. (See also Bar Chart and Point & Figure Chart.)

CLEAN-OUT DAY — See Selling Climax.

CLIMACTIC TOP — A sharp advance, accompanied by extraordinary volume, i.e., much larger volume than the normal increase, which signals the final "blow-off" of the trend, followed by either a Reversal, or at least by a period of stagnation, formation of Consolidation Pattern, or a Correction.

CLIMAX DAY — See One-Day Reversal.

CLIMAX, SELLING — See Selling Climax.

CLOSING PRICE — The last sale price of the trading session for a stock. In a commodity, it represents an official price determined from a range of prices deemed to have traded at or on the close; also called a settlement price.

CLOSING THE GAP — When a stock or commodity returns to a previous gap and retraces the range of the gap. Also called covering the gap or filling the gap. (See also Gap.)

COIL — Another term for a Symmetrical Triangle.

COMMISSION — The amount charged by a brokerage house to execute a trade in a stock, option, or commodity. In a stock, option, or commodity, a commission is charged for each purchase and each sale. In a commodity, a commission is charged only when the original entry trade has been closed with an offsetting trade. This is called a round turn commission.

COMMON GAP — Also called Area Gap. Any hole or gap in the chart occurring within an Area Pattern. The forecasting significance of the Common Gap is nil. (See also Gap.)

COMPARATIVE RELATIVE STRENGTH — Compares the price movement of a stock with that of its competitors, industry group, or the whole market.

COMPLEX HEAD-AND-SHOULDERS — Also called Multiple Head-and-Shoulders. It is a Head-and-Shoulders Pattern with more than one right and left shoulder and/or head. (See also Head-and-Shoulders.)

COMPOSITE AVERAGE — A stock average composed of the 65 stocks which make up the Dow–Jones Industrial Average and the Dow–Jones Utility Average.

COMPOSITE LEVERAGE — In Edwards and Magee, it is a formula for combining the principal factors affecting a given sum of capital used (i.e., sensitivity, price, and margin) into one index figure.

CONFIRMATION — In a pattern, it is the point at which a stock or commodity exits an Area Pattern in the expected direction by an amount of price and volume sufficient to meet minimum pattern requirements for a *bona fide* breakout. In the Dow Theory, it means both the Industrial Average and the Transportation Average have registered new highs or lows during the same advance or decline. If only one of the Averages establishes a new high (or low) and the other one does not, it would be a nonconfirmation, or Divergence. This is also true of oscillators. To confirm a new high (or low) in a stock or commodity, an oscillator needs to reach a new high (or low) as well. Failure of the oscillator to confirm a new high (or low) is called a Divergence and would be considered an early indication of a potential Reversal in direction.

CONGESTION — The sideways trading from which Area Patterns evolve. Not all Congestion periods produce a recognizable pattern, however.

CONSOLIDATION PATTERN — Also called a Continuation Pattern, it is an Area Pattern which breaks out in the direction of the previous trend. (See also Ascending Triangle, Descending Triangle, Flag, Head-and-Shoulders Continuation, Pennant, Rectangle, Scallop, and Symmetrical Triangle.)

CONTINUATION GAP — See Runaway Gap.

CONTINUATION PATTERN — See Consolidation Pattern.

CONVERGENT PATTERN (TREND) — Those patterns with upper and lower boundary lines which meet, or converge, at some point if extended to the right. (See also Ascending Triangle, Descending Triangle, Symmetrical Triangle, Wedges, and Pennants.)

CORRECTION — A move in a commodity or stock which is opposite to the prevailing trend, but not sufficient to change that trend. Called a rally in a downtrend and a reaction in an uptrend. In the Dow Theory, a Correction is a Secondary Trend against the Primary Trend, which usually lasts from 3 weeks to 3 months and retraces from one third to two thirds of the preceding swing in the Primary Direction.

COVERING THE GAP — See Closing the Gap.

CRADLE — The intersection of the two converging boundary lines of a Symmetrical Triangle. (See also Apex.)

DAILY RANGE — The difference between the high and low price during one trading day.

DEMAND — Buying interest for a stock at a given price.

DESCENDING (PARALLEL) TREND CHANNEL — When the Bottoms of the reactions comprising a decline develop along a line (sometimes called a Return Line), which is also parallel to the basic down trendlines (i.e., the line which slopes down across the wave tops in a decline), the area between the two lines is called a Descending or Down Channel.

DESCENDING TRENDLINE — The declining wave in a stock or commodity is composed of a series of ripples. When the tops of these ripples form on, or very close to, a downward slanting straight line, a basic Descending or Down Trendline is formed.

DESCENDING TRIANGLE — One of a class of Area Patterns called Right-Angle Triangles. The class is distinguished by the fact that one of the two boundary lines is practically horizontal, while the other slants toward it. If the bottom line is horizontal and the upper slants downward to an intersection point to the right, the resulting Area Pattern is called a Descending Triangle. The implication is Bearish, with the expectant breakout through the flat (horizontal) side. Minimum Measuring Formula: add the broadest part of the Triangle to the breakout point.

DIAMOND — Usually a Reversal Pattern, but it will also be found as a Continuation Pattern. It could be described as a Complex Head-and-Shoulders Pattern with a V-shaped (bent) Neckline, or a Broadening Pattern which, after two or three swings, changes into a regular Triangle. The overall shape is a four-point Diamond. Since it requires a fairly active market, it is more often found at Major Tops. Many Complex Head-and-Shoulders Tops are borderline Diamond Patterns. The major difference is in the right side of the pattern. It should clearly show two converging lines with diminishing volume as in a Symmetrical Triangle. Minimum Measuring Formula: add the greatest width of the pattern to the breakout point.

DISTRIBUTION — The first phase of a Bear Market, which really begins in the last stage of a Bull Market. The period when farsighted investors sense that the market has outrun its fundamentals and begin to unload their holdings at an increasing pace. Trading volume is still high; however, it tends to diminish on rallies. The public is still active, but beginning to show signs of caution as hoped-for profits fade away.

DIVERGENCE — When new highs (or lows) in one indicator are not realized in another comparable indicator. (See also Confirmation.)

DIVERGENT PATTERN (TREND) — Those patterns with upper and lower boundary lines which meet at some point if extended to the left. (See also Broadening Formation.)

DIVERSIFICATION — The concept of placing your funds in different industry groups and investment vehicles to spread risk. Not to put all your financial eggs in one basket.

DIVIDENDS — A share of the profits, in cash or stock equivalent, which is paid to stockholders.

DORMANT BOTTOM — A variation of a Rounding (Bowl) Bottom, but in an extended, flat-bottomed form. It usually appears in "thin" stocks, (i.e., those issues with a small number of shares outstanding) and characteristically will show lengthy periods during which no sales will be registered for days at a time. The chart will appear "fly-specked" due to the missing days. The technical implication is for an upside breakout.

DOUBLE BOTTOM — Reversal Pattern. A Bottom formed on relatively high volume which is followed by a rally (of at least 15%), and then a second Bottom (possibly rounded) at the same level (plus or minus 3%) as the first Bottom on lower volume. A rally back though the apex of the intervening rally confirms the Reversal. More than a month should separate the two Bottoms. Minimum Measuring Formula: take the distance from the lowest bottom to the apex of the intervening rally and add it to the apex.

DOUBLE TOP — A high volume Top is formed, followed by a reaction (of at least 15%) on diminishing activity. Another rally back to the previous high (plus or minus 3%) is made, but on lower volume than the first high. A decline through the low of the reaction confirms the Reversal. The two highs should be more than a month apart. Minimum Measuring Formula: add to the breakout point the distance from the highest peak to the low of the reaction. Also called an "M" Formation.

DOUBLE TRENDLINE — When two relatively close Parallel Trendlines are needed to define the true trend pattern. (See also Trendline.)

DOW–JONES INDUSTRIAL AVERAGE — Developed by Charles Dow in 1885 to study market trends. Originally composed of 14 companies (12 railroads and 2 industrials), the rails, by 1897, were separated into their own Average, and 12 industrial companies of the day were selected for the Industrial Average. The number was increased to 20 in 1916, and to 30 in 1928. The stocks included in this Average have been changed from time to time to keep the list up to date, or to accommodate a merger. The only original issue still in the Average is General Electric.

DOW–JONES TRANSPORTATION AVERAGE — Established at the turn of the century with the new Industrial Average, it was originally called the Rail Average and was composed of 20 railroad companies. With the advent of the airlines industry, the Average was updated in 1970 and the name changed to Transportation Average.

DOW–JONES UTILITY AVERAGE — In 1929, utility companies were dropped from the Industrial Average and a new Utility Average of 20 companies was created. In 1938, the number of issues was reduced to the present 15.

DOWNTICK — A securities transaction which is at a price that is lower than the preceding transaction.

DOWNTREND — See Descending Trendline and Trend.

DRAWDOWN or RETRACEMENT — The ebb, or loss, of a portfolio's equity from a relative high to a relative low. Maximum drawdown equals retracement from maximum high point to minimum low point.

END RUN — When a breakout of a Symmetrical Triangle Pattern reverses its direction and trades back through axis Support (if an upside breakout) or Resistance (if a downside breakout), it is termed an *end run around the line*, or *end run* for short. The term is sometimes used to denote breakout failure in general.

EQUILIBRIUM MARKET — A price area that represents a balance between demand and supply.

EX-DIVIDEND — The day when the dividend is subtracted from the price of the stock.

EX-DIVIDEND GAP — The gap in price caused when the price of a stock is adjusted downward after the dividend payment is deducted.

EXERCISE — The means by which the holder of an option purchases or sells shares of the underlying security.

EXHAUSTION GAP — Relatively wide gap in the price of a stock or commodity which occurs near the end of a strong directional move in the price. These gaps are quickly closed, most often within 2 to 5 days, which helps to distinguish them from Runaway Gaps, which are not usually covered for a considerable length of time. An Exhaustion Gap cannot be read as a Major Reversal, or even necessarily a Reversal. It signals a halt in the prevailing trend, which is ordinarily followed by some sort of area pattern development.

EXPIRATION — The last day on which an option can be exercised.

EXPONENTIAL SMOOTHING — A mathematical method of forecasting which assumes future price action may be forecast by using a weighted average of past periods; a mathematical series in which greater weight is given to more recent price action. A method of trend identification.

FALLING WEDGE — An Area Pattern with two downward slanting, converging trendlines. Normally, it takes more than 3 weeks to complete, and volume will diminish as prices move toward the apex of the pattern. The anticipated direction of the breakout in a Falling Wedge is up. Minimum Measuring Formula: a retracement of all the ground lost within the Wedge. (See also Wedge.)

FALSE BREAKOUT or FALSE SIGNAL— A breakout which is confirmed but which quickly reverses and eventually leads the stock or commodity to a breakout in the opposite direction. Indistinguishable from premature breakout or genuine breakout when it occurs.

FAN LINES — A set of three secondary trendlines drawn from the same starting high or low, which spread out in a Fan shape. In a Primary Uptrend, the fan would be along the tops of the Secondary (Intermediate) Reaction. In a Primary Downtrend, the fan would be along the bottoms of the Secondary (Intermediate) Rally. When the third Fan Line is broken, it signals the resumption of the Primary Trend.

50-DAY MOVING AVERAGE LINE — Is determined by taking the closing price over the past 50 trading days and dividing by 50. *EN: Simple moving average for n days consists of summing prices for n days and dividing by n. On n+1 drop the first day and add the new day to the formula, etc.*

FIVE-POINT REVERSAL — See Broadening Pattern.

FLAG — A Continuation Pattern. A flag is a period of congestion, less than 4 weeks in duration, which forms after a sharp, near vertical, change in price. The upper and lower boundary lines of the pattern are parallel, though both may slant up, down, or sideways. In an uptrend, the pattern resembles a Flag flying from a mast, hence the name. Flags are also called Measuring or HalfMast Patterns because they tend to form at the midpoint of the rally or reaction. Volume tends to diminish during the formation, and increase on the breakout. Minimum Measuring Formula: add the distance from the breakout point, which started the preceding "Mast" rally or reaction, to the breakout point of the Flag.

FLOATING SUPPLY — The number of shares available for trading at any given time. Generally, the outstanding number of shares less shares closely held and likely to be unavailable to the public. Shares of a company held by its employee pension fund, for example, would not generally enter the trading stream and could be subtracted from the outstanding shares.

FORMATION — See Area Pattern.

FRONT-MONTH — The first expiration month in a series of months.

FUNDAMENTALS — Information on a stock pertaining to the business of the company and how it relates to earnings and dividends. In a commodity, it would be information on any factor which would affect supply or demand. *EN: Also, earnings, profits, profit margins, cash flow, sales, and other statistics sometimes used to obfuscate the value of the issue.*

GAP — A hole in the price range which occurs when either (1) the lowest price at which a stock or commodity is traded during any time period is higher than the highest price at which it was traded on the preceding time period, or (2) the highest price of one time period is lower than the lowest price of the preceding time period. When the ranges of the two time periods are plotted, they will not overlap or touch the same horizontal level on the chart — there will be a price gap between them. (See also Common or Area Gap, Ex-Dividend Gap, Breakaway Gap, Runaway Gap, Exhaustion Gap, and Island Reversal.)

GRAPH — See Chart.

HALF-MAST: — See Flag. Edwards said "The flag flies at half-mast" referring to the tendency of prices to consolidate half way through a surging vertical run.

HEAD-AND-SHOULDERS PATTERN — Although occasionally an Inverted Head-and-Shoulders Pattern (called a Consolidation Head-and-Shoulders) will form, which is a Continuation Pattern, in its normal form, this pattern is one of the more common and more reliable of the Major Reversal Patterns. It consists of the following four elements (a Head-and-Shoulders Top will be described for illustration): (1) a rally which ends a more or less extensive advance on heavy volume, and which is then followed by a Minor Reaction on less volume; this is the left shoulder; (2) another high-volume advance which exceeds the high of the left shoulder, followed by another low-volume reaction which takes prices down to near the bottom of the preceding reaction, and below the top of the left shoulder high; this is the head; (3) a third rally, but on decidedly less volume than accompanied either of the first two advances, and which fails to exceed the high established on the head; this is the right shoulder; and (4) a decline through a line drawn across the proceeding two reaction lows (the neckline), and a close below that line equivalent to 3% of the stock's market price. This is the confirmation of the breakout. A Head-and-Shoulders Bottom, or any other combination Headand-Shoulders Pattern, contains the same four elements. The main difference between a Top Formation and a Bottom Formation is in the volume patterns. The breakout in a Top can be on low volume. The breakout in a Bottom must show a "conspicuous burst of activity." Minimum Measuring Formula: add the distance between the head and neckline to the breakout point.

HEAD-AND-SHOULDERS BOTTOM — Area Pattern which reverses a decline. (See also Head-and-Shoulders Pattern.) *EN: An upside down name for an upside down pattern. See Kilroy Bottom.*

HEAD-AND-SHOULDERS CONSOLIDATION — Area Pattern which continues the previous trend. (See also Head-and-Shoulders Pattern.)

HEAD-AND-SHOULDERS TOP — Area Pattern which reverses an advance. (See also Head-and-Shoulders Pattern.)

HEAVY VOLUME — The expression "heavy volume," as used by Edwards and Magee, means heavy only with respect to the recent volume of sales in the stock you are watching.

HEDGING — To try to lessen risk by making a counterbalancing investment. In a stock portfolio, an example of a hedge would be to buy 100 shares of XYZ stock, and to buy one put option of the same stock. The put would help protect against a decline in the stock, but it would also limit potential gains on the upside. See Natural Hedge.

HISTORICAL DATA — A series of past daily, weekly, or monthly market prices.

HOOK DAY — A trading day in which the open is above/below prior day's high/low and the close is below/above prior day's close with narrow range.

HORIZONTAL CHANNEL — When the Tops of the rallies and Bottoms of the reactions form along lines which are horizontal and parallel to one another, the area in between is called a Horizontal Trend Channel. It may also be called a Rectangle during the early stages of formation.

HORIZONTAL TRENDLINE — A horizontal line drawn across either the Tops or Bottoms in a sideways trending market.

HYBRID HEAD-AND-SHOULDERS — A small Head-and-Shoulders Pattern within a larger Head-and-Shoulders Pattern. (See also Head-and-Shoulders Pattern.)

INDUSTRIAL AVERAGE — See Dow–Jones Industrial Average.

INSIDE DAY — A day in which the daily price range is totally within the prior day's daily price range

INSIDERS — Individuals who possess fundamental information likely to affect the price of a stock, but which is unavailable to the public. An example would be an individual who knows about a merger before it is announced to the public. Trading by insiders on this type of information is illegal.

IPO — Initial Public Offering.

INTERMEDIATE TREND — In Edwards and Magee, the term Intermediate or Secondary refers to a trend (or pattern indicating a trend) against the Primary (Major) Trend which is likely to last from 3 weeks to 3 months, and which may retrace one third to two thirds of the previous Primary Advance or Decline.

INVERTED BOWL — See Rounding Top.

INVERTED TRIANGLE — See Right-Angled Broadening Triangle.

ISLAND REVERSAL — A compact trading range, usually formed after a fast rally or reaction, which is separated from the previous move by an Exhaustion Gap, and from the move in the opposite direction which follows by a Breakaway Gap. The result is an Island of prices detached by a gap before and after. If the trading range contains only one day, it is called a One-Day Island Reversal. The two gaps usually occur at approximately the same level. By itself, the pattern is not of major significance; but it does frequently send prices back for a complete retracement of the Minor Move which preceded it.

KILROY BOTTOM — The Editor's contribution to the nomenclature. A more descriptive term for the undescriptive "Head-and-Shoulders Bottom".

LADDERING — A practice some Wall Street underwriters used in the tulipomania of the 1990s. Consists of selling IPO shares for the pre-opening price to insider customers in exchange for their agreement to buy more in the public offering at higher prices. Caused extreme volatility and big run ups in early days of IPOs. An unethical form of price manipulation.

LEVERAGE — Using a smaller amount of capital to control an investment of greater value. For example, exclusive of interest and commission costs, if you buy a stock on 50% margin, you control $1 of stock for every 50 cents invested or leverage of 2-to-1.

LIMIT MOVE — A change in price which exceeds the limits set by the exchange on which the futures contract is traded.

LIMIT ORDER — A buy or sell order which is limited in some way, usually in price. For example, if you placed a limit order to buy IBM at 100, the broker would not fill the order unless he could do so at your price or better, i.e., at 100 or lower.

LIMIT UP, LIMIT DOWN — Commodity exchange restrictions on the maximum upward or downward movements permitted in the price for a commodity during any trading session day.

LINE, DOW THEORY — A Line in the Dow Theory is an Intermediate Sideways Movement in one or both of the Averages (Industrial and/or Transportation)in the course of which prices fluctuate within a range of 5% (of mean price) or less.

LOGARITHMIC SCALE — See Semilogarithmic Scale.

MAJOR TREND — In Edwards and Magee, the term Major (or Primary) refers to a trend (or pattern leading to such a trend) which lasts at least one year, and shows a rise or decline of at least 20%.

MARGIN — The minimum amount of capital required to buy or sell a stock. The rate, 50% of value in 2005, is set by the government. In a commodity, margin is also the minimum, usually about 10%, needed to buy or sell a contract. But the rate is set by the individual exchanges. The two differ in cost as well. In a stock, the broker lends the investor the balance of the money due and charges interest for the loan. In a commodity, margin is treated as a good faith payment. The broker does not lend the difference, so no interest expense is incurred.

MARKET ON CLOSE — An order specification which requires the broker to get the best price available on the close of trading.

MARKET ORDER — An instruction to buy or sell at the price prevailing when the order reaches the floor of the exchange.

MARKET RECIPROCAL — Normal average range of a stock based on the average range for a number of years, divided by the current average range. The result is the reciprocal of the market movement for the period. Wide market activity, for example, would show a small decimal, less than 1. Dull trading would be a larger number.

MAST — The vertical rally or reaction preceding a Flag or Pennant Formation.

McCLELLAN OSCILLATOR — An Index based on New York Stock Exchange net advances over declines. It provides a measure of such conditions as overbought/oversold and market direction on a short- to intermediate-term basis. The McClellan Oscillator measures a Bear Market Selling Climax when registering a very negative reading like –150. A sharp buying pulse in the market is indicated by a very positive reading, well above 100.

MEASURING FORMULAE — There are certain patterns which do allow the chartist the opportunity to project at least an interim target level of the direction of the Primary Trend. The most important of these patterns are found to be Triangles, Rectangles, Head-and-Shoulders, Pennants and Flags.

> Triangles — When a stock breaks out of a Symmetrical Triangle (either up or down), the ensuing move should carry at least as far as the height of the Triangle as measured along its first reaction.
> Rectangles — The minimum you would expect from a breakout (up or down) out of a Rectangle Pattern would be the distance equal to the height of the formation.
> Head-and-Shoulders Tops/Bottoms — The Head-and-Shoulders Pattern has one of the better measuring sticks. In either a Top or Bottom, the interim target, once the neckline is penetrated, is the distance from the Top (or Bottom) of the head to the level of the neckline directly below (above) the head.
> Pennants and Flags — The one thing to remember about these Continuation Patterns is that they "fly at half-mast." In other words, the leg in equals the leg out.

MEASURING GAP — See Runaway Gap.

MEGAPHONES — Megaphones are Broadening Tops. The Broadening Formation may evolve in any one of the three forms comparable, respectively, to Inverted Symmetrical, Inverted Ascending, or Descending Triangles. The symmetrical type, for example, consists of a series of price fluctuations across a horizontal axis, with each Minor Top higher and each Minor Bottom lower than its predecessor. The pattern may thus be roughly marked off by two diverging lines, the upper sloping up from left to right, the lower sloping down. These Broadening Patterns are characteristically loose and irregular, whereas Symmetrical Triangles are regular and compact. The converging boundary lines of Symmetrical Triangles are clearly defined, as a rule. Tops and Bottoms within the formation tend to fall within fair precision on these boundary lines. In the Broadening Formation, the rallies and declines usually do not all stop at clearly marked boundary lines and are subject to spikes. We could call this a Megaphone Spike because the formation keeps on crowding at the lines to look like a megaphone. It has a tendency to spike down more than up.

MINOR TREND — In Edwards and Magee, the term Minor refers to brief fluctuations (usually less than 6 days and rarely longer than 3 weeks) which, in total, make up the Intermediate Trend.

MOMENTUM INDICATOR — A market indicator which utilizes volume statistics for predicting the strength or weakness of a current market and any overbought or oversold conditions, and to distinguish turning points within the market.

MOVING AVERAGE — A mathematical technique to smooth data. It is called moving because the number of elements are fixed, but the time interval advances. Old data must be removed when new data is added, which causes the average to "move along" with the progression of the stock or commodity. *EN: Simple moving average for n days consists of summing prices for n days and dividing by n. On n+1, drop the first day and add the new day to the formula, etc.*

MOVING AVERAGE CONVERGENCE/DIVERGENCE (MACD) — MACD, an oscillator derived by dividing one Moving Average by another. Basically, it combines three Moving Averages into two lines. In today's computer programs, the Moving Averages are usually exponentially weighted, thus giving more weight to the more recent data. It is plotted in a chart with a horizontal Equilibrium Line.

The Equilibrium Line is important. When the two Moving Averages cross below the Equilibrium Line, it means that the shorter EMA is at a value less than the longer EMA. This is a Bearish signal. When the EMAs are above the Equilibrium Line, it means that the shorter EMA has a value greater than the longer EMA. This is a Bullish signal.

The first line is the difference between a 12-period Exponential Moving Average and a 26-period Exponential Moving Average. The second line (signal line) is an approximate exponential equivalent of a 9-period Moving Average of the first line. The exponential values being 0.15, 0.075, and 0.20. An MACD can be displayed as a line oscillator or a histogram.

Buy signals are generated when the faster Moving Average Line crosses the slower Moving Average Line from below. Sell signals come from the opposite, when the faster line crosses the slower line from above. Beware of mechanically trading every MACD crossover; it can lead to whipsaws and drawdowns with substance. The fact is, narrow trading ranges give many false signals which can be avoided with additional interpretation. (See also Appendix C.)

MOVING AVERAGE CROSSOVERS — The point where the various Moving Average Lines pass through or over each other.

MULTICOLINCARITY — The incorrect procedure of using the identical data to supply different types of indicators. The indicators will all confirm each other since they are based on the same data. Combining RSI, Moving Average Convergence/Divergence (MACD), and rate of change (where all indicators use the same closing prices and relative time periods) should provide the same signals, but they could easily be incorrect. Multicolincarity can be avoided by using one indicator based on closing prices, another from volume, and a third from price ranges. It can also be avoided by using data generated indicators compared to chart patterns. (See also Bollinger Bands, MACD, Wilder RSI.)

MULTIPLE HEAD-AND-SHOULDERS PATTERN — See Complex Head and-Shoulders.

NARROW RANGE DAY — A trading day with a narrower price range relative to the previous day's price range.

NATURAL and UNNATURAL Methods or Systems — Bassetti's half humorous identification of "natural methods" of analysis, such as chart analysis, which looks directly at market data, as opposed to "unnatural methods" which place an algorithm between the data and the analysis, such as moving averages, oscillators, etc.

NATURAL HEDGE — Bassetti's formulation of a technique recommended by Magee whereby a portfolio is always somewhat long and somewhat short. It is an imperfect hedge intended to cushion downside (or upside) risks. E.g., long the DIA and short its members (or their proxies) which are in downtrends.

NECKLINE — In a Head-and-Shoulders Pattern, it is the line drawn across the two reaction lows (in a Top), or two rally highs (in a Bottom), which occur before and after the head. This line must be broken by 3% to confirm the Reversal. In a Diamond Pattern, which is similar to a Head-and-Shoulders Pattern, the neckline is bent in the shape of a V or inverted V. (See also Diamond and Head-and-Shoulders.)

NEGATIVE DIVERGENCE — When two or more Averages, indexes, or indicators fail to show confirming trends.

NORMAL RANGE FOR PRICE — *EN: An analytical tool invented by Magee for measuring the volatility of stocks. Cumbersome in the modern context, but interesting. Cf. Appendix A.*

ODD LOT — A block of stock consisting of less than 100 shares.

ON BALANCE VOLUME (OBV) — OBV is a popular Volume Indicator, developed by Joseph Granville. Constructing an OBV line is very simple: the total volume for each day is assigned a positive or negative value depending on whether prices closed higher or lower that day. A higher close results in the volume for that day getting a positive value, while a lower close results in a negative value. A running total is kept by adding or subtracting each day's volume based on the direction of the close. The direction of the OBV line is watched, not the actual volume numbers.

Formula:

- If Today's Close > Yesterday's Close,
  then OBV = Yesterday's OBV + Today's Volume
- If Today's Close < Yesterday's Close,
  then OBV = Yesterday's OBV – Today's Volume
- If Today's Close = Yesterday's Close,
  then OBV = Yesterday's OBV

ONE-DAY REVERSAL — See Island Reversal.

OPTION — The right granted to one investor by another to buy (called a call option) or sell (called a put option) 100 shares of stock, or one contract of a commodity, at a fixed price for a fixed period of time. The investor granting the right (the seller of the option) is paid a nonrefundable premium by the buyer of the option.

ORDER — See Limit Order, Market Order, and Stop Order.

OPTIONS RESEARCH, INC. — Founded by Blair Hull, later of Hull Trading Co. The first company to computerize the Black–Scholes Model.

OSCILLATOR — A form of momentum or rate-of-change indicator which is usually valued from +1 to –1 or from 0% to 100%.

OVERBOUGHT — Market prices that have risen too steeply and too quickly.

OVERBOUGHT/OVERSOLD INDICATOR — An indicator that attempts to define when prices have moved too far and too quickly in either direction, and thus are liable to a reaction.

OVERSOLD — Market prices that have declined too steeply and too quickly.

PANIC — The second stage of a Bear Market when buyers thin out and sellers sell at any price. The downward trend of prices suddenly accelerates into an almost vertical drop while volume rises to climactic proportions. (See also Bear Market.)

PANIC BOTTOM — See Selling Climax.

PATTERN — See Area Pattern.

PEAK — See Top.

PENETRATION — The breaking of a pattern boundary line, trendline, or Support and Resistance Level.

PENNANT — A Pennant is a Flag with converging, rather than parallel, boundary lines. (See also Flag.)

POINT & FIGURE CHART — A method of charting believed to have been created by Charles Dow. Each day the price moves by a specific amount (the arbitrary box size), an X (if up) or O (if down) is placed on a vertical column of squared paper. As long as prices do not change direction by a specified amount (the Reversal), the trend is considered to be in force and no new column is made. If a Reversal takes place, another vertical column is started immediately to the right of the first, but in the opposite direction. There is no provision for time on a Point & Figure Chart.

PREMATURE BREAKOUT — A breakout of an Area Pattern, then a retreat back into the pattern. Eventually, the trend will break out again and proceed in the same direction. At the time they occur, false breakouts and premature breakouts are indistinguishable from each other, or a genuine breakout.

PRICE EARNINGS RATIO — Price of stock divided by earnings (which may or may not be real) to give the p/e ratio. Sometimes an unnatural, or imaginary, number.

PRIMARY TREND — See Major Trend.

PROGRAM TRADING — Trades based on signals from various computer programs, usually entered directly from the trader's computer to the market's computer system. *EN: Usually indicates large volume transactions on large baskets of stocks by professional traders.*

PROGRESSIVE STOP — A stop order which follows the market up or down. (See also Stop.)

PROTECTIVE STOP — A stop order used to protect gains or limit losses in an existing position. (See also Stop.)

PULLBACK — Return of prices to the boundary line of the pattern after a breakout to the downside. Return after an upside breakout is called a Throwback.

PUT — An option to sell a specified amount of a stock or commodity at an agreed time at the stated exercise price.

RAIL AVERAGE — See Dow–Jones Transportation Average.

RALLY — An increase in price which retraces part of the previous price decline.

RALLY TOPS — A price level that finishes a short-term rally in an ongoing trend.

RANGE — The difference between the high and low during a specific time period.

REACTION — A decline in price which retraces part of the previous price advance.

RECIPROCAL, MARKET — See Market Reciprocal.

RECOVERY — See Rally.

RECTANGLE — A trading area which is bounded on the Top and the Bottom with horizontal, or near horizontal, lines. A Rectangle can be either a Reversal or Continuation Pattern depending on the direction of the breakout. Minimum Measuring Formula: add the width (difference between Top and Bottom) of the Rectangle to the breakout point.

RED PARALLEL — A line drawn parallel to the trendline (Red Trendline) which connects at least two Bottoms. The Red Parallel (basically a Return Line) is started off a high and used to estimate the next high point.

RED TRENDLINE — A straight line connecting two or more Bottoms together. To avoid confusion, Edwards and Magee use a red line for Bottom Trendlines and a blue line for Top Trendlines.

RELATIVE STRENGTH (RS or RS INDEX) — A stock's price movement over the past year as compared to a market index (most often the Standard & Poor's 500 Index). Value below 1 means the stock shows relative weakness in price movement (underperformed the market); a value above 1 means the stock shows relative strength over the 1-year period.

Equation for Relative Strength:

$$\frac{\text{Current Stock Price}/\text{Year-Ago Stock Price}}{\text{Current S\&P 500}/\text{Year-Ago S\&P 500}}$$

(See also Wilder Relative Strength Index.)

RESISTANCE LEVEL — A price level at which a sufficient supply of stock is forthcoming to stop, and possibly turn back for a time, an uptrend.

RETRACEMENT — A price movement in the opposite direction of the previous trend.

RETURN LINE — See Ascending or Descending Trend Channels.

REVERSAL GAP — A chart formation where the low of the last day is above the previous day's range, with the close above midrange and above the open.

REVERSAL PATTERN — An Area Pattern which breaks out in a direction opposite to the previous trend. (See also Ascending Triangle, Broadening Formation, Broadening Top, Descending Triangle, Diamond, Dormant Bottom, Double Bottom or Top, Triple Bottom or Top, Head-and-Shoulders, Rectangle, Rounding Bottom or Top, Saucer, Symmetrical Triangle, and Rising or Falling Wedge.)

RIGHT-ANGLED BROADENING TRIANGLE — Area Pattern with one boundary line horizontal and the other at an angle which, when extended, will converge with the horizontal line at some point to the left of the pattern. Similar in shape to Ascending and Descending Triangles, except they are inverted and look like Flat-Topped or Bottomed Megaphones. Right-Angled Broadening Formations generally carry Bearish implications regardless of which side is flat. But any decisive breakout (3% or more) through the horizontal boundary line has the same forceful significance as does a breakout in an Ascending or Descending Triangle.

RIGHT-ANGLE TRIANGLES — See Ascending and Descending Triangles.

RISING WEDGE — An Area Pattern with two upward-slanting, converging trendlines. Normally, it takes more than 3 weeks to complete, and volume will diminish as prices move toward the apex of the pattern. The anticipated direction of the breakout in a Rising Wedge is down. Minimum Measuring Formula: a retracement of all the ground gained within the wedge.

ROUND LOT — A block of stock consisting of 100 shares of stock.

ROUND TRIP — The cost of one complete stock or commodity transaction, i.e., the entry cost and the offset cost combined.

ROUNDING BOTTOM — An Area Pattern which pictures a gradual, progressive, and fairly symmetrical change in the trend from down to up. Both the Price Pattern (along its lows) and the Volume Pattern show a concave shape often called a Bowl or Saucer. There is no minimum measuring formula associated with this Reversal Pattern.

ROUNDING TOP — An Area Pattern which pictures a gradual, progressive, and fairly symmetrical change in the trend from up to down. The Price Pattern, along its highs, shows a convex shape sometimes called an Inverted Bowl. The Volume Pattern is concave shaped (a bowl) as trading activity declines into the peak of the Price Pattern, and increases when prices begin to fall. There is no measuring formula associated with this Reversal Pattern.

RUNAWAY GAP — A relatively wide gap in prices which occurs in an advance or decline gathering momentum. Also called a "Measuring Gap," since it frequently occurs at just about the halfway point between the breakout which started the move and the Reversal Day which calls an end to it. Minimum Measuring Formula: take the distance from the original breakout point to the start of the gap, and add it to the other side of the gap.

RUNNING MARKET — A market wherein prices are moving rapidly in one direction with very few or no price changes in the opposite direction.

SAUCER — See Rounding Bottom and Scallop.

SCALLOPS — A series of Rounding Bottom (Saucer) Patterns where the rising end always carries prices a little higher than the preceding Top at the beginning of the pattern. Net gains will vary from stock to stock, but there is a strong tendency for it to amount to 10–15% of the price. The total reaction, from the left-hand Top of each Saucer to its Bottom, is usually in the 20–30% area. Individual Saucers in a Scallop series are normally 5 to 7 weeks long, and rarely less than 3 weeks. The volume will show a convex or Bowl Pattern.

SECONDARY TREND — See Intermediate Trend.

SELLING CLIMAX — A period of extraordinary volume which comes at the end of a rapid and comprehensive decline which exhausts the margin reserves of many speculators or patience of investors. Total volume turnover may exceed any single day's volume during the previous upswing as Panic Selling sweeps through the stock or commodity. Also called a Clean-Out Day, a Selling Climax reverses the technical conditions of the market. Although it is a form of a One-Day Reversal, it can take more than one day to complete.

SEMILOGARITHMIC SCALE — Price or volume scale where the distance on the vertical axis (i.e., space between horizontal lines) represents equal percentage changes.

SENSITIVITY — An index used by Edwards and Magee to measure the probable percentage movement (sensitivity) of a stock during a specified percentage move in the stock market as a whole. *EN: More or less equivalent, or with the same intent as beta.*

SHAKEOUT — A corrective move large enough to "shake out" nervous investors before the Primary Trend resumes.

SHORT INTEREST — The number of shares that have been sold short and not yet repurchased. This information is published monthly by the New York Stock Exchange.

SHORT SALE — A transaction where the entry position is to sell a stock or commodity first and to repurchase it (hopefully at a lower price) at a later date. In the stock market, shares you do not own can be sold by borrowing shares from the broker, and replacing them when the offsetting repurchase takes place. In the commodity market, contracts are created when a buyer and seller get together through a floor broker. As a result, the procedure to sell in the commodity market is the same as it is to buy.

SHOULDER — See Head-and-Shoulders Patterns.

SMOOTHING — A mathematical approach that removes excess data variability while maintaining a correct appraisal of the underlying trend.

SPIKE — A sharp rise in price in a single day or two.

STOCHASTIC — Literally means random.

STOCHASTICS — The Stochastic Oscillator, developed by George Lane, compares a security's price closing level to its price range over a specific period of time. This indicator shows, Lane theorized, that in an upwardly trending market, prices tend to close near their high; and during a downward trending market, prices tend to close near their low. As an upward trend matures, prices tend to close further away from their high; as a downward trend matures, prices tend to close away from their low. The Stochastic Indicator attempts to determine when prices start to cluster around their low of the day in an uptrending market, and cluster around their high in a downtrend. Lane theorizes these conditions indicate a Trend Reversal is beginning to occur. The Stochastic Indicator is plotted as two lines, the %D Line and %K Line. The %D Line is more important than the %K Line. The Stochastic is plotted on a chart with values ranging from 0 to 100. The value can never fall below 0 or above 100. Readings above 80 are considered strong and indicate a price is closing near its high. Readings below 20 are strong and indicate a price is closing near its low. Ordinarily, the %K Line will change direction before the %D Line. However, when the %D Line changes direction prior to the %K Line, a slow and steady Reversal is often indicated. When both %K and %D Lines change direction, and the faster %K Line changes direction to retest a crossing of the %D Line, though doesn't cross it, the incident confirms stability of the prior Reversal. A powerful move is under way when the Indicator reaches its extremes around 0 and 100. Following a Pullback in price, if the Indicator retests extremes, a good entry point is indicated. Many times, when the %K or %D Lines begin to flatten out, the action becomes an indication the trend will reverse during the next trading range. (See also Appendix C.)

STOCK SPLIT — A procedure used by management to establish a different market price for its shares by changing the common stock structure of the company. Usually a lower price is desired, and established by canceling the outstanding shares and reissuing a larger number of new certificates to current shareholders. The most common ratios are 2-to-1, 3-to-1, and 3-to-2. Occasionally, a higher price is desired and a reverse split takes place where one new share is issued for some multiple number of old shares.

STOP — A contingency order which is placed above the current market price if it is to buy, or below the current market price if it is to sell. A stop order becomes a market order only when the stock or commodity moves up to the price of the buy stop, or down to the price of a sell stop. A stop can be used to enter a new position or exit an old position. (See also Protective or Progressive Stop.)

STOP LOSS — See Protective Stop.

SUPPLY — Amount of stock available at a given price.

SUPPLY LINE — See Resistance.

SUPPORT LEVEL — The price level at which a sufficient amount of demand is forthcoming to stop, and possibly turn higher for a time, a downtrend.

SYMMETRICAL TRIANGLE — Also called a Coil. Can be a Reversal or Continuation Pattern. A sideways congestion where each Minor Top fails to attain the height of the previous rally and each Minor Bottom stops above the level of the previous low. The result is upper and lower boundary lines which converge, if extended, to a point on the right. The upper boundary line must slant down and the lower boundary line must slant up, or it would be a variety of a Wedge. Volume tends to diminish during formation. Minimum Formula: add the widest distance within the Triangle to its breakout point.

TANGENT — See Trendline.

TAPE READER — One who makes trading decisions by watching the flow of New York Stock Exchange and American Stock Exchange price and volume data coming across the electronic ticker tape.

TEKNIPLAT PAPER — A specially formatted, two-cycle, semilogarithmic graph paper, with sixth-line vertical accents, used to chart stock or commodity prices. Check the web site: www.edwards-magee.com.

TEST — A term used to describe the activity of a stock or commodity when it returns to, or "tests," the validity of a previous trendline, or Support or Resistance Level.

THIN ISSUE — A stock which has a low number of floating shares and is lightly traded.

THREE-DAY-AWAY RULE — An arbitrary time period used by Edwards and Magee in marking suspected Minor Tops or Bottoms.

THROWBACK — Return of prices to the boundary line of the pattern after a breakout to the upside. Return after a downside breakout is called a Pullback.

TOP — See Broadening Top, Descending Triangle, Double Top, Head-and-Shoulders Top, Triple Top, and Rounding Top.

TREND — The movement of prices in the same general direction, or the tendency or proclivity to move in a straight line. (See also Ascending, Descending, and Horizontal Parallel Trend Channels, Convergent Trend, Divergent Trend, Intermediate Trend, Major Trend, and Minor Trend.)

TREND CHANNEL — A parallel probable price range centered about the most likely price line.

TRENDING MARKET — Price continues to move in a single direction, usually closing strongly for the day.

TRENDLINE — If we actually apply a ruler to a number of charted price trends, we quickly discover the line that most often is really straight in an uptrend is a line connecting the lower extremes of the Minor Recessions within these lines. In other words, an advancing wave in the stock market is composed of a series of ripples, and the bottoms of each of these ripples tend to form on, or very close to, an upward slanting straight line. The tops of the ripples are usually less even; sometimes they also can be defined by a straight line, but more often, they vary slightly in amplitude, and so any line connecting their upper tips would be more or less crooked. On a descending price trend, the line most likely to be straight is the one that connects the tops of the Minor Rallies within it, while the Minor Bottoms may or may not fall along a straight edge. These two lines — the one that slants up along the successive wave bottoms within a broad up-move and the one that slants down across successive wave tops within a broad down move — are the Basic Trendlines. You draw an Up Trendline by drawing the line on the inner side. You draw a Down Trendline by drawing it on the outside. You draw a Sideways Trendline on the bottom.

TRIANGLE — See Ascending Triangle, Descending Triangle, Right-Angled Broadening Triangle, and Symmetrical Triangle.

TRIPLE BOTTOM — Similar to a flat Head-and-Shoulders Bottom, or Rectangle, the three Bottoms in a Triple Bottom.

TRIPLE TOP — An Area Pattern with three Tops which are widely spaced and with quite deep, and usually rounding, reactions between them. Less volume occurs on the second peak than the first peak, and still less on the third peak. Sometimes called a "W" Pattern, particularly if the second peak is below the first and third. The Triple Top is confirmed when the decline from the third Top penetrates the Bottom of the lowest valley between the three peaks.

200-DAY MOVING AVERAGE LINE — Is determined by taking the closing price over the past 200 trading days and dividing by 200, then repeating the process each succeeding day, always dropping off the earliest day.

UPTICK — A securities transaction which is made at a price higher than the preceding transaction.

UPTREND — See Ascending Trendline and Trend.

UTILITY AVERAGE — See Dow–Jones Utility Average.

V/D VOLUME — Is the ratio between the daily up-volume to the daily downvolume. It is a 50-day ratio which is determined by dividing the total volume on those days when the stock closed up from the prior day by the total volume on days when the stock closed down.

VALIDITY OF TRENDLINE PENETRATION — The application of the following three tests when a trendline is broken to determine whether the break is valid, or whether the trendline is still basically intact: (1) the extent of the penetration, (2) the volume of trading on the penetration, and (3) the trading action after the penetration.

VALLEY — The V-shaped price action which occurs between two peaks. (See also Double Top and Triple Top.)

VOLATILITY — A measure of a stock's tendency to move up and down in price, based on its daily price history over the latest 12-month period. *EN: See formula in Resources.*

VOLUME — The number of shares in stocks or contracts in commodities which are traded over a specified period of time.

"W" FORMATION — See Triple Top.

WEDGE — A chart formation in which the price fluctuations are confined within converging straight (or practically straight) lines.

WILDER RELATIVE STRENGTH INDICATOR (RSI) — Although relative strength, comparing a security price to a benchmark index price, has been around for some time, this indicator was developed by J. Welles Wilder, as explained in his 1978 book, *New Concepts in Technical Trading*.

Relative Strength is often used to identify price Tops and Bottoms by keying on specific levels (usually "30" and "70") on the RSI chart, which is scaled from 0-100. The RSI can also be useful to show:

1. Movement which might not be as readily apparent on the bar chart.
2. Failure Swings above 70 or below 30, warning of coming Reversals.
3. Support and Resistance Levels appear with greater clarity.
4. Divergence between the RSI and price can often be a useful Reversal indicator.

The Relative Strength Index requires a certain amount of lead-up time in order to operate successfully.

Bibliography

Allen, R.C., *How to Use the 4 Day, 9 Day and 18 Day Moving Averages to Earn Larger Profits from Commodities*, Best Books, Chicago, 1974.

Arms, Richard W., *Volume Cycles in the Stock Market. Market Timing Through Equivolume Charting*, Dow Jones-Irwin, Homewood, IL, 1983.

Arms, Richard W., Jr., The Arms Index, TRIN), Dow Jones-Irwin, Homewood, IL, 1989.

Belveal, L. Dee, *Charting Commodity Market Price Behavior*, 2nd ed., Dow Jones-Irwin, Homewood, IL, 1985.

Bernstein, Jacob, *The Handbook of Commodity Cycles. A Window on Time*, John Wiley & Sons, New York, 1982.

Bernstein, Peter, *Against the Gods*, John Wiley & Sons, New York, 1996.

Blumenthal, Earl, *Chart for Profit Point & Figure Trading*, Investors Intelligence, Larchmont, NY, 1975.

Bolton, A. Hamilton, *The Elliott Wave Principle. A Critical Appraisal*, Monetary Research, Hamilton, Bermuda, 1960, Bressert, Walter J. and James Hardie Jones, *The HAL Blue Book. How to Use Cycles With an Over-Bought/Oversold and Momentum Index For More Consistent Profits*, HAL Market Cycles, Tucson, AZ, 1984.

Chicago Board of Trade, "CBOT Dow Jones Industrial Average and Futures Options," Chicago, 1997.

Cohen, A.W., *How to Use the Three-Point Reversal Method of Point & Figure Stock Market Trading*, 8th rev. ed., Chartcraft, Larchmont, NY, 1982.

Cootner, Paul H., Ed., *The Random Character of Stock Market Prices*, MIT Press, Cambridge, 1964.

de Villiers, Victor, *The Point and Figure Method of Anticipating Stock Price Movements. Complete Theory and Practice*, Windsor Books, Brightwaters, NY, orig. 1933, reprinted in 1975.

Dewey, Edward R. with Og Mandino, *Cycles, the Mysterious Forces That Trigger Events*, Manor Books, New York, 1973.

Dobson, Edward D., *Understanding Fibonacci Numbers*, Trader Press, Greenville, SC, 1984.

Dreman, David, *Contrarian Investment Strategy*, Simon & Schuster, New York, 1974.

Dunn & Hargitt *Point and Figure Commodity Trading. A Computer Evaluation*, Dunn & Hargitt, Lafayette, IN, 1971.

Dunn & Hargitt *Trader's Notebook. Trading Methods Checked by Computer*, Dunn & Hargitt, Lafayette, IN, 1970.

Elliott, Ralph N., *The Major Works of R.N. Elliott*, Prechter, R., Ed., New Classics Library, Chappaqua, NY, 1980.

Emery, Walter L., Ed., *Commodity Year Book*, Commodity Research Bureau, Jersey City, NJ, annually.

Frost, Alfred J. and Robert R. Prechter, *Elliott Wave Principle, Key to Stock Market Profits*, New Classics Library, Chappaqua, NY, 1978.

Galbraith, John K., *The Great Crash 1929*, Houghton Mifflin, Boston, 1961.

Gann, W.D., *How to Make Profits in Commodities*, rev. ed., Lambert-Gann Publishing, Pomeroy, WA, orig. 1942, reprinted 1976.

Granville, Joseph E., *New Strategy of Daily Stork Market Timing for Maximum Profits*, Prentice-Hall, Englewood Cliffs, NJ, 1976.

Hadady, R. Earl, *Contrary Opinion. How to Use it For Profit in Trading Commodity Futures*, Hadady Publications, Pasadena, CA, 1983.

Hurst, J.M., *The Profit Magic of Transaction Timing*, Prentice-Hall, Englewood Cliffs, NJ, 1970.

Jiler, Harry, Ed., *Guide to Commodity Price Forecasting*. Commodity Research Bureau, New York, 1971.

Jiler, William L., *How Charts Can Help You in the Stock Market*, Trendline, New York, 1962.

Jorion, Philippe, *Value at Risk*, John Wiley & Sons, New York, 1996.

Kaufman, Perry J., *Commodity Trading Systems and Methods*, Wiley, New York, 1978.

Kaufman, Perry J., *Technical Analysis in Commodities*, John Wiley & Sons, New York, 1980.

MacKay, Charles, *Extraordinary Popular Delusions and the Madness of Crowds*, Three Rivers Press, New York, 1980.

Magee, John, *Analyzing Bar Charts for Profit*, John Magee Inc. (now St. Lucie Press, Boca Raton FL), 1994.

Magee, John, *Winning the Mental Game on Wall Street*, (2nd edition of *The General Semantics of Wall Street*), edited by W.H.C. Bassetti, St. Lucie Press, Boca Raton, FL, 2000.

Mandelbrot, O., "A MultiFractal Walk Down Wall Street," *Scientific American*, February 1999, June 1999.

McMillan, Lawrence G., *Options as a Strategic Investment*, New York Institute of Finance, New York, 1993.

Natenberg, Sheldon, *Option Volatility and Pricing Strategy*, rev. ed., Probus Publishing Company, Chicago, 1994.

Niederhoffer, Victor, *The Education of a Speculator*, John Wiley & Sons, New York, 1997.

Nison, Steve, *Beyond Candlesticks*, John Wiley & Sons, New York, 1994.

Nison, Steve, *Japanese Candlestick Charting Techniques*, New York Institute of Finance, New York, 1991.

O'Neil, William J., *How to Make Money in Stocks*, 2nd ed., McGraw-Hill, New York, 1995.

Patel, Charles, *Technical Trading Systems for Commodities and Stocks*, Trading Systems Research, Walnut Creek, CA, 1980.

Pring, Martin, *Technical Analysis Explained*, 2nd ed., McGraw-Hill, New York, 1985.

Pring, Martin J., *Technical Analysis Explained*, 3rd ed., McGraw-Hill, New York, 1991.

Schultz, John W., *The Intelligent Chartist*, WRSM Financial Services, New York, 1962.

Schwager, Jack D., *A Complete Guide to the Futures Markets. Fundamental Analysis Technical Analysis, Trading Spreads and Options*, John Wiley & Sons, New York, 1984.

Schwager, Jack, *Schwager on Futures, Technical Analysis*, John Wiley & Sons, New York, 1996.

Schwager, Jack D., *Market Wizards*, HarperBusiness, New York, 1990.

Schwager, Jack D., *The New Market Wizards*, HarperBusiness, New York, 1992.

Shibayama, Zenkei, *Zen Comments on the Mumonkan*, Harper and Row, New York, 1974.

Sklarew, Arthur, *Techniques of a Professional Commodity Chart Analyst*, Commodity Research Bureau, New York, 1980.

Teweles, Richard J., Charles V. Harlow, and Herbert L. Stone, *The Commodity Futures Game — Who Wins? — Who loses? — Why?*, 2nd ed., McGraw-Hill, New York, 1974.

Vodopich, Donald R., *Trading For Profit With Precision Timing*, Precision Timing, Atlanta, GA, 1984.

Wheelan, Alexander H., *Study Helps in Point and Figure Technique*, Morgan Rogers, 1966.

Wilder, J. Welles, *New Concepts in Technical Trading Systems*, Trend Research, Greensboro, NC, 1978.

Williams, Larry R., *How I Made $1,000,000 Trading Commodities Last Year*, 3rd ed., Conceptual Management, Monterey, CA, 1979.

Zieg, Kermit C., Jr. and Perry J. Kaufman, *Point and Figure Commodity Trading Techniques*, Investor's Intelligence, Larchmont, NY, 1975.

Zweig, Martin, *Winning on Wall Street*, Warner Books, New York, 1986.

Index

U

volume action and should be
studied with this in mind.)